PROPERTY AND POLITICS
1870–1914

PROPERTY AND POLITICS
1870–1914
LANDOWNERSHIP, LAW, IDEOLOGY AND URBAN DEVELOPMENT IN ENGLAND

AVNER OFFER

CAMBRIDGE UNIVERSITY PRESS

CAMBRIDGE
LONDON   NEW YORK   NEW ROCHELLE
MELBOURNE   SYDNEY

Published by the Press Syndicate of the University of Cambridge
The Pitt Building, Trumpington Street, Cambridge CB2 1RP
32 East 57th Street, New York, NY 10022, USA
296 Beaconsfield Parade, Middle Park, Melbourne 3206, Australia.

© Cambridge University Press 1981

First published 1981

Printed in Malta by Interprint Limited

British Library Cataloguing in Publication Data

Offer, Avner
Property and politics, 1870–1914.
1. Real property – England – History
2. Great Britain – Politics and government – 1837–1901
3. Great Britain – Politics and government – 1901–1936
I. Title
333.3′2′0942   HD603   80-41010

ISBN 0 521 22414 4

For Leah

CONTENTS

CONTENTS

FIGURES AND ILLUSTRATIONS

TABLES

PREFACE

Like Isaiah Berlin's fox, this book 'knows many things'. It dwells on the manifold relations of land and society in late-Victorian England: the development of land law and the distribution of tenures, the unfolding of political discourse, the certitudes of economics and the constraints of the economy, the development of interest groups, the growth of social movements, and the mental and cultural dimensions of ownership. Behind this diversity of appearances, one senses a stubborn hedgehog, who 'knows one big thing'. This is the pursuit of security and esteem: fleeting possessions that can only be captured and secured by the institutions of property. This pursuit gave an inner coherence to the Victorian and Edwardian 'land question', the topic that was the starting point of my research.

Earlier versions of parts II–V of this book were contained in my Oxford D. Phil. thesis of 1978. Both the text and the quantitative data have been extensively revised, and the thesis is now superseded. Limitations still remain, and the scope of the book should be clearly indicated. The search for origins and explanations has often taken me to earlier times than 1870. Ireland, Scotland and Wales differed from England in their tenurial, legal and fiscal systems. They have been well served by recent studies, and have therefore been largely excluded. Some topics of great importance, such as landlord-tenant relations, the role of aristocratic landowners and the origins of council housing are being pursued by other scholars (D. Englander, D. Cannadine and M. Swenarton, respectively), whose work has either appeared very recently, or is due to be published shortly. These topics are consequently given less emphasis here. I myself have written elsewhere on the aggregate movements of rent, and on the inter-war Law of Property reform, and am still striving to learn other parts of the terrain. This book is an exploration, not a definitive map.

It is a pleasure to thank all those who made research and writing possible. Thanks are due to the Hebrew University of Jerusalem and the Anglo-Israel Association for generous scholarships, and to H. Silver for help in need; also to R. Carr, the Social Science Research Council and

PREFACE

Merton College, Oxford, for assistance with research expenditure. St Antony's College, Oxford, provided a congenial and stimulating environment for research. Most of the text was written while I was a Junior Research Fellow at Merton College, where the Warden and Fellows made me very welcome and comfortable. The final revision was influenced by the suggestions and ideas of students and colleagues at the University of York.

Among individuals, I would like to thank my parents first. Members of the History Department at the Hebrew University of Jerusalem, and particularly Y. Arieli, Y. Elkana, J. L. Talmon and J. M. Winter, initiated me into their discipline. At Oxford, P. Mathias supervised the early stages of research, and has been an unfailing source of encouragement and wise advice. F. M. L. Thompson supervised the later stages, and his influence will be evident throughout. Many friends and obliging scholars have commented on early drafts. They include S. Cretney, H. Ergas, R. M. Hartwell, S. Mendelson, K. O. Morgan, R. Samuel and the *History Workshop* collective, S. Volkov, P. J. Waller, J. M. Winter, M. Zimmeck and (as thesis examiners) T. C. Barker and Lord Briggs. E. W. Cooney and P. Solar have generously and assiduously read through the final draft. I have also derived much benefit from discussions of my papers at seminars at Oxford, London, Leicester, Warwick, Kent and York, and even more from innumerable informal conversations with friends and fellow-workers, especially D. Englander and the late R. Issacharoff. For unstinted assistance and advice I have to thank F. Bendall, J. Weddle, N. Eilan and M. Zimmeck. If I have failed to benefit fully from so much goodwill and good sense, the fault is mine alone. Finally, I am deeply grateful to Leah Offer for years of companionship and many kinds of support, and I wish to dedicate this book to her.

University of York   A.O.
July 1980

ACKNOWLEDGEMENTS

Ownership of copyright in unpublished documents cited or quoted in this book is gratefully acknowledged as follows: Beaverbrook Foundation and Mr A. J. P. Taylor (Lloyd George and Bonar Law papers at the House of Lords Record Office), British Library (Balfour and Halsbury papers), British Library of Political and Economic Science (Charles Booth and Webb collections), H. M. Land Registry (Statistical department Mss.), House of Lords Record Office (Herbert Samuel papers), Museum of English Rural Life, University of Reading (Central Land Association records), Newcastle University Library, the Trevelyan family and Dr Pauline Dower (Walter Runciman and C. P. Trevelyan papers at the Newcastle University Library), the Public Record Office (for various government papers quoted). Special thanks are due to the following custodians of records who also extended generous hospitality: Mrs G. Bence-Jones and Mr G. Pretyman (E. Pretyman press cuttings), Mr Francis Fortescue Brickdale (C. F. Brickdale papers), Mrs H. B. Pease (J. C. Wedgwood papers). For permission to cite and quote from dissertations I am obliged to Drs D. Englander, A. S. King, A. J. Peacock and D. H. Reeder. Copyright in text and illustrations is also acknowledged: Dr H. Pelling (fig. 17.4B), *Punch* (fig. 22.1), the Society of Authors (extracts from the plays of G. B. Shaw) and Prof. P. R. Thompson (fig. 17.4A). My sincere apologies to any owners of copyright in quoted material whom I have inadvertently overlooked or have failed to trace.

ABBREVIATIONS

Add   MSS British Library Additional Manuscripts
A.M.C.   Association of Municipal Corporations
AP   Asquith Papers
App.   Appendix
Auct. Inst.   Occasional paper read at the Auctioneers' Institute
BL   Bonar Law Papers
BP   Brickdale Papers
BLPES   British Library of Political and Economic Science at the
          London School of Economics
Bodl. Lib.   Bodleian Library
Booth   Charles Booth Papers at the BLPES
Brit. Lib.   British Library
CAB   Cabinet Papers (PRO)
C.C.A.   Central Chamber of Agriculture
CLA   Central Landowners' Association
Com.   Committee
CPT   Charles P. Trevelyan Papers
D.N.B.   *Dictionary of National Biography*
Econ. Hist. Rev.   *Economic History Review*
EG   *Estates Gazette*
incl.   including
GLC   Greater London Council Record Office
H.C. deb.   House of Commons debates
H.L. deb.   House of Lords debates
Hist. Journ.   *Historical Journal*
IR   Inland Revenue (PRO)
IRAR   Annual Report of HM Commissioners of Inland Revenue (in the
          P.P.)
Jnl. Econ. Hist.   *Journal of Economic History*
J.R.S.S.   *Journal of the Royal Statistical Society*
LAR   Land Registry (PRO)
L.C.C.   London County Council
LCO   Lord Chancellor's Office (PRO)

ABBREVIATIONS

Lond. Stat.   *London Statistics*
LG   Lloyd George Papers
Lib.   Liberal
LNS   Land Nationalisation Society
LPDL   Liberty and Property Defence League
LS   Incorporated Law Society
LSAR   Incorporated Law Society, *Annual Report*
LSPR   Incorporated Law Society, *Proceedings and Resolutions of the Annual Provincial Meeting*
L.S.E.   London School of Economics
LUJ   *Land Union Journal*
L.T.C.   Local Taxation Committee (C.C.A.)
Memo.   Memorandum
M.B.W.   Metropolitan Board of Works
Mun. Jnl.   *Municipal Journal*
n.p.   no pagination
POJ   *Property Owners' Journal*
P.P.   Parliamentary Papers.*
Pr.P.   Presented Papers (L.C.C.)
PRO   Public Record Office
S.D.   Standard deviation
SH   Small holdings
TLV   Taxation of Land Values
Trans. S.I.   *Transactions of the Surveyors' Institution*
UCTLV   United Committee for the Taxation of Land Values
Webb   Passfield collection at the BLPES
WL   Walter Long Papers
WP   J. C. Wedgwood Papers
WR   Walter Runciman Papers
WRO   Wiltshire Record Office (Walter Long Papers)
YP   Years Purchase

* Parliamentary debates and sessional papers are cited in the forms recommended by P. and G. Ford, *A guide to parliamentary papers* (3rd edn Shannon, 1972), pp. 71–3. Short titles have been used for sessional papers. All books published in London unless indicated otherwise. The term 'Radical' denotes adherence to philosophical radicalism and its political connection in the first four decades (or so) of the nineteenth century, and to the progressive wing of the Liberal party thereafter. The adjective 'radical' denotes a tendency to political extremes.

INTRODUCTION

I

> The first man who, having enclosed a piece of ground, bethought himself of saying *This is mine*, and found people simple enough to believe him, was the real founder of civil society.[1]

It is possible to imagine, like Rousseau, a world in which the disposal of land is free from strife. An assurance that land is humanity's common heritage continues to inspire social philosophers and social movements in the face of contrary realities. But the arrangements which govern the allocation of land to particular people (and people to particular parcels of land) are still among the most potent determinants of the character of social relations, economic activity and political power. What was true before the emergence of capitalist property in land remains true in socialist societies, where it has been abolished. Land remains a principal source of authority and inequality.

Another eighteenth-century writer advanced a forceful utilitarian justification of private property. Jeremy Bentham, in his *Principles of the civil code*, suggested that land was not the gift of God but the gift of the state. He professed to value equality, but unlike Rousseau, he also valued civilisation, and valued it more highly than equality. Property was the pre-condition of subsistence and of abundance, and inequality was a price that had to be paid. Unlike other English and Scottish writers, Bentham did not regard property as an absolute (or 'natural') right which had been acquired solely by individual labour. Property was a social construct which was only justified by expediency; what had been granted could be taken away. Although property was acquired by individuals, it depended upon the sanction of the law and the pleasure of the state. Moreover, possession was precarious, and depended upon the sovereign for protection. 'Law alone', he wrote, 'has been able to create a fixed and durable possession which deserves the name Property ... It

---

[1] J. J. Rousseau, 'A discourse on ... the origins of inequality', in *The social contract and discourses*, ed. and transl. G. D. H. Cole (Everyman's edn 1913), p. 207.

1

requires in the legislator vigilance constantly sustained and power always in action to defend it against his constantly reviving crowd of adversaries ... take away the laws, all property ceases'.[2]

One of the features of private property is its absolute nature: it confers an exclusive right to enjoy or dispose of the object without hindrance. But dependence upon the sovereign dents the perfection of ownership. Bentham observed that rights (including property rights), gave rise to obligations in a *reciprocal* relation.

Rights and obligations, though distinct and opposite in their nature, are simultaneous in their origin, and inseparable in their existence. According to the nature of things, the law cannot grant a benefit to any, without, at the same time, imposing a burden on some one else;[3]

The relation is reciprocal because obligations will generate rights. For example, it follows from the foregoing that owners of property incur an obligation to the legislator, the judge and the lawyer, who safeguard possession. On the reciprocal principle these obligations are transmuted into rights, property rights, vested in the personnel of the law and the state. 'Wealth', wrote Bentham, 'can only be defended at its own expense',[4] and owners are obliged to dilute their sovereignty in favour of officials and lawyers. Landed wealth is especially vulnerable, owing to its visibility, immobility and durability.

A legal guarantee of possession is not sufficient. It must be possible to realise rights and exchange them in a market. So land agents, surveyors, attorneys and other market middlemen also acquire a vested interest in landed property. 'Transaction costs' are like sand in the gears of perfect exchange. They eat into ownership and aggregate into a middleman's interest, which takes on the attributes of a species of property.

A further imperfection of property is imposed by politics. Victorian England was governed by a hierarchy of proprietors. Social standing and political authority were associated with wealth and landed property attracted special esteem. But the corollary of esteem is envy, and the maintenance of landowners and capitalists in dominance entailed a levy on property commensurate with the challenges from within and without. Domestic discontent and foreign powers had to be appeased, bought off or fought off.

[2]J. Bentham, 'Principles of the civil code', *The works of Jeremy Bentham* Bowring edn (1838–43), i, 307, 309.
[3]*Ibid.* 301.
[4]*Ibid.* 313.

Now Bentham's reciprocity principle assumes a conservation (or 'zero-sum') rule, namely that rights lost to one set of proprietors will accrue to another. Without pressing this notion too far, it is clear that the erosion of property rights gives rise to new ones in the process of social, economic and political change. This historical redistribution of property rights between individuals and groups is the main theme of this book. It reveals an unfamiliar view of the transition from a narrow plutocracy to bureaucratic liberal welfare capitalism in Britain before the Great War. The attenuation and emergence of property rights in the nineteenth century was not highly visible, but it was a central mode of internal change, and continued to affect British society into the inter-war years and beyond.

Without thereby embracing its ethical premises and social overtones, Bentham's conception of property must be acknowledged as a good approximation to the dominant assumptions and practice of nineteenth-century English society and it is still serviceable today. But the history of property has also been shaped by the persistence of the collective claim from natural law to which Rousseau gave such powerful vent. Land is the gift of God, and landed property did not enjoy the same legitimacy as property acquired by labour. This idea has been cultivated by a succession of writers, from Thomas Spence, who first published his views in 1775 and acquired a numerous following in the early nineteenth century, through Ogilvie, Paine, Godwin, Dove, J. S. Mill and A. R. Wallace.[5] The doctrine has never been relinquished in the British Radical tradition. It permeated Liberal party politics in the late-Victorian period and was taken up in due course by the Labour party. In David Lloyd George's melodramatic populist campaigns of 1909–14, the Benthamite process of a gradual re-allocation of rights was subjected to a sharp dose of Rousseau's re-distributive prescription.

A third conception of property also pervaded the Victorian scene. Bentham had called it, sarcastically, 'matchless constitution' – referring to the majestic self-image of the English *ancien régime* with its conception of an organic, slowly evolving, hierarchical unity, as expounded by Blackstone and Burke. Unlike Bentham's and Rousseau's radical models, this was not a theory, but a set of institutions and a code of practices, attitudes and habits. It was embodied in the laws of landed inheritance and transfer, and defined, interpreted and enforced by lawyers and the courts. It underlay the living culture of landed society. Natural rights, the

[5]M. Beer, *A history of British socialism* (1940 edn), i, 106–23, ii, 237–45.

utilitarian approach and the aristocratic-legal tradition – these three conceptions of property animated the protagonists who debated the English 'land question' between the 1870s and the Great War. In the background was a secular depression in agriculture, the painful expansion of towns, and the growth of urban forms of landed property. The notion of a 'land question' belongs to the vocabulary of political Liberalism. In order to make sense of its manifold historical manifestations, it is necessary to identify and examine the legal and economic structures, the interests, pressure groups, personalities, attitudes and ideas that made up the universe of landed and urban property.

II

A welter of landed property tenures and interests existed in England at the end of the nineteenth century. They may be sorted out into a number of distinct clusters. Each cluster shared similar legally defined and sanctioned property rights; each deployed distinctive methods of appropriation; each had a characteristic social distribution and gave rise to organisations, pressure-groups and lobbies; each cultivated typical sets of attitudes and values. Ignoring for the moment many finer distinctions and areas of overlap, the main clusters fell under the following heads. (a) Property practitioners, a professional and quasi-professional corps of auctioneers, surveyors, estate agents and solicitors who mediated between other interests and primed the property markets. (b) Freehold groundowners, dominated by corporate bodies, the aristocracy and the wealthy. (c) Entrepreneurial freeholders and leaseholders, mainly builders, house-landlords, rentiers, retailers, farmers and manufacturers. (d) Middle-class mortgagees, lending directly or through solicitors, insurance companies and building societies. (e) Occupiers of dwellings (and consumers of rent-intensive coal, transport, food and beer). (f) 'The guardians of the state' (Bentham) – the agents of the law, and of local and imperial government.

Property relations make up much of the texture of everyday life and lend themselves to artful evocation. But this aspect of the study is subordinated to the task of establishing structural outlines: who owned, how exclusively and how much, in terms of broad tenurial subgroups and measured in money. It is a study of distribution, not production. The intangibles of tenure will also be considered and its structures, subdivisions and significations will be invoked to clarify the course of

4

English politics from the 1870s (and in some cases, earlier) until the Great War. Tenurial clusters interpenetrated and interacted. In response to the cyclical pressures of the regional, national and global economy they generated social tensions and political antagonism. A tenurial thread ran through all the great domestic questions of late-Victorian England: agriculture, industry and employment, education and religion, social welfare, urbanisation and defence. As the clouds gathered in Edwardian skies tenurial contention created much of the thunder. We shall try to place these contentions in a longer perspective. Political paradigms which emerged in the 1880s ran their course within this period, which is long enough to observe two political generations grappling with similar problems. It also spans almost two of the nineteenth-century's long cycles of urban development.

'Property' may be defined as a bundle of rights, comprising of claims enforcible in law. Both Roman law and English common law set land apart as a superior prototype of property, in acknowledgement of its primacy among the assets of agrarian societies. Let us define *tenure* to signify such property rights as pertain to land, minerals and buildings, following the lay construction of the term. Tenure, then, is any claim on land, buildings or minerals. It may be exercised directly by physical or legal occupation, or indirectly as a charge or an expectation in money, labour or kind (corresponding to the legal distinction between 'corporeal' and 'incorporeal' assets).[6] Two qualities mark it out. First, tenure is a pre-condition of physical and moral subsistence. It implies a degree of autonomy, however limited. Regulating access to shelter and food, tenure is rooted in human needs: agricultural landlessness and urban overcrowding likewise proclaim its denial. It makes a convenient instrument of exploitation and control.

Secondly, the objects of tenure are marked off from other forms of property by their rigid and substantial character. The stock of land and buildings cannot be rapidly expanded or reproduced and the extent of the surface is fixed. Lawyers acknowledge this demarcation in the distinction between 'immoveable' and moveable assets (or in English usage, between 'real' and 'personal' property). Before the onset of machine industry tenurial rights made up the bulk of nations' assets. If this was no longer true of late-Victorian Britain, contemporary estimates still

[6] A manor, right of way, a rent-charge or an advowson (the right to present to a church living) are examples of 'incorporeal' tenure. See G. W. C. Paton, *A textbook of jurisprudence* (4th edn 1972), ed. G. W. Paton and D. Denham, ch. XXI. C. R. Noyes, *The institution of property* (New York, 1936) is exhaustive.

assigned more than forty per cent of the national wealth to land and buildings in 1885, and a third in 1912.[7]

The cluster of property rights that we have designated 'tenure' does not constitute an arbitrary category. It was deeply embedded in social and political institutions, and was most clearly demarcated in two realms: the legal and the fiscal. The category of 'real property' (or 'realty') led an independent legal existence with its own peculiar modes of possession, inheritance and transfer.[8] Other, overlapping, operational definitions of tenure were provided by the income tax assessment schedule A ('lands, houses and messuages') and by local government's categories of 'rateable property'.[9] The fiscal and legal systems underscored the distinctiveness of tenurial property rights, kept tenurial categories in currency and broadcast them into the farthest reaches of the polity, mentality and morality of a peculiarly property-conscious society.

Units of tenure are often more durable than bricks and mortar and are constantly transferred as people inherit, marry and move; they are bought, sold and disputed. The ubiquity of tenure presents serious problems of measurement. Formal tenures are not all-pervasive and leave gaps where assets are not explicitly and unambiguously owned. Rooms in a household, for example, are allotted informally and costly benefits like roads and parks are nominally free. Even where tenurial arrangements are explicit they are seldom exclusive or absolute, i.e. vested unconditionally in a single proprietor. Some assets, including village greens and national territories, are held on communal tenures and their disposal is determined by custom or *ad hoc* in law courts, Cabinets, and ultimately, battlefields. The 'imperfection' or 'attenuation' of tenures is one of their fundamental attributes, which arises, as Bentham observed, from the very nature of private property. Some of the more exclusive forms of private property were less perfect than they seemed; and some of the peripheral interests sufficiently tenacious to merit description as property rights.

An example of imperfect but nonetheless real tenure is provided by the relation between the legal professions and the law of property. Part I of the book explores the nature of this tenure; it describes how the state, impelled by landowners and capitalists, attempted to take it over; how it

---

[7] P. Deane and W. A. Cole, *British economic growth 1688–1959* (2nd edn Cambridge, 1967), tables 70, 71, pp. 271, 274.

[8] J. Williams, *Principles of the law of real property*, ed. T. C. Williams (18th edn 1896), pp. 1–35.

[9] J. Stamp, *British incomes and property* (1920 edn), chs. I–IV.

6

failed to do so, and why. Part II is a new survey of the main tenure clusters, with quantitative estimates largely drawn from death-duty returns between 1896 and 1914. It depicts the hierachies of tenure and derives political implications from their relative magnitudes. Part III describes an outline of tenurial politics between 1850 and 1902. Tenurial animosities found an outlet in the rigid doctrines which the Tories and Liberals adopted about the ends and means of local taxation. Municipal enterprise emerged as a creative and combative tenurial presence towards the close of this period. Part IV remains with this theme, and describes the linked Edwardian crises of urban property and municipal finance. Part V probes some cultural sources of tenurial attitudes and takes tenurial politics up to their climax in 1914.

Part I

LAW AS PROPERTY –
SOLICITORS, THE LAND
MARKET AND LEGAL REFORM

1

SOLICITORS: PROFILE
OF A PROFESSION

I

'Property and law are born and must die together', wrote Bentham. 'Before the laws, there was no property: take away the laws, all property ceases'.[1] The organs of the law are symbiotic with property. Of the two branches of the legal profession in England, the solicitors combined a commercial function with their legal role. They were inextricably intertwined into the cluster of property middlemen. Their fees and commissions constituted a permanent rent-charge on the value of land and buildings. The Law of Property may be regarded as another rent-charge, an 'overhead' liability of private property.

The solicitor is a vaguely familiar figure, hovering on the margin of the Victorian visual field. Dickens' novels abound with lawyers but no single stereotype predominates. Alongside the honourable Mr Wickfield stands the abominable Uriah Heep. John Galsworthy drew a memorable portrait of Soames Forsyte, the 'Man of Property', occupying a comfortable and confident universe. A. J. P. Taylor has demoted solicitors into the 'other ranks' of the law in order to enhance the achievement of his hero, David Lloyd George, who emerged from a small-town Welsh practice,[2] but they are more properly regarded as junior officers, subordinate to the Generals of the Bench and the Colonels of the Bar. Another populist politician, Clement Attlee, grew up in the more substantial surroundings of a London solicitor's household.[3] 'By the Edwardian era no one better symbolized the prosperity and respectability of middle-class England than the family solicitor', write two recent historians of the profession.[4] But this veneer of respectability belied some sordid realities. The prosperity of the top echelon of Edwardian lawyers obscured the declining economic position of the profession as a whole. As we shall see, it

[1] Bentham, 'Civil code', Bowring edn, i, 309.
[2] A. J. P. Taylor, 'Lloyd George: rise and fall' in *Essays in English history*, Penguin edn (1976), p. 255.
[3] C. R. Attlee, *As it happened* (1954), pp. 1–4.
[4] B. Abel-Smith and R. Stevens, *Lawyers and the courts* (1967), p. 128.

11

concealed widening inequalities, unfulfilled aspirations, exploitation, anxiety and fears.

Almost sixteen thousand solicitors were active in England and Wales in 1900, of whom more than a third could be found in London, within ten miles of the Central Post Office.[5] The great majority, in London and elsewhere, practised alone or in small partnerships and only knew a limited world of small-time conveyancing, probate, trusts and litigation.[6] London offered a certain scope for specialisation. Earlier in the nineteenth century railway bills had been a great source of income and Parliamentary work remained highly lucrative.[7] Local authorities alone spent about £650,000 a year around the turn of the century in promoting and opposing private legislation, most of it on legal fees.[8] The High Courts attracted remunerative litigation and the City offered commercial work and gave rise to great diversified firms like Freshfield's, which still exists. A few City practitioners specialised in company promotion,[9] while others served the landed aristocracy. Christopher Haedy was chief agent to the Dukes of Bedford, Henry Trelawney Boodle to the Duke of Westminster, Pollock and Co. acted for successive Lords Middleton and Currey's for the Duke of Devonshire.[10] Baxter, Rose, Norton and Co. was one of the largest firms which specialised in election agency. One of the partners, R. Dudley Baxter, was a notable economist and helped to formulate Conservative economic policy and its principal, Sir Philip Rose, administered the business of the Conservative party together with Disraeli's private affairs.[11] At the other end of the social scale, slum lawyers touted among the undefended poor in the police-courts and

[5]15,948 practising certificates. *IRAR* (1900), 71. Ratio of Londoners estimated from the *Law list*.
[6]BLPES, Webb Professional Collection Misc. 248 (henceforth Webb Prof.) IV/4, E. B. V. Christian to S. Webb, 17 Dec. 1915 (this source is discussed below, p. 13); Abel-Smith and Stevens, *Lawyers* (1967), p. 210 and references to experience in advertisements in the Law Society *Registry* (see pp. 15–18).
[7]M. Birks, *Gentlemen of the law* (1960), p. 240.
[8]PRO 30/72/20, Association of Municipal Corporations Minutes and Records (1901), pp. 8, 36–7.
[9]J. W. Reid, 'On the formation of limited companies', *LSPR* 25, (1898), 66–73. Also Webb Prof. IV/4, W. R. Southeard to S. Webb, 21 Jan. 1916, fols 67, 70.
[10]Haedy, see D. Spring, *The English landed estate in the nineteenth century* (Baltimore, 1963), pp. 68–78; Boodle – F. Banfield, *The great landlords of London* (1890), p. 53; Pollock – National Register of Archives, Middleton 7428(IV); Currey – Dr D. Cannadine (oral information).
[11]Baxter, see p. 164. Rose – H. J. Hanham, *Elections and party management* (1959), pp. 244, 357; R. Blake, *Disraeli* (1966), *passim and idem. The Conservative party from Peel to Churchill*, Fontana edn (1972), p. 141.

prowled hospital wards in the hope of persuading injured persons to sue for damages.[12]

Beatrice and Sidney Webb began to collect evidence for a study of the professions in 1914 and a short typescript monograph on lawyers, written in 1915, survives in their papers. It gives a vivid description of stratification in the solicitors' branch.

> The most profitable businesses in the profession are believed to divide among their four or five partners as much as £20,000 or £30,000 a year but these are quite exceptional. The number of London solicitors making, for each partner, as much as £1,000 a year, is believed to be (out of some 5,000 on the roll) not more than a few hundred. In provincial practice, both the usual income and the highest point reached, are considerably lower; though the old established and reputable firms in the principal cities and in the old county centres, by whom nearly all the local appointments are monopolised, still do very well. On the other hand, both in London and the provinces a large number of solicitors become clerks to more prosperous firms, often accepting salaries of £150 a year and even less. The long years of waiting for a sufficiency of clients often constitute a horrible torment: in some cases a demoralizing one, leading to habits of intemperance. Every large provincial city has its small group of solicitors who have failed to come through, and who drag on a disreputable existence ...
>
> [They] often combine with their work the practice of agency for life and fire insurance offices; collect rents, debts on commission; they do some of the work of the public accountant, and occasionally act as house agents and auctioneers ...
>
> [They] frequently hold part-time appointments as secretaries of companies, political agents and managers of property.[13]

Low as a solicitor might fall, he was still separated from the vast majority of black-coated workers by a barrier which could not be surmounted without a large outlay of capital and time. To gain admission as an articled clerk the candidate had to pay a premium of up to £300 to a practitioner, and a stamp duty of £80. Five years of unpaid and often unenlightening apprenticeship then followed. 'The document [of

---

[12] Booth B152 (notes on inquiries about legal occupations in London by G. H. Duckworth), interview with George W. Lay, police and county-court solicitor, 20 Dec. 1895; *POJ*, May 1910, 3.

[13] Webb Prof. XVIII. S. Webb, 'The Organisation of the Legal Profession' (?1915), fols 91–2.

articles] read to me like a sentence of penal servitude', remembered one practitioner; 'a sentence to five years copying out drafts', recalled another.[14] In an interview with one of Charles Booth's assistants, George Lay, a City solicitor, estimated that five years of board and lodgings, books, lectures and examination and admission fees cost at least £700 (more than twice the average value of a working-class house and more than ten times the annual income of a family on the poverty line).[15] One of the Webbs' informants in 1915 put the cost of training at fully £1,000.[16] Men were known by George Lay to have spent £500 on crammers and coaching. Very few passed the final examinations by the age of twenty-one years and Lay himself 'never earned a penny until he was 24'.[17]

Education made another effective social barrier. All candidates for articles (graduates excepted) were made to take a 'Preliminary' examination before proceeding to the 'Intermediate' and 'Final' vocational examinations (taken in mid-apprenticeship and at its end, respectively). 'Prelim' papers covered English composition, algebra, geography, history, Latin and two additional languages. When it was introduced by the Law Society in 1860 one gate was left open for aspirants lacking the requisite polish. Solicitors had sometimes granted articles to long-serving clerks; Uriah Heep had probably climbed by this route. Dispensations for 'ten-year men' (as they were known) were placed in the gift of the Lord Chief Justice and the Master of the Rolls.[18] They were not highly regarded. 'Like men promoted from the rank among soldiers', said George Lay, they 'become the worst of solicitors'.[19] 'They lack education and breeding of the ordinary articled clerk, as well as the needful money and influence', wrote James Dodd, one of the Webbs' correspondents.[20] The Law Society persistently sought to plug this loophole and the number of dispensations was reduced to a trickle in the 1900s.[21]

[14]Premium – Booth B152, Duckworth interviews with F. Higgs (solicitor's clerk), and G. Lay, Dec. 1895, fols 6, 76; Webb Prof. IV/4, James J. Dodd to B. Webb, 18 March 1914, fol. 4. 'The document ...' – M. Letts, *The old house: A generation of lawyers* (1942), p. 49. 'a sentence' – R. Maclean, *Diversions of an articled clerk* (1892), p. 3 (complaint of a 'fellow apprentice').
[15]Booth B152, G. Duckworth, Dec. 1895, fol. 76.
[16]Webb Prof. IV/4, J. G. Godard to S. Webb, 23 Dec. 1915, fol. 34.
[17]Booth B152, fol. 74.
[18]The Solicitors' Act 1860 (23 and 24 Vict. c. 127, s. 4) and 1877 (40 and 41 Vict. c. 25, s. 11).
[19]Booth B152, fol. 78.
[20]Webb Prof. IV/4, 18 March 1914, fol. 4.
[21]LS, *Report by the examination committee* ... (1904), p. 49. 'Ten year men' fell from some twenty a year in the early 1880s to 4–12 a year between 1900 and 1907. See *LSAR* (1904), 68 and (1908), 84.

Returns commensurate with this costly training were by no means certain. Openings were limited and in order to gain experience and contacts clerks would sometimes continue to work unpaid even after the end of their training. A long time might elapse between the final examination and the issue of a practising certificate. Some solicitors found it difficult to raise £9 yearly for the practising licence (less in the provinces and the first three years). Admitted but uncertified clerks formed a large 'reserve army' of as many as two thousand in London alone.[22] A beginner employed in another solicitor's office could expect £100–£120 a year at the age of twenty-five. 'Domestic servants, a fee paying education for the children, the necessary standard of dress, housing, furniture and entertaining could not be procured on a salary of less than £200 per annum', writes F. Musgrove on the authority of the *Cornhill Magazine* of May 1901. 'This figure must be regarded as the bare minimum necessary to maintain a middle middle-class way of life'.[23] A salaried solicitor could only hope to touch this threshold at the peak of his trajectory between the ages of thirty and thirty-five years (see fig. 1.1). An experienced managing clerk rarely earned more than £200 and many older solicitors had to subsist on £130–£160.

Practitioners often plunged prematurely into independence. The Law clerks' monthly magazine described how 'large numbers of men without money or prospects become solicitors carrying on some small apology for a practice in a tumble-down office, the rent of which they have a constant struggle to meet'.[24] A well-informed observer wrote in 1896, 'the utmost that a solicitor can possibly hope to achieve is a competence; not all solicitors do this; few become rich and extremely few become rich as a result of professional exertions alone'.[25] A member of the Law Society council said in 1892 that the average income of solicitors did not amount to £200 a year and at the 1900 meeting of the Solicitors' Benevolent Association Henry Attlee, father of the future Prime Minister, said that 'He had made some inquiries some years ago as to the average income of solicitors on the Rolls, and had been astonished to find that it could not be put higher than £300 a year. In fact a much lower sum would

[22]See LS *Registry* (a monthly advertising publication), July 1906, 576F; July 1909, 209F, 1988F, 1994F, 1999F (advertisement nos); Webb Prof. IV/4, J. Dodd to S. Webb, 18 March 1914; PRO T 172/950, 1893; J. W. Reid, 'Professional problems', LSPR 33 (1908), 237; Leader, *Law clerk and municipal assistant*, June 1912, 25.
[23]F. Musgrove, 'Middle-class education and employment in the nineteenth century', *Econ. Hist. Rev.* 2nd ser. 12 (1959), 100.
[24]Leader, *Law Clerk*, Oct. 1909, 121.
[25]E. B. V. Christian, *A short history of solicitors* (1896), p. 231.

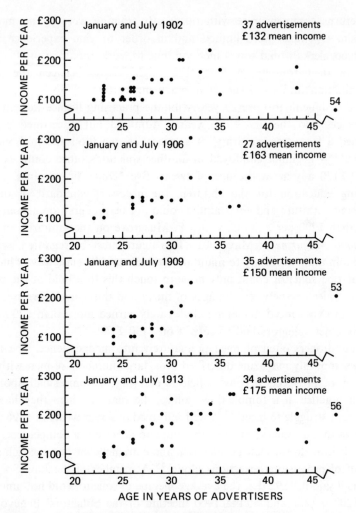

Fig. 1.1. *Desired annual salary and age of solicitors seeking employment through advertisements in the 'F' register, Law Society* Registry; *selected months, 1902, 1906, 1909 and 1913.*

probably represent that income'.[26] James Dodd wrote to the Webbs in 1914 that

It takes a good many six-and-eightpences to pay expenses and build up a livelihood and solicitors' incomes fluctuate from year to year. Those who succeed to rich practices, or have the command of

[26]R. G. Lawson, 'The profession and public opinion', *LSPR* 29 (1903), 215.

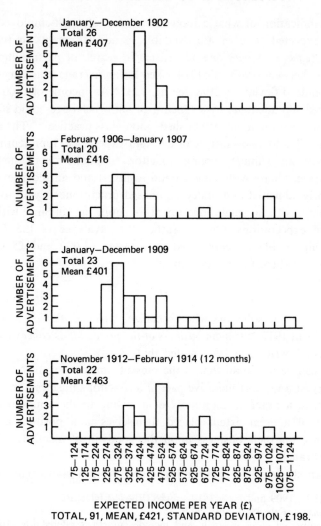

Fig. 1.2. *Advertising for partnerships and practices in the Law Society* Registry, *1902–14: distribution of incomes sought.*

money to lend have no reason to complain, but the average income of the ordinary solicitor cannot be very much above £250 a year. Many are glad to take managing clerkships at £100 a year, and others, becoming despondent at the horribly long wait for clients, turn their attention to mercantile or literary pursuits.[27]

[27]Webb Prof. IV/4, 18 March 1914, fol. 5.

17

Some indication of what a moderately successful self-employed practitioner expected to earn are available in advertisements in the Law Society *Registry*. Ninety-one advertisers in search of partnerships over four years between 1902 and 1914 asked for an average yearly income of £421 (standard deviation £198; see fig. 1.2).[28] An income of £500 a year was considered adequate by a solicitor of self-proclaimed 'good standing and social position' in an 'established, good-class practice'.[29] The advertisements fall into two clusters of age and experience, representing two archetypes: an affluent, young solicitor, a public-school man and University graduate with some capital to invest and an older, experienced, poorly educated and under-capitalised practitioner trying to join a partnership with a small investment or none at all and with very moderate expectations. On the rather thin evidence of the *Registry* partnerships could be capitalised at between £1,000 and £5,000, the equivalent of three to ten years' profits.[30]

II

'Except for a few solicitors who specialize', wrote E. B. V. Christian to the Webbs in 1915, '*the main business of the profession is conveyancing*'.[31] 'A Barrister', writing in 1902, stated that,

> There can be no doubt that at the present time conveyancing forms the largest and most lucrative part of a solicitor's business, and that they have a practical monopoly of it, owing to the senior branch having to a great extent placed themselves in a position of dependence for their business upon the goodwill of members of the lower branch.[32]

A modern study of the eighteenth-century attorney states that 'perhaps

[28]1902, 1906, 1909 and Nov. 1912 – Feb. 1914 (12 months).
[29]LS *Registry*, Feb. 1902, adv. 765F.
[30]The number of cases is small, and includes practices offered for £160, £350 (*Registry*, May 1913, 283E2 and July 1906, 313E2) and larger sums ranging up to £1000. Advertising in the *Registry* was regarded as somewhat disreputable within such a close-knit profession; see 'Prospects in the professions. III. The solicitor', *Cornhill Magazine*, new ser. no. 77, (Nov. 1902), 649. S. Webb valued goodwill at up to six years' purchase but E. B. V. Christian, a contemporary historian of the profession 'never heard of more than 2 or 3 years' purchase of a solicitors' practice except for the big Lincoln's Inn firms'. Webb Prof. IV/4, Christian to Webb, 24 Jan. 1916, fol. 53 and B. H. Drake (another solicitor) to Webb, 19 Jan. 1916, fol. 59.
[31]Webb Prof. IV/4, 17 Dec. 1915, fol. 13. Italics added.
[32]A barrister, *Lawyers and their clients* (1902), pp. 71–2.

the greatest single source of business and profit was his concern with landed property, and all the problems it involved'.[33] A heavy reliance on land and house transfers continues unbroken to this day.[34] Indeed, upholders of conveyancing profitability describe it as vital to the survival of a private legal service outside the metropolis.[35] In 1968 the Prices and Incomes Board found that 55.6 per cent of solicitors' incomes were directly attributable to conveyancing.[36]

A legal maxim states that 'possession is nine-tenths of title'. Many years of undisturbed occupation may pass without any call for legal expertise. It is only when property is released for sale, lease or succession that the owner is placed in the hands of the lawyer, and the latter comes into his own. The official lawyers' monopoly of conveyancing came about almost inadvertently, as a consequence of the mounting fiscal pressure created by Britain's eighteenth-century wars. William Pitt the younger imposed an annual licence duty on attorneys in 1785. Stamp duties were later imposed on articles and on admission certificates. In 1804 the annual duty was doubled to £10 and in order to enforce it, the licence was made a condition of preparing a deed relating to personal or real property, with a penalty of £50.[37]

The monopoly provided lawyers with an indispensable and remunerative role in the management of landed and urban society and was much more valuable to the profession than the sum of transfer fees. In a notoriously imperfect market it gave them privileged access to current information on property values and placed them in an ideal position to serve as brokers between buyers, sellers, auctioneers and surveyors, builders and financiers. As entrepreneurs, mortgage brokers, trustees, executors and property managers they operated in the market on their own account. In local government their contacts were both a lever for election and appointment, and an inducement to put official positions to

---

[33]R. Robson, *The attorney in eighteenth-century England* (Cambridge, 1959), p. 54.

[34]'[Land transfer] now forms the chief occupation of the great body of solicitors ...', N. T. Lawrence, *Facts and suggestions as to the law of real property* (1879; presidential address, Incorporated Law Society). Also Birks, *Gentlemen of the law*, (1960) p. 279 and Abel-Smith and Stevens, *Lawyers* (1967), p. 47.

[35]See H. Kirk, *Portrait of a profession: a history of the solicitor's profession 1100 to the present day* (1976), pp. 144–54.

[36]National board for prices and incomes, report no. 54. Remuneration of solicitors; P.P. 1967–8 Cmnd 3529 XXVII, table 15, p. 49.

[37]Kirk, *Portrait of a profession*, (1976) pp. 128–30.

good use.[38] Town clerkships were practically a professional preserve and solicitors were prominent among occupational groups on municipal councils.[39]

Some fifty thousand subalterns and subordinates were employed in legal occupations in salaried and weekly positions. Together with their dependants and those of the qualified professionals (with whom they slightly overlapped) approximately three hundred thousand people derived a livelihood from the law in the Edwardian period.[40] The mechanics of land transfer were largely in the hands of clerks. Conveyancing and managing clerks ran the offices and the principals concentrated on meeting clients and attracting business.[41] James Dodd, in a letter to the Webbs, has left a description of the pay and prospects of the clerical proletariat, c. 1914.

A very rough computation allows two and a half clerks to every practising solicitor, but this includes office boys and typists. The need for typewriting has introduced girls into solicitors' offices, but it is rare for any of them to rise out of their grading, nor are they ever seen at the Courts, not even in routine work that juniors are entrusted with. They come into the office already trained, and earn from 12/- to 25/- a week, but only those who are quick at shorthand can hope ever to earn more than 15/- a week, out of which there are travelling and luncheon expenses to be paid. Solicitors' clerks must start as office boys if they are to be of any use. They begin at six shillings a week, and if they have grit enough to learn shorthand they can speedily get up to twelve shillings. But there are many to whom shorthand seems impossible, and they are lucky if they are earning eighteen shillings by the time they are 21, and twenty-five shillings at 30. Beyond this it is difficult for them to go. In large offices, where there are half-a-dozen partners, the prospects are brighter. The boys become juniors and sometimes managers, and

---

[38]In London, see D. A. Reeder, 'Capital Investment in the Western Suburbs of Victorian London' (Leicester Univ. Ph.D. thesis, 1965), pp. 202–13, 246–51. C. Fenby, *The other Oxford* (1970) describes a web of legal practice, property development and local politics in pre-war Oxford. R. Jefferies, *Hodge and his masters* (new edn 1890), ch. XVI portrays the country solicitor.

[39]See Lawson, 'The profession and public opinion' *LSPR* 29 (1903), 200. In 1902 solicitors were 11.1 per cent of the Birmingham City Council and 6.1 per cent of Leeds City Council. In 1912 the figures were 14.2 and 12.5 per cent respectively (E. P. Hennock, *Fit and proper persons* (1973), p. 44, 206).

[40]See C. H. Feinstein, *National income, expenditure and output of the United Kingdom, 1855–1965* (Cambridge, 1972), table 7.18, p. 173.

[41]Christian, *Short history* (1896), p. 94. 'Accustomed to work without supervision' was a recurrent formula used by clerks advertising for positions.

managing clerks get from £150 a year up to £350. It is doubtful however if there are more than 500 managing clerks in England earning £200 a year ... A solicitors' clerk with no aptitude is a blind-alley employment – it leads to nothing but disaster in the event of dismissal, for it is the practice in all large offices to promote the juniors rather than take in from outside clerks who have been dismissed ...'[42]

'The factories of the law are noiseless', wrote George Duckworth in the legal section of Charles Booth's survey of London labour in the 1890s. Most legal documents were still copied by hand on paper or vellum by professional law-writers (or 'engrossers') who were paid just over a penny for copying a 'folio' of seventy-two words. They belonged to a skilled trade and served an apprenticeship of five to seven years. One or two could be found in a large solicitors' office but as a class they were employed in the premises of sub-contracting 'Law Stationers'. Work was very seasonal but a good copier could average £2 a week, a good skilled wage, the whole year round. Final copy was produced with an energy and urgency quite markedly in contrast with the dilatory shuffling of deeds between vendor's and purchaser's solicitors. Drafts were sent out in the evening and solicitors expected to receive them copied out the following morning. Long hours were kept and Sunday work was usual, but the fluctuations of business still left room for a sizeable fringe of casual workers, 'known as "the trade", whose life and habits it would require a Dickens to describe'. Supplied with work by middleman 'office keepers' who also let desks, ink, fire and lighting, the 'sitters' were trained men who had fallen out of regular work from a dislike of tedium or the effects of drink. Below them came the 'wallers' who had not served their time but had managed to acquire the skill. 'If wanted they are to be found leaning against the street wall (whence their name) or at the "iron office", as one of the lamp posts in Cursitor Street is known.'

> ... at midnight those men may be found writing away though almost dropping with sleep. One man complained that he had several times broken his glasses, and once almost put out his eye with his pen, through falling asleep while writing in the small hours of the morning. While working, the men drink, and many of them have a bottle of liquid refreshment on the floor beneath their seats ...[43]

[42] J. Dodd to B. Webb, 18 Jan. 1914, Webb Prof. IV/4, fols 11–12.
[43] G. H. Duckworth, 'Law' in C. Booth et al. Life and labour of the people in London (1903), 2nd ser: Industry, iv, 72–8.

A small group of women in 'the trade' only trained for six months or a year, and were accused of undercutting rates by the men. They appeared a poor lot to Duckworth, 'very short, spectacled and bent'.[44]

[44]Booth B152, G. H. Duckworth, interview with Joseph Brown, a 'waller', Dec. 1895, fols 104, 114.

2

A BENTHAMITE PROJECT: LAND-LAW REFORM 1826-1870

I

A luxuriant late-Victorian land transfer industry flourished upon the fertile sub-soil of English land law. Private conveyancing held owners to ransom at their most vulnerable and imposed a heavy transaction cost, in both money and time, on the market for land. Reform was plainly overdue; the prospect hung like a cloud over the prosperity and prospects of the industry. An agitation had begun in the 1820s to bring the land laws into greater harmony with market rationality. It was a tributary of the great Victorian movement for legal, administrative and institutional reform foreshadowed in the writings of Bentham. But land law reform did not run true to type and developed as a distinct and symptomatic variant. By 1870 the main lines of reform had crystallised and the project was well under way; this early phase is described in this chapter.

The complicated mechanics of conveyancing account for its productive role in the legal economy. Procedures remained substantially unchanged during the first three-quarters of the nineteenth century. Title to real property could not be established positively but could only be inferred from the absence of adverse claims in the records of previous transactions. The vendor's solicitor prepared an abstract of all previous deeds which the purchaser's solicitor then scrutinised. Documentation was extensive and its perusal often inconclusive. Searches were protracted, and difficult cases were submitted to specialist barristers in the Temple and Lincoln's Inn. One of them, the mid-Victorian Lord Chancellor Westbury described the deeds as 'difficult to read, impossible to understand and disgusting to touch'.[1] A technically marketable title had to be clear for sixty years (forty after 1875); Joshua Williams, the Victorian conveyancing authority, speculated that the sixty-year rule had emerged to reflect the ordinary duration of human life.[2] Up to 1845 conveyances employed a legal fiction known as 'lease and release' but the simplified

[1] C. H. S. Fifoot, *Pollock and Maitland* (Glasgow, 1971), p. 15.
[2] Williams, *Real property* (1896) p. 555.

deed which replaced it was not noticeably shorter. Solicitors' fees, like those of the copyists, were determined by the length of the documents perused and drawn up and consequently deeds and abstracts were excessively padded with verbiage.[3] The process was harassing, costly and slow and had to be repeated on every sale, mortgage or lease. Nor did it furnish any guarantee of possession. Old deeds were easily suppressed or mislaid. 'Many titles', the Royal Commissioners on Real Property wrote in 1829, 'notwithstanding long enjoyment, are found unmarketable; and if, after tedious delays, the transaction is completed, the law expenses inevitably incurred sometimes amount to no inconsiderable proportion of the value of the property'.[4]

Two great divisions of the land law may be distinguished, the one covering 'transfer', the other 'enjoyment'.[5] Private conveyancing was only the warp of the legal web which enveloped the rights of property in land. The weft was made of elaborate provisions for the creation of tenures, trusts, mortgages and settlements of which the principle of primogeniture and the practice of strict settlement were the keystone. Like conveyancing, the creation of settlements lies well concealed behind a curtain of technicalities and the layman must tread warily among the 'obscure doctrines of seisin and tenure, which no practising lawyer really understands'.[6] The legal artifact of strict settlement had been devised in the seventeenth century and was meant to protect the territorial integrity of landed estates by vesting them in trustees, limiting inheritance to a life-tenancy of the eldest in the male line, restricting the life-tenant's powers of mortgage and sale, and providing for other members of the family from the fruits of the estate. It was habitually renewed every generation.[7]

'Strict settlement' is really a misnomer, since English law, by the 'rule against perpetuities', forbade any bequest extending more than twenty-one years beyond existing lives.[8] So settlements came up for review every generation or two and rigid entails did not exist. Joshua Williams has given a fine sketch of the practice.

> Although strict and continuous entails have long been virtually abolished, their remembrance seems to linger in many country places, where the notion of *heir land*, that must perpetually descend

[3] F. Pollock, *The land laws* (2nd edn 1887), pp. 103–5, 162–4.
[4] Real property. R. com. 1st rep.: P.P. 1829 (263) X, 41.   [5] *Ibid.* p. 6.
[6] C. Sweet, 'The land transfer acts', *Law Quarterly Review* 24 (Jan. 1908), 33.
[7] See e.g. Pollock, *Land laws*, pp. 108–25.
[8] Williams, *Real property*, p. 380.

from father to son, is still to be met with. It is needless to say that such a notion is quite incorrect. In families where the estates are kept up from one generation to another, settlements are made every few years for this purpose; thus in the event of a marriage, a life estate merely is given to the husband; the wife had allowance for pin-money during the marriage, and a rent-charge or annuity by way of jointure for her life, in case she should survive her husband. Subject to this jointure, and to the payment of such sums as may be agreed on for the portions of the daughters and younger sons of the marriage, *the eldest son who may be born of the marriage is made by the settlement tenant in tail*. In case of his decease without issue, it is provided that the second son, and then the third, should in like manner be tenant in tail; and so on to the others; and in default of sons, the estate is usually given to the daughters. By this means the estate is tied up till some tenant in tail attains the age of twenty-one years; when he is able with the consent of his father, who is tenant for life, to bar the entail with all the remainders. Dominion is thus again acquired over the property, which dominion is usually exercised in a re-settlement on the next generation; and thus the property is preserved in the family. Primogeniture, therefore, as it obtains among the landed gentry of England, is a *custom* only, and not a *right* [except in case of intestacy]; though there can be no doubt that the custom has originated in the right, which was enjoyed by the eldest son, as heir to his father, in those days when estates tail could not be barred.[9]

Legal intervention was required at frequent intervals and the practice bound the legal and landed interests in a special relationship. In return for this constant attendance, as one critic of the system saw it,

The family solicitor becomes a regular annuitant on the estate. It is he who holds the title deeds; he alone who understands the state of the property; and it is held by him by a species of customary tenure ... in seeking for a reason for this we find that the profession hold an influence over the minds of the people by reason of the cumbrous and mysterious nature of the system of which they are the exponents, without parallel, unless we except the influence at one time exercised by the Church.[10]

[9]*Ibid.* pp. 98–9.
[10]R. J. Abraham, *A popular explanation of the system of land registration under Lord Westbury's act*, 2nd edn (1864), pp. 2,3.

A welter of jointures, portions, mortgages, partial and contingent interests, diminished estate revenues and reduced even further the limited liquidity of land as a marketable asset.

Like an ill-fitting boot the web of property law combined protection with irritation. Tenurial arrangements, apparently, were sufficiently elastic to accomodate aristocratic requirements of continuity and flexibility and the lawyers who made up the Real Property Commission did not think the law required any substantial additions or alterations. In the manner of Blackstone, they regarded it 'as near to perfection as can be expected in any human institution'.[11] Families were preserved, yet there was always a sufficient supply of land in the market; but the law respecting *transfer* was admitted to be seriously defective, and the Commission devoted the whole of its first report to this question.[12] In the past the solution most commonly canvassed had been the official registration of property rights with a view to decreasing uncertainty and making conveyancing simple and public.

Abortive registries of deeds were established under Henry VIII in 1536; the conveyancing fiction of 'lease and release' had been devised by lawyers in order to evade the obligation to record land transfers on official rolls.[13] A general registry of deeds (the register of Sasines) was established in Scotland in 1607 and Sir Francis Bacon came close to establishing one in England. The question was frequently before Parliament in the seventeenth century and a law commission mooted registration under Sir Matthew Hale during Cromwell's protectorate. Registries of deeds were opened in the West, East and North Ridings of Yorkshire in 1703, 1708 and 1735 respectively and in Middlesex and Ireland in 1708.[14]

These registries contained copies or abstracts of all deeds and only registered deeds were binding. As the register was open to the public (or at least to lawyers) the danger of forgery and fraudulent concealment of documents was removed. Conveyancing was still carried out privately and disputes taken to Counsel or the courts. A novel and more radical principle began to emerge in the 1820s, although it was not fully

[11]Real property. R. com. 1st rep. 1829, 6. And see E. Spring, 'The settlement of land in nineteenth-century England', *American journal of legal history* 8 (1964), 209–23.
[12]Real property. R. com. 1st rep. 1829, 7.
[13]Pollock, *Land laws*, (1887) p. 103.
[14]G. W. Sanders, 'An historical account of the progress of registration in England so far as respects assurances of land', Registration and conveyancing. R. com. rep.; P.P. 1850 [1261] XXXII, 232–44.

developed until the 1850s. This was registration *of title*, not deeds. From a passive repository of deeds the registry would be transformed into a public office actively responsible for ascertaining, granting and certifying title in every transfer. Henceforth the 'historical' basis of title is abandoned and ownership becomes absolute. No retrospective investigations are ever required, registration providing sufficient proof of ownership.[15] Registration of title bore ominous implications for solicitors, since it threatened to deprive them of a creative (and lucrative) function and transfer it to a bureaucracy.

Land law became a dense thicket during the legislative holiday of the eighteenth century, making an ideal subject for the codifying predilections and prolific pen of Jeremy Bentham but even that indefatigable genius seems to have shrunk from the magnitude of the task. He considered the matter in a suppressed section of the *Introduction to the principles of morals and legislation* (1780) and in a manuscript completed in 1782 but not published until 1945.[16] Bentham expressed alarm at the discovery that every conveyance created, in effect, a new law and that the body of laws included, *inter alia*, all conveyances.[17] He sketched out an analysis designed to reduce this infinite multitude of laws to manageable categories, but abandoned the effort and turned his energies to constitutional and penal matters. In 1826 a Benthamite project of codification nevertheless saw the light. It was written by James Humphreys (d. 1830), a successful and respected conveyancing barrister who associated with Austin and other Benthamites. Previous legislative interferences had failed, he claimed, 'and the noxious weed has grown by pruning'.[18] Humphreys' code was inspired by the *Code Napoléon*. He proposed a drastic reduction in the number of tenures and a great simplification of the formulas of transfer. Conveyance was to be effected through a register of deeds which came close in its conception to registration of title.

Any suggestion that land law might fall short of perfection was bound to provoke indignation among conveyancers and sympathy among landowners. Pamphlets, counter-pamphlets, journal articles, books and private-member bills stoked a heated controversy. Humphrey's code was

---

[15] Registration of title. R. com. rep.; P.P. 1857 [2215] XXI.
[16] J. Bentham, *Of laws in general*, ed. H. L. A. Hart (1970), Appendix B, and pp. 176–82. See also Bentham, 'Civil code', *Works*, Bowring edn, i, Pt. II.
[17] Bentham, *Of laws in general*, pp. 177–80.
[18] J. Humphreys, *Observations on the actual state of the English laws of real property with the outlines of a code* (1826), p. 2. See W. A. J. Archbold, 'James Humphreys', *D.N.B.*

27

likened to a destructive earthquake and his election to the Bench of Lincoln's Inn was successfully opposed.[19] In February 1828 the government announced its intention to appoint a commission of inquiry into the law of real property. Despite pleas from Henry Brougham, the great legal reformer, and from other members of parliament, the Home Secretary refused to give Humphreys a seat on the commission.[20] Hence the Royal Commission's complacency, already noted above, regarding the state of the laws relating to tenure. Of the Royal Commission's four reports, the first two were devoted to registration (1829 and 1830), only the third to the manifold questions of tenure (1831–2) and the fourth to wills (1832). Bentham's own response was somewhat ambiguous and possibly tinged with jealousy. He praised Humphreys warmly as a 'star in the horizon of jurisprudence' and set out to out-Humphrey Humphrey in a critique so thorough and searching that it occasionally descended to sarcasm.[21] To the Royal Commission on Real Property he sent a long memorandum on registration of title which, while fully embracing the principle, was mainly concerned with the inefficiency inherent in public offices. Subsequent experience has confirmed the insight of his analysis.[22]

'No measure has been suggested to us from so many different quarters or has been so earnestly pressed upon us as a general registry of deeds',[23] wrote the commissioners in their first report, and proceeded to recommend its establishment in their second. John Campbell KC (1779–1861; afterwards solicitor- and attorney-general, Baron and Lord Chancellor, a legal statesman and prolific, if superficial legal historian) was chairman of the inquiry. On 16 December 1830 he introduced a General Register Bill in a long maiden speech in the Commons. Further bills were introduced in the three following years but to no avail. The Royal Commission had anticipated a contraction of solicitors' incomes and recommended some form of compensatory remuneration,[24] and Campbell anticipated oppo-

---

[19] See e.g. E. B. Sugden, *A letter to James Humphreys* (1826), esp. pp. 5–8; J. Humphreys, *A letter to Edward B. Sugden* (1827), pp. 1–2, R. C. Real prop. 2nd rep. (1830), 4 and Archbold, 'Humphreys', *D.N.B.*

[20] 18 H. C. deb. 2 ser. Feb. 1828, H. Brougham, 130–1; 29 Feb. 1828, 835; 19 H. C. deb. 2 ser. 26 June 1828, Sir J. Mackintosh, 1524; Sir Robert Peel, 1525–6.

[21] J. Bentham, 'Commentary on Mr Humphreys' real property code', *Westminster Review* (October 1826), reprinted *Works*, Bowring edn, v, 387–416.

[22] Real property. R. com. 3d rep.: P.P. 1831–2 (484) XXIII, App. Pt. III, 36–56, J. Bentham, 'Outline of a register of real property', reprinted in Bowring edn, v, 417–35.

[23] Real property. R. com. 1st rep. 1829, p. 60.

[24] *Ibid.* 2nd rep. 1830, p. 65.

sition: 'a notion has gone abroad among solicitors, chiefly in the country, that this measure will materially interfere with their professional profits; and I have reason to know that on this ground they are prepared to oppose it, and get up petitions against it'.[25] In retrospect, Campbell blamed failure on the solicitors:

> my grand scheme of a General Register met with the most lively opposition. This was chiefly caused by the country attorneys, – the most influential class in this Kingdom, – who had taken up the notion without sufficient ground, that the measure would greatly diminish their business and their profits.[26]

Registration was launched with official blessing. It was a Benthamite programme of legal rationalisation of the type designed to improve the 'artificial identification of interests' by creating a State agency to reinforce laisser faire, private property and the market.[27] It enjoyed the prophet's personal imprimatur. The fate of this measure is a test of the power of Benthamite principles to explain change in British society and is relevant to the debate on the growth of government in the nineteenth century.[28] We may say without revealing the plot that if the programme did not fully succeed it was partly owing to disregard for some of Bentham's strictures!

II

In the Victorian period the cost of land transfer began to occupy the propertied classes after a century of relative neglect. Four Royal Commissions considered the subject between 1830 and 1870, a pamphlet and periodical literature kept it in the public eye, and a number of private bills were introduced.[29] Nassau Senior estimated, in evidence to a committee of the House of Lords, that transfer costs diminished the value of real property by three years purchase, or some £240 millions.

[25] *Speeches of Lord Campbell at the bar and in the House of Commons* (Edinburgh, 1852), p. 458.
[26] *Ibid.* pp. 426–7.
[27] Needed because men's egos did not naturally harmonise. See E. Halévy, *The growth of philosophic radicalism* (1972 edn), p. 17.
[28] See A. J. Taylor, *Laissez-faire and state intervention in nineteenth-century Britain* (1972).
[29] F. M. L. Thompson, 'The economic and social background of the English landed interest 1840–70, with particular reference to the estates of the Dukes of Northumberland' (Oxford Univ. D.Phil. thesis, 1955), ch. II (ii), 'the legal diversion', gives an excellent account of this phase.

James Caird placed the depreciation at five years purchase.[30] The Royal Commission report of 1857 marked the swing from the registration of deeds to the more Radical concept of title registration. It aspired to the certainty of ownership and simplicity of transfer provided by the registries of Consols, railway shares and ships, which would make land into a commodity like any other.[31] England was falling behind. Registration of deeds or of title was practised in most of continental Europe, including the Ottoman empire, in most British colonies and in many American states. Resistance in England came mainly from solicitors. Baron Campbell did not live to see the acceptance of the registration; he died in 1859. A Land Registry Office was finally established in London in 1862 by Lord Westbury, a Tory Lord Chancellor. It was an unhappy hybrid of the two systems, registration of deeds and of title. Owners had to register their titles voluntarily, and since solicitors were determined to obstruct them, the office attracted very little business. Moreover, its transactions were hopelessly slow and inefficient and a Royal Commission pronounced the registry a failure in 1870, after a searching inquiry.[32]

In the 1870s, after two score years of agitation, the ambiguities and complexities of real property law still left considerable scope for procrastination, frustration, litigation and cost. Something had been done to mitigate the cumbrous technicalities captured for posterity by Dickens in *Bleak House* but land and house property was still governed by a separate doctrine of law (equity) and contested in special courts (of Chancery) by a specialised set of lawyers (the Chancery bar).[33] Despite a self-evident interest in legal complexity these lawyers did not constitute a coherent interet. Conveyancing counsel were merely a small subgroup within the barristers' profession and conveyancing was only one of their many concerns. Many legal reformers came from within their ranks and their expertise was available to all comers. Of the select few who had achieved professional success and a comprehensive grasp of the land laws, many belonged to 'The Institute', a self-selected elite dining club of

[30] Burdens affecting real property. H. L. sel. com. mins. ev.; P.P. 1846 (411) VI Pt. I, N. Senior, quest. 5,462 (cited Thompson, thesis (1955), p. 92); J. Caird, *English agriculture in 1850–51* (1852), p. 496.

[31] Registration of title. R. com. rep.; P.P. 1857 [2215] XXI, esp. pp. 22–4, 31.

[32] Land transfer. R. com. rep.; P.P. 1870 C.20 XVIII.

[33] F. W. Maitland, 'The law of real property' [1879] in *Collected papers*, ed. H. A. L. Fisher (1911), i, 162–201. The Judicature Act of 1873 merged the Chancery and Common Law courts, but not the respective doctrines.

forty who met five times a year (and were known informally as 'the forty thieves'). 'The Institute' was primarily a club and when it took up professional issues it could rarely speak with one voice.[34] A difficult medium calls for high skill and the expert conveyancer regarded himself as something of an artist. '[Conveyancing] is a fine art', wrote one of them, 'and like other things capable of a high degree of excellence, it is rarely done very well'.[35] Family connections with solicitors were often necessary to gain a foothold even if few were driven, like the barrister in Gilbert and Sullivan's *Trial by jury*, to 'fall in love with a rich attorney's/ Elderly, ugly daughter'.[36] In contrast, the bulk of solicitors' staple conveyancing was routine, semi-skilled, safe and non-contentious.

Solicitors were better organised than conveyancing counsel and their interests were more effectively focussed. Strong local law societies existed in the provinces and the Incorporated Law Society of London (founded in 1823 and incorporated by Royal Charter eight years later) was the profession's acknowledged voice. By the 1870s many practitioners were coming to realise that payment 'by folio' was a mixed blessing. Small properties, which made up the majority of transactions, were prohibitively expensive to transfer while large ones escaped with relatively small fees. Because, as one lawyer put it, 'one acre was old as a thousand',[37] single houses could carry the same bulk of documents as large estates, and attracted the same fees.

No vital interest of the solicitors was served by division of labour with the barristers or indeed, by the whole cumbersome system of real property law. It merely alienated clients and was difficult to defend. A reform would suit solicitors well, provided it could be kept within limits.

Simplification of the land laws would leave the solicitor's function, in a system of private conveyancing, very much as before. Procedures would be easier to carry out, costs and delays reduced, demand would increase, turnover accelerate and clients be more content. Less work would be farmed out to the senior branch, whose expertise would be rendered obsolete. This approach may be called 'the simplification strategy' after the title of a paper read in 1862 by E. P. Wolstenholme, a leading

---

[34]Brickdale Papers, *The Institute* (n.d.; list of members to c. 1887); H. W. Elphinstone, *The Institute* (1897), (extracts from rules); J. S. Vaizey, *The Institute* (1907) (lives of distinguished members); A. Underhill, *Change and decay: the recollections and reflections of an octogenarian bencher* (1938), p. 91.
[35]E. Fry, *Studies by the way* (1900), pp. 107–8.
[36]Underhill, *Change and decay*, (1938) pp. 68–9.
[37]209 H.C. deb. 3d ser. 16 Feb. 1872, C. Wren-Hoskyns, 567.

conveyancing barrister.[38] In contrast with previous schemes, the codification and simplification of the property laws was not put forward as a supplement to registration, but as *an alternative*. Codification would make private conveyancing so simple as to make registration unnecessary. His scheme went unremarked at first, but it was to have the greatest significance and influence in the long run. It embodied two unspoken qualifications. First, that fees in the aggregate should not fall and second, that simplification should not go so far as to make solicitors themselves redundant, or permit the substitution of a public office for the guild monopoly. Reform had to be a plausible alternative to registration.

Land law reform was broadly identified in the 1860s and 1870s with the cause of Radical Liberalism in its conflict with the landowners.[39] James E. Thorold Rogers, the pioneering economic historian who was intimate with Cobden said of his friend in 1869, that

> During the last years of his life, there was nothing which Mr Cobden used to state more frequently than this – that, if youth and leisure could be restored to him, his first political duty would be an agitation for the reformation of the laws which regulate the conveyance, the inheritance and the settlement of land.

Rogers would not divert any political energy into a quarrel with the lawyers and placed the blame squarely on the aristocracy.

> the charges on legal instruments ... arise, I believe, not from the cupidity of lawyers whose interests as a professional class would be furthered by the distribution of land and the multiplication of business, but from the vanity which possesses owners of property ... why should the purchase of land be more difficult and dangerous than that of railway stock and consols? Can we avoid the conclusion that these impediments are created or maintained in the interests of an aristocracy which is resolved at all hazards to entrench its position by the continuance of the most irrational and mischievous expeditions?[40]

[38]E. P. Wolstenholme, 'Simplification of title to land preferable to the introduction of novel modes of assurance, with an outline of a plan', *Papers read before the Juridical Society* 2, no. xxvii (March 1862), 533–52.
[39]See F. M. L. Thompson, 'Land and politics in England in the nineteenth century', *Transactions of the Royal Historical Society* 5 ser. 15 (1965); H. J. Perkin, 'Land reform and class conflict in Victorian Britain', in *The Victorians and social protest* ed. J. Butt and I. F. Clarke (Newton Abbot, 1973).
[40]J. E. Thorold Rogers, *The laws affecting landed property* (Manchester, 1869), pp. 1, 17. Also J. E. Thorold Rogers, *Cobden and modern political opinion* (1873), ch. III.

Registration, like the railways, may be adapted to serve diametrically different regimes. Whether it is oppressive or liberating, collectivist or individualist, depends mainly on the context.[41] In Germany and Austria the register was instrumental in the taxation of land.[42] In Australia it facilitated frontier settlement and urban land speculation.[43] In 1848 it played a role in abortive land reforms in Ireland.[44] In Malaya in the Edwardian period it cleared the way for the extension of rubber plantations at the expense of the peasantry.[45] The Cobdenite agitators for 'Free Trade in Land' who were the strongest public voice in favour of registration in Britain wanted to substitute a class of small capitalists for the large landowners but the front of advocates extended from the Duke of Marlborough through John Stuart Mill to H. M. Hyndman, the Marxian socialist.[46] Gladstone regarded it as a part of the 'common profession of a limited creed' of the Liberal party.[47] For class-conscious Radicals registration was a means of dismantling the instruments of aristocratic identity and separateness. Entrepreneurs, landed and otherwise, desired greater liquidity for their assets: Registration was a prerequisite of an interventionist policy of tenure reform, peasant proprietorship, allotment provision, home ownership for the working classes; it was an accessory of land taxation, sanitary reform and compulsory purchase. These connections are manifest in subsequent Liberal proposals and measures in the 1880s and after.[48] Conversely, solicitors

---

[41] For surveys see C. F. Brickdale, *Land Transfer in various countries* (1894) and 'Land registration', *Encyclopaedia Britannica* (11th edn 1911); J. E. Hogg, *Registration of title to land throughout the empire* (Toronto, 1920); J. R. Simpson, *Land law and registration* (Cambridge, 1976).

[42] C. F. Brickdale, Registration of title in Germany and Austria-Hungary, vol. 1:P.P. 1896 C. 8139 LXXXIV, p. 76.

[43] See R. M. Torrens, *Speeches ... explanatory of his measure for reform of the law of real property ...* (Australia, 1858) and *An essay on the transfer of land by registration* (1882).

[44] W. L. Burn, 'Free trade in land: an aspect of the Irish question', *Transactions of the Royal Historical Society* 4 ser. 31 (1949), 69–71.

[45] Dr. C. E. R. Abraham: oral information (see C. K. Meek, *Land law and custom in the colonies* (1946), pp. 40–1).

[46] Marlborough, see p. 42; J. S. Mill, *Principles of political economy* ed. W. J. Ashley (1909), Bk. 5 ch. viii §3, pp. 886–7; H. M. Hyndman, *England for all* (cheap edn 1881), p. 30.

[47] W. E. Gladstone to Earl Granville, 5 Oct. 1885 in *The political correspondence of Mr. Gladstone and Lord Granville, 1876–1886*, ed. A. Ramm (Oxford, 1962), ii, 401–2.

[48] For a few typical statements, see the Housing of the working classes. R. com. 1st rep.; P.P. 1884–5 C. 4402 XXX, 48–9; the 'Newcastle Programme' of 1891, National Liberal Federation, *Proceedings* of the Annual Meeting (1891), p. 8;

strove to maintain the identification of the mystique of landed society with the mysteries of the land laws, and sought the support of the Conservative party.

EG 7 Sept. 1901, 413 (London County Council circular contemplating legislation for a register of slum owners); E. G. Howarth and M. Wilson, *West Ham: a study in social and industrial problems* (1907), pp. 131–2; A. Offer, 'The origin of the law of property acts 1910–25', *Modern law review* 40 (1977), 507–8 (Lloyd George in 1909–10) and D. Lloyd George, Speech at Middlesbrough, *The Times* 10 Nov. 1913, 4c ('A national house survey').

3

LAWYERS AND LIBERALS
1870–1895

I

The last of the Victorian Royal Commissions on registration reported in 1870. In the next twenty-five years the subject was swept into the mainstream of politics. As the pressures for reform gathered strength, the legal profession had to muster ever-increasing skill to ward them off. Lord Westbury's futile registry of 1862 managed to grant only two hundred and five titles in its first five years. In order to dislodge the opposition voluntary enticement no longer sufficed. Compulsion had become necessary. Selborne, who was Gladstone's Lord Chancellor, introduced a bill in 1873. It adopted the simplified mode of registration recommended by the latest Royal Commission, with a significant new departure: registration was to become compulsory after a trial period of two years. Selborne denied having radical inclinations and justified the bill in commercial necessity.[1] The proposal marked a high point for the prospects of land registration in England and the challenge did much to bring about the emergence of co-ordinated professional action by solicitors.

When the ministry changed in 1874 Hugh Macalmont Cairns became Lord Chancellor. As solicitor-general in 1859 he had introduced a registration bill; and he did not allow Selborne's bill to lapse. But he changed its import by dropping the most essential element, compulsion. He put forward a candid, if curious excuse for defusing the bill. 'However stringent you might make the compulsory clause', he said in Parliament, 'the ingenuity of conveyancers would be able to defeat it'.[2] Cairns was reacting mainly to strong pressure from Birmingham solicitors. 'Compulsory registration', he maintained, 'might excite intense dissatisfaction ... which might lead to an effort to get rid of the new system altogether'.[3] The Lords divided on party lines and passed an emasculated bill on to the Commons, where it was subsequently approved

[1] 215 H.L. deb. 3 ser. 20 April 1873, Selborne, 1119.
[2] 222 H.L. deb. 3 ser. 9 Feb. 1875, 156.
[3] *Ibid.* 23 Feb. 1875, 749 and see 219 H.C. deb. 3 ser. 1 June 1874, 728.

in 1875. In the Commons a Liberal Queen's Counsel (George Osborne Morgan) exposed the measure for what it was. Without compulsion, he said, registration was useless and at best the act would remain a dead letter. Otherwise it could do positive harm by 'unsettling the law for nothing, shelving the issue and appeasing public opinion'.[4] There is evidence that the Law Society strove for just this outcome.[5] On the face of it, the act was a technical, sectional affair. Very few laymen spoke and the bill received the active support of solicitors in the House. But the link with the 'land question' helped to line up the Tories in silent, but effective acquiescence.

Owing mainly to the onset of agrarian depression in Britain and Ireland in the late 1870s 'the land question' grew from the fad of a few Radicals and began to preoccupy the political nation.[6] At the same time the wake of a property market boom exposed a host of forgeries and frauds. In the atmosphere of confidence created by the building boom of the middle 'seventies a solicitor named Dimsdale was able to mortgage forged deeds to the amount of £300,000. This was only the most spectacular of a bumper harvest of frauds in those years. The building societies added their voice to the proponents of registration and began to prepare a bill, *The Times* voiced doubts over the probity of solicitors, and it even managed to attract a letter from a practitioner who appealed, 'register, register, register'.[7] On 14 May 1878 George Osborne Morgan, the critic of Lord Cairns' registration act, moved for a Select Committee 'to inquire and report whether and what steps ought to be taken to simplify the title to land and to facilitate the transfer thereof, and to prevent fraud on purchasers and mortgagees of land'. Under the pressure of public opinion the parliamentary custodians of the solicitors' interests calculated that a registry of deeds on the Middlesex or Scottish model, which left conveyancing to lawyers, might be a lesser evil than compulsory registration of title. G. B. Gregory, a Conservative MP and an officer of the Law Society, seconded the motion.[8]

Forty years of parliamentary agitation for land-law reform, which provoked so many protests and petitions from attorneys and solicitors, also gave rise to a few self-reforming schemes from within the pro-

[4] 224 H.C. deb. 3 ser. 4 July 1875, 1417–25.
[5] 220 H.C. deb. 3 ser. 4 July 1874, Sir Francis Goldsmid, 1234.
[6] See H. Lynd, *England in the eighteen-eighties* (New York, 1945), p. 124 *et seq.*
[7] *The Times*, 18 Jan. 1878, 9–11; 19 Jan., 11; 22 Jan., 5.
[8] See 239 H.C. deb. 3 ser. 14 May 1878, 1885–98.

fession.[9] A number of solicitors gave evidence in favour of reform before the Royal Commission of 1868–70 and one even went so far as to recommend registration on the assumption that the resulting increase in turnover would compensate for the decline in unit value.[10] A link between property values and conveyancing fees appeared to be a step in the right direction, and a number of fee scales were proposed by the central and provincial law societies during the 1870s. These scales would have given the profession the best of both worlds: existing high fees would remain in force for small properties, and fees would be pegged to property values in large transactions. Successive Lord Chancellors rejected them as too high.[11]

George Osborne Morgan, the Liberal QC, was voted chairman of the select committee on land transfer of 1878. Previously a public advocate of registration, he now began to play the solicitors' tune. George Shaw-Lefevre (later Baron Eversley, a leading champion of 'Free Trade in Land') proposed the gradual extension of registration, but his draft was rejected by the majority of Conservatives and solicitors on the committee. The Report that Morgan drafted for the majority conceded reforms the solicitors had long been advocating, in particular the pegging of fees to property values. If a scale of value-related fees was introduced and payment made independent of the length of documents then short standard forms could replace the prolix documents of land transfer.[12] Such forms had been incorporated into Acts in 1845 and 1860, but did not gain acceptance because they threatened to contract earnings.[13] Registration of deeds was recommended, but put off until the completion of the Ordnance Survey Cadastral (property boundary) map, at that time still eleven years off.[14] After the Report was published Morgan wrote an

[9]See e.g. Real property. R. com. 2nd rep. 1830, Memorandum by T. G. Fonnereau, Appendix, pp. 11–12; Registration of title. R. com. rep. 1857, 'Plan of registration proposed by Mr Robert Wilson', Appendix, pp. 83–117 and 'Suggestion and Plan by Mr Cookson', pp. 128–33. Also leaders, *Solicitors' Journal* 6 (1862), 353, 859 (quoted in Kirk, *Portrait of a profession*, (1976) p. 138).

[10]Land transfer act. R. com. report; P.P. 1870 C. 20 XVIII, p. xvii.

[11]Tentative suggestions: Registration of title. R. com. rep. 1857, par. xciii, p. 48 and Land transfer act. R. com. rep. 1870, Appendix, p. 67, q. 39. Proposals: see *LSAR*, 1871–6. Also Land titles and transfer sel. com. rep.: P. P. 1878–9 (244) XI, pp. 167–8. 'Best of both worlds': see scale fees, *LSAR* (1871), App. 26–7 and (1880), 48.

[12]Land transfer and titles. Sel. com. rep. 1879, p. viii.

[13]See Sweet, 'land transfer acts' (1908), 32.

[14]Land transfer and titles. Sel. com. rep. 1879, p. xiii.

article in the *Fortnightly Review* which was apparently an attempt to re-establish his Liberal credentials with regard to the land question. It was apologetic over the committee and the arguments about registration appeared inconsistent and confused when compared to his earlier Parliamentary statements.[15]

On 7 October 1879 N. T. Lawrence, President of the Law Society, introduced the reform proposals to the profession at its annual provincial meeting. Almost one third of his presidential address was taken up by a hostile history of land registration which concluded,

> The proposed system would place the main part of the business of the transfer of land in the hands of a Government officer. For Government to undertake private business is contrary to the principles of our political system. It could not tend to the benefit of the public, because the great business, which now forms the chief occupation of the great body of solicitors, would overwhelm with its weight any office which could be established.

The fraud excitement having safely blown over he withdrew the assent to a deeds registry and proposed a more limited registry, for mortgages only.[16] His other suggestions were either technical, or window dressing, and largely immaterial to the central issue, which was undoubtedly registration.[17]

The Law Society appointed a special committee to work in conjunction with the official draftsmen. One of the latter was E. P. Wolstenholme, originator of the 'simplification strategy' (see above, p. 31) and its recent exponent before the select committee.[18] No wonder then that when the government bills were ready in January 1880 they were found to be 'in remarkable agreement with the suggestions of the Council'.[19] The bills placed conveyancing fees on a value-related scale and substituted short forms for the verbose texts employed in drafting deeds and abstracts. In 1881 they were enacted as the Conveyancing and the Solicitors' Remuneration Acts. A Settled Land Act relaxed some of the limitations on the transfer and sale of settled property. Without going as far as Wolstenholme desired, and clearing away the complicated

[15] Reprinted, G. O. Morgan, *Land law reform in England* (1880), esp. pp. 15–16, 22.

[16] N. T. Lawrence, *Facts and suggestions as to the law of real property* (1879), pp. 19, 34.

[17] See *LSAR* (1880), 8 and *LSPR* (1880), 134.

[18] Land titles and transfer. Sel. com. mins. of ev.; P.P. 1878 (291) XV, E. P. Wolstenholme, esp. questions 2470–9, 2485–8, 2501–12.

[19] *LSAR* (1880), 7–8.

tenures of real property law, the reform was still a notable success for the simplification strategy.

In the years of Lord Cairns (1874–80) the solicitors' profession managed to neutralise threats while maintaining the semblance of welcoming change. The tactic depended on the Lord Chancellor's collusion and remained a model for subsequent leaders of the profession. 'The success of the great measures of 1881 and 1882', remarked the author of a Law Society manifesto in 1886, 'is entirely due to the fact that their provisions were suggested, drafted or corrected by practising conveyancers (barristers and solicitors) ... even with regard to Lord Cairns' Acts, the government of the day was merely passive'.[20]

Payment by folio was ended by the act of 1881 but it remained to tie up some loose ends. Neither Lord Cairns nor his successor (Lord Selborne) could agree with the Law Society about the fee scale or the mode of fixing it. A long wrangle ensued until the Master of the Rolls devised a compromise scale much lower than the one demanded by the Society and even that was delayed (until 1 January 1883) because the President of the Law Society witheld his consent.[21] But the protests soon subsided. Solicitors could still use the previous conventions but the new scale was universally adopted. It was consistently undercut and never called into question until after the Great War. A general increase in solicitors' incomes resulted, as large transfers became more remunerative.

A few years after the new scale had taken effect a conveyancing barrister found occasion to express his misgivings in a letter to the Lord Chancellor.

> Speaking not only as a conveyancer but as a trustee for many years
> ... I have come to the conclusion that the General Order in
> question framed and sanctioned as it was with the best intentions by
> three eminent judges and an eminent country solicitor has in the
> result laid a heavy burden on land and imposed shackles on
> transfers and other transactions which nothing but a repeal of the
> order can strike off. Solicitors' bills for transactions in the way of
> sales and purchases and mortgages for the more usual amounts of
> from £1,500 to £5,000 have been doubled and trebled in amount
> owing to the scale charges ...

[20]Incorporated Law Society, *Statement on the land laws* (1886), p. 16.
[21]*LSAR* (1881), 12–14; *LSPR* (1911), 50; J. S. Rubinstein, *The Conveyancing Acts, 1881, 1882 and the Solicitors' Remuneration Act, 1881* (4th and 5th edns, 1882, 1884), pp. 24, 25–8 respectively.

Many solicitors hesitate to make the scale charges against their own clients feeling that they are in excess of the vaiue of the work done and perhaps feeling that the amount of the charges must operate as a deterrent from future transactions but I fear.it is rarely that a mortgagor or lessee gets the benefit of any such hesitation.

Since the scale charges have been introduced London as well as country solicitors have done more conveyancing work in their own offices and sent less to counsel the reason being that the scale charges are so heavy that they cannot with prudence be increased by the addition of Counsel's fees. The result of which is that the client although paying a heavier bill loses the benefit of the advice of the specially trained practitioner.[22]

He went on to relate instances from experience and concluded, For three or four years I have heard similar complaints on all sides. How the order was made in the form it was is to me an inscrutable mystery. That order and that alone is a sufficient explanation and I think a justification, as regards the legislation of the last few years at any rate of what Lord Salisbury I think remarked that any improvement in the Law seemed always to make it more expensive.

In the decade following the acts the profession manifested remarkable vigour and health. Despite a long slump in construction and the depression in farmland prices it grew by one-fifth while the number of auctioneers, house agents and other property practitioners fell by almost a tenth. At an average two per cent a year it grew more than twice as fast as the general population and employment in the law kept well up with the increase of numbers in other professions.[23] Some of this vitality may well be attributed to the improved fee structure introduced by the legislation of 1881.

II

The revolving stage of politics moved leftwards in the early 1880s and the political props shifted to the right. In the 'Free Trade in Land' literature of the 1870s primogeniture was identified as the root evil. It facilitated the maintenance of large estates and assisted the process of landed concentration. Life-tenants were unable to manage estate finances

[22]PRO Lord Chancellor's Papers LCO 1/56, Walter Morsehead to Lord Halsbury, Memorandum, 19 April 1887, pp. 4, 5.
[23]Solicitors' and property profession licences are enumerated in *IRAR*. Employment in the professions, see Mitchell and Deane, *Abstract*, p. 60.

with complete freedom because of their imperfect tenure and agriculture was consequently under-capitalised and stagnant. If tenure were made absolute and partible inheritance introduced there might be a flow of capital into the countryside and a more equal distribution of land, as urban and rural savings were attracted to agriculture. The object was 'to make the ownership of land accord with the free operation of economic laws'.[24] Prosperous peasant proprietors would then come to replace the great estates.[25] Cheap and simple land transfer was a corollary. As Dicey later pointed out, 'Free Trade in Land' was the pure milk of Bentham, i.e. law reform as reinforcement for private property and laisser-faire.[26] But the notion that law reform alone could bring about such momentous changes of tenure lent an implausible air to the Free-Land literature and new movements in the early 1880s were much less tender to individual tenure. Henry George's single tax on land, A. R. Wallace's scheme of land nationalisation and Jesse Collings' state-sanctioned 'three acres and a cow' were interventionist panaceas for rural regeneration which willingly contemplated the disturbance of property rights. But some measures were common to the old and new Radicalism and the break between them was not complete. Both were antipathetic to aristocracy and both treasured the vision of a peasant proprietary.

While the sanctity of property was being questioned by Radicals individualism began to revive as a creed for modern Conservatives. Spencer's *The man versus the state* (1884) and the writings of W. H. Mallock were conspicuous in a tide of pamphlet and periodical literature. This reasoned resistance to the public mitigation of unbridled competition eventually found its mature voice in that great counter to the Whig interpretation of history, A. V. Dicey's *Lectures on law and public opinion in England* (1905). The Liberty and Property Defence League of employers and landowners, which Lord Wemyss founded in 1883 to fight the socialist menace, gave it a vocal pressure group.[27] Benthamite fundamentalism, having served for a time to challenge landed hegemony, reverted to its other role as a defence of property against the democratic threat. Consequently, as we shall see, the ideology of Free Trade in Land became less repugnant to Conservatives. Land

[24] A. Arnold, *Free land* (1880), p. 12.
[25] *Ibid*. pp. 285–8. And see Thompson, thesis (1955), *passim*.
[26] A. V. Dicey, 'The paradox of the land laws', *Law quarterly review* (1905), 226–228.
[27] See E. Bristow, 'The defence of liberty and property in Britain, 1880–1914' (Yale Univ. Ph.D. thesis, 1970), ch. 3, and K. D. Brown (ed.) *Essays in anti-labour history* (1974), chs. 9, 11–13.

registration, which carried fewer anti-aristocratic connotations than the measures against primogeniture and strict settlement, was even more acceptable. It remained in the arsenal of the Radicals but its Benthamite tinge now made it attractive to intellectual conservatives. Many landowners, however, were slow to adapt and continued to regard any land-law reform with suspicion. Such was the altered ideological climate which solicitors found themselves exposed to in the 1880s.

Gladstone's second government did not question the settlement of 1881; the solicitors had dependable allies in the Liberal camp.[28] It was the Tory party which repudiated the settlement, when its turn in power came again in 1885. A new urgency infused the 'land question' in the early 1880s: agriculture was depressed and Ireland was seething. Building fell to a low ebb in the cities and the middle classes rediscovered the slums. 'Free Trade in Land' was overshadowed, first by the appearance of Henry George and then by the rhetoric of Joseph Chamberlain and his 'Radical Programme', not, like George, on the fringes of public life, but well inside the ruling Liberal Party. Randolph Churchill and the Marquess of Salisbury, who led the Tories, attempted to meet Chamberlain on his own ground and steal some of his thunder. Churchill enrolled in the cause of Leasehold Enfranchisement and Salisbury sat on the Royal commission on the housing of the working classes (see chapter 9). Both were uncomfortable about their party's association with traditional forms of tenure, transfer and inheritance and solicitors could no longer rely on their unquestioning support.

On 9 July 1885 the Duke of Marlborough introduced the second reading of a bill for registration of title in the House of Lords. Lord Salisbury, less than three weeks into his first ministry, sided with the solicitors against the bill.[29] With an election approaching both parties tried to win popularity out of registration. A lively correspondence in *The Times* was precipitated by a letter from the Duke of Marlborough who wrote on 22 September,

> The greatest enemy of the land, and the most deadly friend to the landed interest is to be found in the iron grasp of the legal profession on the title deeds to real property. We do not require the

[28]'it is said that only upon the intercession of Sir Henry Fowler [Liberal MP, solicitor and future Cabinet Minister, later Viscount Wolverhampton] ... were the Bills allowed to pass upon the change of government' (Christian, *Short history* (1896), p. 229). Also PRO 30/51/9 Cairns Papers, Lord Selborne to Cairns, 24 May 1880, fols 150–1 and 252 H.C. deb. 3 ser. 24 May 1880, W. E. Baxter and W. E. Gladstone, 320–1.

[29]299 H.L. deb. 3 ser. 9 July 1885, Salisbury, 108–9.

nationalization of land; we do require to nationalize the title to land.[30]

On 7 October Lord Salisbury announced in favour of registration, in an election speech at Newport.

> We ought to have compulsory registration of titles. (Cheers.) If we cannot achieve the object, no harm will be done ... If it is successful, not only will the lawyers' bill be diminished, but every labouring man who is able to purchase will be able to attach himself to a freehold in land. (Cheers.)[31]

Salisbury had long regarded primogeniture and strict settlement as mere outworks in the landowners' defensive position,[32] and he was willing to give them up in order to encourage Liberal desertions. In December he wrote to Churchill,

> The abolition of primogeniture is in itself of no importance except on strategic grounds – it is not worth the trouble of resistance. But it is a bit of a flag. The concession would be distasteful to a certain number of our people now, and it might be acceptable as wedding-present to the Moderate Liberals whenever the Conservative party leads them to the altar. I would not proffer it, therefore, now; though if carried against us, I should make no serious fight over it.[33]

Lord Halsbury, the new Lord Chancellor, had already begun to prepare a comprehensive bill establishing compulsory and universal registration of title and abolishing primogeniture and the power of creating an entail. Unlike Cairns, Halsbury had not been a conveyancing barrister; he remained unperturbed by the Law Society's opposition and impervious to the influence of its Liberal sympathisers.[34] In November 1886 he received a letter of encouragement from Lord Salisbury, who wrote in words that might have been copied verbatim from Arnold's *Free land*,[35]

> My general view is that the law of settlement and entail, as it now stands, is like armour was to the knights at the close of the middle

---

[30] *The Times*, 22 Sept. 1885, 4b.

[31] *The Times*, 8 Oct. 1885, 7.

[32] See 'The programme of the Radicals' *Quarterly Review* no. 270 (1873), reprinted in *Lord Salisbury on politics*, ed. P. Smith (Cambridge, 1972), pp. 320–22.

[33] W. S. Churchill, *Lord Randolph Churchill* (2nd edn 1907), pp. 437–8.

[34] Professional opposition – LS, *Statement on the land laws* (1886); PRO LCO 1/56 [1886–7], memoranda from lawyers; LCO 1/55, Henry Fowler to the [Liberal] Lord Chancellor (Herschell), 12 Feb. 1886, an example of backstage pressure.

[35] Arnold, *Free land* (1880), p. 28.

ages. It was meant for their defence; but it only prevented them from defending themselves.[36]

Upon its introduction in the Lords, the Land Transfer bill was strongly supported by the Prime Minister. A group of landowners opposed it as 'a sop to the cerberus of Socialism', but the Liberal peers backed the measure. It passed by a small majority, too late in the session, however, to go through the Commons.[37] The following year the diehard landowners were well-briefed by the Law Society and the Liberals withdrew their support. Not a voice was raised in its favour, and it failed again in 1889. But Halsbury was determined to press on and to bypass the Lords if necessary.[38]

A member of the Incorporated Law Society noted large unexplained expenditures in the society's accounts in 1886 and in 1889 the society admitted to considerable expenses in connection with current land transfer bills.[39] Some light on its modes of operation is thrown by the memoirs of Arthur Underhill. He was an underemployed barrister who attempted to supplement his earnings, like many impecunious colleagues, by speculative authorship. In 1879 he started a successful venture by publishing a pamphlet which gave a negative answer to the question *Should entails be abolished?* The result is recorded in his memoir, *Change and decay* (pp. 48–9).

I was not aware at the time that the Law Society, with the assistance of the greatest conveyancing counsel of my time ... had persuaded Lords Cairns and Selborne to father a Bill which subsequently became law under the title of The Settled Land Act 1882. However, I, greatly daring, sent a copy of my pamphlet to Lord Cairns, who forwarded it to Wolstenholme, with the intimation that it was written in popular language and would made good propaganda for their bill. To my astonishment one morning Wolstenholme and the late Nathaniel Tertius Lawrence (then President of the Law Society) called at my chambers and offered to take, at cost price, the whole of a new edition of 2,000 copies (with new references to their Bills) for distribution among peers, members of Parliament and others.

[36]Brit. Lib. Add. MSS. 56371, Halsbury papers, Salisbury to Halsbury, 29 Oct. 1886, fol. 28.
[37]See 313 H.L. deb. 3 ser 25 April 1887, 1875.
[38]See Halsbury papers, Add MSS. 56371, W. H. Smith to Halsbury, 18 May 1889, fol. 125 and 7 Nov. 1889, fol. 128. Also the printed prospectus for a 'Registration of title association' (c. 1890) in the Brickdale Papers.
[39]*Solicitors' Journal*, 8 Feb. 1886, 235–6; *LSAR* (1899), 51.

Note the collusion between the President of the solicitors and the government draftsman! The pamphlet had a marked effect on Underhill's career. He obtained some very valuable clients and a lucrative post as lecturer in the Law Society's lectures. In 1893 he was elected to 'The Institute' and in 1905 became a 'Conveyancing Counsel of the Chancery Court' in succession to Wolstenholme. His practice once more 'increased very greatly'.[40] It was a long-term investment for the Law Society. In 1918, near the end of his career, Underhill was able to repay their generosity with another well-timed appearance in the annals of land law reform.

Salisbury, Halsbury and W. H. Smith presented a firm front to the solicitors and indicated that the profession's alliance with the landed interest, which had stood between them and registration for so long, was approaching the end of its course. It had always been an uneasy alliance. The majority of solicitors, engaged in urban, financial and commercial pursuits, had a greater affinity with the Liberalism of Cobden or the new 1880s Conservatism of Goschen than with the backwoodsmen. Men of this stamp adorned their Parliamentary leadership: Henry Fowler, for example, the Liberal–Imperialist front-bencher and Albert K. Rollit, a 'progressive' Conservative involved in an amazing range of activities from Chambers of Commerce to Savings Banks, who will appear in these pages again as an outstanding champion of municipal enterprise. For such men the old rural connection had always been somewhat forced and the shift was not unwelcome. It presented a belated opportunity for the profession to abandon its role as an accessory of aristocracy and latch on to the fashionable controversy on collectivism and individualism, on the side of the latter.

In 1892 and 1893 the Law Society produced two long ideological statements. The two reports on *Officialism* stated a creed of fundamentalist individualism.[41] In presenting registration of title as an unnatural, inequitable and inefficient interference of the state with the economy the Society sought common ground with the Gladstonian doctrine of minimal government. The reports reflected a sense of increasing despondency.[42] No respite from the building slump was yet in sight and gloom was darkened by the failure of the Liberator building society in 1892. After hovering around two per cent a year in the 1880s the growth of the

[40]Underhill, *Change and decay* (1938), pp. 73, 89, 91, 102–3.
[41]*LSAR* (1892), 85–115; *LSAR* (1893), 77–125.
[42]See W. P. Fullagar, 'Our profession: its present-day position and obligations', *LSPR* (1893), 196–205.

profession virtually came to a halt in 1893.[43] A long campaign to take bankruptcy and company liquidation out of solicitors' hands and place these functions with the Board of Trade culminated adversely for the profession in 1890 with the passing of the Bankruptcy and Companies (Winding-Up) Acts. Demands were being made for the institution of a public trustee. Recurrent abuses and the expense, delay and risk of entrusting business to solicitors animated these campaigns.[44] Members of the profession expressed insecurity about their social standing.[45.] Because the profession's capital asset was goodwill the demand for state supervision, with its implied lack of confidence, added insult to injury. To this calendar of woes was now added the imminent prospect of compulsory land registration.

Gladstone's last ministry of 1892 was even more firmly committed than its predecessors to land-law reform with the result that solicitors in Parliament were increasingly isolated. Herschell, the Lord Chancellor, introduced a land transfer bill in March 1893. On the advice of C. F. Brickdale, a Land Registry official, he left the abolition of primogeniture and entails for a separate bill and succeeded, with this tactic, in forcing the bottleneck in the House of Lords. The primogeniture bill failed to get a second reading but the land transfer bill passed unopposed, 'notwithstanding the very strongest efforts of the solicitors' body, both by deputations to the Lord Chancellor and by private influence on individual peers, to obtain its rejection'.[46] Gladstone joined forces with A. J. Balfour, the Conservative leader, to plead for the bill in the Commons. Solicitors and their Parliamentary supporters used increasingly blatant tactics of harassment and delay both within the House and without, and succeeded in blocking the bill in 1893, 1894 and 1895.[47] Herschell deplored their obstructions and threats, but paid homage to their ideological pretensions. 'With a good deal that is said in reference to

[43]'The Profession is palpably overstocked' (ibid. 196–7). See IRAR, solicitors licences.
[44]See LSAR (1892), 45–6; 'Officialism', LSAR (1893), 85–108 and App. VI, 270 et seq.; LSAR (1894), 61–77; LSAR (1895), 44–85.
[45]Fullagar, 'Our profession' (1893), 196.
[46]PRO LAR 1/71, C. F. Brickdale, 'The recent history of land transfer ...' draft memorandum by the Chief Registrar, c. 1906; also LSAR (1893), 40; 11 H.L. deb. 4 ser. 20 April 1893, Herschell, 738.
[47]See 16 H.C. deb. 4 ser. 21 Aug. 1893, Balfour, 747 and reply by Radcliffe-Cooke; 16 H.C. deb. 4 ser. 24 Aug., Gladstone, 974. Harassment, see Radcliffe-Cooke, as above and 29 Aug. 1107; 17 H.C. deb. 4 ser. 12 Sept. 1893, H. D. Greene, 938–9 and 18 Sept. col. 1472. Also 23 H.L. deb. 4 ser. 24 April 1894, 1207–10 and [48] below.

officialism and its dangers I find myself in sympathy', he said in 1893. 'I think it is in principle objectionable'. The state, he added later, was not out to compete with professionals, only to offer a service which they, as individuals, could not possibly provide.[48] It was an argument that solicitors had been making ready to meet.

E. P. Wolstenholme, the conveyancing barrister and Law Society adviser, had long recommended the divorce of private conveyancing from the defence of primogeniture and strict settlement. In his view, a simplified law of tenure, inheritance and settlement offered a better defence from registration of title than inflexible resistance to change. His strategy was endorsed by the Morgan Select Committee of 1879 and found minority support in the Law Society Council in 1880, at the time of the Cairns reform. It was raised again by John Hunter in 1885, when the Halsbury reforms were threatening.[49] In 1894 the profession was no longer bound by obligations to the landowner stalwarts of the old property law and Hunter, now become President of the Law Society, revived his proposal.

The essentials of the 'Wolstenholme scheme' were simple. Transfer of land would be assimilated to the transfer of 'personal' property. Of the many forms of tenure only two would remain, fee simple (i.e. absolute ownership or 'freehold') and long leasehold. An executor ('real representative') would take charge of inheritance, in the manner of dealing with personal property. Subordinate and equitable interests would no longer encumber the title, but would be listed on a register of *caveats*, which every purchaser would consult to ensure that he was getting a clear and absolute title. 'I believe', said Hunter, 'the result would be a system of conveyancing which would outbid anything a Government office could offer in simplicity and undersell it in cost'. Hunter advocated an explicit return to the 'simplification strategy' and he tried to meet the traditional objections to that course.

The simplification of title and of forms of deeds would of course diminish our professional profits in each individual case, but according to precedent in all other branches of business, increased facilities and diminished cost may be expected to increase the number of

[48] 11 H.L. deb. 4 ser. 20 April 1893, Herschell, 738–9 and 32 H.L. deb. 4 ser. 8 April 1895, 1122–4.
[49] See land titles and transfer. Sel. com. mins. of ev; P.P. 1878 (291) XV, E. P. Wolstenholme, quest. 2475–8, 2537–42; Report; P.P. 1878–9 (224) XI, p. iv; J. Hunter, 'Land law reform' *Solicitors' Journal*, 17 Oct. 1885, 782–3; LS, *Statement on the land laws* (1886), p. 40–1; PRO LCO 1/56, Wolstenholme to Lord Halsbury, 'Land transfer bill 1887; observations', pp. 9–10.

transactions quite sufficiently to compensate us; 'small profits and quick returns' are quite acceptable to the legal as to the commercial community'.[50]

Wolstenholme was asked by the Law Society to draft his scheme in a bill.[51] He was assisted by B. L. Cherry, a young barrister who was soon to take over his mantle of authority in real property law as well as his role as adviser-in-chief to the Law Society. Another conveyancing barrister connected with the Law Society, Horace Davey, introduced the bill in the House of Lords in 1896 and the scheme was established as the Society's official policy. Davey was a long-serving Liberal MP who had acted for the Society in Parliament as early as 1881. He was also the professional mentor of R. B. Haldane, the Liberal politician, then at the height of his success at the Bar.[52] N. T. Lawrence, who had managed the 1881 reforms for the Law Society, welcomed the return to a policy of controlled reform which had been so successful in staving off registration in the 1870s.[53] But despite the commitment of the Law Society Council, this was not to be. Neither rank-and-file practitioners nor the government were willing to listen to such counsels of compromise. But to comprehend the subsequent politics of registration it is first necessary to investigate the legal economy yet more closely.

[50]Presidential address, *LSPR* (1894), pp. 41, 48–9.
[51]*LSPR* (1894), 18.
[52]E. P. Wolstenholme and B. L. Cherry, *A bill intituled an act to simplify the title to and the transfer of land* (1896). Davey's links with the Law Society, see *LSAR* (1882), 11. Also PRO LCO 1/55, Horace Davey (then Solicitor-General), 'Memorandum on land registry', 1 March 1886. Compare pp. 4–7 (not numbered) with LS, *Statement on the land laws* (1886), pp. 23, 31.
[53]*LSPR* (1894), 6–8. Also B. G. Lake, 'Registration of title and conveyancing reform', *LSPR* (1895), 144.

4

SOLICITORS AND THE
PROPERTY CYCLE, 1895–1925

I

This chapter examines the nature and extent of the solicitors' reliance on land transfer. It shows how the cycles of the property market affected the fortunes of the profession in times of boom and slump, of peace and war; and how the long cycle of urban development gave rise to individual, social and institutional stresses in a leading property profession. To begin, we shall examine the mechanism at rest, as an inert system of circulation. Then we shall view it in operation, contracting and expanding in response to economic cycles and external disturbances.

The flow of land revenues into the legal economy may be monitored at a number of gates. A 'plumbing diagram' is given in figure 4.1 for ease of

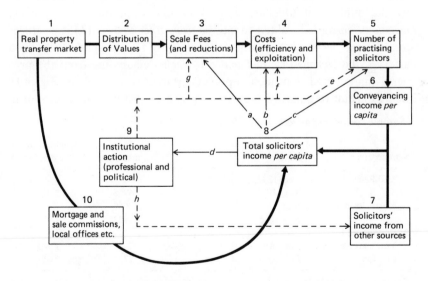

Input (Money), ➝. Feedback: Individual practitioners' adjustments ⟶,
Institutional adjustments − − →

Fig. 4.1. *A model of the effects of the real property transfer market on the solicitors' profession, 1895–1925.*

reference. The *annual turnover of the property market* (no. 1 in Fig. 4.1) was the unmoved mover of the system, its principal independent variable. Inland-revenue stamp-duty returns for sales, leases and mortgages make it possible to follow the fluctuations of the property market with some precision after 1894 (see Fig. 4.2). The financial flows were very large. In 1898, for example (a year of peak turnover), the total of sales, leases and mortgages was £393 millions, comparable, for example, with domestic exports of £233 millions in the same year.

A small percentage of these hundreds of millions of pounds was deflected to the solicitors' profession as land transfer fees, and a rough measure is provided by the Solicitors' Remuneration Act scale fees of 1881. This was a sliding scale, changing with the value of the property and falling much more heavily on small transactions. In order to arrive at a mean percentage some notion of the distribution of property values is required. A number of distributions indicate a combined weighted average conveyancing fee of between 1.9 and two per cent of the value of property transferred or mortgaged.[1]

Both the *distribution of values* (2. in Fig. 4.1) and *scale fees* (3.) remained fixed throughout the period. Rents and subordinate clerical labour made up the main *costs* (4.). Land transfer income is then divided by the number of *solicitors in practice* (5.) to produce *conveyancing income per head* (6.). Added to *income from other sources* (7.) it produces *total income per head* (8.). Another tributary of funds bypassed the main artery – the *commissions and indirect benefits* emanating from the property market and dependent upon its prosperity (no. 10. in Fig. 4.1). Being difficult to quantify, they are largely excluded from this account in

[1]Sample conveyancing fees, 1892–1914.

Sample areas	Dates	No. of transactions	Weighted mean conveyancing fee
1. Middlesex	Dec. 1892, April and Aug. 1893	6735	2.01%
2. North Riding	Aug. 1895– July 1896	2923	1.92%
3. London and Yorkshire	June–Aug. 1907		1.94%
4. London	Jan.–April 1914	1731	2.05%

Sources: (1 and 2) Registration of title in Germany and Austria; P.P. 1896 C. 8139 LXXXIV, pp. 207–8; (3) PRO LAR 1/81, C. F. Brickdale, 'An estimate of the annual saving to the nation to be expected from the establishment of general registration of title under the Land Transfer Acts', 25 March 1919, p. 1; (4) Land Registry statistical dept. Mss 125/1, 'First registration values', 13 June 1923.

spite of their importance. Their hidden mass reinforced the trends we shall describe.

In 1905, 1.9 per cent of the turnover of the real property market gave 16,455 practising solicitors a total of some £5.4 million in transfer fees, or about £328 gross per head. Overhead costs were claimed (in 1917) to have been in the order of 35 per cent before the war.[2] This deduction brings the income per head down to a net figure of £213 a year. Compared with the earning expectations of salaried solicitors (about £150 a year) and solicitors in private practice (£350–£450 net in London; see pp. 16–17 above) this order of magnitude (say 50 per cent of all earnings) gives a crude index of the importance of land transfer to the profession. It was probably higher in small and provincial practices and it excludes commissions and indirect benefits. In the Law Society's *Registry* practices were often advertised in such terms as 'mostly conveyancing' or 'conveyancing and general practice'. Needless to say, the business was not shared out equally. In one sample (Middlesex, all sales, December 1892, April and August 1893) 60 per cent of the fees came out of 20 per cent of the sales.[3] However distributed, the fluctuations of such a major source of income were bound to have a large impact. Even when other sources of income are taken into account, land transfer fee income per head may be regarded as a good guide to the general social and economic well-being of the profession.

With more than 95 per cent of all transactions amounting to less than £5,000 the majority of solicitors found themselves competing in a fairly homogeneous market, particularly in London and the big provincial towns. But the individual's competitive interest in reducing fees was at cross purposes with the professional monopoly interest in keeping them stable and high. Professional organs worked through internal controls or external influences. They could *regulate the number of practitioners* admitted through examinations and fees (*e* in Fig. 4.1). They could negotiate with employees and *promote efficiency* through law reform (*f*). Higher fees were sought through political influence and *scale undercutting* was *controlled* through internal sanctions (*g*). Both political and internal professional action were needed to maintain other sources of income and *protect from encroachment* by other professions and by the State (*h*). There was very little, however, that either individuals or

[2] PRO LCO 2/423, S. Garret [President of the Law Society] to Lord Finlay [the Lord Chancellor], 17 Nov. 1917.
[3] Registration of title in Germany and Austria; P.P. 1896 C. 8139 LXXXIV, pp. 207–8.

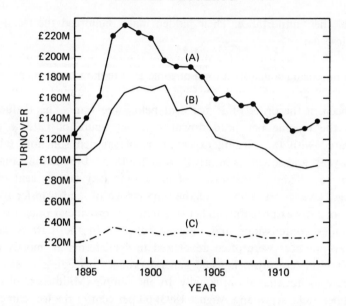

Fig. 4.2. *Property market turnover in England and Wales, 1894–1913.*

(A) conveyances and leases; (B) mortgages; (C) leases. Source: *IRAR*, stamp duties. See Table 4.2.

professional organs could do to influence the movements of the real property market other than by taking a reduction in fees. Land-law reformers asked for just that – in order to boost the circulation and distribution of land, they argued, the drain to solicitors had to be plugged. It was to meet this threat, described in the previous chapter and again in the next, that professional organisations directed their greatest efforts. This chapter is mainly concerned with the 'market reactions' of individual solicitors.

Solicitors' land transfer fees derived directly from property market turnover and the latter conformed to the 'urban cycle', a long cyclical movement which characterised urban growth in the nineteenth century both in Britain and overseas.[4] The last phase of the cycle, from the early 1890s to the Great War, may be followed in stamp duty statistics. Fig. 4.2 shows the movement of the property market in England, broken down to its component elements, from 1894 to 1913. Aggregate turnover rose from £230 million in 1894 to a peak of £394 million in 1899. In 1900

[4]See M. Gottlieb, *Long swings in urban development* (New York, 1976).

52

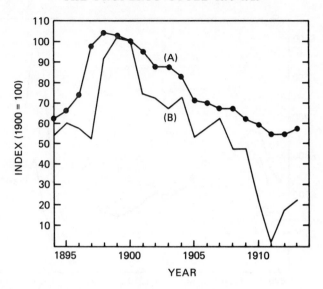

Figure. 4.3. *Solicitors' land transfer fees and the growth of the profession 1894–1913.*

(A), net mean land transfer fee per head. 1900 = £298. (B), annual percentage growth of the profession, 3-year moving average. 1900 = 0.9%. Source: *IRAR*, stamp duties and practising licences.

the cycle turned and decline continued steadily down to £223 million in 1912. A nadir of £132 million was reached in 1917 when the war brought the market almost to a standstill. The post-war boom was partly a reflection of inflated currency. A record turnover of £747 million in 1921 did not recapture the heights of the late 1890s in constant prices, and the market settled down to a level of activity corresponding to the stagnant period of 1904–7.[5]

The profession could not possibly contract sufficiently to adjust for the amplitude of the Edwardian property slump and the market depression was consequently transmitted to the average practitioner's conveyancing income (see Figs. 4.3 and 4.4). The index of a year's average land transfer fees rose from 62 in 1894 to 104 in 1898 and then fell to 55 in 1912. The *growth* of the profession, however, adjusted remarkably to market trends. It rose (on a three-year moving average) when the market rose in the 1890s and came to a standstill at the bottom of the slump, in 1910 (Fig. 4.3). The profession grew when property thrived and stagnated when property sales went down.

[5]See Table 4.2, p. 66.

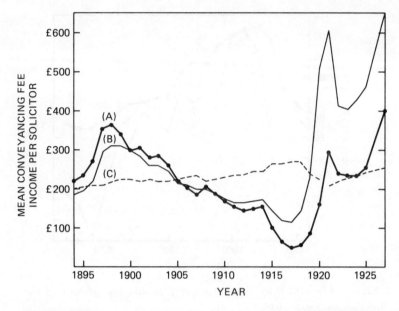

Fig. 4.4. *Mean net conveyancing fee income per solicitor, 1894–1927 (England and Wales).*

(A), constant 1900 prices; (B), current prices; (C), GDP per head, constant 1913 prices (scale/5). Sources: (A) Deflator; Sauerbeck-*Statist* wholesale price index. (B) *IRAR*, stamp duties and solicitors' licences. (C) C. H. Feinstein, *National income and expenditure of the United Kingdom 1855–1965* (Cambridge, 1972), p.T42.

There is no comparable source for estimating the trend of solicitors' earnings from other activities. At the very least, these activities were incapable of filling the gap created by the decline of the land market after 1905. Abel-Smith and Stevens write that 'the growing value and relative simplicity of conveyancing work gave little incentive for solicitors to search for new outlets for their skills or extend their services to a wider section of the population ... nor was the legal profession effective in obtaining a major share of new potential areas of work which developed in the later part of the nineteenth century'.[6] Frauds and malpractice increased the pressure on government to take work out of practitioners' hands. More than two decades of agitation culminated in 1906 in the establishment of a Public Trustee Office. The Land Registry was a growing menace and solicitors were unable to exclude laymen and barristers from

[6]Abel-Smith and Stevens, *Lawyers* (1967), pp. 208, 209.

clerkships to magistrates and local authorities. 'The result has been to direct a broad current of business out of the private channels in which it previously flowed', wrote a contemporary observer.[7] Other professions also encroached. Banks and trust companies took over part of the trustee business.[8] Auctioneers and surveyors competed in the land agency and transfer business.[9] Accountants penetrated the tax and company law field.[10] Arbitration in commercial matters was frequently resorted to in order to bypass the courts. Joseph Chamberlain was reputed to have excluded lawyers from the compensation tribunals of his Workmens' Compensation Act in order to prevent it from becoming a Solicitors' Employment Act.[11] In 1912 the President of the Law Society blamed the plight of the profession on the expense, uncertainty and delay which was turning the public away from litigation.[12] Solicitors were driven out of political and electoral agency by professional agents. 'At least two thirds of [Conservative] agents were still lawyers in 1906, but less than a quarter were lawyers by 1911 ... the day of the lawyer was over.'[13] The divorce and motor accident bonanzas were still in the future.

II

Radical oscillations in the balance of population and resources did not fail to breed their quota of misery and vice. A sense of the profession's tenuous grasp on gentility pervades R. G. Lawson's 1903 paper on 'The profession and public opinion'. After recounting the poor earning prospects of solicitors he reveals that seven lawyers had descended to the workhouse and seventy-three were in lunatic asylums.[14] A persistent persecution complex runs through the *Proceedings* of the annual provincial meetings. 'We are looked upon as a necessary evil', complained W. P. Fullagar in 1893 and again in 1900.[15] R. G. Lawson read out an

[7]P. W. Chandler, 'The battle of the trusts', *LSPR* (1909), p. 89.
[8]*Ibid.* p. 90.
[9]*EG*, 21 Feb. 1903, 308 and 28 Feb. p. 355; Presidential address; *LSPR* (1909), 42; A. G. Watney, 'Presidential address', *Auctioneers' Institute* (20 Oct. 1909), 12.
[10]Abel-Smith and Stevens, *Lawyers* (1967), 87–8, 209–10.
[11]*LSPR* (1903), 207.
[12]*LSPR* (1912), 28–9.
[13]J. Ramsden, *A history of the Conservative party, vol. 3: The age of Balfour and Baldwin, 1902–1940* (1978), p. 52.
[14]Lawson, 'The profession' *LSPR* (1903), 215. There is nothing extraordinary about the figures but the reference is symptomatic.
[15]Fullagar, 'Our profession' *LSPR* (1893), 196; Fullagar, 'Our society: its work, position and benefits', *LSPR* (1900), 116.

anthology of denigrations, with contributions from Walter Savage Landor, John Bright, Lecky and Joseph Chamberlain. He concluded with a quote which he felt reflected a popular image of lawyers – 'Sweep away the lawyers and forthwith there would be an end to triumphant mongery. The lawyer is the typical knave, the arch villain, the president monster, the heartless demon of our social system'.[16] Prosperous solicitors felt a disparity between their income and social status. The road to the judicial bench was barred and there was little prospect of office or honours. The President of the Law Society complained, 'it is seldom that any distinction is bestowed upon a solicitor ... money making, mere money making, is not ennobling, it is very much the reverse'.[17]

Status anxieties were exacerbated by periodic fits of bad conscience. Benjamin G. Lake, a former President of the Law Society and one of the leading warriors against land registration, was convicted in 1900 of defrauding clients of £173,772, and was sentenced to twelve years of penal servitude. His case reverberated through the profession.[18] Solicitors were in fact less prone to bankruptcy than other property practitioners but failures often occurred at the top where they attracted disproportionate attention. Solicitors who went into bankruptcy owed an average of £7,748, about four and a half times as much as the insolvent auctioneer or estate agent. The latter, however, were twice as likely to fail. Collapses did not bunch together in the slump but rather near the top of the boom, and big failures were liable to occur in the first years of a downturn in the building cycle. Both the size and the number of solicitors' bankruptcies increased between 1899 and 1904. After 1905, when the slump really set in, insolvencies dropped to a lower level. An instance of how they came about is given in a Board of Trade return in 1904: 'The largest bankruptcy of the year is that of a firm of solicitors. The practice had been established for over a century; the firm had latterly embarked in large land and building speculation, in order to carry on which they had used money belonging to clients ... ' In this particular case, liabilities were £218,732.[19]

Brankruptcy and fraud brought public disrepute upon the profession

[16]Lawson, 'The profession' (1903), 208–9. Quoted from J. C. Jefferson, *A book about lawyers* (1867), i, 114. See also Presidential address, *LSPR* (1894), 119.
[17]*LSPR* (1905), 36.
[18]See *Solicitors' Journal* 26 Jan. 1901, 214–5; 2 Feb., 232, 236; 9 Feb., 249, 255–6; 16 Feb., 275.
[19]Board of Trade bankruptcy act. 21st rep.; P.P. 1904 (312) LXXXVII, p. 5. These annual reports are also the source of the figures.

and demoralised it from within.[20] There was no *esprit de corps*, complained E. B. V. Christian in 1896, none of the good fellowship kept up by the barristers.[21] At the fringes of the profession, stated a President of the Society in 1906,

> All kinds of shifts are understood,
> All kinds of arts are practised, bad and good,
> All kinds of ways to earn a livelihood.[22]

What he had merely alluded to, the *Property Owners' Journal* made quite explicit in August 1909.[23]

> it must be remembered the out-put year by year of fully qualified practitioners is greatly in excess of the requirements of the population, and as the legitimate business of a lawyer's office must have some limitation, it inevitably follows, when not ordinarily engaged in the work properly appertaining to the office there are many firms *who make work*. It is at this point the lawyer becomes a menace to property owners. One of the first operations in time of slackness is to call in mortgages, not because the money is bona-fide required for other purposes, but for the sake of the costs of being 'paid-off', and reinvesting the fund. Another equally annoying operation is to combine with a surveyor ..., and serve indiscriminately notices of delapidation on the properties on which ground rents are collected in the office ... Speculative actions for wrongful distress, etc., against landlords so readily undertaken by certain of the profession do not endear the lawyers to our body of readers. The sparrow never loves the hawk. Apart from which, however, the profession must realise that the education of the common people, and the trend of modern legislation by the institution of the Land Registry and other kindred institutions, will narrow the scope for their operations, and that they must not look for the fat things secured in the past in these more strenuous times.

The Law Society could not fully reconcile the principle of free enterprise with strictly regulated professional standards, and breast-beating over

---

[20] See LS, 'Report of the special committee on malpractices' (14 June 1900) and 'Special General Meeting on bankrupt solicitors' (17 April 1902) (in the Bodleian law library): Newspaper cuttings and minute books of the committee on malpractices in the Law Society library; J. W. Budd, 'Solicitors and accounts' and W. Godden, 'Clients' monies', *LSPR* (1905), 38–46 and 47–53.

[21] Christian, *Short history* (1896), pp. 234–5.

[22] *LSPR* (1906), 45.

[23] This journal is described in Chapter 18, p. 298.

bad morals was usually followed by exhortations for self-regulation.[24] Failure to separate clients' and practitioner's monies was a frequent cause of bankruptcy. An examination in bookkeeping for articled clerks was introduced in 1906 but the Society tarried long in supporting compulsory auditing and the deposit of clients' funds in separate accounts. Matters reached a head in 1908 when *The Times* was driven to state that 'if the Law Society does not settle the question in its own way, outsiders will attempt to settle it in their way and in one likely to be crude and drastic'.[25] In 1912 a member of the Society (F. Nunn) presented a 'Proposal for the creation of an Inner Circle in the profession'. The Law Society had failed, he said, and the profession was contaminated. 'Now we know that there are solicitors to whom it would be unwise and unkind to entrust a large sum of money. Solicitors are a practically unlimited multitude'. He proposed to establish a professional elite which would guarantee the integrity and substance of its members by imposing an entry fee, an annual subscription, a deposit and an audit.[26]

III

Unlike their employers, solicitors' clerks had no militant trade union to protect their interests and in the Edwardian decade they had to cope with technical change as well as cyclical depression. Mechanical printing began to displace the manual skills of engrossers and law-writers, and female typists began to replace male copying clerks inside the offices. Previously they might hope for a career culminating in a managing clerkship at £200 a year; by 1914 office clerkship was regarded as a dead-end career. In March 1906 the *Law Clerk*, a monthly for unadmitted and unarticled clerks was launched by a private entrepreneur, who identified some 50,000 voiceless constituents. It was avowedly a 'class organ', and in the first year or so it concentrated its attention on exploitation and degradation of workers in law offices. Unpaid overtime, insecurity of employment, low wages and shabby treatment were constituent elements of the experience reflected in the editorial and letter columns of the journal. '[There was] no class of employees who, in a great number of instances, had to put up with more bullying, abusive and insulting

[24]E.g., Fullagar, 'Our society' *LSPR* (1900), 116; Presidential address, *LSPR* (1909), 93–4.
[25]*The Times*, 23 Oct. 1908, 12a. And see *LSPR* (1909), 10.
[26]*LSPR* (1912), 206–16.

behaviour, as well as indignities flung at them by their principals, as law clerks', wrote one correspondent.[27] Combination in a trade union was the remedy constantly reiterated by the editor and his readers. Copying clerks were seen to be a dying breed and women typists were regarded as enemies, not allies.[28]

'Competition from above', from downgraded qualified solicitors, was the most immediate challenge perceived by the seniors who dominated local clerks' associations. In 1907 these clerks consoled themselves that qualified men were not being paid any better than themselves, and believed that 'a good many solicitors will not engage an admitted man owing to the risk of the latter taking away his clients and commencing practice on his own account'.[29] By October 1909 a real slack in employment was becoming evident and the implication of this competition were beginning to sink in.[30] A young qualified solicitor could afford to work as a clerk and supplement an income of £100 a year with support from a middle-class home, in the hope of accumulating experience and contacts. Such men placed an upper limit on the wages of unqualified staff, who were forced to undertake skilled work at wages sometimes lower than the rate for manual labour. They felt 'crushed between the solicitors acting as clerks at the top and the cheap female clerk at the bottom'. It was rare to find a situation advertised in the Law Society *Registry* at more than thirty shillings a week while the majority were for twenty-five shillings or less.[31] 'I would rather be a dustman', wrote one of those who were thus squeezed out, 'who I believe can command a salary of 30s. a week and has no appearances to keep ...'[32]

The clerks' impulse was to break *into* the system, not to break it up. They demanded access to their employers' monopoly. Charles Casey, the honorary secretary of the Northern [Ireland] Law Clerks' Society wrote to the Prime Minister in October 1909, to complain that 'the public reward lawyers upon a much better scale than the lawyers reward their assistants. All unearned increment does not rise from the land', for-

---

[27] *Law Clerk* (Aug. 1906), 79–80. And see Chapter 1, pp. 20–21.
[28] *Law Clerk* (May 1906), 36; (Aug. 1906), 80; (June 1907), 49; (July 1907), 72–3; (Aug. 1907), 88–9; (Sept. 1907), 107–8; (Oct. 1907), 113–4; (June 1909), 73–4.
[29] 'Does it pay to be articled?', *Law Clerk* (March 1907), 6; (Sept. 1907), 104–5 (quote).
[30] 'Does it pay to be a law clerk?', *Law Clerk* (Oct. 1909), 121.
[31] Quoted from A. C. Warwick, 'The law clerk's position', *Law Clerk* (Oct. 1909), 115. See also (Oct. 1907), 115 and 'The "Qualified Clerk" in the solicitor's office' (May 1910), 41.
[32] H. W. Eldred, *Law Clerk* (Oct. 1909), 115.

getting, perhaps, that Asquith was a lawyer himself. Other local clerks' associations joined in agitating for a Law Clerks Bill which proposed to exempt clerks of twelve years' standing from the preliminary and intermediate examinations of the Law Society and from the £80 articles fee.[33] Captain James Craig, the Ulster leader, introduced it as a private bill in 1910, which did not increase its prospects. An attempt to revive the moribund 'ten-year man' (see chapter 1, p. 14) could not be more badly timed. Hard-pressed as it was by the decline of the property market and its struggle against registration of title, the Law Society could scarcely be expected to lower its educational barriers. The solicitors' press dismissed the project with contempt and considering the profession's Parliamentary powers of obstruction, it never stood the smallest chance.[34]

Casey concluded the campaign in an open letter to the President of the Law Society which contained the threat of nemesis.

> The recognition of other people's rights might have saved the solicitors' profession from Official Receivers, the Land Registry and the Public Trustee. Are you now going to repeat the mistakes of the past in regard to your clerks? ... They are not content with the crumbs.[35]

Land registration, however, threatened clerks as much as their employers and the chairman of the Solicitors' Managing Clerks Association did not miss the opportunity to appear before the Royal Commission on land transfer in 1909. He made a claim for a fair allocation of openings in the public service for clerks, in view of the impending decrease in solicitors' work.[36] Declining employment was not conducive to combination. Several local associations continued to exist and the National Union of Clerks tried to woo the unorganised but a general union of law clerks failed to emerge. The *Law Clerk*, having enlarged its title in 1908 to embrace 'the municipal assistant' also faded out after January 1913.

IV

Professional expectations were 'sticky' and failed to diminish in line with real prospects. Statistical evidence is not conclusive but it suggests a

---

[33] *Law Clerk* (Oct. 1909), 115; Feb.–June (1910). The bill: P.P. 1910(12)V, p. 338.
[34] *Solicitors' Journal*, 5 March 1910, 319; *Law Notes* (April 1910), 98–9 and (May), 154.
[35] *Law Clerk* (May 1910), 38–9. The bill appeared again in 1911; see *Law Clerk* (Feb. 1911), 187.
[36] Land transfer acts. R. com. mins of ev.; P.P. 1911 Cd. 5494 XXX, ques. 8145–58.

growing polarisation within the profession, a weeding-out of the weak in line with similar processes in other commercial pursuits and property professions.[37] A 'sound family practice' advertised in January 1909 still promised £400–£500 gross a year, an 'old-established General Practice' was worth £600 to each of the two retiring partners. 'Small practices' and 'junior partnerships' were still worth £200–£300 a year.[38] The mean of partnership advertisements in the Law Society *Registry* did not follow the decline in land transfer income but rather increased somewhat in 1912–13 and the high values (£600–£1000) were more in evidence. Salaried income expectations also rose, yet fewer beginners presented themselves for work at £100 a year and for the first time three advertisements inserted in January were still being printed in July. Sidney Webb reported that 'an advertisement for an admitted solicitor to act as a clerk brought, in 1914, over a hundred candidates'.[39]

Solicitors who would have set up independently before now appeared to opt for the security of salaried employment. The higher expectations of independent practitioners may have reflected the increased size of a viable practice. Steady or even rising expectations continued in a period of declining overall returns, giving rise to a form of frustration termed 'decremental deprivation' by one student of social discontent.[40] The President of the Law Society expressed it in his address for 1912.

> Do we not constantly hear of solicitors leaving the profession? Do we not frequently hear fathers bewailing the fact that they have put their sons into their business? Gentlemen, is £120 or £130 or £140 a year to be the end-all of a solicitor's profession? Do we not constantly find that the work is decreasing and remuneration is becoming smaller?[41]

A disparity between the large amplitude of the property cycle and the narrow margin for adjustment in the number of practitioners lay at the root of the malaise of the solicitors' profession in the Edwardian period. It probably accounts for the bitterness and insecurity so common in the profession's internal and external relations in the decades preceding the First World War. In the professional examinations the Law Society had

---

[37] A. Dobraczyz, work in progress on the urban landlord in the nineteenth century and G. Anderson, *Victorian clerks* (Manchester, 1976), pp. 46–7, 130. Anderson's account of office experience corresponds closely to mine.

[38] LS, *Registry* 'E' register advertisements, Jan. 1909/760, April 1910/564E2, Nov. 1910/1055, Dec. 1912/2289E1.

[39] Webb Prof. XVIII, S. Webb, 'The organisation of the legal profession' (typescript c. 1915), p. 96.

[40] T. R. Gurr, *Why men rebel* (Princeton, 1971), pp. 46–8.

[41] *LSPR* (1912), 28.

a ready-made regulator of the size and standards of the profession. Was education ever approached in this way, as a conscious method of control? Cramming and practical experience sufficed to pass the 'intermediate' and 'final' examinations in legal subjects and the main hurdle for socially 'inferior' candidates was the 'preliminary' examination in general education. In 1886 the Society decided not to impose the University of London matriculation examination as the standard for its 'preliminary' because it had no control over a number of alternative examinations permitted by law, at least one of which (the Oxford and Cambridge local junior certificate) was regarded as a soft option. Latin was retained in the 'preliminary' syllabus in 1904 as a method of keeping up standards. A course of legal study or even a degree were considered as possible methods of regulation, and in 1903 the Society set up a School of Law in London which competed successfully with Chancery Lane crammers.[42] Nevertheless, a period of apprenticeship ('articles') remained the high road into the profession. Articles could not be easily abandoned in the quest for exclusive standards because of their value as a source of indentured labour and periodic cash premiums.[43]

Still, examinations remained a gate. How effective did the Society prove as gatekeeper? Fig. 4.5 records the performance of candidates in its three examinations. It is evident that the 'preliminary' was tightened up as a result of the examination committee report of 1904 while the other two examinations remained at roughly the same level of difficulty. This was another blow to self-help. An older, self-educated clerk could not sit for the Oxford and Cambridge junior certificate which carried an age limit of sixteen years. Otherwise educational policy does not appear to have had much effect on the scale of recruitment. It did tend to raise the class barrier and to restrict senior clerks' opportunities in the decade before the war.

The effect of the Edwardian property slump on the profession may be likened to that of a Malthusian shortfall of resources. The outcome was apparently not a soaring 'death rate' but a species of 'birth control'. At the annual provincial meeting of 1908 J. W. Reid complained of the 'well-to-do firms who are producing solicitors at this alarming rate'. He proposed a 'comparatively mild remedy for strangling at birth a certain proportion of infant solicitors' by having each practitioner limit himself

---

[42]'Report of the legal education committee', *LSAR* (1903), 40–57 and LS, *Report by the examination committee* ... (1904).
[43]H. C. Trapnell, 'The present education of solicitors', *LSPR* (1894), 144–62; Fullagar, 'Our society' *LSPR* (1900), 111; J. Moore-Bayley, 'The solicitor in the making', *LSPR* (1908), 117–25.

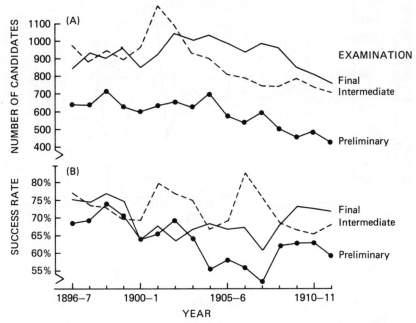

Fig. 4.5. *Number of candidates (A) and success rates (B) at Law Society examinations, 1896–1912. Source:* LSAR.

to one articled clerk instead of the two normally allowed.[44] Professional intake and discharge between 1895 and 1930 are recorded in Fig. 4.6. It corresponds to a demographic chart: the top curve (clerks taking articles) representing conceptions, the next line (admissions) representing births and the bottom curve (withdrawals) the death rate. It shows how recruitment fell steadily before the war, as the withdrawal rate increased (and became less stable). Even before the war mortality had overtaken natality and there were the makings of a Malthusian 'population crisis'. It appears that the reduction in intake which halted the growth of the profession after 1908 was not caused by positive intervention but came rather as a market response, through a contraction of the number of openings combined, perhaps, with a diminished attractiveness of solicitors' prospects.

It required a catastrophic war to restore the fortunes of the profession. In his lament of 1903 R. G. Lawson confided, 'I have heard the opinion gravely expressed by a member of the profession that a plague or war would be an unmixed blessing'.[45] A reduction in admissions could prevent the decline of incomes, but a drastic 'positive check' in the form

[44]J. W. Reid, 'Professional problems', *LSPR* (1908), 236–41.
[45]Lawson, 'The profession', *LSPR* (1903), 209.

63

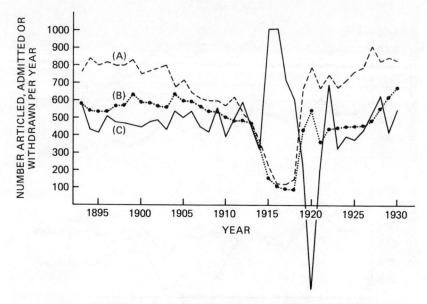

Fig. 4.6. *Demographic trends in the solicitors' profession,1893–1930.*

(A), articles ('conceptions'); (B), admissions ('births'); (C), withdrawals ('deaths'). Sources: *LSAR, IRAR.* Withdrawals equal admissions minus the annual increase of practitioners.

of war was needed to redress the balance of population and resources. This suggests a reason why recruits were so readily enticed to the colours in 1914; in addition to the 'pull', such as it was, of exuberant or earnest patriotism there was also a strong element of 'push': the emptiness, drudgery and frustration of a career in conveyancing, whether as a junior or as a clerk. High competition also characterised the other property professions and only the surveyors, as we shall see (Chapter 22 p. 366) enjoyed an employment boomlet with Lloyd George's Land Valuation. Volunteers for military service between August 1914 and February 1916 included 41.7 per cent of those of eligible age groups employed in the professions, compared with 29.4 per cent in all occupations. Only entertainers produced a higher quota (41.8 per cent).[46]

Table 4.1 summarises the war effort of the solicitors' profession. Mortality was 17.1 per cent among solicitors who served, and 24.1 per

[46]J. M. Winter, 'Britain's "Lost Generation" of the first world war', *Population Studies* 31 (1977), table 6, p. 454.

Table 4.1. *War effort of the solicitors' profession, 1914–1918.*

Period	Solicitors		Articled clerks	
	Joined	Died	Joined	Died
Up to July 1915	2053	47	1098	26
July–December 1915	419	100	167	64
January–December 1916	98	155	20	110
1917	494	149	138	93
1918	260	137	62	65
Total	3324	588	1485	358

Source: LSAR, 1915–19.

cent among articled clerks. The proportion of solicitors killed is equivalent with the proportion killed among Cambridge (17 per cent) and Oxford (16.5 per cent) graduates who served in the forces. The proportion of articled clerks killed is lower than that of the parallel age group ('early twenties and late teens') in King's College, Cambridge (26 per cent) and Balliol College, Oxford (30.6 per cent).[47] These losses amounted to about a year and a half's intake into the profession and no account is taken of the effects of injury and captivity. Even more important was the virtual standstill of new recruitment for four years. Those who stayed at home may have had a hard time for a few years when sales plummeted and retail prices rose enormously,[48] but returning solicitors appear to have found it difficult to resume their practices and many did not survive the collapse of the post-war boom. This is indicated by the high positive withdrawal rate of 1922, shown in Fig. 4.6. In 1920–25 the professional population settled down at a level of about 1500–1700 fewer practitioners than in 1910–14, an overall loss of about ten per cent. After four years of inactivity the land market revived and reached unprecedented heights; the political efforts of prewar years also began to bear fruit. A new equilibrium was established at a higher level of per capita conveyancing income than in 1908–14. The profession did well out of the war.

[47] Winter, 'Lost Generation', table 10; *idem,* 'Balliol's "Lost Generation"', *Balliol College Record* (1975), 22–6; King's College statistics Winter, 'The demographic consequences of the Great War' (unpublished paper).
[48] See J. Matthews, 'The First World War and country solicitors', *Solicitors' Journal,* 13 Sept. 1974, 623–4 (I owe the reference to Mr D. R. Harris).

Table 4.2. *Property market turnover in England and Wales, 1894–1927 (In rounded £ million).*

Year (ending March)	Conveyances	Mortgages	Leases	Total
1894	105	104	21	230
1895	117	104	23	244
1896	134	114	27	275
1897	184	148	36	368
1898	197	164	32	393
1899	192	171	31	394
1900	187	168	30	385
1901	168	173	28	369
1902	161	147	29	337
1903	162	151	29	342
1904	151	143	30	324
1905	133	123	28	284
1906	134	118	28	280
1907	127	115	26	268
1908	129	116	27	272
1909	112	111	26	249
1910	117	100	25	242
1911	103	96	25	224
1912	106	92	25	223
1913	111	95	27	233
1914	114	98	25	237
1915	87	76	21	184
1916	70	56	20	146
1917	68	46	18	132
1918	98	45	17	160
1919	182	64	18	264
1920	436	155	28	619
1921	516	196	35	747
1922	311	161	30	502
1923	294	168	37	494
1924	304	188	36	528
1925	334	205	35	574
1926	350	208	38	596
1927	330	220	41	591

Sources: *IRAR*, 'Stamp Duties', e.g. *IRAR* 1912; P.P. 1912–13 XXIX, table 51, p. 61. Rates in force are listed in Table 45, pp. 52–4.
Reliability and significance
1. *General.* The series used omit small classes of stamps incident on realty (on agreements, settlements, unclassified documents and adhesive revenue stamps) amounting to 4.1 per cent of the total in 1912. A category of 'blank instruments' was merged with the others in 1909. Previous to that year its components were apportioned to their respective categories.
2. *Conveyances.* This was the most straightforward conversion. The duty was 0.5 per

Notes to Table 4.2 continued

cent of the consideration up to the year 1909, when it was doubled for all dealings of more than £500.

3. *Mortgages.* The standard rate of duty was 0.125 per cent, but stamp duty returns also included unspecified sums due to equitable mortgages (at 0.025%) and reconveyances of mortgages at the same rate. Low-security equitable mortgages were not a very popular form of credit (B. Campion, 'Bankers' advances upon title deeds to landed proprietors, Pt. I,' *Journ. Inst. Bankers* 27 (1907), 45–9), and reconveyances do not count as mortgage flows. The effect of including equitable mortgages at the standard rate (0.125%) is to·deflate the total flow, and the inclusion of reconveyances has the effect of inflating it, so they partly cancel each other out. More disruptive was the practice of securing short-term business credit on the collateral of land and houses. These loans are indistinguishable from other mortgages in the returns, but we have estimated them at about 20 per cent of the total (see Chapter 8, p. 143), so the mortgage curve in Fig. 4.2 is best read from the 'leases' curve upwards, and not from the base line.

4. *Leases.* Short-term agreements were stamped at a very low rate and do not, on the whole, figure on the curve. For periods of over a year, a sliding scale was charged on the rent. We have assumed the aggregate to be equivalent to the duty on sales, i.e. 0.5 per cent. Leases granted for a consideration rather than a rent were charged at this rate. Rates were doubled in 1909 and the gap was bridged by extrapolation.

5

BENTHAMISM BLUNTED
1895–1925

I

Property market fluctuations spelt prosperity or famine for solicitors but land registration threatened them with dispossession. Evidence given by their leaders to a Commons select committee in 1895 revealed a deep-seated hostility to registration.[1] Nevertheless, and in spite of remonstrances from provincial solicitors the Law Society was forced by the unanimity of public opinion to enter into negotiations with Lord Salisbury's new government.[2] In 1897 a compromise was reached whereby compulsory registration of title would be introduced as an 'experiment' into the Administrative County of London. Lord Campbell had warned in 1830 with remarkable foresight that a register introduced 'in a single maiden county ... would not be a fair trial and ought not to be attempted: it would be effectively thwarted by the enemies of the measure'.[3] The land transfer bill agreed between Lord Halsbury and the Law Society came up for its second reading in the Commons on 3 August 1897, the penultimate night of the session. Representatives of the provincial solicitors staged a revolt and were only appeased by one further concession, the so-called 'County Veto' – a provision that County Councils would have to approve any extension of registration into their areas. In a letter to *The Times* Lord Herschell voiced the fear (fully justified by later events) that 'opposition to land transfer by registration will be shifted from the House of Commons to County Councils'.[4]

The loss of London was a major breach in the solicitors' defences. Several attributes singled out the metropolis as a suitable target for Lord Halsbury's offensive. In the first place leading metropolitan solicitors were milder in their opposition, owing perhaps to a lesser dependence on conveyancing. Secondly, the Progressive party on the London County

[1] E.g. land transfer bill. Sel. com. rep.; P.P. 1895 (364) XI, R. Hunter, q. 962–3.
[2] See the press welcome to the blue book on registration in Germany, p. 71.
[3] John Campbell, H. C. 16 Dec. 1830, in Campbell, *Speeches* (1852), p. 459.
[4] *The Times*, 5 June 1897, 11; 50 H.C. deb. 4 ser. 1 July 1897, 936–44; 52 H.C. deb. 4 ser. 3 Aug. 1897, 294–306, 4 Aug., 326–36.

Council was keen on land reform and unlikely to make trouble. Sir Arthur Arnold, the veteran advocate of 'Free Land' was Chairman of the L.C.C. from March 1895 to March 1897.[5] Thirdly, London was the largest and most important property market in the country, with more than one-fifth of the rateable value of England and Wales, 45 per cent of Law Society members and more than a third of the solicitors' profession.[6] Fourthly, an embryo Land Registry had existed in London since Lord Westbury's act of 1862. Having barely survived extinction it carried a small traffic of voluntary registrations with a staff of six clerks and two officials, but it was a base for future expansion. The Prime Minister complimented Halsbury on his preseverance in accomplishing an act which 'the bleached bones of many Chancellors had seemingly shown to be impossible'.[7]

A sharp reaction from discontented London solicitors soon threw the Council of the Law Society, the affluent group of practitioners who had made the 'compromise', on the defensive.[8] The act of 1897 released the differences which had long been simmering within the Society,[9] and marked a shift in its confrontation with government. The council would have preferred to continue the pretence of a discreet and mutually advantageous understanding with another estate of the *ancien régime* but this course no longer existed and the profession was gradually pushed into a stance of open defiance, of harping upon a populist rejection of Big Government. Greater militancy had been building up since the early 1890s. It erupted in the Commons 'rebellion' of 3 August 1897, and it threw up an alternative leadership and an alternative style of conflict.

J. S. Rubinstein (1852–1915) was solicitor to the Birkbeck Bank and Building Society, a prominent financial institution of late-Victorian London. A taste for Opera and the music-hall, and an extensive connection among West End proprietors and performers made him a familiar backstage figure in London theatres and music-halls. His Bohemian disposition manifested itself in a mercurial personality, a flair

[5] For his views on registration, unchanged since *Free Land* (1880) see A. Arnold, 'The land transfer bill', *London*, 23 May 1895, 377.
[6] *London Statistics* 8 (1897), cxi; *LSAR* (1898), 31; p. 12, above.
[7] A. Wilson Fox, *The Earl of Halsbury, Lord High Chancellor* (1929), pp. 142–3.
[8] In December 1898, even before the actual introduction of compulsory registration in London the Council made ready to collect evidence unfavourable to the land transfer act. See *LSAR* (1901), 17 and land transfer acts. R. com. mins. of ev. (1911), J. S. Beale, q. 8921.
[9] For long-standing differences between the Council and the rank-and-file see Kirk, *Portrait* (1976), pp. 141–2.

for colourful oratory and the pretensions of authorship. A compulsive activist, he combined a penchant for the platform with the pursuit of professional interests. His gifts were first deployed in the service of the Leasehold Enfranchisement Association in the 1880s. A life-long Liberal, he nevertheless sat on Kensington Vestry as a Conservative. Likewise, membership of Arthur Arnold's Free Land League did not prevent him from agitating against registration of title. He had a special claim to expertise, having compiled and published a guide to the Conveyancing and Solicitors' Remuneration Acts of 1881 and a handbook on conveyancing costs, both of which went through several editions.[10]

'A solicitor who gets a Building Society appointment regards himself as provided for life', wrote James Dodd to the Webbs in 1914.[11] As a Building Society solicitor, Rubinstein had special reason for concern over registration. Building Societies handled a great number of small and often standardised transactions. The societies were well-placed to dispense with solicitors for land transfer work if registration simplified and threw it open to non-professionals. The Building Societies' Association had been among the most persistent advocates of registration since the 1870s.[12] Within the legal profession Rubinstein was something of an *enfant terrible*, standing outside the establishment and not bound by its conventions and etiquette. In 1897 he began to concentrate his political experience and muckraking talents on the Lord Chancellor in an attempt to draw Halsbury into open combat against the entrenched positions of solicitors in the property market, local government and Parliament. The first of a vitriolic series of papers, soon to become a regular feature, was delivered at the annual provincial meeting in 1897.[13] Between October 1897 and February 1898 he used his position on the Kensington vestry as the command-post of a campaign to persuade the other vestries to petition the L.C.C. against the Land Transfer Act.[14] But the L.C.C. persisted.

[10] Based on an interview with his son, the late H. F. Rubinstein, 10 Sept. 1974, and on information in the Law Society records department, See also D. A. Reeder, 'The politics of urban leaseholds in late Victorian Britain', *International Review of Social History* 6 (1961), 422; Land transfer acts. R. com. min. of ev.; P. P. 1911 Cd. 5494 XXX, ques. 4885–7, 4930–1.

[11] Webb Prof. IV/4, J. Dodd to B. Webb, 18 March 1914, fol. 5.

[12] See e.g. PRO LCO 2/8$\frac{18}{1}$, Building Societies' memorandum to the Lord Chancellor, May 1888, or 'Registration of title' (leader), *Building Societies' Gazette*, 1 Jan. 1900, 8–9, censuring Rubinstein.

[13] J. S. Rubinstein, 'The land transfer act, 1897', *LSPR* (1897), 79–90.

[14] *The Times*, 13 Dec. 1897, 9; *LSAR* (1903), 77; land transfer. R. com. evidence (1911), q. 4935.

Rubinstein faced a formidable opponent at the Land Registry. Charles Fortescue Brickdale (1857–1944) was a barrister with a family tradition of conveyancing and land law reform stretching back to Bentham.[15] In the manner of Arthur Underhill he published at his own expense a short book on *Registration of title to land and how to establish it without cost or compulsion* in 1886. The land-question debate was raging and Brickdale sent off copies to leading politicians, barristers and solicitors.[16] It was to prove, he recalled, a 'throughly good investment'.[17] Both the Law Society and the Lord Chancellor approached him with offers of work in support of their respective causes. He took up the Lord Chancellor's offer and after proving himself as a draftsman of the land transfer bill, he was enlisted by Lord Halsbury to help rejuvenate the Land Registry in 1888. It was the start of a life-long commitment to the government service.

Brickdale was an archetype of the late-Victorian reforming official: independent, earnest, opinionated, hard-working and stubborn. He served a long apprenticeship in the tactics of land-law reform under Halsbury and Herschell during the lean years of the Land Registry. His blue book report on registration of title in Germany and Austria–Hungary earned a leader in *The Times*, and approbatory reviews in the *Manchester Guardian*, the *Economist* and twenty-one other metropolitan and provincial papers.[18] Brickdale was a prolific and lucid writer and earned the grudging respect of his rivals.[19] In July 1898 he was placed at the head of the Land Registry. At first the assignment strained his competence; a small office dealing with voluntary registrations at a leisurely pace had to be converted at short notice to the compulsory registration of each and every transaction in the largest market in England, under the critical surveillance of a hostile clientele. He failed to meet the deadline and the beginning of compulsory registration had to be postponed by six months, to 1 January 1899.[20]

[15]His father Matthew J. Fortescue Brickdale, a member of 'The Institute', had been a pupil and associate of C. H. Bellenden Ker, an important early-Victorian law reformer. Brickdale senior had been something of a Radical and contributed to the Christian Socialist press in the 1850s. See Brickdale Papers (BP), C. F. Brickdale, typescript biography of M. J. F. Brickdale (*c.* 1928).

[16]BP, a collection of letters of acknowledgement and comment, 1886–7.

[17]BP, undated note by C. F. Brickdale.

[18]Systems of registration of title now in operation in Germany and Austria-Hungary. Reports of the Assistant Registrar of the land registry; P.P. 1896 C. 8139 LXXXIV and 1897 C. 8319 LXXXVIII. Press cuttings volume in BP.

[19]'Grudging respect', see presidential address, *LSPR* (1905), 27.

[20]An outline of his career is in the BP. See also T. B. F. Ruoff, *H. M. land registry centenary 1862–1962* (multigraph, c. 1962), p. 5 and Add MSS 56370, Halsbury Papers, K. M. Mackenzie to Halsbury, 15 Sept. 1898, fols. 123–4.

It was greeted with opposition of unprecedented shrillness. The *Law Notes* of November 1899, for example, took its cue from Rubinstein with such passages as follow (pp. 335, 343),

As we have said over and over again in the interests of the public, it is the duty of the profession to make the registration of title so unpalatable to those who register in the parts where registration is already compulsory that at the end of the probationary period of three years, there will be no chance of the compulsory area being extended.

'Chats with Young Solicitors' in the same number asked:

Are we encouraging the registration of titles under the Acts of 1875 and 1897? Well, what do you think? Are we likely to do anything to bring about professional suicide? ... No, no; we are doing our level best to thwart registration of title ... If the registration of title in the present compulsory area is made as inconvenient, troublesome and expensive as possible, there will be little likelihood of the area being extended. Our view is, that every solicitor owes a duty to the profession, and also to the public, to throw every obstacle in the way of registration of titles, i.e., in the way of encouraging the government doing the conveyancing work of the country; for, in simple truth, this is what registration of title really means.

The Registrar and the lawyers remained locked in combat for the following decade. Space rules out a full narrative account of this episode, so rich in the detail of manoeuvre and counter-manoeuvre, abuse and counter-abuse. Rubinstein relied on direct action and his propaganda combined ideology with innuendo. 'To rely on Parliament', he wrote in *The blight of officialdom*, 'is to rely upon a broken reed'.[21] He used permeation tactics to obtain resolutions, representations and deputations to the Lord Chancellor from local authorities, building societies, bankers and property-owners' associations. In one audacious action he even captured the Land Law Reform Association, which was committed to registration as the third item in its manifesto. All this activity failed to prevent the extension of compulsory registration into the City of London in 1902, but kept it out of Northamptonshire in 1903.[22] Let some stanzas

[21]*LSPR* (1903), 128.
[22]See PRO LCO 2/183 (1902) for corporate representations; for Land Law Reform Association, memorandum to the Lord Chancellor, 23 July 1901 and 'Report of the executive committee of the Land Law Reform Association on the administration of the land transfer acts by the Land Registry' (Aug. 1902),

tell the stirring tale. A saga entitled 'The Limpet and the Registrar' appeared in the *Law Notes* for February of 1903, preceded by these remarks: 'Lord Halsbury has refused an inquiry into the working of the Land Registry in London, and characterized the opposition to its extension as a self-interested one. The Registrar has reported the experiment a complete success. No other county has as yet, however, adopted the system'.

From 'The Limpet and the Registrar':

> The Limpet and the Registrar
> Were walking in the Strand.
> They wept to think of lawyers' fees
> On the transference of land.
> "If we could run a Registry,"
> They said, "it would be grand."

> "The time has come," the Limpet said,
> "To talk of many things:
> "Officialized conveyancing
> "And the blessings that it brings,
> "Red tape, routine and sealing-wax,
> "And clipping lawyers' wings."

> Then London County hurried up
> All eager for the prize,
> And donned her red-tape harness
> Before their wondering eyes.
> She was *quite* the *youngest* County
> (As you might perhaps surmise).

> "A stately pile," the Limpet said,
> "Is what we chiefly need,
> "And sinecures for relatives
> "Are very nice indeed!
> "We'll incorporate each County,
> "We are certain to succeed."

> "Oh, pray not *me*, each County cried,
> Turning a little blue;
> "To extend without inquiry

p. 1. For the City of London, LCO 2/183 *passim* and Add MSS 56370, Halsbury Papers, K. Muir Mackenzie to Halsbury, 20 Nov. 1901, fol. 153; Northamptonshire – PRO LAR 1/183 (1902–3), *passim* and land transfer R. com. ev.; P.P. 1909 Cd. 4510 XXVII, quest. 2136–54.

"Were a shabby thing to do."
"I'VE REPORTED," said the Registrar,
"That's *quite* enough for you!"

"Come, Counties," said the Registrar,
"A boon for every one!
"Pray share the blessings London owns,
"And do as she has done!"
Each County shrewdly winked his eye,
But answer came there none.

II

Rubinstein was assisted by the state of affairs at the Land Registry. There were teething troubles and inefficiencies. As Bentham had feared, registration of title, which could only be justified by cheapening the transfer of property, had actually made it more expensive. Compulsory registration only provided 'possessory titles' which were not guaranteed in any way. When registered titles came on the market they had to be investigated all over again and the cost of registration was added to the normal conveyancing fees. This weakened the position of the Registry with its Building Society friends. Edward Wood, Chairman of the Building Societies Association and a personal friend of Brickdale warned and remonstrated repeatedly.[23] Brickdale believed that if the Registry could only grant 'absolute' (i.e. fully guaranteed and legally indefeasible) titles its superiority would be demonstrated.[24] The Society on its part renewed the attack on 'Officialism' and continued to agitate for a public inquiry to expose the Registry's shortcomings.[25]

At the end of 1907 both sides sought a way out of the deadlock. The Law Society began to revert to the conciliatory strategy of reform and simplification and commissioned T. Cyprian Williams, a conveyancing barrister, to draft an updated version of the Wolstenholme scheme. A Society-inspired article by the barrister Charles Sweet flew yet another old kite, the extension of registration not of title, but of deeds.[26] Brickdale however was thinking of attack, not retreat. He concocted a

[23]PRO LAR 1/91, E. Wood to C. F. Brickdale, 25 Nov. and 9 Dec. 1902.
[24]Land registry. Report of the Registrar on the first three years; P.P. 1902 Cd. 1111 LXXXIII, p. 31.
[25]Between 1886 and 1907 the Law Society published at least one long statement against registration every year in *LSPR* or separately. And see LCO 2/185, E. G. Hill (President of the Law Society) to the Lord Chancellor, 16 Jan. 1904.
[26]Williams was the son and editor of Joshua Williams. His bill is in PRO LAR 1/26. See also LCO 2/360, C. F. Brickdale, 'Memorandum on Wolstenholme's scheme', 20 June 1908 and C. Sweet, 'The land transfer acts', *Law Quarterly Review* 24 (1908), 37–9.

scheme for an advance on the lines of 1896; a bargain with the bankers and building societies against the 'desperadoes of Chancery Lane'. With the help of those interests he considered it possible to rush through in one session a bill for the substitution of absolute for possessory titles in all ordinary cases of first registration, and for the abolition of the County Veto as the first step in extending compulsory registration to the whole country. No full-scale inquiry was required, because '... it could not prevent an attempted "block" in the House of Commons by the solicitors, which is all we have to fear'. He felt he could certainly hold his own in an enquiry:

> I should dearly love to have had the solicitors out in the open and to have exposed their abominable tactics in the sight of all men but it would take a long time, and it would arouse more bad feeling than ever, and I am quite willing to take my revenge in a swifter though less sensational manner.[27]

Lord Loreburn, the Liberal Chancellor, was sympathetic to Brickdale but could not afford to ignore the solicitors' opposition. He took Brickdale at his word and granted the Law Society their inquiry in return for a concession: equalisation of Land Registry fees for possessory and absolute titles.[28] More important, the Registrar was given powers to grant absolute titles automatically, without special application and without incurring delay. After ten years of compulsory registration it became possible for the first time to begin the construction of a true registry of title granting indefeasible, absolute titles requiring no subsequent investigation. Despite solicitors' obstructions the number of absolute titles on the register began to rise rapidly.[29] A set-piece rehearsal of four decades of conflict took place at the hearings of the Royal Commission which lasted from October 1908 to November 1909. Brickdale, the Law Society, the provincial associations, the bankers, the building societies, even the solicitors' managing clerks, all had their innings. Encouraged by the unfolding of Lloyd George's radicalism, Brickdale put forward a maximalist demand for the rapid extension of compulsory registration to the whole country at government expense.[30]

[27] PRO LAR 1/27, Brickdale to Muir Mackenzie, 12 Oct. 1907. The scheme is outlined in LAR 1/12, Brickdale to the Lord Chancellor (Loreburn), 8 Jan. 1906.

[28] BP, K. Muir Mackenzie to Brickdale, 11 May 1906 and Brickdale's comments on *verso*; PRO LAR 1/86 and LCO 2/260, *passim*.

[29] PRO LCO 2/259, Brickdale to Loreburn, 6 March 1907, 5 May 1909 and LAR 1/81, C. F. Brickdale, 'Observations on the Law Society's resolutions of 8 Sept. 1911'; C. F. Brickdale 'Report on the recent increase of registration with absolute title' (printed, 4 pp. May 1912).

[30] Land transfer acts. R. com. ev. (1909), q. 12719a.

III

In 1910 the conflict entered its most critical phase; by 1922 it had been resolved. I have already recounted the story in detail elsewhere; this section will retell it in outline, and complement it with additional evidence and some general conclusions.[31] Land registration combined the older Benthamite Radical appeal with the more recent Liberal preoccupation with social 'efficiency'. Brickdale had laboured long to publicise the efficiency and fiscal utility of registration in Germany and found a willing pupil in Lloyd George. Registration of title was also associated with the Liberal feud against the landed interest which flared up with the introduction of the 'People's Budget' of 1909. In 1910 Lloyd George accepted Brickdale's proposals to create one grand 'Domesday Office' out of the Land Registry, the Ordnance Survey and the valuation department of the Inland Revenue, to carry the burden of his challenge to the landlords. In 1913 the project was revived as the 'Land Ministry', one of the props of the unfinished 'land campaign' which Lloyd George launched in anticipation of the elections of 1915, and which forms the subject of chapter 22. Solicitors were generally indifferent to the 'People's Budget' and its land values taxation, which could only bring them additional business. But their reaction to Liberal support for registration was comparable to the doctors' attitude to health insurance. After fighting a spirited rear-guard action they rejected Rubinstein's militancy and came to the verge of capitulation in 1912. The Liberal thrust lost its impetus, however, and petered out with the resignation of Loreburn and the accession of R. B. Haldane to the woolsack in 1912.

R. B. Haldane (1856–1928) has been enjoying a good press recently. One study depicts him as 'Public Spirit personified' and he serves as patron saint to the Haldane Group of Labour Lawyers.[32] His role in the land transfer saga does not fully harmonise with this wholesome image. Haldane had trained as a conveyancer and, in his own words, 'practised conveyancing down to nearly the end of my time at the Bar'.[33] He had been a pupil in the chambers of Horace Davey, a Liberal in the House of Commons and later in the Lords, who had a long and close connection

[31]A. Offer, 'The origins of the Law of Property Acts, 1910–25', *Modern Law Review* 40 (Sept. 1977), 505–22, where full references to undocumented statements in this section may be found.
[32]E. Ashby and M. Anderson, *Portrait of Haldane at work on education* (1974), p. 2. Also S. E. Koss, *Lord Haldane: scapegoat for Liberalism* (1969).
[33]R. B. Haldane, *An autobiography* (1931), p. 66.

with the Law Society. The Society had long cultivated a group of conveyancing barristers with briefs, drafting commissions and business connections. In addition to Davey, the group included such people as Arthur Underhill, E. P. Wolstenholme and B. L. Cherry.[34] Haldane held a nostalgic, almost lyrical view of the old conveyancing, as he told the House of Lords in 1920.

> I was brought up as a Lincoln's Inn conveyancer, and in the early days when I went to the Bar I spent many laborious days and nights in a garret in Lincoln's Inn reading, I should not like to say how many thousands of the old pages of abstracts of title ... we lived laborious days because we had to watch at every turn for technicalities, a good many of which have since been swept away, but which in those days constituted pitfalls. I do not wish your Lordships to understand that lawyers did not take an immense interest in those pitfalls. Sometimes they loved them ... The old path, whatever its difficulties, was very familiar to lawyers of the old school. One cannot help have a certain love for things that follow from a logical principle ...[35]

His autobiography contained a passage in similar vein.[36]

Haldane spoke out in support of registration in the House of Commons in 1891, as befitted an 'advanced' Liberal of his generation.[37] In 1895 he was a member of the select committee on the land transfer bill. He helped to arrange the 1897 compromise with the Law Society and was one of its sponsors in Parliament. In 1905 he wrote an encouraging letter to Brickdale.[38] Later he changed his tone. Subsequent letters to Brickdale were aloof and non-committal.[39] During a House of Lords debate on registration in 1911 Haldane alone stood up to defend the solicitors against an all-party attack.[40] After his elevation to the woolsack he was invited to dine with the conveyancers of 'The Institute', an honour most rarely granted, by a body which he held in high regard.[41] Haldane had clashed with Loreburn before, and their rivalry was exacerbated when the latter was preferred over Haldane for the Lord

---

[34] See pp. 44–5, 47–8.
[35] 39 H.L. deb. 5 ser. 3 March 1920, 263–4.
[36] Haldane, *Autobiography*, pp. 66–7.
[37] 356 H. C. deb. 3 ser. 24 July 1891, 340.
[38] BP, Haldane to Brickdale, 8 June 1905.
[39] BP, Haldane to Brickdale, 14 Feb. 1914 and PRO LCO 2/407, Brickdale to Sir Claude Schuster, 10 June 1917.
[40] 9 H. L. deb. 5 ser. 19 July 1911, 561–3.
[41] Loreburn was never invited. See 'The Institute', *List of past and present members* (1968), p. 17 and Haldane, *Autbiography*, p. 67.

Chancellorship in 1905.[42] Loreburn had been a warm supporter of Brickdale,[43] and plans for extending registration were well advanced when he retired due to illness in 1912. Haldane was quick to abandon, indeed to reverse his policies.

The Law Society soon confirmed that Haldane was a friend. He let Loreburn's plans fall by the wayside and set up a new drafting team for conveyancing reform which started work on the lines of the 'simplification strategy' devised by Wolstenholme and Cherry and adopted by the Law Society some eighteen years before (see pp. 47–8). The plan for reforming the land laws, wrote Haldane in his memoirs, 'had been more or less worked out by an eminent conveyancer, the late Mr Wolstenholme. His chief disciple, Mr, afterwards Sir, Benjamin Cherry, was ready to place his knowledge and experience at my disposal ... the Primary draftsman was Sir Benjamin Cherry'.[44] Cherry was possibly even closer to the Law Society than Wolstenholme. He had drafted Society bills and represented the Society at public inquiries throughout the Edwardian period.[45] In 1913 he prepared two bills for the simplification of the property laws modelled on the bill he had drafted for the Law Society with Wolstenholme in 1895–6. Needless to say, the bills were warmly endorsed by the Society.[46]

Haldane reversed a policy of support for registration of title which successive Lord Chancellors had consistently pursued since 1885 and reverted to the Cairns approach of reform in agreement and co-operation with the Law Society. He repudiated a time-honoured land-reform principle and moreover, one explicitly modelled on German practice, of which he was an important advocate. He appears to have placed his loyalties to a professional clique higher than his Liberal principles. His motives were hardly consistent with the principles of a land-reforming ministry, but perhaps they represent a more profound appreciation of the values of Wilhelmine Germany than the superficial admiration of bureaucratic efficiency which his colleagues professed. His policy explains

---

[42]R. F. V. Heuston, *Lives of the Lord Chancellors, 1885–1940* (1964), pp. 167–8.
[43]BP, Loreburn to Brickdale, 18 Sept. and 31 Dec. 1910, and 18 Feb. 1914.
[44]Haldane, *Autobiography*, p. 250.
[45]For evidence of Cherry's ties with the Law Society see E. P. Wolstenhoeme and B. L. Cherry, 'Observations on land transfer and conveyancing bill' (1896, Lincoln's Inn library); PRO LAR 1/86, H. Percy Harris to C. F. Brickdale 10 Dec. 1907; *LSAR* (1908), 27; land transfer R. com. ev. (1911), quest. 6782–820, 7220–83; *LSPR* (1914), 136; PRO LCO 2/443, B. L. Cherry, 'Law of property bill, memorandum' (c. 1919), p. 1; LCO 2/445, Malcolm Macnaughten to Claude Schuster, 5 Aug. 1920.
[46]*LSAR* (1914), 47, 113.

the absence of land transfer and registration from the Liberal Land Enquiry of 1913–14.[47] But the reactionary project was not consummated; European war interfered with the progress of the bills.

During the war years Brickdale attempted to enlist emergency collectivism and reconstruction planning into the service of registration.[48] A Ministry of Reconstruction land policy committee undertook to examine the land laws in September 1917. The potential of registration in a controlled economy was demonstrated by a series of initiatives in 1918. Registration was wanted to enforce the compulsory shift from pasture to wheat under the Corn Production Act and to identify alien property; a great future role was predicted for it in the impending post-war land and housing programmes. In response to these initiatives the Ministry of Reconstruction finally set up a land transfer sub-committee, but only in January 1919.[49] By then, however, the opportunity had been missed: the war was over and so was the thrust of Liberal Radicalism. A Coupon Parliament was installed in Westminster.

The land transfer sub-committee was dominated by advocates of the solicitor interest. Arthur Underhill, a conveyancing barrister who had been closely associated with the Law Society since 1880 produced a pamphlet which equated registration of title with bolshevism.[50] His proposals were reprinted by the committee and adopted as the basis of its report. B. L. Cherry, the draftsman of Haldane's pre-war bill and still in the Law Society's pay, was commissioned to draft a Law of Property bill. He began work on yet another version of the Wolstenholme scheme.

When F. E. Smith became Lord Chancellor early in 1919 he was impatient for a rapid and spectacular accomplishment and sought for it in land-law reform.[51] At first he considered following in the footsteps of Halsbury and becoming the champion of registration. In June 1919 he entered into negotiations with the Law Society for the removal of the 'County Veto' (see p. 68). The solicitors were evasive and obdurate and Brickdale warned of the futility of appeasement: 'Our old experience of

[47] Land Enquiry Committee, *The land: the report of the land enquiry committee*, ii. urban (1914), xxx.
[48] PRO LCO 2/407, Brickdale to the Lord Chancellor, 10 Dec. 1917.
[49] The documentation is too extensive to cite and this account is very compressed. See PRO LCO 2/508, 'Acquisition and valuation of land committee' (c. March 1919).
[50] A. Underhill, *The line of least resistance* (c. 1919). Typescript, PRO LCO 3/43; pamphlet, LCO 2/509; reprinted Acquisition and valuation of land committee 4th rep. Transfer of land; P. P. 1919 Cmd 424 XXIX, app. I, esp. p. 34.
[51] This and the following paragraphs are abstracted from Offer, 'Origins' (1977) where sources are cited.

the Law Society is that it is not much use making concessions to them. There is always someone who gets up afterwards and asks for more'.[52] Lord Birkenhead (as Smith had become) recognised where real power lay and in his ruthless drive for results soon abdicated his principles. B. L. Cherry, the draftsman of the law of property bill, was highly instrumental in this result. He admitted that the existing system of private conveyancing did not stand, as he put it, 'a dog's chance' against registration.[53] His appointed task was to restore the competitiveness of private conveyancing by effecting a drastic simplification of the whole of the law of real property. He took over the management of the bill with the full assent of the Lord Chancellor and the permanent secretary, remaining in close consultation with the Law Society, steering the bill according to its requirements, and constantly urging concessions on the permanent secretary.

Such single-minded pursuit of reform disturbed many vested interests: conveyancing barristers, provincial solicitors, owners of manors and the Commons Preservation Society. Some opposition was obviously simulated in order to force further restrictions on the Land Registry. Overt opposition came mostly from the right. Trades unions, who were indifferent anyway, were granted an amendment which permitted them to extend their ownership of land beyond one acre. Leslie Scott, the Liverpool Conservative who proposed the amendment in a letter to the Cabinet, argued that 'it was very desirable that the Labour Party and the Trades Unions in particular should own as much land as possible in order to give them a proprietary interest which would disincline them to revolution'.[54]

Josiah Wedgwood, a veteran Liberal disciple of Henry George and a recent adherent of the Parliamentary Labour party, led the surviving rump of land reformers in the House of Commons. 'This Parliament of 1918–1922', he wrote in his memoirs, 'was quite the wickedest I have known'.[55] By 1921 he was apparently not above a little wickedness himself. He had met F. E. Smith at Winston Churchill's 'other club' during the war and in 1919, when Smith became Lord Chancellor, he obliged his friend by overlooking the contempt of court implied in Wedgwood's scandalous attack on divorce procedure.[56] In response to a

[52]PRO LCO 2/444, Brickdale to Claude Schuster, 17 May 1920.
[53]LCO 2/449, B. L. Cherry to Lord Birkenhead, 23 June 1922.
[54]PRO LCO 2/449, Cabinet Home Affairs Committee circular CP 4004, 31 May 1922, including letter from L. Scott to H. A. L. Fisher, secretary, 30 May 1922.
[55]J. C. Wedgwood, *Memoirs of a fighting life* (1940), p. 146.
[56]*Ibid.* pp. 117, 150.

letter from Birkenhead, Wedgwood failed to deploy his formidable talents for obstruction against the Lord Chancellor's elaborate and vulnerable bill. The letter merits a long quotation.[57]

Secret.

My Dear Josh,   13 July 1921

... The Bill is in no sense a party measure and raises no controversial issues ... it touches indirectly the question of the single tax. You know that although I have never completely agreed with your view on this matter, I have understood it and have perhaps even looked at it with the sneaking sympathy of the Liverpool school. I realise, therefore, that it is a subject which might at any time become of urgent and practical importance.

The principal and almost the only effect of the Bill would be to sweep away an enormous mass of technicality affecting the ownership of land whose very existence is a bar to any revised system of taxation. If you can imagine yourself as Chancellor of the Exchequer introducing your single tax bill, you would find yourself hampered by masses of feudal law ...

Naturally I do not want to point out in any loud voice to the world at large some of the advantages of simplicity as they may appear to you. So long as you see a step taken in the direction which you desire your astute mastery of Parliamentary tactics will teach you how best to assist it. It may be – I hope it will be that judicious silence will help me most. But of this you will judge.

The Law of Property bill was enacted in 1922. It promised a free run of ten years for a greatly simplified form of private conveyancing. The extension of registration was postponed for that length of time and made conditional on a public inquiry and an affirmative vote in both houses of parliament. It gave the solicitors as much forward security as was practicable in the period, expressed in a time horizon of ten years.[58] A further extension of this horizon was achieved when the application of the act was postponed until 1925, to pass consolidating legislation and enable Cherry to write not one, but three textbooks.[59] Notwithstanding

[57]Original of letter in Wedgwood papers, copy in PRO LCO 2/448. Capacity for obstruction, Wedgwood, *Memoirs*, pp. 71–2. Lukewarm remonstrances, 154 H.C. deb. 5 ser. 15 May 1922, 119–23.

[58]Recalling the same government's 'ten-year rule' on armaments. See A. J. P. Taylor, *English history 1914–1945* (1965), p. 228.

[59]See Offer, 'Origins' (1977), 520, n. 99.

the post-1922 deflation, solicitors also received a 33.5 per cent rise in the conveyancing fee scale in 1925, and a 50–350 per cent rise (on a sliding scale) in registration fees. These rises restored net conveyancing income per head to the record levels of the late 1890s. In 1926–7, the first year in which the new scales came into effect, net income per head (after deducting 35 per cent for overheads and taking account of the fee scale for registered land in London) was £653 a year. This was equal to £401 in 1900 prices, or an index figure of 135. The previous record was 122, reached in 1898 (1900 = 100) (see Fig. 4.4). In 1925 the profession was secure and profitable as never before. The war relieved it of the surplus of practitioners; the Law of Property Act of 1922 secured its monopoly; conveyancing costs were considerably reduced for the solicitors and raised for the client. After 1925 there was a big expansion in building activity.[60] These factors must have been the basis of the renewed attraction of the profession after 1925.

IV

Conclusion and Epilogue

In order to explain the course of land law reform the Law of Property must itself be considered as a species of corporate property. It was a vested interest of the legal profession. Its value was subject to the fluctuations of the long cycles of the property market, and the legal fraction of the English middle classes did not thrive in the years of the Edwardian property slump. Some scores of thousands of black-coated workers partook in this experience, together with a broader fringe of other property professionals. To make things worse, government began to encroach upon the same market and crude conflicts of interest were sometimes starkly expressed. Business in HM Land Registry declined by some 40 per cent between 1904 and 1912. The spokesman for a deputation of third class clerks (who carried out routine tasks in the department) complained in 1912 'that he and most of his colleagues had attained their maximum pay for some time, [and] that their prospects of promotion were very poor'. The official who had come to hear their grievances blamed the solicitors: 'When their opposition is overcome, as we hope and believe it will be the present difficulty will be at an end'.[61]

[60] H. W. Richardson and D. H. Aldcroft, *Building in the British economy between the wars* (1968), table 1, p. 56.
[61] PRO LAR 1/91, 'Notes of interviews at the Land Registry', 25 June 1912, pp. 1, 3.

The Great War literally decimated the solicitors' profession but the purge laid the ground for its inter-war prosperity. This experience may not be untypical of inter-war bourgeois retrenchment.

Competition with private conveyancing had a distorting effect on the Land Registry so it may be misleading to compare the economic performance of the two methods. When the 1897 act was introduced in the House of Commons the attorney-general of the day promised 'a saving of perhaps as much as four fifths of the charges which existed at the present time', and was received with cheers.[62] In its first years the Registry offered a few enterprising individuals a service at one-fifth the cost of private conveyancing but procedural defects within the registry and a solicitors' boycott rendered it unavailable to the great majority of proprietors. At this level, moreover, the Registry's fees were producing a loss and they had to be raised in 1908.[63] In 1912 the Registrar abandoned his attempt to price solicitors out of existence. Instead, he offered to accommodate them with exclusive or privileged access to the Registry and higher solicitors' scale charges for registered property. This principle was incorporated into the settlement of 1925.[64] It is idle to speculate on the potential performance of the Land Registry in the absence of private competition. It might have become less sharp and helpful than it is today, and the danger of bureaucratic aggrandisement, arrogance and inefficiency cannot be dismissed. On the other hand the absence of a centralised register of ownership has handicapped land-use and planning policies, at both local and national levels. It has kept ownership under a veil of secrecy and the procedures of transfer under a mantle of mystery, to the advantage of the monopolisers of this information in the estate agency and land-transfer professions. The register is not open to the general public (it is selectively open to government agencies) and is still not universal at the time of writing.

Knowledge of property law and a corporate influence on its formulation were crucial for the solicitors' success. Wolstenholme's long-term 'simplification strategy' was a successful adaptation which proved more effective than die-hard obstruction. It enabled the profession to rationalise its procedures and retain the productivity gains. The settlement of 1922–5 has proved to be very durable and survives in its essentials up to the present day. Registration was very slowly extended.

[62] 50 H.C. deb. 4 ser. 1 July 1897, 938.
[63] PRO LCO 2/259, C. F. Brickdale, 'Memorandum', 6 March 1907.
[64] PRO LAR 1/26, C. F. Brickdale, Memorandum on a meeting with the President of the Law Society, 11 Jan. 1912.

The Law Society removed its opposition in 1952 while managing to exclude other professions from the Land Registry and keeping the monopoly intact.

Mystification was one of the profession's important weapons. Birkenhead wrote in his covering letter to the Cabinet in 1920, 'The matters dealt with in the [Law of Property] Bill are highly technical and I should not serve any useful purpose by discussing them at length.'[65] The Acts of 1925 made up an enormous body of legislation, reputed to be the largest enacted as one unit in English legal history. 'They have done', the textbook claims, 'much to infuse simplicity and reason'.[66] Be that as it may, they were only pushed through to satisfy the vested interest of a determined group in a lucrative and largely superfluous function. Nor was this outcome a foregone conclusion. Not all contemporary tenure groups were so successful. House-landlords for example, another middle-class tenure interest, never fully recovered from the effect of wartime and post-war rent controls.

The solicitors' struggle against compulsory registration is comparable in certain respects to the private-bill legislation which served to establish property rights in Victorian England. Like most of the great volume of private legislation it did not have any great impact upon party politics. Nonetheless it was a political triumph. My 1977 article invoked Max Weber's idea of 'rationalisation' as a key to the conflict between an emergent bureaucracy and an entrenched monopolistic guild. Weber assumed that bureaucracy would follow upon democracy.[67] Why then did bureaucracy falter in this case? Solicitors were never a very large group nor always a unanimous one in Parliament. Between 1900 and 1919 there were usually fewer than twenty-five of them in the Commons of whom some, like Lloyd George, were not sympathetic (on the other hand, some barristers were effectively part of the solicitors' lobby).[68] In pre-war Parliaments Radicals commanded much larger numbers. The success of the solicitors' resourceful and ungentlemanly parliamentary tactics highlights the failure of Radical land policy even in this uncontroversial sphere. Then again, perhaps the political neutrality of registration militated against its forceful prosecution.

[65] PRO LCO 2/443, Duplicated note signed by Birkenhead, 27 Jan. 1920.
[66] R. Megarry and H. W. R. Wade, *The law of real property*, 4th edn (1975), p. 1.
[67] *From Max Weber*, ed. H. H. Gerth and C. Wright Mills (1948), ch. 7, esp. p. 231.
[68] Solicitors in Parliament were counted by the *Solicitors' Journal* after general elections. They averaged nineteen between 1900 and 1919.

Personalities also played a part. The accession of Haldane was the most important turning point. As Birkenhead aptly understated, 'Lord Haldane exhibited a very informed but slightly adverse interest [in registration of title]'.[69] After the war it was the abdication of Radicalism which more than anything provided the solicitors with the freedom of action which led to the Law of Property Acts. An element of desperation in their tactics again calls attention to the nature of land law as property. Why did Brickdale's and successive governments' strategy of reform end in such a miserable failure? Arguably, because of a misconception of the problem. Registration, which appeared on the face of it to be a rather mild measure of legal and administrative reform was really a measure for *nationalisation without compensation*. Brickdale's proposed 'Domesday Office' of 1910 (see p. 76) would have made the land transfer profession redundant, destroying the livelihood of a substantial component of the middle class together with many scores of thousands of employees and dependants. The strategists of land-law reform gave little thought to the need for alternative employment for this multitude. The social cost of change was overlooked and registration was evaluated as a costless saving.[70] The solicitors may have fought so resolutely because they had their backs to the wall and were shown no line of retreat. Nationalisation without compensation was far removed from the political postures of the would-be reformers, who ranged from the reactionary Lord Halsbury, who led the Lords' rebellion against the Parliament Act in 1911, to the mildly Liberal Loreburn and Brickdale. Even land nationalisers and Fabians did not propose to appropriate private property without any compensation in the Edwardian period (although the Henry Georgians did) and such a course was even less acceptable in the political climate of the early inter-war years.

Bentham would not have fallen into this error. He reserved his greatest eloquence to condemn the analogous case, 'Suppression of places and pensions, without indemnifying the individuals who had possessed them', not only on grounds of utility, but also of justice. The rentier in his make-up probably shuddered at the thought.

Envy is never more at ease than when it is able to conceal itself under the mask of the public good: [he wrote] but the public good

[69] 44 H.L. deb. 5 ser. 17 March 1921, Birkenhead, 654.
[70] See e.g. PRO LAR 1/81, C. F. Brickdale, 'An estimate of the annual saving to the nation to be expected from the establishment of general registration of title under the land transfer acts', 25 March 1919.

only demands the reform of useless places – it does not demand the misery of the individuals holding the place reformed.

The principle of security requires, that in all reforms the indemnity should be complete. The only benefit that can be legitimately derived from them is limited to the conversion of perpetual into transitory charges ...

Individual interests are the only real interests. Take care of individuals; never injure them, or suffer them to be injured, and you will have done enough for the public.[71]

What would have been required of a practicable policy of land law reform? The solicitors came closest to capitulation at the bottom of the property slump, in 1911–12. In a market society, it seems, proprietors will resist administrative, legal or fiscal assault, but they will abide by the adverse decisions of the market. Is this not the essence of liberal freedom? The business of private conveyancing could have been run down first by making it less lucrative, by diluting the professional monopoly and throwing the field open, or by regulating fees. Some provision would have to be made for older and less adaptable practitioners. The able would not have stayed. Expropriation by main force of middle-class interests was not practicable in Edwardian England and may still not be so today.

Controversy over conveyancing costs flared up again in the 1960s and 1970s. A number of cut-price conveyancing firms began to compete with lawyers and to challenge the monopoly, meeting with furious opposition from the Law Society.[72] In 1972, in a curious act of historical blindness, the Lord Chancellor (Hailsham) abolished scale fees in the expectation that market forces would bring them down. Instead, there was a general upwards drift of fees in relation to property values, amounting in some places to more than a third in less than four years.[73] Compulsory registration continued to expand, adding a massive land transfer bureaucracy numbering more than 5,000 on top of the solicitors' profession, and making the latters' work simpler than ever before. In 1978 three-quarters of the population of England and Wales lived in the areas of compulsory registration, where double-decker conveyancing (private below, official above) prevailed.[74] The most devastating exposure ever of

---

[71]Bentham, 'Civil code', Bowring edn i, 320, 321.
[72]Kirk, *Portrait*, (1976) pp. 146–52.
[73]R. Bowles and J. Phillips, 'Solicitors' remuneration: a critique of recent developments in conveyancing', *Modern Law Review* 40 (Nov. 1977), 647.
[74]*H. M. Land Registry. Report to the Lord Chancellor 1977–8* (1978), pp. 3, 14.

private land transfer·was published in 1976 by a onetime conveyancing solicitor. Michael Joseph's scathing book, *The conveyancing fraud*, was published privately, but nevertheless soon went through a number of editions. In 1977 the Law Society ran a national advertising campaign in the press which advised the public, 'don't listen to Whatsisname, see a solicitor'. In a one-man crusade, a law lecturer from Worcester changed his name by deed poll from Reynolds to Whatsisname after carrying out cheap conveyancing in defiance of the Society, for which he was taken to court by the humourless lawyers' trades union and given a well-publicised legal trouncing (£150 fine and £600 costs).[75] Late in 1979 top-heavy conveyancing was given another lease of life by a Royal Commission on legal services. Five out of fifteen members dissented.[76]

The Benthamite thrust for rationalisation seems fully spent in Britain at the time of writing (1979), at least so far as vested property interests are concerned. With the spread of owner-occupation and the prevalence of 90 per cent mortgages, house buyers may find themselves spending a good part of their cash outlay, as much as a quarter or more, on professional fees, whenever they need to occupy a house for a few years. The property booms of the early and late 1970s have periodically jacked up conveyancing incomes. It seems fully consonant with the temper of the times that the country is reconciled to a comfortable, respectable and cynical monopoly.

[75]See *The Times*, 29 Nov. 1977, 3; 10 Jan. 1978, 4; 11 Jan., 2; 12 Jan., 2; 19 Jan., 2: 20 Jan., 2; 21 Jan., 2.
[76]Legal services. R. com. rep.; P.P. 1979 Cmnd. 7648, vol. 1, pp. 243–86 and 808–16.

Part II
DIMENSIONS OF TENURE

6

CLERGY, CORPORATIONS AND JUNIOR PROPERTY PROFESSIONS

A miscellany of imperfect impropriators existed in circumstances loosely analogous with those of the solicitors. Clergy, dons, City guildsmen, surveyors, auctioneers, lowly house agents: what these disparate occupations shared was a comparable mode of appropriation. Like the solicitors they only exercised limited control over the principal and subsisted, at least in their corporate or professional capacity, largely on a flow of land revenues from tithes, rents, rent-charges, commissions and fees. This chapter is mainly concerned to find how much they each managed to drain off the national rent and whether their share increased or fell (a rent time-series for England and Wales is printed in Table 6.3, p. 102). Subsequent chapters will move up the ladder of tenurial perfection to establish the nature, distribution and fluctuations of the dominant species of tenure, the property of landowners and capitalists and also their burden of debt, the character of their creditors and the national political forces constraining their interests. To begin, however, let us move for a while from the sordid spheres of the property marketplace.

I

Tithe

The parish clergy may be considered as a 'property profession'. In numbers, status, social function and average income they were comparable with lawyers. About twelve thousand Anglican clergymen (in England alone) in the late 1870s made up a class of 'resident landowners' who mediated between the upper and lower orders and subsisted (at an average of £300 a year) on their glebes and on commuted tithes payable as a rent-charge by farmers (from 1891, by landowners) in the parish.[1] The comparison with lawyers has been made by Bentham, who valued religion in strictly utilitarian terms.

[1] James Caird, *The landed interest and the supply of food* (4th edn 1880), pp. 135–6.

The ministers of religion ... are a body of inspectors and teachers of morals who form, so to speak, the advanced guard of the law; who possess no power over crime, but who combat with the vices out of which crimes spring; and who render the exercise of authority more rare, by maintaining good conduct and subordination.

'The expense of their support', he said, 'ought to be referred to the same head as the expenses of police and justice – to that of internal security'.[2] In other words, tithe was a title to property earned in the protection of property.

Collection of tithes in cash or kind had become increasingly vexatious in the first third of the nineteenth century and commutation in 1836 seemed to place the clergy on a secure basis.[3] Tithe was linked in 1836 to a moving average of grain prices in the previous seven years. For tax purposes it was regarded as a species of landed property, i.e. assessed to Schedule A of the income tax. As agriculture entered its sixty-year crisis in the late 1870s the fickleness of indexation began to affect the clergy's inheritance. Commuted tithe amounted to £4.05 million in 1886–7, or 2.5 per cent of all rental (see Table 6.3).[4] The grain-price index stood at 87.4 in 1887 (1836 = 100) and having fallen from a peak of 112.8 in 1875 it continued to decline until 1901 (66.5), and then rose into the low 70s in the years before the war, producing little more than three million depreciated pounds a year. Of this only some 60 per cent was payable directly to parochial incumbents and almost twenty per cent had devolved to lay impropriators.[5] It was 'the Church's worst financial crisis since the middle of the sixteenth century', wrote the historian of her finances.[6] Spiritual fires were also burning low, but the collapse of grain prices and of rural rents may have facilitated the contraction of the clergy which took place in the Edwardian decade.[7]

What is more, the tenurial nature of tithe ensnared the parsons in a peculiar fiscal net. Tithe rent-charges were assessed for local rates at their full value, which was often in excess of the incumbent's disposable income, subject as it was to curates' stipends and other inescapable

[2]Bentham, 'Civil code', *Works*, Bowring edn, i, 316.
[3]See E. J. Evans, *The contentious tithe* (1976).
[4]Strictly speaking about 9% less, since tithe included rates, and Table 6.3 does not.
[5]Parochial incumbents 59.5%, clerical impropriators 16.8%, lay impropriators 18.9%, schools and colleges 4.8%. About £260,000 of tithe remained uncommuted. Return of all tithes commuted; P.P. 1887 (214) LXIV, p. 294.
[6]G. F. A. Best, *Temporal pillars* (Cambridge, 1964), p. 471.
[7]Musgrave, 'Middle class education' (1959), table 2, p. 105.

expenses and obligations. In 1887, for example, tithe rates came to £357,000, representing a local income tax on the clergy equal to some 8.7 per cent of tithe incomes, and this at a time that national income tax stood at a mere 3.3 per cent.[8] An agitation was got up and the 'Tithe Rent-Charge Owners Union and Church Property Defence Association' persuaded the Royal Commission on Local Taxation in 1899 that there was 'no other class of ratepayers whose basis of assessment results in the contribution of so large a proportion of income towards local taxation'. The government of the day, as we shall see, was particularly partial to the Church, and granted a rate rebate of 50 per cent in 1899.[9] But in the long run the parsons were not as successful as the solicitors. As their secular authority diminished, their title depreciated. In 1936 tithe rent-charge was commuted again, this time into government stock. The redemption issue amounted to £70 million, no mean sum in the 1930s, with three per cent interest and redeemable at par in sixty years.[10] Inflation soon ate deeply into this nest egg and the parish clergy were finally and peacefully dispossessed not by revolution or reform, but by the retail price index.

II

Corporate bodies

The corporate institutions of pre-industrial England still maintained a considerable foothold on British soil in the last third of the nineteenth century; enough to give them some five per cent of the total aggregate (Schedule A) rental.[11] Functionally considered, they fell into three broad groups: oldest and most firmly established were the Monarchy, the Church, the Oxford and Cambridge colleges, the old public schools, the Inns of Court, the City of London and the Livery Companies, the Clubs,

---

[8]*IRAR* (1888), Appendix, p. xx.
[9]Local taxation. R. com. 2nd rep.; P.P. 1899 C. 9142 XXXV, pp. 26–9. See Chapter 14, p. 213.
[10]Evans, *Tithe*, pp. 166–7.
[11]Excluding rates. Schedule A source, see Table 6.3, p. 102. Corporate land and urban property revenues were assessed at £6.234 million in 1870 (5% of schedule A rentals, excluding rates). See Corporate bodies Schedule A property return, 1870; P.P. 1872 (122) XXXVI, p. 145. A roughly comparable estimate in 1882 gave rents of £8.79 million (5.6% of schedule A). See Real property held in mortmain or for charitable, public or perpetual uses. Abstract of return; P.P. 1882 (274) L, p. 445.

learned societies and academies of the arts. All were committed in their various ways to the preservation and development of upper-class codes and culture, symbols and values, means of coercion and modes of control. For these purposes, landed property provided both financial resources and an environment of elaborate dignity; in the emphatic surroundings of cathedrals and quads religious and secular priesthoods officiated in the rituals of status and class, while middle-class recruits to gentility absorbed the ethos of the old landed and professional elites and made their own contributions to its evolution.

Corporate tenure was a mediaeval relic. Corporations were immortal legal personalities and their exemption from feudal obligation excited the jealousy of the nobility. In 1273 Edward I enacted the statute *De Viris Religiosis* to prevent the transfer of land into the 'dead hand' (mortmain) of religious orders, an act followed by many others to the same effect.[12] By the eighteenth century the distrust of religious bodies and the dislike of death-bed bequests had not abated, and was augmented by next-of-kin fears of disinheritance. A Mortmain Act was passed by large majorities in 1763, forbidding the bequest of land to corporations, and the principle was retained in amending legislation in 1888 and 1891.[13] Yet the Acts were evaded by secret trusts and by special Acts of Parliament,[14] and the Crown granted a steady stream of exemptions, an average three every two years between 1837 and 1887.[15] The abuse of charities and individualist hostility to corporations gave rise to a certain amount of reforming zeal between the 1860s and the 1880s, notably from W. E. Gladstone; he attempted to tax them in 1863, and succeeded in imposing an annual corporation duty, in lieu of probate duties, in 1885.[16]

Towards the end of the nineteenth century the property holdings of corporations still reflected their pre-industrial origins: their wealth was still overwhelmingly invested in land. In 1882 they held some 5.7 per cent of all agricultural acreage in England and Wales.[17] Two great surveys,

[12]Texts printed in L. Shelford, *A practical treatise on the law of mortmain* (1836), app. pp. 809ff. The book is a lode of charity lore.

[13]G. L. Jones, *History of the law of charity* (Cambridge, 1969), pp. 109–13.

[14]See W. F. Finlason, *An essay on the history and effects of the law of mortmain* (1853), pp. 86–7, 191.

[15]Mortmain licences granted to bodies corporate. Return; P.P. 1888 (348) LXXX, p. 689.

[16]See, e.g. A. Hobhouse, *The dead hand* (1880); L. T. Hobhouse and J.L. Hammond, *Lord Hobhouse: a memoir* (1905), pp. 26–32; 297 H.C. deb. 3 ser. 30 April 1885, 1153–4, 1192–8. More recently, D. Owen, *English philanthropy 1660–1960* (Cambridge, Mass. 1965), pp. 322–29.

[17]Mortmain. Abstract of return; P.P. 1882 (274) L, p. 5.

compiled around the end of the first and third quarters of the nineteenth century showed the extent of landed revenues in charity incomes to be 72 and 66 per cent respectively and much of the residue was invested in mortgages.[18] Non-charitable corporations took 90 per cent of their incomes from realty.[19] In 1902 70.8 per cent of the charitable incomes exempt from income tax were derived from landed and urban property.[20] Crown revenues from the Duchies of Cornwall and Lancaster came largely out of rents, like the endowment incomes of Oxford and Cambridge colleges.[21] The Ecclesiastical Commissioners reduced their dependence on rents from a very high level of 91 per cent in 1885 to 72 per cent in 1914, but like the charities, they also kept a large portfolio of mortgages.[22]

Another category of trusts and charities included in the totals quoted above was not designed for the consumption of the upper classes but for the discharge of paternalist and philanthropic obligations. An income of about £2.2 million a year was available for such purposes in the 1870s, of which roughly 42 per cent was earmarked for poor relief. Education received 35 per cent, religion 11 per cent, medicine 9 per cent and public amenities 3 per cent.[23] This category of funds was particularly open to frivolous and misdirected benefactions and was most often subject to the whims of long-deceased donors. Sometimes the opposite happened and the living contrived to frustrate the intentions of the dead, as when charity funds were diverted from the poor to middle-class scholarships and schools. Misappropriations of this kind were popular with Radical 'land question' agitators in the 1870s and 1880s. The City guilds and the Dauntsey charity (1889–90) were among the outstanding cases.[24] A third

[18]The 'General digest of charities' of 1840 was compiled between 1819 and 1837; that of 1876, between 1861 and 1867. See Endowed charities. Explanatory memorandum and tabular summaries; P.P. 1877 (261) LXVI, pp. 13–22.
[19]Produce of corporation duty 1886–7. Return; P.P. 1887 (195) LXVI, p. 341.
[20]I.e. assessed to schedule A. See *IRAR* (1903), pp. 181, 192.
[21]The Duchies of Cornwall and Lancaster and the Crown Woods and Forests produced £0.803 million in 1906 (0.36% of all rent); P.P. 1907 XLVII, pp. 140, 148, 552, 554. Oxford and Cambridge colleges took in £0.526 million in 1903, of which 93% came from land, houses and tithes. See J. P. D. Dunbabin, 'Oxford and Cambridge college finances 1871–1913', *Econ. Hist. Rev.* 2 ser. 28 (1975), table 4, p. 638.
[22]Best, *Temporal pillars* (1964), app. VII, table B, pp. 553–4, col. 1 as a percentage of col. 3.
[23]Endowed charities; P.P. 1877 (261) LXVI, Table II, pp. 13–15.
[24]E.g. G. J. Holyoake, *Sixty years of an agitator's life* (1902), ii, ch. XCVI; see J. F. B. Firth, *Reform of London government and of city guilds* (1888), pt. III, p. 90ff; J. Collings and J. L. Green, *Life of the right honourable Jesse Collings* (1920), ch. XXVI.

class, of more truly social tenures, was established through municipal responsibility. Schools, parks, libraries, hospitals and other municipal education and welfare assets in England were only worth some £0.7 million a year in 1870 (0.6% of all rental and 12.2% of corporate property).[25] It was this category that was to undergo the most remarkable growth. Finally, friendly societies and trades unions were debarred from owning more than an acre of land, in the spirit of the laws against mortmain. Still, they managed to keep about a third of their assets in realty (mostly mortgages) in 1877 and raised the proportion to more than one-half by 1910.[26]

Traditional corporate bodies may have required special dispensations from the law of mortmain in order to acquire land but once in possession it was even more difficult for them to sell.[27] So the stream of income, the rents, usually mattered more to them than the movement of capital values. An overview of corporate and social welfare tenures is given by Table 6.1, which summarises the movement of those rents in England in the two decades preceding the Great War. Almost all the tenure of old-established *non*-charitable corporations (col. 1) was vested in London bodies and distributed among them in the following proportions. City companies and guilds owned about one-half (51%), the City corporation itself under a third (28%), the Inns of Court (and the Law Society) had eight per cent and the London clubs seven. Only incomes not applied to 'charitable' purposes are counted.[28] Like Oxbridge colleges, but unlike the Ecclesiastical Commissioners, these custodians for the London patriciate just managed to hang on to their share of the nation's landed incomes (about 0.4%).[29] Although they lost about ten per cent of their share of the national rent the Ecclesiastical Commissioners (col. 3) actually performed better overall than some of their corporate peers. They

[25]Corporate bodies; P.P. 1872 (122) XXXVI, p. 145.
[26]Trade union act 1871, s. 7; Friendly societies act 1875, s. 16(2). Friendly society mortgages were 25.1% of £12.7 millions total assets in 1877; land and houses made up another 4.9% (P. J. H. J. Gosden, *Self-help* (1973), Tables 4.1 and 4.2, pp. 91, 94–5). In 1910 the total had risen to £60.2 million of which £33 million were invested in mortgages, buildings and land (Registrar of friendly societies. rep ... 1911; P.P. 1912–13 (123-XII) LXXXII, Table 1(A), p. 13.).
[27]Williams, *Real property* (1896), pp. 282–4.
[28]Produce of corporation duty 1886–7; P.P. 1887 (195) LXVI, p. 341.
[29]For Oxbridge, see Dunbabin, 'College finances' (1975), 646–7. It does not follow, as he writes, that they enjoyed 'an untypical prosperity in the years before the First World War', since the share of tenure in the national income declined somewhat in those years. See A. Offer, 'Ricardo's paradox and the movement of rents in Britain, 1870–1910' *Econ. Hist. Rev.* 2nd ser. 33 (1980), 236–52.

Table 6.1. *Corporate and social welfare rents in England and Wales, 1895–1910, In £1 million and as a percentage of the aggregate (schedule A) rental*

	(1) Non-charit-able corpor-ations[b]		(2) Charities, hospitals, schools[c]		(3) Ecclesiastical Commissioners[d]		(4) Total[e]	
Year[a]	£M	%Sch.A	£M	%Sch.A	£M	%Sch.A	£M	%Sch.A
1895	0.70	0.40	4.44	2.52	1.51	0.86	6.65	3.77
1900	0.78	0.40	5.06	2.58	1.59	0.81	7.43	3.79
1905	0.85	0.39	6.91	3.18	1.71	0.79	9.47	4.35
1910	0.90	0.39	8.06	3.46	1.81	0.78	10.77	4.62

[a] Fiscal year starting April, except col. (3) which is for the year ending on the 1st of November.
[b] Source: corporation duty, *IRAR*. Net revenue multiplied by 20, with 10 per cent deducted for the value of personalty. See Produce of corporation duty, 1886–7; P.P. 1887 (195) LXVI, p. 341.
[c] Source: Total income tax schedule A exemption in respect of charities, hospitals, schools etc, *IRAR*. Multiplied by 1.2 to restore repairs deduction and adjusted for change of system in 1900 (multiplied by 1.45 in 1895). See J. C. Stamp, *British incomes and property* (1920 edn), pp. 65–6 and *IRAR* (1901), p. 118.
[d] Source: Ecclesiastical Commissioners' annual reports, P.P.
[e] Source for schedule A rental: table 6.3, p. 102.

diversified into other assets probably on the proceeds of land sales and their London estates were well situated for capital gain.[30]

Schools, hospitals, parks, colleges and universities, almshouses and asylums, and their landed endowments, were all impartially exempted from income tax irrespective of whether they were financed by philanthropy or by local government, provided they accepted no fees and made no profits, and were not overtly religious institutions (they make up col. 2, Table 6.1).[31] The Inland Revenue drew a line between good works and public works. No exemption was given to sewers, gasworks, waterworks, town halls, etc; of which, more anon. Due to agricultural depression the corporate estates which had been so valuable in the 1860s became 'white elephants' in the mid-1880s, difficult to let and impossible to sell.[32] The

[30]See p. 95 and Best, *Temporal pillars* (1965), p. 471.
[31]T. C. Jarvis, *Income tax* (1912), pp. 22–3; J. H. Redman, *Pratt and Redman's income tax law* (10th edn 1923), pp. 49–50. Of more than 300 applications for charitable status *rejected* between August 1887 and July 1888 the great majority were religious endowments. Income tax on charities. (3) Claims rejected; P.P. (H.L.) 1888 (289) XIX, p. 10ff.
[32]Lord Salisbury's metaphor, Newport speech, *The Times*, 8 Oct. 1885, 7d.

return of 1870, which assessed corporate and social welfare tenures at five per cent of the total rental, is not strictly comparable with the figures for 1895 (Table 6.1, col. 4) in which their value fell to 3.7 per cent of the total. Nevertheless the latter figures appear low in comparison and their fall may well reflect the heavy reliance of corporations and charities on agricultural land. A high tide of urban land values in the 1890s, a revival of agriculture in the 1900s and, most important, the 'expansion of municipal education in the 1900s are the most likely reasons for the subsequent revival, which brought the totals almost back to the levels of 1870. Municipal tenure, for social welfare, education and for sanitary, transport and administrative infrastructure was the great new tenurial factor of our period. From very small beginnings, its holdings grew to overshadow the paternalistic, pre-municipal system of welfare.

III

Property professions

Back to the property market, now; let us examine a few more middlemen, all of them aspirants to professional status. 'Many lawyers are half land agents, many land agents are half lawyers', wrote a legal journalist in 1903.[33] Despite frequent boundary disputes, solicitors clearly predominated in the quasi-professional corps of general practitioners, the surveyors, auctioneers, valuers, estate-, house- and land-agents who primed the circulation of property.[34] Auctioneers were advised in a handbook of 1909 that 'such business is usually in the hands of solicitors, and, therefore, a beginner will do well to secure an early introduction as possible to so useful a body of men'.[35] The market also made work for a host of more specialised architects, civil engineers and surveyors.[36] A specialist press, dominated by three substantial weeklies vied for custom – the *Estates Gazette* (established 1857), the *Land Agents' Record* (established 1879, with an agricultural bias) and the *Property Market Review* (established 1893). A vast traffic of advertising spilled over and helped to sustain the daily and weekly press. Property dealing had its share of worthies, the equivalents of Galsworthy's Swithin Forsyte, whose potted

[33]*Land and Law* (Feb.–March 1903), 1.
[34]Boundary disputes, see e.g. *EG*, 26 May 1900, 902; *POJ*, April 1912, 3.
[35]A chartered surveyor, *Auctioneering as a profession* (1909), p. 55.
[36]A list of occupational associations is given in in the Institute of Auctioneers and Estate Agents' *Yearbook*, e.g. (1913), 494.

biographies and full-page bearded portraits graced the pages of the *Estates Gazette*. It also had its share of quacks: anyone could set up as a house agent or valuer, subject only to a small yearly licence fee.[37]

Occupational boundaries were not strictly observed and professional associations only embraced a minority, so the return of licences is the best guide to the number of practitioners. There were fewer auctioneers and estate agents than solicitors in England and Wales: 11,075 of the former against 16,845 of the latter in 1910.[38] If bankruptcy is any guide, they were also lesser men. The (hypothetical) average bankrupt solicitor was in debt to the tune of £7748 between 1891 and 1913. The insolvent auctioneer or estate agent only owed a fifth as much, but was twice as likely to fail.[39] The number of licences fell by about eight per cent during the 1880s, possibly reflecting the agricultural depression; it rose some thirteen per cent in the 1890s, in the wake of the property boom and thereafter, in line with the solicitors' rate of growth, remained stagnant up to 1910.[40]

Like the solicitors' incomes, property practitioners' remuneration was made up of two elements: service fees and trading commissions. The fee level for most services (i.e. auction and valuation) was approximately double a single solicitor's fee: about two and a half per cent on small and medium properties.[41] Commissions, of course, are impossible to estimate.[42] It is only possible to suggest an order of magnitude for the property practitioners' cut. Five to ten per cent (say seven per cent) of all property market turnover (except mortgages) is a reasonable guess; this to cover both fees and commissions, solicitors as well as surveyors, estate agents, valuers and auctioneers. Table 6.2 sets out the result. The reader may vary the percentage without altering the pattern: in 1910, compared with the beginning of the Edwardian decade, a slightly increased body of practitioners was chasing after a much reduced volume of work.

'One class of business eagerly sought after, and considered a great

[37] £10 for auctioneers, £2 for appraisers and house agents.
[38] Auctioneers, see H. M. Customs and Excise. 1st rep.; P.P. 1910 Cd. 5302 XXII, p. 67, tables 67–8. Solicitors, *IRAR* (1911).
[39] Solicitors, standard deviation (s) = £4321; Auctioneers mean debt £1731 (s = £500). Mean bankruptcies per year: solicitors 40 (s = 9); auctioneers etc. 56 (s = 10). Bd. of Trade bankruptcy act reports 1896–1914, e.g. P.P. 1914 (413) LXVII, Annex no. VI, pp. 65–6.
[40] *IRAR*, 1880–1905, Excise (B) tables;[38] above.
[41] See e.g. Auctioneers and Estate Agents Inst. *Yearbook* (1913), 344ff.
[42] A scale of London commissions ranging between 5 and $1\frac{1}{2}$ per cent (on a sliding scale) may be found in R. Ernest, *How to become a successful estate agent* (1904), pp. 47–8.

Table 6.2. *Professional property incomes in England, 1900 and 1910, at seven per cent of market turnover*[a]

Year ending 31 March	Practitioners (of whom solicitors)	Property market turnover (sales & leases)	7% of turnover	Per cent of all rent (sch. A)[b]	Mean annual income
1900	26,773 (15,948)	£217M	£15.2M	8.0%	£567
1910	27,920 (16,845)	£142M	£9.9M	4.3%	£355

[a] *Source:* Inland Revenue and Customs and Excise annual reports, P.P.
[b] Table 6.3, p. 102.

asset in a business, is that of rent-collecting', the prospective auctioneer was advised in 1909.[43] In a cyclical, seasonal competitive sector, the steady flow of rent-collection and property management income was a useful counter to uncertainty. 'Owing to the trouble of management which it involved, weekly property could hardly be called an investment, but really almost amounted to a business', said a practitioner at a Surveyors' Institute meeting in 1893.[94] It was undertaken by agents, he added; people in the country invested through him and never saw their properties from year's end to year's end. An advertisement in the *Land and House Property Year Book* for 1900 announced that 'Messrs. Philip and George Geen relieve the owner of all trouble, and help to keep the tenants in good humour'.[45] They charged five per cent of the rent for their trouble, and undertook repairs as well, another source of steady profit. Whether the growth of this line of work was sufficient (together with eviction, foreclosure, distrain and other slump business) to compensate for the collapse of the property market after 1905 is not clear.

The maturing professional image of the surveyors, who offered a mix of technical skills and commercial services, was confirmed when their institute was granted a Royal Charter in 1881.[46] Its junior, the Auctioneers' Institute, sometimes managed to project an air of nonchalant confidence from its imposing headquarters in Russell Square. 'Its position is assured', declared the President in 1908, 'its high ideals are

[43] *Auctioneering as a profession* (1909), p. 52.
[44] H. Griffin, in a discussion of his paper 'Weekly property as an investment'. *Trans. S.I.* 26 (1893–4), 375–6.
[45] *Land and House Property Year Book* 9 (1900), p. iii.
[46] F. M. L. Thompson, *Chartered surveyors: the growth of a profession* (1968), chs. VIII, IX.

common knowledge'.[47] Inside the building, however, prominent members were giving vent to their disquiet. James Boyton, past President of the Institute, a member of the L.C.C. and later a Conservative MP, complained about the intensity of competition.

> The great trouble we are in these competitive and hard times is this question of fees ... knowing the great cutting that is going on, and the small fees daily being taken for valuation, in the future there should be a greater endeavour on the part of the profession to stand shoulder to shoulder in order to maintain a proper standard of fees, which at the moment are a disappearing quantity ... of course, I do not want to suggest that in any way we should be a Trades Union.[48]

A closed shop of property professionals was out of the question given the superior attitude adopted by solicitors whose president, in his address of 1909, accused the junior professions of trespass.[49] The president of the auctioneers felt bound to remonstrate and to ask that solicitors 'will take care not to so unduly expand as to interfere with the legitimate work of our profession'.[50] The Incorporated Law Society presented an ideal that other self-styled 'landed property practitioners' could aspire to. The auctioneers copied the solicitors' three-tiered examination system in 1891 and the surveyors adopted it in 1913. And if they were powerless against the monopoly position of solicitors, at least they could try to establish the same control over their own part of the pasture. A common front was mooted in 1907 and after prolonged negotiations the auctioneers amalgamated in 1912 with the Estate Agents' Institute in order to establish statutory registration for all those dealing with real property. They were still struggling towards this goal in the 1960s, and finally achieved it in 1979.[51]

IV

Recapitulation and conclusion

Genteel dons and devout parsons, aspiring lawyers and enterprising middlemen – all these landed property-related occupations, professions

[47]A. G. Dilley, 'Presidential address', *Auct. Inst.* (14 Oct. 1908), 9–10.
[48]In discussion of a paper by E. H. Blake, 'Mortgages – some notes on law and practice', *Auct. Inst.* (11 Nov. 1908), 36. More on the keenness of competition, *Auctioneering as a profession* (1909), pp. 5–15.
[49]'President's address', *LSPR* (1909), 42.
[50]A. G. Watney, 'Presidential address', *Auct. Inst.* (20 Oct. 1909), 12.
[51]D. H. Chapman, *The chartered auctioneers and estate agents' institute: a short history* (1970), pp. 81–4: the Estate Agents Act was passed in 1979.

Table 6.3. *Gross rents (in £M), excluding rates, in England and Wales, 1855–1910*

(1) Year[a]	(2) Total schedule A[b] rent	(3) 'Lands'[c]	(4) 'Houses'[d]
1855	91.3	43.931	47.390
1856	92.9	44.315	48.601
1857	94.5	44.700	49.811
1858	96.0	45.058	50.939
1859	97.5	45.416	52.068
1860	99.0	45.775	53.196
1861	100.5	46.133	54.324
1862	103.2	46.594	56.571
1863	105.9	47.055	58.818
1864	108.6	47.516	61.065
1865	110.9	47.486	63.381
1866	113.2	47.457	65.697
1867	115.4	47.427	68.013
1868	118.2	47.740	70.444
1869	120.9	48.052	72.876
1870	123.7	48.365	75.307
1871	127.6	48.678	78.965
1872	129.8	48.991	80.799
1873	127.7	46.616	81.039
1874	133.9	50.276	83.580
1875	137.3	50.951	86.301
1876	141.2	51.641	89.536
1877	144.6	51.659	92.955
1878	148.0	51.670	96.375
1879	151.5	51.678	99.794
1880	153.1	50.535	102.572
1881	154.8	49.406	105.360
1882	156.4	48.277	108.147
1883	158.0	47.457	110.575
1884	159.7	46.659	113.005
1885	161.3	45.825	115.434
1886	161.7	44.661	117.024
1887	162.1	43.417	118.657
1888	162.4	42.173	120.271
1889	164.2	41.744	122.497
1890	166.0	41.308	124.723
1891	167.4	40.871	126.578
1892	168.9	40.434	128.432
1893	170.3	39.997	130.285
1894	172.8	39.520	133.274
1895	176.2	39.936	136.243
1896	178.7	38.366	140.321
1897	183.2	38.797	144.400

Table 6.3 continued

(1) Year[a]	(2) Total schedule A[b] rent	(3) 'Lands'[c]	(4) 'Houses'[d]
1898	185.7	37.227	148.478
1899	190.8	37.124	153.724
1900	196.2	37.255	158.960
1901	201.1	37.150	163.934
1902	206.0	37.074	168.899
1903	210.9	36.999	173.866
1904	214.2	36.984	177.238
1905	217.6	36.969	180.609
1906	220.7	36.954	183.734
1907	223.8	36.939	186.858
1908	226.9	36.924	189.982
1909	230.0	36.909	193.106
1910	233.1	36.854	196.196

Sources: IRAR
[a] Fiscal year beginning in April.
[b] Total of cols. 3 and 4.
[c] Income tax schedule A 'Lands' gross assessments, including farmhouses and tithes, less rates on tithes. Interpolated from valuation years (Stamp, *British incomes* (1920), pp. 31–6d).
[d] Income tax schedule A 'houses and messuages' gross assessments, separately interpolated for London and the rest of England.

and subclasses of rentiers – fared rather poorly in the Edwardian period.

Collectively, each of these groups had to adapt to contractions in their sources of livelihood, whether from cyclical depression of construction and effective demand for housing, from the secular depression of agriculture, or from both. Overall, these groups claimed a sizeable proportion of the national rent, ranging, say, between one-tenth and one-seventh.

That workers suffered from an inflationary earnings squeeze in 1900–14 is a well-known feature of the period and has been given some of the credit for the pre-war wave of 'labour unrest' ever since.[52] But with economic growth as a whole being cut after 'the climacteric of the 1890s' is there any reason to suppose that professional and propertied classes as a whole did any better?[53] A great surge of overseas investment after 1905

[52] G. D. H. Cole, *The world of labour* (3d edn 1917), pp. 35–6.
[53] Gross national product increased 21.5% between 1899 and 1913, and 35.4% in the preceding fifteen years (C. H. Feinstein, *National income, expenditure and output of the United Kingdom 1855–1965* (1972), Table 5 col. 10, pp. T14–15).

is sometimes invoked to demonstrate the prosperity of the middle classes in that period but there is plenty of evidence to show that the malaise was not restricted to the real property markets. Did middle-class employment opportunities keep up with the expansion of education? The debate between F. Musgrove and H. Perkin has not been fully resolved but Musgrove has presented a strong case for pessimism.[54] 'Home securities' – the bulwarks of Victorian portfolios – all depreciated sharply: Consols, municipal bonds, railways and utilities lost up to a third of their value after the mid-1890s,[55] and recent research. seems to indicate that the net returns to capital, both domestic and overseas, fell to an historically low level during this period; the years 1909–13 saw a particularly precipitate decline.[56] The point of this digression, which is also the agenda for new work already in progress, is to suggest that the prospect (or even the experience) of straitened circumstances may have contributed to the disruptive political inclinations of the respectable classes between 1909 and 1914.

Within occupational associations the squeeze gave rise to some half-hearted measures for restricting competition, to some boundary disputes and to a few successful interventions at the political level, in particular the parsons' rate subsidy of 1899 and the solicitors' long-term 'simplification strategy' which only reaped its reward after the war. Only one member of this cluster of imperfect tenures fared markedly better. These were the administrators of social welfare tenures, i.e. charity and municipal bureaucrats. This divergence carries a profound structural significance which merits, and will receive, much closer investigation. First, however, we resume our progress from imperfect and indirect forms of tenure to the main forms of private property, where the appearance and reality of possession were less ambivalent.

[54]Musgrove, 'Middle class education' (1959), H. Perkin, 'Middle class education and employment in the nineteenth century: a critical note' Econ. Hist. Rev. 2 ser. 14 (1961), 122–30 and The origins of modern English society, 1780–1880 (1969), pp. 252–79, 428–9.

[55]See A Stockbroker, 'The depreciation of British home securities', Economic Journal 22 (1912), 219–30.

[56]See M. Edelstein, 'Realized rates of return on U.K. home and overseas portfolio investment in the age of high imperialism', Expl. Econ. Hist. 13 (1976), graph 3, p. 312.

7

LANDOWNERS AND
ENTREPRENEURS:
DOMESDAY REVISITED

I

Introduction and summary

In the course of economic development rent is expected to claim an ever-decreasing share of the national income, as the economy creates productive forces that are less dependent than agriculture on the use of land. Were nineteenth-century Radicals justified then when they warned that land was fixed in supply and landowners were bound to increase their share of society's produce? Yes and no. On the face of it, rent grew somewhat less than the national income between 1855 and 1914 but this aggregate trend is partly belied by closer investigation. Agricultural land fell sharply in relative terms after the 1870s while urban rents increased their share of the national income as the towns expanded. The supply of land was not fixed, as some economists have assumed, but was elastic in response to the demand for farms and building sites, and to the development of transport technology. Furthermore, the railway, tramway and road networks which increased the supply of land and acted to depress rents in central locations were voracious land users and claimed their own substantial rents. Even the decline of agricultural rents is not entirely clear-cut since much of the outlay was merely shifted from rent rolls to food import bills, and paid rents overseas. Except for agriculture, therefore, which became an increasingly peripheral source (see Table 6.3), rents kept up their overall share (at about 12–14 per cent of the national income) quite well in the latter half of the nineteenth century. Different sub-classes of proprietor were not all equally favoured.[1]

'Land monopoly' was a rallying cry of Victorian and Edwardian Radicalism. The contours of monopoly were delineated by John Bateman in 1883 on the basis of the 'new domesday' Parliamentary return of landowners of 1873. On Bateman's calculations, barely one-half

[1] This paragraph is elaborated in Offer, 'Ricardo's paradox' (1980), *passim*.

of one per cent of all proprietors, the owners of more than 1,000 acres, owned almost sixty per cent of the land.[2] Such figures may convey a misleading impression. Bateman estimated only the acreage, not capital values, and excluded the metropolis. Urban land is therefore underrepresented in his magnitudes. No other estimate has yet been put forward to test his figures and this chapter probes the structure and distribution of tenures in order to present a new and different estimate. Taken one generation later, over the period 1896–1914, this estimate is based not on acreage but on capital values derived from death-duty assessments and includes London and urban property in general at its full value. Unlike Bateman's tables, it takes in the whole UK, not only England and Wales. So the two estimates are not strictly comparable; they complement each other and refract similar realities through different prisms. The later estimate does not alter the emphasis on gross inequality in the distribution of real property. As many as seven-eighths or more of English households enjoyed no more tenure than a working-class dwelling held at a week's notice. But the new estimate substantially modifies the distribution *among proprietors*, and tends to moderate the degree of concentration presented by Bateman. An acreage distribution gives rise to different social and political implications than a distribution of capital values. Instead of 60 per cent being concentrated in the hands of the very rich only some 30 per cent are now identified in upper-class or wealthy hands.

With ownership so highly concentrated historical attention has tended to focus on the aristocrats at the top. The toe of the distribution, however, is a much more populous district and was of great but neglected political and social significance. Two clusters of tenure are examined in this chapter – landowners and entrepreneurial capitalists. Landowners owned the ground of both farmland and urban sites which they leased to capitalists on various terms. The latter farmed, built houses, let them, and carried out a variety of commercial, industrial and professional occupations in their own and in rented premises. Functional, social and economic distinctions within each cluster will be described; the incidence of each tenure on the ground and its distribution between classes of proprietors will be measured. Some readers may not care for the detailed calculations and the main conclusions are summarised here for their benefit.

The core of wealthy landowners, defined alternatively as the proprietors of settled land or the bequeathers of more than £50,000, appear

[2] J. Bateman, *The great landowners of Great Britain and Ireland* (4th edn 1883), 'Summary table of England and Wales', p. 515.

to have held, as noted above, somewhat less than one-third of British tenure. Towards the end of the period their share began to decline in both country and town. Landowners were still a rural tenure, with two-thirds of their holdings in farmland and only the residue in urban sites, and agriculture was depressed. Urban ground rents were potentially more lucrative but were also becoming more precarious in the Edwardian period, both economically and politically. They were the most socially exclusive form of private tenure. Residential and commercial buildings accounted for two-thirds of all tenure. Their ownership was much more equally distributed, and was diffused among large numbers of petty entrepreneurs. Capital values fared rather worse even than rents in the Edwardian period and the fraction of land in all property passing at death fell quite remarkably from about 29 to 23 per cent, underscoring the impression of tenurial crisis sketched out in previous chapters.

'Land monopoly' is a misleading slogan if it suggests a socially isolated plutocracy. The legal and fiscal framework of tenure set up bonds of common interest which acted across social and income class barriers and tied small proprietors into the web of plutocracy. Subsequent chapters will show how the multitude of small proprietors was discovered (by the Radicals even before the Conservatives) as a source of strength for the few at the top. Small owners in both country and town were potential bulwarks for the rich. And a deceptively egalitarian design for a property-owning democracy could be woven into a defence of inequality, out of two strands: plutocratic preponderance of wealth and middle-class preponderance of numbers.

II

Sources and methods

The tax system embodied a rough-and-ready social analysis in the death-duty returns (*IRAR*) which contain two separate sources on tenure in the U.K. before the Great War. Both consist of time-series; the first begins in 1896 and shows the distribution of property passing at death *by tenure*. The second starts in 1904 and shows the distribution of tenure *by wealth*.[3] They describe capital values. Unfortunately no source is readily

[3] E.g. *IRAR* (1906), 'Estate duties'. First distribution, table XC, pp. 110–1. Second distribution, table LXXXII, pp. 96–7. Totals are some 10% higher in the former due to a more inclusive definition of 'realty'. See note[66] to this chapter for details.

available to provide a social and tenurial breakdown of income flows (i.e. rents) comparable to the professional, corporate and aggregate series given in preceding chapters. Nor are the series fully comprehensive; many classes of property holders are excluded: charitable and public bodies, the Crown, local government, partnerships and joint-stock companies. Most are treated elsewhere in this study and only joint-stock corporations will detain us here.

Joint-stock company tenure was embodied in stocks and shares, which fell under personalty in the death-duty returns. Most of it belonged to railway, mining and utility firms which were not assessed to schedule A, and amounted to 15–20 per cent of the total rental.[4] Joint-stock company property within schedule A only amounted to 1.6 per cent of the total in 1870,[5] though it probably increased substantially by the 1900s.[6] Most of London's public houses, for example, were acquired by the breweries between 1895 and 1903.[7] In contrast, the grocery chains which began to multiply outlets during the same period, preferred to operate from rented premises.[8] Private companies occupied, but did not necessarily own, a large share of urban property – almost a third in a sample taken in 1906 and made up of the main provincial towns and two metropolitan boroughs.[9] But the bulk of urban and rural tenure was still vested in private individuals, and these owners are the subject of the remaining part of this chapter.

The death-duty samples which we propose to use were not a perfect proxy for the prevailing distribution of property and contemporary attempts to project them with the aid of multipliers on to the whole population did not meet with conclusive success.[10] As a distribution of property at death they tended, if anything, to exaggerate the actual degree of the concentration of wealth. Moreover, when a very large

[4]Offer, 'Ricardo's paradox', table 2, p. 247.
[5]Corporate bodies; P.P. 1872 (122) XXXVI, p. 145.
[6]Stamp, *British incomes* (1920), p. 75.
[7]D. M. Knox, 'The development of the tied house system in London', *Oxford Economic Papers*, 10 (1958), 68, 71, 73, 77–8.
[8]P. Mathias, *Retailing revolution* (1967), pp. 58, 64, 65, 78, 152.
[9]Birmingham, Leeds, Liverpool, Manchester, Sheffield, West Ham and the borough of Holborn. 30.7 per cent of the aggregate rateable value (i.e. including railways and other non-schedule A property) were occupied by 9280 corporations, joint-stock companies and other companies (presumably including charities and local authorities). Boroughs (rateable value) return; P.P. 1906 (215) CII, p. 345.
[10]B. Mallet and H. C. Strutt, 'The multiplier and capital wealth' *J.R.S.S.* new ser. 78, pt. 4 (1915), 555–99.

landowner died his estate made an exceptional 'bulge' which increased the variance of the death-duty series. In 1902 the effect was so marked that it has had to be smoothed out of some of the tables which follow.[11] Not all data were equally reliable. Debt liabilities, for example, were real quantities but other figures were only valuations scrutinised by the Inland Revenue department. Valuations other· than actual sales were bound to be more or less arbitrary due to the imperfection of the property market, and more so in the case of large and valuable estates. The exercise was more art than science. 'You just fired your shot in the dark and stood to your guns the best way you could, swearing you had hit the very bull's eye, whether you knew it or not', is how one practitioner described it.[12] It is only to be hoped that Inland Revenue valuers were consistent in their bias. In 1909 their procedures were tightened up to produce an increase of the yield but as a measure of detection this may well have been cancelled out by greater incentives for tax avoidance created by the increased duties of the 'People's Budget' the same year.[13] To conclude, death-duty data are best considered as a source for orders of magnitude, not for year-to-year trends, and for most purposes the time-series have been averaged and the distributions converted from real quantities to percentages. When all is said, however, the data provide new detail and a substantial revision of previous analyses derived from Bateman (1883) and the 'new domesday' of 1873.

III

Landowners

This cluster embraced the traditional tenures of the established landed aristocracy and gentry, of more recent adherents to their values and life-style, and of a fringe of other social groups. One possible definition of the core of this cluster is given by the incidence of settled land. Strict

[11] J. Wedgwood (*The economics of inheritance* (Pelican edn. 1939), ch. VII) shows that the size of estates rose substantially with age in 1911–14, but the distribution of wealth was relatively constant at different ages. Two great estates could have affected the 1902 data: the third Marquess of Bute died in 1900 and the sixth Earl Fitzwilliam in 1902 (W. D. Rubinstein, 'British millionaires, 1809–1949', *Bulletin Inst. Hist. Research* 47 (1974), 211).

[12] J. J. Done, 'Valuations for mortgage'. *Trans. S.I.* 38 (1905–6), 79.

[13] 52 H.C. deb. 5 ser. 22 April 1913, D. Lloyd George, 276, and Harold Cox, *Land Agents' Record*, 7 March 1914, 312.

settlements were meant to keep estates intact from generation to generation and to endow them (in the words of F. M. L. Thompson) with a 'semi-corporate' quality.[14] Nineteenth-century estimates of the extent of settled land in Britain ranged from one-quarter to three-quarters of the whole, and most concentrated at the higher end. Thompson has made a provisional estimate based on a large sample of landed estates that 'just under half the area of England was subject to settlement'.[15] He noted, as did Eileen Spring later, that aristocratic land frequently went into and out of settlement.[16] Life-tenants' powers of sale were greatly increased by the Settled Land Act of 1882, which may have encouraged the release of land.[17]

Death-duty returns indicate that settled land was still a ubiquitous tenure around the turn of the century but that it was also on a definitely declining trend. They measure capital values, not area, and the U.K., not England, so the magnitudes are not incompatible with Thompson's estimate. But settled land definitely presents a lower profile than it does in most previous estimates. Table 7.1 shows how much capital passed at death every year between 1898 and 1914, and the respective shares of realty and of settled land. Realty, as noted above, decreased its share of the total from about 29 to 23 per cent. Settled land lost about one-third of its share of realty, from approximately 32 per cent of all land and houses in 1898 to about 21 per cent in 1914. Defined in this way the 'hard core' of landowner tenure contracted from one-third to one-fifth of all landed property and estates passed out of settlement, gradually at first and more rapidly after 1909.

The apparent shift away from tenure in general and from settled land in particular was compounded of a number of factors. The total capital subject to duty increased by a mere average 0.5 per cent a year between 1898 and 1914, even less than the rate of growth in the economy. Two reasons may be proposed (a) a remarkable decline in the crude death rate (from 17.5 to 13.8 per thousand between 1898 and 1913)[18] and (b) a general decline in the value of tenurial, gilt-edged and other 'strong' securities.[19] What about tax evasion? This is perhaps best regarded as a

---

[14]F. M. L. Thompson, *Hampstead: building a borough, 1650–1964* (1974), p. 369.
[15]*Idem, English landed society in the nineteenth century* (1963), p. 68.
[16]*Ibid.* pp. 66–9; Spring 'Settlement of land' (1964).
[17]See T. E. Scrutton, *Land in fetters* (Cambridge, 1886), pp. 134–9.
[18]Mitchell and Deane, *Abstract*, p. 37. None of the reasons is sufficient. The death rate decline most probably centred on the young and the poor, rather than the rich and old in our sample.
[19]See p. 104.

Table 7.1. *Gross capital passing at death and the distribution of realty and settled realty in the U.K. 1898–1914*[a]

Year ending 31 March	Settled realty in £M	as % of total realty	Realty in £M	as % of total capital	Total capital in £M personalty and realty
1898	21.97	29.2	75.20	27.5	273.77
1899	22.47	29.7	75.70	27.0	280.10
1900	28.26	31.3	90.18	27.6	326.20
1901	26.69	31.3	85.32	28.9	294.84
1902	45.95	43.8	106.80	32.8	320.30
1903	24.93	29.4	84.87	28.4	298.46
1904	21.80	27.0	80.71	27.5	293.18
1905	23.79	28.9	82.28	27.9	293.32
1906	23.50	28.0	83.97	27.7	303.72
1907	22.83	27.0	84.59	25.8	328.33
1908	24.71	29.0	85.19	27.1	313.90
1909	20.42	26.4	77.38	25.6	301.81
1910	17.51	23.3	75.07	24.0	312.35
1911	14.62	20.8	70.19	23.4	300.49
1912	17.95	25.0	71.67	23.4	306.67
1913	16.08	21.9	73.33	23.9	306.97
1914	12.03	16.7	71.83	21.9	327.70
Least-squares trend (1902 omitted)					
1898		32.0		29.2	293.40
1914		21.1		23.1	316.30
Annual growth rate ($\log Y = \log a + \log b\, t$)		−2.73%		−1.42%	0.5%
R^2		0.69		0.73	0.23
Smoothed 1902 value		30.3		28.7	−

[a] *IRAR*, 'Estate duties', e.g. (1914) table 22, p. 25. Excluding insolvent estates and those not liable to duty (i.e. valued at less than £100 net). The total of the two classes in 1914 was £4.9 millions, or 1.5% of all property. Property held in partnership, an average 2.9% of the gross total, is assigned in this table to personalty.

constant, although increased death-duty rates after 1910 created new incentives. How far was the duty avoided by gifts *inter vivos*? Stamp duties were imposed on such transfers in 1910, and revealed an irregular flow of gifts (2.6% of realty passing at death in 1911, 5.3% in 1913, 3.0% in 1914).[20] A large variance was the signature of large estates, which were the most likely avoiders of the tax. So the effect of avoidance should be

[20] *IRAR*, e.g. (1912–13), 'Stamp duties', table 51, p. 61.

borne in mind: it is to underestimate the concentration of realty in large estates by 2–5 per cent in relation to all tenure. Trusts were another popular refuge, and it was estimated by the Inland Revenue in 1919 that 12 to 15 per cent of property in the hands of individuals was settled or in trust.[21] Tenurial investments, particularly ground rents, were very popular with trustees.[22]

A more important reason behind the apparent decline of tenure in the capital passing at death was the general fall in urban property values which took place during the Edwardian decade. Inland Revenue valuations, which reacted only sluggishly to market trends, revealed a decline of 20.4 per cent in the Years Purchase (YP; i.e. the ratio of capital value to rent) of ground rents between 1898 and 1914, and of 14.1 per cent in the Years Purchase of freehold house property and business premises.[23] The trend of London property prices which is discussed in chapter 17 points to an even greater decrease. In a review of the property market in 1910 the surveyor J. G. Head told an audience of auctioneers,

Unhappily there will be no difficulty in every one of us recalling instances of land, houses, shops, factories, or some other form of property having fallen thirty per cent or even fifty per cent, below the value at which it stood ten years ago. Throughout the country, in large city or small town, you hear the same story of low prices and few buyers. My own experience is chiefly among town properties ... I understand that in some districts farm lands have shown a surprising recovery in value.[24]

Agricultural land valued for estate duty had indeed risen about a fifth in Years Purchase (from 17.0 in 1895–6 to 21.6 in 1913–14), but this was very far from enough to compensate for urban declines.[25]

Yet another explanation is compatible with these trends: sales of tenure by landowner rentiers to active farmers and capitalists (who were presumably younger) or, in the case of urban land, to trustees and companies. Such transfers would postpone the appearance of property in estate duty returns. F. M. L. Thompson's account of a surge in the

[21]PRO IR 63/86, Board of Inland Revenue, 'General capital levy', 19 May 1919, fol. 276.
[22]See e.g. C. R. Dowsett, *Buy English acres* (1905), p. 31. And this despite legal discouragement (R. D. Urlin, *A handy book on the investment of trust funds* (3d edn 1902), p. 17).
[23]*IRAR* (1906), table XC, pp. 110–1; (1914), table 28, pp. 32–3.
[24]J. G. Head, 'The property market – retrospect and outlook' *Auct. Inst.* (12 Jan. 1910), 42.
[25]See note[23] above.

dissolution of large estates after 1910 accords with this explanation.[26] It is too early to pronounce a verdict at this stage of the study. One conclusion is nevertheless clear: whether for economic, social, political or fiscal reasons private tenure contracted in late Edwardian Britain, both in relative and in absolute terms, and settled land contracted even more. The crisis of the property professions, which was examined in previous chapters, was only a reflection of serious difficulties affecting property owners themselves.

IV

Conversion rent

The incidence of settled land provided one definition of the scale of landowner tenure. A second definition arises from function, not from legal form. It refers to the agricultural and location value of land and embodies the classical–economic distinction between land and capital. The landowner farmed out economic opportunities (and risks) to agricultural and urban entrepreneurs; they provided skills, management and working capital and took their chances; the landowner took the residue. The distinction was never complete in practice. Aristocrats developed mines, docks and canals and others farmed on their own account; urban landowners were not immune to the risks of urban development.[27] But these exceptions do not upset the rule. Traditional tenurial arrangements still dominated the countryside. Eighty-eight per cent of the holdings in England were cultivated by tenants in 1908.[28] 320,000 farm tenants rented the land and the fixed capital from 10–15,000 landowners.[29] After a period of strife in the late 1870s and early 1880s the two interests increasingly presented a common agricultural front in England. In Wales

[26]Thompson, *Landed society* (1963), p. 322ff. See however the qualification, p. 359, below.

[27]See J. T. Ward and R. G. Wilson (eds) *Land and industry* (Newton Abbot, 1971).

[28]Rounded. See Agricultural statistics, 1908; P.P. 1909 Cd. 4533 CII, tables 11–13, p. 70ff. The proportions had not changed appreciably in thirty years (Small holdings. Sel. com. rep.; P.P. 1889 (313) XII, q. 4975 (Jesse Collings) and app. 6, p. 503).

[29]Agricultural statistics, 1908, Pt. I, table 12, p. 72. Bateman (*Great landowners* (1883), p. 515) identified 13,805 owners of 300-plus acres in England and Wales in 1873, and the structure of ownership had not changed much.

and Scotland relations were more troubled and Ireland was in a class of its own. Some 40,000 landowning peasant proprietors in England assumed an ideological importance out of all proportion to their numbers.[30] After the severe depression of land values and incomes in the 1880s the bottom was touched in the mid-1890s and the Agricultural Rates Act of 1896 signified the start of a modest revival.[31]

To compensate for the decline of agricultural property there was the prospect of a change of use, from farmland to urban land and later on, from residential to commercial uses. Capital gains were potentially of one order of magnitude in the first instance and one more in the second. For example, the conversion of farmland to building land on the outskirts of Birmingham in the 1750s increased its value from six to twelve times, and the rateable value of an acre in the City of London was about fifteen times as much as the average for London as a whole in 1912.[32] Let us call such realised gains a *conversion rent*: this was the great prize which urbanisation offered to the traditional owners of the land. Conversion rent, however, was not an increase in the factor share. It was the way in which groundowners retained their share of the national income.

As a group, urban landowners more than succeeded in keeping up their share of the national income. Urban composite rents (i.e. both buildings and sites) in England and Wales which stood around seven per cent of total domestic (U.K.) income in 1870 rose to over ten per cent by 1885 and remained at that level until the war. Site rents, which accounted for less than 30 per cent of the composite rent in the 1870s rose to almost 40 per cent by the late 1890s and did not fall below one-third in the 1900s.[33] But individual landowners could not be sure of reaping windfalls and the wait could be protracted by the long depressions and unpredictable spatial propensities of the long cycle of urban development. Urban development was a speculative undertaking and the development value of much urban land was akin to that of a lottery ticket. Bankers accepted urban land as collateral only with the greatest misgivings and placed it among the lowest grades of security.[34] A popular

[30]See chapter 21.
[31]A. H. Rhee, *The rent of agricultural land in England and Wales* (1949), diagram II, p. 48.
[32]Birmingham, C. W. Chalklin, *The provincial towns of Georgian England* (1974), p. 145. London – *Lond. Stat.* 23 (1912–13), 46–7, 667.
[33]Offer, 'Ricardo's paradox' (1980), figs. 1 and 2, pp. 240–1.
[34]J. W. Gilbart, *The history, principles and practice of banking*, revised by A. S. Michie (1905), i, 253–4.

handbook advised the would-be banker in a chapter called 'Securities which are not Security',[35]

> For a Bank to hold this description of property, for better times and a higher price, is virtually to speculate in it. Its sale is of all things the most uncertain, and the demand for it the most capricious. There is not a town in England where you may not find secluded plots of building-land, which the tide of building has passed by on either side, from no apparent cause, and left in abandoned sterility.

Charles Henry Sargant, who was a lawyer and a spokesman for the landowner interest in London, described the preliminaries to development in 1886.[36]

> As London, or one of the greater provincial towns, gradually spreads its network of houses over a larger and larger area, the owner of land lying for the time being on their outskirts is placed in a position of considerable perplexity and anxiety ... he has probably received and rejected numberless tempting offers from land speculators, land companies and others, to purchase his land at prices which would yield him an income many times the rent he has been receiving from his agricultural tenants. And now, having preferred to forgo a large portion of this income, in the expectation of the ultimate profit to be derived from personally superintending the development of his land as a building estate, he finds a good deal of difficulty in in deciding how best to realise this profit.

He had a number of methods to choose from. First, the owner could sell the freehold outright and pocket the increment. The rent was then cut away from the site and set free to find its best return in the general pool of private capital. In other words, it ceased to be a distinctive *land* rent. Secondly, the owner could retain an interest in the land by clamping a rent-charge on the property at the time of sale, or, what amounted to the same thing, granting a very long lease, of more than 100 and normally closer to 1000 years. The 'conversion rent' was appropriated as a perpetual annuity, secured on the value of the land and the buildings. Or he could create so-called 'short' building leases, of anything from around fifty to ninety-nine years, with the right of re-possessing the land (and the buildings erected upon it) when the lease fell in. The groundowner received a ground-rent annuity or a lump sum, or sometimes both, and the opportunity to reclaim the conversion rent every

[35]G. Rae, *The country banker: his clients, cares and work* (4th edn 1885), p. 115.
[36]C. H. Sargant, *Ground rents and building leases* (1886), pp. 9–10.

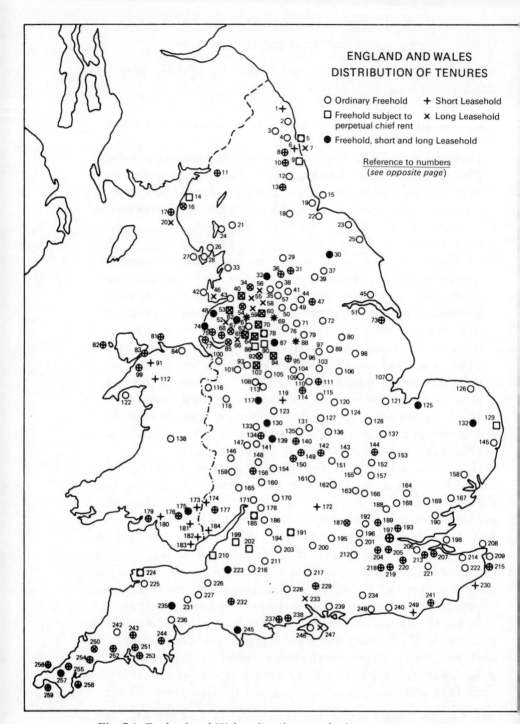

Fig. 7.1. *England and Wales: distribution of urban tenures, c. 1914.*
Source: The land (1914), ii, *facing p. 352.*

1 Belford	66 Warrington
2 Alnwick	67 St Helens
3 Rothbury	68 Prescot
4 Morpeth	69 Huddersfield
5 Tynemouth	70 Oldham
6 Jarrow	71 Barnsley
7 South Shields	72 Doncaster
8 Newcastle	73 Grimsby
9 Sunderland	74 Bootle
10 Gateshead	75 Liverpool
11 Carlisle	76 Denby
12 Durham	77 Birkenhead
13 Willington	78 Ashton
14 Maryport	79 Rotherham
15 Hartlepool	80 Gainsborough
16 Workington	81 Llandudno
17 Whitehaven	82 Holyhead
18 Darlington	83 Bangor
19 Stockton	84 Rhyl
20 St Bedes	85 Widnes
21 Kendal	86 Stockport
22 Middlesbrough	87 Glossop
23 Whitby	88 Sheffield
24 Bowness	89 Retford
25 Scarborough	90 Stalybridge
26 Ulverston	91 Bethesda
27 Barrow	92 Macclesfield
28 Dalton	93 Crewe
29 Ripon	94 Buxton
30 Malton	95 Bakewell
31 Knaresborough	96 Chesterfield
32 Skipton	97 Worksop
33 Lancaster	98 Lincoln
34 Clitheroe	99 Carnarvon
35 Shipley	100 Chester
36 Harrogate	101 Nantwich
37 York	102 Congleton
38 Otley	103 Mansfield
39 Marston	104 Matlock
40 Blackburn	105 Leek
41 Leeds	106 Newark
42 Blackpool	107 Boston
43 Preston	108 Newcastle-under-
44 Normanton	Lyme
45 Hull	109 Belper
46 Lytham	110 Ilkeston
47 Pontefract	111 Nottingham
48 Southport	112 Blaenau Festiniog
49 Wakefield	113 Stoke-on-Trent
50 Dewsbury	114 Derby
51 Barton-on-Humber	115 Loughborough
52 Wigan	116 Oswestry
53 Chorley	117 Stafford
54 Darwen	118 Shrewsbury
55 Accrington	119 Burton-on-Trent
56 Burnley	120 Melton Mowbray
57 Bradford	121 Spalding
58 Todmorden	122 Pwlheli
59 Rawtenstall	123 Lichfield
60 Rochdale	124 Oakham
61 Bury	125 King's Lynn
62 Bolton	126 Cromer
63 Middleton	127 Leicester
64 Manchester	128 Peterborough
65 Salford	129 Yarmouth
	130 Walsall

131 Hinckley	196 Uxbridge
132 Norwich	197 London
133 Wolverhampton	198 Sheerness
134 Dudley	199 Bristol
135 Nuneaton	200 Newbury
136 Market	201 Staines
Harborough	202 Bath
137 Chatteris	203 Devizes
138 Llanidloes	204 Malden
139 Birmingham	205 Croydon
140 Coventry	206 Gravesend
141 Kidderminster	207 Chatham
142 Daventry	208 Margate
143 Wellingborough	209 Ramsgate
144 Huntingdon	210 Weston-Super-
145 Lowestoft	Mare
146 Leominster	211 Westbury
147 Stourport	212 Working
148 Worcester	213 Rochester
149 Leamington	214 Whitstable
150 Warwick	215 Deal
151 Northampton	216 Frome
152 St Neots	217 Andover
153 Cambridge	218 Redgate
154 Evesham	219 Redhill
155 Bedford	220 Sevenoaks
156 Malvern	221 Maidstone
157 Biggleswade	222 Canterbury
158 Ipswich	223 Wells
159 Hereford	224 Ilfracombe
160 Tewkesbury	225 Barnstaple
161 Banbury	226 Bridgwater
162 Buckingham	227 Taunton
163 Dunstable	228 Salisbury
164 Saffron Walden	229 Winchester
165 Ross	230 Folkestone
166 Luton	231 Wellington
167 Colchester	232 Sherborne
168 Bishop's Stortford	233 Southampton
169 Braintree	234 Pulborough
170 Cheltenham	235 Tiverton
171 Gloucester	236 Exeter
172 Oxford	237 Bournemouth
173 Merthyr	238 Christchurch
174 Tredegar	239 Portsmouth
175 Aberdare	240 Brighton
176 Rhondda	241 Hastings
177 Pontypool	242 Launceston
178 Painswick	243 Tavistock
179 Swansea	244 Newton Abbot
180 Neath	245 Weymouth
181 Pontypridd	246 Newport
182 Cardiff	247 Ryde
183 Penarth	248 Worthing
184 Newport	249 Eastbourne
185 Stroud	250 Bodmin
186 Minchinhampton	251 Devonport
187 High Wycombe	252 Liskeard
188 Hertford	253 Plymouth
189 Barnet	254 St Austell
190 Maldon	255 Redruth
191 Swindon	256 St Ives
192 Watford	257 Camborne
193 Leyton	258 Falmouth
194 Malmesbury	259 Penzance
195 Reading	

two or three generations. These arrangements signified a robust commitment to the persistence of property relations far into the distant future and bound the landowners to a permanent stake in the urban landscape.

The regional distribution of urban tenures at the end of the nineteenth century reflected patterns established in the eighteenth century and earlier.[37] An archaic system of leases for lives persisted in Devon and Cornwall and 'feu duties', a form of rent-charge, prevailed in Scotland. The distribution of urban tenures in England and Wales was described and mapped in evidence presented to the Select Committee on Town Holdings in the 1880s and brought up-to-date by the Liberal Urban Land Enquiry of 1914, whose map is reproduced as Fig. 7.1.[38] Freehold, the majority tenure, was to be found in some proportion in most towns. It was dominant in the Northern, Midland and Eastern counties. Perpetual leases and chief-rents (sometimes known as 'fee farm rents') prevailed in Lancashire, some towns in the North and in Bristol. Short leases were dominant in Jarrow and Newcastle (municipal corporation leases), Sheffield, Southport, Birmingham, Grimsby, Oxford and in the South, the West and South Wales. Liverpool was partly short leasehold and in London, as we shall see, some two-thirds of the buildings were subject to this tenure.

V

Capitalists and entrepreneurs

House-landlords, traders and shopkeepers, publicans, small master artisans and large manufacturers all came into the 'capitalist' category, a term sanctioned by contemporary usage. The bulk of land in domestic and commercial use was subject to capitalist tenure. Bateman counted 825,272 proprietors of up to ten acres in England and Wales in 1873 (outside the metropolis) and in London, forty years later, there were 38,200 owners.[39] But the number of tenurial capitalists was larger.

[37]Chalklin, *Provincial towns* (1974), *passim*. See the bibliography for titles on the formation of urban estates in the nineteenth century by Dyos, Reeder, Olsen and Thompson.
[38]Town holdings. Sel. com. evid. & app.; P.P. 1887 (260) XIII, pp. 664–816. Tenure map of England and Wales, facing p. 816; also *ibid*. Rep. & evid.; P.P. 1889 (251) XV, pp. 6–9. Also *The land* (1914), ii, 348–52.
[39]Bateman, *Great landowners* (1883), p. 515 and chapter 17, p. 273.

Bateman did not count leasehold proprietors, and leasehold accounted, as we shall see below, for approximately one-fifth of U.K. urban tenure, most of it in small units and most of it in England. So there must have been rather more than a million small proprietors. In 1894 there were 1.209 million properties in England and Wales, the owners of which earned less than the taxable income (£160 a year);[40] in 1909 there were said to be 2.5 million of these 'small fry' in Britain.[41] Each proprietor owned an average seven or eight units: there were 7.8 million houses and other premises in England and Wales in 1909, and about 9.1 million 'hereditaments' (i.e. tenurial units).[42] More than a million proprietors barely deserved to be called 'capitalists'. The average annual value of tax-exempt property was merely £9 a year.[43] This characteristic of capitalist tenure was of great importance: urban property was held, for the most part, in small parcels by a multitude of small and medium-scale owners. This house-owning multitude (between, say, one-seventh and one-tenth of all households) let out their properties at rack-rent, or occupied their own shops, dwellings, workshops and factories.

A reliable figure for the scale of owner-occupation is difficult to come by, but it is thought to have been low (a recent study quotes an unsupported figure of 10.6 per cent in 1914).[44] House-ownership was rare among the working classes but not uncommon among middle-class occupiers, if only because a great many business premises doubled as dwellings. Twenty-three per cent occupation by (leasehold) owners on the Russells' Bloomsbury estate in 1889 was claimed to be a typical figure. In Cardiff, owner-occupation of the most highly valued dwellings (more than £35 rateable value a year) rose over one-quarter in 1884 and in the best ward of Leicester it was 17.3 per cent during the same period.[45] House-ownership was an aspiration of well-paid workers in

[40]Stamp, *British incomes* (1920), p. 67.
[41]PRO IR 73/4 (Private office papers) G. R. Harrison to Fisher [both revenue officials], 16 June 1909. 2.5 million properties, not owners.
[42]Houses and premises, see Mitchell and Deane, *Abstract*, p. 237. 'Hereditaments', see PRO CAB 37/117/96, Inland Revenue, '[Taxation and rating of land values]', 24 Dec. 1913, p. 10.
[43]Stamp, *British incomes* (1920), p. 67.
[44]M. J. Boddy, 'The structure of mortgage finance: building societies and the British social formation', *Trans. Inst. Brit. Geographers* new ser. 1 (1976), 60. Also M. Bowley, *Housing and the state 1919–1944* (1945), p. 85.
[45]Bloomsbury, see Town holdings. Sel. com. rep.; P.P. 1899 (251) XV, pp. 9–10, 35; Cardiff, M. Daunton, *Coal metropolis: Cardiff 1870–1914* (Leicester, 1977), p. 108; Leicester, R. M. Pritchard, *Housing and the spatial structure of the city* (Cambridge, 1976), p. 71.

regular employment.[46] Apparently one-fifth of the workers in Kenricks, a Birmingham hardware firm, were freeholders in the 1850s;[47] a few of the skilled legal copiers interviewed for Charles Booth's survey in London were house-owners.[48] West Yorkshire and Tyneside, where the building society movement was better developed, appear to have had a higher proportion of home-ownership.[49] 'In Oldham,' said the preamble to the Unionist housing bill of 1912, 'out of 33,000 inhabited houses, over 10,000 or about a third, are owned, or in the course of being purchased by artisan proprietors.'[50] The South Wales coalfield apparently had a very high incidence of working-class home-ownership, coming up to 60 per cent in some localities, and Cardiff had an overall percentage of 9.6 falling to 7.2, between 1884 and 1914.[51] In York, at the turn of the century, 608 working-class house-owners (occupying almost six per cent of working-class housing) were headed by 120 widows, 30 spinsters and 58 retired men, and tailed by eight labourers.[52]

Capitalists' tenurial profits came mostly out of fixed stock, i.e. dwellings and commercial structures. The potential value of the land would have largely been anticipated by 'conversion rents' of past and present landowners, and by mortgage interest charges. If the urban house-capitalist was a freeholder he stood to gain from secular rises in property values, provided he acquired and sold his property at the right point in the cycle (recall that property values declined sharply between 1900 and 1910). If he was a leaseholder there were only short-term gains and personally-created goodwill. The rest was appropriated by landowners in ground rents and renewal premiums. Depressions in value could not, however, be shifted back to the landowner. Landowners secured an income and capital gains primarily from the fact of possession; entrepreneurs had to rely on judgement, effort, skill and luck.

[46]Barrow, see E. Roberts, 'Working-class standards of living in Barrow and Lancaster, 1890–1914', *Econ. Hist. Rev.* 2 ser. 30 (1977), 318. For a trenchant analysis, see Daunton, *Coal metropolis* (1977) chapter 7.
[47]R. A. Church, *Kenricks in hardware: a family business 1791–1966* (Newton Abbot, 1969), pp. 277–8.
[48]Booth B152, interview with J. Brown, March 1896, fol. 108.
[49]C. F. Saunders, 'Building societies in the United Kingdom: what they have done and what they are doing', *Building Societies Gazette*, 1 Jan. 1915, 2.
[50]Housing of the working classes (no. 2) bill, 'memorandum'; P.P. 1912–13 (311) II, p. 718. And see A. Shadwell, *Industrial efficiency* (one-vol. edn 1909), p. 63. Also chapter 23, below, p. 388.
[51]Daunton, *Coal metropolis* (1977) p. 108.
[52]B. S. Rowntree, *Poverty: a study of town life* (4th edn 1902), p. 166.

About 23 per cent of the aggregate rental was produced by straight-forward industrial and commercial premises and another 15 per cent by hotels, pubs and residential shops.[53] It is difficult to generalise about the importance of rental expenditure in commercial enterprise. The question was studied by W. B. Cowcher, an Oxford tax inspector who read for a part-time research degree at the University and submitted one of its early B.Litt. theses in 1914, on the incidence of local taxation. His witty but muddled dissertation included a survey of the impact of rent on retail profits in Oxford, based on the taxman's privileged information. The pattern he found shows how much the importance of tenure varied from one establishment to another. Rents in his sample of 72 shopkeepers ranged from six per cent of the profits to 180 per cent with a mean of 36 per cent and a median of 24 per cent. He could discern no relation at all between rent and profits.[54] A much more comprehensive survey was carried out in 1914 by the Inland Revenue in connection with the fiscal controversies which form the subject of our last chapter. A sample of 3340 individuals and firms (needless to say, not a 'scientific' sample) in 23 sectors provided data on the relations between local rates (a tax on rent) and business income or profits. It shows that shopkeepers and small manufacturers had a much larger relative rental outlay than big commercial and financial firms. Unfortunately there was no separate category for dwelling-house capitalists in the survey, but they were obviously a more markedly tenurial class than high-street traders, and some 62 per cent of all house property was made up of dwellings.[55]

Provision of housing for the mass of the population was left to the most disreputable section of entrepreneurs. Property investments were nicely graded by risk: sound freehold property occupied by the middle classes was in greatest demand and the same kind of leasehold property only slightly less so. Investors were warned off working-class housing, particularly weekly property.[56] On the whole they heeded the advice and the middle- and upper-class households who occupied the top fifteen per cent of houses commanded more than half of the country's housing resources. Any cut-off point is arbitrary, but the exemption limits of

---

[53]Great Britain, average of inhabited house duty assessment years, 1894 to 1911 (Mitchell and Deane, *Abstract*, p. 238).

[54]W. B. Cowcher, 'A dissertation upon the incidence of local rates and taxes upon the unearned increment of land', (Oxford Univ. B. Litt. thesis, 1914), app. table 6 and notes.

[55]See table 7.2, p. 122, and note[53].

[56]Dowsett, *Buy English acres* (1905), pp. 32–3.

Table 7.2. *Rent and rates as a percentage of profits in selected urban sectors, 1914[a]*

Sector	Metropolitan (M) or provincial (P)	Number in sample	Rates as % of profit[b]	Rent as % of profit[c]	Mean unit Profit per year[b]
Small retailers	M	201	14.0%	70%	£321
Small retailers	P	527	9.5%	48%	£340
Large retailers	M + P	189	7.1%	36%	£3,850
Miscellaneous manufacturers	M	82	6.7%	34%	£980
Medical practitioners	M	55	6.3%	32%	£899
Miscellaneous manufacturers	P	220	4.7%	24%	£785
Engineering	P	90	4.3%	22%	£577
Legal practitioners	M	39	3.9%	20%	£904
Legal practitioners	P	92	2.9%	15%	£585
Finance and stockbrokers	M	33	0.8%	4%	£66,869
Miscellaneous firms	M	44	0.4%	2%	£199,615
Grand total	M + P	3340	2.3%	11%	£7,278

[a] *Source:* PRO T171/70 (Chancellor of the Exchequer's private office papers), 1914 Budget, c. April 1914 (n.p.). The table is extracted from a very extensive and detailed Inland Revenue report. Grand total includes unlisted categories.
[b] Profit, i.e. net income from trade sources alone.
[c] Notional rent, i.e. rates × 5 (see chapter 18, pp. 288–9 for an account of the relation between rent and rates).

inhabited house duty (less than £20 annual rental net of rates) would take in the vast bulk of working-class and lower-middle-class housing in Britain. Allowing for higher rents and multiple occupation a comparable figure for London would be £41 a year. In 1904 (an assessment year) 6.11 million dwellings in this class made up 85 per cent of the housing stock in Britain but only 45 per cent of its value – figures which highlight the unequal distribution of accommodation. A London house agent wrote in 1886 that 'Investors of the better class will not touch a kind of property which brings them into such unpleasant relations with a class below them'.[57]

[57]Sargant, *Ground rents* (1886), p. 94.

Landlords and agents, equipped with suitable aptitudes and a specialised knowledge of their terrain, manned the trenches of the class war. It was not a game for the tender-hearted. 'Small capitalists, by personal attention might make it more profitable than others who employed even experienced and careful agents ... larger capitalists had better leave it alone', said an estate agent (W. H. Hudson) at a discussion at the Surveyors' Institution in 1893.[58] Gross rates of return on dwelling property in poor working-class districts of London rose to between 25 and 30 per cent in London in a sample taken in 1912; in Stepney in 1906 it reached the amazing average level of 36 per cent![59] Hudson in 1893 'did not think that such a rate of interest as 8 per cent would repay anybody for the trouble and anxiety of such property' and another participant in the discussion explained why. 'The margin of profit would rapidly disappear in the event of either the sanitary inspector or the freeholder making himself at all unpleasant'.[60]

The slum landlord was cast as the monster of social literature, both documentary and fictional. A chain of skinflint entrepreneurs exploited the desperate housing need of the submerged third of the working class. In *How the poor live* (1883) George Sims described an outing to London's East End.

we descend the crazy staircase and get out into as much light as can find its way down these narrow alleys.

Outside we see a portly gentleman with a big gold chain across his capacious form, and an air of wealth and good living all over him. He is the owner of a whole block of property such as this, and he waxes rich on his rents. Strange as it may seem, these one-roomed outcasts are the best paying tenants in London. They pay so much for so little, and almost fight to get it (pp. 9–10; Sims is described in chapter 18, p. 305).

Sartorius, the capitalist in Bernard Shaw's *Widowers' houses* explained to Trench, his mortgagee:

What Lickcheese [the rent-collector] did for me, I do for you. He and I are alike intermediaries: you are the principal. It is because of the risks I run through the poverty of my tenants that you exact interest from me at the monstrous and exorbitant rate of seven per

[58]H. Griffin, 'Weekly property as an investment', *Trans. S.I.* 26 (1893–4), discussion, 364.
[59]Chapter 17, fig. 17.7 and table 17.3, pp. 269 and 270.
[60]Griffin, *Trans. S.I.* 26 (1893–4), 365, 370.

cent, forcing me to exact the uttermost farthing in my turn from the tenants.[61]

Late-Victorian landlords acquired a fearsome reputation because of the high cost of housing relative to wages, and because of their power to evict at a week's notice in case of non-payment. 'The chief item in every poor budget is rent', wrote Maud Pember Reeves in a report of a survey of South London households in 1908. Working-class rents came to more than one-third of the unskilled wage of 'round about a pound a week'. The poor, she showed, paid more for their inferior space than the rich for theirs, and the rent frequently ate into the family's food. The precarious incomes of the poor meant that eviction was an ever-present menace. 'On the whole', she observed, 'the actual landlord is by no means the monster he is popularly represented to be. He will wait rather than change a good tenant. He will make no fuss if the back rent is paid ever so slowly'. Some of the risk, however, was transferred to the poor, who often had to sub-let or take in lodgers in order to secure suitable accommodation. A woman who could barely afford a rent of seven shillings might suddenly have to find ten shillings or more because she was forced to take unsatisfactory tenants. 'Turned into a landlord in her own person', wrote Mrs Pember Reeves, 'she is wonderfully long-suffering and patient, but at the cost of the food of her family. If ejectment has to be enforced, she, not the real landlord, has to enforce it'.[62] The poor were not only consumers of housing, but also reluctant and poorly-paid property professionals.

VI

How much did each class and cluster own?

A graphical description of the distribution of landed and urban property among tenure clusters and social classes is set below in a series of simple diagrams, which largely speak for themselves. All the diagrams are derived from the means of distributions of property passing at death between the 1890s and 1914. Each of them is followed by a short

[61]G. B. Shaw, 'Widowers' houses' (1893), *Plays unpleasant* (Penguin edn 1946), p. 72.

[62]M. Pember Reeves, *Round about a pound a week* (1913), ch. III; See D. Englander's comprehensive 'Landlord and tenant in urban Britain: the politics of housing reform, 1838–1924' (Warwick Univ. Ph.D. thesis, 1979), which appeared to late to be fully utilised in this study.

explanatory comment and has a matching table of data at the end of the chapter.

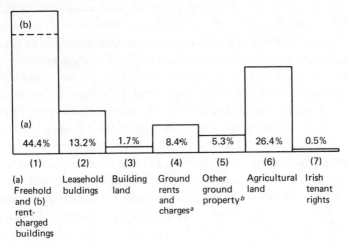

Fig. 7.2. *Distribution of tenures in the .UK, 1896–1914 (mean percentages)*.

Capital values, from death-duty valuations. *Sources: IRAR* (1906) table XC, pp. 110–11 and (1914), table 28, pp. 32–3. Time-series and dispersal data, Table 7.3, below.
*a*Ground rents, chief rents, fee farm rents, feu duties, ground annuals, rent charges, tithe rent charges and cessers of annuities.
*b*Mines, minerals, quarries, timber, interests in expectancy, sporting rights, proceeds of sale of settled realty, and miscellaneous, including brickfields, common and manorial rights and property not defined.

Fig. 7.2. Distribution of tenures. Capitalists owned most of the *value* of land and buildings but their tenure partly overlapped with *imperfect* landowner tenures which still extended over some two-thirds of all realty. Freehold buildings and leasehold buildings were typical capitalist tenures. Building land was an almost pure instance of 'conversion rent' and therefore falls by definition among landowner tenures. Ground rents were overwhelmingly urban although Scottish 'feu duties' extended into the countryside. An assortment of other ground property (block 5) also belonged to the landowner tenures: coal royalties, timber and sport; manorial dues and fines; reversions, expectancies and other residual or contingent interests. Agricultural land made up just more than a quarter of the total and Irish tenant right was a tiny residue.

Capitalist property (blocks 1 and 2) added up to more than half of all tenure, an average 58 per cent. The value of property owned outright under *landowner* tenures (agricultural land, ground property and build-ing land, blocks 3–6) was rather less than one half, i.e. 42 per cent. But landowner tenure was exposed to social and economic friction far beyond its actual share of the tenurial cake which is one reason why it made such a convenient political adversary. Leasehold tenure (block 2) was subject to loose landowner control and rent-charged property (block 1b) to a residual landowner interest. Added on to the straightforward landowner tenures (blocks 3–6) they extended the sway of the landowner class of tenures, both full and attenuated, to some 63 per cent, or almost two-thirds of all landed and urban property. If the full landowner tenures alone are examined (blocks 3–6) then landowners are seen to have remained a prevailingly rural interest. Two-thirds of their tenure was still in agriculture (block 6) and only a third was in urban ground rents and other ground property (blocks 3–5). Socially the landowner tenure was not all of a piece and carried a sizeable fringe of peasant cultivators and of bourgeois owners of ground rents, of whom more below.

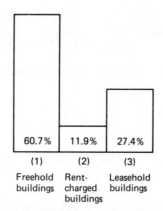

Fig. 7.3. *Tenure of buildings in the UK, 1896–1914 (mean percent-age distribution).*

Capital values, from death-duty valuations. *Source*: as for Fig. 7.2. The time-series are given in Table 7.4.

Fig. 7.3. Tenure of buildings. Owing to the frequent overlap of capitalist and landowner tenures, the tenure of urban *buildings* was differently distributed from urban tenures overall. 61 per cent of urban buildings were freehold (1) and another 12 per cent were subject to rent-charges (2); 27 per cent were held on short leasehold (3). The Liberal land enquiry of 1914 arrived at similar conclusions for England and Wales, using Town Holdings Committee returns from 1889. They estimated the incidence of dwelling tenures on the population (a slightly different measure) as follows.

> Substantially more than one-half of the urban population of England is living under ordinary freehold tenure; about one-twentieth under freehold subject to some form of perpetual annual payment; somewhere about one-tenth under long leasehold; and rather under one-third on short leasehold.[63]

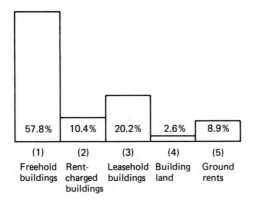

Fig. 7.4. *Urban tenures (including site tenures) in the UK, 1896–1914 (mean percentage distribution).*

Capital values, from death-duty valuations. *Source*: as for Fig. 7.2. The time-series are given in Table 7.5.

Fig. 7.4. Urban tenures (including site tenures). This is a distribution of property rights, not of bricks and mortar. Ground rents, the main landowner tenure in the towns (5) amounted only to nine per cent of the total or perhaps a little more.[64] But it involved the landowners in leasehold and rent-charged property which comprised another 31 per cent (3 and 2). Altogether then, with the addition of vacant building land, the landowner interest embraced (imperfectly) more than 40 per cent of all *urban* property rights.

---

[63] *The land* (1914), ii, 349.
[64] The second death-duty series gave 10.1 per cent for 1904–14 and 10.9 per cent for 1904–12, but excluded some residual property rights. See note[66].

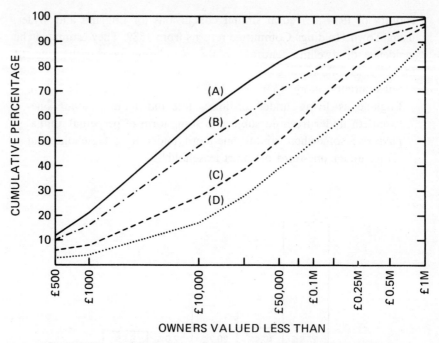

Fig. 7.5. *Social distribution of tenures: distribution of property in each tenure, by wealth of owners, U K 1904–14 (mean percentage). (A) house property and business premises; (B) all tenures; (C) agricultural land; (D) ground rents.*

Capital values, from death-duty valuations. *Source*: see Table 7.6.

Fig. 7.5. Social distribution of tenures Agricultural landowners were still a much more affluent class than urban capitalist house-owners and urban groundowners were the most affluent of all. Distribution profiles of the three tenures show their breakdown by wealth of owner (owners' total wealth, not their landed wealth alone). The closer the curve to the bottom right-hand corner, the greater the inequality of distribution. Urban groundowners (curve D) come out as a distinctly unequal, wealthy and by inference, upper-class group. Persons leaving more than £50,000 at death owned 61 per cent of urban ground rents. In contrast, urban house-proprietors were just as distinctly middle class and consequently registered a convex profile (curve A). Of their assets, 59 per cent belonged to owners of *less* than £10,000 and a full 82 per cent to owners of less than £50,000. Most of the residue was no doubt in industrial premises or in town and country residences held by the rich for their own occupation.

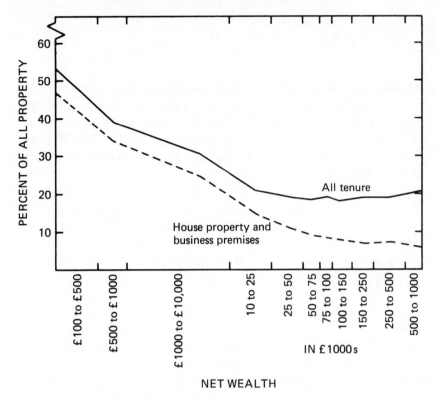

Fig. 7.6. *Tenure as percentage of wealth, UK 1904–14 (mean).*
Capital values, from death-duty valuations. *Source:* Table 7.7.

Fig. 7.6. Tenure as a percentage of wealth This figure reinforces the impression already formed by Table 7.2, that the middle-class users and owners of buildings were a more truly landed interest than the rich. In other words, small capitals were more deeply committed to tenure than large ones. Among the small and middling farmers, entrepreneurs, rentiers and professionals who left estates of between £1,000 and £10,000, tenure was the largest single asset, accounting for almost a third (31 per cent) of all their property. One-quarter was in bricks and mortar (table 7.7, cols. 2 and 4, row 6). The proportion of tenure increased as affluence decreased and it touched 50 per cent among the smallest proprietors. British smallholders were predominantly urban and the small and medium owners of up to £10,000 held almost half of all tenure (table 7.6, col. 4, row 6).

129

VII

Conclusion

Settled estates, which embraced about one-quarter of all tenure, provided us (in section III of this chapter pp. 109–11) with one definition of the core of landowner tenure. Let us now venture another definition, namely all the tenure of estates assessed for death duty at more than £50,000 capital value (mean, 1904–14). This is a roughly comparable and probably lower threshold than Bateman's 'Squires', the owners of between one and three thousand acres.[65] Farmland and urban ground rents in the possession of these large estates amounted to 18 per cent of all tenure; house property and business premises brought their holdings up to 30 per cent of all tenure in the UK, or slightly more than the share of settled land.[66] Thirty per cent of *the value* of tenure was the share of tenure owned by the rich in the Edwardian period, as opposed to Bateman's sixty per cent of the acreage.[67] The number of proprietors in each class gives a general idea of the social stratification of property. For every patrician worth more than £50,000 there were 116 smaller men of property. Four owned between £10,000 and £50,000, thirty-eight between £500 and £10,000 and seventy-four less than £500.[68] In other words, fewer than one per cent of all proprietors (0.86%) owned 30 per cent of the land, by value.

The social distribution of agrarian and house-capitalist tenure showed little change in the last decade before the Great War (table 7.8). Not so the rich man's tenure, urban ground rents, which showed signs of commercial change or social dilution. The proportion of ground rents

---

[65]Bateman, *Great landowners* (1883), p. 515. 'Squires', 'Great landowners' and 'Peers', his upper categories, formed a smaller proportion of all proprietors (0.44 per cent) than the owners of more than £50,000 in our sample (0.86 per cent).

[66]These data, like Figs. 7.5–7.6 and tables 7.6–7.8 are based on the second of the death-duty series which gives slightly lower totals for tenure because residual ground property ((5) in Fig. 7.2) was transferred into an undifferentiated general-purpose category ('other property'). The mean covers a shorter and later period (1904–14) and therefore reflects the shift away from tenure. Mean tenure shares in this source are as follows (Fig. 4.2 data in brackets): Agricultural land – 28.2 per cent (26.4 per cent); house property and business premises – 64.5 per cent (59.3 per cent); ground rents – 7.3 per cent (8.4 per cent). They are calculated from the bottom row, Table 7.7 below, with differences due to rounding.

[67]The rich (i.e. owners of more than £50,000) owned one-half of all *agricultural* land, a figure not too far from Bateman's 60 per cent (table 7.6, (1) row 8). Bateman's figure is reached if £25,000 is taken as the threshold.

[68]Mean 1909–14. *IRAR* (1914), table 18, p. 20.

belonging to estates of more than £50,000 decreased (on trend) from about three-quarters (73 per cent) in 1904 to one-half in 1914. It is difficult to say whether the tenure was being taken over by corporations and institutions, or whether it was passing into the hands of smaller proprietors, since the series has the large variance typical of the large owners' fractions.[69] Traditional owners were apparently abandoning this tenure in favour of more liquid forms of property. Thus, for example, the estate of Baron Kensington disposed of £560,000 of London ground rents at one sale in December 1902, of which the *Estates Gazette* proclaimed that it 'creates a record in the annals of the land market'.[70] Three years later a portion of the Burrage estate, Woolwich, 'which comprises nearly 4,000 properties, extends to 400 acres and has boundaries along 20 miles of streets near the royal arsenal' obtained £553,450 in four sales of ground rents. The *Estates Gazette*, blessed with a short memory and a long view, hailed it again as 'a sale the like of which has not been equalled in England for over half a century'.[71]

To conclude then – tenure in Edwardian England presented a *dual aspect*. More than a million house proprietors co-existed in the shade of a few thousand landowners with very large concentrations of tenure. If property professionals and mortgagees are taken into account, the tenurial interests of the small and medium bourgeoisie are seen to have been even more numerous and substantial. Before we proceed to examine the political implications of this two-tiered tenurial structure, there is one more fraction of property to consider, the mortgagees.

[69] Mean 61.2, standard deviation 11.2 (the inverse of (3) row 8, Table 7.6).
[70] *EG*, 3 Jan. 1903, 12.
[71] *EG*, 30 Dec. 1905, 1162.

Table 7.3. (See fig. 7.2.) *Percentage distribution of the gross capital value of realty subject to estate duty, U.K. 1896–1914, by tenure. (Year ending March. Sources: See fig. 7.2)**

Year	(1) Freehold and other buildings	(2) Leasehold buildings	(3) Building land	(4) Ground charges	(5) Other ground property	(6) Agricultural land	(7) Other	Total
1896	47.0	15.2	1.4	5.9	3.6	25.0	0.8	100.00
1897	42.1	12.6	1.1	7.7	6.4	29.3	0.8	100.00
1898	42.2	12.8	1.6	8.0	8.0	26.6	0.7	100.00
1899	43.9	12.5	2.0	8.2	4.3	28.5	0.7	100.00
1900	42.3	12.8	2.1	10.0	4.0	28.1	0.7	100.00
1901	43.3	12.5	1.7	8.0	5.3	28.6	0.7	100.00
1902	42.5	11.4	2.1	8.4	5.5	29.5	0.5	100.00
1903	44.4	12.3	2.5	9.1	4.4	27.1	0.3	100.00
1904	45.0	13.4	1.8	8.9	4.4	26.1	0.4	100.00
1905	44.9	12.1	1.6	10.2	5.7	25.0	0.5	100.00
1906	44.7	12.4	1.8	8.3	5.1	27.5	0.3	100.00
1907	43.0	12.3	1.8	11.3	5.5	25.8	0.4	100.00
1908	43.0	13.0	1.8	9.3	6.4	26.1	0.4	100.00
1909	44.8	14.6	1.4	7.9	4.5	26.4	0.4	100.00
1910	43.3	13.7	1.3	9.7	6.5	25.2	0.3	100.00
1911	46.5	13.0	1.1	7.7	6.8	24.4	0.4	100.00
1912	46.6	13.2	2.1	8.6	5.9	23.0	0.5	100.00
1913	48.7	14.3	1.2	5.9	5.1	24.4	0.4	100.00
1914	47.0	17.5	1.3	5.5	4.2	24.2	0.4	100.00
Mean 1896–1914	44.4	13.2	1.7	8.4	5.3	26.4	0.5	100.00

Table 7.4. (See fig. 7.3.) *Percentage distribution of the capital value of houses and business premises subject to estate duty, by tenure, U.K. 1896–1914.* (Source: *see fig. 7.2*).*

Year	(1) Freehold	(2) Leasehold	(3) Other[a]	Total
1896	59.56	26.10	14.34	100.00
1897	59.12	27.61	13.27	100.00
1898	60.42	27.53	12.05	100.00
1899	60.69	25.87	13.43	100.00
1900	57.65	31.16	11.19	100.00
1901	59.30	27.01	13.69	100.00
1902	60.70	26.23	13.07	100.00
1903	60.19	27.33	12.47	100.00
1904	59.51	28.81	11.78	100.00
1905	60.48	27.23	12.29	100.00

*Totals do not add up to 100.00 due to rounding.

132

Table 7.4 contd.

1906	60.33	26.75	12.92	100.00
1907	58.72	30.18	11.10	100.00
1908	59.64	29.56	10.79	100.00
1909	59.19	·29.14	11.67	100.00
1910	58.61	30.43	10.96	100.00
1911	63.09	25.33	11.59	100.00
1912	60.42	26.97	12.61	100.00
1913	62.30	25.41	12.28	100.00
1914	59.05	29.47	11.48	100.00

Mean 1896–1914

60.38	27.43	11.88	100.00

[a] Other – long leasehold (over 100 years) and rent-charged property.

Table 7.5. (See fig. 7.4.) *Percentage distribution of urban realty subject to estate duty, by tenure, U.K. 1896–1914.* (Source: *see fig. 7.2.*)*

Year	(1) Freehold buildings	(2) Leasehold buildings	(3) Other buildings[a]	(4) Building land	(5) Ground rents	Total
1896	58.3	22.7	11.8	2.1	5.2	100.00
1897	57.8	20.7	11.4	1.8	8.2	100.00
1898	58.7	20.8	9.9	2.6	8.0	100.00
1899	58.7	19.8	11.0	3.1	7.4	100.00
1900	55.8	19.6	9.2	3.2	12.2	100.00
1901	57.5	19.8	11.2	2.7	8.8	100.00
1902	58.5	18.6	10.5	3.4	9.0	100.00
1903	57.7	18.8	10.4	3.8	9.2	100.00
1904	57.4	20.1	10.0	2.7	9.9	100.00
1905	57.8	18.4	10.8	2.4	10.6	100.00
1906	58.1	19.1	11.2	2.8	8.8	100.00
1907	55.9	18.6	9.5	2.7	13.3	100.00
1908	57.0	20.1	9.3	2.7	10.8	100.00
1909	57.5	22.2	10.5	2.1	7.8	100.00
1910	56.8	21.2	10.0	2.0	10.0	100.00
1911	60.9	19.9	10.2	1.7	7.4	100.00
1912	56.9	19.3	11.1	3.1	9.7	100.00
1913	61.0	21.0	10.7	1.7	5.5	100.00
1914	57.6	25.3	10.4	1.9	4.7	100.00
Mean 1896–1914	57.8	20.2	10.4	2.6 ·	8.9	100.00

[a] Other buildings – long leasehold and rent-charged property.
*Totals do not add up to 100.00 due to rounding.

Table 7.6. (See fig. 7.5.) *Percentage of tenure held by owners of different wealth, U.K. 1904–1914 (mean). Based on the gross capital passing at death*

Row no.	Proprietors valued up to[a]	(1) Agricultural land	Cumulative percentage (2) House property and business premises	(3) Ground rents	(4) All realty
1.	Insolvent Proprietors	(2.2)[b]	(2.2)	(2.2)	2.2
2.	£100–£500 (Gross)	3.2	5.7	2.3	4.7
3.	£100 (Net)	(4.1)	(6.6)	(3.2)	5.6
4.	£500	5.7	12.1	3.5	9.7
5.	£1,000	8.2	20.6	4.2	16.0
6.	£10,000	27.6	59.8	17.1	47.7
7.	£25,000	39.2	73.3	27.9	60.4
8.	£50,000	50.5	82.0	38.8	70.0
9.	£75,000	58.1	86.0	45.1	75.2
10.	£100,000	64.7	88.4	49.7	78.2
11.	£150,000	72.0	91.3	55.7	83.2
12.	£250,000	80.8	94.1	65.7	88.2
13.	£500,000	88.8	97.2	76.4	93.2
14.	£1,000,000	95.7	98.9	90.4	97.2
15.	More than £1,000,000	100.0	100.0	100.0	100.0

[a] Proprietors are ranked by their *net* wealth (both real and personal), unless otherwise indicated. The cumulative percentage, however, refers to gross values.
[b] Figures in brackets are extrapolated from 'All realty' figure (col. 4).
Source: IRAR, 'Estate Duties', e.g. P.P. 1914 XXXVI, tables 20, 21, 30, pp. 22, 23, 35. For dispersion data, see table 7.8.

Table 7.7. (See fig. 7.6.) *Tenures as a percentage of all property in the U.K., at different levels of wealth, 1904–14 (mean)*

Row no.	Proprietors' net wealth in pounds	Percentage of all property							
		(1) Agricultural land	S.D.[a]	(2) House property and business premises	S.D.[a]	(3) Ground rents	S.D.[a]	(4) All realty	S.D.[a]
1.	Insolvent proprietors	2.7	(0.4)	21.1	(2.2)	0.07	(0.05)	51.7	(4.5)
2.	100–500 (Gross)	6.3	(0.8)	46.7	(1.4)	0.3	(0.08)	23.9	(1.9)
3.	Less than £100 (Net)	4.5	(0.6)	34.1	(0.8)	0.3	(0.06)	36.5	(3.5)
4.	100–500 (Net)	5.3	(0.4)	24.6	(0.7)	0.9	(0.08)	53.3	(1.4)
5.	500–1,000	5.3	(0.6)	14.5	(1.6)	1.2	(0.3)	38.9	(0.8)
6.	1,000–10,000	6.4	(0.9)	11.2	(1.2)	1.5	(0.3)	30.7	(1.1)
7.	10,000–25,000	7.8	(1.7)	9.1	(0.7)	1.6	(0.5)	21.0	(1.4)
8.	25,000–50,000	9.2	(2.1)	8.2	(1.4)	1.7	(0.5)	19.1	(2.1)
9.	50,000–75,000	8.7	(1.7)	7.7	(1.3)	1.8	(0.5)	18.5	(2.3)
10.	75,000–100,000	9.5	(3.0)	6.8	(0.9)	2.7	(1.2)	19.1	(2.9)
11.	100,000–150,000	8.0	(2.5)	7.1	(3.2)	2.9	(2.0)	18.1	(2.3)
12.	150,000–250,000	9.1	(4.3)	5.8	(2.5)	5.5	(3.7)	19.0	(4.0)
13.	250,000–500,000	5.8	(5.9)	2.6	(1.9)	4.7	(8.3)	18.1	(6.0)
14.	0.5M–1,000,000							20.4	(6.7)
15.	More than 1,000,000							13.1	(15.4)
	All proprietors	6.6	(0.8)	15.1	(0.8)	1.7	(0.5)	23.5	(1.8)

Source: Death duty valuations, e.g. *IRAR*; P.P. 1914 XXXVI, tables 20, 21, 30, pp. 22, 23, 35.
[a]Standard deviation.

Table 7.8. (See fig. 7.5 and table 7.6.) *Percentage of tenure held by owners of different wealth, U.K. 1904–1914 (mean)*

Row No.	Proprietors' net wealth in pounds	Percentage of all tenure held by proprietors of each class							
		(1) Agricultural land	S.D.[a]	(2) House property and business premises	S.D.[a]	(3) Ground rents	S.D.[a]	(4) All realty	S.D.[a]
1.	Insolvent proprietors	(2.2)		(2.2)		(2.2)		2.2	(0.4)
2.	100–500 (Gross)	1.0	(0.1)	3.5	(0.7)	0.1	(0.03)	2.5	(0.5)
3.	Less than £100 (Net)	(0.9)		(0.9)		(0.9)		0.9	(0.2)
4.	100–500 (Net)	1.6	(0.2)	5.5	(0.5)	0.3	(0.1)	4.1	(0.3)
5.	500–1,000	2.5	(0.3)	8.5	(0.6)	0.7	(0.2)	6.3	(0.6)
6.	1,000–10,000	19.4	(1.9)	39.2	(1.6)	12.9	(3.9)	31.7	(1.9)
7.	10,000–25,000	11.6	(2.7)	13.5	(0.8)	10.8	(4.4)	12.7	(1.0)
8.	25,000–50,000	11.3	(1.1)	8.7	(1.0)	10.9	(3.4)	9.6	(0.9)
9.	50,000–75,000	7.6	(0.3)	4.0	(1.5)	6.3	(1.5)	5.2	(0.6)
10.	75,000–100,000	6.6	(1.7)	2.4	(0.4)	4.6	(1.4)	3.6	(0.5)
11.	100,000–150,000	7.3	(1.2)	2.9	(0.6)	6.0	(1.9)	4.4	(0.7)
12.	150,000–250,000	8.8	(2.6)	2.8	(0.5)	10.0	(3.8)	5.0	(1.1)
13.	250,000–500,000	8.0	(2.6)	3.1	(1.1)	10.7	(5.8)	5.0	(1.4)
14.	0.5M–1,000,000	6.9	(4.7)	1.7	(0.7)	14.0	(7.3)	4.0	(1.2)
15.	More than 1,000,000	4.3	(2.4)	1.0	(0.9)	9.6	(11.1)	2.7	(2.1)
Total[b]		100.0		100.0		100.0		100.0	

Source: See Table 7.5.
[a] Standard deviation.
[b] Total does not add up to 100.0 due to rounding.

136

8

MORTGAGEES

I

The pattern of debt

Legal mortgage was the most common lender's tenure. In return for a loan, the full legal title was conveyed to the mortgagee. The deed specified repayment in six months' time, and after this had elapsed, the lender could call the loan in, subject to three months' notice. The borrower was entitled to repay the loan and regain his title at any time, subject to six months' notice or a fine of six months' interest in lieu. This right, the 'equity of redemption', was itself a marketable tenure and its value was the difference between the market price of the property and the oustanding value of the loan. Custom limited the advance to two-thirds of the estimated value of the property; if the market value declined below the amount of the loan, the 'equity of redemption' became negative and the borrower lost the incentive to repay.[1]

The flow of mortgage loans was related to the cycle of new construction. A new building had to be financed at least twice: the builder needed short-term credit to construct and the landlord then required long-term credit in order to purchase. Fig. 4.2 has shown the scale and fluctuation of mortgage lending, and how closely it moved with the turnover of the property market. Mortgage lending was also well correlated with the number of new houses in Great Britain, as calculated by B. Weber.[2] In addition to the annual *flow* of lending from stamp duties, the *stock* of outstanding landed loans may also be estimated, from the mortgage debts of the deceased which are recorded in death-duty returns. Agricultural, ground-rent and urban capitalist debts can be separately measured and the debtors ranked by wealth. Fig. 8.1 presents the essence of these data and Table 8.1 lists them.

[1] E. H. Blake, 'Mortgages – some notes on law and practice', *Auct. Inst.* (11 Nov. 1908), 13–28.
[2] Correlation coefficient of the number of new houses (Great Britain) and the annual flow of mortgages (England and Wales), 1893–1913, $r = 0.82$ (Weber, see Mitchell and Deane, *Abstract*, table 4, p. 239).

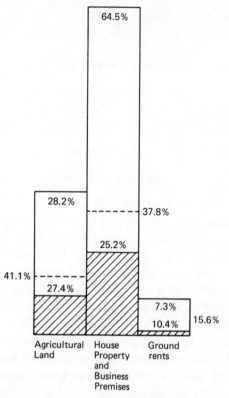

Fig. 8.1. *Mortgage debt as a percentage of tenure in the UK, 1904–14 (mean: overall mean debt 25.9 per cent).*

In each block, the shaded area represents the mortgage debt, the top figure is the percentage of all tenure, the bottom figure the percentage of debt and the external figure is the approximate percentage of tenure securing the debt. *Source:* Death duty valuations, gross and net capitals passing at death, *IRAR* (1904–14), e.g. (1914), tables 20, 21, 30, pp. 22, 23, 35. See Table 8.1, p. 139. For differences between percentages in this figure and in Figs. 7.2–7.4 see n.[66], p. 130.

Table 8.2. The social distribution of debt. Mortgage debts amounted to an average one-quarter (25.9%) of the value of tenure in the U.K. between 1904 and 1914 (col. 4, bottom row). This means that more than a *third* of land and house property was mortgaged, since advances did not exceed two-thirds of the value. Smaller proprietors were more deeply in debt: mortgage liabilities tapered off from 30.6 per cent among owners of between £500 and £1,000, down to about 15 per cent among those with more than £50,000. Agricultural property was the most heavily

Table 8.1. *Mortgage debt in the U.K., 1904–14 (mean)*

	Agricultural land	House property and business premises	Ground rents	Total (T) or weighted mean (M)	
1. Category's share of all tenure	28.2%	64.5%	7.3%	100.0%	(T)
2. Debt as percentage of value	27.4%	25.2%	10.4%	25.9%	(M)
3. Approximate proportion of property mortgaged (debt × 3/2)	41.1%	37.8%	15.1%	37.1%	(M)

Source: see Fig. 8.1.

encumbered (27.4 per cent); buildings a little less (25.2 per cent). Ground rents carried less than half this level of debt, only 10.4 per cent. Not only were they concentrated in the fewest hands, they were also the least encumbered of all tenures. For rich proprietors, of more than £100,000, the size of the debt varied considerably from year to year, without revealing any clear upwards or downwards trend. This only reflected the small numbers and the divergence of circumstances among the wealthy: even a fairly comprehensive sample, such as this, does not make it possible to generalise about them. In some years, the returns showed no landed debt at all among the wealthy; when in debt, however, their aggregate liabilities rarely rose above the national average.

Insolvent owners accounted for 2.2 per cent of all tenure (see table 7.6). Oddly, and in common with the nearly-solvent owners of less than £100, they had by far the largest stake in realty: more than half their assets were invested in tenure, compared with about one-quarter for all proprietors (see table 7.7). So much for the wisdom of the property press, which never tired of repeating that nothing was safer than bricks and mortar: 'Land, it has been said most truly, is the basis of all security', wrote the *Estates Chronicle* on the first page of its first issue, on 15 April 1898. Edwardian experience was at variance with its intuition, as the figures demonstrate.

Legal mortgages made up a stable core of long-term credit at a moderate rate of interest, advanced as perpetual annuities and discharged at the borrower's convenience. If a loan was called in, there was time enough to arrange another. Even in a slump 'there [was] no difficulty in

Table 8.2. *Mortgage debts as a percentage of tenures at different levels of wealth, U.K. 1904–1914 (mean).*

Row no.	Proprietors' net wealth in pounds £[a]	Debt as a percentage of tenure							
		(1) Agricultural land	S.D.	(2) House property and business premises	S.D.	(3) Ground rents	S.D.	(4) All realty	S.D.
1.	Insolvent proprietors							105.2	(5.0)
2.	100–500 (Gross)	2.2	(1.5)	6.7	(7.7)[b]	0.3	(0.6)	6.3	(7.2)
3.	Less than £100 (Net)							68.5	(5.1)
4.	100–500 (Net)	57.1	(3.0)	54.6	(1.4)	31.5	(10.3)	54.8	(1.2)
5.	500–1,000	34.9	(4.2)	30.1	(1.4)	13.5	(4.7)	30.6	(1.2)
6.	1,000–10,000	26.4	(2.5)	22.2	(1.0)	8.8	(2.2)	22.5	(1.1)
7.	10,000–25,000	24.0	(4.7)	16.4	(2.0)	5.4	(3.6)	17.8	(2.0)
8.	25,000–50,000	23.7	(5.9)[c]	13.8	(2.9)	7.1	(3.9)	16.6	(3.0)
9.	50,000–75,000	21.5	(6.5)[d]	12.5	(4.2)	6.0	(5.5)	15.8	(3.0)
10.	75,000–100,000	23.7	(6.4)	13.6	(6.4)	5.3	(5.1)	17.8	(4.5)
11.	100,000–150,000	17.7	(7.4)	12.7	(8.4)	8.3	(8.2)	15.1	(5.3)
12.	150,000–250,000	23.1	(10.3)	7.6	(3.6)	13.1	(10.5)	15.8	(7.7)
13.	250,000–500,000	16.6	(8.0)	9.1	(6.2)	9.2	(9.9)	13.0	(5.3)
14.	0.5M–1,000,000	17.2	(10.7)	9.4	(6.7)	9.3	(9.3)	13.0	(6.1)
15.	More than 1,000,000	5.0	(4.3)	3.0	(2.7)	3.3	(6.0)[e]	4.4	(3.6)
16.	Sub-total (excluding 1 and 3)	22.8	(2.7)	21.0	(2.1)	8.7	(3.4)	20.7	(1.8)
	Total indebtedness	27.4		25.2		10.4		25.9	(1.9)

Sources: See Fig. 8.1.

[a] Inclusive of lower, but not higher figure; s.D. is standard deviation.
[b] Mean 2.5 (s.D. 0.8) up to 1911. A sharp rise from 1911 to 13.4, 16.8 and 24.2.
[c] Mean is 25.9, s.D. equals 3.2 if 1911 (16.8) and 1914 (10.8) are omitted.
[d] Mean equals 24.7, s.D. is 3.4 if 1912 (7.7), 1909 (15.0) and 1904 (16.1) are omitted.
[e] Three values of 12.6, 16.5 and 7.1. The rest 0.0.

140

obtaining reasonable advances on good landed securities'.[3] Landowners borrowed to finance agricultural improvements, mining and industrial investments, family jointures and portions, and conspicuous consumption.[4] A classic instance were the debts incurred by W. E. Gladstone on the security of Hawarden, to salvage a disastrous mining venture and keep up family appearances. 'I earnestly entreat,' wrote the Prime Minister to his son on the 23 October 1882, 'that you will never, under any circumstances, mortgage any of your land'. He also wrote, on 3 October 1885, that 'to mortgages I am greatly opposed ... as a general rule they are mischievous, and in many cases, as to their consequences, anti-social and immoral'.[5]

Tenurial capitalists sank much borrowed money into dwellings and business premises; 65 per cent of all mortgages were secured in this way (see Fig. 8.1). In Glasgow, 90 per cent of the dwellings were estimated to be mortgaged in 1915.[6] Second and third mortgages were also available, with less security for the lender but a higher return.[7] Credit was readily available to builders and developers to bridge the period between the initiation of housing projects and their successful disposal.[8] Yet another form of mortgage, often a less binding 'equitable mortgage', was the revolving credit provided by banks to manufacturers and traders on the collateral of plant and premises.[9]

On the assumption that entrepreneurial vitality declined with age it is likely that mortgage indebtedness at death included a smaller share than normal for overdrafts and working credit. Table 8.2 therefore represents the lower limits of landed debt in the U.K. and omits some of the more volatile elements. Proprietors are ranked by their net, not gross assets, so that an estate commanding, say, £10,000 worth of land but mortgaged to the hilt will appear in a low rank. As a result, smaller estates appear to

[3]Blake, 'Mortgages' (1908), 13.
[4]On aristocratic indebtedness, see F. M. L. Thompson, 'The end of a great estate', *Econ. Hist. Rev.* 2 ser. 8 (1955), 36–52; D. Spring, 'English landownership in the nineteenth century: a critical note', *Econ. Hist. Rev.* 9 (1957), 472–84 and D. Cannadine, 'Aristocratic indebtedness in the nineteenth century: the case reopened', *Ibid.* 30 (1977), 624–50.
[5]J. Morley, *The life of William Ewart Gladstone* (1903), i, 347, 349.
[6]Increases in rental of small dwellings in Scotland. Dept. com. rep.; P.P. 1914–16 Cd. 8111 XXXV, p. 6.
[7]Blake, 'Mortgages' (1908), 15–16.
[8]See H. J. Dyos, 'The speculative builders and developers of Victorian London', *Victorian Studies* 11 (Supplement, 1968), 663–7.
[9]See B. Campion, 'Bankers' advances upon title deeds to landed proprietors. Pt. I', *Journal of the Institute of Bankers* 27 (1907), 26–53.

be more encumbered than they really were and larger estates somewhat less.

The cost of servicing the debt was even more significant than its absolute size. With the yield on Consols down to 2.5 per cent in 1896, an increase of 1 per cent in the interest rate meant an addition of more than a third to finance charges. Consols rose from an average 2.5 per cent between 1895 and 1899 to 3.3 per cent between 1910 and 1914.[10] In Glasgow, 'the rate on first mortgages was generally 1 per cent above the rate on Consols ... it fell to as low as 3 per cent or even $2\frac{3}{4}$ per cent in 1896; by 1904 it had risen again to $3\frac{1}{4}$ per cent and by 1912 to 4 per cent [on private mortgage bonds]'.[11] Such increases had serious repercussions for proprietors, quite apart from aggravating factors such as rising labour and material costs, and the decline of property values. As in other instances, groundowners enjoyed a positive advantage: not only was their capital liability lower; owing to the greater security offered to the lender by freehold land, their interest rates were also lower.[12]

II

Providers of credit

Banks did not normally lend long on mortgage but provincial banks provided substantial sums of short-term working credit to their clients on the security of title deeds and this form of credit was not unknown in London.[13] Frederic Seebohm, President of the Country Bankers' Association, estimated in 1895 that £100–£150 millions, about half of all short-term bank credit, were secured in this way.[14] A somewhat lower magnitude was estimated by an informed observer in 1912: '24.3 per cent of the total loans and advances made by six of the largest London Clearing Banks are secured on real property. The advances of purely country banks would stand in a higher proportion'.[15] These credits have

[10]Mitchell and Deane, *Abstract*, p. 455.
[11]A. K. Cairncross, *Home and foreign investment 1870–1913* (Cambridge 1953), pp. 35–6.
[12]Blake, 'Mortgages' (1908), 14; Urlin, *Trust funds* (1902), pp. 42–7.
[13]Gilbart, *Banking*, rev. Mitchie (1905), i, 253–4; Dyos, 'Speculative builders' (1968), 665; D. H. Reeder, 'Capital investment in the western suburbs of Victorian London' (Leicester Univ. Ph.D. thesis, 1965), pp. 151–2.
[14]Land transfer bill. Sel. com. ev.; P.P. 1895 (364) XI, ques. 3882–7.
[15]BL 27/4/6, Lord George Hamilton to A. Bonar Law, 5 Nov. 1912.

the effect of inflating the mortgage investment flow that we have deduced from stamp duty returns. By how much? The loans were known to bankers as 'dead loans' – credit was constantly renewed but the deeds were held for longish periods. Let us assume a turnover period of six years (comparable to building society mortgages, discussed below). One-sixth of the (approximately) £125-million-worth of deeds on deposit in 1895 would account for 18 per cent of the mortgage flow in that year, say 20 per cent for the whole period.

Building societies, insurance companies, friendly societies and charities were the other institutional mortgagees. Building societies lent an average £9.3 million a year between 1901 and 1912, rising from 6.1 per cent to 8.9 per cent of the total mortgage flow between 1901 and 1912 but keeping their annual lending fairly stable (s.d. £0.4 million). Their mortgage *stock* increased from £47.9 million to £60.6 million in the same period.[16] Insurance company mortgage assets were almost twice as large – £109 million at the end of 1912. Given the same stock/flow relation as building societies (an average 6.1) they would have lent £14 million in 1900 and £18 million in 1912, 9.5 and 18.5 per cent respectively of all mortgage loans in those years, which were a peak and a trough of the urban cycle.[17] Friendly societies and charities contributed another 3–4 per cent.[18] Despite their impressive growth, building societies still accounted for only a small part of mortgage lending before the war, and insurance companies, which held a larger share, were in the process of reducing their commitment.[19] Disregarding the 20 per cent we have assigned to the banks, institutions lent less than one-quarter of the mortgages (23 per cent) around the turn of the century, at the height of the boom, and more than a third (39 per cent) in 1912, at the bottom of the slump. Only if the share of banks is added did institutions as a class provide more than a third of mortgage credit around 1900 (39 per cent) and over half (51 per cent) in 1912.

'The general public' was the largest lender of conventional legal mortgages.[20] A large number of investors of purely local horizons were

[16]Sanders, 'Building societies' (1915), 3, and table 4.2, p. 66, above.
[17]Calculated from D. K. Sheppard, *The growth and role of U.K. financial institutions 1880–1962* (1971) table (A) 2.5, col. 2, pp. 154–6.
[18]*Ibid.* table (A) 2.8, pp. 162–3. Extrapolated backwards from 1920.
[19]£70.9 million of mortgages made up 45.7 per cent of insurance company assets in 1880; by 1914 a mortgage stock of £114.1 million was only 20.7 per cent of their portfolios (see n.[17]).
[20]Blake, 'Mortgages' (1908), 14.

glad to place their money in the hands of those, like the Forsytes, who had 'a talent for bricks and mortar' and 'no dread in life like that of 3 per cent for their money'.[21] Estate-duty returns show that private individuals supplied an average 82 per cent of the credit used by individual mortgagors between 1904 and 1914.[22] When mortgages were authorised for trustee investment in 1859 they provided executors with a more remunerative security than Consols. 'The general result has been that trustees have largely availed themselves of "real securities", i.e. mortgages.'[23] A few colonial securities were added by the Trustee Act, 1893; The Colonial Stock Act, 1900 greatly extended the authorised list and admitted municipal and railway securities as well;[24] But the pattern of trustee investment was already firmly set.

Solicitors were able to tap an apparently inexhaustible reservoir of loan capital which they made available at 5 or $5\frac{1}{2}$ per cent. This part of the market appears to have been little influenced by the competing uses for capital in the commercial metropolis or overseas.[25]

A line of credit from middle-class professionals, traders, manufacturers and rentiers into bricks and mortar, which had characterised the eighteenth and early nineteenth centuries was still very much in evidence at the beginning of the twentieth. Many building societies, often based in solicitors' offices, were only a slightly corporatised version of the same mode of finance.[26]

III

Mortgagees and the Edwardian property slump

What did mortgagees forgo in their attachment to bricks and mortar? No comprehensive indicator of mortgage interest is available, but the rate of return on long-term or perpetual loans could not be very flexible.

[21]J. Galsworthy, *The man of property* (1906, Penguin edn 1951), p. 25.
[22]*IRAR* (1904–14), 'Estate duties', e.g. (1914), (a) table 26/6, 'Money out on mortgage', pp. 28–9. (b) Mortgage debts, calculated from tables 20, 21 and 30, pp. 22, 23 and 25. The mean of (a) was £13.9 million a year (s.d. 0.7); the mean of (b) was £16.9 million a year (S.D. 1.9).
[23]Urlin, *Trust funds* (1902), p. 28.
[24]Trustee Act 1893, 56 & 57 Vict. c. 53 s. 1; Colonial Stock Act, 63 & 64 Vict. c. 62, s.2.
[25]Reeder, 'Capital investment' (1965), p. 213; also pp. 175, 203–13.
[26]*Ibid.* p. 203; Fenby, *The other Oxford* (1970), p. 62ff.

Building societies gave their depositors very little more than Consols. They found it possible to attract a large amount of capital 'at rates varying from 3 per cent upwards, usually not more than $3\frac{1}{2}$ per cent and very rarely exceeding 3 per cent'.[27] From around the turn of the century the differential in favour of mortgages was continuously under pressure from rising interest rates and from high-yield investment opportunities in municipal and overseas securities. Converting mortgages to higher rates of return was fraught with risk; it threatened to wipe out the margin of security. After 1905 construction became depressed, rents did not rise, property values fell and higher interest charges could only push borrowers closer to insolvency. 'The landlord', says Cairncross of Edwardian Glasgow 'was caught between rising interest rates and falling demand'.[28] The mortgagee was in the same boat. Demands for simplification of foreclosure procedure began to appear in the legal press in 1910, a periodic symptom of hard times.[29] But entering into possession was a doubtful remedy in a property slump. 'Within the last year many mortgage securities and other properties have had to be realised at a loss – often a serious loss – to the people interested', said the President of the Auctioneers' Institute in his address on 20 October 1909.[30]

A report from the estate agents Whitton and Laing, of Exeter, concludes a doleful survey of the property market, printed in the *Property Market Review* on 1 January 1910.

> We have found that shop and business properties, residences and dwelling houses have been practically unsaleable except at sacrificial prices, and we have sold properties this year for about half what we realised for them ten or twelve years ago.

Messrs. Provis and Company, of Manchester, declared:

> This has been a disastrous year, and one which would have been more pronounced had not far fewer properties been offered during 1909 than in former years. Building operations are being curtailed in every district, the recent scarcity of money possibly accounting for this.

On the same page (4), the next item was a report on 'Building activity in Sydney'.

[27]Sanders, 'Building societies' (1915), 4; see J. P. Lewis, *Building cycles and Britain's growth* (1965), pp. 152–4.

[28]Cairncross, *Home and foreign investment* (1953), p. 36.

[29]J. Indermaur, 'Suggestions for amendments in foreclosure practice', *LSPR* (1910), 192–201, esp. 197. Other references, J. Hunter, 'Presidential address' *LSPR* (1894), 46; *LSAR* (1913), 37 and (1914), 42–3.

[30]A. G. Watney 'Presidential address 1909–10', *Auct. Inst.* (20 Oct. 1909), 10.

A great building boom is in progress in Sydney. Never has there been greater activity in that city and throughout New South Wales generally. Materials cannot be supplied fast enough to meet the demand. As a result there is a dearth of labour in certain departments, and the trade unions are taking advantage of the situation by demanding an increase of wages.

Had Sydney siphoned off the money from Manchester?

In other words, were mortgage funds mobile between home and foreign investment? Did they flow overseas when property was low at home? Estate duty returns indicate that mortgage loans granted by *individuals* constituted a distinctly immobile capital. This does not rule out the possibility or indeed the probability that the actual possessors, i.e. landowners and capitalists, were pulling out of realty and investing overseas. This is the evidence (Table 8.3). Mortgagees retained a constant (slightly increasing) share of the capital passing at death between 1898 and 1914, an average of 4.42 per cent. During the same period the share of realty fell by more than 20 per cent, largely, it appears, in response to the depression of urban property values. Investment in colonial and foreign government bonds increased by 24 per cent and as much or probably more was sent abroad by private companies, whose shares and debentures also increased their share of the capital passing at death by 24 per cent, mostly in the last three years before the war. The large shift into

Table 8.3. *Mortgages and other property as a percentage of capital passing at death, U.K. 1898–1914*

	[Per cent of capital at death, 1898–1914 (log trend)]				
Fraction	1898	Mean	1914	Annual growth	R^2
Mortgages	4.26%	4.42%	4.58%	0.45%	0.15
Realty	29.9%	26.5%	23.3%	−1.55%	0.64
Foreign government bonds	3.17%	3.54%	3.93%	1.35%	0.44
Shares and debentures of public companies	26.3%	29.4%	32.7%	1.38%	0.57
Consols	3.88%	2.93%	2.13%	−3.67%	0.84
Total	67.4%	66.8%	66.6%		

Source: IRAR, e.g. (1914), tables 26 and 30, pp. 28–9 and 35.

bonds and shares was largely accomplished at the expense of realty and to a lesser extent at the expense of Consols, which depreciated even more than tenure.

So existing mortgages were apparently not recalled, but new investors in mortgages were not forthcoming. Quite possibly they sought more secure and profitable outlets overseas. The *flow* of mortgages began to ebb after 1902 (see Fig. 4.2). The building societies, which offered investors better security, were not so badly affected. They received repayments of principal as well as interest, so that property rarely depreciated below the value of the outstanding balance. The *Liberator* building society collapse of 1892 was not repeated but the failure of the Birkbeck Bank and Building Society in 1911 was followed by a 10 per cent contraction in building society lending.[31]

Private lenders, however, were more exposed than institutions. About one-fifth of all mortgage liabilities recorded in the death-duty returns had been incurred by bankrupt or nearly insolvent borrowers, and the mortgage debts of insolvent estates rose by more than two-thirds between 1899 and 1908. Concurrently, the deterioration of tenurial collateral was echoed in the decline of another species of property, commercial goodwill. Goodwill was a locational asset, created by commercial or professional enterprise and rarely detachable from the site. From a high of £1.3 million in 1903 its share of the capital passing at death fell by more than 50 per cent to £669,000 in 1912, tracing the erosion of small capitalist security and that of the capitalists' creditors as well.[32] To conclude, the title deeds to more than one-third of U.K. tenure were held by private and institutional lenders, whose assets were literally bound up with those of their borrowers. The pre-war property slump jeopardised the security of outstanding loans and lenders, and strongly discouraged new lending.

[31] E. J. Cleary, *The building society movement* (1965), pp. 142ff., 156–8; Sanders, 'Building societies' (1915), 2–3.
[32] *IRAR* (1898–1914), e.g. (1914), tables 26 and 30, pp. 28–9, 35.

9

THE RAMPARTS OF PROPERTY

I

To conclude Part II, let us recall the dual nature of tenure in Britain at the beginning of the twentieth century. About thirty per cent of all realty was highly concentrated in the hands of a few thousand wealthy proprietors. But a substantial part of the late-Victorian middle classes was also committed to houses and land: a million or more middling and small landlords, shopkeepers, manufacturers, farmers and rentiers, their employees and dependants; solicitors, auctioneers, surveyors, land agents; parish and cathedral clergy, the dons of Oxbridge, the administrators and inmates of a hundred charities and clubs. About one-third of all middle-class property was sunk in tenure,[1] and a third of all tenure was mortgaged to a set of middle-class mortgagee rentiers. As we have shown, most forms of tenurial property, both direct and indirect, became severely depressed in the Edwardian period. The fluctuations of the property market and the turnings of government tenurial policy could affect the fortunes of a large and numerous social and political property-owning constituency.

The property-less made up a much larger constituency, and here lay the problem. 'Tenants', said George Head in his lecture of 1910, 'outnumber landlords by a hundred to one, and a very large number of them have votes; anything therefore which affects them is bound to find a voice in the ballot box to a very greater extent than anything which affects the landlords'.[2] How could a property-less electorate be reconciled to the unequal distribution of property? The cumulative lesson of a succession of social and political upheavals on the continent of Europe presented the Free Trade Radicals with a solution to this dilemma. Joseph Kay, one of the progenitors of Free Trade in Land, commended in 1850 (just as Karl Marx was to condemn one year later) the way in which 'throughout all the excitement of the revolutions of 1848, the peasant proprietors of France, Germany, Holland, and Switzerland, were almost

[1] See Table 7.7, col. 4, rows 1–6, p. 135.
[2] Head, 'The property market' (1910), 66.

148

universally found upon the side of order, and opposed to revolutionary excesses'.[3] But the dissemination of property as a social prophylactic among the republican operative population of ten millions which he foresaw in Lancashire and Yorkshire was no more than a Utopian remedy and Kay was content to rely mainly on education and religion 'to enlist as many as possible of our poorer classes on the side of order, and to increase as much as possible the conservative feelings of our people'.[4]

It was somewhat more realistic to hope that a dose of landed property would stiffen the petty bourgeoisie in its loyalty to the prevailing order.

In a country like our own [wrote Kay], where the accumulation of enormous masses of uneducated workmen is going on with such a rapidity, it is doubly important for us to consider, how we may render our small shopkeeper class as conservative as possible, in order thereby to create a counterpoise for the influence of the increasing multitudes of the labourers of our great cities. It is impossible to attain this end more surely or more quickly than by encouraging the subdivision of the land, and by teaching the small shopkeepers to feel, that they may become proprietors, if they will only save capital enough for the purchase of a farm. On this ground I repeat what I have said before, that if it were thought inexpedient to encourage the general subdivision of land, yet it would seem to be highly expedient to introduce, at least into the crowded manufacturing districts, some such system, in order thereby to create among the shopkeepers, and among those who would become owners of gardens or of farms, a strong conservative class, capable of counterbalancing the immensely powerful democratic class, which is now nursing in those districts, and which is increasing there every day in strength and numbers.[5]

Small peasant and artisan property in cottages and plots was widely diffused in Western Europe, where democracy appeared to have been effectively tamed. A plebiscitary universal franchise became the bulwark of authority, first in Napoleon III's France and later in Bismarck's

---

[3] J. Kay, *The social condition and education of the people in England and Europe* (1850), i, 273.
[4] *Ibid.* 286.
[5] *Ibid.* 298–9. And see Cobden's speech at the inaugural meeting of Metropolitan and National Freehold Land Association, 26 Nov. 1849, in R. Cobden, *Speeches on questions of public policy* ed. J. Bright and J. E. Thorold Rogers (1878), pp. 540–8.

Germany. The first series of Cobden Club essays, published in 1871, included an essay by the Belgian economist and agrarian writer Emile de Laveleye. The ordeal of the Paris Commune lent weight to his warning: 'The inevitable progress of ideas of equality must put property in peril in countries in which it is held by a small number of families'. He compared the Flemish peasant proprietor with the Irish tenant.

In the public-house peasant proprietors will boast of the high rents they get for their lands, just as they might boast of having sold their pigs or their potatoes very dear. Letting at as high a rate as possible comes thus to seem to him to be quite a matter of course, and he never dreams of finding fault with either the landowners as a class or with property in land. His mind is not likely to dwell on the notion of a caste of domineering landlords, of "bloodthirsty tyrants", fattening on the sweat of impoverished tenants, and doing no work themselves; for those who drive the hardest bargains are not the great landowners, but his own fellows. Thus the distribution of a number of small properties among the peasantry forms a kind of rampart and safeguard for the holders of large estates; and peasant property may, without exaggeration, be called the lightning conductor that averts from society dangers which might otherwise lead to violent catastrophes.

The concentration of land in large estates among a small number of families is a sort of provocation of levelling legislative measures. The position of England, so enviable in many respects, seems to me to be in this respect full of danger for the future.[6]

A 'rampart and safeguard for the holders of large estates'. This passage was approvingly quoted in 1881 by Arthur Arnold in *Free land* (p. 287). When the Conservatives adopted the principles of Free Trade in Land in the 1880s (Chapter 3, pp. 40–2), they also began to realise the power of Laveleye's formula. It underlay the policy of state-aided peasant-land purchase with which they managed to pacify rural Ireland starting in the late 1880s. In England as well the multitude of smaller proprietors began to assume a role in Conservative schemes, of Laveleye's 'ramparts' – a protective band of middling and small capitalists, professionals and rentiers huddled together for mutual support and forming a shield for large estates and capitals. These ideas of Tory democracy which were planted in the 1880s were the germ of a social process which is still working itself out.

[6]E. de Laveleye, 'The land system of Belgium and Holland', *Systems of land tenure in various countries*, ed. J. W. Probyn (1871; new edn 1881), pp. 444, 484.

II

Two kinds of issue dominated relations between landowners and capitalists. Both went far back into the past, and acquired new life in the 1880s. The first grew out of the traditional contentions and collusions of tenurial interests, and the cyclical swings and strains of tenurial incomes and values. Insecurity of tenure and the consequent risk to leaseholders' 'improvement' outlays animated the Farmers' Alliance and the leasehold enfranchisement movement, both of them directed by small capitalists against the landowners in the early 1880s, a period of agricultural and urban depression.[7] The second issue which divided proprietors and set them against each other was the cost and benefits of government. Both issues raised questions of distribution. In the first, of apportioning the benefits of tenure among different proprietors. In the second, of paying for what may be termed the 'overheads' of the tenurial system. As in all such contentions, the antagonists appealed to a number of different and sometimes incompatible principles of utility and justice. Most individuals and pressure groups knew their own interest well enough, but the range of positions did not always fit into the conventional demarcations of Victorian and Edwardian politics. Obfuscation and ignorance, unintended and wilful, must also be given their due. The claims of subordinate tenures, of working-class occupiers and construction workers, of agricultural labourers and Irish tenant farmers also began to be heard and the men of property had to take notice.

The immobility of urban groundowner tenure and its long-term commitment to particular sites rendered it vulnerable to currents of social and political change. It had been forged in the seventeenth and eighteenth centuries in a society dominated by landowners, and was implicitly based upon their social and political prestige. Great urban fiefs like the Bedford, Grosvenor and Portman estates tried to perpetuate the pattern of tenurial relations by imposing physical controls on the buildings and social controls on the tenants.[8] These controls created and conserved the architectural dignities and amenities of Bloomsbury, Belgravia and Mayfair, but at a price that many occupiers were beginning to regard as excessive. For capitalist leaseholders the old-

[7] Leasehold enfranchisement, see below. Farmers' Alliance, see F. J. Fisher, 'Public opinion and agriculture 1875–1900' (Hull Univ. Ph.D. thesis, 1972), pp. 157–209 and *idem*. 'The Farmers' Alliance: an agricultural protest movement of the 1880's', *Agricultural History Review* 26 (1978), 15–25.

[8] D. J. Olsen, *Town planning in London in the eighteenth and nineteenth centuries* (New Haven, 1964), pp. 99–125.

established landowner tenure fulfilled no self-evidently necessary social or economic function. With commercial goodwill accumulated on and tied to the landowner's site, the urban capitalist leaseholder considered himself to be faced with monopoly power. Urban landowner tenure was mainly secured by the continuity of old contracts. Ultimately it relied on the coercive power of the state; but in the last quarter of the nineteenth century the state was no longer so securely at the landowner's bidding. Although the value of leasehold buildings was discounted in the property markets in comparison with freehold, leasehold remained disagreeable to the capitalist mentality. Unlike freehold tenures, leaseholds were not waxing but wasting assets and as large numbers of long leases were due to fall in in the 1880s the prospect of renewal premiums and revised rents presented an outlook of gloom. The first shot of resistance was fired in 1879, in a periodical article which gave vent to middle-class resentment and placed the blame for a host of urban ills on leasehold tenure. Leasehold gave rise to slipshod construction, profiteering, an unhealthy preference for the fleeting over the permanent, in short, to a general weakening of social and moral fibre.[9]

Landowners needed to break their isolation and seek a closer relation with other species of proprietors. This strategy was initiated in 1882 by the Earl of Wemyss, a large landowner in Scotland and Gloucester, who brought landlords and capitalists of all shades into his anti-socialist organisation, the Liberty and Property Defence League, the organ of the new 'individualism'.[10] In March 1883 Joseph Chamberlain reinforced the long-standing Radical challenge to landed hierarchy with attacks on the class of landowners 'who toil not neither do they spin'. In June he advocated manhood suffrage, to include the agricultural labourers.[11] In October the Marquess of Salisbury responded with sombre reflections:

the members of the classes who are in any sense or degree holders of property are becoming uneasy at the prospect which lies before

[9][J. T. Emmet], 'The ethics of urban leaseholds', *British Quarterly Review* 69 (April, 1879), 301–33 (I owe this reference to R. E. Quinalt). Leaseholder grievances are given at length in the literature produced by the Leaseholds Enfranchisement Association.

[10]See N. Soldon, 'Laissez-faire as dogma: The Liberty and Property Defence League 1882–1914', in *Essays in anti-labour history* ed. K. D. Brown (1974), pp. 208–33 and E. Bristow, 'The Liberty and Property Defence League and Individualism', *Hist. Journal* 18 (1975), 761–81.

[11]J. L. Garvin, *The life of Joseph Chamberlain* (1935), i, 391–4.

them. The uneasiness is greatest among those whose property consists in land, because they have been the most attacked; but this feeling is not confined to them. No one will say that this anxiety is without foundation. Things that have been secure for centuries are secure no longer.[12]

It was not Free Trade in Land that he feared. If a real demand for small holdings existed he would meet it from the surplus land of corporations and charities. The great estates would not be broken up. Lord Salisbury professed to believe that the laws of political economy favoured large holdings even more after the onset of the agricultural depression and the shift from arable into grass.[13] But he was apprehensive about the social viability of hierarchy and wealth; in remarkable coincidence, by the way, with the private views of Gladstone, who wrote to his son in 1885:

An enemy to entails, principally though not exclusively on social and domestic grounds, I nevertheless regard it as a very high duty to labour for the conservation of estates, and the permanence of families in possession of them, as a principal source of our social strength, and as a large part of true conservatism.[14]

A direct challenge to the landowners of London and of other leasehold towns was mounted in 1884 by the Leaseholds Enfranchisement Association, an organised pressure group which advocated legislation to entitle leaseholders to purchase the freehold.[15] The shopkeepers, professional men and small capitalists who made up the movement were vexed by restrictions on the free disposal and use of their premises and resented the erosion of their capital as leases approached their termination. For the prosperous trader this meant a sharp increase in rents, a costly bill for 'dilapidations', a hefty premium, and a set of lawyers' and surveyors' fees. For example, on Sunday, 25 March 1888, 1786 ninety-nine-year leases on the Portman estate in Marylebone fell in. Rents were raised seven and eightfold, and substantial premiums were extracted. Renewals were only offered for much shorter periods. An unearned increment of some £1.25 millions was harvested in Baker Street and its precincts alone.[16]

---

[12]'Disintegration', *Quarterly Review* no. 312 (Oct. 1883), rep. in *Lord Salisbury on politics*, ed. P. Smith (Cambridge, 1972), pp. 343–4.
[13]Above, Chapter 3, p. 43 and Newport Speech, *The Times*, 8 Oct, 1885, 7d.
[14]Morley, *Gladstone* (1903), i, 348.
[15]See D. A. Reeder, 'The politics of urban leaseholds in late-Victorian England', *International Review of Social History* 6 (1961), 413–30.
[16]F. Banfield, *The great landlords of London* (1890), pp. 34–9.

In working-class districts the value of property dwindled to nothing in the last years of the lease. Unscrupulous entrepreneurs leased or bought these 'fag-ends' cheaply for quick profits; they allowed houses to run down and sometimes assigned them to 'men of straw' (workhouse inmates) in order to evade the obligation to repair.[17] Henry Broadhurst, the Liberal working-man MP, sponsored a series of enfranchisement bills. He held out the promise of better working-class housing, and the prospect of ownership for more than two million leaseholders.[18] Few workers were in a position to benefit directly, since the overwhelming majority occupied their dwellings on weekly or quarterly tenancies, not long leases. As for 'fag-end' leases, they undoubtedly accounted for much suffering in London slums, but overall they could only affect a very small minority of tenants, since less than a third were in leasehold property, of which only a small proportion could have been approaching the end of its term, even in London (and see Fig. 18.3, p. 293).

On the Tory side Randolph Churchill, like his opposite number Chamberlain, was prospecting for a new political constituency and courting displeasure of his party leader. He realised that leaseholders were potential ramparts of property, and introduced one of the first leasehold enfranchisement bills in March 1884, when he declared in Parliament that,

It has been calculated that if the principle of the Bill became law, upwards of 2,000,000 of freeholders would be created and enfranchised in a short time. The Prime Minister was even now asking Parliament to add 2,000,000 of votes to the electoral roll and he [Churchill] would ask hon. Gentlemen on the Conservative side of the House would it not be better that that number of electors should be freeholders, than that they should be men liable to be turned out of their houses and subject to every kind of injustice and extortions? Who was more likely to be a contented citizen, the man who was a freeholder and who was safe in his property, or the man who was at the mercy of a colossal landowner?[19]

The statistics were faulty, and the politics proved abortive. But it was a challenge to the party leader Lord Salisbury, himself one of London's wealthy landowners.

Early in December 1885 Churchill, who had become a member of

[17]See e.g. Housing of the working classes. R. com. rep.; P.P. 1884–5 C. 4402 XXXI, pp. 21–2, 85, and under 'leases' in the index.
[18]286 H.C. deb. 3 ser. 19 March 1884, 212–21.
[19]286 H.C. deb. 3 ser. 19 March 1884, 240.

Lord Salisbury's government, submitted a long memorandum on policy and tactics to his Prime Minister. As a central item of the domestic programme Churchill proposed to enfranchise *future* leaseholders (to avoid interference with existing contracts), copyholders and occupiers of mortmain lands; to introduce registration of title and to abolish primogeniture and entails.[20] Salisbury replied on 9 December. We have already quoted that part of his reply which contemplated the sacrifice of primogeniture and entails (p. 43). He explained:

the Moderate Liberals will require some such concession as a condition of their joining us and as a proof to their own friends that they have not been guilty of any *apostasy* in so doing. That being so, the extra tinge of Liberalism in our policy will be part of the bargain when it comes, and must not be given away before that time comes.[21]

As for enfranchisement, Salisbury could appreciate the force of the 'ramparts' strategy, but not when it directly threatened the urban ground tenure which was the heritage of his family and class. His own view was that the cost of the ramparts should not be borne by the property they were meant to protect. He put forward an important principle, that was to become the mainstay of Conservative policy, first in Ireland and later in England; namely, that if re-distribution of property was desirable for political reasons, then the landowner should get the fullest compensation and the state should bear part of the cost and assume the whole financial risk.

The proposition of Leasehold Enfranchisement in the future requires more thrashing out. I doubt whether it would effect your object, which is that more occupiers should be owners of the houses they inhabit. I quite agree in the object. I should be more disposed to follow the Irish precedent and give local authorities the power of advancing (on the security of the tenement) some large fraction of its value at low interest, limiting the advance to cases where the occupier was owner of the whole lease – and of course, confining it to voluntary purchase. This for existing leaseholds. For future buildings the most effective plan would be to allow exemption from the rates and house tax for five years in all cases where the occupier was also the owner.[22]

[20]Churchill, *Lord Randolph Churchill* (1907), p. 435.
[21]*Ibid.* p. 437.
[22]*Ibid.* p. 438.

Here, in the last sentence, is an anticipation of the policies which allowed income-tax relief on mortgage interest to become a state subsidy for owner-occupation after the First World War.[23]

As we have already seen, Salisbury was also quite willing to sacrifice the lawyers' mainstay, private conveyancing, and to introduce compulsory registration of title. Defending the Land Transfer Bill that he had introduced in the Lords, his Lord Chancellor Halsbury said that

If there is to be an attack on property it will be resisted with much greater force if it is possible to say that it includes all property, not merely property which has any peculiar privilege, because then it can be said that an attack on property is an attack on property of all kinds.[24]

This was one method of breaking out of the landowners' isolation, in agreement with the principles of the Liberty and Property Defence League: extending a hand to owners of other species of property by breaking down the legal singularities of tenure. The other method was the 'ramparts' strategy: to enlist numbers of small proprietors into the defences of property and create popular bulwarks for property, founded upon the democratic franchise. Lord Salisbury defined the policy in an apt phrase during the Land Transfer Bill debate: 'When you talk of the diffusion of property for maintaining the principle of property you mean *the diffusion of small quantities among large masses*. I entirely concur in that view'.[25]

His outstretched hand did not extend to leaseholders. Their agitation was gathering force. A Select Committee was appointed in 1886 to inquire into 'the terms of occupation, and the compensation for improvements, possessed by the occupiers of town leases and holdings'.[26] Morley, Gladstone and other dignitaries of the Liberal party subscribed to the goals of the movement in 1887 and 1888.[27] In attacking long-established contracts, Salisbury warned, the leasehold enfranchisers subverted the very foundations of economic activity. In 1889 he declared,

If you come in and break contracts which already exist, if you come and tell men practically by a great example that, make what agreements they will, they shall not be secure from some political agitation which may cut those agreements for a political object; if

[23]See A. A. Nevitt, *Housing, taxation and subsidies* (1966), ch. 5.
[24]313 H.L. deb. 3 ser. 31 March 1887, 31.
[25]*Ibid.* 25 April 1887, 1771. Italics added.
[26]Town holdings. Sel. com. rep.; P.P. 1886 (213) XII, p. iii.
[27]Leaseholds Enfranchisement Association, *Fifth annual report* (1888), pp. 5, 13–14.

they feel that there is no security in the law for the investment of their money for the building of houses they will not build houses but they will take their money elsewhere.

Contracts were the foundation of business confidence, he continued, and added, 'if I wanted a definition of Conservative policy, I should say that it is the policy of a party who preaches confidence. (Cheers.)'[28] Perhaps one may detect a wavering of confidence in the Prime Minister himself. One year previously, in 1888, he sold outright £200,000 worth of property in the Strand for a new commercial development, instead of creating new leases.[29]

Leasehold enfranchisement was avowedly a lower middle-class movement and at the end of the 1880s it found itself immobilised by cross-fire coming from both right and left.[30] The landowners of London put up a formidable opposition and the Town Holdings committee report of 1889 agreed with Salisbury's view that owner-occupation for artisans was a chimera which did not justify Parliamentary interference with existing contracts.[31] From the left, the Fabians invoked the danger of the 'ramparts' to argue that enfranchisement was a retrograde step, a reinforcement for property and an obstacle to land nationalisation. In 1891, when an enfranchisement bill finally reached a second reading, they persuaded leading Liberals to vote against it and were proudly instrumental in its defeat.[32]

Leaseholder resentment continued to simmer in London and the provinces but the agitation was exhausted for the time being. It flared up once again shortly before the Great War, in another period of tenurial depression.[33] It may be mere coincidence, but the enfranchisers largely fell silent when property values began to rise again in the 1890s. Although it raised a considerable stir in the 1880s, leasehold enfranchisement, like the analogous movements for allotments and small holdings, could only tap a limited reservoir of discontent. Only a fraction of all tenure was affected, and a smaller fraction of proprietors in a limited number of localities, namely capitalists and landowners with expiring leases. The strength of popular demand may also be questioned. In 1893

---

[28]Speech at Nottingham, 26 Nov. 1889, *The Times*, 27 Nov. 1889, 6d.
[29]*The Times*, 7 May 1888, 8f.
[30]Leaseholds Enf. Assoc. *Seventh ann. rep.* (1890), Howard Evans, pp. 13–17.
[31]Town holdings. Sel. com. rep.; P.P. 1889 (251) XV, pp. 39–40.
[32]See S. Webb, *The truth about leasehold enfranchisement* (Fabian tract no. 22, 1890) and A. M. McBriar, *Fabian socialism and English politics 1884–1918* (Cambridge, 1962), pp. 27, 187, 239, 242.
[33]See below, p. 390.

the ecclesiastical commissioners offered 999-year leases to their short leaseholders and did not find many takers.[34] It was a restricted but not unworthy movement, whose modesty of aims militated against success. 'It is the old story of the chartists who opposed Free Trade, lest it should make the condition of the people so tolerable, that they would cease to agitate for the charter', complained Howard Evans, a veteran Radical and one of the movement's main spokesmen, of the Fabian opposition.[35] Like many Victorian agitations it was motivated by a legitimate grievance and its goals were partially realised in the 1960s.[36] Even in its heyday it was overshadowed by a question which offered much greater scope for the 'ramparts' strategy; which affected proprietors all over the country, on the land and in the cities, and involved vast numbers of house-tenants as well: the increasing burden of local rates and its impact on relations between different classes of tenure and between them and the state.

[34]*EG*, 25 Feb. 1893, 177; Thompson, *Hampstead* (1974), p. 368, n. 1.
[35]Leaseholds Enf. Assoc. *7th Ann. rep.* (1890), p. 14.
[36]By the Leasehold Reform Act, 1967.

Part III

TENURE AND TAXATION 1850–1900

10

BANNERS OR SPOILS?
THE DOCTRINES OF TAXATION

The Land Tax, wrote J. S. Mill, 'ought not to be regarded as a tax, but as a rent-charge in favour of the public'.[1] Seen in this aspect 'the public', or rather the organs of local and national government, were a very substantial rentier: a 'sleeping partner' (as Marshall called them)[2] of other tenures, comparable in magnitude with agricultural landownership. Government appropriated some 23 per cent of the annual rental in rates and taxes at the end of the Edwardian period, say £80 million out of £350 million.[3] In addition to this income of £80 million, government owned valuable chunks of property outright in the form of land, schools, baths, libraries, town halls, sewers, gasworks, waterworks and tramways. The annual loan charges on the local government debt is a crude proxy for the annual value of this property. They came to some £30 million in 1910.[4] When added on top of central government taxes and local rates, the total value of government tenure, direct and indirect, capital and annual, came to between a quarter and a third of the annual rental in England and Wales.

A great tenurial interest had established itself by the Edwardian period. Like the original ground-owning aristocracy, government levied its tribute primarily by political edict, and not through the market. Landlord–tenant relations dominated the politics of tenure in the peasant country of Ireland, in the farming districts of Wales and in the Highlands of Scotland. Taxation overshadowed tenure as a political

[1] J. S. Mill, *Principles of political economy*, ed. W. J. Ashley (1909), p. 820.
[2] A. Marshall, *Principles of economics* (8th edn 1920), p. 637.
[3] *Local and central taxation of tenure in England and Wales, fiscal year beginning in 1910* – £79.2M. Made up as follows: (a) *local taxation*, £65.2M; (b) *central taxation*: income tax sch. A (85% of U.K. total), £7.9M; estate duties, £2.4M; inhabited house duty, £1.7M; stamp duties, £1.4M; land tax, £0.6M.
  Total gross rental – £346.6M. Made up as follows: sch. A gross rental – £233.1M; property rated but not assessed to sch. A (20% of Sch. A) – £46.6M; local rates and inhabited house duty – £66.9M. Sources: *IRAR* (1911, 1912); Mitchell and Deane, *Abstract*, p. 415; Offer, 'Ricardo's paradox' (1980), table 2 and app. I, cols. (3) and (4). Note that the rental base here is wider than the one used in 'Ricardo's paradox', p. 248, n. 5.
[4] £31.1M in the fiscal year starting 1910. (Mitchell and Deane, *Abstract*, p. 417).

issue in Victorian and Edwardian England. Local Taxation 'occupied more of the attention of the Chambers of Agriculture than all other questions put together,' wrote their Secretary in 1915.[5] The historians' neglect of the question belies its importance as a medium of property relations in national and local politics. The Victorians knew better. Memorable words of a past master of the subject, the third Marquess of Salisbury, recall that finance was the substance of politics.

The chief object of Government, in England at least, is the protection of property ... the main business of Parliament is to make laws to define and to secure in some form or other the distribution of property ... Finance, which has been the main battle-field of so many conflicts, is a contest between various classes waged for the purposes of resisting the imposition of what each considers an unfair proportion of that contribution from property by which the service of the State is carried on ... As property is in the main the chief subject-matter of legislation, so it is almost the only motive power of agitation.[6]

The incidence of local taxation was one of the great and constant preoccupations of Victorian and Edwardian politics. Emerging in the 1840s (with much earlier antecedents) the issue persisted unchanged in its essentials for more than fifty years. As originally formulated, it helped to demarcate between the nascent creeds of political Conservatism and Liberalism. In time, attitudes on both sides hardened into dogmas and doctrinal slogans became cues of political alignment through the rest of the century. Indeed, these dogmas became truly essential elements of respective party identities. Like every great political issue, contention over the incidence of local taxation reflected fundamental differences, deeply rooted in the social, economic and mental realities of Victorian England.

Incidence can be confusing because more than one question was involved. First, there was the division of obligations between local and central (or in contemporary usage, 'imperial') government. Second, the comparative burden of taxation in the country and the city. Third, the distribution of the burden of *local* taxation between the tenures, or more simply, between occupiers on the one side, and owners on the other. Fourth, the inequality of incidence between poor and affluent local taxation districts. The formal liability for the poor rate and other local taxes fell on the occupiers of land and houses in the parish. Some drainage and paving rates were levied from

[5] A. H. H. Matthews, *Fifty years of agricultural politics* (1915), p. 53.
[6] 'The House of Commons', *Quarterly Review* no. 231 (1864), rep. in *Lord Salisbury on politics*, ed. P. Smith (1972), pp. 182–3.

owners, and commercial stock-in-trade had been liable in a few districts, but both practices had largely fallen into disuse by 1840.[7] A large proportion of the rates on working-class houses let weekly were paid quarterly by the landlords, a practice known as compounding.[8] Otherwise, landlords (and particularly, urban groundowners under the leasehold system) were not *formally* liable to the rates. *Effective incidence* was something different. Did rates stick to the point of collection, or could they be shifted down the ladder of tenures? This was but one bone of contention between Conservatives and Liberals. Each party held fairly coherent (if not always internally consistent) views on incidence and these are set out in the following three paragraphs. For the sake of clarity they are reduced to 'ideal types', stripped of the accumulated verbiage and variation of sixty years. They reflect the state of the question in its late-Victorian maturity, and may be compared, for example, with the House of Commons debate on 23 March 1886, one out of many Parliamentary set-piece debates on the subject.[9]

Two slogans contained the essence of the Conservative position: 'The special burdens of land' was the grievance; 'equalisation of taxation' the remedy. Owing to the restricted incidence of local taxation, tenure (both land and houses; the fundamental unity of the two categories was a central tenet of Conservative doctrine) was paying more than its fair share of taxation. In the Conservative scheme, taxes fell under three heads. (a) Customs and excise, taxes on consumption falling on the population at large (except for the malt tax which fell on the landed interest). (b) Direct national taxes on property and income (income tax, probate duties, house duty, land tax, etc.). (c) Local taxation, a direct tax falling on realty alone. Tenure paid its share of national taxation, but had to bear an *additional* burden of local taxation as well. In 1868–9, for example, ordinary incomes paid five pence in the pound income tax, or 2.1 per cent. Tenurial incomes paid another 12.1 per cent in local taxation, almost seven times as much as owners of personalty![10]

Despite the formal immunity of ground property from local taxation, Conservatives argued that it was effectively liable. Ricardian economics

[7] E. Cannan, *The history of local rates in England* (2nd edn 1912), chs. IV and V.
[8] See W. C. Ryde, *The law and practice of rating* (3d edn 1912), pp. 81–3.
[9] 303 H.C. deb. 3 ser. 23 March 1886, 1643ff. For other proximate debates, see chapter 11, pp. 181–2.
[10] £16.2 million local taxation on realty in 1868–9 (see Table 10.1) divided by gross schedule-A rental plus local taxation (£134.4 million). For the Conservative view, see R. D. Baxter, *Local government and taxation and Mr Goschen's report* (1874). Baxter calculated the rate of taxation at 12 per cent on real property, 5 per cent on personal property and 3 per cent on personal incomes (*ibid.* p. 22).

deduced that a tax on land fell ultimately on the landowner's rent. Proof being, argued Conservatives, that if rates came down, rents would go up. 'Local' or 'beneficial' taxation for paving the streets, laying sewers and similar expenditure was admissible; it increased the value of land and was therefore a legitimate charge on tenure. Not so the poor rates and the costs of prisons, asylums, hospitals, trunk roads and schools. These were 'national' obligations and therefore 'onerous' when limited in their incidence to tenure alone. Conservatives proposed to shift the burden two ways. First, they would make 'personal' property liable to local taxation; i.e. merchants' stock-in-trade and the capital of industrialists, professionals, bankers and shipowners. But this was not in earnest. What they insisted on was a transfer of 'national' services to the central Exchequer by means of grants-in-aid from Whitehall to local government.

Liberals denied the unity of land and houses. Local taxation, they showed, fell increasingly on urban houses, not on rural land, and was therefore paid by urban capitalists and occupiers. The working class, not the landowners, bore the fiscal brunt, as indirect taxation on con-

Table 10.1. *Incidence of local and central taxation in England and Wales, 1851 and 1869*

Part I Tax category	[*1851*]		[*1869*]	
1. Local tax on *Realty*	£9.9M		£16.2M	
National tax on *Realty*	£5.7M		£7.1M	
Total	£15.7M	27.5%	£23.3M	33.2%
2. National and local tax on *Personalty*	£10.8M	19.0%	£15.8M	22.5%
3. Customs, excise and post office profits	£30.4M	53.4%	£31.0M	44.2%
Total taxation	£56.9M	100.0%	£70.1M	100.0%
Part II				
Real property: Income tax assessment (Schedules A and B) 1. In £M	£115.1		£174.5	
2. As % of total income tax assessment	52.6%		42.9%	

Sources: Part I. Local taxation. Rep. of G. J. Goschen; P.P. 1870 (470) LV, Appendix, Pt. III, tables VI and X, pp. 121, 126–7. *Part II.* Mitchell and Deane, *Abstract*, p. 430.

sumption. Except for duties on beer, which was a proper object for taxation, they proposed to reduce both customs duties and the excise. Liberals denied that rates were shifted on to the owners. Taxation stuck at the point of collection and was effectively paid by the occupiers. Urban landowners' rent-rolls swelled owing to the public spending of rates they did not pay. Alternatively, Liberals were willing to admit that some taxation was shifted to the groundowners but claimed this was no cause for complaint. The so-called special burdens of land were 'traditional' or 'hereditary' obligations that landowners had assumed together with the titles to their property. And if a share of the rates fell on the landowner's rent this was only just and proper, since rent was a pure surplus which did not contribute to production, and was fair game for taxation. Liberals sometimes argued that landowners had wriggled out of their traditional fiscal obligations. In particular they mentioned the land tax, which had been four shillings in the pound on the true rental in the eighteenth century. But demands to revive this tax were made in the same half-hearted spirit as Conservative demands for rating stock-in-trade. Government grants-in-aid were rejected by Liberals as disguised 'doles'; invitations to local extravagance and maladministration. For the next instalment of taxation, Liberals looked to the separate rating of ground property, preferably on its capital value.[11]

The two opposing doctrines reflected the classic cleavage of English capital; indeed, they underscore its historical reality. Of the two, Conservative doctrine grew out of the grievances of agriculturists and the Liberal programme stood for the interests of industrial, mercantile and finance capital. Between the landed interest on one side and the mill-owners and merchants on the other lay another fraction of capital: urban house-capital, made up of a mass of property owners who assumed most of the rate burden and lacked a definite political attachment. Their interest was commensurate both with the Conservative complaint about finance-and-mercantile capital's immunity from the poor rates, and with the Liberal outrage at the landowners' evasion of the municipal burden.

What were the respective doctrines designed for? Was fiscal reform an end in itself, a straight expression of economic interest? Or was it mainly a ruse for helping its advocates into power, the true end of politics? In other words, did the doctrines mainly serve as political banners or did they constitute claims for spoils? Conservative and

---

[11] R. Giffen, 'Taxes on land' (1871) in *Essays in finance* (1880), pp. 234–58 was a sophisticated Liberal statement; S. Webb, *A plea for the taxation of land values* (1887) was a concise Radical statement.

Liberal fiscal doctrines were often described by their adherents as 'non-political' (a common form of Victorian special pleading) which suggests that their value as banners, carrying a political appeal across the parties, came before any immediate economic interest. Is this the reason why spoils often failed to materialise when power was captured?

Both parties clung to well-defined policies for five or six decades. The dogmas of local taxation, whether as banners or as claims, both in and out of power, remained important elements of political identity and their changing usages and meanings marked the progress of political self-definition. For the Parliamentary origins of the issue, which form the subject of the next chapter, it is again necessary to revert to the first half of the nineteenth century.

11

THE COUNTRY VERSUS THE CITY IN PARLIAMENT, 1850–1885

I

Conservative rating doctrine crystallised as a reaction to the repeal of the Corn Laws. In 1836 'the agricultural interests' succeeded in getting the first grants in aid of local taxation.[1] In 1845 they clamoured again for budget surpluses to be applied to the same purpose.[2] Agriculturists regarded protection as an indemnity for their 'special burden' of local taxation, and the claim was backed by the authority of Ricardo.[3] On 27 January 1846 Sir Robert Peel conceded that the end of protection gave the agriculturists a claim for compensation (he spoke of 'recognition'). He promised a reform of the Law of Settlement to prevent indigent labourers from being returned to their rural parishes and offered to transfer criminal prosecutions, and the salaries of some poor law officers, from the ratepayer to the Treasury.[4]

On 1 February 1849 the Corn Laws finally expired. Five weeks later Benjamin Disraeli rose in the Commons to propose a motion on Local Burdens. He alluded to 'severe and terrible' distress amongst the agricultural class, whose misery was compounded by £12 million of taxes a year that no other form of property had to bear. Deprived of protection, agriculture deserved relief from its special obligation. Support for the poor, he said, was 'either a matter of police or a social duty'.[5] Either way, it was properly an obligation of 'personal' as well as 'real' property. He proposed to shift half the sum, £6 million, to the Consolidated Fund. Although he spoke for the landed interest, Disraeli shrewdly perceived

---

[1] Sir E. Hamilton, 'Memorandum on imperial relief of local burdens and on the system of imperial and local taxation', Local taxation. R. com. memoranda; P.P. 1899 C.9528 XXXVI, pp. 11–12.
[2] 78 H.C. deb. 3 ser. 17 March 1845, W. Miles, 963ff. Also Burdens affecting real property. H.L. sel. com. rep.; P.P. 1846 (411) VI, Pt. I, pp. xiii–xiv.
[3] See W. Smart, *Economic annals of the nineteenth century 1821–1830* (1917), pp. 5–6.
[4] 83 H.C. deb. 3 ser. 27 Jan. 1846, 272, 264–76.
[5] 103 H.C. deb. 3 ser. 8 March 1849, 424, 426–7, 432 (£10 million in local taxation and £2 million land tax).

that the urban ratepayer could also be attracted, with consequent damage to the Radical constituency, whose strength, Cobden wrote to a friend the same year, lay with the 'shopocracy'.[6] Disraeli had discovered a slogan with which to separate the shopkeeper and house-capitalist from the mill-owner and merchant, thus isolating the urban patriciate within its own bastions.

I quite sympathise with the owners of real property in towns as to their grievances and heavy assessments. The measure, however, which it is my intention to propose, ... will relieve the suffering towns from this burden. It will put an end to those complaints of which we have heard so much from Manchester, Bradford and other great seats of manufacturing industry. I sympathise with their sufferings, I acknowledge their grievance; and I say it is a vital question to the owners of real property in towns, whether only one-fourth of the property of the country should have the whole burden of local taxation thrown upon it.[7]

His motion, however, was lost by a majority of 119.

Disraeli toured the Southern Counties in the autumn of 1849, speaking to meetings of farmers and landowners, trying to wean them from protection and to win them for a miscellaneous set of alternative policies. Of these, rate relief proved the most alluring, and other proposals were dropped.[8] Come the new session, Disraeli introduced a motion for the relief of local taxation and concluded a two-night full-dress debate on 21 February 1850 with a dazzling speech charged with sarcastic invective against urban capitalism, political economy and free trade. Even Gladstone acknowledged the ratepayers' grievance and marched into his rival's lobby; and the government majority dropped to twenty-one.[9] The slogan had demonstrated its power to sway loyalties in Parliament.

[6] J. Morley, *The life of Richard Cobden* (1881), ii, 61, letter dated 13 Dec. 1849.
[7] 103 H.C. deb. 428–9.
[8] W. F. Moneypenny and G. E. Buckle, *The life of Benjamin Disraeli Earl of Beaconsfield* (1914), iii, ch. VII, esp. p. 230. Other proposals were to equalise the land tax in favour of the more heavily taxed districts and to create a new sinking fund which, by improving government credit, would also reduce commercial interest rates and make credit easier for agriculture. He also had to reckon with a resurgence of protectionist agitation which received the tacit support of the party leader Lord Derby (*ibid.* p. 214).
[9] 108 H.C. deb. 3 ser. 21 Feb. 1850, Gladstone, 1204–12; Disraeli, 1264–72. Disraeli's proposal of 1850 was less extravagant and only asked for the transfer of Poor Law establishment charges (some £1.5 million) to the Exchequer (108 H.C. deb. 3 ser. 21 Feb., 1040).

So novel was Disraeli's challenge that the Radicals were at a loss for an effective response. Cobden was taken off his guard: the experienced war-horse was confused by Disraeli's unaccustomed fanfare. 'The hon. gentleman', he complained, 'has talked of every subject except protection to native industry. Well, here I am, ... anxious to argue with him [about protection]'.[10] Radicals and Peelites denied that there could be any community of interest between farmers and landowners, let alone the country and the city. Relief, they said, would redound to the landowners at the expense of working men. Grants-in-aid would be wastefully spent, and prolong the life of the income tax. John Bright understood the purpose of the motion better than others, and did not deny that there was an interest common to rural and urban landowners.

> The great point has been to get up a cry – and that has been your great difficulty during the recess – a cry by which you could unite landlord and tenant in one general assault upon the country and resources of the Chancellor of the Exchequer... It is not then, a question between land and the towns, but it is a question between the owners of property, who have something, and the great masses, 'the have-nothings', as they are called...[11]

But except for greater economy, Liberals had no positive proposals of their own to offer.

Conservative rating doctrine was a product of Disraeli's political genius. It helped to forge the modern Conservative party and to consolidate Disraeli's leadership. Looking back, he wrote in 1860,

> I found the Tory party in the House of Commons, when I acceded to its chief management, in a state of great depression and disorganisation... By a series of motions to relieve the Agricultural Interest by revising and partially removing the local taxation of the country, I withdrew the Tory party gradually from the hopeless question of Protection, rallied all those members who were connected either personally or by their constituencies with the land, and finally brought the state of the parties in the House of Commons nearly to a tie.[12]

Disraeli had raised the banner, but allowed it to fall from his hands when the first turn in power came. His budget of 1852 failed to honour his

[10]108 H.C. deb. 3 ser. 19 Feb. 1850, 247.
[11]108 H.C. deb. 3 ser. 21 Feb. 1850. The Home Secretary (Sir George Grey), 1052, 1059, 1061; T. Hobhouse, 1092–3; Sir James Graham, 1193–4; J. Bright, 1102–3.
[12]Moneypenny and Buckle, *Disraeli*, iii, 196.

promises to the farmers or the towns. The malt tax was repealed, but local taxation was left unchanged. The exemption limit on inhabited house duty was lowered, creating an additional rate on houses. Resistance to the house duty in the towns helped to bring about the rejection of the budget,[13] and the defeat of the government, and demonstrated the political potency of the question.

The defeat of Lord Derby's government in 1852 also laid the issue to rest for the time being, and local taxation did not seriously impinge upon national politics again until the later 1860s. But rate revenues began to rise very steeply in the mid-1850s, after some two decades of relative stability in absolute terms (and decline in relative terms). The increase (some two-thirds between 1851 and 1869) was not out of line with economic growth during this period, but it was nevertheless perceived as a growing burden. Revenues were increased by two mechanisms: first, by improvement rates to finance urban capital, mainly sewers and roads; and second, by a tighter system of poor law assessment and rating. The Parochial Assessments Act of 1862 provided for more realistic valuations which brought assessed values much closer to the real ones and produced a one-off increase of revenue from the same rates in the pound. In 1865 a prolonged agitation for a more equitable distribution of poor law burdens culminated in the Union Chargeability Act. This act extended the unit of rating from the parish to the Poor Law Union. It destroyed the fiscal advantages of forcibly depopulated 'close' parishes in the countryside and the relative immunities of many affluent town parishes. In other words, it undermined some of the fiscal privileges of tenurial wealth in both town and countryside. Poor rates rose very sharply after these reforms. Needless to say, both acts were strongly resisted by the landed interest in Parliament. They form a prelude to the re-emergence of local taxation on the national stage.[14]

II

It took the Liberals more than a decade to move beyond mere opposition to agricultural subsidies and evolve a positive rating doctrine of their own. Like its Conservative counterpart, this was not a product of

[13]*Ibid.* chs. XI–XII, esp. p. 436.
[14]See M. Caplan, 'The new poor law and the struggle for union chargeability', *International Review of Social History* 23 (1978), esp. 285–300; Baxter, *Local government* (1874), *passim.*; and table 10. 1, p. 164.

detached meditation but a straight expression of a particular social and economic conjuncture. Liberal rating doctrine emerged from the growing pains of the metropolis and the doctrine was to bear the imprint of London for three decades. Unlike Paris, London did not have a Baron Haussmann; on a more modest scale the Metropolitan Board of Works (hereafter M.B.W.) began in 1856 to carry out a series of capital projects that culminated, in the mid-1860s, in the Thames Embankment and the Main Drainage schemes. Heavy compensation for landowners was added to the considerable costs of construction. Finance placed the main constraint on this badly-needed enterprise.[15] An improvement rate on the whole metropolis paid for the state-guaranteed loans that provided the bulk of the funds, and the balance was found from special London duties on coal and wine.

By the mid-1860s both these resources were running short. Coal duties were a tax on the poor and their continued existence was a reproach to Free Trade. The M.B.W. improvement rate was also regressive in its incidence. It came on top of the poor and other local rates, which had reached high levels in the poorer districts. London's balkanisation into a large number of corporations and vestries perpetuated a pattern of gross inequality: assessments were lenient in the wealthy districts and rigorous in the poor. Nominal rates in the pound on these non-comparable valuations varied between 2s. 1d. in St George's, Hanover Square, a wealthy West End parish, and 6s. 9d. in St George the Martyr, Southwark, on the South side of the Thames.[16] Sitting on top of the national rent heap, London, and the City of London in particular, possessed large accumulations of unrated ground property. For the leaseholder, even in the City with its low valuation, rates 'approach a confiscation of property [and] check and impede the progress of improvement in the construction of dwellings for the middle and working classes'.[17]

Liberal rating doctrine was essentially a reaction to the predominance of the leasehold system in London. Two principles ran through it. (a) The need to extend local taxation to ground property, and (b) to equalise the rate burden between the London parishes. Both principles, but parti-

---

[15] See the reports of the two Select Committees on local taxation and government in the metropolis; (a) P.P. 1861 VIII, and (b) P.P. 1866 XII, and 1867 (135) XII.

[16] Metropolitan local government. Sel. com. 1st rep. and mins. of ev.; P.P. 1866 (186) XIII, p. xi.

[17] Metropolitan local government. Sel. com. 1st rep.; P.P. 1866 (186) XIII, W. E. Hickson (ratepayer and house-owner). q. 6720.

cularly the latter, depended on a concomitant principle (c), the reform of London government.

A movement to equalise metropolitan poor rates began in 1855 and a bill was introduced by A. C. Ayrton in 1858.[18] The rating of ground property, which was to hold such enduring fascination for the Liberal party, made its Parliamentary entrance on the 27 February 1866. A. C. Ayrton, MP for Tower Hamlets, a tactless and tireless municipal reformer (and later Commissioner of Works in Gladstone's government) moved the appointment of a Select Committee to consider the finance of London's capital projects. Harvey Lewis (Liberal, Marylebone) seconded; 'those who had the strongest interest in metropolitan improvements', he said, 'were in reality those most free from taxation. In point of fact the taxation fell principally upon the occupiers of the metropolis, while the freeholders, who derived immense revenues from their property, scarcely paid anything'.[19] Sir John Thwaite, Chairman of the M.B.W., later gave evidence before the Committee, where he claimed that the landowners' immunity from rates was a recent evasion of a long-standing legal obligation.

> Our rate is, in point of fact, a sewers' rate ... That, in itself, is a landlords tax, but it has been the practice, for many years, for the landlords to dislodge that liability by covenanting with their tenants that the tenants shall pay the sewers' rate, and thus casting the charge upon the occupiers.[20]

Eighteenth-century private legislation bears him out.[21]

The Select Committee reported firmly in favour of an equalisation of rates between districts, and the rating of landowners. Such were the beginnings of the great cause. Ayrton introduced a private bill for the rating of owners in 1867, in the face of strong resistance from the City of London corporation. But the City soon saw the light and introduced a bill of its own, imposing a sixpenny rate on owners. This was rejected by the Select Committee in its next report, in favour of Ayrton's M.B.W. bill which was not, however, enacted. Next to raise the Liberal rating banner was the MP for the City, George Joachim Goschen (1831–1907) who had previously, as a banker, intervened personally to support the M.B.W.'s credit.[22] Goschen's speech on 21 February 1868 marked the extension of

[18]Caplan, 'Union chargeability' (1978), 282–4.
[19]181 H.C. deb. 3 ser. 27 Feb. 1866, 1213.
[20]Metropolitan local government and taxation. Sel. com. 1st rep.; P.P. 1866 (186) XIII, q. 309.
[21]See Cannan, *Hist. rates* (1912), pp. 112–14.
[22]190 H.C. deb. 3 ser. 21 Feb. 1868, Ayrton, 1034.

Liberal front-bench support for the policies introduced two years previously by Ayrton and Lewis. The speech took its text almost entirely from the Committee report. 'What,' asked Goschen, 'would be the view taken in Bethnal Green as to the Thames Embankment?' In reply to this rhetorical question, he said,

it was not fair, when an improvement was to be made, which might be thought most important by the wealthy, that it should be carried out at the expense of the whole metropolis while at the same time the burdens at the East End were to be borne partially and locally.

Equalisation of burden between the districts and the rating of land-owners held the solution.[23]

'Would the State increase its contributions for municipal purposes?' Not a chance, said Goschen. In central London ground property was surrounded by the mercantile and financial wealth of an empire. It was unreasonable to single out groundowners alone for additional taxation, and understandable that Goschen would consider how to bring other capital into the net. A local income tax was rejected for the reason usually given against such schemes, that 'personal' property was difficult to localise. Instead, he proposed to surrender the House Duty to the municipalities and compensate the Treasury with an additional penny on the Income Tax.[24] Despite an external similarity, this was no concession to the Disraelian principle of Exchequer grants in relief of the rates, which some City Conservatives were demanding.[25] Quite the contrary: about half the house duty was collected in the metropolis and the rest came from a few large towns. No subsidy would reach the agricultural districts or the country towns.[26] And Goschen's other proposal (to surrender to London the tax on hackney carriages) would benefit the metropolis alone.

III

Another lobby was formed in 1866 whose impression on the local taxation issue was to be even more lasting than that of London Liberals.

[23] *Ibid.* 1021.
[24] *Ibid.* 1025, 1027.
[25] Metrop. loc. govt. Sel. com. 1st rep.; P.P. 1866 (186) XIII, W. E. Hickson, q. 6720.
[26] Matthews, *Fifty years of agricultural politics* (1915), p. 88. Inhabited house duty was only paid by some 15 per cent of the houses, shops and farmhouses in England and Wales. The rest were below the exemption limit of £20 gross value a year. See Mitchell and Deane, *Abstract*, pp. 236 and 239.

This was the Central Chamber of Agriculture (hereafter C.C.A.). Dominated by large farmers and landowners, it became the acknowledged spokesman for the agrarian interest in England soon after its foundation. In 1868 the C.C.A. began to deploy an effective and well-drilled pressure-group in the House of Commons and embarked on a policy of consistent opposition to any bill that imposed additional burdens on the rates. Its positive principles were inherited from Disraeli's parliamentary agitations: first, to make 'personal' property liable to local burdens, and second, to secure government grants in aid of 'national' services. In 1869 the C.C.A. formed a semi-independent organ, the Local Taxation Committee (L.T.C.).[27] From then on, not a year passed without some obstructive Parliamentary activity on behalf of the Committee, and some sessions were very busy indeed. Practically every interventionist bill brought grist to the Committee's mill and its history parallels the course of social legislation in Britain.[28] Its leaders participated in urban politics as well. Albert Pell (1820–1908), first chairman of the C.C.A., was a Conservative MP for South Leicestershire, a large farmer and also a property owner and Poor Law Guardian in St George in the East, Stepney; as chairman of the annual Central Poor Law Conferences between 1877 and 1898 he persistently advocated the reduction of outdoor relief.[29] Two other persons closely associated with the L.T.C. were Michael Hicks Beach (1837–1916), a Gloucestershire landowner who rose to senior Cabinet rank in Lord Salisbury's governments, and Massey Lopes.

Lopes (1818–1908) was a Devon landowner, a keen agriculturist and a powerful Parliamentary speaker. On 12 May 1868 he delivered a speech that was as significant, in its own way, as Ayrton and Lewis's London site-rating speech had been two years before. Poor rates, not capital improvements were the object of his concern. Until exempted by an Act in 1840, he reminded the House, stock-in-trade had been liable to the rates. Six out of every seven pounds of income in the kingdom escaped local taxation, he asserted, and followed with a quasi-Marxian attack on urban capital.

From labour – from labour of poor men – people make wealth. All capital was acquired by labour; why, then, should not wealth thus created contribute to the exigencies of the state and the relief of the

[27]Matthews, *Fifty years* (1915), pp. 77–83, 124; *EG* 31 Dec. 1898, 1133.
[28]Matthews, *Fifty years*, pp. 81–124 is a chronicle of the L.T.C.
[29]E. Clarke, 'Albert Pell', *D.N.B.*

poor, to the comfort of the afflicted and the maintenance of the aged, many of whom had worn themselves out, and spent the best part of their lives in acquiring for others wealth and affluence? ... they were, in fact, robbing one pauper to pay another.[30]

For the next four years every session was marked by one or more long debate initiated and dominated by Lopes. His message fell on willing urban and Liberal ears. Boards of Guardians in Liverpool, Birmingham and Leeds asked to be relieved of the exclusive cost of treating sickness, lunacy and imbecility, and urban Ratepayers' Associations formed a connection with the C.C.A. Local Taxation Committee.[31]

IV

One of the persistent features of Victorian urbanisation was the increasing reluctance of many manufacturing and commercial magnates to reside in the toiling and poverty-stricken urban neighbourhoods where their fortunes were made. Removal to the suburbs and beyond released them from irksome social and municipal obligations and also from the localised tax burdens of poor law expenditure. William Rathbone (1819–1902), Liverpool merchant and shipowner, a philanthropist, a city councillor and 'a decided Liberal' (*Dod's*), sounded the authentic voice of embattled Guardians in the towns.[32] On 22 June 1869 he moved a resolution to provide State grants to Poor Law authorities, which demonstrated the attractions of the Conservative rating banner. His speech began with an explicit acknowledgement of Massey Lopes' contention that 'a large portion of the wealth of this country escaped altogether from contributing to local taxation', which 'pressed with far more cruel injustice upon the small householders of large towns' and was largely evaded by commercial, manufacturing and trading interests.

... as their wealth increased, and large towns were extended, those

[30] 192 H.C. deb. 3 ser. 12 May 1868, 139–40. His speech was followed by John Stuart Mill's only sustained Parliamentary contribution to the subject (although Mill was a member of the metropolitan government select committee). Mill thanked Lopes for an able speech, gave a fair-minded account of both sides of the question, conceded the need for rate support, and came down in favour of Goschen's plan (*Ibid.* 152–4).

[31] 197 H.C. deb. 3 ser. 22 June 1869, W. Rathbone (see note[32]), 437; Matthews, *Fifty years* (1915), pp. 73–4. The bodies in question were a Metropolitan Poor Rate League, and Ratepayers' Associations from Leicester and Norwich.

[32] See E. Rathbone, *William Rathbone, a memoir* (1905) and P. J. Waller's forthcoming book on Liverpool politics (read in typescript).

classes escaped more and more from the contributions. They did not pay on their capital, because that capital, consisting mainly of personalty, was not subject to local taxation. Nor did they contribute in the towns on their domestic establishments, because now the merchant, the banker, or the broker, instead of living on the spot where his business was conducted, resided out of town, beyond the area of taxation. The fact that men of the class to which he referred paid so insignificant an amount towards the relief of the poor had, he was convinced, a good deal to do with their withdrawal from a discharge of the duties of Poor Law Guardian ... in the larger towns the richer a man was the smaller was the proportion he contributed, and the poorer a man was the larger was the proportion which he paid. A merchant doing a large business in a moderately large office and warehouse only paid rates for those premises, whatever might be the extent of his transactions ... Upon the class of small tradesmen the poor rate operated most oppressively, and with especial severity upon those who were in the humblest circumstances.[33]

Rating reform came high among the priorities of the Liberal government that took office in December 1868. As President of the Poor Law Board, Goschen took charge. Early in 1869 he informed Gladstone that Lopes' motions had raised expectations among Liberal agrarians and that there was strong pressure for a commission of inquiry into local taxation. The Conservatives intended to occupy the field, but 'many of our own side are equally hot upon the subject'.

I think it will be absolutely necessary for the Government to take some distinct line of policy with regard to the whole matter and above all to prevent that rush upon the Consolidated Fund on the part of local tax payers, in which the towns are unlikely to join the country gentlemen. I am working on a plan ... I think we might succeed in taking the wind out of the Conservative sails and at the same time accomplish the much more important object of throwing [?] aside the attack on the Consolidated Fund...[34]

Goschen's plans and actions still revealed a metropolitan bias. London was given machinery to increase local taxation in line with rising rents, by the Valuation of Property (Metropolis) Act of 1869. Re-assessment was to take place every five years on the same basis as the Income Tax

[33] 197 H.C. deb. 3 ser. 22 June 1869, 430-2.
[34] Gladstone Papers, Brit. Lib. Add. MSS. 44161, G. J. Goschen to W. E. Gladstone, 15 Jan. 1869, fol. 150 *et seq.*

(Schedule A), and rate claims were consolidated.[35] In November 1869 a Cabinet Committee was appointed to consider the 'Local Taxation Plan for 1870',[36] but no bill was ready for introduction within the session. Instead, Goschen prepared the ground with a Report on Local Taxation (compiled for him by Robert Giffen, the statistician) that made a highly partisan case. It was designed to demonstrate that there was no call for state subsidies to the country interest. The Report conceded that local rates had doubled in twenty years from £8 million to £16 million (see Table 10.1) but claimed that the increase had mainly occurred in the urban districts. House property in England was indeed heavily taxed. Rural rates, however, had remained constant. In those rural districts where they were high, they had always been high and constituted 'an hereditary burden which has at all times been heavy'. Of the additional urban rates only some £2 million were 'a lamentable increase of burden' owing to higher Poor Law expenditure. The rest (£5 million) was largely to pay for public works, 'not so much a burden as an investment'.[37]

An important Liberal slogan came into currency in 1870 – 'the division of rates between owners and occupiers'. A Select Committee was elected in March to investigate the expediency of this policy. It reported that a part of the rate already devolved indirectly on the owners and recommended their subjection to a formal liability as well, in order to involve them more deeply in local affairs.[38] Goschen did not introduce his bills until April of 1871.[39] They were ambitious, perhaps too ambitious. The whole existing structure of local government and taxation was to be swept away. A single local rating authority and one single consolidated rate were to be substituted for the many that existed before. New Parochial and County Boards were to become the organs of local government, posing a threat to the existing structure of landed hegemony in the countryside.

The consolidated rate merely extended the benefits of the London

[35] 32 & 33 Vict. c. 67. Another urgent task undertaken by Goschen was to restore the compounding system, abolished by the Representation of the People Act of 1867. See the Assessed Rates Bill, committee stage 197 H.C. deb. 3 ser. 21 June 1869, 360–430.

[36] Gladstone Papers, Add MSS. 44637, fol. 110. I owe this reference to Dr Agatha Ramm.

[37] Local taxation. Report of G. J. Goschen; P.P. 1870 (470) LV, pp. 40–1. For Giffen's role, see loc. cit. p. 41 and A.E.B., 'Obituary' [Sir Robert Giffen], J.R.S.S. 73 (1910), 529–30.

[38] Local taxation. Sel. com. rep.; P.P. 1870 (353) VIII, p. iii.

[39] 205 H.C. deb. 3 ser. 3 April 1871, 1115ff.

Valuation Act to the country as a whole and was a rationalisation long overdue; it had been initiated by B. W. Hunt, the Conservative Chancellor (in 1867) and approved by a Select Committee in 1868.[40] So far so good. But Goschen's own innovation, the 'division of rates', was taken by the Country interest as a gratuitous attack upon themselves, and yet failed to generate any great enthusiasm among urban members. Why were reactions so negative? In Scotland and Ireland, after all, division of rates was already in force without any obvious harm to landownership.[41] As if to give credence to agrarian suspicions, the boroughs were excused from the division of their rates and its full rigour was only to be applied to rural county rates.[42] Nor was there much for the boroughs in the Rating and House Tax Bill. At some future unspecified date, the house duty was to be surrendered by the Treasury to the local authorities (i.e. the metropolis and a few large towns). Smaller towns would get nothing, and the great urban centres – only promises. The bills may have safeguarded the Exchequer, but they failed to please. Landowners in particular regarded the plan as a party attempt to divide them from the farmers.

Goschen's Select Committee Report had been carried by the minister's casting vote, Lopes claimed, when he introduced his annual motion in 1871. '[Goschen] knew that owner and occupier were united upon this question, and that when united they were very strong; but he thought he might throw a bone of contention among them and so divide them'.[43] Gladstone's speech confirmed the charge. 'I deny', said the Prime Minister, 'that for the purpose of this argument houses and land are one description of property'.[44] Lopes could only posit the unity of tenure in comparison with the exemptions and immunities of 'personal' capital, and he made the case with great skill. '... if there were not a poor rate', he asked, would [there] be any protection for either persons or property?'

A poor rate, in his opinion, was as essential to internal defence against the dangerous classes as our Army and Navy were for the purpose of external defence; and for both descriptions of defence it was, he contended, equally the duty of the Government to provide

[40] Poor rates assessment. Sel. com. rep.; P.P. 1867–8 (342) XIII, pp. iii–v.
[41] 205 H.C. deb. 3 ser. 3 April 1871, Goschen, 1134.
[42] See Rating and local govt. bill; P.P. 1872 (106) V, p. 317, Clause 5(4.) (a).
[43] 204 H.C. deb. 3 ser. 28 Feb. 1871, 1060.
[44] *Ibid.*, 1108.

... lunacy was a national calamity ... it was no special creation of land and houses.[45]

He went on to develop an underconsumptionist critique of local taxation: House-capital was 'sentenced to transportation, so that it might do in other countries what it ought to do in this in the way of developing national resources'. Local rates were a direct and indirect cause of urban misery and overcrowding. They led 'to withdrawal of capital, to less demand for labour, less wages, more pauperism and consequently higher rates'.[46] Sclater-Booth, another landowner, specified the demands: an increase of government grants for police from one-quarter to one-half the expenditure and half the cost of lunatic asylums.[47] Goschen reserved his reply but later stated emphatically that subsidies were out of the question.[48]

Whatever the merits of Goschen's projected reforms, they failed completely as political banners. Lopes' motion was defeated in 1871 but Goschen's bills had to be withdrawn without debate. One of their clauses threatened to extinguish yet another landowner privilege: it provided for the rating of country mansions not on their notional letting value (commonly assessed very low) but on four per cent of their capital value.[49] In addition, an imprudent threat by Robert Lowe (the Chancellor) to tax farm horses discontented country members so much that Disraeli expected a dissolution.[50] In 1872 Massey Lopes' annual resolution succeeded, and the government was defeated by 259 votes to 159. In the same year there was a majority of 92 against the government on a resolution for placing election expenses on the rates.[51] The C.C.A. Local Taxation Committee continued to obstruct a large number of bills,[52] and its determined resistance to any legislation which entailed an addition to the rates was one of the main frustrations of Gladstone's economy-minded administration.

Contemplating the dissolution of Parliament, Gladstone admitted as much in a letter to Lord Granville, on 8 January 1874.

[45]*Ibid.*, 1045–6.
[46]*Ibid.*, 1058.
[47]*Ibid.*, 1066.
[48]205 H.C. deb. 3 ser. 3 April 1871, 1138.
[49]Rating and house tax bill; P.P. 1871 (105) III, p. 263, cl. 6, p. 2. See also 205 H.C. deb. 3 ser. 3 April 1871, Goschen, 1133.
[50]William Rathbone to his wife, 29 April 1871, printed in Rathbone, *William Rathbone* (1905), p. 276.
[51]210 H.C. deb. 3 ser. 16 April 1872, Lopes resolution and debate, 1331–1404; election expenses, *ibid.*, 1876.
[52]Matthews, *Fifty years* (1915), p. 90.

I am convinced it is not in our power to draw any great advantage, as a party, from the subject of Local taxation ... the rate payers are a good deal demoralised, as such, partly by the working of our present law as to the incidence of new burdens [which fell on occupiers alone], partly by the nature of the agitation which has been so astutely and ably prosecuted. They want money; and are at present rather indifferent about anything except money. Now in the game of offering money, first the Tories are completely beforehand with us, secondly they will outbid us if we enter into a competition. I have no doubt that if we must deal with the chief difficulties of the case, I do not abandon the hope that we may do it solidly and with credit; but I am certain we cannot make it an effective means of taking the weights out of the other scale, and putting them into ours.[53]

The party of economy had little to offer to ratepayers. Nevertheless, Liberal rating doctrine (dressed in rather ambiguous phrasing) stood first among the boons promised by Gladstone in his address to the Greenwich electors. Disraeli replied in kind and the election may be regarded as the first fought on the Victorian doctrines of local taxation, among other issues.[54]

Soon after Disraeli's victory a deputation of agriculturists and urban ratepayers arrived at his door to claim the spoils, in the form of government grants in relief of the rates. Disraeli re-affirmed the doctrine, but refrained from any promises, He was not entirely free from the assumptions of Gladstonian finance and realised perhaps that by giving away the prize he placed the banner at risk. 'I was most careful', Disraeli told the deputation, referring to the origins of the agitation, twenty-five years before, 'to make the issue broad, and to make our claims for relief upon a large and general foundation'; to appeal, in other words, to country and city alike.[55] All-too-real differences between Town and Country, and between landowners and house-capitalists, might come into the open if their common grievances were removed. Stafford Northcote's 1874 budget raised the police grant, introduced a 4s. weekly allowance for every pauper lunatic and transferred the cost of prisons to the national purse. The total Exchequer grant to local authorities

[53]A. Ramm (ed.), *The political correspondence of Mr Gladstone and Lord Granville, 1868–1876* (1952), ii, 439.
[54]See *The Times*, 24 Jan. 1874, 8c; 26 Jan. 8a, 2 Feb. 5a, 6b.
[55]Deputation of the Central Chamber of Agriculture and the Metropolitan Poor Rate and Local Taxation League, *The Times*, 24 March 1874, 8b.

doubled from £1.15 million in 1872–3 to £2.24 million in 1875–6. But it did not increase much further.[56] When faced by the onset of agrarian depression Disraeli told his rural clients in 1879 that the limits of the rate-support policy had been reached and that no more grants could be contemplated.[57] In retrospect, then, 1874 marked the maturity of the two doctrines, and the point where party dogmas had hardened.

V

The agrarians regained the initiative during Gladstone's second government, as they had during his first. On 28 March 1881 they narrowly lost a resolution to remove the maintenance of main roads from the rates.[58] The Queen's speech for 1882 promised a debate on imperial relief for local rates.[59] The agrarians returned to the attack, and forced Gladstone to concede a grant of £250,000 for the maintenance of main roads, in place of local expenditure.[60] The Prime Minister made no more promises in 1883 but a resolution introduced by Albert Pell was amended for the government by a majority of only ten in a house of 450. After the division, thirty-one Liberals, led by Thomas Duckham, chairman of the C.C.A., submitted a memorial to Gladstone in which they demanded urgent relief for the ratepayers.[61] In 1884 Pell succeeded in passing a resolution with a majority of eleven against the government.[62]

The 'local taxation party' lost a division on 5 May 1885 but had the satisfaction, one month later, of knocking the last nail into the Gladstone government's coffin. On 8 June 1885 Michael Hicks Beach (another past chairman of the C.C.A.) moved, on the second reading of the Customs and Excise Bill,

That this House ... declines to impose fresh taxation on real property until effect had been given to the resolutions of 17th April, 1883, and of 28th March, 1884, by which it had been acknowledged that further measures of relief were due to the ratepayers in counties

[56]Ten years later it was only £3.4M, despite the expansion of many local services (J. W. Grice, *National and local finance* (1910), table 1, pp. 364–5).
[57]244 H.L. deb. 3 ser. 28 March 1879, 1977–8.
[58]260 H.C. deb. 3 ser. 28 March 1881, 42–85.
[59]266 H.C. deb. 3 ser. 7 Feb. 1882, 5–6.
[60]*Ibid.*, Gladstone, 39–41, for promise; Matthews, *Fifty years* (1915), p. 96; Gladstone's admission of being forced to concede the grant, 313 H.C. deb. 3 ser. 25 April 1887, 1810.
[61]Matthews, *Fifty years* (1915), pp. 97–8.
[62]286 H.C. deb. 3 ser. 28 March 1884, 1023–1102.

and boroughs in respect of local charges imposed upon them for national services.[63]

On losing the vote (by a majority of twelve) Gladstone resigned. Each of these motions provided ample opportunity to discuss fiscal views on both sides of the House, and both Liberal and Conservative dogmas were given extended expositions by their advocates. But the inactivity of Gladstone's government robbed Liberal doctrine of its credibility. It needed new men from outside the House to breathe new life into the tired doctrine.

In promoting their programme of rating reform, Goschen and Gladstone had refrained from invoking the full authority of classical political economy. The advocates of Free Trade in Land, in the Cobden–Kay–Arnold–Brodrick lineage, also held back. For classical political economy contained a remedy for landowners' privilege that had already acquired a subversive tinge in the 1870s. Adam Smith, who was otherwise favourably disposed to landed proprietors, had identified rent as a monopoly price. Ricardo had gone further, and argued that the rent of land strangled profits and slowed down growth, and that the interests of the landowner were inimical to those of the rest of society.[64] Probably under the influence of the Physiocrats, Adam Smith deduced from the monopoly nature of rent that 'Ground rents and the ordinary rent of land are, ... perhaps, the species of revenue which can best bear to have a peculiar tax imposed upon them', a proposition that Ricardo also admitted.[65] John Stuart Mill (following his father, James Mill), concurred, and deduced that the Ricardian increase of rent in the progress of society could legitimately be intercepted. Having satisfied himself that the trend of the relative share of rent was indeed upwards,[66] he finally, towards the end of his life, offered this insight to the promoters of a radical re-distributionist organisation. Speaking from the chair at the inaugural meeting of the Land Tenure Reform Association in 1871 he said that,

[63] 298 H.C. deb. 3 ser. 8 June 1885, 1421. The other issue was the raising of duty on spirits and beer (in which barley and hop growers were interested) without a corresponding increase on wine.

[64] Adam Smith, *An inquiry into the nature and causes of the wealth of nations*, Cannan edn (Chicago, 1976), i, Bk I, ch. xi, p. 162; D. Ricardo, *On the principles of political economy and taxation*, ed. P. Sraffa and M. H. Dobb (Cambridge, 1951), ch. ii.

[65] Smith, *The Wealth of Nations*, ii, Bk V, ch. ii, p. 370; Ricardo, *Principles*, p. 204.

[66] J. S. Mill, *Principles of political economy*, ed. W. J. Ashley (1909), Bk. IV, ch. ii, 1–3 (pp. 701–4), ch. iii, 4–5 (pp. 715–24) and Bk. V, ch. ii, 5 (pp. 817–9).

Land is limited in quantity while the demand for it, in a prosperous country, is constantly increasing. The rent, therefore, and the price, which depends on the rent, progressively rises, not through the exertion or expenditure of the owner, to which we should not object, but by the mere growth of wealth and population. The incomes of landowners are rising while they are sleeping, through the general prosperity produced by the labour and outlay of other people.

Mill intended no harm to the present recipients of rents. He proposed that all *future* increment be appropriated by the State.[67] This reformulation of natural rights doctrine, with its qualified assertion of the collective title of tenure, became one of the inspirations of the Radical and socialist revivals of the 1880s.

[67] Land Tenure Reform Association, *Report of the inaugural public meeting ...* (1871), pp. 9–10; see also R. Harrison, *Before the socialists* (1965), pp. 215–26.

12

HENRY GEORGE AND LOCAL TAXATION 1885–1895

I

Henry George (1839–1897) appeared on the English scene in 1882 as a transatlantic menace, following on the influx of underpriced grain and the American funds that fed unrest in Ireland. He was indubitably a man of the left: 'Like Marx, George turned the guns of the classical economy on the fortress they were supposed to defend'.[1] Marx acknowledged George's priority and deplored it. '... it is a first, if unsuccessful attempt at emancipation from the orthodox political economy', he wrote to Sorge in 1881.[2] 'The real importance of Henry George', wrote another heretic, J. A. Hobson, 'is derived from the fact that he was able to drive an abstract notion, that of economic rent, into the minds of "practical" men and generate therefrom a social movement'.[3]

At one level, the doctrine that Henry George professed was merely an extreme form of Cobden's political creed. '... the antagonism of interests,' he wrote, 'is not between labour and capital, as is popularly believed, but is in reality between labour and capital on the one side and landownership on the other'.[4] This was the point of the graft on the old Liberal stock. George was antagonistic to rent, but not to profit. In his theory, land hoarding and speculation were the root causes of economic depressions, of unemployment, of urban overcrowding and of poverty. A tax on the entire value of rent would liberate both capital and labour from taxation, make land freely available to labour and usher in an era of unfettered free trade. Written in vivid and vigorous language, the book made a great impression on many in the Radical wing of the 'party of progress'. Some found their way into socialism and ultimately into

---

[1] A. Birnie, *Single-tax George* (1939), p. 70.
[2] K. Marx to Friedrich A. Sorge, 30 June 1881, K. Marx and F. Engels, *Selected correspondence 1846–1895* ed. and transl. D. Torr (1936), p. 396.
[3] J. A. Hobson, 'The influence of Henry George in England', *Fortnightly Review* 68 (1897), 836–7.
[4] Henry George, *Progress and poverty* (Everyman's edn 1911), p. 142.

labour politics. Others helped to form the single-tax movement and its Siamese twin, the Land Nationalisation Society.[5]

Progress and poverty went deeper than political economy or fiscal doctrine. It reaffirmed the gospel of 'natural rights', revived its Rousseauian undertones and challenged the utilitarian respect for property rights. It penetrated even deeper, and carried a message of spiritual regeneration. With compelling literary power it evoked a metaphysic that resonated with values and needs of the middle-class mentality of its time (more about this in chapter 20). A tension between pragmatism and Utopia runs throughout the book. Ultimately the tax on rent was designed to bring about a reversal or urbanisation, a return to nature, an end to alienation and inequality and the full development of men's innate powers.[6]

> The great cause of inequality in the distribution of wealth is inequality in the ownership of land[7] ... to relieve labour and capital from all taxation, direct and indirect, and to throw the burden upon rent, would be, as far as it went, to counteract this tendency to inequality, and, if it went so far as to take in taxation the whole of rent, the cause of inequality would be totally destroyed ...[8] The destruction of speculative land values would tend to diffuse population where it is too dense and to concentrate it where it is too sparse; to substitute for the tenement house homes surrounded by gardens, and to fully settle agricultural districts ...[9]

The Georgian organisations founded in Britain in the 1880s adopted the name of 'Land Restoration League', Scottish and English respectively. The title does not signify whether land is to be restored to the people, or the people to the land. This ambiguity enabled romantic 'back to the landers', pragmatists and those like Sidney Webb who welcomed machine industry, to work together, and gave Londoners a common cause with Welsh and Scottish peasants. The life of the movement has already been exhaustively described in a number of unpublished theses.[10]

[5]For the reactions to Henry George, see C. A. Barker, *Henry George* (New York, 1955), ch. XIII, pp. 378–416.
[6]*Progress and poverty*, p. 331–2.
[7]*Ibid.* p. 211.
[8]*Ibid.* p. 311.
[9]*Ibid.* p. 319.
[10]See esp. P. Ho, 'Land and state in Great Britain 1873–1910' (Columbia Univ. Ph.D. thesis, 1952); A. J. Peacock, 'Land reform 1880–1919' (Southampton Univ. M. A. thesis, 1961); S. B. Ward, 'Land reform in England and Wales 1880–1918' (Reading Univ. Ph.D. thesis, 1976). I am particularly indebted to Dr Peacock's excellent thesis.

Here we are concerned with a different problem: what was the impact of the land reformers on the politics of local taxation in England?

The period of Henry George's greatest influence, 1883–5, coincided with depression in arable farming, agrarian unrest in Scotland and Ireland and increasing ruling-class concern with the magnitude of poverty in the metropolis. The 'bitter cry' press campaigns of 1883–4 were given official recognition with the appointment of the Royal Commission on the Housing of the Working Classes in 1884. A celebrated passage in its Report is usually taken to demonstrate the decisive influence of George on English Land Policy.[11] It was repeatedly invoked and quoted in Edwardian Liberal policy documents.[12] The passage in question merits a close reading, for it encapsulates the problem of the links between the Sage of San Francisco and Liberal rating doctrine.

At present, land available for building in the neighbourhood of our populous centres, though its capital value is very great, is probably producing a small yearly return until it is let for building. The owners of this land are rated not in relation to the real value but to the actual annual income. They can thus afford to keep their land out of the market, and to part with only small quantities, so as to raise the price beyond the natural monopoly price which the land would command by the advantages of position. Meantime, the general expenditure of the town on improvements is increasing the value of their property. If this land were rated at, say, 4 per cent on its selling value, the owners would have a more direct incentive to part with it to those who are desirous of building, and a two-fold advantage would result to the community. First, all the valuable property would contribute to the rates, and thus the burden on the occupiers would be diminished by the increase in the rateable property. Secondly, the owners of the building land would be forced to offer their land for sale, and thus their competition with one another would bring down the price of building land, and so diminish the tax in the shape of ground rent, or price paid for land which is now levied on urban enterprise by the adjacent landowners, a tax be it remembered which is no recompense for any industry or expenditure on their part, but is the natural result of the industry and

[11]Henry George, Jnr., *The life of Henry George* (1900), p. 453; Barker, *Henry George* (1955), p. 414; Peacock, 'Land reform' (1961), p. 68.

[12]Quoted e.g. in PRO CAB 37/97/16, D. Lloyd George, 'Taxation of land values', 29 Jan. 1909, 3–4; Papers bearing on land taxes; P.P. 1909 Cd. 4750 LXXI, p. 239; *The land* (1914), ii, 552–3.

activity of the townspeople themselves. Your Majesty's Commissioners would recommend that these matters should be included in legislation when the law of rating comes to be dealt with by Parliament.[13]

Taken at face value, the statement appears to open revolutionary perspectives. Four per cent, as Henry George's biographer points out, represents a return approximating to the full economic value of land.[14] With such a high tax, towns could intercept the whole capital gain arising on the margin or urban expansion, i.e. the 'conversion rent' (see Chapter 7, section IV, p. 114). Benefits would diffuse in the form of lower land prices, making for less overcrowding and a better urban environment. Now the Royal Commission report was signed by seventeen pillars of the Victorian establishment, including the Prince of Wales, the leader of the Conservative party and an heir apparent to the Liberal party (Lord Salisbury and Sir Charles Dilke). Yet historians of the land reform movement have failed to register surprise at such a remarkable conversion.[15]

On closer examination the notion appears to be based on a misunderstanding. Four per cent of the capital value is *not* the tax payable but the taxable assessment. That is to say, the four per cent of the capital value were to be the *assessable value*, from which local taxes would be raised at the prevailing rate.[16] The Commissioners did not want to impose penal taxation on ground property, merely to end its immunity to *ordinary* local taxation. In his dissent from the Report G. J. Goschen complained that 'The suggestion involves an entirely new principle in the law of rating, namely taxation of capital instead of annual value ...'[17] He should have known better. The principle had formed part of his own Rating and House Tax Bill, introduced fourteen years previously.[18] What is more, the rating of capital values, and even the separate assessment of land and buildings were common practice in the met-

---

[13]Housing of the working classes. R. com. 1st rep.; P.P. 1884–5 C.4402 XXX, p. 42.

[14]As he put it, 'to propose a tax rate at a level at all near the interest rate on capital was of course to enter entirely within the premises and expectations of land-value taxation' (Barker, *Henry George* (1955), p. 414).

[15]Admittedly Lord Salisbury, R. A. Cross and G. J. Goschen dissented from the passage.

[16]See e.g. 303 H.C. deb. 3 ser. 23 March 1886, J. Chamberlain, 1687.

[17]'Memorandum by the Right Hon, G. J. Goschen, M.P.', Housing of the working classes. R. com. 1st rep. (1884–5), p. 66.

[18]See chapter 11, p. 179.

ropolis, in cases where no measure of annual value was available, e.g. on owner-occupied property, hotels, public houses and schools. The latter were separately assessed on the value of the land and the buildings in at least five districts (Camberwell, Holborn, Islington, St Saviour's and Shoreditch). Holborn extended the practice to other property as well.[19]

So the banker's protest only demonstrated how much he had moved from the Liberal position he had been instrumental in formulating. Lord Salisbury protested less than Goschen and with reason. For the passage only expressed a familiar and long-standing Liberal doctrine, and one that Gladstone's government had done nothing to enforce. And it was balanced by the preceding paragraph, which contained the *Conservative* doctrine of local taxation. The Commissioners, this passage stated,

> are of the opinion that until some reform is introduced which shall secure contribution to local expenditure from *other sources of income* received by residents in the locality,[20] in addition to the present rateable property, no great progress can be made in local improvements.[21]

The crucial report turns out to be no more than a ritual ventilation of the two doctrines.

And yet the report cannot be written off entirely, for it signified the revival of Liberal rating doctrine as an active force, in response (in no small measure) to the influence of Henry George.[22] On 16 March 1886, George's closest associate in England, William Saunders, tabled a motion in the House of Commons for the direct assessment of ground rents, in which he cited the passage in the Royal Commission's Report.[23] A long debate ensued and the question was finally referred to the Select Committee on Town Holdings (which had been appointed a short time before to examine leasehold enfranchisement). Seven days later James Thorold Rogers, the old Cobdenite Professor of Political Economy moved a resolution in favour of the division of rates, and the rating of country mansions at their true value. Rogers. offered the 'division of rates' as a moderate alternative to Georgian doctrine and promised it would be 'a

---

[19]GLC, L.C.C. Local govt. and taxation com. *Pr.P.* 1 (1889). Lewisham Union assessment com. 'Statement containing an analysis of the replies to certain questions submitted to metropolitan assessment committees' (Jan. 1885) [printed].

[20]i.e., from 'personal' property. Italics added.

[21]Housing of the working classes. R. com. 1st rep. (1884–5), pp. 41–2.

[22]See e.g. G. Shaw-Lefevre's speech at Bethna! Green, 7 Oct. 1885, in *The Times*, 8 Oct. 1885, 8a.

[23]303 H.C. deb. 3 ser. 16 March 1886, 999.

great concession to popular sentiment, and a very considerable means of stifling public discontent'.[24] In a house of 392 the resolution was approved with a majority of forty.

Why did the landowners resist the division of rates with the lessees? Did not the proposal originate with Goschen, a City banker with no reputation for radicalism? And did the landowners not argue that the rates were theirs to pay (indirectly, through lower rents) anyway? One of the keys to Conservative obstruction was contained in their watchword 'existing contracts', which came into currency in the 1880s. Conservatives agreed that local taxation was taken into account when leases were created. But town leases ran for up to a century and all the while the lessee absorbed the increases in local taxation. When leases finally fell in the landowner had to take the new level of rates into account when fixing the rent of the new lease, but was compensated many times over by capital gains. To subject owners to local taxation in mid-lease overturned one of their fundamental immunities – hence their insistence on the sanctity of 'existing contracts'. 'Division of rates' began as a London doctrine, and resistance also came mainly from London landowners and their spokesmen in the property professions.[25] 'Existing contracts' remained a high hurdle on the road to rating reform, a shibboleth of Conservative rating doctrines.

In the countryside leases were negotiated at much shorter intervals, often from year to year, and consequently rates (in theory at least) were reapportioned between owners and farmers at frequent intervals. Dividing the liability would only formalise an existing relationship and give landowners a greater voice in the expenditure of local revenues. So Scotsmen (who already had division of rates), agriculturists and Conservatives outside the London ground interest were ready to tolerate the division of rates. 'Indeed', wrote Albert Pell, a leading member of the C.C.A.'s Local Taxation Committee, 'the proposal to divide the payment between owners and occupiers is a truly conservative one'.[26] Agrarians could not ignore the popularity of the Liberals' attack on the landed interest. In the Commons debate on 23 March 1886, agrarian Conserva-

---

[24]*Ibid*, 23 March 1886, 1647; see also 1648 and J. E. T. Rogers, *The economic interpretation of history* (1888), pp. 162, 498.

[25]See e.g. Lord Salisbury's speech at the National Union meeting at Nottingham, *The Times*, 26 Nov. 1889, 6e (and chapter 9, p. 157) and C. H. Sargant, *Urban rating* (1890), p. 66ff. Lord Salisbury also invoked freedom of contract against Liberal land reform in Ireland ('Disintegration', *Quarterly Review* 156 (1883), 580).

[26]W. Rathbone, A. Pell and F. C. Montague, *Local government and taxation* (1885), p. 128.

tives conceded the principle of the division of rates. They insisted, however, on coupling it with their own remedy of national relief for local taxation.[27] We have already referred to this debate as a set-piece rehearsal of the rating doctrines of the two parties (p. 163). The agrarian concession followed the example of 'the balance of doctrines' in the Royal Committee Report, and marked the limits of Conservative willingness to compromise.

II

Liberal rating doctrine was associated from its origin with the cause of a single municipal government for London. In the early 1880s, hastened no doubt by the 'bitter cry' agitations and the promise of a Liberal government, the movement for London government blossomed into life under the leadership of the London Municipal Reform League.[28] London finances had not improved since the agitations of the 1860s: the burden of the rates had increased and the coal and wine duties were due to expire in 1890. Lord Hobhouse (1819–1904), a leading member of the Municipal Reform League, regarded ground rents as a suitable substitute. 'Make the owners of property pay rates,' he wrote to the *Star* in 1888, 'and you will replace the coal-tax without burdening the occupier. Let us go to Parliament for that'.[29] On the eve of the formation of the London County Council, Lord Hobhouse became the chairman of a joint body of the Municipal Reform Council and the Georgian 'English Land Restoration League'. This was the United Committee for the Taxation of Ground Values. Sidney Webb wrote the Committee's first pamphlet, *A Plea for the Taxation of Ground Values* (1887), and Lord Hobhouse added a preface.

Webb brought a unique combination of passion and expertise into the question of local taxation. Like his contemporaries at the Fabian Society he had fallen under the spell of Henry George during his first visits. Unlike them, he kept in touch with the master after his departure.[30] He

[27]303 H.C. deb. 3 ser. 23 March 1886. Paget, 1651–6 R. Jasper More, 1656–60; Sir John Kennaway, 1666; Captain E. Cotton, 1674–7.
[28]See J. Lloyd, *London municipal government* (1911).
[29]L. T. Hobhouse and J. L. Hammond, *Lord Hobhouse: a memoir* (1905), p. 167. See also interview with Hobhouse, 'Is much to be got out of ground rents?', *Pall Mall Gazette*, 25 Jan. 1888, summarised in Hobhouse and Hammond, pp. 174–5.
[30]S. Webb to H. George, 8 March 1889, in *The letters of Sidney and Beatrice Webb*, ed. N. Mackenzie (Cambridge, 1978), i, 125–6.

also had extensive first-hand administrative experience of local taxation in London, having, as an Inland Revenue Surveyor of Taxes, sat on three district assessment committees in the London valuation of 1881.[31] It was there that he realised that,

> The income which the owners of London are receiving from rent is not only the annual rental, but the average unearned increment of London ... It comes to about one per cent for the year on their properties, so that in addition to 37 million of rent, we have four or five millions in unearned increment.[32]

'This Committee,' wrote Sidney Webb of the United Committee in 1890, 'presenting its aims in the moderate and practical way dear to the English mind, has already exercised a most potent influence, and at least two-thirds of the members of the London County Council adopt its programmes'.[33]

In fact the policy adopted by the Progressives on the County Council, and by Lord Hobhouse in particular was an explicit rejection of Webb's programme. The Georgians had got off to a· good start. On 26 February 1889, barely a month after its first meeting, the London County Council appointed a Land Valuation Committee with distinctly Georgian terms of reference: 'to consider the best method of ascertaining the value of land throughout the metropolitan area, irrespective of the value of the buildings'.[34] These terms are traceable to *Progress and Poverty*, where George stated categorically that 'the value of land can always be readily distinguished from the value of improvements'.[35] George was invited to give evidence about American practice, Sidney Webb drew up a draft bill for the separate valuation of land and houses, and the Committee reported cautiously in favour of the principle.[36] About the same time John Fletcher Moulton, QC, a former Liberal MP (1885–6) and amateur scientist, published the second United Committee pamphlet, more advanced in the Georgian direction than Webb's, which elaborated a scheme for bringing groundowners into local taxation through a separate assessment of land and houses, and the assessment of land on capital

---

[31]GLC L.C.C. *Pr.P.* 2 (1889), *Report of the land valuation committee* (June, 1889), pp. 49, 56.
[32]*Ibid.* p. 68.
[33]S. Webb, *Socialism in England* (1890), pp. 58–9.
[34]GLC L.C.C. *Pr.P.* 2 (1889) *Report of the land valuation committee* (1889), p. 3.
[35]*Progress and poverty*, p. 301; see also p. 302.
[36]Henry George's evidence, L.C.C. *Report of the land valuation com.* (1889), pp. 18–20; Webb's draft bill, *Socialism in England* (1890) pp. 105–6.

value, not annual income. How much local taxation should fall on the landowners was left unstated, save for saying that it ought to do so 'to a large extent'.[37]

Starved of funds for essential public works and services, and tantalised by the vision of untaxed ground wealth accumulating all around, the Progressive Party at the London County Council raised high the banner of rating reform. Not, however, the flag of socialism or even of Henry George, but that old battle-standard, 'the division of rates'. The Land Valuation Committee's report was not acted upon, but merely referred to another committee, of more orthodox membership. Lord Hobhouse was chairman, and his brother-in-law, Sir Thomas, Baron Farrer (1819–1899; Permanent Secretary to the Board of Trade, 1856–86, and a writer on financial and economic affairs) was the other dominant member. Although he wanted to bring in ground property under local taxation, Hobhouse had no use for Fletcher Moulton's proposals. At seventy years of age he was no longer receptive to novel formulas.[38] Farrer was no more a disciple of George than his fellow septuagenarian Hobhouse. His own favourite device for intercepting capital gains was a municipal death duty.[39]

Hobhouse's memorandum was the basis of the Committee's report, submitted to the L.C.C. in 1891. Its central principle was the division of rates. The form it suggested was a landowner's rate on *income* not capital, on the same lines, (and possibly using the same machinery) as Schedule A of the income tax.[40] In a book published the same year Farrer re-stated the case for Liberal doctrine as an antidote to more radical reforms, and appealed to the landowners' self-interest.

Those who have anything to do with the public business of our large towns know how bitter is the feeling on the subject of the incidence of urban rates; how much this feeling interferes with the physical and social improvements on which we have all set our hearts; and how dangerous this feeling may become to the ownership of land. We are not far from an Irish land question in London.

... The confiscation of the unearned increment, the nationalisation

[37]J. F. Moulton, *The taxation of ground values* (1889), p. 7.
[38]GLC L.C.C. Local govt. and taxation com. Sub-committee on incidence of taxation, bound minutes (1889), draft 'Memorandum of Lord Hobhouse', Dec. 1889, pp. 3–5. Discussions of the committee, July–Dec. 1889, fols. 1–18.
[39]*Ibid.* 17 July 1889, fols. 5–6.
[40]Compare Hobhouse's 'Memorandum', loc. cit. and L.C.C. meeting, 3 Nov. 1891, report of the incidence of taxation sub-com. as reported in W. Saunders, *History of the first London County Council 1889–1890–1891* (1892), pp. 556–8.

or the municipalisation of land, or Mr George's single tax may be absurdities, injustices and impossibilities; but they are scarcely more unjust than a state of things in which land, and especially urban land, is exceptionally relieved from taxation.[41]

Meanwhile, L.C.C. committees beavered away at other reforms and L.C.C. MPs initiated and introduced a wide variety of rating bills.[42] The Valuer's department began to challenge the chronic under-assessment of wealthy districts. In one-third of the metropolis it revealed under-assessment amounting to £900,000 but the legal challenges produced meagre results.[43] The Improvements Committee produced a plan for the special rating of landowners who stood to gain from particular public works. This principle, known as 'betterment' was embodied in an L.C.C. bill but dismissed by a House of Commons' committee in 1890.[44] An L.C.C. election manifesto of 1892 demonstrates the amplitude of Radical commitment to rating reform independently of single-tax doctrine. John Benn (1850–1922, a leader of the Progressive party on the L.C.C.) promised his electors the division of rates, application of the betterment principle, appropriation of City charity funds and the equitable rating of land and houses. More than thirty years later Benn's biographer would write – 'Hardly any item of that bold programme has been completely carried out even to-day'.[45]

When the L.C.C.'s local government and taxation committee agreed to introduce a Rating of Owners Bill in 1893 it stopped far short of an equal division of rates between owners and occupiers. A mere fourpence in the pound (out of an average London rate of about five shillings) was to be levied by the Inland Revenue as a surcharge on Schedule A in London. It was introduced as an ordinary local authority private bill, but was torpedoed by the agrarians. At the insistence of James Lowther, chairman of the Central Chamber of Agriculture, the speaker ruled the bill out of order.[46] A betterment bill was stopped in the Lords. Next session (1894), as a small measure of compensation, the Liberal government agreed to help pass an Equalisation of Rates Act, which authorised a

[41]Lord Farrer, *Mr. Goschen's finance* (1891), pp. 136, 139–40.
[42]On 23 April 1891 for example, the L.C.C. local govt. and taxation com. considered 12 private bills, including rating of machinery, taxation of ground rents, equalisation, leasehold enfranchisement etc. See its *Pr.P.* 3 (1891) (GLC).
[43]Saunders, *History of the 1st L.C.C.* (1892), p. v.
[44]London streets (Strand improvement) bill. Sel. com. rep.; P.P. 1890 (239) XV, pp. iii–iv.
[45]A. G. Gardiner, *John Benn and the progressive movement* (1925), p. 152.
[46]B. F. C. Costelloe, *The incidence of local taxation* (1893), p. 32.

uniform sixpenny rate over the whole metropolis. A. J. Balfour, the Conservative leader, then introduced a betterment bill for Manchester, the location of his constituency. Despite its misgivings the House of Lords passed it and also had to concede the L.C.C.'s betterment bill.[47] But the L.C.C. did not proceed with betterment. Instead, it financed the Strand–Kingsway improvements by purchasing property adjoining the project, and letting it at its increased value. This was the system previously employed by Birmingham in the Corporation Street development and was the method of 'recoupment' urged upon the council by its critics in 1890.[48] In 1895 the Liberals fell out of power at Westminster and the Moderates (i.e. Conservatives) achieved electoral parity at the L.C.C. Rating reform, in London at least, sank from view for two years.

III

Gladstone revived the memory of the injustices of the London Embankment finances in a speech in 1887.[49] At Birmingham in 1888 the Liberal Party pledged itself to the taxation of ground rents. The same commitment was undertaken by subsequent conferences, culminating in the Newcastle Programme of 1891, where it appeared twice, in both the 'London' and the 'omnibus' resolutions.[50] R. B. Haldane stated in Parliament in 1891 that 'it is not proposed to put a 20s. in the pound on ground value. To do that would only be distinguishable from confiscation in the same way as putting one to death in a warm bath is distinguishable from hanging'.[51] Together with Asquith, Sydney Buxton, Arthur Acland and Sir Edward Grey he introduced in 1892 a modest bill designed (like John Stuart Mill's proposals twenty years before) to intercept London's *future* unearned increment, without touching existing assets.[52] It fell short of Mill's plan in being limited to sites actually required for use by local authorities.

I bring forward this Bill [said Haldane] not because I agree with Mr

[47]Gardiner, *Benn* (1925), pp. 164–70.
[48]See London streets sel. com. rep. (1890), p. iv and Sir G. Shaw-Lefevre, 'The cost of the Holborn and Strand improvement schemes' *The Times*, 29 April 1905, 4d–c.
[49]*The Times*, 30 July 1887, 12a. See pp. 171–3, above.
[50]See e.g. National Liberal Federation annual meeting, Birmingham, *The Times*, 8 Nov. 1888, 10b; Manchester, *The Times*, 5 Dec. 1888, 12c; Newcastle, *The Times*, 2 Oct. 1891, 10b and 3 Oct., 10b.
[51]352 H.C. deb. 3 ser. 29 April 1891, 1709.
[52]See pp. 182–3.

Henry George, but because I disagree with him. If you are able to stop the agitation which then began, and which, it seems, has been acquiring force ever since, something must be done. The mind of the people is awakened on this subject; and I think in this connection we owe something to Mr George instead of having a grudge against him. He has made the people see that something must be done; and what we seek in this Bill is to do that something, not in the unjust form he proposed, but in a just form.[53]

The debate began after midnight and soon became acrimonious and personal. 'One of the coolest and most impudent attacks upon the security of property which I think has ever been submitted to the legislature of a civilised country', ejaculated one opponent from the right.[54] On the left Cunninghame-Graham, the Scottish socialist, made vocal objections to Haldane's distinction between landed and other capital, and was suspended from the House.[55] Shortly before sunrise there were still 371 members in the chamber and they rejected the bill by a majority of 75.[56] After succeeding Gladstone as Premier in March 1894 Lord Rosebery re-affirmed Liberal rating doctrine. From the platform of a great public meeting, he pledged loyalty to the L.C.C., whose first Chairman he had been. 'It has laid down some principles which will not be allowed to die until they are carried into effect,' he declared in somewhat ambiguous wording. 'The first of these is the taxation of ground values (Cheers).'[57]

There was a fundamental difference between Fabian rating doctrine (laced as it was with Henry Georgian principles) and the Liberal doctrine. Liberals merely desired the equitable re-distribution of the incidence of local taxation; the Fabians (and the single-taxers) wanted to use local taxation for the extinction of rent. When pressed on the point, Sidney Webb admitted as much. He did so in 1890, giving evidence before the Town Holdings Committee,[58] and again in 1893, in sharper terms, when Michael Hicks Beach, leader of the landed interest, interrogated him for the Royal Commission on Labour.

Q. 3857. You wish the burden to be shared between owner and occupier? – In some form yes; but I do not mean what is ordinarily called 'the division of rates' ...

[53] 4 H.C. deb. 4 ser. 4 May 1892, 72.
[54] *Ibid.* A. A. Baumann, 84
[55] *Ibid.* 107–8.
[56] *Ibid.* 136.
[57] *The Times*, 22 March 1894, 7b.
[58] Town holdings. Sel. com. rep. & min. of ev.; P.P. 1890 (341) XVIII, q. 497.

Q. 3887. Supposing it had to go so far as to amount to 20s. in the pound, what then? – That is a consummation I should view without any alarm whatsoever.[59]

Lord Hobhouse explicitly underlined the difference between Liberals and Fabians in an 'Eighty Club' speech in 1892.

Mr Sidney Webb [he said] is a gentleman whose ability and uprightness I wish to speak of with every respect, and I have no doubt that when he is returned to the Council he will do excellent work in it. But he does take some very far-reaching views, in which he is not followed by me, and, so far as I know, he is not followed by the majority, or any member of the Progressive Party.[60]

In 1894 he wrote in the *Contemporary Review* of 'the cranky-headed men who, professing the desire for reform, do all they can to hinder it, unless it is laid out in every jot and tittle according to their own fancies; perhaps not a very numerous class but a troublesome one'.[61]

It is important to stress that Liberal doctrine on the one hand, and Fabian and single-tax doctrine on the other, kept their identities separate and aimed at entirely different destinations. Webb invested his hopes in the inevitability of collectivism; but he had no misgivings about marching down the road in formation with the Liberals, and blowing the L.C.C. Progressive trumpet. Such apparent duplicity troubled contemporaries on both the right and the left, and has led historians to question Webb's good faith.[62] On their side, the Liberals could hardly avoid being tainted by association with single-taxers and socialists. Haldane might protest,[63] but the stigma stuck, to be repeatedly used by extremists on both sides of Liberalism; to be exploited, on occasion, by the Liberal leaders themselves.

IV

The first significant instance of the contamination of Liberal doctrine with Georgian language was the single-tax slogan 'the taxation of land values' (the concept 'land values' was taken directly out of *Progress and*

[59]Labour. R. com. (sitting as a whole). Min. of ev.; P.P. 1893–4 C.7603–I XXXIX, Pt. I.
[60]Lord Hobhouse, *London government* (29 Feb. 1892), p. 18. And see his preface, S. Webb, *A plea for the taxation of land values* (1887), pp. 5–6.
[61]Quoted in Hammond and Hobhouse, *Lord Hobhouse* (1905), p. 156.
[62]See e.g. P. Thompson, *Socialists, Liberals and Labour* (1967), pp. 141–5.
[63]4 H.C. deb. 4 ser. 4 May 1892, 97.

Poverty).[64] This slogan (henceforth designated TLV) universally displaced 'division of rates' as the Liberal catch-phrase from the late 1880s,[65] without any fundamental alteration of doctrinal substance. The new slogan reflected a change of generations, and the effect of Fabian and single-tax propaganda. It was the first of Henry George's permanent legacies to the rating question.

Henry George's second legacy was a movement; a body of 'faddists' on the left wing of the Liberal Party, counting among their numbers a clique of Radical MPs (William Saunders, Professor James Stuart and J. F. Moulton were the most outstanding of the first generation). Writing in 1897, J. A. Hobson observed,

> The spirit of humanitarian and religious appeal which suffuses *Progress and Poverty* wrought powerfully upon a large section of what I may call typical English moralists. In my lectures upon Political Economy about the country, I have found in almost every centre a certain little knot of men of the lower-middle or upper-working class, men of grit and character, largely self-educated, keen citizens, mostly nonconformists in religion, to whom Land Nationalisation, taxation of unearned increment, or other radical reforms of land tenure are doctrines resting upon a plain moral sanction. These free-trading Radical dissenters regard common ownership of land and equal access to the land as a "natural right," essential to individual freedom. It is this attitude of mind which serves to explain why, when both theoretic students of society and the man in the street regard Land Nationalisation as a first large step in the direction of Socialism, organized Socialists regard the followers of Henry George with undisguised hostility and contempt.[66]

For the initiated, rating reform took on the dimensions of political myth (in Sorel's sense of the term). Liberal rating doctrine, bogged down in lethargy and a mess of conflicting interests, was energised by the conviction and vitality that single-taxers and socialists brought into their propaganda. Their example was infectious, and played a part in revitalising the Liberal party after 1900.[67]

The third, and probably the least fortunate legacy, was the project of a

[64]*Progress and poverty*, pp. 136, 161, 187.
[65]See e.g. the National Liberal Federation resolution at Manchester, *The Times*, 5 Dec. 1889, 12c.
[66]Hobson, 'Influence of Henry George', 841–2.
[67]See chapter 16, p. 245ff.

separate valuation for land and buildings. Its elegance may have appealed to the scientific mind of Fletcher Moulton; its tidiness, to the bureaucratic predilections of Sidney Webb. Experienced officials like Baron Farrer and Lord Hobhouse suspected it was too complicated for practical application.[68] Three interconnected weaknesses characterised the project. First, it called for the separation of land value from the value of the buildings erected upon the land, and the valuation of a fictional entity, the 'bare site'. Secondly, the valuation of capital, as opposed to the assessment of rental income, was bound to be at once more difficult, and more arbitrary, since capital values, unlike rents, are not a question of fact, but of expectation, except in the case of actual sales. Thirdly, taxation affects expectations of profit, and therefore depresses capital values. A tax on land values would therefore nullify the valuation on which it was based. Given political goodwill, none of these problems was fatal. Site value tax systems were established in the 1890s and 1900s in Australia, New Zealand and in some German and American cities. Rating practice tolerated even stranger fictions than 'bare sites' (the rating of railways was one example). But for a politically contentious doctrine, complexity and cost were to prove a serious and eventually fatal handicap.[69]

Edgar Josiah Harper (1860–1934) was Assistant Valuer to the London County Council from 1890 to 1900 and Statistical Officer between 1900 and 1911. Simplicity of valuation was the cardinal pre-condition of TLV and Harper's expert authority lent more credibility to the separate valuation of sites and structures than perhaps any other single factor. Harper was an undercover single-taxer,[70] with a vested personal interest. Starting at eighteen years of age as clerk in the Architect's department at the Metropolitan Board of Works, he was earning £162 a year ten years

[68]Farrer, *Mr. Goschen's finance* (1891), p. 146 and GLC, Hobhouse, 'Memorandum' (1889), pp. 3–5 (see[38], p. 192).

[69]This is anticipatory. For a sympathetic discussion of the project, see A. W. Fox, *The rating of land values* (2nd edn. 1908); a collection of documents covering the whole period – Papers bearing on land taxes; P.P. 1909 Cd. 4750 LXXXI; a good critique – H. Cox. *Land nationalization and land taxation* (2nd edn. 1906), pp. 95–125. Foreign experience – PRO CAB 37/117/91, 'Memorandum on colonial and foreign land taxes', Dec. 1913, and Yetta Scheftel, *The taxation of land value* (Boston, 1916), chs. II–IV, VI, VIII, X.

[70]Charles Trevelyan Papers, CPT 9, Crompton Lewellyn Davis [Secretary of the English Land Restoration League] to C.P. Trevelyan, a single-tax MP (see p. 246), 16 Nov. 1902, referring to the recruitment of London County Councillors: '... of course *Harper's* name *must not be mentioned* [underlined in the original] as it would never do for him to have been conspiring in a matter in which the Councillors will join'. See also CPT 9, A. Billson MP to C. P. Trevelyan, 22 Jan. 1902.

later in 1888. In 1889 he gave evidence to the L.C.C.'s Land Valuation Committee and was soon promoted to the Valuer's office. Thereafter he rose, not without controversy, and reached £1100 a year before he left the L.C.C. in 1911, to become the head of Lloyd George's Land Valuation.[71] From the first, he made light of the difficulties and cost of a separate valuation, and went on to do so whenever the opportunity presented itself, inside the L.C.C., and before professional bodies and Commissions of Inquiry.[72] In 1895–6 he carried out a pilot valuation of London.[73] Of his persuasiveness there can be no doubt: he left a favourable impression on many contemporaries. Sidney Webb invited him to be one of the London School of Economics' first lecturers in 1895.[74] Without disparaging the energy or the ability of this admirably self-made man, it will be seen that he created misplaced confidence by dismissing difficulties too easily; and that he confounded the problems with a certain obscurity of thought and expression.

All things considered, Henry George loomed larger in England as bogeyman than prophet. Outside a small band of loyalists, he inspired more fear than respect. Hyndman the Marxist soon fell foul of him.[75] Liberal economists (except Sidgwick) accorded the compliment of serious attention, but only in order to knock him down.[76] Samuel Smith, an old-style Gladstonian Liverpool MP recorded the consternation George excited in orthodox Liberal ranks in his first visits, and took the platform against him in the last visits.[77]

It was association with Irish 'crime' and not socialist theorising which

[71]L.C.C. *Minutes*, 8 Oct. 1889, 18 Feb. 1890, 13 March 1894; H. Haward, *The London County Council from within* (1932), pp. 218–20; *Who was who.*

[72]See e.g. GLC L.C.C. *Land valuation com.* (1889), ques. 238–65; E. J. Harper, 'Incidence of rates upon landed property', *EG* 3 April 1897, 519–20; Local taxation. R. com. vol. IV min. of ev.; P.P. 1900 Cd. 201 XXXVI, ques. 22,201–22,524; *ibid.* final rep. Engl. & Wales; P.P. 1901 Cd. 638 XXIV, p. 169.

[73]Printed in *Lond. Stat.* 8 (1897–8), 208–11.

[74]For testimonials, see the letters,[70] and Wedgwood Papers, C. Lewellyn Davies to J. Wedgwood, 29 Jan. 1906; also the following documents, cited in Papers bearing on land taxes (P.P. 1909) (page nos. refer to this collection): (a) L.C.C. Report on the rules for deduction, 11 Dec. 1893, p. 298. (b) Local taxation. R. com. separate report on urban rating and site values; 1901, p. 268. Fox, *Site values* (1908) frequently invoked Harper's authority. Sidney Webb, see 'A school of economics', *London*, 29 Aug. 1895, 278. Efficiency and ability, see Haward, *L.C.C. from within* (1932), p. 205.

[75]See H. M. Hyndman, 'Introduction', *The single tax versus social democracy* (public debate between Henry George and Hyndman, 2 July 1889, rep. 1906), pp. 3–4.

[76]Alfred Marshall, Arnold Toynbee, Henry Fawcett, J. E. Thorold Rogers, Thomas Farrer; see Barker, *Henry George* (1955), pp. 389–94.

[77]S. Smith, *My life work* (1903), pp. 148–51.

first invested George with menacing qualities,[78] and he made a handy brush to tar the Liberal party. In a memorable and oft-quoted phrase, Salisbury described his opponents as being 'on an inclined plane leading from the position of Lord Hartington to that of Mr. Chamberlain and so on to the depths over which Mr. Henry George rules supreme'.[79] Salisbury skilfully whipped up his supporters' fears in order to pull the Conservative party behind the London groundowners, of whom he became even more representative after the Whig defections of 1886. As the owner of land wedged between the old improvements on the Embankment and the projected new ones in the Strand (in the 1890s the Hotel Cecil was erected on this site, sold by then to the Duke of Norfolk),[80] he spoke frequently on local taxation, with passion and knowledge. The subject recurs in his major political speeches of the 1880s and 1890s: he disseminated the pure milk of Conservative doctrine, opposed the disturbance of existing contracts, damned the L.C.C. and all its works.[81] After 1886, in the years of their late-Victorian ascendancy, the Conservatives pressed the logic of their rating doctrine to the limits of practical politics. In the first years of the twentieth century the doctrine was exhausted, and this hastened the collapse of Conservative political hegemony. This course of events is the subject of the next two chapters.

[78]See *The Times*, 12 June 1882, 6c; 4 Sept. 1882, 5a–d, 7b (leader); 6 Sept. 1882, 6a (letter from H.G.), 7c–d, 3d (Leader on 'The nationalization of land').
[79]Speech at Dorchester, 16 Jan. 1884, quoted Garvin, *Chamberlain* (1932), i, 462.
[80]'London's largest hotel', *London*, 9 Jan. 1896, 23.
[81]Local taxation, see *The Times*, speech at Newport, 8 Oct. 1885, 7b; Nottingham, 27 Nov. 1889, 6e; Exeter, 3 Feb. 1892, 6c. Attacks on L.C.C., Queen's Hall speech, 8 Nov. 1894, 4b–c; Albert Hall, 17 Nov. 1897, 10b–c.

13

MR GOSCHEN'S FINANCE
1887–1892

Soon after taking office in 1885, the agrarians in Lord Salisbury's first administration made ready to gather the harvest sown eighteen years before. Michael Hicks Beach became Chancellor of the Exchequer and submitted a plan to impose a local income tax in relief of local rates.[1] A year of political turbulence followed. Randolph Churchill, who replaced Beach in the next Conservative government, held Gladstonian views on finance,[2] so it fell to G. J. Goschen, who was called in after Churchill's resignation, to assume his old mantle of rating reformer, this time in a Conservative Cabinet. In the process of changing his political stripes, Goschen substantially modified his local taxation doctrine as well, thereby demonstrating its party-political nature. The principle behind his new policy was to redress the alleged inequality of incidence between real and personal property, an inequality he had strongly denied eighteen years before. The method he chose resembled the one he had essayed in 1868 and 1871 – assigning national taxes to local authorities in relief of the rates. The first instalment was modest, £280,000 granted in 1887 in anticipation of larger measures.[3]

Goschen's budget of 1888 was, he said, as much a ratepayers' as a taxpayers' budget.[4] An attempt to raise some of the necessary revenue by a wheel and van tax and a duty on horses ended in farcical failure.[5] Probate duty was the other source. One-half was assigned to the Local Taxation Account. It was the one tax, Goschen said, which fell exclusively on realised personalty, 'and it was always the dream of [Conservative] reformers of local taxation to make personalty contribute thereto'.[6] Publicans' and other excise licences were also assigned to the local authorities, and in 1890 local councils were compensated for the loss of horse and cart taxes with a surcharge on beer and spirits, the

[1]PRO CAB 37/16/70, M. Hicks, Beach, 'Local taxation', 21 Dec. 1885.
[2]See Churchill, *Lord Randolph Churchill* (1907), ch. XVIII.
[3]B. Mallet, *British budgets 1887–88 to 1912–13* (1913), pp. 7–8.
[4]See 324 H.C. deb. 3 ser. 26 March 1888, 268–9, 287.
[5]F. M. L. Thompson, 'Nineteenth-century horse sense', *Econ. Hist. Rev.* 2 ser. 29 (1976), 67–9.
[6]324 H.C. deb. 3 ser. 26 March 1888, 288–9.

renowned 'Whiskey Money', some of which was made available for technical education. In five years, despite the abolition of most pre-existing grants, the support for local authorities doubled, from four million pounds in 1887 to eight millions in 1892.[7]

Not all the agrarians were satisfied that Goschen had undergone a genuine conversion. To allay their suspicions, he circulated in May 1889 a document which affirmed his new convictions. In correspondence with Henry Chaplin (President of the Board of Agriculture) that he laid before the Cabinet, Goschen wrote,

> We have parted with millions of Imperial money to keep our pledge to the ratepayers, of whom those connected with land were the most conspicuous in demanding this concession. ... All that I have said to you is not an *ex post facto* argument, used to meet the objections of yourself and your friends. I contend that my policy throughout my three Budgets has been favourable to the landed interest, and will prove to be so, when regarded as a whole ... There was a time – some twenty years ago, when I held and contended that land hardly contributed its fair share to the Imperial revenue; but I fully realize how great has been the change since then, and how the disastrous fall in the revenue derived from land has altered the proportion which it may be justly expected to bear both of local and national burdens. In all my financial policy I have borne this fact in mind.

Goschen concluded, however, with a warning. 'I do not think that any further diversions of Imperial resources to the relief of rates would be possible.'[8]

In Parliament as well, Goschen invoked the severity of the farming depression to justify the break with previous parsimony. 'Land', he said, 'has depreciated enormously in value'.[9] A new horizon of public expenditure was opened up by his grants. In them, the historian may recognise an unsuspected link between the agrarian depression of the 1880s and

---

[7]Mitchell and Deane, *Abstract*, p. 414. In addition to other sources cited, this chapter is based on a number of studies that were more or less polemical contributions to contemporary controversies. The first, second and last were London School of Economics monographs: (a) Cannan, *Hist. rates* (1912). (b) Grice, *National and local finance* (1910). (c) E. Hamilton, 'Memorandum on imperial relief of local burdens', Local taxation. R. com. memoranda; P.P. 1899 C.9528 XXXVI. (d) Mallet, *British budgets* (1913). (e) S. Webb, *Grants in aid: a criticism and a proposal* (1911).

[8]PRO CAB 37/24/25, [Correspondence between G. J. Goschen and H. Chaplin], 6, 7, and 9 May 1889, pp. 2, 5.

[9]324 H.C. deb. 3 ser. 26 March 1888, 289.

the British welfare state. In Protectionist countries such as Germany and (much later, in the 1930s) the United States, agriculturists were pioneer claimants of state aid.[10] Goschen's budgets conform to the same pattern.

Yet the device most favoured by Goschen, of assigning national revenues to local authorities, was originally designed by him (in the 1860s) to favour London and the large cities, and this bias was preserved in his new proposals: the distribution of the new grants was meant to conform with the distribution of indoor pauperism. This principle was not acceptable to the agrarians; on their demand, the grants were distributed on the same pattern as the Exchequer grants they replaced, thereby perpetuating the advantages of the countryside and gravely discriminating against the metropolis. Londoners of all political complexions never tired of complaining about this bias, and calculated London's loss in hundreds of thousands of pounds.[11] Even if London failed to get its just share, Disraeli's principle of recognition of urban claims for rate relief was still respected. Goschen rejected suggestions 'that this relief of local taxation is simply to be a gift to the squirearchy. On the contrary, a very large proportion of this relief will go to some of the poorest ratepayers in some of the poorest towns in the kingdom'.[12] Subsequent grants for technical education (1890) and free primary education (1891) were also distributed without an overt bias in favour of town or country.[13]

How did the Liberals react? A Treasury memorandum placed before Gladstone's cabinet in 1884 had made a strong argument in favour of state intervention: 'The national conscience', it stated, 'is more easily aroused than the local conscience'.[14] In Gladstone's view, however, it was the duty of the national conscience to protect the national purse. His observations were made on the occasion of Goschen's first budget in 1887, when Goschen introduced an increased road grant. Gladstone now repudiated his own road grant of 1882, saying it had been forced upon him. Gladstone's speech set the tone of Liberal reaction to Conservative

---

[10]H-J. Puhle, *Politische Agrarbewegungen in kapitalistischen Industriegesellschaften* (Göttingen, 1975), p. 12.

[11]*London*, leaders, 8 March and 19 April 1894, 143 and 239; 30 May 1895, 410; 16 Jan. 1896, 66; Hamilton, 'Memorandum' (P.P. 1899), p. 21; Haward, *L.C.C. from within* (1932), pp. 212–17.

[12]324 H.C. deb. 3 ser. 26 March 1888, 289.

[13]For the former, see p. 202, the latter, G. Sutherland, *Policy-making in elementary education* (Oxford, 1973), p. 287ff.

[14]CAB 37/13/48, R. G. C. Hamilton, 'State interference with industrial enterprise', 1 Dec. 1884, p. 2.

grant policy in the subsequent fifteen years, with the argument that grants-in-aid were merely doles for the landlords.[15]

At one level, Gladstone's strictures were merely ratepayers' cheese-paring elevated into national finance: grants supposedly undermined economic management and strict administration. They also raised an old question of principle: grants drawn from the Exchequer, said Gladstone, were ultimately a charge on labour, not on property. To evade this particular charge, Goschen made his grants out of the probate duties, which were undoubtedly a charge on personal capital. Now the Liberal Party had long been associated with the demand for the substitution of direct for indirect taxes; and for lower rates of tax on 'earned' and smaller middle-class incomes (the principles of 'differentiation' and 'graduation').[16] But Gladstone held back from committing for local purposes the most readily available source of additional revenue, the income tax.[17] Retrenchment was the only solution he offered for the crisis of local revenue. Both parties admitted that the ratepayer deserved relief.[18] One intractable problem remained: who pays? Liberals and Conservatives clung to comfortable doctrines that placed the sacrifice on the other side. Landowners were prepared to charge the capitalists, by way of the Exchequer; industrialists were perfectly willing to make landlords and rentiers bear the burden. As *theories* of incidence there was not, at this stage, much to choose between the two. In practice, however, Conservative doctrine was innovative and opened the way for novel modes of expenditure.

One instance of the contest between industrial capital and land-and-house owners in the late 1880s was the local taxation of machinery. Manufacturers and local Chambers of Commerce claimed that such rates were a tax on labour. House owners and town councillors replied that machinery itself was an enemy of labour. Feelings ran strong on Tyneside, with its extensive shipyards and works, and even more extensive workmen's dwellings. Any relief of the former, said opponents of the measure, would have to be borne by the latter. 'Is it reasonable to cry out for relief to a firm like Sir W. Armstrong's (whose £100 Shares are now quoted at £200) at the expense of the artisan, or the small shopkeeper who can scarcely make both ends meet?' asked a Gateshead Broadsheet.[19] After failing to settle the question in the courts, a private

[15]313 H.C. deb. 3 ser. 25 April 1887, 1810–11.
[16]F. Shehab, *Progressive taxation* (Oxford, 1953), pp. 90–6, 189–93.
[17]313 H.C. deb. 3 ser. 25 April 1887, 1813.
[18]*Ibid.*, 1810.
[19]Broadsheet signed by Henry Wallace, F.S.I., Gateshead, 17 March 1890, in

member's bill for de-rating machinery was introduced every year for a few years after 1887 and received a majority on second reading in 1890. But the status quo was too strong, and industrial demands were not satisfied until the inter-war industrial depression.[20]

Unequal incidence of death duties had been a standing Liberal grievance since the 1850s.[21] Probate duty on personal wealth was three per cent, the succession duty on realty a mere one per cent of a more lenient valuation.[22] In 1888 Goschen raised the succession duty to $1\frac{1}{2}$ per cent and assigned half the probate duty to local taxation, thereby 'equalising' the death duty on both forms of property for 'imperial' (i.e. national) purposes. This juggling of words still left the probate duty more than twice as high as succession duty. When the agrarians protested against the increase of succession duty, Goschen defended the higher tax as 'a most diplomatic act', that would pre-empt more radical reforms.[23]

Government expenditure had increased by almost a third in the twenty years after 1874. The increase (some £24 million) was almost equally divided between the Army and Navy on the one side, and education and grants-in-aid on the other.[24] The Liberals came in again in 1892, and when Harcourt began to frame his budget for 1894 it appeared that an additional £2.3 million would be required to pay for Lord Spencer's Naval programme. Armaments and local subsidies were equally repugnant to Liberals. They also upset the delicate balance of Gladstonian finance. An armament drive was more than the ageing and ailing Gladstone could countenance, and he resigned early in 1894. Sir William Harcourt was determined to make his budget for that year an

Walter Long Papers, Wilts. Record Office WRO 947/12, 'Rating of Machinery bill, 1890'. See also Rating of machinery bill. Sel. com. rep.; P.P. 1887 (231) XI; and Local taxation. R. com. final rep.; P.P. 1901 Cd. 638 XXIV, pp. 53–6.

[20] U. K. Hicks, *British public finances: their structure and development 1880–1952* (2nd impression, 1958), pp. 57–8; G. D. H. and M. I. Cole, *The condition of Britain* (1937), pp. 342–3.

[21] A succession duty on realty was introduced by Gladstone in his 1853 budget. See 125 H.C. deb. 3 ser. 18 April 1853, 1394–8.

[22] The valuation was a capital sum representing the value of an annuity yielding the actual rental for the life of the heir. Older heirs paid on less than the full market value and so did proprietors of land with low rentals in relation to the capital value, e.g. of building land ripe for development.

[23] CAB 37/24/25, G. J. Goschen, ['Succession duties'], 9 May 1889, p. 2. Another reason for agrarian displeasure was the transfer of two-thirds of the valuation from annuity to market value. See CAB 37/32/54, [G. J. Goschen], 'Attacks made on the finance of the government', n.d. [1892], pp. 13–14.

[24] Mallet, *British budgets* (1913), p. 78.

occasion, quite literally, for the settling of accounts between Liberalism
and the landed interest. Ignoring Lord Rosebery's remonstrances, he
proceeded to use the death duties for this purpose. All the different death
duties were assimilated into one, graduated from one to eight per cent, and
assessed on the market value of the estate. By blending all capital passing at
death in one common pool, Harcourt undid the purported basis of Goschen's
grants, namely the contribution of personalty to local taxation. The
agrarians were thoroughly aroused, and the incidence of taxation was once
again ventilated at great length in Westminster. Landowners predicted the
end of great houses and great estates; a campaign of obstruction was carried
out against the bill in Parliament, a campaign of propaganda outside.[25]
Harcourt gilded the pill with a concession on one of the agrarians' old
grievances (strongly expressed by urban proprietors as well); a deduction
from their income tax assessments for depreciation and maintenance, one-
sixth for houses, one-eighth for land.[26]

[25]A. G. Gardiner, *The life of William Harcourt* (1923), ii, ch. XVI.
[26]i.e., from schedule A assessments. Credit for the measure was claimed by the
United Property Owners and Ratepayers Association of Great Britain, of
which more below (chapter 18, p. 238ff). See 'The protection of property
owners', *EG* leader, 15 June 1901, 1045. Other claimants, see EG, 25 Dec. 1897,
1025 and 20 May 1899, 842.

14

DOLES FOR SQUIRE AND PARSON
1895–1902

By a quirk of political patronage, one of the officials who assisted in the preparation of Harcourt's death-duty reform was Sir Alfred Milner. After serving Goschen as private secretary between 1884 and 1889 (and a three-year stint in Egypt) the future pro-consul had been given a berth in the Inland Revenue, as Chairman of the Board. Milner had the fullest sympathy for the claims of the great landowners, but did not share their apocalyptic view of the new duties. He regarded the reform as a tactical concession, *reculer pour mieux sauter*; as he wrote to Harcourt's successor, Hicks Beach, in 1896,

> It always seemed to me that land suffered more from its inability to make good its just claims with regard to Local Taxation and Land Tax than it gained from clinging to its indefensible advantages in respect of Death Duties. They were invariably cast in its teeth whenever its advocates raised the question of the exceptional burdens on land, and being greatly exaggerated in the popular imagination created a prejudice which effectively prevented land from getting relief in the directions in which it is clearly entitled to it.[1]

This was no mere expression of sympathy. In the immediate aftermath of Harcourt's budget, Milner had been instrumental in getting an unprecedented subsidy for the landed interest.

Apart from the very modest equalisation and betterment bills in London, the Liberal ministry's record on local taxation had been almost purely negative.[2] Sir Henry Fowler, President of the Local Government Board, produced a report that merely reprinted and updated Goschen's effort of 1870. It reiterated Goschen's conclusions that rates had practically doubled in the previous two decades, but that increases had fallen on the towns, not on agriculture.[3] But wheat prices had touched

---

[1] PRO IR 74/2. M1.2, Sir Alfred Milner to the Chancellor of the Exchequer, 'Experience of the first year of the new estate duty', 12 Aug. 1896.
[2] The Fabian Society [S. Webb and G. B. Shaw], 'To your tents, oh Israel!', *Fortnightly Review* 60 (1893), 578, 580, 584–5, complained that even those modest measures had been obstructed by the government.
[3] Local taxation. H. H. Fowler. Report; P. P. 1893–4 (168) LXXXVII, p. li.

their lowest point for more than two centuries during the Liberal ministry and the government could not entirely ignore the extent of the farming depression. They chose a standard evasion and appointed a Royal Commission, which began to collect evidence on a grand scale. When the Unionists won the elections in July 1895 with a majority of 152, they proceeded to turn the Royal Commission to their own use. In the autumn of 1895 Milner was called to give evidence. His presentation was carefully prepared. It was designed to show not only that land was excessively encumbered with local taxation, but that it paid more than its fair share of *imperial* taxation as well. Out of every pound of income, he contended, the respective heads of property were liable as follows (in pence):[4]

Lands	19.42 d
Other rateable property (i.e., houses)	15.6 d
Non-rateable property	14.41 d
Weighted Average	15.426 d

In January 1896 the Commission presented a hasty interim Report, which recommended a remission of local rates on agricultural land.[5] The Report was followed in April by the Agricultural Land Rating Bill, which became the most controversial legislative measure of 1896.

The bill proposed to assess agricultural land at one-half of its rateable value for local taxation. The shortfall, estimated at £1.56 million, was to be made good by the Exchequer, and paid to local authorities from estate-duty revenues derived from personalty. Now that all death duties were pooled the formula was devoid of any practical meaning but it gave a doctrinal underpinning to the measure.[6] Agricultural depression was invoked as justification for the subsidy but the opponents of the bill refused to be taken in. They attacked it as an example of 'legalised robbery'.[7]

The bill, and the government's rating policy in the subsequent nine years, represented a new departure in Conservative rating doctrine. Disraeli's principle of equal consideration for town and country was

[4]See Bodl. Lib. Add. Milner Papers, Ms. Eng. Hist. c. 695, Manuscript tables for submission, 19 Dec. 1895, f. 16. For his evidence, see Agricultural depression. R. com. ev. Pt. IV: P. P. 1896 C. 8021 XVII, ques. 63,071–520 and 63,937–64,036; and App. A, XXXIII, pp. 576–86.
[5]Ag. depression. R. com. 2nd rep; P.P. 1896 C. 7981 XVI; summary of Milner's evidence, pp. 10–12.
[6]On this point, see 42 H.C. deb. 4 ser. 1 July 1896, H.H. Asquith, 452.
[7]41 H.C. deb. 4 ser. 24 May 1896, H. Lewis (a Welsh Liberal), 152.

discarded. Instead, grant funds were reserved for the Party's special clients; agriculture and the Church. William Harcourt observed quite accurately in debate:

Formerly your help was given to everybody alike, but the conception of picking out one class and giving to that class, and that alone, the assistance of the rates, never entered into the hearts of even the Tory party to conceive until they had a majority of 150. (Laughter and Cheers.)[8]

To grasp the prize Conservatives had to release the banner. For more than twenty-five years their appeals on behalf of ratepayers in general had attracted members from the other side of the House. Now the position was swiftly reversed. George Whiteley, Member for Stockport, led an urban Unionist revolt. Town members resented the bill for two reasons. First, they rejected the claims of agriculture, as an industry, for special relief. Some of their own industries were no less depressed. In Oldham alone, they claimed, there were 600,000 fewer spindles than three years before; in Lancashire, half-a-million less in one year. Secondly, the bill discriminated against local government in the towns. '. . . a gross and cruel act of injustice to the boards and urban districts of the country,' said Whiteley, 'Up to the present, all those grants in aid had been shared and distributed alike amongst all real-property owners'. He demanded a limit of two or three years on the subsidy and a strong Royal Commission of experts, otherwise urban support would be withdrawn.[9]

Henry Chaplin, the veteran agrarian, was President of the Local Government Board and in charge of the bill. In 1913 he recalled:[10]

it was met with so much opposition from the borough members in the House of Commons on both sides, quite irrespective of party ... that it was found to be impossible [despite an overwhelming Unionist majority] to carry that Bill without coming to an understanding with the borough members upon that question. In consequence the whole burden of that duty of coming to an understanding fell upon me, and after numerous conversations and discussions what happened was this. An understanding was come to by which the Bill should be made of a temporary character only, and it was made to last for five years ... Another concession was

[8]42 H.C. deb. 4 ser. 1 July 1896, 491.
[9]39 H.C. deb. 4 ser. 20 April 1896, G. Whiteley, 1327, 1329–31.
[10]PRO PRO 30/72/44, Minutes and reports of the Association of Municipal Corporations (1913), annual meeting, 28 May 1913, H. Chaplin's speech, p. 112. For his concession see 40 H.C. deb. 4 ser. 13 May 1896, 1295.

that a Royal Commission should be immediately appointed to inquire into and report upon all the grievances that the boroughs had to complain of ...

This was the origin of the Royal Commission on Local Taxation.

It was especially galling to town members that accommodation land, market gardens and even vacant building land should be relieved of half the rates. Asquith pointed out that there was no agrarian depression in the metropolis and its environs.[11] Urban land values were soaring. Vacant land, which Radicals had considered grievously under-taxed was now to receive even greater remissions.[12] The opposition attacked the bill with relish. William Harcourt recognised 'the same spirit which inspired the Corn Laws'.[13] Liberal parsimony also had its say. Henry Fowler, for example, detected 'the first step towards making the poor rate a national charge'.[14] Imputations of personal corruption were freely made. David Lloyd George gained notoriety for accusing Henry Chaplin of a personal interest. The President of the Local Government Board, he claimed, would gain £700 from the bill. Taking the capital value of their land, the Cabinet ministers as a group 'would benefit to the extent of two and a quarter millions by this Bill ("Hear, hear" and cries of "No!")'.

Having bled the farmer to the last drop of his blood, the landowners were now seeking to bleed the taxpayers, who were to be driven into the landlords' leech pond ... There were misery and actual hunger in the Welsh tin-plate districts, but where was the bill for the relief of the tin-plate industry?[15]

Not content with verbal protest, he refused to vacate the chamber for a division, and, with four like-minded comrades, was suspended from the House.[16]

Why did the Unionists embark on a policy of selective subsidies that threatened their urban support? One answer lies in the agrarian complexion of the ministry. Veteran agrarians held key positions: Hicks Beach was at the Treasury, Walter Long at the Board of Agriculture and Chaplin in the Local Government Board. Salisbury was not apathetic to their claims and A. J. Balfour was concerned about the Church and its schools. For politicians in intimate contact with rural life, carrying a

[11]42 H.C. deb. 4 ser. 1 July 1896, 457.
[12]See fig. 15.2 below, p. 226 for the actual impact of the Agricultural Rates Act.
[13]42 H.C. deb. 4 ser. 1 July 1896, 497.
[14]*Ibid.* 467.
[15]40 H.C. deb. 4 ser. 30 April 1896, 241–2.
[16]41 H.C. deb. 4 ser. 24 May 1896, 151ff.

burden of local paternalist obligation, the farming depression was a more pressing reality than urban suffering. Tithe rent charge, rural educational trusts and voluntary-school incomes were all linked with the price of corn, and the latter's decline exacerbated the hardships of the clergy and deepened the crisis of church schools in the countryside. Liberals also detected a reluctance among the agrarians to meet the crisis of rural education with support from local rates; many rural districts were not rated for education at all.[17]

Finally, the government laboured under a growing sense of financial stringency, created in no small part by the fiscal myopia of its Treasury advisers. Sir Edward Hamilton sounded the alarm in July 1895, before the new Cabinet had warmed their seats. Expenditure, he warned, was rising by leaps and bounds, and there was no ready source of additional revenue. 'Unless the brake is applied to the spending propensities of the State, the Government may ere long find themselves confronted with a choice of evils involving serious changes in our fiscal system, and consequently formidable Parliamentary difficulties.'[18] Hamilton's memorandum set the tone of Treasury advice over the subsequent ten years. By endorsing its tenets, Salisbury's Cabinet gradually abdicated their domestic political sovereignty.

Disraeli once said (in 1872, in a debate on local taxation) that 'The Consolidated Fund is spoken of as if it was to be shut up in a box and never used for any purpose, whereas our duty is to see that it is used for purposes conducive to the public welfare'. As late as 1895 A. J. Balfour printed at the head of his election card 'Poor Law and School Board rates to be charged on the Imperial Exchequer'.[19] Old-style Liberals might still fear that the Conservatives could evolve a 'national poor rate', and rank-and-file Unionists still hoped they would.[20] But the new policy of selective subsidies set a limit to the scope of Conservative doctrine as an instrument of political mobilisation. Old-Age Pensions, for example, were ruled out. Hamilton regarded both expenditure and taxation as positive evils; he exceeded his brief by repeatedly underscoring the

[17]See T. J. MacNamara, 'The local support of education', Nineteenth Century no. 238 (Dec. 1896), 919–24.
[18]PRO CAB 37/39/38, E. Hamilton, 'Some remarks on public finance', 24 July 1895, pp. 15–16.
[19]Disraeli, 210 H.C. deb. 3 ser. 16 April 1872, 1396–7. Balfour, see 107 H.C. deb. 4 ser. 6 May 1902, T. J. MacNamara, 905.
[20]Liberals – Henry Fowler, 42 H.C. deb. 4 ser. 1 July 1896, 467; others – see London, the L.C.C. Progressive weekly, 6 June 1895, 426; 4 July, 528; 12 Dec. 1082.

political dangers of additional taxation, but remained blind to the political and social advantages open to a spending government. In short, his fiscal advice was bad politics. But then, his political masters were under no obligation to take it: their Liberal successors knew how to get different advice when they wanted it.[21]

Except for a Utopian counsel of economy, Hamilton had nothing to offer but a choice of evils. Income tax at 3.3 per cent (8d in the £) he regarded as too high for a time of peace. His strictures on the fiscal potential of beer duty were animated by a deference to the brewing interest unbecoming in a civil servant.[22] He warned of alienating the working classes with food taxes, but the balance of his advice was subtly tilted in favour of the old heresy of import duties on sugar and corn.[23] His prediction of 'a gradual and insidious growth of public charges outstripping the natural increase of revenue'[24] was grotesquely falsified the very same year by an emergent budget surplus of some £5 million.[25] It was the prospect of this surplus that enabled the Conservatives to envisage aid for agriculture and the voluntary schools *without* any recourse to new taxation.[26]

Conservative partiality for the Church was the source of their second special subsidy. Three out of five primary schoolchildren in England and Wales were educated in voluntary schools, a vast majority of them in Church of England schools largely unsupported by local rates. These schools, which had a virtual monopoly in most rural areas and a solid hold in many urban ones, fared badly in comparison with rate-supported board schools: expenditure on a scholar in the former was an average £1 18s. 11d in 1895, in the latter £2 10s. 2d.[27] The financial crisis of the Church and the depression in rural districts added to the voluntary schools' troubles.

The religious and educational ramifications of this problem were manifold, but they lie beyond the scope of this study; the education

[21]Compare the two Treasury memoranda by W. Blain, CAB 37/66/61, 'Direct and indirect taxation', May 1903 (printed 25 Sept.) and CAB 37/87/22, 'Supertax', 26 Feb. 1906.

[22]CAB 37/39/38, E. Hamilton, 'Some remarks on public finance', 24 July 1895, p. 9.

[23]*Ibid.* pp. 10, 13, 15.

[24]*Ibid.* p. 15.

[25]CAB 37/40/67, E. Hamilton, 'How to dispose of the surplus of 1895–6', 31 Dec. 1895. The actual surplus was £5.8 million.

[26]The Queen's speech, 37 H.C. deb. 4 ser. 11 Feb. 1896, 5–6; also Financial statement, M. Hicks Beach, 39 H.C. deb 4 ser. 16 April 1896, 1055, 1077–84.

[27]Sutherland, *Education* (1973), tables 1 and 5, pp. 350, 356.

problem impinged heavily on Conservative rating policy. Aid for education was promised in election manifestoes in 1895, and reiterated in the subsequent Queen's speech. An education bill introduced in 1896 coupled a measure of re-organisation, with state subsidies for voluntary schools. It raised too many passions, both fiscal and religious, and had to be abandoned. In October 1896 Cabinet was again searching for a way to support the voluntary system. A general subvention for all schools was considered and rejected, in favour of a subsidy as deftly selective as the Agricultural Rates Act: a grant of £600,000, and de-rating, for voluntary schools, and another £100,000 or so for the most necessitous Board Schools.[28] The thrust of the bill was again unmistakeable. Sir John Gorst, in charge of the Bill, confided to Beatrice Webb: 'we are on the eve of a crisis: there will be a revolt of the urban Tories. They can't go on watching their seats being taken from under them. As for social reform: all chance of that is gone'.[29]

'We have a government,' said Fletcher Moulton in the Finance Bill debate of 1899, 'which dare not tax the poor and will not tax the rich'.[30] The point was well made. By the end of the 1890s the policy of selective subsidies was reaching its practical limit. The Royal Commission on Local Taxation became the instrument of a third substantial dole. Cabinet decided, and the Commissioners agreed, to recommend a rebate of one-half the rates for the resident parsons of the Church of England, on the lines of the Agricultural Rates Act.[31] But the Chancellor's self-imposed tax constraints meant there was little money available, even for the most deserving of the government's clients. While expressing his sympathy with the parsons' plight, 'Black Michael' refused to make a grant for their relief. Notwithstanding the Agricultural Rates Act, he informed the Cabinet,

> I submit that such a grant would be a most dangerous precedent – for it is perfectly possible that in the course of the inquiry some other classes of ratepayers may establish a case of over-assessment under the present system – and would have an irresistible claim to be aided in the same way.

Instead, he argued, their grievances should be met 'by readjustment

[28]CAB 37/43/44, A. J. Balfour, [Education bill: grants-in-aid to voluntary schools], 8 Nov. 1896 (and subsequent memos). These proposals were enacted as the Voluntary Schools Act and the Necessitous Board Schools Act, 1897.
[29]Beatrice Webb's diary, 3 Feb. 1897 (*Our partnership* (1948), p. 137).
[30]Mallet, *British budgets* (1913), p. 143.
[31]See chapter 6, pp. 92–3.

between the ratepayers, not at the cost of the Exchequer'.[32] In other words, the clergy should be relieved locally, at the ratepayers' expense. Throwing down the gauntlet to the ratepayer (not least the agrarian ratepayer) was an act of parsimony bordering on political foolhardiness. Hicks Beach was overruled; but the principle was to re-appear, as the financial basis of the great Education Bill of 1902.

The South African war belied the Chancellor's pessimism˙ and, paradoxically, reinforced it. An ample margin was revealed for new borrowing, and for increasing the income tax, but the obligations of war ruled out any additional subsidies for voluntary schools. Sir Robert Morant's conversation with Joseph Chamberlain on 12 December 1901 is revealing:

Chamberlain: 'Why not do as was done in 1870, and promise additional grants to Voluntary Schools out of State funds, thus avoiding recourse to the rates?'

Morant: ˙'Because your War has made further recourse to State grants impossible'.[33]

On 31 January 1901 Edward Hamilton produced another alarmist memorandum, modelled very closely on his document of 1895. Its velvet prose was still enthralled by the mirage of retrenchment. It was 'impolitic' to interfere with the manufacture of brewers, who were so powerful a class; death duties 'are quite as high as they would be tolerated'. Income tax it was dangerous to increase. In his judgement it was more acceptable to 'broaden the base of taxation', i.e. to tax the consumption of the working classes.[34] This expert advice was really no more than an expression of political preferences. In embracing 'a broader base of taxation', Hicks Beach also embraced the political consequences. Sugar duties were introduced in 1901 and in October of that year Customs and Excise submitted an elaborate plan for taxing imported meat and corn.[35] The budget of 1902 incorporated a registration duty on wheat. Recall (p. 167) that Conservative rating doctrine had been formulated in response to the repeal of the Corn Laws; that it was a demand for compensation to landowners for the loss of protection. No wonder then that when Conservatives decided that their rate-relief policy

[32]CAB 37/49/21, M. Hicks Beach, 'Rating of tithe rent-charge', 14 March 1899, pp. 1, 5.

[33]B. M. Allen, *Sir Robert Morant* (1934), p. 168, quoted in Amery, *Chamberlain* (1969), v, 87.

[34]CAB 37/56/14, E. Hamilton, 'The financial problem', 31 Jan. 1901, pp. 3, 10–14.

[35]CAB 37/58/93, G. L. Ryder, J. A. Kempe and R. T. Prowse, 'Extension of the basis of indirect taxation', 7 Oct. 1901.

was exhausted, they looked to protection once again as a source for State subsidies. In a curiously symmetrical historical trajectory, Conservative doctrine relapsed into protection when its momentum was lost.

Looking forward to 1902, Hicks Beach sounded a note of despair. He demanded from his Cabinet colleagues 'a real check on the continued increase of ordinary expenditure ...' Education estimates had grown by £2.5 million since 1895–6. 'This might, at any rate, warn us against imposing new liabilities on the Exchequer for University, secondary or commercial education.' 'With regard to the large increase in payments to local taxation,' he continued, 'I will only say that I think we are not now in a position to hold out hopes of additional grants from the Exchequer either in aid of rates, or for old-age pensions'.[36] This was the fiscal background of the 1902 Education bill. The Budgets of 1901 and 1902 started the Unionist Party down the politically disastrous road to tariff reform. The Education bill was this policy's counterpart in the sphere of local taxation.

Rather than allow the church schools to be extinguished, Balfour determined to unload them on the ratepayers.[37] It was the local equivalent of 'broadening the base of taxation'. To have given special grants to church schools (in 1897) was bad enough. To place them on the rates was politically much worse, for it forged a strong popular coalition against the government. '[A] Bill to put Christianity on the rates',[38] cried Lloyd George, and the moribund Nonconformist conscience awoke from its slumbers. The controversy restored the Welshman's reputation, and he made the most of the religious issue.[39] Urban school boards were aroused by the threat to their independence, and the projected education authorities, the urban and county councils, viewed with dismay a new obligation designed to increase the education rate by up to 45 per cent at a stroke.[40] Country members were aghast at having to pay education rates for the first time.

A Devon member described grass-roots Unionist defections;[41] the member for South-East Essex led Conservatives voting against the bill.[42] A massive deputation waited on Balfour on 15 June 1902, and on 23

[36]CAB 37/58/109, M. Hicks Beach, [Financial difficulties: appeal for economy in estimates], Oct. 1901, pp. 3, 5, 7.
[37]113 H.C. deb. 4 ser. 2 June 1902, 1149.
[38]114 H.C. deb. 4 ser. 11 Nov. 1902, 665.
[39]See e.g. 107 H.C. deb. 4 ser. 8 May 1902, 1098ff.
[40]107 H.C. deb. 4 ser. 6 May 1902, T. J. MacNamara, 905–7.
[41]113 H.C. deb. 4 ser. 2 June 1902, G. Lambert, 1147.
[42]114 H.C. deb. 4 ser. 11 Nov. 1902, Major F. C. Rasch, 667.

June he finally backed down and promised a grant of £900,000.[43] Michael Hicks Beach resigned in disgust.[44] The grant was mainly intended as compensation to local authorities for the prospective loss of voluntary contributions. In the end, the government was forced to find as much as £1.2 million.[45] It now bore almost one-half of the cost; London Radicals and the agrarians both demanded that the government assume three-quarters, but Balfour declined such an open-ended commitment.[46] Further expansion would fall on the local authorities. Generous financing at the outset might have defused the bill. Balfour's concessions came too late, however: the Liberal party was given a tremendous boost, which started it down the road to 1906.

Much has been made of the Fabian support for Balfour's education bill. Sidney Webb had been instrumental in constructing the London County Council's system of secondary and higher education, which earned him a measure of ill-will on his previous stamping ground, the London School Board. His sponsorship of Balfour's bill, which proposed to end the independence of school boards and transfer their work to county councils alienated many of his old allies in London's Liberal party.[47] Of greater significance however than those sectarian jealousies was the convergence of men of the left and of the right to realise a possibility which had been latent in Disraeli's rate support doctrine, i.e. to join together to introduce an étatiste measure.

At a London School of Economics lecture in 1899 Webb praised grants-in-aid as a unique invention of the British genius, an excellent combination of carrot and stick. Webb's conversion to this Tory doctrine marked another step away from the vestiges of his early Radicalism and the start of a strong commitment to government grants as deliberate instruments of social administration, thus presaging the long trend of social policy in twentieth-century Britain.

No subject [he said] except, perhaps, war, so annoyed Mr Gladstone as that of grants-in-aid, and he consistently fulminated

[43] 109 H.C. deb. 4 ser. 23 June 1902, 1401–7.
[44] V. Hicks Beach, *The life of Sir Michael Hicks Beach* (1932), ii, 170, 171ff. He was also influenced by pressure to increase Naval expenditure.
[45] 115 H.C. deb. 4 ser. 2 Dec. 1902, Walter Long, 955.
[46] 114 H.C. deb. 4 ser. 12 Nov. 1902, Henry Chaplin's amendment, 797ff. Government grants covered one-half (50.8%) of the cost of primary education in 1904–5, the first year of the full application of the Act in England and Wales. See Education rates. Dept. com rep.; P.P. 1907 Cd. 3313 XXI, p. 15.
[47] See e.g. B. Simon, *Education and the labour movement* (1965), pp. 203–7, 225–35; McBriar, *Fabian socialism* (1962), pp. 215–17.

against them as iniquitous, and 'a positive excitement to extravagance'. What he did not realise is that sometimes it is desirable to encourage expenditure.[48]

In this, as in so much else, he could feel the future in his bones.

[48]S. Webb, 'The evolution of local government – VI', *Mun. Jnl. & London*, 8 Dec. 1899, 1313. The centrality of grants-in-aid in Webb's thinking on social administration is further discussed in chapter 23, p. 386.

Part IV

MUNICIPAL ENTERPRISE AND PRIVATE CAPITAL

15

TOWNS AGAINST THE TORIES
1890–1902

I

The influence of town governments in national affairs was enhanced in the 1880s by their new responsibilities. In opting for selective subsidies in 1896 Salisbury's Cabinet effectively disowned the towns. This section describes the urban reaction, its economic motivations and political consequences. To begin with, the urban interest needs to be defined. In the 1880s local affairs were still managed by a plurality of overlapping elected authorities, falling under three main heads: Poor Law Unions, School Boards and municipal authorities with responsibility, respectively for welfare, education and the urban infrastructure. Division of labour was not so clear-cut in practice, and political fragmentation militated against efficient administration.[1] The multiplication of authorities was sometimes carried to absurd lengths. Goschen, who had laboured long to reduce it, used to tell how one of his suburban properties, assessed at £1,100, attracted eighty-seven separate rate demand notes in one year.[2]

Of the three sets of institutions, municipal corporations were the main repositories of civic identity. Town halls gave a symbolic focus to the Victorian city and town councils monopolised the rituals of mayoralty and conducted the main business of civic deliberation. As effective proprietors of streets, sewers, buildings, gas, water and transport systems, in short, as owners of public capital, the councillors held greater assets and assumed greater liabilities than other local bodies. By the 1880s they had long displaced the Poor Law guardians as the largest local spenders.[3] The obligation to provide massive fixed capital placed great financial responsibility on the council leadership. It also presented them with levers of power, patronage and prestige. Great aqueducts, broad

[1] Often one or another of the elements was missing, and municipal functions were undertaken by more than one authority, e.g. sanitary commissioners, improvement boards etc. See G. C. Brodrick, 'Local government in England' in *Local government and taxation in the United Kingdom*, ed. J. W. Probyn (1882), pp. 8–87.
[2] G. J. Goschen, 'On local rates' (n.d. ?1882) [leaflet, Bodleian Library].
[3] Mitchell and Deane, *Abstract*, pp. 416, 420.

thoroughfares, libraries and University Colleges reflected greater glory than primary schools and work-houses. Large funds were handled, important contracts awarded, great works undertaken. At a Birmingham banquet in 1896 Joseph Chamberlain delivered a set speech:

> I have always compared the work of a great corporation like this to that of a joint-stock company, in which the directors are represented by the Councillors of the City, in which the shareholders are every ratepayer, and in which the dividends are to be found in the increased health and wealth and happiness and education of the community.[4]

Corporations were great capitalists and gave rise to a new bourgeoisie of contractors and civic servants. Of the latter Chamberlain said, 'There is no economy more disastrous than the economy which endeavours to make cheeseparing savings in the remuneration of men whose services may be priceless'.[5]

The urban interest was dependent on Parliament for both legal and financial powers, and it crystallised as a Parliamentary pressure group. An Association of Municipal Corporations was formed in 1872 (henceforth A.M.C.).[6] Four or five times a year the Council of the Association assembled in London. Most of the representatives were Town Clerks: salaried, not elected officers; a minority were mayors or councillors. Once a year (from the late 1890s, twice) the delegates (usually town clerks, mayors or councillors) of more than a hundred urban councils would get together for a week-end, usually in the London Guildhall. By 1895 the A.M.C. embraced all but an insignificant minority of the urban councils in Britain; it maintained a permanent office, disposed of some £1000 a year, and wielded considerable influence in Parliament.[7] Urban interests were deliberated and articulated in other

[4]*London*, 16 July 1896, 679; almost identical with his 1892 statement quoted by A. Briggs, *History of Birmingham* (1952), ii, 74, whose preceding pages are most illuminating on the rise of municipal mentality.
[5]*London*, 16 July 1896, 679.
[6]A.M.C. records were bound into annual volumes of printed and duplicated minutes, reports, circulars etc., now deposited in PRO class PRO 30/72. Volumes are paginated but not always consistently. I have tried to use the most helpful form of reference.
[7]PRO 30/72/24 A.M.C. (1895), Ann. meeting Pres. address, 22 March 1895, pp. 1–2. Funds available to the A.M.C. were intermediate between those commanded by the land reform groups (the English Land Restoration League disposed of £200–£250 a year in the late 1880s) and those of the London Municipal Society, the Conservative pressure group (£2,476 official 'above board' expenditure, 1895–6; see Ward, 'Land reform' (1976), pp. 221, 238 and K. Young, *Local politics and the rise of party* (Leicester, 1975), p. 74.)

places as well, at the annual central Poor Law conferences, for example. But the A.M.C. was the representative voice of urban collective capital, and is therefore the natural vehicle for its history.

The A.M.C. possessed a leader of exceptional calibre. Sir Albert Kaye Rollit, LL.D. (Lond.) (1842–1922) hailed from Hull, where he was a shipowner and solicitor, and the town's mayor between 1883 and 1885. Rollit was a powerhouse of energy and activity, a compulsive collector of offices, accomplishments and honours. In 1886 he was elected Conservative MP for South Islington, which seat he continued to hold for twenty years. In London he developed a thriving legal practice, sat on the Council of the Law Society and served as its President, and founded and presided over the Associated Chambers of Commerce. A list of his multifarious activities and interests could easily fill a whole page. In photographs Rollit appears as a man of striking presence: stout, bull-necked, bald-headed; his pointed mustachioes gave him the appearance of a Balkan warlord. He was a tireless politician and in 1889, Chairman of the National Union of Conservative Associations. To this central organ of Unionism he presented a well formulated philosophy of Conservative pre-emption. 'The statesman's duty', he said, 'is to effect peacefully what may otherwise become a social revolution'.[8] In 1888 Rollit was elected Vice-President of the Association of Municipal Corporations and two years later he rose to the Presidency, a position from which he exercised a dominating influence on municipal politics for the subsequent sixteen years. He was an ardent municipal capitalist, and cultivated at the A.M.C. a creed of 'municipalism', a gospel of civic spending that ran counter to the orthodoxy of retrenchment and economy.

Rollit was a powerful public speaker, and his orations make a memorable record of the municipal cause in its formative years. Like Sidney Webb, he was a prophet of welfare capitalism. Unlike Webb, who was an unwitting prophet, Rollit preached collectivism as a safeguard, not an alternative, for private property. So long as the individual remained insecure, he insisted, property could not be safe.

> Men must even meet Socialism itself [he said]. It stalks abroad, and we must look it in the face – not shirk it as a spectre only to be

[8]Besides Rollit's record of activity at the A.M.C. and the Law Society this paragraph is derived from T. T. Wildridge, *An account of the honorary freedom of the town ... of Hull* (Hull, 1891), pp. 11–26; *Our shipping headlights* (Hull, 1900), pp. 148–9; H. O. Horne, *A history of savings banks* (1947), p. 247 et seq.; *Who's who* and *Who was who*; the quote is from The National Union, *Speech by Sir A. K. Rollit ... on organization and social reform*, 26 Nov. 1889, p. 8.

avoided. In its one sense of the State, Municipality or public bodies, doing what men cannot do, or do so well, for themselves, its principle has been adopted in many of those statutes which are our own work, and of which our party has no reason to be ashamed.[9]

A man of humanitarian values and humanistic education, Rollit liked to evoke the analogy of ancient Rome, 'the eternal city which survives not only in its literature and its laws, but also in those great public works which are your business today,' as he said to the assembled municipal officers, '– its streets, its pavements, its aqueducts, its cloaca, and its catacombs'.[10] Public Works were not merely prudent responses to necessity; they were an embodiment of virtue, and would advertise virtue to posterity. 'And if it be said that such a programme is socialistic,' he said in another speech, 'I reply that, as in all else, there is both good and bad in Socialism; that the adoption of what is good is the best preventive of what is bad'.[11]

The essence of 'municipalism' was expressed in a speech delivered by Rollit in 1898 at the annual meeting of the A.M.C. It was the antithesis of the voguish 'individualism' propagated by Spencer, Mallock and Dicey, and particularly by the Liberty and Property Defence League on behalf of business, banking and property.

> The necessary complement of Individualism [he said] is, for political and social stability and safety, some wise Collectivism, and municipal channels are best for this purpose. *The strongest security for person and property is to make, as far as possible, life worth living for all*, and there is still truth, and as much truth as ever, in the answer of the Greek sage to the question, 'What is the ideal State?' – 'One in which the rich are not too rich nor the poor too poor.' Danger, political and social, still lurks in each of these extremes, and they may best be modified by a wise and enterprising appreciation and application of the municipal spirit. (Cheers).[12]

How to adjust the sacrifices to the benefits: that was the fundamental dilemma of urban finance. The balance of urban opinion concurred in refusing to leave paving, sewering and lighting to the goodwill of

[9]National Union, *Speech by ... Rollit* (26 Nov. 1889), p. 9.
[10]PRO 30/72/25 A.M.C. (1896) Pres. address, p. 62.
[11]A. K. Rollit, *Municipalism* (an address to the ... British Institute of Public Health at Hull, 9 Aug. 1895), p. 10.
[12]PRO 30/72/27, A.M.C. (1898) Pres. address, 26 March 1898, pp. 64–5; italics added. For 'individualism' see p. 41.

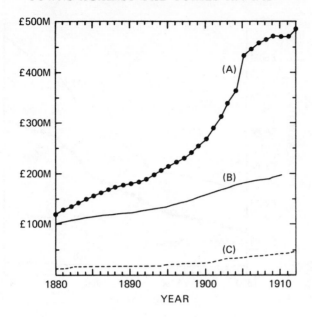

Fig. 15.1. *Local debt and non-farm rental in England and Wales, 1880–1912.*

(A) outstanding loans, urban; (B) annual non-farm rental; (C) out-standing loans, rural and mixed rural and urban. Sources: (A), (C), as Fig. 15.2; (B), Offer, 'Ricardo's paradox', app. II, col. 3.

individual landowners.[13] So long-term capital formation had to be financed by short-tenure ratepayers for the ultimate gain of the permanent landlords. The towns were not deterred: they borrowed and invested, and the rates increased inexorably. But local politics and local improvements were fouled by ratepayers' economy movements, which were given effective powers of obstruction by the Borough Funds Act of 1872. Single ratepayers could and did force a poll of the ratepayers on municipal expenditure bills, at considerable expense to local authorities.[14] The Act was a standing complaint at the A.M.C. and appeared on its agenda almost every year, but the corporations' Parliamentary power was not sufficient to effect its repeal. A rate on

[13]PRO 30/72/9, A.M.C. (1880–1), 'Private improvement expenses', 9 Aug. 1880, pp. 242–7. Same title, 7 Jan. 1881, pp. 247–9 (circulars by the Secretary, A. G. Pritchard).

[14]The Act did provide a deterrent and an occasional check to municipal maladministration. Dr R. M. Pankhurst used it in the 1890s to defeat a Manchester sewage scheme (S. Pankhurst, *The Suffragette movement* (1932), pp. 143–5).

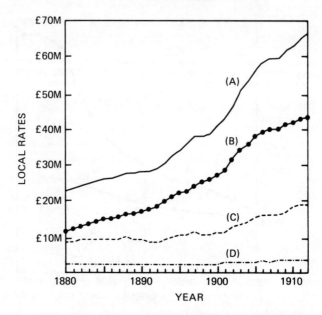

Fig. 15.2. *Local rates in England and Wales, 1880–1912.*

(A), all rates; (B), urban rates; (C), mixed rural and urban rates; (D), rural rates. *Sources: (1880–91)* Local taxation. H. H. Fowler. Report; P.P. 1893–4(168) LXXXVII, app. A, table I, pp. 6–7 and app. C, table VII, pp. 138–9. *(1892–1900)* Local govt. bd. annual rep. (P.P.). *(1901–12)* Local taxation returns; P.P. Pt. VII (occasionally Pt. VIII), 'Summary and index'.

owners, general or particular, was an enticing release from the dilemma. It was attempted, as we have seen, by the Metropolitan Board of Works, and carried further by Liverpool Corporation in the late 1860s.[15] Improvement rates were levied in particular streets, and incorporated into Housing Acts. A practical expression of this demand were the London and Manchester betterment bills of 1890, 1893 and 1894 (p. 194).

Fig. 15.1 and 15.2 illustrate the constraints of local finance. Fig. 15.1 compares the urban debt (A) with the rental income from urban property (B). The magnitude of the debt is an indicator of urban enterprise. The urban debt grew from a little more than the annual rental income to more than twice its size in 1912. In other words, the mounting of the debt far exceeded the growth of urban property yields. Incidentally, this figure also shows that the rural and semi-rural debt (C) was a very small

[15]p. 172 and R.H.I. Palgrave, *Local taxation* (1871), p. 68.

fraction of the whole. Not all the debt was contracted in the formation of new capital. Much was incurred in the purchase of private companies at the end of their concessionary periods. The massive leap in curve (A) in 1904–5 represents the transfer of the London water system from private companies to the Metropolitan Water Board.

Fig. 15.2 shows the increase of rates. Urban rates (B) grew in the same way as the urban debt, demonstrating the close connection between the two. *From property owners' point of view the increase of rates was almost entirely 'onerous' (see p. 164) because it failed to increase property yields.* Ratepayers, however, experienced a constant increase in their obligations.[16] Municipal enterprise was blunted on the one side by the government, which became reluctant to authorise new loans, and on the other by the ratepayers, who had to repay them. Rural and semi-rural rates did not grow in the same way, but generated the same complaints, that the rate burden was 'onerous' since rural and semi-rural ratepayers paid a large share of the aggregate rate but only partook in a small part of the new capital formed. A small dent in the overall growth of rates (A) after 1897 marks the impact of the Agricultural Rates Act (some £1.3M, only about one-quarter of which went to purely rural authorities).

The majority of a special A.M.C. committee endorsed the London and Manchester betterment bills in 1894 as 'fair and reasonable proposals'. A minority went further and proposed a scheme for assessing houses and sites separately, the latter at market (i.e. capital) value.[17] Council adopted the majority view and reserved the question of Land Value Rating for further consideration.[18] Taken for pragmatic reasons and not out of political idealism, this temperate decision was more significant than any number of land reform leaflets, because it spoke for the concensus of urban officials possessing a broad local mandate. It was part of the towns' struggle for greater control over their own affairs; for release from dependence on Parliament for their powers and from the expensive compensation for compulsory purchase which Parliament specified. In 1895 Rollit demanded a wide extension of local jurisdiction under which, among other benefits, 'the municipalities would soon practically solve for themselves the question of Betterment and Worsement much better than Parliament has yet shown its ability to do so; which would remove the

---

[16]Not all the social gain represented by the debt was attributable to rate expenditure; some was created by self-financing 'trading' services such as trams and gasworks.

[17]PRO 37/72/23, A.M.C. (1894), 'Betterment and ground values. Special committee report', p. 8.

[18]*Ibid.*, Council minutes, 14 June 1894, p. 58.

great obstacle to public improvements'.[19] But for two more years the urban interest held back and left the field to the single-taxers; the question was held in suspension while urban resentment mounted. It re-emerged in 1897, gathered momentum in 1898 and gradually swept the municipal movement into a strong antagonism to the Unionist government. The reasons were complex, political as well as economic. Let us consider the politics first.

II

In January 1896 the Earl of Onslow, leader of the Moderate [Conservative] Party on the London County Council, conducted a deputation of vestrymen to see the Chancellor and plead for a fairer distribution of Exchequer grants.[20] *London*, the Progressive weekly, met the Agricultural Land Rating and the Education bills with a leader 'A Raid on London'. 'Three hundred thousand pounds a year is the amount which London will have to contribute to the agricultural interest,' it wrote, '... London is already over-taxed in comparison with the rest of the country ...'[21] At the A.M.C. annual meeting, Sir Albert Rollit expressed similar sentiments.[22] We have already documented how urban Unionist opposition led to the appointment of a Royal Commission (p. 210). The very existence of the London County Council was threatened by Unionist policy in London, which began to strive in 1894 for the devolution of Metropolitan government to municipal boroughs.[23] As the L.C.C. election of 1898 began to approach, Lord Salisbury renewed his attacks on the competence and integrity of the Progressive leadership on the Council.[24] Dr T. J. MacNamara, a schoolteacher and leading left-winger in the Progressive Party, unerringly exposed the purpose behind 'tenification', the plan to devolve London government to ten separate boroughs.

What is at the bottom of Lord Salisbury's proposal to dismember London? It was not so much to increase the dignity of local authorities as to enable the rich to shake off their obligations to the poor. The rich with their few needs want to cut themselves adrift

[19]Rollit, *Municipalism* (1895), p. 5.
[20]*London*, 16 Jan. 1896, 66.
[21]*London*, 23 April 1896, 393.
[22]PRO 30/72/25, A.M.C. (1896), Pres. address, p. 61.
[23]See Young, *Local politics* (1976), ch. 2.
[24]See his speech at the Albert Hall, *The Times*, 17 Nov. 1897, 10.

from the poor parishes with their low rateable value and many needs.[25]

In October 1897 the Progressives warmed for the fight by raising the banner of taxation of land values (abbreviated in this study to TLV). After a series of motions and debates the L.C.C. approved an 'owner's tax' by a large majority, despite the near-equality of the parties on the Council.[26] The offensive at Spring Gardens (the location, adjoining Trafalgar Square, of L.C.C. offices) was backed up by a grass-roots agitation. One such event was reported in *London* on 9 December 1897. It conformed to a general pattern: the initiative coming, perhaps, from land-reform militants, but attracting broad support for a standard proposal on the general lines of Fletcher Moulton's scheme; without, however, any suggestion of penal or extraordinary levels of land value taxation. A conference was convened under the auspices of the Land Nationalisation Society, 'representing all shades of opinion on land reform'. After a long discussion standard resolutions were agreed: a separate valuation of land and houses, based on 4 per cent of the capital value, with an option for compulsory purchase by the town at the same valuation. Steps to be taken to secure the unearned increment, and working-class housing to be the first charge on the receipts.[27] The *Estates Gazette* saw red; 'it is, of course, impossible to be angry with people who are obviously suffering from mental aberration . . .'[28]

TLV was much bandied about in the L.C.C. election which re-established the Progressive majority in 1898.[29] In the next two years a rash of TLV resolutions and conferences swept the country. A separate wave of agitation originated in Glasgow, where the Council also committed itself to a TLV bill in October 1897. Delegates from 150 rating authorities were sent to Bradford in January 1898 to draft a TLV petition to Parliament. Battersea vestry convened 100 delegates in March.[30] A resolution by the Cardiff Poor Law Union in September was endorsed by 95 Boards of Guardians and the Land Law Reform Association held a large conference at the Westminster Palace Hotel in

[25] At a TLV meeting; see *London*, 9 Dec. 1897, 963. This aspect is elaborated in 'London government bill', *Mun. Jnl. & London*, 31 March 1899, 395.
[26] L.C.C. Proceedings, reported in *London*, 7 Oct. 1897, 813; 21 Oct. 846; 18 Nov. 917–18; 9 Dec. 965.
[27] *London*, 9 Dec. 1897, 963.
[28] 'Land restorers or land grabbers?' (leader), *EG*, 8 Jan. 1898, 56.
[29] See e.g. 'Make it hot for them' (leader), *EG*, 5 Feb. 1898, 218; 'The Moderates and their friends' (leader), *London*, 10 Feb. 189, 88.
[30] Peacock, 'Land reform' (1961), p. 104ff.

December.[31] In October 1899 216 delegates from 112 local authorities came to Glasgow and a well-attended conference took place in Huddersfield in November;[32] the list is not exhaustive. Large numbers of municipal officials, councillors and MPs attended such conferences along with delegates from land-reform societies, trades unions, the co-operative movement and a miscellany of progressive groups.

The Association of Municipal Corporations took up TLV almost simultaneously with the L.C.C. in October 1897 and adopted it unanimously in the following March. It did not enter into details but asserted that 'it is urgent to provide some means by which owners of land (whether occupied or vacant) shall contribute directly to the local revenue'.[33] Its officers struggled to prevent the identification of TLV with Liberal politics in order to canvass the widest possible support.[34] But the rising men of the Liberal front bench (including Grey, L. Harcourt and Campbell-Bannerman) frequently sent their blessings.[35] In two long Parliamentary debates, in February 1899 and May 1900, Asquith, Haldane and Lloyd George placed themselves in the van of the municipal agitation and claimed it for their own.[36]

Even bastions of reaction were becoming restive. One of the oldest and strongest ratepayers' associations in the country, the Liverpool Property Owners' Association, flirted with the idea of leasehold enfranchisement, and for two years running, gave a hearing to a speaker who suggested the taxation of Lord Derby's ground rents.[37] In January 1899 Bradford Corporation decided to append a TLV clause to its annual bill.[38] Manchester Council followed; Glasgow and Salford actually introduced such a clause.[39] Liverpool came over in 1901.[40] The A.M.C. re-affirmed

---

[31]*London*, 15 Sept. 1898, 597; Land Law Reform Association, *The rating of ground values* (Conference ... 8 Dec. 1898), pp. 1–3.

[32]*Mun. Jnl. & London*, 27 Oct. 1899, 1169; *Property Market Review*, 2 Dec. 1899, 1019.

[33]PRO 30/72/26, A.M.C. (1897), General meeting, 22 Oct. 1897, p. 2; quote from PRO 30/72/27, A.M.C. (1898) Annual meeting, 26 March 1898, p. 40.

[34]J. T. Woodward, Vice-President of the A.M.C. at the Huddersfield TLV conference, *Property Market Review*, 24 Nov. 1899, 1019; PRO 30/72/29, A.M.C. (1900), Proceedings of the annual meeting, 31 March 1900, pp. 61–2.

[35]See e.g. Land Law Reform Assoc., *Rating* (Conference, Dec. 1898), p. 4; *Estates Chronicle*, 15 April 1898, p. 5, speech by Asquith.

[36]See 66 H. C. deb. 4 ser. 10 Feb. 1899, 522–624 and 82 H.C. deb. 4 ser. 1 May 1900, 433–88.

[37]*EG*, 28 Sept. 1898, 528; 27 May 1899, 909.

[38]*Mun. Jnl. & London*, 19 Jan. 1899, 77.

[39]PRO 30/72/29, A.M.C. (1900), pp. 61–66, 92; *EG*, 12 Jan. 1901, 60–1.

[40]*Mun. Jnl.*, 19 April 1901, 292.

its support and decided to proceed with a bill, and in 1901 Glasgow, the London County Council and Battersea vestry each introduced one.[41] By the turn of the century a popular front was being forged, embracing the broad ranks of Liberalism, nascent Labour and the municipal interest, leavened by a core of committed Radicals from the land-reform societies.

III

Underlying the municipal politics of the period was the great domestic investment boom of the late 1890s, with local authorities as its leading sector.[42] Private investment in suburban development sharpened the dilemma of public finance, by obliging the towns to accelerate the formation of collective capital: roads, sewers, water, illumination, police stations, schools etc. (see fig. 15.3). It also generated massive private gains in land values, as vacant land was developed for building and landowners pocketed large conversion rents. The discord between public burdens and private gains was one of the powerful sources of the anti-landlord feeling that emanated from TLV conferences, and spread far beyond the ordinary Radical circles. In Bury, to cite one example, a newly-formed Property Owners' Association complained that Lord Derby took £85,000 out of the town every year, one third of its annual value, without contributing to its expenditure. His Lordship withheld land from building in order to increase its value; he had to be rated in order to bring down local taxation.[43] Municipalities were not alone, however, in rushing to cater for the surge of urban expansion; private capital vied with them to develop the municipal frontiers. Low interest rates, a rise in purchasing power, and the temporary eclipse of overseas opportunities, meant that urban investment had become particularly attractive in Britain in the late 1890s. Gas, water and urban transport had long been provided by private firms in many towns. Riding on the last great tide of pre-war urban investment, a new technology was maturing for deployment, based on a new source of power, electricity.

Two distinct applications of electricity were involved: first, generation of current for power and light. Secondly, traction for urban transport, either street tramways, or, in London, in underground railways. Municipalities and private companies experimented with the new technology in the 1880s and began to develop them in earnest in the

[41] PRO 30/72/29 A.M.C. (1900), Ann. meeting, 31 March 1900, pp. 23–4.
[42] Cairncross, *Home and foreign investment* (1953), p. 168.
[43] *EG*, 27 May 1899, 905.

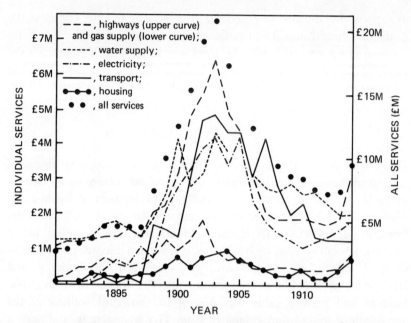

Fig. 15.3. *Municipal capital expenditure in England and Wales, 1890–1914.*

Individual services (transport, housing, electricity, gas, water supply, highways), left hand ordinate; all services, right hand ordinate. Source: Mitchell and Deane, *Abstract*, pp. 420–1.

early 1890s.[44] Sufficient promise had been shown by the end of the decade to attract the financial brokers of the City. Transport and power were forms of investment these men understood, with more than half-a-century of experience in railways and gasworks, at home and overseas. Traction and generating technique had been perfected in the United States, where large sums were already invested, and experience had accumulated in design, manufacturing and commercial operation. Vast profits had been made, and Britain appeared ripe for the same kind of development.[45] Expertise, enterprise and funds came from the United States. Money raised in the City often came from groups like the Exploration Company, which normally specialised in overseas

[44] A detailed record is contained in E. Garcke's annual *Manual of electrical undertakings* (1896ff.); see vol. 12, (1908) p. 41 for a chronological list of electric tramways, 1883–99.
[45] Two recent monographs: J. P. Mackay, *Tramways and trolleys* (Princeton, 1976) and I.C.R. Byatt, *The British electrical industry 1875–1914: the economic returns to new technology* (Oxford, 1979).

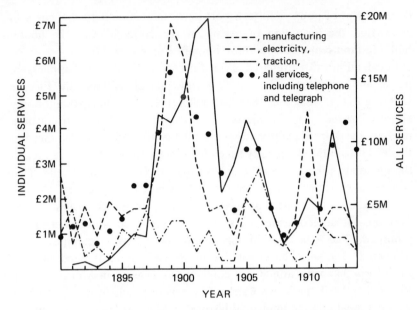

Fig. 15.4. *Electrical companies. Nominal capital registered in the UK, 1890–1914 (including overseas companies registered in London).*

The filled circles represent all services, including telephone and telegraph which are not separately plotted. Source: *Manual of electrical undertakings*, 18 (1915–16), 71.

investment. Finance-capitalist giants contended over particular projects. In the case of London's underground tubes, the money and enterprise of the Speyer Syndicate (mostly raised in Europe and America) took on and defeated the resources of Wall Street's House of Morgan.[46] In Brinley Thomas' model of the Atlantic Economy, capital flowed to the periphery when investment was slack at home.[47] The diffusion of electric technology in Britain demonstrates the obverse: a flow of investment and technology from the 'periphery' to the metropolis, to exploit a domestic boom. Yet Britain was not the virgin land that investors had contemplated. Municipal capital was well entrenched, and not always willing to become subservient to finance-capital.[48] Figs. 15.3 and 15.4 reflect the respective roles of municipal and private capital in the

[46]T. C. Barker and M. Robbins, *A history of London transport* (1975), ii, chs. 3–5.
[47]B. Thomas, *Migration and urban development* (1972), chs. 2–4.
[48]See M. Falkus, 'The development of municipal trading in the nineteenth century', *Business History* 19 (1977), 134–61.

development of power and transport between 1890 and 1914. They also show that the formation of urban infrastructure *followed* the house-building (and real estate) boom (compare Fig. 4.2, p. 52).

Local authorities exercised a measure of control over suppliers of power and transport under the Tramways Act of 1870 and the Electric Lighting Acts of 1882 and 1888. In 1898 a threat to municipal autonomy appeared in the form of projects to generate and distribute current on a regional basis, from giant stations situated at the pitheads. The General Power Distribution Company asked for powers to supply a large area in the midlands, taking in Sheffield, Nottingham, Derby and Lincoln. Two companies were projected to embrace the whole of Lancashire, Mersey-side and Chester. Others applied for powers in South Wales and in London. Great economies of scale were predicted and lower prices promised. 'The Attack on Municipal Electricity,' cried headlines in the *Municipal Journal*; 'The Great Towns Roused'. Several hundred dele-gates from 34 towns attended a conference convened in Manchester on 10 January 1899; the Town Clerk of Liverpool proclaimed that the bills 'raised a great crisis in municipal history'.[49] Alarmist language abounded at the Annual Meeting of the Association of Municipal Corporations. 'We have gone to huge expenses in endeavouring to supply the public need for this particular illuminant,' said the mayor of Nottingham, 'I appeal to your own instincts of self-preservation ... tomorrow it may be your turn'. The Lord Mayor of Sheffield hinted that the threat was not merely commercial. 'That Company,' he said, alluding to the General Power Distribution Company, 'backed by a league which may, I think, be fitly called the Liberty and Licence League, have set to work to try and set back the clock of municipal progress for a quarter of a century, and that, and nothing less than that, is the question which we are asked to settle and discuss to-day'.[50]

The organisation which attracted the wrath of the Mayor of Sheffield was the Liberty and Property Defence League, one of the main vehicles of anti-labour and anti-municipal propaganda in the previous two decades.[51] *London*, Robert Donald's Progressive Party weekly drew blood in June 1898 when it exposed corrupt dealings in the City of London Electric Lighting Company, and won a libel case against Joseph Savory, Lord Mayor of the City. Savory was a large shareholder in the

[49]See *Mun. Jnl. & London*, 5 Jan. 1899, 11 for the Midlands scheme; 12 Jan. 1899, 40–41 for headlines, p. 41 for Manchester conference; 19 Jan. 1899, 75, for the Lancashire and the South Lancashire and Cheshire schemes.
[50]PRO 30/72/27, A.M.C. (1898), General meeting, 19 Oct. 1898, pp. 97, 99–100.
[51]See chapter 3, p. 41.

company (the largest was N. M. Rothschild), and a stalwart of the League.[52] In two public meetings in February 1899 the League launched an anti-municipal crusade.[53] The propaganda engines of the financial and commercial establishment were turned out in force.

At the instance of the League, between four and five hundred petitions were presented to Parliament, signed by railway, tramway, gas, engineering, electric lighting, water etc. companies, by Chambers of Commerce, and by associations of employers, traders, property owners, and Ratepayers throughout the United Kingdom, presented in the House of Commons by Sir John Lubbock, in the House of Lords by the Earl of Wemyss.[54]

Books were published, pamphlets printed, articles filled the press.[55] The London Municipal Society also entered the fray: large financial interests were involved. For in addition to sundry electric power and lighting projects, the metropolis was the scene of conflict over the L.C.C.'s plans to take over and electrify the tramways; of heroic underground railway projects; and of the long-festering issue of the terms of compensation for municipalisation of the water companies.[56] The same issues were replicated all over the country.

Leading the anti-municipal campaign was Sir John Lubbock (1834–1913; created Baron Avebury, 1900), a polymath naturalist, author, banker, leader of London Conservatism, past chairman of the L.C.C., Unionist MP and himself an investor and director of the City of London Electric Lighting Company.[57] His L.C.C. election pamphlet of 1898, 'On the Real Issues of the London County Council Elections', concentrated on the question of municipal enterprise. It was the beginning of a running critique of the municipal movement, kept up by

[52]'How the City sold its municipal birthright', *London*, 30 June 1898, 414–15 and subsequent issues; *Mun. Jnl. & London*, 5 Jan. 1899, 27–8.

[53]For verbatim reports of the meetings see D. H. Davies, *The cost of municipal trading* (1 Feb. 1899) and LPDL, *The dangers of municipal trading* (9 Feb. 1899).

[54]LPDL, *Dangers of municipal trading* (1899), p. 27.

[55]For anti-municipal publications, see pp. 236–7. A comprehensive early treatment is in L. Darwin, *Municipal trade* (1903). For the left-wing view see e.g. G. B. Shaw, *The commonsense of municipal trading* (1904) and R. B. Suthers, *Mind your own business* (1905). An important source is the Municipal trading joint sel. com. min. ev.; P.P. 1900 (305) VII. An extensive economic appraisement, D. Knoop, *Principles and methods of municipal trading* (1912).

[56]See Gardiner, *John Benn* (1925), chs. XIV, XVI.

[57]A. G. Duff (ed.), *The life work of Lord Avebury* (1924), esp. ch. III, B. Mallet, 'Political and economic', pp. 35–66. For Lubbock's shareholding see Lord Avebury, 'Municipal trading', *Mun. Jnl.*, 20 April 1900, 314.

Lubbock in speeches, articles, pamphlets and books.[58] Lubbock turned
Chamberlain on his head: the L.C.C., he said, was in danger of becoming
a sort of 'London, Ltd.', with the ratepayers as shareholders and the
County Councillors as directors.[59] Urban enterprise was condemned by
the anti-municipalists on economic, social, political and moral grounds.
The towns competed unfairly with private capital; they accumulated
unhealthy amounts of debt; rates increased to intolerable levels;
municipal bureaucracy was inefficient and conservative, and obstructed
technical progress. It endangered freedom, cossetted labour and gave
municipal workers an undue influence, as voters, over their employer.
Finally, it opened the way to socialism. On 26 June 1899 Lubbock
presided over a meeting of MPs who demanded a Parliamentary inquiry
into municipal trading. Balfour promised to appoint one in the following
session,[60] and the promise was kept.

Lord Avebury was the public figurehead of the anti-municipal crusade.
Emile Garcke (1856–1930) was one of its principal wire-pullers.
German by birth, naturalised British, an electrical engineer and a
remarkable industrial, commercial and political entrepreneur, Garcke
had risen by the mid-1890s to become one of the managers of the Brush
Electrical Engineering Company, one of the largest British manufacturers
of generating and transmission equipment. In 1896 he organised the
British Electric Traction Company, to exploit the new electric tramway
technology. The Brush Company and a mysterious City millionaire, Mr
George Herring, were the main interests behind this conglomerate of
some fifty to sixty tramway and generating companies, known to the
Liberal press as 'the octopus' or 'The Trust'.[61] The B.E.T.'s tentacles
stretched to Clydeside, the North-East, Lancashire, East Anglia, North
London, Croydon, Brighton and Wales. Its largest interests were in the
Black Country and the Potteries. Garcke claimed at one time to control
some 15 per cent of all tramways in the United Kingdom. He also
operated overseas, in Bombay, Vienna and Auckland, New Zealand. (His
annual *Manual of electric undertakings*, a comprehensive source of

[58]See Lord Avebury, 'The growth of municipal and national expenditure ...',
Presidential address, *J.R.S.S.* 64, Pt. I (1901), esp. 73–8; *Essays and addresses
1900–1913* (1903), pp. 206–36; *On municipal and national trading* (1906);
'Municipal and government trading', in M. H. Judge (ed.), *Political socialism: a
remonstrance* (1908), pp. 106–21.
[59]Sir John Lubbock, *On the real issues of the London County Council elections*
[London Municipal Society pamphlet no. 4] (16 Jan. 1898), p. 14.
[60]LPDL, *Dangers of municipal trading* (1899), pp. 28–9.
[61]Abstracted from R. Fulford, *Five decades of B.E.T.* (1946), pp. 9–42; 'Octupus',
loc. cit. p. 42; 'The Trust', see e.g. *Mun. Jnl.* for 1903, which devoted 23 index
entries to the B.E.T.

information, made no distinction between home and foreign statistics.) Deploying his companies brought 'the Oligarcke', as the *Municipal Journal* called him, into recurring friction with local authorities.[62] In autumn 1902 he established the Industrial Freedom League to carry out anti-municipal propaganda and to undermine municipal initiative with ratepayer militancy. The league was active in the midlands late in 1902 and in early 1903, with uneven success. It was still in existence in 1909.[63] Garcke was present at the 1899 Society of Arts meetings with Lubbock; the Industrial Freedom League provided Lubbock with platforms, printed his speeches and made him a Vice-President.[64]

The anti-municipal campaign reached its climax between August and November 1902, when *The Times* published a series of 16 articles under the title 'Municipal Socialism', which evoked strong displeasure in Town Halls. The first article, on 19 August, began with a reds-under-the-bed-style *exposé*, linking municipal enterprise with the Social Democratic Federation, the I.L.P. and extreme socialistic theories. Over the following months, the anonymous writer ran through the whole gamut of anti-municipal arguments in great detail, hinting at corruption, and singling out Glasgow, West Ham and Halifax for particular censure.[65] Subsequently published as a book, the articles were distributed by Garcke's Industrial Freedom League. A close relation existed between Garcke and this main trumpet of establishment opinion. Garcke wrote six articles on electricity for the eleventh edition of the *Encyclopaedia Britannica*, which was edited from Printing House Square. In 1906 he also contributed a series of articles directly to *The Times*.[66]

The Select Committee appointed in 1903 in the wake of *The Times*' articles could only confirm the municipalities' success. It declined to enter the minefield of 'municipal trading' and its investigation of auditing practices was more damaging to the Local Government Board than to the towns.[67] Throughout the crisis Rollit had stood as firm as a rock,

[62]Fulford, *Five decades* (1946). '15 per cent', p. 38; 'Oligarcke', p. 44.
[63]*Mun. Jnl.*, 26 Sept. 1902, 787, 795; 31 Oct. 1902, 893; 14 Nov. 1902, 934–5; 2 Jan. 1903, 11; 19 March 1909, 227; Fulford, *Five decades* (1946), pp. 43–5. There is a set of League pamphlets in the Bodleian Library, cat. no. 24831 e 10 (5–12).
[64]See Lord Avebury *et al.*, *Speeches delivered at the annual meeting of the Industrial Freedom League* (30 June 1903).
[65]*The Times*, 19, 23, 28 Aug.; 2, 5, 8, 10, 16 (West Ham), 18, 22, 25, 30 (Glasgow) Sept.; 6 (Glasgow), 13 (Halifax), 21, 30 Oct.; 11 Nov. 1902. *The Times*' archivist, Mr G. Phillips, confirms that they were written by E. A. Pratt.
[66]Reprinted as E. Garcke, *The progress of electrical enterprise* (1907).
[67]Municipal trading. Joint sel. com. rep.; P.P. 1903 (270) VII, p. vi.

taking up the challenge in Parliament and inspiring municipalist meetings.[68] He had spoken up against 'trusts' and 'rings' as early as 1889[69] and continued to do so; Parliamentary attacks on municipal autonomy came to naught. At the A.M.C. annual meeting in March 1903 Rollit exuded defiance at *The Times'* insinuations.

I deny the allegations and despise the allegator [he proclaimed]. When I was in the United States recently, I was brought into contact a great deal with the exuberance of private enterprise, with the excesses of private enterprise, with what I venture to call the tyranny of the trusts ... the necessaries of life are cornered by combines in corn and coal, famine and starvation is the lot of many of the people ...[70]

The contest between municipal and private capital ended in a tie. The towns provided more power, and more miles of tramways, than the companies. Regional power bills were mostly defeated; private profits in urban transit fell, at a time when interest rates were generally increasing (see Fig. 15.5). The new electrical investment at the end of the Edwardian decade (see Fig. 15.4) went largely overseas. The B.E.T. ran into financial difficulties towards the end of the 1900s and had to be restructured (John Clapham, the economic historian, was one disappointed investor).[71] London's ambitious underground railways found it difficult to break even.[72] On the other hand, public enterprise was forced into stricter economic discipline than would otherwise have been the case. The L.C.C., for example, had to scrap the Thames steamboats that it had equipped on a lavish scale.[73] Great and lasting assets were created under both systems of investment. Public vigilance countervailed against blatant super-profits, but it also prevented the economies of a regional scale of operation. The attack on municipal enterprise could not be translated into political censure; two select committees were inconclusive and the towns demonstrated their parliamentary muscle; but municipal enterprise was blunted for a generation. We shall go over the ground

[68]See e.g. 79 H. C. deb. 4 ser. 26 Feb. 1900, 1072–3; *Mun. Jnl.* 13 April 1900, 294–5 and the speech at an A.M.C. meeting (*Mun. Jnl.,* 29 March 1901, 239–40) which concluded, 'to do good and to be spitefully entreated is kingly'.
[69]National Union, *Speech by ... Rollit* (26 Nov. 1889), p. 10.
[70]PRO 30/72/33, A.M.C. (1903), Report and proceedings of the annual meeting, 21 March 1903, pp. 53, 56.
[71]J. Clapham, *The economic history of modern Britain* (1938), iii, 138; Fulford, *Five decades* (1946), pp. 48–50; E. Garcke, 'Tramways', *Enc. Britannica* (11th edn 1911).
[72]Barker and Robbins, *London transport* (1976), ii, ch. 7.
[73]Gardiner, *John Benn* (1925), pp. 310–15, 371–2.

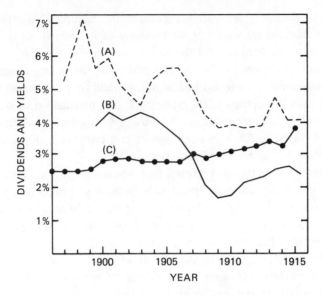

Fig. 15.5. *Electrical companies registered in the UK, dividends on ordinary capital and the yield on Consols, 1896–1915.*

(A) electricity supply; (B) traction; (C) Consols. Sources: A, B, *Manual of electrical undertakings*, 18 (1915–16), 5, 22; C, Mitchell and Deane, *Abstract*, p. 455.

again, in chapters 17 and 18; the significance of the 'municipal trading' controversy here is in giving yet another reason why the urban interest was alienated from private capital and its political organs, Conservatism in London, in Parliament and in the Government, and why it was prepared to join forces with Conservatism's opponents.

Another link between the building cycle and the radicalisation of municipal politics between 1898 and 1902 was the shortage of accommodation that was acutely felt in London and elsewhere during those years. Housing distress had long festered close to the surface of London politics.[74] After 1898 it rose once again. Conferences, reform schemes, pamphlets and press articles formed a tide of comment and complaint. Even the *Estates Gazette* acknowledged the problem in a large number of articles, symposia and reports.[75] Shortage of house-room was the keynote of the agitation. The title of a Fabian tract,

[74]See A. S. Wohl, *The eternal slum* (1977).
[75]e.g., *EG* 31 Dec. 1898, 1092–3; 14 Oct. 1899, 663; 4 Aug. 1900, 205; 23 March 1901, 483.

The house famine,[76] accurately expressed the nature of the problem, although the authors were but dimly aware of its immediate causes. In contrast with the hardships of the early- and mid-eighties this crisis was kindled not by depression but by prosperity; not by unemployment but by full employment. Demand had begun to build up from the mid-1890s together with the upturn of the trade cycle and had helped to stimulate the expansion of home-building. A housing boom and a housing crisis coincided owing to the high employment and buoyant incomes induced by the onset of the South African War.

The Fabian investigator reported that 'house-agents and landlords ... have answered me that never previously have they been so deluged with applications for housing'.[77] Builders were unable to meet the surge of demand and great pressure was placed on existing accommodation. George Haw, a Radical journalist, wrote in 1900,

> For the first time, then, in the history of cities, we see skilled and sober workmen with good jobs, willing to pay even a high rent, failing utterly to find houses at any price.[78]

Those whose incomes did not expand were forced to endure aggravated over-crowding or extortionate rents. 'If you won't pay the rent,' the poor were told, 'plenty of other people will'.[79] The middle classes were also affected. In Wimbledon, 'hundreds of people willing to pay £80 to £150 per annum' were said to be searching in vain for proper accommodation.[80]

True to the embattled spirit of municipal enterprise, town councils in many parts of the country acknowledged a duty to step in and mitigate the housing famine (see Fig. 15.3).[81] West Ham, for example, prepared to spend one million pounds in erecting cottages for three thousand working-class families.[82] The housing of the people, Rollit told the annual meeting of the A.M.C. in 1901, 'is the municipal problem of the day, and the municipalities must solve it'.[83] This agreed with the sense of the meeting; the Mayor of Plymouth gave a moving description of

---

[76] *The house famine and how to relieve it* (Fabian tract no. 101, 1900).

[77] Dr Edward Bowmaker, 'III. The facts as to overcrowding', *The house famine* (1900), p. 11.

[78] *The Daily News* [later editions, George Haw], *No room to live* (1900), p. 12.

[79] *Ibid.* p. 64.

[80] *EG* 14 Sept. 1901, 486.

[81] See *Houses for the people* (Fabian tract no. 76, 1899 edn) for details of municipal housing projects.

[82] *EG*, 14 Oct. 1899, 663.

[83] PRO 30/72/30, A.M.C. (1901), Annual meeting, 21 March 1901, Pres. address, p. 42.

housing deprivation, and of his frustrated efforts to relieve it. Rollit insisted again that his purpose was the very opposite of subversive; that 'The Home' was the great social centre and its well-being the key to all progress. Underlying his vision of social harmony was, as usual, a practical demand: local authority housing was largely financed from government loans and the towns asked for a longer period of re-payment: an extension from sixty, to eighty, or even one hundred years. A deputation went to see Walter Long, President of the Local Government Board on 29 November 1901.[84]

Long was gripped in the vice of Unionist finance, and arguments for social cohesion could not budge him.[85] An extension, he replied, would not bring housing within the means of the poor, and would open the door to other demands. He warned of placing too many burdens on posterity.[86] The housing agitation gathered force, however, with the formation of Radical and Labour pressure groups.[87] The indefatigable MacNamara introduced repayment-period extension bills into Parliament in 1901, 1902 and 1903. Long capitulated in 1903 and introduced a government bill to extend the period of repayment to eighty years.[88] But the breach was not healed. In 1905 Rollit still bore the grudge. He suggested collusion between the government and the banks to deny loan funds to the towns.[89] The political upshot of the housing question, then, was to estrange the urban interest yet further from the government and to align these reluctant socialists with Radicals, Liberals and Labour.

[84] *Ibid.*, Appendix.
[85] PRO 30/72/30, A.M.C. (1901), Rollit's account of Long's visit to Hull, A.M.C. Autumn gen. meeting, 23 Oct. 1901, p. 131.
[86] *Ibid.*, Appendix. A.M.C. deputation to Long, 29 Nov. 1901, Long's reply, pp. 212–13.
[87] See D. Englander, 'The workmen's national housing council, 1898–1914' (Warwick Univ. M.A. thesis, 1973), pp. 69–143.
[88] See E. Gauldie, *Cruel habitations* (1974), p. 303.
[89] PRO 30/72/35, A.M.C. (1905), Ann. meeting, 1 April 1905, pp. 52, 56. He also complained that the period of repayment had not in practice been extended (PRO 30/72/34, A.M.C. (1904), p. 61).

16

FORGING A WEAPON –
THE TAXATION OF LAND VALUES
1901–1906

I

All this time, the Royal Commission on Local Taxation beavered away, hearing evidence and issuing interim papers. Much of the TLV agitation was carried out with one eye on the Commissioners, whose final report was issued in May 1901.[1] Before we consider it, it is necessary to revert to the vexed question of incidence. Readers may wish to refer to the outline of party doctrines in chapter 10. To recapitulate the gist of that chapter, Conservative *parti pris* boiled down to the claim that tax burdens bore excessively on (1) direct taxpayers (2) ratepayers (3) agriculture (4) groundowners (i.e. shifted from occupiers) and (5) 'onerous' rates, which ought to be transferred to central government.

The Royal Commissioners' terms of reference adhered to the Conservative formula: 'to report whether all kinds of real and personal property contribute equitably to local taxation'. Their first report surveyed valuation practices and condemned the complexity, duplication and inequity which they found. A single, county-based valuation was recommended instead of the patchwork of existing jurisdictions and practices.[2] Six separate documents made up the final report. A majority report, signed by twelve members out of fifteen, including the Chairman (Lord Balfour of Burleigh), remained within the limits of Conservative orthodoxy. It endorsed Goschen's system of 'assigned revenues' and recommended its extension, bringing in the House Duty and increasing thereby the grants to local authorities by more than one third, from £7.1 to £9.7 million. Funding the grants out of assigned revenues assured that they would increase with the expansion of the revenue. The majority stressed 'national' responsibility (i.e. the State's ultimate obligation) to

[1] See *London*, 3 Feb. 1898, 77 and 10 Feb. 1898, 93.
[2] Local taxation. R. com. 1st rep. Local rates in England and Wales, valuation and collection; P.P. 1899 C.9141 XXXV, pp. 40–43.

242

support the 'onerous' services undertaken by local government: police, asylums, poor relief and main roads.[3] The two Balfours (Balfour of Burleigh and Blair Balfour) advocated direct Exchequer grants and reformed principles of distribution.[4]

This question of incidence was one of the most inconclusive topics of economic investigation in the nineteenth century. The Royal Commission on Local Taxation circulated a questionnaire to economists and financial experts in 1897.[5] In his reply Alfred Marshall advised:

Any analysis that is offered of the incidence of rates, must be taken to refer to general tendencies rather than actual facts. The causes which prevent these tendencies from being applied in prediction resemble those which prevent mathematical reasonings from being applied to the course of a ball on the deck of a ship that is rolling and pitching in cross seas.[6]

Fifteen other replies went through the whole gamut of opinion, and raised an understandable scepticism on the part of interested laymen.[7] It is not part of our task in this chapter to essay an independent judgement, though we shall try to do so in the next two. Despite the bewildering diversity of opinions, a thread of agreement runs through the theory of incidence from Ricardo in 1817, through Alfred Marshall in 1899 and up to Ursula Hicks in 1955.[8] It was succinctly expressed by the Town Holdings Committee in 1892:

The real as opposed to the apparent incidence of Local Taxation in towns falls partly upon the owner of the land, partly upon the house owner, and partly upon the occupier. The proportions in which the burthen is distributed are difficult to determine, and depend upon a variety of circumstances, among which the demand for and supply of houses is the most important.[9]

When demand for houses increased, the tax could be shifted on to the occupier. When demand fell, the tax stuck to the owner. Contractual

[3] Local taxation. R. com. final rep. (England and Wales); P.P. 1901 Cd. 638 XXIV, pp. 11–32.
[4] *Ibid.* 'Separate recommendations by Lord Balfour of Burleigh', pp. 67–85.
[5] Classification and incidence of imperial and local taxation. R. com. local taxation memoranda etc.: P.P. 1899 C.9528 XXXVI.
[6] *Ibid.* 'Answers by Professor Marshall', p. 118. The passage (slightly revised) is quoted from Marshall, *Principles* (1920), pp. 795–6.
[7] See H. Samuel, *Liberalism* (1902), p. 203.
[8] D. Ricardo, *Principles of political economy and taxation*, ed. P. Sraffa and M. H. Dobb (Cambridge, 1951), pp. 201–3; Marshall, see[6]; U. Hicks, *Public finance* (2nd edn 1955), chs. IX–XI.
[9] Town holdings. Sel. com. rep.; P.P. 1892 (214) XVIII, p. xxxvi.

rigidities also exerted a strong influence on the effective incidence: no shifting to owners could occur until leases fell in.

In a minority report the two Treasury men, Sir George Murray and Sir Edward Hamilton, abided by their professional consciences and refused to support increased grants. No transfer of local services to the state, or of central taxes to local authorities was possible in their opinion. Conceding the principle of 'national' obligations, their proposal was designed effectively to *reduce* the relative value of grants-in-aid by freezing them for ten years at existing levels, and re-distributing according to need. Diplomatically, the two experts declined to express an opinion on true incidence and took refuge behind the confusion of other experts, the economists whose opinions Murray had published in 1899.[10] It was probably fiscal pessimism (and sneaking Liberal sympathies?)[11] which led them to sign the fourth document, a Separate Report on Urban Rating and Site Values, which also carried the names of the two Balfours and of Professor James Stuart, a veteran land taxer. Unlike the majority report, this document endorsed the separate valuation of urban sites and structures, and the apportionment of rates between the two, with a somewhat heavier rate on site values.[12] Judge Arthur O'Connor, a single-taxer, proposed to transfer all local taxation on to the site value.[13]

The Royal Commission embarrassed the government in more ways than one. For four long years the Commission had provided an excuse for inactivity.[14] Now the Majority Report, based on long-acknowledged party principles, held out a promise of relief to the towns that the Cabinet could not see their way to honour. And the Separate Report on Site Value Rating, as the majority admitted, derived from the schemes of Fletcher Moulton, Costelloe and Harper, in other words, from the doctrines of the government's antagonists in London.[15] The departure was not really so momentous. Ten years earlier the Town Holdings Committee had contemplated the direct rating of groundowners. For Lord Balfour of Burleigh, who signed both majority and minority reports, it was merely the old 'balance of doctrines'. Moreover, as a Scot,

[10] R. com. local taxation memoranda etc.: P.P. 1899 C.9528 XXXVI, 'Report by Sir Edward Hamilton and Sir George Murray'; incidence, see ch. II, pp. 108–11; policy, ch. IV, pp. 121–31.
[11] See H. Roseveare, *The Treasury* (1969), p. 220.
[12] *op. cit.* 'Separate report on urban rating and site values', pp. 170–6.
[13] *Ibid.*, 'Report by his honour Judge O'Connor, K. C.', pp. 177–84.
[14] See e.g. 66 H.C. deb. 4 ser. 10 Feb. 1899, H. Chaplin, 539.
[15] Loc. tax. R. com. final rep. (1901), pp. 39–41.

he knew there was no harm in rating the groundowner; division of rates was already in force,north of the border.[16]

Balfour of Burleigh and his minority co-signatories took double care to dissociate themselves from Moulton, Costelloe and Harper.

> We feel bound [the Separate Report said] to condemn unhesitatingly all the schemes which have been put before us in connexion with the rating of site values ... We should be sorry to lend any countenance to the crude and violent theories which some witnesses have put before us on the subject of the taxation of land. But a cause which is reasonable in itself ought not to be prejudiced by the excesses of its unreasonable advocates, and a careful consideration of all the particular circumstances of urban local taxation has led us to the conclusion that a *moderate* rate proportionate to site value ought to be imposed.[17]

The five commissioners proposed to divide this rate between owner and occupier, and strictly to limit the rate in the pound.[18] Harper convinced the commissioners that the separate valuation of land and houses could be done easily and cheaply.[19] They approached the question pragmatically, and their adoption of the principles of separate valuation indicated how broadly it had spread in the wake of the TLV agitations. But whatever the commissioners might say and however moderate their intentions, 'site value' had become a Radical banner, and could not be used neutrally. TLV was polarising London politics and the Liberal left hailed the Separate Report as the edge of the Radical wedge.

II

Charles Philip Trevelyan (1870–1958) represented the new breed of Edwardian Liberals. Son of George Otto and brother of George Macaulay, the historians, he entered Parliament in 1899. Like other Liberals of his generation, he was attracted by social reform, but stopped short of socialism. It was a mistake, he said in a speech at Newcastle in 1896, to treat socialists as enemies; they were 'creating the sort of public opinion reformers wanted'. Liberals, Trevelyan insisted, 'recognised as truly as any socialist the evils surrounding them'. He believed that free competition was preferable to State Socialism if equality of opportunity

[16]*Ibid.*, p. 157, and see above, p. 190.
[17]*Ibid.*, pp. 165, 166.
[18]*Ibid.*, p. 172.
[19]*Ibid.*, p. 169.

could be assured.[20] On the municipal front, the two movements could co-operate. Like his friend and contemporary Herbert Samuel, Trevelyan entered the TLV agitation with ardour, and made a special study of local taxation. He spoke repeatedly, wrote a pamphlet against Conservative 'doles' and called for the gradual, painless introduction of TLV.[21] Samuel, despite his commitment to land reform, kept to this moderate position but Trevelyan's idealistic and passionate personality was increasingly attracted to the mysteries of Georgian theory and to the Georgian sect.

The minority's Separate Report of May 1901 on local taxation appeared to bring Georgian doctrine closer to the realm of the possible. With scant regard for accuracy but with good political sense, Trevelyan began to stress the revolutionary aspects of TLV and to present the report as a clean break with the past. Speaking in Brighouse in December 1901 he said, 'Those who advocated the taxation of land values were generally denounced as unpractical and revolutionary souls, and no bill to tax land values had yet been seriously discussed in Parliament ...'[22] Four months later he said, 'A year ago the reform was regarded by a large part of the population as a proposal of fanatics and faddists'.[23]

Trevelyan did not appreciate how weak the government's position was. 'We are running a great risk,' he said soon after the publication of the Royal Commission's Final Report, 'that very soon the Government will come down and say: "We dare not fail to attend to the demands of the towns. We will give them subsidies on the same principle as we are giving them to agricultural districts".'[24] Early in 1902 he set out to board the municipal engine and hitch it to the Liberal and single-tax wagons. On 19 February 1902 he introduced an urban site-value rating bill which was explicitly derivative from Balfour of Burleigh's minority report. In his speech, Trevelyan betrayed a weakness which bedevilled Liberal rating doctrine:

[20]*Newcastle Leader*, 21 Jan. 1896.
[21]See Land Law Reform Association pamphlet by H. Samuel, *The ratepayer and the landowner* (1898) and idem. *Liberalism* (1902), pp. 98–100; C. P. Trevelyan and F. W. Hirst, *The renewal of the doles* (1901). Trevelyan's unfolding views may be studied in an album of cuttings of speeches, CPT 37 (1896–1903). See also A. J. A. Morris, *C. P. Trevelyan 1870–1958: portrait of a Radical* (Belfast, 1977).
[22]CPT 37, fol. 46.
[23]CPT 37, fol. 55, Land Law Reform Association, 15th annual meeting, 24 April 1902.
[24]98 H.C. deb. 4 ser. 29 July 1901, 428.

nearly two-thirds of the towns in England [he said] are freehold towns to which this question has no applicability whatever. The same person will pay the new rate as pays the old one, but the essence of this legislation is to put the tax upon a new kind of property and not upon a new person.

This was not accurate and demonstrates how difficult the subject could be even to those who had made a special study of it. Rented accommodation, and the distinction between owner and occupier, predominated in freehold as well as in leasehold towns. But only in leasehold towns did site-value rating carry a doctrinal, specifically Liberal anti-landowner appeal. Trevelyan also revealed his underlying Henry Georgian assumptions:

the result of a universal land tax for local purposes [he continued], a tax which will bring into use a great deal of land which is now vacant, will be that it will be absolutely impossible for the landlord to shift that tax on to his tenant, because the tenant will be constantly able to go to fresh ground. The inner rings of the town will move out the outer rings, and the outer rings will push the population still further outwards.[25]

The bill was lost by a majority of seventy-one.

In the autumn of 1902 Trevelyan corresponded with the secretary of the English League for the Taxation of Land Values with a view to permeating the L.C.C. and the Eighty Club, recruiting Liberal politicians and forming a Yorkshire branch of the Georgian organisation.[26] Five private TLV bills were introduced in 1903.[27] The most successful, brought in by Dr MacNamara, contemplated a penny rate in the pound on the capital value of land; it missed a second reading by a mere 13 votes.[28] In December Glasgow Corporation, which had retained a leading (and the most extreme)[29] position in the municipal TLV movement, convened another conference of local authorities this time in London. The Council of the A.M.C. was also in session and conference delegates proposed a joint bill. The Council's law committee agreed, and a joint deputation went to see Walter Long, President of the Local

[25]103 H.C. deb. 4 ser. 19 Feb. 1902, 483.
[26]CPT 9, Crompton Llewellyn Davies to C. P. Trevelyan, 20 and 24 Nov. 1902; CPT 13, 17 Feb. 1903.
[27]PRO 30/72/33 A.M.C. (1903), Ann. meeting, pp. 163–5.
[28]120 H.C. deb. 4 ser. 27 March 1903, 532.
[29]Glasgow's bill was the only one which did not respect 'existing contracts' (Cox, *Land nationalization* (1906), p. 97).

Government Board, on 4 February 1904.[30] Sir Albert Rollit led the deputation and a large number of MPs from both parties was also present. Trevelyan had been active behind the scenes.[31]

Rollit was an important parliamentary convert: a proven politician from the Unionist side, wielding the muscle of the municipal contingent. Long was willing to consider the rating of vacant land, but shrank from the possibility of TLV.[32] The very next day Rollit joined C.P. Trevelyan, and eight other Liberal MPs, in sponsoring a Land Values (Assessment and Rating) Bill.[33] On 11 March the bill came up for second reading. Trevelyan described it as a non-Party bill, supported by Conservative town councils, Liverpool in particular. Rollit spoke strongly in favour and demanded a free vote. The government fought back with all the traditional arguments, but was forced to concede a free vote, if only to save face. The bill was read a second time with a majority of 67, thirty-six of them supporters of the government.[34] At the A.M.C. Annual Meeting on 7 May Rollit declared that 'the assessment and rating of land values',

has been raised recently from the rank of a political, or party, to that of a municipal question by the Minority Report of Lord Balfour of Burleigh ... and by the action of the Association and some of its largest city councils, like that of Liverpool. (Hear, hear.).[35]

A similar bill, introduced in 1905 by Sir John Brunner, achieved a majority of ninety against the government.[36]

The *Estates Gazette* realised that municipal support was turning TLV into a real possibility and tried to alert the government. On 25 March 1905 it wrote,

Already great numbers of municipalities have turned eagerly to unjust and visionary schemes of rating ground values, in the desperate hope of obtaining a heavy addition to their incomes. Every year will increase the pressure upon them, and it is absolutely clear that unless it is relieved the rates will reach an intolerable poundage, while possibilities of further borrowing will be very much cir-

[30]PRO 30/72/33 A.M.C. (1903), Council minutes, 10 Dec. 1903, pp. 175–8; 30/72/34 A.M.C. (1904), Council minutes, 4 Feb. 1904, pp. 6–17.
[31]See CPT 13, C. P. Trevelyan to Glasgow Corporation, 6 Feb. 1904 (draft).
[32]PRO 30/72/34 A.M.C. (1904), Report of the deputation, pp. 15–17.
[33]128 H.C. deb. 4 ser. 4 Feb. 1903, 480.
[34]131 H.C. deb. 4 ser. 11 March 1904. Conservative councils' support, Trevelyan, 858; free vote, Rollit, 882; granted reluctantly, G. Lawson, 898ff; division, 912. Government supporters, see Peacock, 'Land reform' (1961), p. 112.
[35]PRO 30/72/34 A.M.C. (1904), Ann. meeting, 7 May 1904, Pres. address, p. 73.
[36]145 H.C. deb. 4 ser. 14 April 1905, 264.

cumscribed .... This matter of local taxation is, indeed, far more urgent than the Fiscal question.[37]

One month later, it wrote,

What the present government has never recognised is that the rating question is the most pressing and important problem of the day ... it is far more important than improvement of education or the reform of licensing.[38]

Rollit might describe the TLV bills as non-political. Trevelyan knew better; and one of the subscribing authors of the bills, together with Rollit, was David Lloyd George. In a Liberal propaganda periodical published in anticipation of the coming general elections Trevelyan described the genesis of the 1904 and 1905 measures, 'the Municipal Bills'. Looking into the future he envisaged 'A National Land Values Tax' in aid of the rates. It would solve the municipal problem at a stroke: a penny in the pound (on a capital land value of £3750 million) would produce £15.6 million a year, nearly double the current grant in aid to the rates. 'It would be a national tax which the House of Lords could only reject at their peril,' he wrote, anticipating the strategy of Lloyd George's 'People's Budget' of 1909, 'while they could mutilate local bills without fear of popular revolt'.[39]

III

In the winter of 1902–3 the tide of war-time prosperity began to recede and with the onset of the following winter, the towns were faced with the prospect of serious unemployment for the first time since 1895. Labourers demonstrated in the streets of the great cities, demanding employment in public works. London's charitable relief agencies were moved to act and the Mansion House Fund was resuscitated. At the A.M.C's December meeting, however, a motion demanding government help could not find a seconder.[40] By the following winter, the problem could no longer be ignored. Local guardians were faced with the need to open stoneyards and distribute money and food. On 14 October 1904 Walter Long met representatives of the London Boards of Guardians and proposed a scheme of relief. Joint Committees of Guardians and

---

[37]'The growth of rates' (leader), *EG*, 25 March 1905, 521.
[38]'The Agricultural Rates Act' (leader), *EG*, 22 April 1905, 715.
[39]C. P. Trevelyan, 'Land taxation and the use of land', *Coming Men and Coming Questions* no. 20 (1905), pp. 9, 15–16.
[40]PRO 30/72/33 A.M.C. (1903), Council minutes, 10 Dec. 1903, p. 179.

Councillors would sift relief claims, and the boroughs would set the deserving to work. A Central Committee would co-ordinate policy across the metropolis; it would raise voluntary contributions, but could fall back on an equalised rate across the metropolis. Long dismissed the possibility of Exchequer subsidies.[41]

A few days after Long's meeting with the Guardians, at the A.M.C. General Meeting, Rollit devoted a large part of his address to Unemployment. His views were conventional. He endorsed the principle of less eligibility, argued that poverty was hereditary, proposed land colonies and emigration, and opposed wage subsidies out of the poor fund. But the crisis could not be denied, and he accepted the need for public works. The cost, however, was too heavy for local resources.

> If every effort is made locally there will be not only a strong claim but an absolute necessity for some supplementary action on the part of the State ... I repeat that mere local contributions out of rates will not be sufficient, in my opinion, for the purpose, and that we shall have to resort to national assistance – (hear, hear) – though the funds must be administered locally, with some proper check upon them.[42]

Five years before, at the Central Poor Law Conference in 1899, Will Crooks summed up the moral problem embodied in Conservative policy. 'You assist necessitous schools, you assist necessitous parsons, and you assist necessitous landlords; then what have the necessitous poor done that they should be denied assistance!'[43] The will to assist was emerging in the municipal bosom, but the means were denied by Balfour's government. Indeed, the municipalities were to be penalised by higher rates. 'Sound finance' had led the government into moral quicksands, and threatened it with political bankruptcy. Two days before Christmas 1904 the Prime Minister reprimanded Walter Long in a letter which bore out Crook's accusation of 1899.

> I have absolute confidence that you will do nothing to endanger

---

[41] This account is based upon the following sources: *London unemployed* (Reports of the proceedings at the conference between W. H. Long MP and representatives of the Metropolitan Boards of Guardians ... 14 Oct. 1904), bound with PRO 30/72/34 A.M.C. (1904); *The Unionist Record 1895–1905* (n.d. ?1905), pp. 74–82; W. Beveridge, *Unemployment: a problem of industry* (*1909 and 1930*) (new edn 1930), p. 154ff.; J. Harris, *Unemployment and politics* (Oxford, 1972), pp. 154–62.

[42] PRO 30/72/34 A.M.C. (1904), Autumn gen. meeting, 19 Oct. 1904; unemployment, pp. 168–71; quote, p. 170.

[43] *Mun. Jnl. & London*, 24 Feb. 1899, 247.

the working of the Poor Law or to yield unduly to sentimental demands, which in the long run may do more harm than good to the persons on whose behalf they are made. At the same time, is it not a very novel departure, on this side at least of St George's Channel, to give Imperial aid to local authorities for the purpose of enabling them to deal with their own special problem of pauperism?

I understand that you think you may be driven to give certain London areas either facilities for obtaining money on loan, or else cash advances presumably at a rate of interest lower than that at which they could borrow. Was anything of this kind ever done for the unemployed before? Was it done, for instance, in the Lancashire Cotton Famine? and can we now do it for West Ham unless we are prepared also to do it for any district in the country which finds itself in difficulties?

You will understand that my fear is not that the money will be improperly used, for this I am certain you will prevent. My anxieties rather arise from what seems to me, perhaps wrongly, to be the novelty of your proposal, and from the dangerous extensions which this new principle may have in hands less firm and expert than your own.[44]

Recall that just one year before, Balfour's government had committed over £100 million of its credit to buy out the Irish landowners.

On 6 November 1905, 50,000 unemployed marched on Westminster and a deputation was admitted to see the Prime Minister. It included a separate contingent of women. 'One after the other,' wrote the *Evening News* in its late edition,

The destitute women of Poplar themselves stood up and pleaded for their sisters and brothers in despair. All told the same tale of want of work, heart-rending poverty, miserable homes, and starving children. One went so far as to threaten that there would be bloodshed unless something was done ... Afterwards representatives of the London Trades Council addressed Mr Balfour, one declaring that if society owed nothing to the workless, the latter had no duty towards society. Another pointed out the danger to the possessing classes of a great strike of the workers such as has occurred in Russia. A third remarked, "You can vote money to stop swine fever; vote it to stop hunger fever".

[44] Brit. Lib. Add. MSS. 49736 (Balfour Papers), A. J. Balfour to Walter Long, 23 Dec. 1904, fols. 40–41. (Typed carbon copy.)

Even at the twilight of his administration, Balfour upheld his reputation for toughness. 'The Government,' he was reported to say, 'would do everything in their power. They could do nothing beyond last year's Act.'

IV

The conundrum of local taxation may be simply stated. Urbanisation gave rise to social costs as well as real estate windfalls. The direct cost was unquestionably borne by the poverty-stricken labouring population. Property's minimum, self-regarding obligation was to maintain the productive capacity of the population and to contain its discontent. As Bentham so clearly perceived, property needed to set aside part of its increment in order to safeguard the rest. This, indeed, was all that the Liberals asked of the landowners. As Lord Hobhouse put it,

> what we ask is, that the dirty acres which the presence and industry of the people have transmitted into gold shall bear their proper share – not the whole, but their fair share – of the expenses which are necessary to keep that population in being … The people give the value; the people create the necessity for expense.[45]

The nub of the matter, then, was 'who pays?' Disraeli made a splendid political banner out of local taxation by offering to transfer the fiscal obligations of social welfare from tenurial proprietors to the State. Although carried aloft by the agrarians, this policy secured the Conservatives wider urban support than their natural sway permitted, and brought Liberal governments several times to the point of defeat. Goschen's finance in the 1880s was a cautious implementation of the policy. What began as a contest between the different factions of urban and rural property was gradually overshadowed by the emergence of a massive new tenure, consisting of municipal property rights, which took its rightful place alongside the old-established ones on the tribunes of politics. To snub this tenure after 1895 was a lapse of political judgement on the part of the Tories. The Cecil leadership neglected the political possibilities opened by 'municipalism' and its variants, the policies of urban amelioration and social paternalism outlined by Tory progressives.[46] Instead they pandered to their clients: the church, agriculture, City finance, London's groundowners. It appeared as if the

---

[45]Hobhouse, *London government* (1892), pp. 15–16.
[46]See Lord Salisbury's favourable remarks on 'Paternal Government', United Club dinner, *The Times*, 16 July 1891, 10b.

252

Unionist leaders lacked the will to bear the fiscal cost of prolonging their political ascendancy. Chamberlain warned Hicks Beach in 1901,

> there is no necessity for any declaration of a "policy of economy" as a supreme object at the present time but on the contrary ... undue stress on this point would be misconstrued and would seriously endanger the position of the Government or Minister that gave to it an exceptional and special prominence.[47]

So the banner passed into Liberal hands. It was effective in drawing urban Conservatives and giving the Liberals a reputation for social concern. The Liberals' special slogan, the taxation of land values, was only made into a banner by the unreasonably ferocious reaction of the landowners. To redeem its promise, the Liberal party would have to forget some of its cherished tenets of 'economy' and break out of the Tories' self-imposed fiscal straitjacket. TLV was a main weapon in their armoury, albeit untested and possibly double-edged. We now abandon high politics, in order to observe property relations more closely, at street level, and to examine property owners interacting with town, not national, government.

[47]J. Chamberlain to M. Hicks Beach, 30 Sept. 1901, in V. Hicks Beach, *M. Hicks Beach* (1932), ii, 156.

17

THE PROPERTY CYCLE IN
LONDON 1892–1912

Summary

This chapter centres on the collapse of property values in London (and by extension, in other urban centres) between about 1905 and 1912. Records of London auction sales are used to reconstruct the movement of market values and the distribution of tenures. Property market activity conformed with the long cycle hitherto identified in the building industry. House rents rose somewhat during the 1890s upswing of the cycle, and kept up during the Edwardian downswing. But rent movements were relatively limited. Property values were already high in 1892, and fell by some 40 per cent during the Edwardian period. This Edwardian property slump was symptomatic of a serious crisis in the supply of housing in the large urban centres. The reasons for the slump are examined in the second part of the chapter. They included, on the supply side, the rise in interest rates and in the costs of construction and repairs. On the demand side there was a demographic contraction, stagnating incomes and the extension of cheap and rapid urban transport. But market economics do not exhaust the causes of the crisis. The next chapter goes on to assess the impact of politics, and stresses the mounting burden of local taxation, and the failure of tenurial pressure groups to arrest the process of tenurial decline.

I

No single location is more suitable than London for a close look at property relations before the Great War. Not that it was typical in every respect; but the sheer mass of London tenures dominated national trends, and claimed a disproportionate share of public and political attention. In 1899, the escalating trend of rent in the County of London crossed the descending trend of agricultural rent in England and Wales (£39.3 million for the town, £37.2 million for the country).[1] London

[1] Gross rents (assessed for income tax, sch. A) (*IRAR*).

254

accounted for some 21 per cent of the rent in England and Wales in 1901, with only 14 per cent of the population.[2] Near the tip of the national rent pyramid, a built-up acre in the City of London rented on the average for about four thousand times as much as an acre of farmland.[3] The tip itself was literally plated with gold. Near the Bank of England a plot was sold in 1905 for the equivalent of £3.25 million an acre, about one-tenth of the bullion in the vaults;[4] at this price, land around the Bank was worth 32,500 times more than typical farmland.

London's splendour and London's slums were both unequalled in magnitude in Britain. The rent of average working-class dwellings was 70 per cent higher in London than in Birmingham, twice as high as in Wigan, three times higher than in Macclesfield.[5] A large fraction of the Ricardian, or pure Rent in England and Wales accumulated in London. At Spring Gardens and Westminster, London tenure was the subject of endless political debate. Chancery Lane, Bloomsbury and Parliament Square contained the headquarters of the Property Professions, at an easy distance from the Law Courts in the Strand and the barrister's Inns. The City also harboured the principal organs of the property press. At Tokenhouse Yard, adjacent to the Bank of England and the Stock Exchange, was the largest and most important property clearing house in the United Kingdom, the London Auction Mart.

Like other London exchanges, the Mart had its origins in an eighteenth-century City coffee house, Garraway's in Cornhill. At the beginning of the nineteenth century the leading auctioneers combined to erect a new auction room, which was to possess 'the characteristics of a national edifice', and an imposing building was opened in Bartholomew Lane, facing the Bank. In 1864 a move was effected to less spacious premises close by at Tokenhouse Yard. The Auction Mart was a profitable undertaking, owned by a group of leading auctioneers.[6] In the 1890s it was the focus of the London property market, with a large provincial turnover as well. In 1898, its best year before the Great War, the Mart had a total turnover of £12 million – a smaller proportion of

[2] *Ibid.*, and *Lond. Stat.* 12 (1901–2), x.
[3] In 1901 the mean gross annual value of an acre in the city was £8,694 (*ibid.*, xi, 8).
[4] *EG*, 9 Sept. 1905, 466. The Bank itself was assessed (gross) at £109,000 in 1912, making a capital value of £2.18 millions at 20 years purchase (*POJ*, Feb. 1912, 8).
[5] Cost of living. Bd. of Trade rep.; P.P. 1908 Cd. 3864 CVII, p. xv.
[6] 'Busy centres of City life: Tokenhouse Yard, the headquarters of the real estate market', *London*, 27 June 1895, 501–2.

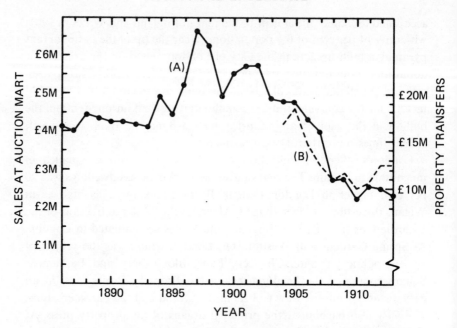

Fig. 17.1. *Real property sales and transfers in London, 1886–1913.*

Full line, property in the London postal districts sold at the Auction Mart, (Source: *Estates Gazette*, 1887–1914); Interrupted line, property transfers in the Administrative County of London registered at HM Land Registry (Source: H. M. Land Registry Statistical Dept. MSS, 'Monthly return of transactions and fees', 1904–14, comprising all property transfers in the County of London, mortgages excluded).

national sales than contemporaries imagined.[7] Within London (as defined by its postal districts) Mart sales rose from £4.3 million in 1890 to £6.6 million in 1898, reverting to a low of £2.3 million in 1910.[8] This was consistently about one-quarter of all property sales in the County of London (a smaller area) as recorded by the Land Registry.[9] Fig. 17.1 shows how good the fit was, and Mart sales may be regarded as representative of London trends. Like other security and commodity exchanges the ideal of a perfect market was rarely attained. Large traders dominated the Mart and rings sometimes combined to rig prices.[10]

[7] For their views, see F. M. L. Thompson, 'The land market in the nineteenth century', *Oxford Econ. Papers*, new ser. 9 (1957), 296–300.
[8] *Ibid.* table II (ii), 297. The first column refers to the postal districts; data before 1896 are available in the *Estates Gazette*.
[9] Between 1904, when reliable figures begin, and 1913. See Fig. 17.1.
[10] *London*, 27 June 1895, 501–2. See also *EG* leader, 12 Sept. 1896, 386–7.

Nevertheless the volume of sales was sufficient to reflect (if not actually to determine) the level of property values in the metropolis. Edgar Harper, The L.C.C. valuer, acknowledged the Mart's pre-eminence in his definition of 'Site Value' as 'the annual equivalent of the capital value which the site in question would fetch at Tokenhouse Yard'.[11]

An inner circle of auctioneers at the Mart formed the Estates Exchange 'for the purpose of supplying its members with information on the rise and fall of property values'. The society kept meticulous registers of property sales (not only in the Mart) for the benefit of its 130 members.[12] For non-members, the *Estates Gazette* printed weekly lists of auction sales. Frank Wilson, its publisher, went further to undermine the Exchange's monopoly of information. In 1892 he began to publish a *Land and House Property Year Book*, recording the year's business on the Mart, and details of additional metropolitan sales. Far from making a better market for land, the Estates Exchange aspired to restrict it. The number of members declined to 117 by 1921. In that year the Auctioneers' Institute, the profession's association (see pp. 100–1) tightened its grip on the property market by acquiring the Auction Mart and excluding non-members from its sales. Frank Wilson's *Year Book* was also taken over and market data reverted to secrecy. Circulation was restricted to members of the Institute and the new editor warned them: 'it is hardly necessary to suggest that members should not allow the Year Book to be inspected by non-members'.[13] In this furtive format the volume continued to appear annually until 1972. It is the main statistical source for this chapter.[14] The first page of the 1897 edition is reproduced as Fig. 17.2. Each sale was described in one or two lines, giving standard bits of information: the district, the address, the number of properties, the tenure, the weekly, quarterly or yearly rent, unexpired term and ground-rent if leasehold, the type of property (land, dwellings, commercial etc.), the date and the sale price.

Of the large amounts of detailed information that can be gleaned from the records, four main indicators suffice to define the structure and trend

[11]Quoted by Fox, *Site values* (1908), p. 34.
[12]*London*, 27 June 1895, 502. The origins of the Estates Exchange are described by Thompson, 'The land market' (1957), 294–5.
[13]'Preface', *Estates Exchange Year Book* (1923), whence the quote; also Chapman, *Auctioneers' Institute* (1970), p. 58.
[14]The *Year Book* ceased publication in 1921 and was privately printed with one year's gap as the *Estates Exchange Year Book* (1923–60) and *Results of Auction Sales* (1961–72). E. A. Vallis, Treasurer of Oriel College, Oxford, kindly placed the volumes at my disposal.

SALES AT THE LONDON AUCTION MART

AND

IN THE METROPOLIS

TOGETHER WITH MANY OF THE

CHIEF PROVINCIAL SALES

DURING 1897.

ABBREVIATIONS.

F—Freehold. **C**—Copyhold. **ut**—Unexpired Term. **GR**—Ground Rent. **R**—Rent. **YR**—Yearly Rent. **QT**—Quarterly Tenancy. **MT**—Monthly Tenancy. **WR**—Weekly Rent. **WT**—Weekly Tenants (or more than one tenant). **FGR**—Freehold Ground Rent. **CGR**—Copyhold Ground Rent. **LGR**—Leasehold Ground Rent. **IGR**—Improved Ground Rent. **ER**—Estimated Rent. **P**—Possession. **pa**—Per annum. **P-h**—Public-house. **B-h**—Beerhouse. **Shares**—Fully paid unless otherwise stated.

LONDON AND SUBURBAN.

ACTON	When Sold.	Price Realised.
12, Antrobus Road, F, R £23 8s.	Dec 21	290
4, Apsley Villas, ut 70 years, GR £12 10s., YR £52 10s.	June 1	425
Avenue Road, 17 plots of building land, F	Mar. 10	800
Berrymead Road, a plot of land, 60ft. by 117ft., F	June 17	135
Berrymead Road, Three plots of land, F	Mar. 10	183
21, 23, 25 and 27, Berrymead Road, F, WR £88 8s.	July 21	700
22, Birkbeck Road, F, R £45	Nov. 11	540
Bollo Bridge Road, Two plots of land, each 19ft. by 100ft., F	June 1	170
46. Burlington Gardens, ut 70 years, GR £8, R £40	Nov. 11	300

B

Fig. 17.2. *The first page of the 'Land and House Property Year Book' for 1897.*

of the property market. These are: (a) the turnover of the property market, in relation to metropolitan and national trends; (b) the movement of rents; (c) the trend of capital, or selling values; (d) the distribution and balance of tenures, that is to say, how much property was appropriated by ground-landlords, how much by leaseholders, and how much by freeholding house-capitalists and owner-occupiers. A total of 4,489 sales were abstracted from the *Year Book*, containing particulars of 12,150 parcels of property: houses, shops, ground-rights etc. The details were transferred to punched cards.[15] To cover as long a period as possible, the samples were taken at five-year intervals, starting in 1892, and then in 1897, 1902, 1907 and 1912. In the following sections, each of the indicators is examined in detail, followed by a discussion of their wider significance.

Property market turnover

The total volume of sales in the sample, on the Mart, in the County of London and in England and Wales is shown in table 17.1. All four variables went through the same cyclical movement, rising in the 1890s, peaking early in the Edwardian period and collapsing towards its end. Two additional features stand out. First, the London indicators (for the Mart and the County) stand lower (at 8–9% of the national total for the latter) than the dominance of London in rental values would lead us to expect. One reason is probably that Mart transactions, and London County sales as well, largely excluded new construction. New buildings circulate more rapidly than the old, as the property goes successively through the hands of developer, builder, purchaser and possibly one or two middlemen.[16] A sample made up largely of second-hand property is bound to show up as a smaller fraction of the total turnover than an equivalent one which includes new construction. The second feature is this: the sample formed a consistent percentage of Mart and national turnover up to 1902, but subsequently declined more sharply. To see why, it will be necessary to disaggregate the sample into its component districts.

First, however, let us translate table 17.1 into graphics, and reduce all its sectors to the same scale. In Fig. 17.3, A, on the left, superimposes the national and the London trend, in an annual series. On the right, B shows the same two curves, but at five year intervals, and superimposed upon them are the *Year Book* sample curves for dwellings and for total

[15]Coding was efficiently undertaken by Miss N. Eilan, financed by an SSRC grant; I gratefully acknowledge both. For details, see A. Offer, 'Property and politics: a study of landed and urban property in England between the 1880s and the Great War' (Oxford Univ. D. Phil. thesis, 1978), pp. 219–20.

[16]Taking a mean new-house value of £250 in 1902, new construction would account for some £38.4 million in Great Britain (20.3 per cent of all sales and leases). New construction probably claimed an even larger slice of property-market turnover on account of a more rapid circulation. Average house value, see Feinstein, *Nat. income* (1972), p. 195; construction, Mitchell and Deane, *Abstract*, p. 239.

Table 17.1 *Property sales, 1892–1912. (See Fig. 17.3)*

Area		Year				
		1892	1897	1902	1907	1912
1. London sample (dwellings)	£M	0.542	0.684	0.654	0.451	0.221
	per cent	(0.43)	(0.30)	(0.34)	(0.29)	(0.16)
2. London sample (total)	£M	0.88	1.47	1.31	0.69	0.49
	per cent	(0.70)	(0.64)	(0.69)	(0.44)	(0.36)
3. London Postal districts (Mart)	£M	4.23	5.26	5.75	3.34	2.55
	per cent	(3.4)	(2.3)	(3.0)	(2.1)	(1.8)
4. London County (total)	£M	–	–	–	13.1	12.6
	per cent	–	–	–	(8.4)	(9.1)
5. England and Wales Conveyances and Leases	£M	126[a]	229	191	156	138
	per cent	(100)	(100)	(100)	(100)	(100)

Sources: (1) and (2) *Land and House Property Year Book.* (3) *Estates Gazette.* (4) 'Monthly return of transactions and fees' (Ms statistics, HM Land Registry). (5) *IRAR*, stamp duty returns. See Table 4.2, p. 66 (year starting in April).
[a] Data for 1893 (no earlier figures available).

sales. A comparison between left and right shows that the main features are preserved in the five-year series and that the discontinuity of five-year intervals is well worth the advantage of a longer time-scale. Returning, then, to Fig. 17.3 A, London and the nation are seen to move together, except that London peaked much higher in the late 1890s. Most of the excess can be attributed, as we shall see, to a public-house speculative boom. Likewise, the London excess around 1902 was mainly caused by a continued boom in commercial and ground-rent property. After 1903 London's decline was more marked. One reason for divergence between London and national sales data was the inclusion of agricultural land in the latter. This acted to depress the national property sales curve in the early 1890s, which were years of agricultural depression, and to raise it above London levels in the later Edwardian years, when both agricultural land prices and land sales looked up, and urban property was increasingly devalued. The fit between *Year Book* samples and the London and national curves in Fig. 17.3 B is also tolerably good.

In conclusion, then, our reasoning is as follows: London Mart data followed national trends quite closely. Auction sales data conformed with the London Mart trend. Ergo, auction sales trends are broadly in line, not only with London, but with urban experience in the rest of England. Property values were strongly depressed in London during the Edwardian building cycle downturn. By extension, therefore, we may assume a similar downturn affecting urban property wherever (as in most of the country) building cycle indicators fell (and see p. 280ff. below), even if the amplitude and timing varied.

Ten London districts were chosen for investigation as giving a good social and locational cross-section of the metropolis, with some duplication for purposes of control. Following Dr H. Pelling's classification of voters in London, the districts fall into one or more of the following categories: (*A*) predominantly middle or upper class; (*B*) mixed middle and working class; (*C*) poor and predominantly working class. Districts have been assigned to a class on the basis of a general impression derived from Pelling's classification (which relied on Charles Booth's researches),

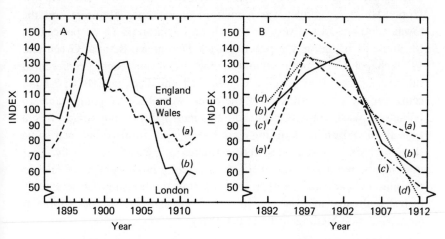

Fig. 17.3. *Property sales in London and in England and Wales.*

(A) annual and (B) quinquennial series compared, 1892–1912. *a*, conveyances and leases, England and Wales; *b*, London sales, postal districts (total Mart sales); *c*, London sales, sample districts total; *d*, London sales, dwellings only (sample districts). The sources are listed in Table 17.1. 100=data mean.

261

the Board of Trade's Cost of Living Inquiries of 1905 and 1912, and a number of standard works.[17] Districts and sub-districts in the *Year Book* corresponded to historical neighbourhoods, and only approximately to administrative divisions (boroughs, parishes or Parliamentary constituencies as the case may have been); they reflected the auctioneer's notion of locality and not the politician's. The maps (Fig. 17.4) show administrative boundaries, not those of the *Year Book*, which would be difficult to establish (subdistricts are listed with the maps). The districts are listed below in the order they appear on the subsequent graphs, so as to give a rough cross-section of the metropolis, from West to East in a generally clock-wise direction. Letters denote the social classification of the district and the percentage of servants to population in 1891 (taken from Booth's surveys) where such a figure is available.

A selection of West and North-Western suburbs (B), outside the County of London, represented the conurbation's expanding margin. Hammersmith and Fulham (B; 4.3 per cent) were western suburbs largely constructed in the second half of the nineteenth century. Hampstead (A–B; 16.3 per cent) was a typical middle-class residential district. Upper-class London is represented by a group of neighbourhoods collectively termed 'Fashionable' (A) including such sub-districts as Bayswater, Belgravia and Mayfair. Holloway (B–C; 4.5 per cent for Upper Holloway alone) was a mixture of artisans, labourers and the lower middle-class not very different from Islington (B–C; 2.1 per cent in SE and SW Islington, the poorer parts). Two areas, Bethnal Green and Whitechapel (C; 0.8 per cent) and Stepney (C; 1.2 per cent)[18] represented the core of East End poverty. Camberwell and Peckham (B–C; 3.2 per cent), on the Southern side of the river, were broadly comparable to Islington. West Ham (C), outside the metropolitan boundary, was a typical outer-London working-class borough. A total of between some three and six hundred sales were extracted in each district, at five-year intervals between 1892 and 1912. A sufficiently large number of sales in the sample years was another consideration in choosing districts. Only districts already in existence in 1892 were chosen, so the sample is somewhat weighted against the periphery.

[17]See H. Pelling, *Social geography of British elections 1885–1910* (1967), pp. xii–xiii, 26–67; C. Booth *et al.*, *Life and labour of the people in London* (1903), religious series, vi, 205ff. (servant statistics); Cost of living. Bd. of trade reports (a) P.P. 1908 Cd. 3864 CVII, pp. 1–59; (b) P.P. 1913 Cd. 6955 LXVI, pp. xiv–lv. Standard works, listed in the bibliography, are by Dyos, G. S. Jones, Reeder, Thompson (*Hampstead*), and Wilson *et al.* (*West Ham*).
[18]Booth, *Life and labour* (1903 edn), religious influences, vi, 210–15.

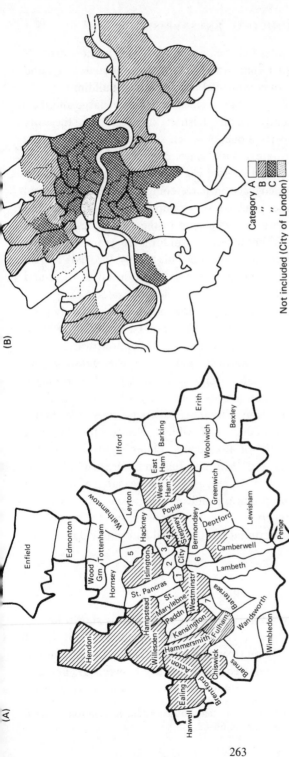

(A)

(B)

Category A
" B
" C

Not included (City of London)

Fig. 17.4 A. Sample districts, approximate boundaries (shaded areas).

Fig. 17.4 B. London: social class of constituencies.

Key: 1, Holborn; 2, Finsbury; 3, Shoreditch; 4, Bethnal Green; 5, Stoke Newington; 6, Southwark; 7, Chelsea. Holloway is included in Islington. The map is adapted from P. R. Thompson, Socialists, liberals and labour – the struggle for London, 1885–1914 (1967), p. 363.

From H. Pelling, A social geography of British elections, 1885–1910 (1967), p. xiii.

A List of the Districts and Sub-Districts from the Land and House Property Year Book used for Quantitative Analysis.
1. North-West Suburban: Acton, Brondesbury, Chiswick, Cricklewood, Ealing, Gunnersby, Harlesden, Hendon, Kensal Rise, Mill Hill, Turnham Green, Willesden Green. 2. Hammersmith and Fulham: Fulham, Hammersmith, Shepherd's Bush, 3. Hampstead: Chalk Farm, Cricklewood, Hampstead, Haverstock Hill, Kilburn. 4. 'Fashionable': Bayswater, Belgravia, Bloomsbury, Hyde Park, Knightsbridge, Mayfair, Portman Square, St. James, Westminster, Regent's Park. 5. Holloway. 6. Islington: Barnsbury, Canonbury, Islington. 7. Bethnal Green: Bethnal Green, Spitalfields, Whitechapel. 8. Stepney: Aldgate, Commercial Road East, Limehouse, Mile End, Ratcliff, Stepney, Wapping. 9. Camberwell and Peckham: (excluding Dulwich). 10. West Ham, Canning Town, Forest Gate, Plaistow, Silvertown, Stratford, Tidal Basin, Upton Park West Ham.

263

The overall volume of sales followed a standard cycle in most districts (Fig. 17.5). Properties other than dwelling houses consisted of ground rents (mostly residential), of commercial and industrial buildings, and of plots of land. The value of each of these sales tended to be large and their numbers were consequently small. District analyses are therefore confined to dwelling property alone, of which sufficiently large numbers were sold. This was no great loss, since commercial and dwelling property tended to move together (see Fig. 17.5, 'total' column). In the late 1890s the big brewers engaged in fierce competition for the control of London's public houses, carried out campaigns of purchase and renovation and pushed beerhouse values up to the sky. Prices in excess of fifty times the annual rent became the norm for a few years. The boom broke around 1900 and public houses ultimately proved a bad investment.[19] The beerhouse boom was in evidence in all districts and largely accounted for the 1897 surge in non-residential sales. Commercial property was still in demand in 1902, and the boom broke sharply soon after. In five out of ten districts dwelling sales peaked earlier, in 1897. In all but two, the overall trend from 1892 to 1912 was downwards.

The north-west suburbs conformed loosely to the national and London cycles, but their secular trend was upwards. The property market as a whole was more heavily weighted with new residential suburbs than our sample. But the inner districts convey a better impression of the market conditions which affected the life and environment of the majority of Londoners. Outer suburbs attracted higher classes of residents and their housing and infrastructure were more up-to-date. Except for the inequality between suburb and town they posed fewer social and political problems. The existence of an outer belt of more favourable experience is not overlooked, but the balance of districts in the sample is appropriate to the social and political questions under consideration.

Rents

Dwelling rents were fairly stable, and rather high. This is shown in Fig. 17.6. Except for two districts, where the median is shown, 'rent' is the landlord's gross mean yearly rent per house, and the level in all but the poorest and richest districts hovered approximately between £35 and £45 a year. Mean house rents were high because buildings were often

[19]D. M. Knox, 'The development of the tied house system in London', *Oxford Economic Papers*, new ser. 10 (1958), 66–83.

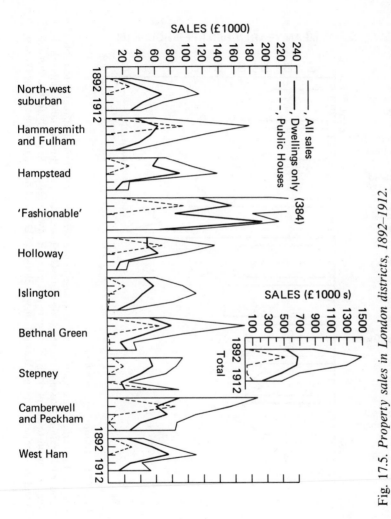

Fig. 17.5. *Property sales in London districts, 1892–1912.*

Thin lines, all sales; thick lines, dwellings only; interrupted lines, public houses. Source: *Land and House Property Year Book.*

265

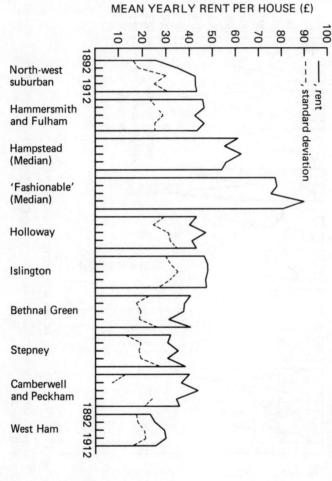

MEAN YEARLY RENT PER HOUSE (£)

North-west suburban

Hammersmith and Fulham

Hampstead (Median)

'Fashionable' (Median)

Holloway

Islington

Bethnal Green

Stepney

Camberwell and Peckham

West Ham

———, rent
– – –, standard deviation

Fig. 17.6. *Annual rent per house, 1892–1912.*

Landlord's average gross annual rent per house, at five-year intervals. Full lines, rent; interrupted lines, standard deviation. No standard deviation plotted for Hampstead and 'Fashionable', where the median was used owing to exceptionally high rents for a few multi-dwelling units. Similarly, for Camberwell; 1902, except that the mean, and not the median, was plotted (S.D. £46). Source: *Land and House Property Year Book.*

266

sub-divided between two or more households in the working-class districts. In the late 1890s only about a quarter of the dwellings in the County of London were valued at less than £20 a year.[20] Too much should not be read into the fluctuations of rent. The variance was large and most of the apparent movement fell within the range of sampling error. Except for one district: in the North-Western Suburbs there was a significant increase in house rents, mainly caused, it would seem, by the onset of rapid transit by tram, tube and train. Otherwise, the curves indicate that rents fluctuated within bands representing some 15 per cent of the total, with a slight rising tendency in some districts.

Table 17.2. *Working-class rents in London and elsewhere, 1890–1912: percentage increase or decrease*

| | [Period] | |
	1890–1900[a]	1905–1912[b]
(*1*) *London boroughs*	per cent	per cent
Acton ⎫ (North-West		+6
Chiswick ⎬ Suburbs)		+3
Willesden ⎭		+1
Hammersmith	8.9	−2
Fulham	20.0	−3
Hampstead	6.7	−
Islington	8.7	−3
Bethnal Green	12.9	−7
Stepney	24.8	−10
Camberwell	10.0	−
West Ham[c]	17.1	−4
(*2*) *Other series*		
20 London boroughs (mean)	9.4	
County of London – all houses under £50 annual value (including rates)	9.9	
'Middle zone' London (mean)		−4
Great Britain (excluding London)	16.0	
20 large provincial towns	12.7	
'Residential' outlay per head, England and Wales[d]	16.2	+1.8 (1904–10)

[a] British and foreign trade and industry. Memoranda etc. 2 ser. Bd. of Trade; P.P. 1905 Cd.2337 LXXXIV, pp. 35, 42, 48.

[b] Cost of living. Bd. of Trade rep.; P.P. 1913 Cd.6955 LXVI, pp. 6–7.

[c] E. G. Howarth and M. Wilson, *West Ham* (1907), table III following p. 48.

[d] See Offer, 'Ricardo's paradox' (1980), Fig. 3, p. 244.

[20] British and foreign trade and industry. Memoranda etc. 2 ser. Bd. of Trade; P.P. 1905 Cd. 2337 LXXXIV, p. 36.

Other sources confirm this impression. Inquiries into the level of working-class house-rent were carried out by the Board of Trade in 1903, 1905 and 1912.[21] Their conclusions may be summarised as follows: house-rents in London rose about ten per cent between 1890 and 1900 and remained level or declined marginally between 1905 and 1912 (see Table 17.2).[22] Most districts conformed to this order of magnitude but in West Ham the increase between 1890 and 1900 was some 15 per cent and in Stepney as much as 25 per cent. Working-class rents outside London rose by 12–16 per cent in the 1890s and then continued to creep upwards between 1905 and 1912.[23]

Capital values

Houses come in all shapes, sizes and locations. A common denominator of value is provided by the *Years Purchase* (YP), the ratio of capital value to annual rent. YP reduces a bewildering variety of non-comparable units to a compact and manageable range. The ratio may react to changes in rent as well as in capital values but in view of the stability of rents observed between 1892 and 1912 (particularly in the second decade) most of the YP movement must be ascribed to capital values. Fig. 17.7 describes the trend of property values (in YP) during this period. It is the most important trend to be discussed in this chapter. Altogether the pattern is only too clear, and resembles the cyclical movement of turnover. Years Purchase of leasehold houses fell by forty to fifty per cent over a short period of time in the late 1900s and house-owners saw up to one-half of their capital dissolving within the space of a few years (freehold values moved the same way). How is it that values declined so dramatically in such a short period? Unlike the decrease of sales this was not entirely a cyclical decline. Values stood high in 1892. And in contrast with the inconclusive movement of rents, the trend of YP was sharp and statistically significant in all districts (see table 17.3).

There were two distinct markets for housing: a market for investments and a market for accommodation. The first was volatile and dealt in capital values, the second was much more stable and its currency was

[21]See table 17.2, notes *a*, *b*.
[22]Trade and industry memoranda, 2nd ser. (P.P. 1905), p. 42 and Cost of living. Bd. of Trade rep. (P.P. 1913), statistical tables, p. 4.
[23]*Ibid.* (1905), p. 35 and (1913), pp. 3–5.

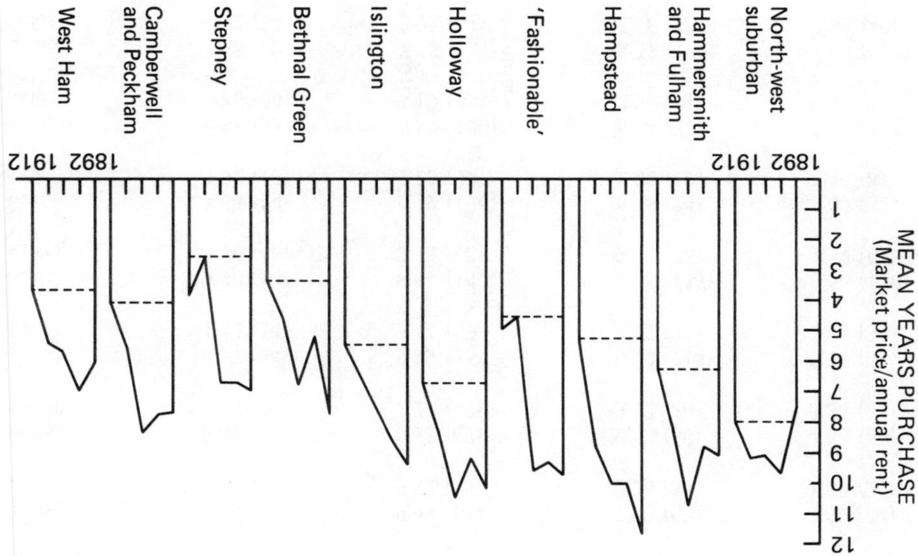

MEAN YEARS PURCHASE
(Market price/annual rent)

Fig. 17.7. Leasehold property values in London, 1892–1912, at five year intervals.

Mean Years-Purchase of dwelling houses sold at the Auction Mart. Interrupted line indicates the lowest level reached. Source: Land and House Property Year Book.

269

Table 17.3. *Leasehold property values in London, 1892–1912: Mean Years Purchase of occupied leasehold dwelling houses sold at the Auction Mart (see Fig. 17.7). Source: Land and House Property Year Book.*

District, Years Purchase (YP) and standard deviation (S.D.)	1892	1897	1902	1907	1912
1. North-west suburban					
YP (and no. of units)	7.46 (16)	9.66 (81)	9.05 (145)	9.15 (75)	7.97 (99)
S.D. (and no. of sales)	3.42 (7)	2.45 (35)	2.85 (55)	2.93 (47)	3.55 (46)
2. Hammersmith and Fulham					
YP (and no. of units)	9.08 (39)	8.84 (137)	11.25 (109)	8.32 (125)	6.38 (36)
S.D. (and no. of sales)	2.09 (24)	2.39 (76)	5.02 (63)	2.82 (55)	2.79 (21)
3. Hampstead					
YP (and no. of units)	11.65 (33)	9.98 (61)	9.98 (63)	8.80 (34)	5.27 (26)
S.D. (and no. of sales)	3.90 (22)	3.72 (48)	2.26 (36)	1.69 (24)	2.70 (15)
4. Fashionable					
YP (and no. of units)	9.66 (41)	9.33 (67)	9.55 (58)	4.58 (56)	5.03 (28)
S.D. (and no. of sales)	3.88 (26)	3.27 (47)	3.12 (40)	3.56 (38)	2.71 (22)
5. Holloway					
YP (and no. of units)	10.17 (94)	9.19 (154)	10.53 (114)	8.26 (40)	6.74 (39)
S.D. (and no. of sales)	1.42 (54)	3.44 (89)	2.77 (72)	2.46 (34)	2.48 (24)
6. Islington					
YP (and no. of units)	9.40 (80)	8.61 (142)	7.58 (117)	6.53 (100)	4.00 (46)
S.D. (and no. of sales)	1.70 (46)	3.12 (98)	3.42 (76)	4.39 (66)	2.06 (28)
7. Bethnal Green					
YP (and no. of units)	7.84 (44)	5.19 (126)	6.79 (74)	4.69 (32)	3.41 (12)
S.D. (and no. of sales)	1.92 (13)	2.23 (33)	2.02 (19)	1.46 (8)	1.40 (6)
8. Stepney					
YP (and no. of units)	6.98 (65)	6.67 (140)	6.74 (74)	2.74 (58)	3.93 (81)
S.D. (and no. of sales)	3.86 (24)	3.19 (63)	2.50 (31)	1.84 (14)	1.61 (34)
9. Camberwell and Peckham					
YP (and no. of units)	7.68 (80)	7.75 (137)	8.37 (172)	6.46 (121)	5.12 (64)
S.D. (and no. of sales)	2.12 (34)	2.91 (61)	2.76 (70)	2.83 (49)	1.97 (33)
10. West Ham					
YP (and no. of units)	7.06 (36)	7.95 (156)	6.72 (290)	6.38 (55)	3.68 (52)
S.D. (and no. of sales)	1.88 (8)	2.78 (40)	1.67 (53)	2.33 (18)	2.50 (19)

rents. Bricks and mortar were a repository of value and a storehouse of expectations, the most popular single category of investment for small capitalists, as we have seen in chapter 7 (pp. 129, 135). Demand for house-property depended on the expectations of such men and on alternative investment opportunities open to them. The collapse of the property market after 1905 marked a decline in the attractions of housing as an investment. The market for *accommodation* was less volatile because it depended on factors which were not as elastic as the expectations of investors. On the supply side, the stock of housing cannot be rapidly increased. On the demand side, usage and contract ruled out violent fluctuations of rent. The stock of humanity changes rather slowly and does not easily shift. Disposable incomes, although subject to trade-cycle fluctuations, were a fairly stable aggregate quantity and a fairly stable proportion was earmarked for housing at every level of affluence. Workers would pay between one-eighth and one-third of their incomes in rent, the middle classes between five and fifteen per cent (chapter 18, pp. 283, 288). Given a stable currency, such constraints ruled out any violent fluctuations of rents.

The Victorian landlord performed a couple of vital functions. The first was to mediate between the two kinds of demand. Housing needs to be financed twice, over a short and a longer term. Developers and builders bore the risk over one or two years, until the finished dwelling was disposed of. The capitalist who bought it only got his capital back after a much longer period: ten, fifteen or twenty years. He also undertook some of the management: collecting the rents, arranging letting and insurance and keeping the property in a state of repair. Some of the risks were devolved to mortgagees, the landlords' 'monkey on the roof'; some of the management was farmed off to agents. The functions of the landlord were not superfluous even if the cost may have been excessive. If they fell into neglect, distress was bound to follow, or another agency would have to step in.

From high values and large sales to low values and low sales – that was the dominant trend of the property market between 1902 and 1912. In other words, for most of London, there were few takers for houses after 1907 and owners could not sell them even at greatly reduced prices. When they sold, they sacrificed much of their capital, and the purchaser was a different kind of person. Ten years purchase represent, undiscounted, a ten per cent gross rate of return. Four years' purchase, as in Stepney, Bethnal Green or West Ham after 1907, is a return of 25%. The 25 per cent investor was a different animal from the person who held government securities at 3%, or let a house at a gross 8%. The late-Edwardian rate of return made housing into a highly speculative investment. House property after 1905 was increasingly cut off from the mainstream of investment, to become a precarious speculation on a par with Mexican mines, offering abnormal returns to hard-faced men. This will also come in for explanation.

Ground rents

Apologists for the landowners often insisted that urban ground property was broadly distributed.[24] Small owners, recall, played an important role in the emergent Conservative doctrine of property. Lord Salisbury foresaw in 1892 that they could become bulwarks for the citadel of property.[25] 'The bulk of the soil of London is held not by bloated aristocrats' proclaimed an *Estates Gazette* leader in 1890, 'but by small or smallish capitalists and the administrators of trust funds ... the outcry against unearned increment is so much ignorant rubbish'.[26]

Conversely, London's ground rents were a great Radical bogey; but solid evidence on the extent of London estates was nowhere to be found. In the middle of the 1880s the secretary of the Municipal Reform League, John Lloyd, began to prepare a ground plan of London on the scale of 25 inches to the mile.[27] Howard Evans, the Radical journalist, compiled a map for his fellow militant in the leasehold enfranchisement movement, the solicitor Charles Harrison.[28] Frank Banfield attached a crude sketch-map of central-London estates to his book against *The great landlords of London* (1890). Another map, of seventeen great estates, survives in Tower Hamlets Public Library. In 1894 the L.C.C. took over the task begun by its Radical progenitors and Lloyd's sheets were transferred to the valuation department, then effectively under the management of Edgar J. Harper. £20,000 were assigned to the project and in 1910 it was almost complete, in the form of 111 sheets on a large scale, delineated in red ink. A revision was undertaken, only to be abandoned in 1915.[29] The sheets repose at present in the G.L.C. Record

[24]E.g. C. H. Sargant, *Ground-rents and building leases* (1886), pp. 146–7.
[25]Speech at Exeter, *The Times*, 3 Feb. 1892, 6c.
[26]*EG* 21 March 1890, 272.
[27]J. Lloyd, *London municipal government* (1911), p. 63.
[28]H. Evans, *Radical fights of forty years* (n.d. 1913), pp. 88–9.
[29]For a rather incomplete account of the map and its antecedents see R. Hyde, 'Mapping London's landlords: *the ground plan of London: 1892–1915*', *Guildhall Studies in London History* 1 (1973), 28–34. For a recent map, see E. Jones and D. J. Sinclair, *Atlas of London and the London region* (Oxford 1968), map 7, showing the location of 137 estates in inner London.

Office and are much the worse for wear. Except for a few sheets which only cover a small part of North London, the key which listed owners by name has been lost and the parcels are only denoted by number.

Interpreting the map's spatial pattern is a task for geographers. It is by no means easy to generalise from it; extreme fragmentation in some sub-districts alternates with broad acres in others. A few general figures on the social distribution of the surface were laboriously compiled in the summer of 1913, in response to a series of questions in the London County Council.[30] They do not add up precisely to known totals, and undoubtedly contain margins of overlap and error. Nevertheless, they constitute an advance on previous ignorance, and, despite a generation elapsed, they complement J. Bateman's distributions of acreage *outside* the metropolis. In the whole County of London, with its 4.5 million inhabitants, there were 14,000 individuals who each owned one house,[31] and 24,200 who owned the ground underlying more than one house. If one-house owners are left out, there was one groundowner, on the average, for every twenty-six dwellings in the County of London (not counting commercial property): 24,200 owners and 620,157 dwellings in 1911.[32]

The surface was distributed in the following way:

Category	Approximate sq. miles	Approximate per cent of L.C.C. area
Public roads and highways[a]	23.	20
Parks and open spaces	10.5	9
Public property: L.C.C., the Crown, etc.	12.	10
Public corporations, railway companies etc.	22.	19
Eleven large estates of more than 1/2 sq. mile each	9.	8
700 owners of more than 5 acres each	38.	33
Total	114.5	99
L.C.C. Area	116.	100

[a] 23–24 square miles (L.C.C. *Questions* 5 (1913), q. 347).

[30] GLC L.C.C. *Questions* 5 (1913), ques. 339, 346–8, 363, 369, July 1913.
[31] One of them was 'Shaw, Geo. Bernard', who owned the miniscule plot no. 52 in Dresden Road, Hornsey Rise, on Ground Map sheet no. 2.
[32] Calculated from 1911 Census housing statistics. See Cost of living report (P.P. 1913), pp. 320–3.

The total adds up to 114.5 sq. miles. The area mapped was 114.75 sq. miles.[33] Of course value counted for more than size, and of the great ducal estates, only the Duke of Westminster's Pimlico fief (3/4 sq. miles) was included among the 'big eleven'.[34]

The map gives rise to a number of striking impressions: first, the large part of London taken up by roads and highways (transport claimed even a larger share, if railways and docks are included). Second, the large area of the metropolis in public and corporate hands. Third, 38,200 ground and house-owners, while making up only some six per cent of London's households (as reckoned by the number of dwellings), were nevertheless not a negligible electoral force. Fourth, while the map was undoubtedly useful (and much used) for administrative work, it was almost useless for political purposes. A mass of detail and an ungainly format garbled its intended message. A valuation would have been of greater use, for it was the value of ground property that mattered, not its precise spatial form, acreage or location.

How did the turnover and value of ground rents compare with other London tenures? One-fifth of all London property sold at the Mart in 1890–2 was in ground rents. 80 per cent of those were straightforward freehold ground rents, the rest were a second tier of leasehold ground rents, for a fixed term of years. The YP of freehold ground rents was high: in 1890–2 it was 28.3 YP, about three times as much as the value of leasehold houses.[35] Ground rents gave better security, and a lower return: they were a first charge on the house, and as a rule, rarely exceeded one-sixth of the rack-rent.[36] Their capital value included the prospect of the reversion at the end of the lease. The movement of ground rents (freehold only) in the sample districts is shown in Table 17.4. Years Purchase rose (significantly) from 26.2 in 1892 to 30.6 in 1897, and dropped from this level to 23.6 in 1912, following the property cycle,

[33]The categories do not add up to this total. Measurement was difficult (see q. 348) and there must have been some overlap. Assuming one-fifth of an acre for each single-house owner, the area owned by them comes to 4.3 sq. miles (3.7 per cent of the L.C.C. area).

[34]These were Lord Northbrook and Dulwich College (more than 2 sq. miles); Lord St. Germans, H. W. Forster, Sir H. P. T. Barron, Sir Spencer Maryon Wilson (more than $1\frac{1}{2}$ sq. mile); Paddington trustees, Mr. Cator (more than one sq. mile); the Duke of Westminster (more than $\frac{3}{4}$ sq. mile); Lord Dartmouth, Prudential Assurance Company, Mercer's Company, Magdalen College, Oxford (more than $\frac{1}{2}$ sq. mile).

[35]'Summary of sales at the London Auction Mart', EG, 16 July 1892, 29 and 7 Jan. 1893, 13.

[36]Sargant, Ground rents (1886), p. 16.

Table 17.4. Sales of freehold ground rents, sample districts, London 1892–1912 (Source: Land and House Property Year Book). See Fig. 18.3, p. 293

Year	1892	1897	1902	1907	1912
Total turnover in pounds	119,385	82,364	121,026	81,584	64,712
Number of sales (and number of units)	122 (124)	64 (64)	106 (725)	96 (698)	90 (543)
Mean Years Purchase	26.18	30.60	28.13	30.25	23.56
(Standard deviation)	(7.14)	(6.69)	(6.43)	(10.70)	(5.66)
Mean unexpired term	60.54	68.60	63.25	53.68	55.62
(Standard deviation)	(26.38)	(25.13)	(20.93)	(22.18)	(23.24)

Fig. 17.8. (p. 277). Method of construction

Columns were made up in the following way. Leasehold and freehold sales in each district were added up, and so was the total annual ground rent on leasehold property. The ground rent was then capitalised on the basis of Years Purchase derived from the separate sales of ground rents in the district. Each tenure's percentage of the total was then calculated. Capitalisation of ground rents was the weak link in the procedure because the number of separate ground rent sales in each district was small and the YP sometimes erratic, so tenure boundaries have been smoothed into trend lines, and should be regarded as orders of magnitude, not precise observations.
Source: Land and House Property Year Book.

with a smaller amplitude than other variables. Perhaps the most remarkable trend was the tremendous fragmentation of ground rents which the sample shows after 1902. Note also that the number of owners on the L.C.C.'s ground map increased between 1897 and 1913,[37] and that estate duty showed a trend towards a somewhat more equal distribution of ground-ownership. The Conservative project for a wider ownership, and for building bulwarks for property, was making slight, but visible progress.

Distribution

How was property distributed among the tenures? For the first time it is possible, using *Year Book* sample analysis, to estimate the actual distribution of tenures in the different districts of London and to arrive at some notion of the respective shares of landowners, and of freehold and leasehold capitalists. The shares are measured as a percentage of the capital value in a particular district (Fig. 17.8) and there is no reason to doubt that they are broadly representative of conditions within the districts. The method of construction is given in the caption to the figure. Three main tenures are distinguished: freehold house property, leasehold house property and ground rents. At the top of each column in Fig. 17.8 is a small fraction of value made up of sales in which the tenures could not be separated. Freehold property is below, demarcated in its turn by a thick boundary line from leasehold tenure. The lowest segment represents the capitalised ground rents of leasehold property. The figures on the boundary show what percentage the ground rents made up out of the total value of leasehold property.

Leasehold lay heavy on the ground in west and north London, embracing sixty to ninety per cent of all dwellings (by value). A lower level of fifty to sixty per cent prevailed in East and South London. Landowners, in their turn, claimed between thirty and fifty per cent of the capital value of leasehold dwellings. Excepting two districts (Hammersmith and the north west suburbs) the landowner's share of leasehold property was either maintained or increased, rising over fifty per cent of the value in three cases. This is only another way of saying that ground rents kept their value better than leasehold houses in the Edwardian property slump, giving the landowners an even greater claim

[37] An interim report in 1897 showed only 1670 groundowners in 3/5ths of the L.C.C. area (*EG*, 11 Sept. 1897, 437).

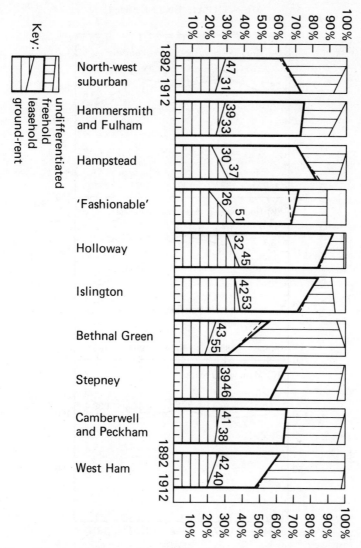

Key: undifferentiated / freehold / leasehold / ground-rent

Fig. 17.8. *Distribution of dwelling tenures in London, 1892–1912.*

Capital values of property sold at the Auction Mart. Boundaries are trend lines, 1892–1912 (five-year intervals). Ground rents were capitalised from incomes using multipliers derived from separate sales of ground rents in the districts. All values are gross. Interrupted lines represent the share of freehold and undifferentiated property, calculated separately. The figures on the columns are the ground-rent capital value as a percentage of the total value of leasehold property (land *and* house) at the beginning and end of the trend line (contd. p. 275).

Source: *Land and House Property Year Book.*

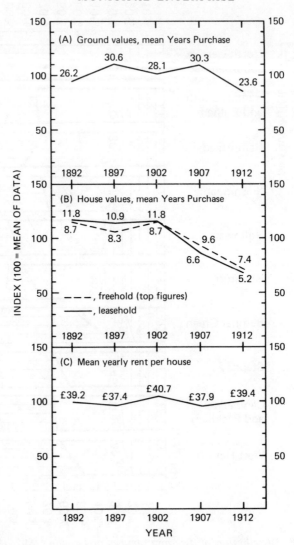

Fig. 17.9. *Ground values, dwelling-house values and rents in London, 1892–1912.*

All the values have been reduced to the same scale, where 100 is the mean of the data. Absolute values are displayed on the curve. (A) ground rents, mean Years Purchase, for ten districts; (B) Houses, mean Years Purchase (leasehold, full line, lower figures; freehold, interrupted line, upper figures) for ten districts; (C) rents for seven districts, excluding Hampstead, 'fashionable' and suburban, the mean yearly rent per house (frequently in multiple occupation).

278

on urban property in a period of decline, and fuelling the fires of agitation. To sum up, Fig. 17.8 gives the following overview: dwelling property in London could be divided into three roughly equal parts. Two were held by capitalists, freehold and leasehold respectively, and the third by a small class of landowners with few obligations, but committed to the sites by a long-term expectation of capital gains. Finally, Fig. 17.9 summarises the course of the property cycle, and compares the movements of all three tenures on the same scale. Sections B and C of this Figure demonstrate the contrast between the sharpness of capital value movements and the stability of rental incomes. In Section B, freehold is juxtaposed with leasehold tenure. Despite a better tenure and a higher YP, freehold declined just as much as leasehold during the property slump. Section A illustrates how much less ground rents declined.

VII

At the turn of the century voices in the property professions were already decrying the 'wild and fabulous prices' and warning that 'a panic is not far off'.[38] In 1905 the *Property Owners' Journal* complained that in the previous ten years weekly, i.e. working-class, housing had lost fully 20 per cent of its value. 'House property will cease to be an investment into which men of moderate means will put their money, as being too uncertain in yielding a return, and too precarious in realisation when required.'[39] By the end of the decade the slump preoccupied the property professionals, and formed the subject of Presidential Addresses at their associations. The historian who peruses these dusty records will be pleased to find that his attentions have been anticipated. 'A great drop in capital value has occurred', said the surveyors' President, '... it must lie with the statistician of the future to show this by tables and curves.'[40] A perceptive attempt to make sense of the slump was made by a prominent surveyor, George Head, in two papers read before the Surveyors' Institution in 1909 and the Auctioneers' Institute in 1910. Head laid down five conditions for a healthy property market. First, an abundance of capital and cheapness of money; second, 'good trade' which made the accumulation of savings possible; third, peace; fourth, political security;

[38] *EG*, 6 Jan. 1900, 21.
[39] *POJ*, Sept. 1905, 1–2.
[40] L. Vigers, Pres. address, *Trans. S.I.* 43 (1910–11), 16; see also A. G. Watney, 'Presidential address', *Auct. Inst.* (20 Oct. 1909), 9–10.

and fifth, concentration of population. Each of these conditions, he considered, had been violated during the previous decade.[41]

Economic historians have generally taken a narrower view than Head. Long and massive swings in the movement of property values have been studied, but only at one remove, through the fluctuations of construction activity and the 'building cycle'. A. K. Cairncross, E. W. Cooney, M. Gottlieb, H. J. Habakkuk, J. P. Lewis, S. B. Saul, and B. Thomas, in works listed in the Bibliography, have all essayed descriptions and explanations of these long swings, approaching them as mainly economic phenomena and framing their explanations largely in economic terms. Before proceeding to widen the field of explanation, let us examine the factors most frequently invoked to explain the building slump after 1905, and see how they affected the property market.

Interest rates were an important influence on the supply of new houses and the value of old ones. Loan charges (or imputed opportunity costs) were one of the largest claims on the house capitalist's income.[42] Between 1897 and 1907 the basic riskless rate of return, the yield on Consols, rose from 2.5 per cent to 3 per cent, an increase of some twenty per cent. To the extent that rents were stagnant after 1900 and real estate was therefore also a fixed-income security, the shift from cheap to dear money acted to depreciate it in the same way, by approximately the same amount (Consols fell from 112 to 82 between 1897 and 1907).[43] Cheap money in the 1890s had stimulated the building industry; once it was mobilised and set into motion, it was very difficult to stop. 'I remember no time when prices ruled so high as they did in 1897-8-9', said Head. 'The demand was great, building was pushed forwards and suburbs were overbuilt – the boom preparing the way for the inevitable slump'.[44] By 1907 the supply of new houses glutted the market and property owners were crying out for a moratorium on new construction. In June of that year, their journal complained that,

the builders go on building, notwithstanding the 90,000 empty houses

[41]G. J. Head, 'Giant London: the evolution of a great city in size and value', *Trans. S.I.* 41 (1908-9), 309-38 and 'The property market – retrospect and outlook', *Auct. Inst.* (12 Jan. 1910), esp. p. 43.

[42]For some Glasgow data, see 'Problems in housing', *Mun. Jnl.* 21. April 1899, 493. For a macro-economic perspective, Offer, 'Ricardo's paradox' (1980), pp. 239-42 and Fig. 2.

[43]See R. G. Hawtrey, *A century of Bank Rate* (1938), pp. 159-62 and 292-3; *The land* (1914), ii, 87-91. The yield on Consols understates the real increase of interest rates (C. K. Harley, 'Goschen's conversion of the national debt and the yield on Consols', *Ec. Hist. Rev.* 2nd Ser. 29 (1976), 101-6).

[44]Head, 'The property market' (1910), p. 46.

and tenements in London. If halt were cried for three years, some of these nonproductive investments would fill up, and the present owners would again think that property after all was not such a bad investment.[45]

Dearer money was coupled with higher maintenance and repair costs or alternatively, a lower standard of upkeep.

Demand for accommodation within the County of London contracted for a number of reasons. The first was the deployment of new means of transport in the Edwardian decade – the tube, the tram and the motor omnibus. Pre-existing underground railways were electrified and the main deep-tube network was in operation by 1908. On the surface the most popular conveyance was the electric tramway which soon began to face competition from motor buses.[46] Cheap and rapid transit increased the attractions of the suburbs, thinned out the city centre and reduced the value of a central location. 'Cheap travelling', said Head, 'has enabled many a dweller in the crowded slums to move away to a neat and convenient cottage, large numbers of which have sprung up on every hand in the outer suburbs'. The middle classes, of course, were even more prominent among deserters from the centre. Head also blamed the telephone, which enabled financiers and merchants to keep in constant touch with their business from afar; the growing preference for 'huge palace hotels' in the place of town houses for the London season, and servants' dislike of cellar accommodation.[47] Population in the County of London ceased growing between 1901 and 1911. Suburban expansion proceeded apace.[48]

A demographic shortfall of demand has also been adduced. Migration from the countryside came to an end towards the close of the Victorian era, and the birth rate of the middle classes, who were the greatest consumers of housing, dropped during the last third of the nineteenth century.[49] A wave of overseas emigration in the late Edwardian period was accompanied by a cyclical shortfall of new marriages, in itself an echo of a similar exodus twenty years before. Brinley Thomas, the chief proponent of the demographic factor, ties it up with better opportunities

[45] POJ, June 1907, 2.
[46] Barker and Robbins, London transport (1976), ii, chs. I–VIII.
[47] Head, 'Giant London' (1908–9), 336; for the process of suburban development see A.A. Jackson, Semi-detached London (1973), chs. 1–4.
[48] See Cost of living. Bd. of Trade rep. (P.P. 1913), p. xiv.
[49] See D. Friedlander and R. J. Roshier, 'A study of internal migration in England and Wales, Pt. I: geographical patterns of internal migration 1851–1951', Population Studies 19 (1965–6), 251–66, esp. 259; J. A. Banks, Prosperity and parenthood (1951), ch. 1.

for investment overseas, which drew capital away from domestic investment in housing.[50] Furthermore the Edwardian period witnessed a slowdown in economic growth and in the increase of real incomes. Real wages actually declined, if the higher incidence of unemployment is taken into account. After unbroken prosperity between 1895 and 1902, the three subsequent years were years of unemployment and depression, and 1908 was also bad for employment and trade. Occupiers of all classes had less to spend on accommodation, and this was particularly true of the poor, the better-paid workers and the lower middle class.[51]

For two or three years around the turn of the century economic prosperity generated a demand that existing accommodation could not meet. Despite an increase of rents, a 'house famine' was experienced in many districts, and property owners extracted a premium of 'key money' over and above the rent.[52] But as the tide of prosperity receded, the tide of occupancy also fell back, and the loss of income forced families to double up, exacerbating previous overcrowding. A house agent in Islington wrote that,

> whereas the houses were formerly occupied by members of one family only, the present class either underlet or take paying guests and, therefore, considerably more people are crowded together than formerly ... in some roads, where a few years ago prospective tenants were waiting for the houses, there are now several vacant.[53]

Head said in 1909: 'Large numbers of premises are vacant in every locality, and there are suburban roads where house agents' boards are almost as plentiful as chimney pots'.[54] This was how the Edwardian housing distress asserted itself – as want in the midst of plenty: 'Overcrowding to-day is not the result of a house-famine; it co-exists in the same districts with a superfluity of empties'.[55] This distress was not produced by market economics alone. The political dimension of the property slump has not received much attention. It forms the subject of the next chapter.

[50]B. Thomas, *Migration and urban development* (1972), ch. 2.
[51]Cost of living. Bd. of Trade rep. (P.P. 1913), pp. i–ix.
[52]Haw, *No room* (1900), pp. 57–63.
[53]*EG*, 29 April 1905, 762; see also *EG*, 22 April 1905, 716.
[54]Head, 'Giant London' (1908–9), 335.
[55]'Housing', *The Times*, 6 April 1912, 7f. For the anti-cyclical movement of dwelling vacancies see J. C. Spensley, 'Urban housing problems', *J.R.S.S.* 81 (1918), 162–71.

18

PROPERTY VALUES, LOCAL
TAXATION AND LOCAL
POLITICS

I

Local taxation was an important influence on the Edwardian property slump, but is only glanced at in passing by economic historians, when they mention it at all.[1] Local rates rose between thirty and fifty per cent everywhere in London between 1891 and 1906 (Fig. 18.1). The highest levels of local taxation were to be found in the poorest districts, where the largest increases and the most stringent valuations took place.[2] Rates were a regressive tax, falling with excessive severity upon the working- and lower-middle classes. Regressive incidence operated in several ways. First, the poor spent a larger proportion of their outlays on rent, and, therefore, a higher proportion for rates as well. Skilled workmen in London could reckon on paying between twenty and thirty per cent of their wages in rent; labourers and the poor even more, and while the outlay was continuous, incomes were not.[3] Around the poverty line, Charles Booth found expenditure on rent, fire, light and insurance to be as high as 40 per cent of the total.[4] At the height of the 'house-famine' George Haw described families paying fully half their incomes in rent; he supposed the average to be one-third.[5] The proportion in the provinces was lower, because rents accounted for almost the whole of the higher cost of living (and the higher wages) of London as compared with the provinces. A. L. Bowley estimated working-class rents at one-sixth of earnings.[6] Furthermore, the tax base was many times less ample in the

[1]See e.g. H. J. Habakkuk, 'Fluctuations in house-building in Britain and the United States in the nineteenth century', *Jnl. Econ. Hist.* 22 (1962), 230.
[2]Chapter 11, p. 171.
[3]See Housing of the working classes. R. com. rep. (P.P. 1884–5), p. 17; Cost of living. Bd. of Trade rep. (P.P. 1908), pp. 6–7, 60, 590–3, 606–13; also Englander, 'Workmen's National Housing Council' (1973), p. 25.
[4]See C. Booth, *Labour and life of the people* (2nd edn 1889), i, 133–8.
[5]Haw, *No room* (1900), pp. 55–6.
[6]See Cost of living. Bd. of Trade rep. (P.P. 1913), p. lviii; A. Shadwell, *Industrial efficiency* (one-vol. edn 1909), pp. 434–6; Stamp, *British incomes* (1920), pp. 458–9; A. L. Bowley, *Wages and incomes in the United Kingdom since 1860* (Cambridge, 1937), p. 119. A recent revision of Bowley's data has increased the

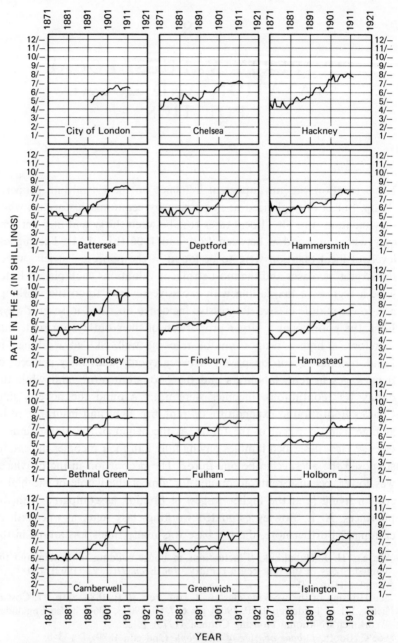

Fig. 18.1. *Rate increases in London, 1871–1912.*

Source: *London Statistics* 23 (1912–13), 608–9.

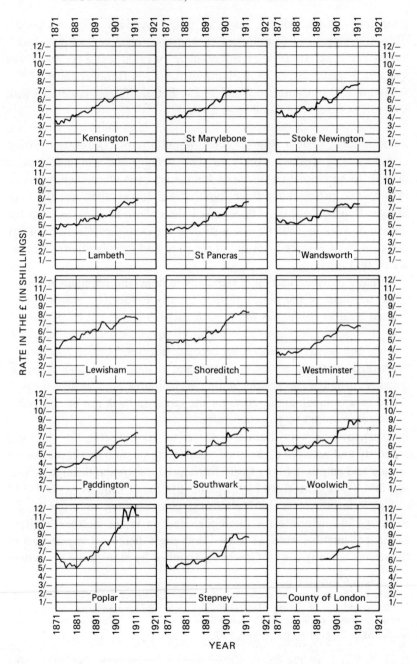

RATE IN THE £ (IN SHILLINGS)

YEAR

poor than in the affluent districts. Rates ascended in working-class districts owing to large poor-law expenditures charged to low rateable values per head. In 1910–11 for example rateable value per head was £40.1 in Westminster, £12.8 in Hampstead, £7.2 in Hammersmith, £5.8 in Islington, £5.2 in Camberwell and £4.2 in Bethnal Green, compared with £9.9 in the County of London as a whole.[7]

A large section of the working classes paid rates indirectly, under the 'compounding' system. Rate-collectors found it impracticable to confront a multitude of workers weekly for their pennies and workers found it difficult to accumulate a quarterly lump-sum, even when they remained in the same premises for three months, which was often not the case. Sturges-Bourne's act of 1819 legalised the collection of rates from the owners of working-class houses, instead of the occupiers. It was explicitly designed to raise more taxes out of the poor and their landlords. The act stated that

> In many parishes, and more especially in large and populous towns, the payment of the poor's rates is greatly evaded, by reason that great numbers of houses within such parishes are let out in lodgings, or in separate apartments, or for short terms, or are let to tenants who quit their residences or become insolvent before the rates charged on them can be collected; and it has been found that in many instances the persons letting such houses do actually charge and receive much higher rents for the same, and will not be charged with or required to pay such rates.[8]

In effect, owners were drafted in to act as tax collectors for the local authority and received a generous commission (as well as allowances for arrears and empties). Many towns introduced the system through private acts and it was generalised by the permissive Small Tenants Act of 1850.[9]

The Reform Act of 1867 abolished compounding in order to get working-class men into the rate-books and on to the electoral register. Municipal finances were threatened and angry tenants demonstrated in the streets of many towns. Goschen responded by re-instating the system

Footnote 6 (*continued*)

share of rent in working-class expenditure to 25–30 per cent (T. R. Gourvish, 'The standard of living, 1890–1914' in *The Edwardian age: conflict and stability 1900–1914*, ed. A. O'Day (1979), p. 17.

[7] *Lond. Stat.* 21 (1910–11), 579–80, 590–1.

[8] Poor Relief Act, 1819, 59 Geo. III c. 12, s. 19.

[9] 13 & 14 Vict. c. 99. The system was examined at length in the wake of the 1867 Reform Act, see e.g. 190 H.C. deb. 3 ser. 19 March 1868, 1893–1922; for a short overview, see Local taxation. R. com. rep. (P.P. 1901), pp. 50–2.

in 1869 and his act fixed the principles and practice of compounding.[10] Application was left to the discretion of local authorities; the upper limit fixed was a rateable value of £20 in London, £13 in Liverpool, £10 in Manchester and Birmingham and £8 elsewhere. Allowances ranged between 15% and 30%. The contours of compounding bring out a vital feature of Victorian and Edwardian towns: lower-class occupiers of compounded housing accounted for a small share of the urban surface, as measured by rateable value. In 1897 the A.M.C. compiled a report that provides a quantitative outline of compounding; 160 boroughs responded, with £34.7 millions rateable value and three-quarters of them practised compounding. Houses worth less than £10 a year (i.e. £2 *above* the compounding limit in most towns) accounted for only one-quarter of the total rateable value. Compounding was allowed in 123 boroughs, forbidden in 26 (11 failed to reply). Allowances ranged between 20 per cent of the rateable value, with empties added (24 boroughs), 30 per cent or one-third (24 boroughs) and 50 per cent inclusive of empties (26 boroughs). 24 failed to answer.[11]

London presents an apparent contradiction. Witnesses before commissions of inquiry commonly reckoned that two-thirds to three-fourths of the population were compounders, embracing a majority of the working classes.[12] This is difficult to reconcile with the fact that the majority of *houses* in London were above the compounding limit. The difficulty is resolved by evidence that rating practice was quite loose and that a great many landlords in London paid the rates without receiving any allowances from the local authority.[13] Recognised compounding accounted for only some six per cent of London's rate revenues at the close of the Edwardian period.[14]

Occupiers who paid their rates directly accounted for most of the rates

[10] Poor Rate Assessment and Collection Act, 1869, 32 & 33 Vict. c. 41. The Public Health Act of 1875 also regulated compounding, together with local private acts. For evidence on the crisis of 1867–9 see 190 H.C. deb. 3 ser. 19 March 1868, 1893–1922; 194 H.C. deb. 3 ser. 25 Feb. 1869, 315–30; 197 H.C. deb. 3 ser. 21 June 1869, 360–98.

[11] PRO 30/72/26 A.M.C. (1897), *Local rating* (March 1897).

[12] Town holdings. Sel. com. min. ev.; P.P. 1890–1 (325) XVIII, G. Beken, p. 65 and ques. 953 et seq.; Local taxation. R. com. min ev.; P.P. 1898 C.8763 XLI, C. H. Sargant, ques. 23, 353–5; *Ibid*. P. P. 1900 Cd. 201 XXXVI, pp. 214, 217.

[13] See e.g. *POJ*, Dec. 1909, Supplement; Feb. 1912, 2; Jan. 1914, 4; C. P. Hall, 'Local taxation and the compounding householder', *Trans. S.I.* 42 (1909–10), 87.

[14] Assuming a 20% allowance. Calculated from L.C.C., *Comparative municipal statistics 1912–13* (1915), pp. 144–5.

Table 18.1. *Rent (and rates) as a percentage of income in middle-class Oxford (year ending 5 April 1912)*[15]

Incomes	Number	Rent (rates) Mean per cent of income	Median per cent of income
£160–£200	165	15.7 (3.5)	14.4 (3.2)
£201–£250	172	14.3 (3.2)	12.5 (2.8)
£251–£300	103	12.9 (2.9)	11.3 (2.5)
£301–£400	160	11.8 (2.6)	10.7 (2.4)
£401–£500	100	10.9 (2.4)	9.2 (2.0)
£501–£749	131	10.1 (2.2)	8.8 (2.0)
£750–£999	82	9.6 (2.1)	9.5 (2.1)
£1000–£1500	96	7.6 (1.7)	7.5 (2.1)
£1501 upwards	55	6.5 (1.4)	5.8 (1.3)
Total	1064	Mean 11.8 (2.6) (weighted)	Median 10.5 (2.3) Mode (9%)

collected in the large and medium towns of England. Not all of them were middle class. Recall the trepidation in the home of Easton, the hard-up house painter in Robert Tressel's *Ragged trousered philanthropists* at the arrival of the quarterly Mugsborough rate demand notes.[16] For affluent ratepayers an inverse relation between income and incidence continued to hold, as table 18.1 demonstrates. It was compiled in 1914 by W. B. Cowcher, a Surveyor of Taxes, in an early Oxford B.Litt. thesis. Residential rates were a heavier burden in the lower middle class than the income tax! (which allowed an abatement of the first £160).

Business rates were much heavier, and a more serious matter than the income tax. Small retailers in London paid an average 14 per cent of their profits, their provincial brethren paid 9.5 per cent, and small master artisans an average 5–7 per cent and more (see Table 7.2). Shopkeepers never tired of complaining about excessive and unjust valuations.[17] For the large merchant or financier the rate, like the rent, was trifling charge. This is why they occupied the costliest premises. But rates weighed upon workshop profits, particularly in the printing (8.2 per cent), shipbuilding (8.7 per cent) and iron and steel industries (7.4 per cent). They were even heavier for enterprises with large land requirements, such as railways,

[15]Cowcher, 'Incidence of local rates' (1914), p. 172 and app. table 1.
[16]R. Tressel, *The ragged trousered philanthropists* (Panther paperback edn 1965), pp. 55–6.
[17]See e.g. *POJ*, May 1912, 3; *The land* (1914), ii, 512–21.

mines, docks and large works in urban districts. An average 9.8 per cent of their profits was paid by 20 coal companies in rates.[18] Railways paid about 15 per cent.[19] The secretary of the London and India Dock Company complained that a third of their dock profits went in rates.[20] High rates encouraged firms to emigrate from town centres to outlying low-rate districts. Yarrow, the big Thames shipbuilders, removed from Tower Hamlets to Clydeside in 1906, allegedly in order to escape the high rates of Poplar.[21] Printing was another industry seeking cheaper sites.[22] The chairman of the Great Eastern Railway invited industrialists to apply for rural sites.

Realising there was a tendency on the part of great manufacturing firms to remove their works from the oppression of the London rates, the company's land agent was entering into negotiations with landlords who had likely sites on the line for the erection of factories and workshops.[23]

To sum up then, the incidence of rates was very unequal. Middle- and upper-class occupiers were very lightly affected, as were the premises of finance and commerce. There was an ample margin for additional revenue from those quarters. The lower middle class paid proportionately higher rates on their dwellings, and their shops and workshops were quite heavily rated. Some land-using sectors of industry, transport and mining paid heavily. House-capitalists' liabilities were even higher, and could only be shifted downwards to the workers and the poor whose liability, in the last count, was the greatest of all. The Conservative doctrine of grants-in-aid as a substitute for the rates could be seen in two lights, depending upon where the money was to come from. If it came from indirect taxation, from a food tariff or from taxes on tobacco and beer the doctrine was nothing more than an expression of upper-class

---

[18]PRO T171/70, 1914 Budget papers, c. April 1914, (n.p.). These are average figures for small samples of small provincial units, except for the coal companies (mean profit £65,421).

[19]Assuming railway rates at 10 per cent of the total GB rate (they were 12.4% of English rates in 1915 – E. J. Harper, 'The bases of local taxation in England', *J.R.S.S.* 81 (1918), 429–32. Rates and railway receipts, see Mitchell and Deane, *Abstract*, pp. 226, 415.

[20]*The Tribune*, 17 Aug. 1906.

[21]See *POJ*, Nov. 1905, 2; *EG*, 4 Nov. 1905, 825; E. C. Barnes (Lady Yarrow) *Alfred Yarrow: his life and work* (1924), ch. XIX, esp. p. 193.

[22]Rising urban site-rents were also to blame. See F. W. Lawrence, 'Housing', in C. F. G. Masterman et al., *The heart of the empire* (new edn 1902), pp. 90–1; P. W. Wilson, 'The distribution of industry', *ibid.* pp. 211–14.

[23]Lord Claude Hamilton, quoted in *POJ*, Aug. 1906, 1.

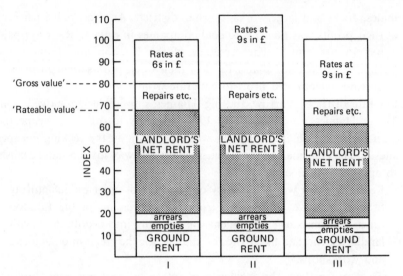

Fig. 18.2. *Effect on the landlord's rent of an increase of rates from 6s to 9s in the pound.*

Columns represent the occupier's rental outlay.

selfishness, an attempt by the most lightly taxed to shift their obligations to those paying the most. But if the grants entailed the extension of direct taxation (which the Conservative party opposed) then it was a responsible, even a statesmanlike policy, substituting a middle and upper-class income tax and a progressive death duty for the regressive and unjust rates. This ambiguity in the doctrine was not fully resolved and the Tories succeeded in implying something of both possibilities. And the prospect of rate relief was a very considerable enticement for an electorate in which the better-off workers and the lower middle class predominated.

II

How much did the increase of rates affect house-property values? Let us look a little closer into this matter. Landlords retained less than one-half of the tenants' rental outlays. Local taxation claimed more than 20 per cent; consequently, any increase in the rates was bound to affect adversely the landlord's share. This is demonstrated in Fig. 18.2.

Fig. 18.2, col. I. The relation between rent and rates. Each dwelling in London was assessed every five years by a district assessment committees. The assessment corresponded to the actual rent received ('taking one year with another'), less rates, with repairs on the landlord. Technically this assessment was called the 'gross value'.[24] A deduction of some 15 per cent was conventionally allowed for maintenance, repairs and insurance. The residue was the 'rateable value'.[25] Liability for taxation was expressed as a 'rate in the pound' on the rateable value. The occupier's actual outlay included rates added *on top* of the gross value. Landlords had to meet additional costs out of the rateable value: arrears could not always be recovered and houses sometimes stood empty. Current magnitudes for these costs were 10 per cent of the gross rent for empties and arrears, and 15 per cent for ground rents.[26] In this example the landlord's net rent came to 48 per cent of the occupier's effective rental outlay. Six shillings in the pound, a common level of taxation in London in the early 1890s, made up 42.5 per cent of the landlord's net rent, 30 per cent of the rateable value, 25.5 per cent of the gross value and 20 per cent of the occupier's rental outlay.

Fig. 18.2 col. II. Let us now increase the rates by one-half, from six shillings to nine shillings in the pound. An increase of exactly this magnitude was registered in Stepney, Camberwell and Bermondsey between 1890 and 1905; and increases of this order took place in many other boroughs (Fig. 18.1). In some, like Fulham they were lower; in others, like West Ham and Poplar, they were higher. Heightened demand for accommodation was pushing rents upwards in the 1890s. Take the direct ratepayer, the lower-middle-class clerk or the small shopkeeper. If he increased his rental outlay by ten per cent (as in this typical example) there would still be no benefit for the landlord. Occupiers bid rents up in their competition for housing, and rent increases of ten per cent or more were widespread (see Table 17.2, p. 267). But the growth of rates absorbed all (or a large part) of the additional revenue. Landlords were able to shift these higher rates on to the tenants, but in most districts they gained little for themselves from the housing shortage. In West Ham, for example, the only district for which detailed annual data are

[24]Ryde, *Rating* (1912), p. 196ff.
[25]Allowances varied and were frequently on a sliding scale but there was a trend towards fixed deductions. See Ryde, *Rating*, pp. 241–2, 909; GLC L.C.C. Loc. govt. com. Minutes 1 (1889–92), 'Draft suggestions for promoting uniformity in the assessment of metropolitan properties' (n.d. May 1890).
[26]Howarth and Wilson, *West Ham* (1907), diagram I, p. 72 and table III, following p. 84 (empties and arrears); ground rents at 15 per cent of the rack rent were the order of magnitude generally found in London B and C districts.

available, the average family increased its rental outlay by 15 per cent between 1892 and 1902.[27] The rise was captured entirely by higher rates. Local taxation was already intercepting and creaming off most or all of the landlords' unearned increment in the 1890s.

By 1905 the increase of rents in London had been well and truly checked, and in some districts it was actually reversed.[28] In West Ham rents fell back to the level of 1892 (as illustrated in Fig. 18.2, col. III). The Outer London Inquiry (1907) aptly summed up the experience of the preceding seventeen years: 'during the whole period 1888–1905 rents had first risen, and then reached the level at which they started, while rates have almost doubled'.[29] In these changed conditions of falling effective demand, the incidence of rates shifted back on to the owners. This is shown in column III.

Fig. 18.2, col. III. This may also be read differently, as describing the re-distribution of rental income between the rate-collector, the landlord and the landlord's creditors, after a 50 per cent increase of taxation. Column III shows that the landlord's share of the rent would fall by some ten per cent when rates went up by one-half, other things remaining equal. But equal they did not remain. Most costs of house-ownership tended upwards, including maintenance and repairs, vacancies, the backlog of rent arrears, the level of ground rents, not to mention interest rates. Already heavily indebted, small house-capitalists fell more deeply into debt after 1910 (table 8.2, footnote *b*).

To conclude this section, let us return to consider the question first posed in chapter 17, about the reasons for the depression of property values in the Edwardian period. But first, one more reason must be examined: this arose out of the nature of leasehold tenure. The remaining life-span of leases was contracting as they ran their course, and London was slowly reverting back to the landowners (Fig. 18.3). Political tempratures may well have been raised as a result, but the gradual shortening of leases which occurred throughout the sample districts apparently had little effect on property values. Freehold property fell in value just as much as leasehold (Fig. 17.9). And because the unexpired terms were more than four times the years purchase on average, they still ran well beyond the time horizons of investors.

[27] Howarth and Wilson, *West Ham* (1907), table III following p. 84.
[28] 'In 1904 and 1905 the influence of bad trade seems to have a marked effect on rents, which fell considerably ...' (*Ibid.* p. 64; and see Cost of living. Bd. of Trade rep. (P.P. 1913), tables, pp. 6–7).
[29] *West Ham*, p. 64.

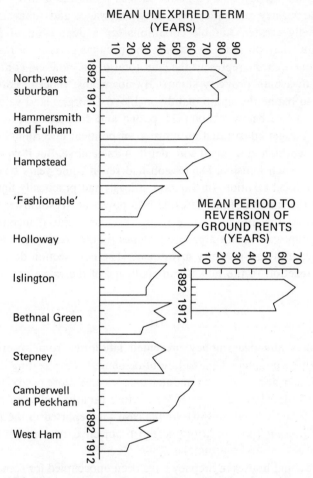

MEAN UNEXPIRED TERM
(YEARS)

MEAN PERIOD TO
REVERSION OF
GROUND RENTS
(YEARS)

North-west
suburban

Hammersmith
and Fulham

Hampstead

'Fashionable'

Holloway

Islington

Bethnal Green

Stepney

Camberwell
and Peckham

West Ham

Fig. 18.3. *Mean unexpired term of leases and years to reversion of ground rents in London, 1892–1912 (five-year intervals).*

Leasehold dwellings in selected districts sold at the Auction Mart 1892, 1897, 1902, 1907, 1912.
Source: *Land and House Property Year Book*: see Table 17.4 for mean reversion periods.

The Edwardian property slump was of an order of magnitude of some 40 per cent (table 17.3). The rise of rates, as we have seen above, would account directly for 10 per cent, or about one-quarter of this decline. Which is not to say that economic factors alone accounted for all the rest. Dear money, unemployment, stagnant wages and suburban trains undoubtedly created suitable conditions for a depression of property values. But they do not fully explain the peculiar severity of the crisis.

Does one-quarter represent the sum total of the political contribution to the Edwardian property slump? By no means. Indeed, Tories were inclined to blame the slump mainly on Lloyd George's land value duties of 1909–10 (see below, chapter 22, p. 368 and chapter 23, p. 391). The People's Budget constituted an infusion of political uncertainty into the property world, and we shall consider it in due course. But it was already the second such infusion. Depression had set in some years before, and the rise of local taxation, (in London at least) had practically finished its work by the time the Liberals came into power at Westminster in 1906. And beyond the direct effect of rising rates on tenurial incomes, how much bloom was taken off property values by the consequent decline of confidence in house-property investment? The next section describes the tenurial reaction to the Edwardian challenge of the rates.

III

Rising rates and dear money prevented landlords from lowering rent sufficiently to counteract the failure of demand. Overcrowding increased wear and tear at a time when maintenance became more costly. If houses remained unlet they deteriorated even more rapidly and were prone to dereliction and vandalism. An extreme case was reported in the *Property Owners' Journal* (possibly not the most objective of sources) in May 1913.

> Twelve small houses in Stepney have been unoccupied for some time past, and on a recent visit to the neighbourhood the owner was unable to find the houses. In fact five of them had entirely disappeared, certain inhabitants of the district having taken the opportunity to raze them to the ground and to remove the bricks, timber, fittings and other materials piecemeal, the owner being just in time to save the main walls and roofs of the seven remaining houses.[30]

Landlords complained of stringent sanitary bye-laws and of increased

[30] *POJ* May 1913, 1–2.

harassment by sanitary inspectors.[31] The stress of bad housing and of insecure tenure exacerbated landlord–tenant relations and helped to give property ownership a bad press, which in its turn eroded the commercial goodwill of house-capitalists, depressed the value of their assets and deterred new investment. Tenants who did not fall into arrears were penalised with an inflated price for an inferior commodity, and provided very high returns to capital in the poorest districts. In this way the accommodation market undermined the proclaimed values of Edwardian society and placed a surcharge on the very households which exemplified its virtues of sobriety and thrift.

Overcrowding and migration to the suburbs contracted the rating base and forced councils to push rates ever upwards in a vicious spiral which generated further overcrowding and migration. In their desperation some boroughs resorted to advertising in railway stations in an attempt to entice residents back to the inner districts.[32] Local authorities also strove to raise the yield of existing rates by reducing the compounding allowances to landlords, or ending them altogether. In effect this meant a higher tax on the occupiers of weekly tenancies. 'Both the extent of compounding and the amount of rebate allowed exhibit a steady tendency to decline', wrote Edgar Harper in a survey of compounding practice in 1907.[33] Plumstead vestry pressed for the abolition of compounding in 1894 and cut the allowance, Southwark followed in 1898, St Pancras in 1900 and 1902, Hackney in 1901, Poplar and Westminster in 1902, Paddington in 1905. Southwark repeated the expedient in 1908 and in 1909 Islington, after fighting a case through a number of appeals, succeeded in doing away with allowances for compounding in all subdivided houses, the most common form of accommodation in the borough, an act soon emulated by Hackney. Lewisham, the only borough that did not compound, was widely admired.[34]

Water mains and sewers; poor relief; schools; police – the means for the physical and social infrastructures had to be found mainly from the proceeds of a tax on the rental value of realty. And this was only a small and declining fraction of the nation's taxable assets. The resistance that ratepayers put up against additions to local taxation had the effect of

[31]*POJ* Sept. 1905, 1–2.
[32]*Ibid.* and *POJ*, Oct. 1911, 3.
[33]E. Harper, 'Memorandum on the practice of compounding for rates in the administrative county of London' (1907), in House letting in Scotland. Dept. com. rep. vol. II, min. ev. App. I; P.P. 1908 Cd.3792 XLVII, pp. 274–6.
[34]Derived from the property and local press.

starving vital services and affected both production and reproduction. Let us remove to the London borough of Islington where on a January evening in 1908 a meeting of the borough council was in progress. A report was lying on the table. The Medical Officer disclosed that infant mortality, at 146 per thousand, was no lower than it had been in the 1840s, sixty years before.[35]

Also lying on the table was a letter from the Holloway and district Ratepayers' Association, which proclaimed that the association was 'strongly opposed to the appointment of paid health visitors to give advice to mothers with regard to the feeding and rearing of infants'. Councillor Cowling, chairman of the Public Health Committee, moved a resolution to employ three health visitors. 'It is a question', he said, 'which affected them not only as members of the council, but as ratepayers and citizens, and also as a nation and a people'. Councillor Harwood replied that,

if they were going to try and rule the people by sentiment alone, they would most assuredly find disaster. He loved children, and had had a great deal to do with children, but at the same time he wished the Council to face the question in a business-like manner (Hear, hear) ...

Councillor Dey also opposed the motion, but made a telling point:

Their hearts bled for the children, and there was not one amongst them who would not do everything he could to help them, but the health visitors would do nothing to feed the starving or relieve existent poverty. It was not that mothers would not nourish children as they ought, but because they could not ... he knew as a fact that the poor dreaded official visits (Hear, hear).

Let Alderman Mills have the last word.

the spectacle before them was that of a Council haggling with a grizzly skeleton while they clutched at the money bags to see if they could save a sovereign. He did not know whether the Council were in a serious mood or if it was bent on clowning. The fact that they countenanced voluntary help showed that they realised that something should be done, and there were sound reasons why the council should do it. They were the custodians of the public health, their responsibilities were just as great as if they had actually the children under their direct control. He hoped the Doctor's proposals would be carried out.

[35]The following account is taken from a report in the *Holloway & Hornsey & Muswell Hill Press*, 10 Jan. 1908.

The borough had a strong Ratepayers' Association and the party of economy were in power. The motion was lost, 36 votes to 17.

IV

Ratepayers' associations remain a neglected subsidiary of the British political tradition. Most were ephemeral creatures, set up *ad hoc* and disbanded just as abruptly after fighting a local election or resisting a capital project for a season or two.[36] A list of two or three score can be compiled from the sources perused for this chapter and any sustained investigation will turn up a great many more. National federations were always cropping up, and one of them, in 1909, claimed three hundred affiliates.[37] Activists professed puzzlement as to why it should be so difficult to mobilise such a substantial property interest.[38] House-capitalists and shopkeepers may have had good reasons to combine but their common interest proved too diffuse. Dispersal acts as a buffer to political organisation and consciousness, as in the case of peasants, farmworkers and housewives. Many had a range of interests and for some, house-ownership was incidental to their main occupation and concern. Many house-owners were absentees. Some 60 per cent of house-property was owned by persons with capitals of less than £10,000 (table 7.6, col. 2, row 6). House-capitalists were small men and women. Among investors, they were bound by the narrowest horizons and the same reasons which made them prefer houses over other securities also prevented them from transcending the immediacies of their localities.

When ratepayers achieved more permanent organisation this was often the work of elements outside house-ownership proper, and particularly of four interests, either separately or in conjunction: property professionals, the ideological and finance-capitalist opponents of municipal enterprise, the big urban landowners and the Unionist party. In other words, the same coalition that sustained the Liberty and Property Defence League. For surveyors, auctioneers, house-agents, and for many solicitors, property was a full-time occupation and an exclusive concern. Their firms and offices provided suitable bases for local political activity.

[36]E. P. Hennock, 'Finance and politics in urban local government in England, 1835–1900', *Hist. Journ.* 6 (1963), 212–25.

[37]Founded 5 June 1907. See *POJ* July, 1907, 3; *POJ* June 1909, 3.

[38]See e.g. the report of the lecture by G. Billings, Vice President of the Property Owners' Association at a LPDL meeting on 'Property owners in danger', May 1906 (*POJ* July 1906, 2–3).

The role of property professionals is exemplified in the Incorporated Association for the Protection of Property Owners, formed as a limited liability company in 1902 by a group of surveyors and auctioneers in north London. The society aspired to national status and eventually achieved it, but after seven years of existence it had only reached 500 members, less than some of the larger borough ratepayers' associations. It spent about £450 a year before 1909, a scale of operation almost exactly matched to that of the Land Restoration League. Like the latter, which derived its finance from the Radical millionaire Joseph Fels, it depended largely on one individual benefactor (E. Yates, d. 1907), and published a monthly journal of 8–12 pages. This organ, the *Property Owners' Journal*, provides a rare window into the world of the small house-capitalist in Edwardian London.[39]

One of the most persistent of ratepayers' groups was the Liverpool Land and House Owners' Association, the embodiment of municipal reaction on the Mersey. It came into being in 1860, in order to resist a clause in the Public Health Act of 1858 which prescribed a measure of open space in front of new buildings. In the 1860s it stood against sanitary reform. In the 1880s, it obstructed municipal slum clearance and rehousing. In the 1890s it agitated for a national poor rate and opposed the expansion of education. In 1887 it branched outside Merseyside, and formed the United Property Owners' Association. By 1900 the new association had established some two score branches, mainly in Merseyside, South Lancashire and the north-east. A permanent parliamentary agent was kept in London. A kindred organisation, the Manchester, Salford and District Property Owners' Association spent thousands of pounds in resisting municipal enterprise both locally and at Westminster. Despite repeated attempts, the United Property Owners failed to gain a foothold in London or the south, and kept within their provincial stamping grounds.[40]

Tramway and railway companies took an understandable interest in local politics, in view of their position as large ratepayers and as competitors of municipal enterprise. They often acted through existing ratepayers' associations, or created new ones especially for the purpose. The activities of the Industrial Freedom League in the interests of the

[39]Society pamphlets and leaflets 1902–15, see Brit. Lib. 1891.C (main catalogue); E. Yates, see *POJ* Sept. 1907, 2. The next two sections may be complemented by Bristow, 'Defence of liberty and property' (1970), pp. 171–3, 328–30.
[40]Annual meetings of the Liverpool and the United Property Owners' associations were extensively reported in the *EG* after 1897. See also B. D. White, *A history of the corporation of Liverpool* (Liverpool, 1951), pp. 51, 60, 134.

electrical industry have already been noted. Soon after the formation of the League, the *Municipal Journal* exposed the new model ratepayers' association.

> We cannot help regarding with suspicion – though, perhaps, in some cases unjustly – the formation of so many ratepayers associations. Curiously enough the inception of these organisations is usually coincident with unusual activity on the part of companies. We learn this week, for instance, that a Ratepayers Defence Committee has been formed in Hove 'for the purpose of opposing the introduction and working of trains by the Corporation without first obtaining the consent of the ratepayers and especially the introduction and working to trams'.[41]

Political subscriptions by railway companies caused considerable concern in the Liberal party, and the question was raised in the Commons and the Cabinet in 1907.[42] A Parliamentary return of contributions was made in 1908.[43] Nevertheless, in 1909 the London and South Western Railway still subscribed to the Battersea Ratepayers' Defence Committee; the London, Tilbury and Southend Railway contributed to the West Ham, East Ham and Poplar Municipal Alliances, and the Taff Vale Railway supported the Cardiff Ratepayers' Association.[44] The Secretary of the Cardiff Association had been the director of the Tramway Company.[45] Naturally, the companies denied that the associations were political organisations.[46]

Ratepayers' associations were miserable affairs, and a spirit of despondency and dejection runs through their publications. At its annual conference in Leicester in 1897, the United Property Owners' Association was boycotted by the local Liberals, including the mayor.[47] And the London association had to promise its members to keep their identities secret.

> As some members request that their membership be kept private from fear of boycott or persecution, names of members are never

[41]'Ratepayers' associations', *Mun. Jnl.* 26 Sept. 1902, 795.
[42]173 H.C. deb. 4 ser. 25 April 1907, 349–70; PRO CAB 37/90/116, D. Lloyd George, 'Subscriptions by railway and other companies for election purposes' (1907).
[43]P.P. 1908 (312) XCV, 155. For whatever it is worth, this return stated that contributions to Ratepayers' and Free Labour associations amounted to £594, a mere 4.1 per cent of all external contributions.
[44]CPT 23, C. P. Trevelyan to Winston Churchill, 21 Oct. 1909.
[45]*Mun. Jnl.*, 28 Nov. 1902, 975.
[46]CPT 23, Churchill to Trevelyan, 29 Oct. 1909. See also 171 H.C. deb. 4 ser. 19 March 1907, 761–2, and 173 H.C. deb. 4 ser. 25 April 1907, 355–6.
[47]*EG*, 15 May 1897, 794.

published without their express consent, owing to the apathy of
property owners as a class having made it in many ways unpopular
to own house property.'[48]
Unlike the Radical societies, with their scores of Parliamentary Vice-
Presidents, the association could not boast of a single member of
parliament on its masthead until the election of James Boyton in 1910.[49]
The movement was an uneasy coalition containing many contradictions.
The groundowner and house-capitalist elements were sometimes at odds
with each other: while the landowners advocated an end to compounding, the house-owners resisted any reduction of compounding allowances, and even demanded a higher compounding threshold.[50] And while
the British Electric Traction Co., an important sponsor of ratepayers'
associations, attempted to consolidate its tramway network, the West
End groundowners successfully resisted the incursion of tramways, and
Lord Kinnoul, head of their West End Tramways Opposition Association made his stand on the grounds that 'the introduction of tramways
into well-established districts almost inevitably brings about great depreciation in the value of residential and other property as well as many
other disadvantages'.[51]

The politics of ratepayers' associations also suffered from a mixture of
motives. In Liverpool, for example, the Land and House Owners'
Association (whose offshoot, the United Property Owners, had been
boycotted by Liberals in Leicester) was led by R. A. Bellwood, a
Gladstonian auctioneer; it advocated leasehold enfranchisement in order
to spite the Conservative council, which was the largest land-owner in
the town centre. The Association's Unionist Parliamentary agent
threatened to resign in consequence.[52] A dash of old-fashioned anti-
government Radicalism survived in some localities. The *Islington
Mercury* was published weekly (later fortnightly) in the winter of 1902/3
by a ratepayers' association which counted Henry Seymour among its
shopkeeper supporters. He was a master glass and sign writer ('the
cheapest house in London', his advertisement proclaimed) who had
published a refutation of Marx from an anarchist viewpoint, which he

[48]*POJ*, Feb. 1903, 1.
[49]*POJ*, March 1910, 1, 8.
[50]Compare Lord Avebury, *On municipal and national trading* (1906), pp. 157–61
and *POJ*, March 1910, 7–8.
[51]*EG*, 16 Feb. 1902, 262.
[52]*EG*, 13 Feb. 1897, 250; *1898*–14 May, 852–3; 24 Sept., 528; 8 Oct., 623; 22 Oct.,
687; 29 Oct., 773; *1899* – 20 May, 842; 27 May, 901, 909.

advertised in the paper.[53] Lord Rosebery regarded ratepayers' associations as potential Liberal auxiliaries (and possibly as bulwarks against the New Liberalism) and called, in 1902, for an extension of the movement.[54] The historical high-water mark of ratepayer militancy, the 'passive resistance' of Non-Conformists to the education rate after 1902, was carried out under Liberal auspices. Yet by the middle of the Edwardian decade, and with the gradual replacement of the old Liberalism by the new, the potential of the movement was increasingly mobilised in the interest of the Conservative party in London.

V

Lurking in the background of the ratepayers' movement at the end of the nineteenth century were the great groundowners, the City financiers, the Liberty and Property Defence League and the London Municipal Society, the Conservative organ in the metropolis. In their struggle against the Municipal Reform League in the 1880s the City Corporation had furtively employed a band of rogues and rowdies to disrupt meetings and to agitate under the banner of a bogus 'Metropolitan Ratepayers' Association'.[55] In 1890 the Liberty and Property Defence League formed a short-lived 'London Ratepayers' Defence League' to resist TLV and defend the integrity of ground rents.[56] The same year saw the formation of the Property Protection Association, which agitated for the same ends in numerous leaflets and pamphlets. Its Vice-Presidency was crowded with dukes, agrarians and financiers.[57]

A powerful combination began to emerge from behind the 'municipal trading' agitation of the early 1900s and in anticipation of the London borough and Council elections of 1906 and 1907. The West End whales gave money, publicity and organisation; the urban and suburban minnows contributed electoral numbers. Metropolitan Conservatism began to construct a new populist platform, under the banner of a 'non-political' 'Municipal Reform Society'. The old ratepayers' association was rejuvenated as a basic cell for a new kind of political organism. Opposition to 'municipal socialism' and civic expenditure was raised as the flag

[53]H. Seymour, *The fallacy of Marx's theory of surplus value* (1897).
[54]*Mun. Jnl.*, 24 Jan. 1902, 64; *The Times*, 2 Oct. 1902, 7e.
[55]John Lloyd, *London municipal government* (1911), pp. 30, 54.
[56]*EG*, 21 Nov. 1890, 497.
[57]For reactions to the first and eleventh annual reports see *EG*, 4 July 1891, 10 and *Property Market Review*, 30 Nov. 1901.

of a mass movement of the right, and middle class fears of working-class encroachment were stirred up for political ends. Lord Avebury, the polymath scientist, banker, politician and author preached the creed of economy in this newly energised and venomous form.[58]

Lord Avebury led a capitalist counter-attack on Labour. More definitely, the political forces of capital and commerce singled out the compounding working-class ratepayer for their target. Municipal spending had to be cut. The working-class ratepayer and the municipal employee stood in the way. They were to be taught that public extravagance was not in their interest; if they could not be persuaded, they would have to be silenced. The London press between 1905 and 1907 was largely arrayed behind the Municipal Reform programme. The line of argument was this: under the compounding system occupiers had no idea what part of their rent was committed to rates and could not realise by how much rates had risen. They had no reason to oppose profligate collectivist candidates and as municipal employees, good reasons to support them. A convenient and compact précis of this doctrine was published in 1905 by the Association for the Protection of Property Owners.[59]

The Property Owners' pamphlet protested against the paralysing combination of high rates and business competition from local authorities. It went directly to the heart of the matter: '[the] amount of rates', it began, '... has so increased during recent years as to become oppressive and unjust'. It decried the 'grave scandal' of 'increased municipal expenditure, in some cases with distinct socialist design'. Then it ran through a gamut of remedies: an upper limit on rates of seven shillings in the pound, reimposition of the coal and wine duties, stricter government auditing, curtailment of municipal parliamentary lobbying, no further equalisation of rates between districts, de-rating of industry. It proposed lower pay and longer hours for road-cleaners, dustmen and other municipal employees, recruitment of cut-price labour from the unemployed, an end to municipal works and trading (i.e. gas, water and transport), a limit on municipal housing – even a charge on library books. It wished to end municipal borrowing from the public, which provided the finance for municipal trading. Retrenchment alone would not suffice, and the Property Owners fell back on the long-established

[58]E.g. Avebury, *On municipal and national trading* (1906), chs. IV, IX–XI.
[59]Incorporated Association for the Protection of Property Owners, *A practicable and equitable scheme for reducing the rates on house property and providing new sources of revenue* (1905) (Brit. Lib. 1891.C).

Conservative doctrine of exchequer subsidies. They asked for substantial grants in aid of poor relief, asylums, education and highways, and for cheap government loans.

The most innovative part was an attack on the working-class franchise. This consisted of a set of proposals, each more severe than its predecessor. Municipal employees were to be struck off the electoral register because of their vested interest in municipal extravagance. Rates were to be entered in a special column in rent books, in order to impress compounding occupiers with their magnitude and to mobilise their indignation against spendthrift politicians. Even better, compounding was to be abolished altogether and the rates thrown directly on the tenants, thereby bringing home to them, quite literally, the need for public economy. As in Disraeli's Reform Act of 1867, voting would again become conditional on direct payment of rates. Occupiers would have to choose between compounding and voting. All compounders (who made up much if not most of the existing working-class constituency) would lose the vote. Finally, the pamphlet advocated the restoration of multiple votes for property owners and the extension of the franchise to ratepaying companies and corporations. Far from being the product of an isolated group on the political fringe, the pamphlet expressed the considered response of London's land-owners and house-proprietors to the challenge of collectivism, and its principles were endlessly reiterated in the Unionist and the property press. 'The community is exploited for the benefit of one class, who do not contribute directly to the rates at all', concluded the pamphlet, 'It is impossible for the more substantial ratepayers to obtain fair representation on the local authorities in many parts of London and they have practically become victims to an organised system of plunder'. It is interesting to note that Albert K. Rollit, who led the forces of 'municipalism', supported the municipal franchise for corporations also demanded by his arch-rival, Lord Avebury. Both men introduced bills to this end.[60]

'Poplar' became a Conservative rallying cry in the last years of Progressive government in London. Under the leadership of Will Crooks and George Lansbury the Poplar Guardians promoted a policy of improved workhouse conditions and generous out-relief, financed by the highest rates in London. In 1904 the slump forced an increase in out-relief, and the Guardians' capital projects for Poor Law Schools and Unemployed Colonies foundered in the face of high indebtedness. Local

[60]PRO 30/72/35, A.M.C. (1905), pp. 63. 115.

ratepayers counter-attacked with complaints to the Local Government Board, and an official investigator was appointed to inquire into the alleged misapplication of public funds.[61] As the borough and municipal elections of 1906–7 began to draw closer, the increase of rates, and its effect in conditions of declining prosperity, began to pervade the public discussion of municipal affairs. The Liberal *Daily News* and the *Estates Gazette* agreed on the severity of the problem, although they differed on solutions.[62] New associations of ratepayers sprang up in many districts and dormant ones were revived. This movement was subsumed in the Conservative front, often under the new-fangled name of Municipal Alliances. Ostensibly non-political, these organisations were a device for transcending the political cleavage that split the middle classes nationally and for mobilising their fears to contain the working-class advance on municipal institutions.

The Poplar Municipal Alliance was the archetypal new model Conservative front organisation. An undercurrent of discontent against high rates had long existed, but the Municipal Alliance was only formed in November 1905. George Bartholomew, managing director of Bryant and May's, the match makers, presided over the meeting. He denounced the feeding of rump steaks to paupers from outside the parish, and called on all ratepayers to join. The meeting carried a motion against extravagance and Bartholomew stressed the demand for a separate column for rates in compounding rate-payers' rent books.[63] The Alliance, which conducted the campaign against the Poplar Guardians, got five 'facing-both-ways' Progressives elected, and acted in co-operation with the Industrial Freedom League.[64] By September 1906, the London Municipal Society, the Ratepayers' Associations and Municipal Alliances were everywhere 'girding their loins for the approaching borough elections on November 1st'.[65] An expensive and skilful propaganda campaign was whipped up in leaflets, pamphlets, posters and the press, concentrating almost exclusively on municipal waste and rising rates. The icons of

[61]J. S. Davy. Poplar union. Report of inquiry; P.P. 1906 Cd.3240, Cd.3274, CIV. Also, R. Postgate, *The life of George Lansbury* (1951), pp. 62, 80ff. and G. Haw, *From workhouse to Westminster: the life story of Will Crooks M.P.* (1907), ch. XXXI.

[62]*DailyNews*, 10 July 1905, 12; 'London's rising tide of rates', *EG*, 15, 22 and 29 April 1905, pp. 658–9, 716 and 762 respectively.

[63]*EG*, 4 Nov. 1905, 825.

[64]Letter from G. Lansbury, *Justice*, 10 Nov. 1906; G. Haw, *Will Crooks* (1907) pp. 274, 281.

[65]*POJ* Sept. 1906, 1. See *POJ*, Aug. 1906, 1–4 for the scale of Conservative–Ratepayer interpenetration.

Fig. 18.4. *An election poster, 1907, from Haward, L.C.C. from within (1932) facing p. 31.*

socialist, progressive, anti-trust and Pro-Boer propaganda were cleverly reversed. Progressives were portrayed as greedy money-grabbers in top hats with 'semitic' features, often driving around in the vehicle of arrogance, the motor car. 'The Harmsworth–Pearson gang are shovelling out money, using their daily and evening papers as great advertisement sheets for the Municipal Reformers and against the Progressives', recorded Beatrice Webb in her diary.[66] London had seen nothing like it before; but its success cannot be attributed to clever advertising alone.

How much rising rates disturbed the equanimity of London's middle classes, and how Conservatives exploited their disquiet, is illustrated in a round of readers' letters written in response to a series of articles in the Liberal daily *Tribune* in July 1906. Their author George Sims was a colourful London *bon vivant*, a prolific and popular playwright, novelist and balladeer, who was also a journalist of undoubted flair. In 1883 he published *How the poor live*, a powerful exposure of slum life in East London which started off the 'bitter cry' agitation. In the course of a long career Sims turned to many expedients, including sponsorship of the 'George R. Sims Hair Restorer'.[67] In 1906 his fertile pen was employed again, this time to bewail 'The bitter cry of the middle classes'.[68] Perhaps he gained entry to the pages of the Radical paper on the strength of his old reputation; maybe more sinister influences were at work. Be that as it may, the series was an outright attack on the London County Council's municipal socialism. Appealing to the crudest emotions of class hatred and envy, Sims encouraged the small trader, the clerk and the struggling professional to blame their hardships on the twin evils of rising rates and the rise of labour, and pointed to the vital connection between them: 'Millions of public money are spent annually,' he declared, 'to the grave injury of the ratepayer, in endeavouring to combat the great natural law of the survival of the fittest'.[69] The poor were pampered at the ratepayers' expense.

George Sims perceived a threat in Will Crooks' progress from the workhouse to Westminster.

It is a grand thing for the boy who was brought up on the rates to rise

[66] B. Webb, *Our partnership* (1948), p. 372 (24 Feb. 1907).
[67] 'This preparation has been largely used for the past fifteen years, and with invariable success' (advertisement, *London*, 7 Oct. 1897, 815).
[68] *Tribune*, 17, 19, 21, 24–6, 28 July, 1906. Sim's anecdotal autobiography *My life* (1917) does not discuss Edwardian politics.
[69] *Tribune*, 26 July 1906, 3.

to Parliament, but it is not pleasant for the ratepayers to reflect that they are being compelled to clothe, feed, educate, house and provide with magnificent libraries a generation which will in process of time crush out their own children and form the majority in the Legislative Assembly – a majority which will be pledged to load the middle-class camel to the last straw, even at the risk of the proverbial result.[70]

He exhorted the readers to join the Middle Class Defence Association and the Association for the Protection of Property Owners. In the large correspondence that ensued, the majority of letters printed showed what a raw nerve the rates agitation had touched. Many readers endorsed Sims' observations and added their own. Coming, as they did, from a middle-class Liberal readership, the letters showed how deeply the combination of economic stagnation and rising rates had affected the shop-keepers, clerks and professionals of London; deeply enough to shake their established local political allegiances. Ratepayers' rebellions had consistently disrupted and frustrated municipal improvement in nineteenth-century provincial towns.[71] The Progressive defeat in the London boroughs in November 1906 and in the L.C.C. in March 1907 was the greatest ratepayer-revolt of them all, whipped up and successfully driven by the Conservatives against the tide of national politics. Incidentally, it managed to fulfil its promise: both the rates and the municipal debt levelled off during the Conservative tenure at Spring Gardens up to the Great War.

One correspondent reminded Mr Sims that 'the middle classes have only themselves to thank if they are now being ruined ... Middle-class men hold the best-paid offices under local governing bodies, and if, as is sometimes asserted, these officials are responsible for the extravagant expenditure, again the blame attaches to the middle class'.[72] Articles and advertisements in the *Municipal Journal* and half-a-dozen other local government weeklies (indeed, those weeklies themselves) told the story of suppliers, contractors and civic servants dependent upon municipal socialism. The surveyors who combined to fight rising rates also competed for employment (by local authorities) on the valuation of those very rates.[73] An army of officials controlled municipal departments; splendidly mustachioed engineers deployed the trams which a municipal

[70] *Ibid.*
[71] Hennock, 'Finance and politics' (1963).
[72] A. Cooke, *Tribune*, 25 July 1906.
[73] See 'Dispute between rating surveyors', *EG*, 1 Sept. 1900, 367.

bureaucracy administered. Civic architects designed the schools in which a growing force of teachers officiated. Rates produced large transfer payments into and within the middle classes and the only anxiety in many middle class minds was whether revenues would hold up.

Conclusion

Three main effects combined to depress property values in Edwardian cities: dear money, failing demand for housing and rising taxation. But these are only proximate causes. The true nature of the slump must be sought beyond the purely economic universe, in the struggle for power at the local, national and even global levels. Rising interest rates, failing demand and rising rates: each of these developments appears to have gained some impetus from politics.

The rise of interest rates was a symptom of a complex of developments which exercised many contemporary minds and is still not fully understood. It signalled the emergence of the European economies from the last stage of the 'Great Depression' in the mid-1890s and some observers correctly identified 1896 as the turning point. Others pointed to the Boer War with its high rates of Government borrowing.[74] The expansion of gold production, the revival of overseas investment opportunities, the extension of the approved list of trustee investments to municipal and colonial government securities were all cited as causes.[75]

For some the rise of interest rates presented a feverish symptom of insecurity. The growth of overseas investment coincided with the rise of imperial contention and with growing international discord. Those were the years of Fashoda, of Milner and Kruger, of the Boxer uprising in China, the Russo-Japanese war and the abortive revolution in Russia, of growing unrest in India, of Morocco, of wars in North Africa and the Balkans, of Franco-German tension, of Anglo-German naval rivalry. Germany not only rattled sabres; it also overtook Britain as a manufacturing nation. Joseph Chamberlain's Tariff Reform campaign, which highlighted competitive weakness and import penetration in many industries, was an expression of growing insecurity. Money saved by not fighting in South Africa, wrote Harold Cox, could have lowered interest

[74]See A Stockbroker, 'The depreciation of British home investments', *Economic Journal* 22 (1912), 226.
[75]See e.g. 'Sir Edward Holden on the fall of Consols', *Statist*, 27 Jan. 1912, 164–5 and 'Consols.-II', *Statist*, 10 Feb. 1912, 295–7.

rates by one per cent, enough to solve the housing question.[76] George Head told surveyors, 'it is evident that any check to our supremacy in trade cannot fail to have a downward bearing on property values'.[77]

Demand for housing also began to fail in the aftermath of the Boer War boom. Economic growth stagnated in the 1900s in Britain, with an adverse effect on purchasing power of both the middle class and the workers. In addition to the direct effect of stagnant (or declining) real incomes on the ability to pay for housing, and the lure of lucrative foreign and municipal securities for investors in housing, the mild inflation and bouts of full employment which characterised the period also fed the labour movement and fired the labour unrest of those years. Indirectly, through its implied challenge to the established order, this helped to undermine the security of property owners and to depress the value of their assets. Substantial overseas migration, which also affected demand for housing, was another symptom of disaffection. Transport technology, another element in failing demand, is perhaps a more autonomous factor. But the timing and form of its diffusion, as we have seen, was strongly affected by local political configurations. The predominance of municipal over private enterprise meant that there was less scope in Britain than in the United States for entrepreneurs to maximise real-estate windfalls from transport development and the net effect of electric and motor traction must have been to keep the aggregate of property values in check.[78]

Rising rates was the third factor, and the one most directly affected by politics. The increase of local taxation could account directly for about one-quarter of the decline of property values in London. But the impact was no doubt magnified in investors' minds by the Conservative propaganda of 1905–7 and the mobilisation of ratepayers into municipal politics. At the beginning of the fourth year of Liberal government the *Property Owners' Journal* opened with words of dark foreboding.

Nineteen hundred and nine opens upon owners of House Property with beclouded prospects. A depression like Egyptian darkness has settled upon every market, so that nothing save the "choices of the choice" will sell, and then only at a price that spells loss of capital. The outlook from the Parliamentary point of view is distinctly discouraging. To murmur the word "site values" impales a quivering shaft into the heart of possessors of ground rents, notwithstanding

[76]Cox, *Land nationalisation* (1906), p. 106.
[77]Head, 'Giant London' (1909), 336.
[78]See Offer, 'Ricardo's paradox' (1980), pp. 245–9.

the government assurance that existing contracts are to be respected. With a savagery suggestive of cannibals, the medical officers of health are relentlessly prosecuting the owners of houses for non-compliance with notices involving trivial alterations, or breaches of ridiculous bye-laws. With trade as bad as it can conceivably be, and tenants out of work in consequence, the current coin of rent is replaced with an unsatisfactory promise to pay, date and place unnamed, hereafter. With empty houses right and left, with rates ascending to the giddy heights of Everest and Kichinjuga, look where he will, the Property Owner for the time being is, and must be, a pessimist.[79]

Political insecurity continued to boost the impact of taxation on property values. 'As beauty is in the eye of the beholder, so value is in the mind of the person who contemplates it', said George Head in 1910. 'Fluctuations of value are largely dependent on the feelings of security and insecurity which prevail in the minds of investors'.[80] He was expressing the tenurial community's disquiet at the impending land value taxes then hanging in suspension together with the rest of Lloyd George's 'People's Budget'.

Socialistic schemes are in the air which, although unlikely to come in the advanced form in which they are promulgated by their advocates, yet tinge and colour the policy of the great party with which they are most nearly allied. Some discern in the bills brought before the Houses of Parliament by H.M. Government more than a mild flavour of socialist confiscation.[81]

Local taxation embodied a fundamental dilemma of Edwardian *Sozialpolitik*. If the production of goods and the maintenance of labour were to be kept at a level of competitive efficiency, urban conditions had to be ameliorated and improved. Revenue from local rates fell short of satisfying these pressing requirements, but taxation of houses was already high enough to choke off the market supply of new housing and cause existing accommodation to be run down. Public works to relieve unemployment indirectly pushed up the rents of the unemployed; better classrooms meant inferior homes; health visitors exacerbated the conditions they were meant to cure, because they were paid for by rates on the poor. Moreover, the geographical inequality of incidence localised the problem in areas already deprived. As George Lansbury said in 1906,

[79] *POJ*, Jan. 1909, 1.
[80] Head, 'The property market' (1910), 48.
[81] *Ibid.* 45.

'when the cost of all-out relief in Poplar falls on Poplar alone ... it is quite evident that Poplar's burden is too heavy'.[82] These were the problems that local taxation placed before the Liberal government and in a more general form, before its European competitors as well.

The armaments race of the first decade of the twentieth century, and the persistent demands for social amelioration, placed a severe strain on the fiscal structure of the European states. In England, France, Austria, Italy, Holland, even in the United States, there were crises in State financing. In England and Germany the issue of the distribution of the tax burden developed into a major constitutional crisis.[83] In 1885 Chamberlain had asked, prematurely, 'what ransom will property pay for the security it enjoys?'[84] In the Edwardian period the payment could no longer be postponed. One interest, the small house-capitalists, had already paid a heavier ransom than it could afford.

In effect, the increase of rates acted as a capital levy on house-property. A government concerned to ameliorate urban conditions could scarcely find a less suitable sector in which to condone such an impost. The Liberals were caught on the horns of a Benthamite dilemma. They were a party of property and order no less than the Conservatives and after 1906 they were called upon to adjudicate on the re-apportionment of the costs of upholding the social order. But past principles and past policies lay heavy on their hands. Liberal doctrine had prescribed independence and self-sufficiency for local administration; it regarded tenure as a fruitful source of revenue. Conservative doctrine, on the other hand, was centralising. So was Fabian doctrine. George Bernard Shaw, like his friend Sidney Webb (above, p. 216) proclaimed that Liberal doctrine was obsolete and that the Tory principle of grants-in-aid, even the reviled Agricultural Rates Act, the dole for landlords, showed the way forward. Moreover, he committed the Fabian Society to this position.

Shaw stated this view in the Fabian 'Election Manifesto' for 1900 with inimitable clarity:

we ... continue to raise our local revenues by a method of rating which is, in effect, a heavy tax on houses. Imagine the effect of shifting this tax to any other necessity of life: say bread, or matches. Popular resistance would be overwhelming: the tax would have to

[82]George Lansbury, in a letter to the *Daily Chronicle*, 21 March 1906.
[83]The last three sentences are taken from C. F. Schorske, *German social democracy 1905–1917* (Cambridge, Mass. 1955), p. 147.
[84]Garvin, *Chamberlain* (1932), i, 549.

be shifted to income. But as we are accustomed to our rating system, we tolerate the taxation of houses, and never think of its effect on the supply.

We therefore suggest that the socialistic policy of Grants in Aid, which the anti-Socialist Liberals have opposed as a policy of doles, can be extended to the housing industry. In the Parliament now being elected [1900], the five years period of the Agricultural Rating Act will expire. By that time the erroneous opposition to its principle, having received no popular encouragement, will have lost countenance; but the objection to its evident favoritism towards the country landlords will remain, and will lead to a demand for extending its benefits. It will then be quite possible to provide for the payment by the Treasury of rates, or half rates, on well-built sanitary houses ... Such an arrangement would stimulate both municipal and private enterprise in the matter of housing.[85]

The principle of grants-in-aid effected a Fabian–Tory convergence against the Liberals which remained in force during the Edwardian period. Bernard Shaw's proposals were to find their most effective expression in a Tory initiative, which will be described in due course (pp. 388, 405).

Tory grant-in-aid doctrine was motivated by the interests of landowners, by the Conservative 'ramparts of property' project of building up a protective belt of small proprietors, and by an opportunist appeal to urban ratepayers. Fabians supported it as a harbinger of State intervention. Shaw and Webb grasped the logic of local taxation as early as 1889 and welcomed the transfer of tenure from house-capitalists to the towns as the making of a trend towards socialism – in the first instance, as an element of 'municipal socialism'. Sidney Webb predicted that rising taxation would gradually expropriate the urban landlords and house-capitalists and force the State to undertake their functions. In 1890 he wrote,

> municipal socialism has ... the effect of absorbing in 'rates' a constantly increasing share of the rental of the country. Our progressive municipalization of rent by increase of local rates, is clearly only an unconscious form of Land Nationalization.[86]

[85]G. B. Shaw, *Fabianism and the empire: a manifesto by the Fabian Society* (1900), pp. 69–70.
[86]S. Webb, *Socialism in England* (1890), p. 190. Webb was typically ambiguous as to whether it was the ground rent alone or the buildings as well that he wished to confiscate through the rates. On the one hand he expressed approval of a rate of twenty shillings in the pound, on the other he said it was impractical to confiscate the whole of the unearned increment (see Chapter 12[58, 59]). Else-

In a lighter vein, the story is told of the Christian Socialist, the Rev. Stuart Headlam. When the rate-collector at his door said, 'Rates are up, Sir', the Reverend answered, 'thank God!'[87]

It was against this background of house-capitalist despondency and a crisis of local taxation that the Liberal government of 1906 began to sort out its plans for additional taxation of tenure, in the form of TLV.

where he claimed that economic friction placed the incidence of local rates on occupiers, not owners (see Webb, *A plea* (1887), p. 11 and Town holdings sel. com.; P.P. 1890 (341) XVIII, e.g. q. 331). The Fabian notion of rent extended beyond ground-rent proper and embraced all forms of costless surplus; there was no reason why house-rents above the replacement cost and the 'normal' profit should not be included (see G. B. Shaw, 'Transition' in *Fabian essays in socialism*, ed. Shaw (1908 rep.), pp. 179–99).

[87] J. W. R. Scott, *England's green and pleasant land* (rev. Penguin edn 1947), p. 106.

Part V

EDWARDIAN CLIMAX 1906–1914

19

TOWARDS THE PEOPLE'S BUDGET
1906–1909

I

The bye-roads of local rating converged again upon the high road of national politics in the years of Campbell-Bannerman, Asquith and Lloyd George. The distribution of tenure in those years, the malaise of urban proprietors and the crisis of local finance have been assessed in foregoing chapters. The narrative of tenurial politics has been carried up to 1906. A large literature has grown up around the Liberal governments of 1906–1914 and there is no point in recapitulation. What stands to be considered is the coherence of policy and the assumptions and attitudes from which it arose. The task calls for the use of both the wide-angle and telephoto lenses, in order to place those familiar landmarks, the great budget crises of 1909 and 1914, in a broader historical perspective; and also to unravel obscure chains of events that gave rise to such great consequences.

A new generation of Liberal MPs, more radical than its predecessors, arrived in Westminster in 1906. Land reform and the taxation of land values were writ large in its election manifestos. Land reform was endorsed by 68 per cent of English Liberal candidates and 52 per cent mentioned TLV.[1] Two engines propelled the TLV bandwagon, often acting at cross-purposes. The municipal interest was energised by the crisis of local finance. The land-reform militants were motivated by a vision of redistribution from landowners to capitalists. Together, the two interests mobilised an impressive Parliamentary presence. Municipal agitation had raised TLV to prominence. In November 1905 (to cite but one instance) a national conference of rating authorities drew up a TLV petition and in February 1906 a deputation of 150, from 118 municipal bodies, presented it to the new Liberal Chancellor, H. H. Asquith.[2] But A. K. Rollit lost his seat in the Liberal landslide and the A.M.C., while

[1] A. K. Russell, *Liberal landslide: the general election of 1906* (Newton Abbot, 1973), pp. 65, 79.
[2] P. Wilson Raffan, *The policy of the land values group in the House of Commons* (address delivered at the National Liberal Club political and economic circle, 25 Nov. 1912), pp. 7–8.

continuing to press for rate-support grants for education, police, roads and unemployment, fell silent on TLV.[3] So for the first two years of Liberal government the land reform movement had the field largely to itself; its doctrines permeated deeply into the body of Liberal opinion. In the Commons, a 'Land Values Group' was formed around a committed core of single-taxers (including P. W. Raffan, C. P. Trevelyan, A. Ure, Josiah Wedgwood, J. Dundas White and J. H. Whitley). By Easter, it claimed as many as 280 adherents.[4]

The land reformers had earned their spurs in the municipal TLV agitations around the turn of the century, and they realised that their schemes for the taxation of tenure had to be reconciled with urban alarm over rising rates. They endeavoured to point out that TLV was not an additional burden, but a shift of taxation from over-taxed buildings and industry to under-taxed (or in some cases, untaxed) sites; from a productive tenure, houses, to a parasitical one, land. An official Liberal leaflet of April 1905 put the argument at its most succinct:

... 2. Under the present system of Rating, for every brick that is laid, and for every improvement that is made, the rate-collector increases his demand. The tax on house-building is in some ways as bad as a tax on bread.

3. The taxation of Land Values would enable us to reduce, and eventually to abolish, the tax on buildings, and thus remove one of the causes which make houses dear and bad.

SUPPORT THE LIBERAL PARTY

AND THE

TAXATION OF LAND VALUES

Note the old Liberal doctrine that tenures were separable for taxation, in direct contrast with the Tory insistence that they were not (see pp. 163–65). Time would soon tell which doctrine was tenable. The leaflet held out even greater hopes from TLV, and blamed land hoarding for economic stagnation.

4. Landowners, by holding out for rents or prices which cannot be paid, are preventing the employment of workmen, the better housing of the people, and the expansion of all kinds of industry.[5]

Two land societies dominated the Liberal field, each with its tight cluster of Parliamentary activists and a loose fringe of more than one

[3] PRO 30/72/36 and 37, A.M.C. minutes (1906, 1907).
[4] Raffan, Land values group (1912), p. 8.
[5] Liberal Publication Department leaflet no. 2041.

hundred sympathisers, some of whom adhered to both groups.[6] On several occasions the societies mustered more than 200 Parliamentary signatures and in December 1906 a joint Liberal and Labour deputation of nearly 150 MPs handed Campbell-Bannerman a memorial signed by as many as four hundred members.[7] The Land Nationalisation Society (hereafter LNS), the smaller of the two, advocated land nationalisation, with compensation for owners.[8] The Land Values Group, Parliamentary spearhead of the English and Scottish Leagues for the Taxation of Land Values, looked forward to the taxation of pure rent to extinction, with no compensation.[9] Both societies denied the legitimacy of Ricardian rent, and pinned their hopes on the same tactic: *a valuation of property separating the site from the buildings, and assessed on capital values.* The LNS saw valuation as a preliminary to its strategy of 'tax or buy'. Owners would be required to place a value on their property. In order to induce a true self-valuation, the declarations could be used for either compulsory purchase (if low) or as a basis for taxation (if high). The Land Values Group wanted the valuation in order to separate the value of sites from the improvements.

Liberal leaflet no. 2041 (quoted above) arrived in Asquith's office like an endorsed bill due for payment.[10] Municipal and parliamentary deputations kept up the pressure for early redemption; and TLV activists submitted proposals for ways and means. Trevelyan elaborated his plan for a penny tax on capital values (see p. 249) and C. Llewellyn Davies, Secretary of the English League for the Taxation of Land Values, presented a scheme for de-rating houses and transferring the burden exclusively to land.[11] Asquith submitted the plans to Treasury officials. Sir Edward Hamilton, the Joint Permanent Secretary, put pen to paper: 'both proposals are to my mind ridiculous', he wrote, and on second thought substituted 'impossible'. He then ran through a list of objections, raising points of practice and principle. They ranged from perverse to prophetic, but the prophecy was of a self-fulfilling quality. As he made

[6] Parliamentary membership, see Ward, 'Land reform' (1976), pp. 461–3.
[7] Raffan, *Land values group* (1912), p. 9; *The Times*, 19 Dec. 1906, 10b–c.
[8] J. Hyder, *The case for land nationalisation* (2nd edn 1914), ch. XVIII.
[9] Raffan, *Land values group* (1912) p. 10; For a manifesto, see C. H. Chomley and R. L. Outhwaite, *The essential reform: Land values taxation in theory and practice* (1909).
[10] It is in T 168/95, the Joint Permanent Secretary's Papers (E. W. Hamilton).
[11] T 168/95; The Davies memo is undated and unsigned, but apparently from Aug. 1906. The Trevelyan memorandum is referred to in a letter from 'WB' (W. Blain?) to Hamilton, 30 July [1906].

amply clear, the veteran civil servant was none too keen. 'I need not say that it would invite violent opposition', he concluded his assessment of the schemes, 'so violent, that the idea could not be proceeded with'. He advised Asquith to take the slow road of valuation reform, and Asquith complied.[12] But if this was meant to be a diversion, it was not sufficient to last the whole of the government's tenure.

The need for valuation reform was not questioned. Goschen had rationalised valuation in London in 1869 but failed to reform the rest of the country two years later (p. 176ff). At the turn of the century the Royal Commission on local taxation recommended, in effect, that the omission be put right. 'Uniformity of valuation', Walter Long explained to the Cabinet in 1901, 'is the first requisite in connection with any improvement in the present system of local taxation'.[13] A valuation bill was finally introduced in 1904, but the moment was not opportune: rating authorities were still smarting from the Education Act fracas. Long proposed to entrust valuation to county and borough councils, subject, as in London, to Inland Revenue supervision. This, complained a Conservative Guardian in a letter to The Times, would sweep out of existence over 600 Union assessment committees and inflict 'another serious wrench to the loyalty of the Conservative party'.[14] In addition to the loss of local dignities (although the writer did not mention it) assessments also stood to be raised, especially in the more affluent districts. So Boards of Guardians and the City of London joined forces to defeat the bill and it fared no better the following year.[15] Valuation reform was a vague enough policy, and yet it held out promise to the restive single-taxers. Asquith committed himself to a separate assessment of site values as early as February 1906 and in December Campbell-Bannerman promised a valuation bill in the following session.[16]

A wind of Radicalism blew in from the north. The single-tax monthly Land Values had been transferred to Glasgow in 1902 and the city's TLV bills had been intermittently introduced starting as far back as 1893.[17] In 1906 one was introduced as a matter of course. It conformed in essentials

[12]T 168/95, Hamilton to Asquith, 9 Sept. 1906. The file opens with an extract from the minority report of the local taxation R. com., followed by a long disapproving letter from Hamilton, dated 25 May 1906.
[13]CAB 37/59/140, W. Long, 'Valuation', 24 Dec. 1901, p. 3.
[14]'A Conservative', The Times, 26 May 1904, 10e.
[15]See The Times, e.g. 15 June 1904, 12f; CAB 37/90/114, J. Burns, 'Valuation (England and Wales)', 28 Dec. 1907, pp. 8–9.
[16]Raffan, Land values group (1912), pp. 7–8; The Times, 19 Dec. 1906, 10b–c.
[17]See 184 H.C. deb 4 ser. 19 Feb. 1908, J. M. Henderson, 880–1 and Scottish land. The report of the Scottish land enquiry committee (1914), pp. 509–11.

to TLV ideas of the 1890s, i.e. a separate valuation of land and houses, and an *additional* rate on owners equivalent to 2s. in the pound, on a rental assessment derived from capital values. The bill was sent to a Select Committee packed with single taxers, who proceeded to transform it root and branch. They proposed a sweeping innovation: all buildings and machinery to be de-rated, and the rating base contracted to sites alone. 'Existing contracts' were boldly brushed aside, as were other theoretical and practical difficulties. The reasoning invoked was undiluted Henry George: land values were created by the labour of the community, not by the owners, and ought to bear the whole rates, which should not be a burden on enterprise and industry. The benefits promised were 'to stimulate buildings and improvements, to bring more building land into the market, to lower rents and to diminish overcrowding'. 'A complete redistribution of the principle of rating' was the avowed aim.[18]

Alexander Ure (1853–1928), a committed single-taxer, was chairman of the Select Committee and also Solicitor-General for Scotland. His superior, the Lord Advocate Thomas Shaw was of only slightly more moderate cast of mind.[19] Next year the proposals appeared as a Land Values (Scotland) Bill, to which the Liberal party became officially committed. It attracted the most vehement opposition from Conservatives, and came to grief in the House of Lords. Never before had such re-distributionist ideas enjoyed wide currency in the Commons. Henry George had suddenly (like Marx in the late 1960s and early 1970s?) become reputable. 'It was noteworthy', one opponent remarked, 'that when the name of Henry George was mentioned in this House it should find on the Liberal benches so many cheers'. Balfour made the same observation.[20] The Liberal leadership was also perturbed. Strong misgivings were voiced both on the right of the party (by Harold Cox) and on the left (by L. Chiozza Money). To allay fears, not least among his own adherents, Asquith tied his own hands with a promise, repeatedly made, to respect 'existing contracts'.[21] The Cabinet nevertheless proceeded with plans for a valuation bill for England and Asquith reiterated his commitment to the principle of separate valuation of sites

[18]Land values taxation etc. (Scotland) bill. Sel. com. special rep.; P.P. 1906 (379) X, p. vi.
[19]H. P. MacMillan, 'Alexander Ure', *D.N.B.*; 184 H.C. deb. 4 ser. 19 Feb. 1908, T. Shaw, 837–45.
[20]177 H.C. deb. 4 ser. 10 July 1907, J. F. Remnant, 1633; A. J. Balfour, 1652.
[21]181 H.C. deb. 4 ser. 20 Aug. 1907, H. Cox, 485ff; L.C. Money, 502ff; H. H. Asquith, 494.

and buildings. The Scottish bill was re-introduced in 1908 and the Lord Advocate hinted darkly that should the Lords reject it, valuation and taxation might be combined in one scheme.[22]

Unionists professed to be dumbfounded by this show of class treachery. Liberals seemed to think, said Bonar Law, that 'because they and their friends do not own any land, that, therefore, they can apply socialism to the land without any danger to themselves'. But wasn't Ure's forensic skill also a rent, created by the community? 'Put the best lawyer in the world out on a moor and what is his value?' Derating of improvements was 'the political economy of the madhouse'.[23]

Municipal pressure for rating reform was building up again,[24] and some Unionists, having learnt the lessons of 1904–5, recognised a political opportunity. Not all of them shared Balfour and Bonar Law's intransigence. In the summer of 1908 'a small group of Unionists, including several leading members of the party', (apparently led by Alfred Milner) drew up an unauthorised programme for a positive Unionist policy.[25] *Inter alia*, they proposed to allow town councils to rate sites separately from structures.[26] Law accepted the text in principle, objecting only to women's suffrage and TLV.[27] In 1900 he had captured the Blackfriars constituency of Glasgow from A. D. Provand, a card-carrying single taxer, and would brook no concessions.[28] So far as groundowners were concerned, his caution was justified. The Liberal party, it seemed, was no longer attempting to get them to make an ordinary contribution to the rates. It wanted site-owners to pay much more, proportionately, than the other interests.

II

After Asquith became Prime Minister in April 1908 he again committed the government to a separate valuation of land and buildings.[29]

[22] 184 H.C. deb. 4 ser. 18 Feb. 1908, Asquith, 743–4; H.C. deb. 4 ser. 19 Feb. 1908, T. Shaw, 843.
[23] 184 H.C. deb. 4 ser. 19 Feb. 1908, A. Bonar Law, 878–9.
[24] E.g. 184 H.C. deb. 4 ser. 18 Feb. 1908, motion on local taxation, 727–37.
[25] A galley proof, untitled and undated, is in BL 18/8/7. The sponsors were Milner, A. Chamberlain, J. W. Hills, L. Amery and F. Ware, editor of the *Morning Post*. See BL 18/4/75, Ware to Bonar Law, 29 Sept. 1908.
[26] BL 18/8/7, manifesto galley no. 3.
[27] BL 18/8/10, Law to Ware, 8 Sept. 1908.
[28] See R. Blake, *The unknown prime minister* (1955), pp. 38–9; 38 H.C. deb. 4 ser. 8 March 1895, A.D. Provand, 700–6.
[29] 188 H.C. deb. 4 ser. 12 May 1908, Asquith, 1058.

But the summer vacation appears to have weakened his resolve. Through the medium of William Robson, the Attorney-General, Asquith informed the Cabinet of the difficulties and dangers inherent in shifting the rates on to the sites, as the single-taxers advocated. 'Land values alone', warned Robson, 'would not suffice for the burden of the rates. In districts where they are worth considering at all, it has been estimated that they amount to one-third of the present rateable value'. Rates also constituted about one third of the rent.

> It would, therefore, amount to a complete confiscation of the owner's interest if the rate were laid on him. It would often amount to more than 20s. in the £, and in that case the owner would not pay it. He would abandon the land, ... and thus the rate would, in effect, be levied on buildings after all.[30]

Robson wrote that a more moderate course, of merely placing an *additional* rate on sites, if applied to agricultural land, 'would inevitably destroy any chance whatever this Bill may have in the House of Lords'. He nevertheless proposed to proceed with the taxation of vacant land and other forms of 'conversion rent' (p. 114) on the outskirts and in the centres of towns.[31] This recalled Mill's proposal of 1871 for taxing future unearned increments. In the meantime Lloyd George, newly installed in the Treasury, evinced much greater enthusiasm for his namesake's nostrums than did the attorney-general. Even before Robson's memo had circulated he by-passed recalcitrant Treasury officials and wrote directly to Sir Robert Chalmers, chairman of the Board of Inland Revenue:

> My mind has been working on a Land Tax – either uniform or graduated according to the size of the estates. A special tax on ground rents and on all lands situated within the area of towns or within a certain distance of towns – graduated according to the size of the towns. I feel that if there is to be an extension of the pension system on contributory lines the property which is improved by the labour of the community should contribute its share. Mining royalties ought also to be taxed for the same reason. I have also a proposal to make about the taxation of waste land.[32]

The letter shows that Lloyd George was probing the possibilities of TLV

---

[30]Bodl. Lib. L. Harcourt Papers dep. 576, W. S. Robson, 'Valuation bill', Sept. 1908 [a Cabinet memorandum], p. 2 (covering letter from Asquith to Cabinet, 21 Sept. 1908).

[31]*Ibid.* pp. 3, 7–8.

[32]PRO IR 73/2, Private office papers, Budget 1909, land tax proposals up to budget speech, Lloyd George to Chalmers, 5 Sept. 1908 (copy).

on his own, although not without the benefit of advice from the organised pressure groups.

A variety of discordant motives animated Liberal valuation proposals. First came the chronic problem of local finance; second, the old Liberal belief that shifting some of the rates on to the landowners would go some way towards a solution. Third, the accumulated anger at the Lords' provocations; fourth, pressure from the land reformers. The single-taxers kept Lloyd George well supplied with memoranda and briefs in that autumn of 1908. What they imagined, in line with Henry George, was a sweeping redistribution from land to capital and labour.

> All productive work is the application of labour to land [wrote Josiah Wedgwood to Lloyd George]. To deal with the Unemployed problem on sound lines we must increase *productive* work, that is we must make it easier for labour to get to the land. Short of a revolution this can only be done by using the compulsion of this land values tax to induce the owners of land and minerals to allow development by labour ... this is not a new tax ... but only the diverting into public pockets of a tax which at present goes into the private pockets of the landlord as rent.[33]

Brave words from a rentier who took up full-time Radicalism on the proceeds of an inherited share in Armstrong's armament works.[34]

Details of the proposed tax were settled in the Inland Revenue by the end of November 1908, but to present it to the Cabinet, the authority of Edgar Harper was invoked. A Cabinet paper carrying his name was constructed with typical ingenuity. What Harper effectively proposed was a land tax equal to (and deductible from) the income tax (Schedule A), but assessed not on income but on capital value. In cases where market value greatly exceeded the capitalised income, the difference would be taxed.[35]

The single-tax rating proposals invoked the principle of 'efficiency'. Land lay underutilised for speculative reasons and a tax would force the owners to put it to the most remunerative use. In its extreme forms, such

---

[33]IR 73/2, J. Wedgwood, 'Memo. on taxation of land values' (n.d.; 'C of Ex 25/9/08' pencilled on verso of p. 4 (f. 318) in Chalmer's hand), f. 316. This was followed by other memoranda from Wedgwood, J. D. White (of the Land Values group) and C. Llewellyn Davies.

[34]Wedgwood was nephew of Hamilton Rendel, bachelor and youngest son of William Armstrong's original partner, J. M. Rendel. See C. V. Wedgwood, *The last of the Radicals: Josiah Wedgwood, M.P.* (1951), pp. 33, 64.

[35]CAB 37/96/164, 'Memorandum by Mr. Edgar Harper on the imposition of a national tax on land values', 5 Dec. 1908.

utilitarian zeal invited ridicule. 'We were staying with the R. C. Trevelyans near Dorking a week ago', a friend wrote to J. C. Wedgwood in 1909, 'and they showed us one of the most beautiful views I have ever seen, which they told us you had exclaimed upon as a magnificent piece of "undeveloped land"'.[36] It was an instance of a clash between the puritanical and the romantic strains of the single-tax creed. In a perceptive memorandum, the Lord Chancellor (Loreburn) argued that economic efficiency did not always coincide with social utility and that a maximum economic return on land could make overcrowding worse and lead to loss of open space.[37] A distrust of the market was also expressed in the same government's Town Planning Act of 1909. The single tax provided an incentive to make the full 'economic use' of land, but zoning and town planning were an indispensible antidote if building was really to be 'set free'.[38] There was also truth in Loreburn's argument that vacant land values were partly 'lottery ticket' values which it would be unjust to tax. Bankers had long taken this view.[39]

Loreburn made other pertinent points. The tax, he said, was potentially regressive; it 'is not in proportion to wealth, but may and indeed must fall upon many comparatively poor people and let the rich go free'. He was sceptical about the practicality of valuation and feared it would prove costly. Moreover, he foresaw that 'In any provisions, however carefully prepared, great litigation will arise'. He asked why the whole country had to be valued in order to tax only undeveloped land.[40] Other Cabinet members also expressed strong reservations.[41] Agricultural MPs and Liberal property owners communicated their misgivings to Asquith, who laid them before the Cabinet. Perhaps the most telling political point was made by an anonymous correspondent, who complained that Asquith and Lloyd George could not see the difference between a legitimate urban site tax, and the Henry George scheme. 'It is this confusion of thought which makes what is reasonable, and by itself doubtless not unpopular, detestable and a source of dread to the loyal voter of all classes'.[42] In a dismissive reply, Lloyd George made short shrift of all objections. He made a telling point against agrarian com-

---

[36]WP1 (1905–14), Philip Morrell [?] to J. C. Wedgwood, 31 Aug. 1909.
[37]IR 73/2, 'Lord Chancellor's Memo', ?17 Jan. 1909, f. 124.
[38]See The land, ii (1914), 559.
[39]IR 73/2, f. 125; Rae, Country banker (1885), pp. 113–15.
[40]IR 73/2, 'Lord Chancellor's memo', f. 126.
[41]Inside Asquith's cabinet: from the diaries of Charles Hobhouse, ed. E. David (1977), pp. 74, 76–8.
[42]CAB 37/97/10, H. H. Asquith, 'Taxation of land values', 22 Jan. 1909, p. 1.

plaints. 'Large sums', he wrote, 'must be raised by this Budget for the financing of proposals which must inevitably relieve agricultural land of a large share of the burdens now imposed upon it for the maintenance of the poor'.[43] The single taxers had pressed the argument that land values should be made to pay for social welfare and that local taxation would be relieved thereby.[44] The whole programme was thoroughly imbued with the spirit (and the technical detail) of their proposals of 1906. There was no immediate expectation of large revenues but the Chancellor held out the (very reasonable) prospect of future windfalls.[45]

The land taxes which appeared on budget day 1909 were an outcome of prolonged and muddled deliberations in which tactical considerations played a considerable part. By imposing the land values tax as a surtax on the income tax, Schedule A, Lloyd George thought he could evade one of the main obstacles, the Prime Minister's pledge to respect existing contracts. Contracts to evade Schedule A assessments had always been void.[46] But this subterfuge carried a political penalty. After years of agitation municipalities had come to regard the site tax as rightfully theirs, and forcefully reminded the government of their grievances by means of a mammoth deputation in March 1909. They would feel cheated of their entitlement if deprived of the fruits of the tax.[47] Moreover, a valuation bill standing alone stood no chance in the House of Lords, so valuation had to be incorporated into the budget. In order to be admitted into the budget, the land taxes had to raise revenue the same year – but no revenue could be raised before the valuation was available. This conundrum was the underlying reason for the variety of taxes finally proposed, on vacant land, on mining royalties and on ground rents. On 13 March 1909 Lloyd George told the cabinet of yet another tax, a 20 per cent capital gains tax ('increment value duty') on land transfers (including death). This had been proposed ten years before to the local taxation Royal Commission by his cabinet opponent Reginald McKenna, and may have been introduced in order to neutralise McKenna's influential opposition. L. Chiozza Money, a left-wing Liberal

[43]CAB 37/97/16, D. Lloyd George, 'Taxation of land values', 29 Jan. 1909, p. 2.
[44]T 168/95, [C. Llewellyn Davies?], 'Memorandum on the taxation of land values', (n.d. ?Aug. 1906), p. 2.
[45]WR 30/27/2/1, W. Runciman, 'Lloyd George's first sketch of his *land tax* proposals – notes dictated by him to the cabinet, March 1909' (holograph). A revenue of £3 million was anticipated for the third year.
[46]CAB 37/97/16, D. Lloyd George, 'Taxation of land values', 29 Jan. 1909, pp. 5–6.
[47]See *The Times*, 19 March 1909, 6c. Chalmers had warned the Chancellor; see IR 73/2, Sir R. Chalmers, 'The budget and site values', 27 Nov. 1908, f. 24.

opponent of the single tax, had commended it in 1907, calling attention to its successful application in Frankfurt and Bernard Mallet, then a Treasury official, brought back a favourable report on the operation of the 'Frankfort Tax' in 1908.[48] It was more far-reaching than Harper's scheme, since it took in all sites, irrespective of the quality or value of the buildings. In effect, it realised Mill's 1871 proposal for the taxation of future increments. Much more than the 'Harper tax' on vacant land it held a promise of constantly increasing revenues, and could have become a major source of revenue. And once the tax was established, the screw could always be turned.

What was Lloyd George trying to achieve? The cumulative effect of sectarian pressure, of aristocratic obstruction, of a long-standing commitment to rating reform, and a shortfall of revenue, had brought about a scheme for fiscal re-distribution that was potentially far in advance of anything ever projected by a Liberal government. The Land Values section of the People's Budget singled out not real property, not rental incomes, but pure Rent, a theoretical entity, for special taxation. The scheme was designed to provoke; but it grew out of a long tradition of resentment and out of a peculiar vision of British society. Antecedents have been amply alluded to. The plan appealed to the instincts of British Radicalism in its extremist mood and threw down the gauntlet to the opposition. But it was more than a mere device.

[48]See local tax. R. com. min. ev. etc.; P.P. 1901 Cd. 201 XXXVI, App. XIX, pp. 225–35; 181 H.C. deb. 4 ser. 20 Aug. 1907, L.C. Money, 503; IR 73/2, 'Report by Mr. Bernard Mallet ... upon taxation of site values in Frankfort, Hamburg, Cologne and Dresden ...' 19 Oct. 1908 (printed for the cabinet, 29 Dec. 1909), ff. 49–63; Also Prussian assessment of real estate. Translations; P.P. 1906 (173) XCIV.

20

ROMANTIC RESIDUES

'solitude in the presence of natural beauty and grandeur, is the cradle of thoughts and aspirations which are not only good for the individual, but which society could ill do without'. (Mill, *Principles*, Bk IV, ch. VI, § 2.)

I

Following the delphic guidance of his intuitions, Lloyd George attempted to revive the latent energies of British romanticism and to harness them to his political vehicle. To comprehend this endeavour it is necessary to digress into the mental history of those sections of society, in the middle classes and among artisans, that actively assimilated, propagated and lived out Liberal attitudes and ideals. Following Vilfredo Pareto, such latent energies may be regarded as 'residues', while their cultural and political expressions are 'derivations'. S. E. Finer explains these concepts:

Non-logical theories contain a constant element and a variable element. The constant element is called a *residue*, which (it is assumed) manifests human sentiments or states of mind. It lies at the root of otherwise very dissimilar theories, being tricked out and masked by a logical or pseudo-logical element called a *derivation*. The residue is non-logical and manifests some basic human principle or attitude; as the unvarying element in multitudinous theories or activities, it is the true object of sociological enquiry, the derivations being mere masks or veils.

The 'residues' examined in this chapter belong to Pareto's class III, 'manifestations of sentiments by activity', which embraces transcendental phenomena.[1] It is impossible to do full justice to the subtlety and richness of the tradition that Lloyd George wished to tap in the space of a short chapter, yet this dimension must not be overlooked in an account of property and politics before the Great War.

[1] V. Pareto, *Sociological Writings* (1966), ed. S. E. Finer, pp. 14, 223.

328

Superimposed upon conventional market valuations and sloping inversely to them was a 'moral valuation', with its troughs in the highly rented centres of the big towns, which were sinks of mental and physical pollution; and rising through the lush English countryside to peaks beyond the margin of cultivation in the sublimity of mountains and moors. Adam Smith regarded investment in agriculture as more attractive than the insecure enterprise of manufacture and commerce, for 'residual' reasons.

> The beauty of the country besides, the pleasures of a country life, the tranquillity of mind which it promises, and wherever the injustice of human laws does not disturb it, the independency which it really affords, have charms that more or less attract everybody; and as to cultivate the ground was the original destination of man, so in every stage of his existence he seems to retain a predilection for this primitive employment.[2]

The moral value of the intermediate zone was acknowledged by the market: Victorian and even Edwardian landownership conventionally provided low economic returns, and set an implicitly high value on the intangibles of squiredom.[3] The profound attraction of the rural pole was also revealed in the preference of middle-class generations whose unceasing migration to the urban periphery continues to this day.

An inverted moral rent gradient had to be perceived by individuals. Culture expressed it as a nominal duality with a simple polarity of values. The city, secular and sordid, carried a negative charge. The surrounding surface conveyed a positive sensation of innocence, beauty and repose. Moreover, it was transcendentally charged and intrinsically sanctified; it stood on a morally superior level. The root source of the moral valuation was religious impulse. Ambivalence towards the dominant commercial ethos was a common Victorian attitude; engendered, perhaps, by the preponderance of inherited wealth in the southern centres of culture.

Middle-class sensibility learned to react to the outdoors with religious arousal between 1780 and 1830 or so.

> Everything seems full of blossom of some kind and at every step I take, and on whatever subject I turn my eyes, that sublime ex-

---

[2] A. Smith, *The wealth of nations* Bk. III, ch. i (Cannan edn Chicago, 1976), p. 403.
[3] See 'Real estate and politics', *EG* 2 Jan. 1909, 11; A.D. Hall, *A pilgrimage of British farming 1910–1912* (1913), p. 433.

pression of the Scriptures, 'I am the resurrection and the life', seems as if uttered near me.

Thus John Constable, the painter, to his fiancée in May 1819. 'The art of seeing nature is a thing almost as much to be acquired as the art of reading the Egyptian hieroglyphics', he told an audience in Hampstead in 1836.[4] The transcendental experience (which the painter expressed as exquisitely in his letters as in his paintings) was defined and propagated in a set of paradigmatic works, differing in range from the patient, detached observation of Gilbert White of Selborne to the inner resonance of the lake poets.[5] From a vantage point early in the twentieth century the exponents of English *transcendentalism* (if it may thus be called) might appear as isolated peaks protruding out of a mass of clouds. A middle-class schoolboy would be familiar with the great names: Thomson, Gray, Wordsworth, Shelley, Byron, Keats. The plains below concealed the social seedbeds of late eighteenth- and early nineteenth-century romanticism. No need to dwell here on the social and mental developments that led eighteenth-century literati to construct in nature a mirror of the Deity. It will suffice to recall that the subversive claims of the Rationalists and Deists and of their romantic descendants (say, Rousseau and Wordsworth) were countered by orthodoxy in the same coin, in Canon Paley's *Natural Theology* (1802), an influential treatise that depicted complexity in nature as evidence for the veracity of scripture.[6]

The great exemplars were merely outcrops of a coherent culture which embraced, without demarcations, the whole field of experience and inquiry, of leisure and work. Breeding cattle overlapped with breeding racehorses; scientific observation with landscape art; aesthetic appreciation with religious experience. William Stubbs, the anatomist of horses, engraver, publisher, painter of the turf, the hunt and the harvest, a scientist, a romantic and an innovative collaborator of Wedgwood the potter, exemplified the effortless movement between the scientific, artistic and technical modes which characterised this intensely *visual* culture at its best.[7] Gilbert White of Selborne, the country parson and author of

[4]C. R. Leslie, *Memoirs of the life of John Constable* (2nd edn 1845), ed. J. Mayne (1951), pp. 73, 327.

[5]On the literary strand see e.g. M. H. Nicolson, *Mountain gloom and mountain glory* (Ithaca, NY 1959), esp. 'Epilogue', pp. 371–93.

[6]W. Paley, *Natural theology: or evidence of the existence and attributes of the Deity* (1802); e.g. 'Conclusions', *The works of William Paley* (1828) ii, 197.

[7]See B. Taylor, *Stubbs* (1971) and C. A. Parker, *Mr Stubbs the horse painter*

the naturalist classic wrote: 'Without system, the field of nature would be a pathless wilderness; but system should be subservient to, not the main object of, our pursuit'. Constable loyally copied this down. He drew on Thomson (*The seasons*), Milton and Martin Luther to explain his conception of landscape; but he also stated that 'Painting is a science, and should be pursued as an inquiry into the laws of nature'. Archdeacon John Fisher, his friend and patron, sent him two volumes of Paley's sermons 'which you may read to your family of a Sunday evening. They are fit companions for your sketches; being exactly like them, full of vigour, fresh, original, warm from observation of nature, hasty, unpolished, untouched afterwards'.[8]

Botany, entomology, ornithology, geology: the peculiar mental intensity of the natural history that emerged after the turn of the century is regarded by its historian as 'in its whole essence an Evangelical creation'.[9] The ultimate symbol of social attainment was also expressed in landscape, imposed upon whole environments by haughty landowners in the form of gigantic parks, in a tradition of gardening which was itself refined, elaborated and developed in relation to a succession of landscape artists culminating in Constable and J. M. W. Turner.[10]

In Turner, the virtuoso of landscape, John Ruskin recognised the acme of modern art; and art, for Ruskin, was infused with moral energy. 'Man's use and purpose', his creed proclaimed, '... is to be the witness of the glory of God and to advance that glory by his reasonable obedience and resultant happiness'. The act of witness was the experience of nature. Truth, the test of art and the wellspring of beauty, was made manifest in landscape: 'every vista a cathedral, every bough a revelation'.[11] The reverse was also true. The age of faith was the age of nature and the sublime gothic cathedrals were made in nature's image.

to the Gothic workman the living foliage became a subject of intense affection, and he struggled to render all its characters with as much

(1971). The absence of a deep analytical dimension and a penchant for classification and detail created the *itinerary* and the *inventory* as typical repositories for this culture (a typical inventory is W. Howitt, *The rural life of England* (3d edn 1844); Cobbett's *Rural rides* is a classic itinerary). J. R. Abbey's three catalogues of *Travel* (1956–7), *Life in England* (1953) and *Scenery of Great Britain and Ireland* (1952) 'in Aquatint and lithography, 1770–1860' are the great sources of inventories and itineraries.

[8] Leslie, *Constable*, pp. 273, 328–30, 323, 139.

[9] D. E. Allen, *The naturalist in Britain* (Pelican edn 1978), p. 76 and ch. 4, *passim*.

[10] C. Hussey, *The picturesque: studies in a point of view* (1927), and L. Parris, *Landscape in Britain, c. 1750–1850* (Tate gallery exhibition catalogue, 1973).

[11] J. Ruskin, *Modern painters* (popular edn 1906), v, 389; i, 81.

accuracy as was compatible with the laws of his design and the nature of his material ... The proudest architecture that man can build has no higher honour than to bear the image and recall the memory of that grass of the field which is, at once, the type and the support of his existence; the goodly building is then most glorious when it is sculptured into the likeness of the fields of Paradise.[12]
Morality and nature were synonymous. This was the message that Ruskin transmitted from the early to the late-Victorians. Transcendentalism came under pressure in the mid-Victorian period from the effects of the Darwinian revolution in natural history (of which more below), the vulgar philistinism of an expanding urban civilization and ironically, from Sabbatarian Puritanism. Zoological and botanical gardens in Leeds, Liverpool and Manchester were closed on Sundays. In Liverpool the cemeteries were opened to the public every day of the week except Sunday.[13] Extreme devotional forms of nature-worship remained a minority taste but there was an extensive latent appeal.[14]

Ruskin helped to keep this appeal in being, and gave it a radical turn. Life itself, he affirmed, arose out of nature, and capitalist accumulation was a denial and negation of life. 'Men can neither drink steam, nor eat stone', he wrote in *Unto this Last*, his critique of political economy. '– so long as men live by bread, the far away valleys must laugh as they are covered with the gold of God, and the shouts of his happy multitudes ring round the winepress and the well'.[15] Ruskin's influence is attested by the circulation of his books, printed in the scores of thousands. Howard Evans, the archetype Radical journalist of the 1880s relates how he copied out favourite passages from *The Seven Lamps of Architecture*.[16] A transcendentalist himself, he used a newfangled tricycle to compile *The London Rambler* (1884), a guide to rural footpaths on the metropolitan fringe. In response to an informal survey, sixteen out of 45 in the 1906 cohort of Labour MPs volunteered evidence on the lasting influence of Ruskin and *Unto this Last*.[17]

Transcendentalism was not merely faith, but faith justified by works –

[12]J. Ruskin, *The stones of Venice* (Everyman edn 1907), ii, 183, 185.
[13]J. L. and B. Hammond, *The bleak age* (Pelican edn 1947), pp. 128–9.
[14]See U. C. Knoepflmacher and G. B. Tennyson (eds), *Nature and the Victorian imagination* (Berkeley, Calif. 1977).
[15]J. Ruskin, *Unto this last* (Everyman edn 1907), pp. 189–90.
[16]Evans, *Radical fights* (1913), p. 107. Evans was a spare-time Congregationalist minister for thirteen years (ibid. pp. 103–5).
[17]Eleven attested to the influence of Henry George. See [W. T. Stead], 'Character sketches I. The labour party and the books that helped to make it', *Review of Reviews* 32 (1906), 568–82.

an ascetic ritual undertaken by large numbers of middle-class youths. The extended tramp, first in England, then in France and Germany, finally in the Alps and into Italy was apparently *de rigeur* for the aspiring young Radical. Charles Dilke walked from London to Brighton in a day, and roved over the north of France. Joseph Chamberlain took the magic road to Chamonix. Asquith walked strenuously in the Lake District.[18] His papers contain a transcendentalist poem, dated 1902, which opens with the words 'I am God in Nature ...'[19]

Almost every political and intellectual biography of this period describes the emotional or metaphysical impact of youthful communion with nature. The Alpine Club of the 1860s brought together the flower of the British professional and intellectual elite in a brotherhood of mental and muscular excellence, providing them with a testing-ground of moral qualities and a source of inward inspiration.[20] Leslie Stephen (1832–1904), prince of the Victorian intellectual aristocracy, may serve as archetype. An advocate by example of Muscular Christianity, he brought his Cambridge college boat to the head of the river and excelled as a mountaineer. Between 1865 and 1868 he was President of the Alpine Club and his mountaineering book, *The playground of Europe*, was published in 1871. Having taken Holy Orders, Stephen suffered a crisis of faith and became an 'agnostic'. In place of Christianity he put 'The ethics of Wordsworth', which he explained in these terms: '... there is in fact a Divine order in the universe; ... conformity to this order produces beauty as embodied in the external world, and is the condition of virtue as regulating our character'.[21] In 1879 he set on foot the 'Sunday Tramps', a walking club of mostly Liberal intellectuals and professionals who met every other Sunday for a twenty-mile hike. After its demise in the 1880s the club was rejuvenated around the turn of the century by G. M. Trevelyan, Charles' historian brother.[22]

[18]S. Gwynne and G. M. Tuckwell, *The life of the Rt. Hon. Sir Charles W. Dilke* (2nd ed. 1918), i, 18–21; Garvin, *Chamberlain* (1932), i, 73–4; J. A. Spender and C. Asquith, *Life of Herbert Henry Asquith, Lord Oxford and Asquith* (1932), i, 213.

[19]AP 92, fols. 1–2. The poem is typewritten, unsigned and dated Quiberville [on the Normandy coast], 9 July 1902. It evokes the majesty of the sea:
The wind, the clouds, are they all not divine?
Awake and share their splendour, they are thine.

[20]D. Robertson, 'Mid-Victorians amongst the alps', in Knoeplflemacher and Tennyson (eds.), *Nature* (1977), pp. 113–36.

[21]L. Stephen, 'Wordsworth's ethics' in *Hours in a library* (3rd ser. 1879), p. 223.

[22]F. W. Maitland, *The life and letters of Leslie Stephen* (1906), pp. 57–79, 280–1; N. G. Annan, *Leslie Stephen* (1951), pp. 80–91, 162; J. Grigg, *Lloyd George, the people's champion* (1978), p. 102.

One of the most moving memoirs of the Edwardian generation is Bertrand Russell's *Autobiography*. Russell was emotionally involved in post-Gladstonian Liberalism.[23] He came under the influence of his first wife's brother-in-law B. F. C. Costelloe, the motive force of TLV on the London County Council;[24] Crompton Llewelyn Davies, secretary of the English League for the Taxation of Land Values, was one of his closest Cambridge friends;[25] under the impact of Henry George, Russell became a convinced land nationaliser.[26] Perfectly true to type, the autobiography is suffused with Wordsworthian sentiment.[27] Russell tramped with George and Charles Trevelyan, those 'terrific walkers';[28] went mountaineering in the Alps;[29] wandered in Italy on foot and bicycle.[30] The outdoors was a source of 'inexpressible delight'. A favourite walk would lead 'up to the crest of Hunt Hill. Quite suddenly, when I expected nothing, I came upon an enormous view, embracing half of Sussex and almost all of Surrey. Moments of this sort have been important in my life'.[31]

What function did these rituals serve? A perceptive explanation is contained in H. G. Wells' *A modern Utopia* (1905). His Platonic alternative to Edwardian England was administered by a self-selected elite of 'samurai'. Each member of this caste was required to undergo an annual solitary, strenuous, seven-day pilgrimage in uninhabited mountains, deserts or woods. This annual dose of sublimity provided a spiritual core for a utilitarian discipline.[32] The Fabian social service state depended implicitly upon the virtue of its administrators. How could virtue be guaranteed under an agnostic and utilitarian ethos? Beatrice Webb thought that a state religion would still be required and reserved the role for the established church.[33] Wells set up the transcendental ordeal as a fountain of virtue, a source of moral grease for the modern utopia. It was the antidote to the temptations of power, the secret of the Guardians' 'detachment from immediate heats and hurries'. 'It pleased me strangely', wrote Wells, 'to think of this steadfast yearly pilgrimage of solitude, and

[23] *The autobiography of Bertrand Russell* (one-vol. edn 1975), p. 158.
[24] *Ibid.* p. 72.
[25] *Ibid.* pp. 55–6.
[26] *Ibid.* p. 41.
[27] *Ibid.* pp. 35, 41–2, 148, 195, 392 etc.
[28] *Ibid.* pp. 61–2.
[29] *Ibid.* p. 39.
[30] *Ibid.* p. 137.
[31] *Ibid.* p. 42.
[32] H. G. Wells, *A modern Utopia* (1905, Nelson pop. edn n.d.), pp. 290–8.
[33] B. Webb's diary, 15 Jan. 1901, Webb, *Our partnership* (1948), pp. 209–10.

how near men might come then to the high distances of God'.[34] Wells was not indulging in idle fancy, but merely extrapolating from a discipline already undertaken by a section of the elite.

As Tom Paine said, the sublime and ridiculous are often so nearly related that it is difficult to class them separately. Sir Edward Grey, the Liberal Foreign Secretary, used to set aside the second Sunday of May for an act of nature-worship:

There are a few days in the first part of May [he recalled] when the beech-trees in young leaf give an aspect of light and tender beauty to English country which is well known but indescribable. The days are very few ... the second Sunday in May was the perfect day. In my calendar it was known as "Beech Sunday", a day set apart and consecrated to enjoyment of the beauty of beech-leaves and to thankfulness for it. It was my habit on that morning, each year, to bicycle to a beech-wood some nine miles from the cottage. There I lunched once every year on that day at the foot of a certain tree ... I thought of it, looked forward to it, counted upon it.

On the appointed Sunday in 1906 an ultimatum to Turkey was set to expire at noon. Grey was forced to remain in the office; the Turks delayed their reply until the very last moment, and the magic moments were lost. 'I remained', Grey wrote, 'so far as ultimatums to Turkey were concerned, a sadder and wiser man'; with what ultimate consequences for war and peace we can only guess. 'I had now to wait another twelve months to see the great Beech wood as I knew it in its greatest beauty.'[35]

Nature-worship was embraced by members of a generation that was losing its Christianity but retaining a conditioned need for metaphysics. C. F. G. Masterman, for example, had gone down from Cambridge in 1898 to live in a South London tenement block in response to a religious call, subsequently making a name for himself as a writer on social questions. Elected to Parliament in 1906 and made an under-secretary in 1908, he published his evocative book, *The condition of England* in 1909. After 1912 he became financial secretary to the Treasury and Lloyd George's right-hand man in the pre-war 'land campaign'. By 1909 he was no longer drawing inner strength from Scripture, but from Wordsworth, Walt Whitman, Henry Thoreau, Richard Jefferies and William Morris. Concluding a chapter on these authors, he wrote,

This unquestioning love of the Earth and the children of it [referring to Jefferies] is perhaps the most hopeful element for future progress.

[34]Wells, *A modern Utopia*, p. 298.
[35]Viscount Grey of Fallodon, *Twenty-five years, 1892–1916* (1925), i, 127–9.

335

In a century of doubts and scepticisms it may serve to bridge the gulf between the old and the new. Whilst men are still confused concerning the purposes of Nature, and still doubtful concerning any definite or intelligent progress towards a final end, it is much that inspiration and content can be found in its present beauty and appeal ... man can accept the summer day, from dawn to sunset, as an 'Eternal moment', something that is good in itself apart from remembrance of what has been or anticipation of what shall be.[36]

Transcendentalist culture may be understood as a sublimation, feeding on instinctive needs that bodily effort out-of-doors can satisfy in those not compelled to undertake it for a living. The values propounded by Masterman were, on this construction, the refined products of a primary exhilaration compounded of movement, colour and strain sometimes almost sexual in its intensity (and as Russell suggests, sometimes sexual in its origin);[37] a mental ecstasy catalysed by physical exertion and easily provoking mystical experience. It is revealing that Bertrand Russell chose to evoke it as a metaphor for philosophical fecundity:

The time was one of intellectual intoxication. My sensations resembled those one has after climbing a mountain in a mist, when, on reaching the summit, the mist suddenly clears, and the country becomes visible for forty miles in every direction.[38]

But in what sense was this kind of elation peculiarly Liberal at the beginning of the twentieth century? Was it not Edmund Burke who made the classic identification of vastness with sublimity?[39]

It would be possible to attempt a quantitative demonstration of how much the recreation of the elite, irrespective of party, gravitated out-of-doors. A browse through *Who's Who* for, say 1900, will amply confirm this. Of 252 notables listed under 'A' and resident in the U.K. 98 gave their recreations as walking, riding, cycling, angling, hunting, shooting, cricket, tennis etc. Of the rest, a significant group (37) was made up of self-proclaimed large landowners.[40] The same landscape that drove Liberals to ecstasy gave rise to a culture that was less self-conscious, more extravert, and less romantic, the culture of the country house.

[36]C. F. G. Masterman, *The condition of England* (1909), ed. J. T. Boulton (1960), p. 197.
[37]Russell, *Autobiography*, p. 35; and see Constable's letter, pp. 329–30, above.
[38]*Ibid.* p. 148.
[39]E. Burke, *A philosophical inquiry into the origin of our ideas of the sublime and the beautiful* (1757), ed. J. T. Boulton (1958), pp. 72–3.
[40]The bias of the sample is to play down outdoor activity since short entries tended to be silent about recreations.

Liberal transcendentalism was, at its heart, a rejection of the city from *within*. Tory outdoors culture was organically rooted in the countryside, centred on the mansion, sustained by a hierarchy of servants, labourers, farmers, parson and squire, gentry and aristocracy. Its rituals were not those of solitary rambling, but of blood sports; its symbols were the gun, the hounds and the horse. In his autobiographical novels (and in his memoirs) H. G. Wells expressed the tension between the two cultures with an authenticity confirmed by his Liberal contemporaries. Against the dynamic, superficial and alienating environment of London he set, with a social upstart's mixture of admiration and antipathy, the self-assured solidity and coherence of country-house paternalism.[41]

A secret empathy linked the two cultures. In Paretian terms, they may be regarded as 'derivations' of the same 'residue'. Feeding on the same instinctual resources, they pursued in different ways a similar ideal of social harmony and personal fulfilment. The 'Liberal' variant stressed potentiality, the Tory defended actuality. But the affinities made it easy to move across the divide. 'In England', Basil Willey has remarked, 'emotional naturalism turned almost inevitably into Toryism or some-thing akin to it';[42] Wordsworth was transformed from a radical into a reactionary. William Morris crossed the same divide in the other direc-tion. In *Culture and anarchy* Matthew Arnold wrote,

> I myself am properly a Philistine ... Nevertheless, I never take a gun or a fishing rod in my hands without feeling that I have in the ground of my nature the self-same seeds which, fostered by circum-stances, do so much to make the Barbarian; and that, with the Barbarian's advantages, I might have rivalled him.[43]

A singular illustration is given in the Trevelyan family circle's annual 'Man Hunt', begun in 1897, and loosely modelled on the Harrow game of 'hare and hounds'. For three days a brilliant entourage, made up of journalists, dons, politicians, a galaxy of 'New Liberals' with a seasoning of other persuasions, would descend on the Lake District. The party then divided into 'hares' and 'hounds' and hunted each other over the hills to their hearts' content, assembling in the evenings before a fire to sing 'John Peel' before dispersing to bed.[44]

---

[41]See L. Masterman, *C. F. G. Masterman: a biography* (1939), p. 119; H. C. Wells, *Tono-Bungay* (1909), pp. 9–18; idem, *Experiment in autobiography* (1934), i, 135–7.

[42]B. Willey, The *eighteenth-century background* (Penguin edn 1962), p. 201.

[43]M. Arnold, *Culture and anarchy* (1869), pp. 106–7.

[44]House of Lords Rec. Office, H. Samuel papers B/7 [The man hunt], including [?Mary and C. P. Trevelyan], *The man hunt* (privately printed, 1937).

This section opened with the words of John Stuart Mill. Let G. M. Trevelyan, another star in the Liberal firmament, state the transcendentalist credo in its last phase:

Through the loveliness of nature, through the touch of sun or rain, or the sight of the shining restlessness of the sea, we feel

Unworded things and old to our pained heart appeal.

This flag of beauty, hung out by the mysterious Universe, to claim the worship of the heart of man, what is it, and what does its signal mean to us? ... whatever its interpretation may be, natural beauty is the ultimate appeal of the Universe, of nature, or of the God of nature, to their nursling man. It and it alone makes a common appeal to the sectaries of all our religious and scientific creeds ... and to many more besides these. It is the highest common denominator in the spiritual life of to-day.[45]

II

Both literally and figuratively, Tories and Liberals contested the same terrain. The Tories, as landowners, were in possession and the Liberals mounted the challenge. One of its forms was the long struggle for public access to open spaces, commons, forests and footpaths. George Shaw-Lefevre (Lord Eversley), Henry Fawcett, Charles Dilke and James Bryce: a succession of Cabinet-rank Liberals led the struggle for almost half a century. The third Marquess of Salisbury consistently gave opposition. The Commons Preservation Society, which those worthies established in 1865, fought to preserve open spaces in and around London and extended its attentions to threatened commons all over the South of England. Wimbledon and Wandsworth Commons, Hampstead Heath and Epping Forest were among the assets saved by the Society for the public.[46]

The Commons Preservation movement marked an early instance of the Radical swing away from Benthamism. Bentham conformed with contemporary 'modernisers' and welcomed enclosures as 'Happy conquests of peaceful industry'; he applauded the consolidation of private property rights which enclosure effected.[47] The Cobdenite Radicals who combined to save surviving commons from enclosure appealed to the

[45]G. M. Trevelyan, 'The call and claims of natural beauty' (1931) in *An autobiography and other essays* (1949), p. 106.
[46]Lord Eversley, *Commons, forests and footpaths* (rev. edn 1910), *passim*.
[47]Bentham, 'Civil law', Bowring edn (1838–43), i, 342.

natural rights vested in the community. Resuscitation of ancient rights was their strategy. Obsolete privileges such as turbary and pasture were converted into means for satisfying the needs of masses crowded in the growing cities. The Tories based their claims on the rights of property and on age-old possession. The Commons Preservation Society rejuvenated popular claims of greater antiquity. The Radical belief that property in land was an illegitimate offspring of the original sin of conquest was infused with legal substance and given a practical application. The Society breathed new life into the Radical myth of a lost era of equity and communality.[48]

These myths stimulated the inquiries of at least two generations of scholars, whose writings on the origin and nature of the mediaeval manor, the process of enclosure, the decline of the peasantry and the disinheritance of the labourer gave an historiographical dimension to the conflict of cultures.[49] By 1914 historians had been recruited to participate directly in the political debate. Gilbert Slater contributed a polemical 'historical outline' to the first volume of the Liberal land enquiry report and R. E. Prothero, who gave a strong partisan slant to the concluding chapter of his *English Farming Past and Present* (1912), was an active adviser and agitator on the Tory side, whose services were recognised with a seat in Parliament, and the Presidency of the wartime Board of Agriculture.[50]

In extremis, the Commons Preservation Society did not shrink from violence to enforce popular rights of access. Berkhamsted Common, for example, was enclosed without notice by the Lord of the Manor in 1866. A force of 120 navvies was hired by the Society, and left Euston by special train on 6 March, 1866, shortly after midnight, bound for Berkhamsted. On arrival,

> A procession was formed at the station. A march of three miles in the moonlight brought them to Berkhamsted Common, and the object of the expedition was then first made known to the rank and

[48]See e.g. Rogers, *Cobden* (1873), pp. 75–9.

[49]The first generation included Sir Henry Maine, F. W. Maitland, J. E. T. Rogers and F. Seebohm; the second, W. J. Ashley, E. C. K. Gonner, J. L. and B. Hammond, A. H. Johnson, R. E. Prothero, G. Slater, R. Garnier, R. H. Tawney and P. Vinogradoff. For a contemporary assessment, see J. A. R. Marriot, *The English land system: a sketch of its evolution in its bearing upon national wealth and national welfare* (1914), with bibliographies on pp. 32, 53 and 80.

[50]G. Slater, 'Historical outline', *The land* (1913), i, lxi–lxxxiii; Lord Ernle [R. E. Prothero], *Whippingham to Westminister* (1938), chs. XI–XIII (and this volume, pp. 383, 399).

file. The men were told off in detachments of a dozen strong. The substantial joints of the railings were then loosened by hammers and chisels, and the crowbars did the rest. Before six a.m. the whole of the fences, two miles in length, were levelled to the ground ...

The action, repeated elsewhere, was successfully upheld in court. Oddly, and typically, it had been organised by a Liberal squire.[51]

No rights of Common had survived in Scotland, and the Highlands had been fenced off for private grouse moors and deer forests. James Bryce (an intrepid walker and a member of Stephen's Sunday Tramps) raised the question in a bill and a resolution, respectively, in 1888 and 1892. His peroration on the second of these occasions contains the very essence of the Liberal challenge to landowner control of the countryside, and its transcendentalist underpinning.

the exclusion of the people from the enjoyment of the mountains of Scotland began just at the time when the love of nature and of the sciences of nature had been most widely and fully developed. The scenery of our country has been filched away from us just when we have begun to desire it more than ever before. It coincided with the greatest change that has ever passed over our people – the growth of huge cities and dense populations in many places outside these cities – and this change has made far greater than before the need for the opportunity of enjoying nature and places where health may be regained by bracing air and exercise and where the jaded mind can rest in silence and solitude ... Man does not live by bread alone. The Creator speaks to his creatures through his works, and appointed the grandeur and the loveliness of the mountains and glens and the silence of the moorlands lying open under the eye of heaven, to have their fitting influence on the thoughts of men, stirring their nature and touching their imagination ...[52]

Country-house splendours and country-house culture spread a civilising patina over the crudities of rural appropriation. In transmuting riches into culture the country house and its appurtenances endowed the landowners with a priestly function as patrons of civilisation. Country-house culture legitimised country-house plunder, and in the later nineteenth century both the artifacts and the acts of appropriation had mellowed with time. But the park, the mansion, the objets d'art and the

[51]Eversley, *Commons* (1910), pp. 46–7; J. A. Froude 'On the uses of a landed gentry' (1876), *Short studies on great subjects* (Fontana paperback edn 1963), Ed. D. Ogg, pp. 756–7.
[52]H.A.L. Fisher, *James Bryce* (1927), i, 280–2.

calf-bound library were not an effervescent superstructure; they were a cement that fortified the very base. Landed culture had been nurtured behind the ramparts of landed property. In the 1880s and 1890s the position begain to change. In a climate of broadening democracy the universal values of culture were pushed forward to stiffen particularist claims of property.

The Duke of Devonshire had already thrown Chatsworth open in 1850, when crowds of artisans and their families came up in excursion trains from the black country, and were allowed to walk through the apartments and the grounds.[53] The landowners' claims as curators of national treasures were aired in 1884 by Richard Jefferies, the Tory transcendentalist writer. Great estates, he argued, did not pay any more. They were not to be valued on their profits alone, but also as the source of the nation's vitality and energy. They created environments of exceptional beauty, and Democracy was urged to sustain the landowner for the sake of the landscape.

> ... the South Wood and the park, the hamlet and the fields, had a value no one can tell how many times above the actual money rental, and the money earned by the operatives in factory and workshop could not have been better expended than in supporting it ... the beauty of these woods, and grain-grown hills, of the very common, is worth preservation at the hands and votes of the operatives in factory and mill.[54]

A harbinger of this new line of defence appeared, incongruously, in a Parliamentary speech that Joseph Chamberlain made in March 1886. This would-be spoliator of landlords accepted that mansions were under-taxed but warned that conventionally-assessed local rates 'would lead to the destruction of many of the most splendid historical places in the country (cheers)'.[55] (Did members cheer the warning or the prospect?) The landed interest warmed up to this theme during the death-duty budget debates of 1894. Chamberlain had described Blenheim (which he had never visited) as a white elephant; in the budget debate of 1894 Henry Chaplin gave Chatsworth as an example of 'scores of estates which occupy a similar position'.

> They employ hundreds of people and labourers of every description, and they give amusement and enjoyment to thousands. In the

[53]J. Caird, *English agriculture in 1850–51* (1852), p. 401.
[54]R. Jefferies, 'A king of acres', *Fraser's Magazine* (Jan. 1884), rep. in idem. *The hills and the vale* (1909), pp. 102–3.
[55]303 H.C. deb. 3 ser. 23 March 1886, 1687.

summer months the means of conveying the people who go to see these places becomes absolutely an industry in itself. But if properties like these, which are blessed or encumbered with a Chatsworth, are to be mulcted in the manner which you propose, the inevitable consequence will be that one after another they will be shut up, their contents will be sold and dispersed ...[56]

The preservation of the country-house ethos required a new form of tenure in conditions of rising taxation. Surely it is no coincidence that the first steps were taken in the death-duty summer of 1894 when the constituent meeting of the 'National Trust for Places of Historical Interest and Natural Beauty' took place in London. The trust was created in order to acquire land and houses by purchase and gift, and it embodied the affinity between the transcendentalist and the country-house ideal. James Bryce and G. Shaw Lefevre were among the founders, and so was the Duke of Westminster, Britain's richest landowner, who occupied the chair of the meeting which took place in his London residence, Grosvenor House.[57] Among the active promoters of the trust, the names of Octavia Hill, of housing fame, and of Robert Hunter, stand out. Hunter (1844–1913), solicitor to the Post Office, was a remarkable tenurial innovator. For many years he was an inventive and resourceful legal adviser to the Commons Preservation Society.[58] In 1907 he drafted the National Trust Act, in which Parliament set aside its age-old aversion to mortmain and consented to render Trust property inalienable.[59] By 1913 the Trust was off to a good start with 62 properties, but its latent function was fully revealed only in the inter-war years and afterwards when it became a repository for the country-house heritage of Britain, which it acquired under a tenure of dual ownership which guaranteed the continued occupation of previous owners. The artifacts of a socially obsolete tenure were thus kept in being for their cultural value; and this was done by keeping a vestige of the old tenure. Thus were the roles reversed, and tenure came to shelter behind culture. The Trust has grown into one of the largest public landowners in the country, with custody over more than 400,000 acres in 1968.[60]

[56]24 H.C. deb. 4 ser. 8 May 1894, 684.

[57]See R. Fedden, *The continuing purpose: a history of the National Trust, its aims and work* (1968), chs. 1–2.

[58]Lord Eversley, *Commons* (1910), *passim*.

[59]7 Edw. VII c. 136, s. 21.

[60]National Trust, *Report by the council's advisory committee on the Trust's constitution, organization and responsibilities* (1968), p. 20.

III

The nascent 'religion of socialism' of the 1880s was thoroughly permeated by the religion of nature. Edward Carpenter, a prophet of both, wrote of 'the great Socialist and Humanitarian and Nature movements which are destined to play such an important part in the new Democracy'.[61] However much they differed on other things, William Morris and Carpenter agreed in their love of the countryside and rejection of the town. Another nature mystic, James Hinton, inspired the Fabian pioneers of the Fellowship of the New Life.[62] Robert Blatchford's immensely popular *Merrie England* expressed the same preference in its title and substance, and country outings were the essence of the Clarion movement. Keir Hardie, as Sylvia Pankhurst relates, 'missed the rural joys which his nature profoundly craved', and was keen on Home Colonisation and on Land Reform.[63] Ramsay Macdonald dabbled in natural history in his youth, and it continued to influence his political thinking. Co-operation, not conflict, was his paradigm of evolutionary development – an organic view of society which owed more to Prince Kropotkin's *Mutual Aid* than to Charles Darwin's 'preservation of favoured races in the struggle for life'.[64] A benevolent evolutionism was central to the social credo of the 'New Liberalism'.[65] But it owed as much to the transcendentalist tradition as to biological science. Hobson looked to Ruskin, not to Darwin.[66]

Natural history had been congenial to the relaxed Anglicanism of the early nineteenth century, and made a seductive parson's pleasure for educated incumbents oppressed by isolation and a surfeit of leisure. Darwin's *Origin of Species* was a rude shock to the Christian naturalist; and a threat to religion itself.[67] Some clung to the transcendentalist

---

[61] E. Carpenter, *My days and dreams* (1916), p. 237. And see S. Yeo, 'A new life: the religion of socialism in Britain, 1883–1896', *History Workshop Journal* no. 4 (1977), 9, 29, 34, 37–8.

[62] Carpenter, *Days* (1916), 216–18, and *passim*; J. and N. Mackenzie, *The first Fabians* (1977), p. 21.

[63] Pankhurst, *Suffragette movement* (1931), p. 177; K. O. Morgan, *Keir Hardie* (1973), pp. 33–4, 47–8, 51, 59, 77, 91–2, 94, 144–5, 200, 211, 214, 222.

[64] J. R. Macdonald, *Socialism and society* (1905), pp. 34–5; D. Marquand, *Ramsay Macdonald* (1977), pp. 12, 17.

[65] M. Freeden, *The new liberalism* (Oxford, 1978), ch. 3.

[66] J. A. Hobson, *Confessions of an economic heretic* (1938), pp. 23, 38–42.

[67] The classic instance is described in E. Gosse, *The life of Philip Henry Gosse* (1890), pp. 273–83.

conception of natural harmony and others adapted their transcendentalism to the 'life force' they discerned in the struggle for existence. George Bernard Shaw was such a 'Vitalist', a self-proclaimed believer in 'transcendental metabiology', who drew on a profound childhood experience of disenchantment with religion to reject the Darwinian disenchantment of Nature.

> There is a hideous fatalism about it, a ghastly and damnable reduction of beauty and intelligence, of strength and purpose, of honor and aspiration ... To call this Natural Selection is a blasphemy, possible to many for whom Nature is nothing but a casual aggregation of inert and dead matter, but eternally impossible to the spirits and souls of the righteous. If it be no blasphemy, but a truth of science, then the stars of heaven, the showers and dew, the winter and summer, the fire and heat, the mountains and hills, may no longer be called to exalt the Lord with us by praise: their work is to modify all things by blindly starving and murdering everything that is not lucky enough to survive in the universal struggle for hogwash.[68]

He might have lifted this message from the final part, Book X, of Henry George's masterpiece.

For such was also the message of *Progress and poverty*, concealed from our generation but perfectly audible to his own. The book reveals its religious purpose in the final chapters. Its faith is the faith of Paley; natural selection and its 'hopeful fatalism' are firmly rejected. George set himself against the 'martyrdom of man' on the altar of progress.[69] Malthusian and Darwinian doctrines, he said, 'reduce the individual to insignificance'.

> They destroy the idea that there can be in the ordering of the universe any regard for his existence, or any recognition of what we call moral qualities.
>
> It is difficult to reconcile the idea of human immortality with the idea that nature wastes men by constantly bringing them into being where there is no room for them. It is impossible to reconcile the idea of an intelligent and beneficent Creator with the belief that the

[68]C. B. Shaw, 'Preface: the infidel half century', in *Back to Methuselah* (1921, Penguin edn 1977), p. 32; 'vitalism', see p. 52; 'transcendental metabiology', 'Postscript' (1944). p. 311.

[69]George, *Progress and poverty* (Everyman's edn), pp. 338–9 *et seq.* George was reacting against a popular and powerful social-darwinian metahistorical treatise by Winwood Reade, *The martyrdom of man* (1872).

wretchedness and degradation which are the lot of such a large proportion of human kind result from His enactments.

So the refutation of political economy was also the salvation of true belief.

We have seen that population does not tend to outrun subsistence; we have seen that the waste of human powers and the prodigality of human suffering do not spring from natural laws, but from the ignorance and selfishness of men in refusing to conform to natural laws ....

Thus the nightmare which is banishing from the modern world the belief in a future life is destroyed.[70]

The pantheistic religion of *Progress and poverty* became, for those who embraced it, a buffer against the alienating corrosion of Darwinian dogma. It answered the religious impulse of men like George Lansbury, who was deeply committed to land settlement and TLV.[71] Joseph Fels, the Jewish industrialist who financed the single-tax movement in England in the Edwardian period impressed Lansbury as

the finest example of a Christian I have ever known ... to listen to him was like listening to one who had seen a great light, to one for whom the small and mean things of life had no meaning ... the freeing of land did not mean simply more potatoes or more strawberries, to him it represented the means by which the whole human race could be made free.[72]

Lansbury subscribed to the same vision and so did many in the Liberal and Labour elite, whose mental formation had conditioned them to perceive 'that there was a man from God, and his name was Henry George'.[73]

IV

Not content to confiscate rent, Henry George proposed to abolish it altogether. *Progress and Poverty* rejected diminishing returns and the advantages of concentration, and advocated the same equalised no-rent land surface that was such a persistent theme of Utopian socialism, of Robert Owen, the young Marx, Proudhon, William Morris, Prince

[70]George, *Progress and poverty*, pp. 395–6.
[71]E. g. G. Lansbury, 'The unemployable. State labour colonies. How to deal with the problem', *Standard*, 16 Dec. 1905.
[72]M. Fels, *Joseph Fels* (1920), pp. 32–3.
[73]J. C. Wedgwood, *Memoirs of a fighting life* (1940), p. 60.

Kropotkin and Robert Blatchford. 'We discourage centralisation all we can', wrote William Morris in *New from Nowhere* (1891). He envisaged a thatch-and-timber landscape, undistrubed by the law of rent, bathing in the sunlight of contentedness, 'Like the medievals ... everything trim and clean, orderly and bright'. Paradoxically, it was the new electric and transport technologies that were to make it all possible. Both Morris and Kropotkin regarded electric power as an agent of de-centralisation.[74] Transport technology provided a means to decentral-ise industry and introduce the transcendental values into working-class lives. This notion exercised great and lasting influence upon the develop-ment of architecture and town planning.[75] No one did more to promote it than a small band of Liberal industrialists: William Lever, George Cadbury and Joseph Rowntree, whose suburban industrial housing estates at Port Sunlight (1888), Bourneville (1893) and New Earswick (1902) embodied the Ricardian-rent-less Liberal Utopia. Ebenezer Howard's *Garden cities of to-morrow* (1902) was tremendously influential both in precept and through the successful example of Letchworth garden city (1903). His vision was likewise founded upon a new urban beginning on agricultural (and hence virtually rent-free) land. Some Conservatives also pinned their hopes on technology to release the populace from the urban vice. A. J. Balfour proposed what amounted to double-decker motorways as a solution to urban overcrowding (1901) and Charles Booth looked to the 'improvement in the speed and cheapening in the cost of travel, as a first and essential step towards the solution of the housing problem in London'.[76]

The uplift of nature was also put forward as a substitute for the intoxication of drink. Moral probity and religious inspiration were paramount among Victorian society's bulwarks against drink and in the housing-reformers' scheme nature was assigned a similar strategic role. Octavia Hill regretted that the working-class Sunday outing into the countryside was often made into an opportunity for drinking, but she believed that 'these days in the country ought to lessen the number of

[74]W. Morris, 'News from nowhere' (1891) in *The collected works of William Morris*, ed. M. Morris (1912), xvi, pp. 68–9, 73, and ch. X *passim*. P. Kropotkin, *Fields, factories and workshops* (1899), pp. 219–27. The book was a gospel of de-centralisation and an earlier version influenced Blatchford's *Merrie England* (1894; see pp. 29–30).

[75]W. Ashworth, *The genesis of modern British town planning* (1954), *passim*.

[76]Booth, *Life and labour* (1902), xvii, 183. And see P. W. Wilson, 'The distri-bution of industry' in *Heart of empire*, ed. Masterman (1902), pp. 223–4.

drunkards every year'.[77] Hence, among other motives, was her militancy in the causes of Commons Preservation and the National Trust. Patrick Geddes, high priest of the English town planning school, underscored the same substitution when he cited the old adage that drink was 'the quickest way of getting out of Manchester'.[78] Abandon Manchester and all it stood for, he implied, and beer would become redundant. On the Cadbury and Rowntree housing trust estates no public houses were permitted, and not only because their patrons manufactured cocoa. Port Sunlight, Letchworth Garden City and Hampstead Garden Suburb imposed similar prohibitions. It was rather that the income liberated from drink made possible the payment of an economic rent.[79] It was an enticing prospect, since expenditure on drink was reckoned to equal expenditure on house-rent among the poor. That there was some scope for substitution there is not any doubt, as the aggregate consumer expenditure on drink in the Edwardian period roughly equalled the outlay on house-rent.[80] Here then was one key to the housing problem. The loss of social communion in the public house (whose human value even B. S. Rowntree grudgingly admitted) was to be replaced by communion with nature. Recreation was a substitute for intoxication. In looking back upon forty years' progress in York Rowntree felt himself vindicated by the validity of this substitution, in the decline of drunkenness and the growth of sport and rural recreation.[81]

Liberating technology was also objectified in the bicycle, which came into wide popular use in the 1890s. 'Bicycling, and what was later called hiking, was another item in the early progressive package', writes Malcolm Muggeridge of his Edwardian 'socialist upbringing' in lower middle-class Croydon. 'There were Clarion Clubs and specially organised rambles; a love of nature was proclaimed as an enlightened alternative to religious worship ...'[82] Another instance of the spiritual substitutions made possible by the cycle is given in Charles Booth's description of a west-London parish:

in the church itself, the working-class is practically unrepresented,

[77]O. Hill, *Our common land (and other short essays)* (1877), p. 2.
[78]P. Geddes, *Cities in evolution* (1915), p. 76.
[79]For drink and housing, see J. Rowntree and A. Sherwell, *The temperance movement and social reform* (7th edn. 1900), pp. 39–42; A. G. Gardiner, *Life of George Cadbury* (1923), pp. 47, 141–66.
[80]C. H. Feinstein, *National income, expenditure and output of the United Kingdom, 1855–1965* (Cambridge, 1972), table 24, p. T61.
[81]B. S. Rowntree, *Poverty and progress* (1941), pp. 370–2.
[82]M. Muggeridge, *Chronicles of wasted time* (1972), i. *The green stick*, p. 57.

and the indifference to church matters is spreading, the clergy say, in the class above. Of this, Sunday bicycling is said to be 'a symptom rather than a cause. It only makes neglect easier.'[83]

'The bicycle', H. G. Wells wrote in his recollections of the mid-1890s, 'was the swiftest thing upon the roads in those days, there were as yet no automobiles and the cyclist had the lordliness, a sense of masterful adventure, that has gone from him altogether now'. Like other progressive couples of their generation Wells and his wife spent their holidays cycling in the countryside.[84] Herbert Samuel relates how Graham Wallas and C. P. Trevelyan taught the Webbs, Bernard Shaw and himself to ride the safety bicycle. Long cycle excursions became one of his favourite recreations, taking him all over England and several times to the Continent.[85] Grey, we may recall, reached his secluded beech trees on bicycle. D. Rubinstein has recently described the cycle's role in breaking down some of the social, mental and geographical boundaries of the late Victorians.[86] He does not explicitly mention the transcendental experience which cycling made more widely accessible; and to the way in which it encouraged young progressives to penetrate into the Tory countryside. Samuel the cyclist, for example, involved himself in the politics of rural Oxfordshire after going down from Balliol in 1893. On election day, 1900, his farmworker electors were harangued with these typically urban Liberal stanzas:

Look here at the barbed wire fences
Enclosing both path and field!
Think of Commons now lost to your children
These are crops that the Tories yield.[87]

From a social point of view, transcendentalism must be judged as a refuge from unpleasant realities. Politically, it suffered from a fatal flaw: like ecological ideas today, it was not made to mobilise masses. Its essence was individualistic, introspective, escapist and exclusive. In a charming lampoon, Canon Scott Holland contrasted the working-class railway outing with the solitary Wordsworthian wanderer.

Once a year the vast, blind, welded masses that have coagulated into cities, let themselves loose, to swarm out over sea and land, for the

[83] Booth, *Life and labour* (1902), Religious influences, iii, 164.
[84] Wells, *Autobiography* (1934), ii, 543.
[85] Viscount Samuel, *Memoirs* (1945), p. 30.
[86] D. Rubinstein, 'Cycling in the 1890s', *Victorian Studies* 21 (1977), 47–71.
[87] H. Samuel papers A/13 (3), 'The general election stakes: a tip for Friday, Oct. 5 1900'.

brief rapture of a Summer Holiday ... Whenever the trip comes in, Wordsworth is gone.

The Canon condescended to welcome the masses into the countryside, and could even empathise with their needs, but he also tendered practical advice to those of his own kind:

Avoid those few chosen spots, consecrated to them: and not a trace will you find of them. Not an 'Arry will be heard to cry; not a giggle of M'ria will reach you. Sheer off a few yards from the beaten tracks, and you will find yourself in uplands as lonely and still as they were in the day when the morning stars sang together. You can wander at will: and not even guess that, down there in the dip, all London is streaming past, with lunch-baskets and bottled beer.[88]

For truth was, the majority of urban manual workers, and their families, had but little use for precious Wordsworthian idealism. Lacking in mobility, they perforce had to cultivate other values, as Lady Bell observed in her study of the steel town, Middlesborough. Cycles and trams could provide an outlet for a few on summer weekends.[89] Otherwise,

Many of the dwellers in the place have as deeply rooted an attachment to it as though it were a beautiful village. There are people living in these hard-looking, shabby, ugly streets, who have been there for many years, and more than one who has left it has actually pined to be back again. It is not, after all, every man or woman who is susceptible to scenery and to the outward aspect of the world round him; there are many who are nourished by human intercourse rather than by natural beauty.[90]

In June 1902 R. C. K. Ensor, then a Fabian journalist, conducted a group of workers to a field outside Manchester. He was sorry to find that 'None of them knew or could name forget-me-nots, daisies, dandelions, clover, pansies or lilies of the valley'. The story was told by C. F. G. Masterman, who concluded sadly, 'They experience no exultation in Nature because they are cut off from the experience of Nature'.[91] The urban worker was not converted by the romantic impulse of Liberalism. The rural labourer was a more promising prospect.

[88] H. Scott Holland, *A bundle of memories* (1915), pp. 241–2, 246–7. I owe this reference to M. Zimmeck.
[89] Lady Bell (Mrs Hugh Bell), *At the works* (1907), p. 126.
[90] *Ibid.* pp. 15–16.
[91] Masterman, *Condition of England* (1909), p. 203; and see R. C. K. Ensor, 'The English countryside' in *England: a nation* (1904), ed. L. Oldershaw, pp. 107–8.

21

BACK TO THE LAND

I

In 1921 Bernard Shaw proposed that romantic vitalism might serve for a new state religion.[1] The notion was not far-fetched, for the Liberals had long integrated a kindred 'derivation' into their ideological armoury. In one of the land campaign speeches of 1914 Lloyd George expressed this doctrine in a telling metaphor:

> The peasantry of a country is like a gold reserve. It is something that is very little in evidence when things are going well with a concern, but at the moment there is a run on the bank you begin to realize the true value of that resource.[2]

The Liberal party had taken over a long-established vitalist vision of a reconstructed countryside.

The advantages of large-scale production were persistently questioned in the face of the consolidation of large landed estates and a commercial and industrial mode of production during the eighteenth century. Adam Smith, who was otherwise an advocate of scale, remained sceptical of its benefits in agriculture, and wrote the classic argument for small ownership:

> A small proprietor ... who knows every part of his little territory, who views it with all the affection which property, especially small property, naturally inspires, and who upon that account takes pleasure not only in cultivating but in adorning it, is generally of all improvers the most industrious, the most intelligent and the most successful.[3]

From Arthur Young in the 1770s to A. Daniel Hall after 1910, expert agricultural and economic opinion tended in the opposite direction. The case for small holdings rested on the arguments of justice as much as the arguments of utility. To mitigate the deprivations of enclosure Arthur Young came (together with many other observers) to favour the provision of allotments and small holdings for dislocated labourers and

[1]Shaw, 'Preface', *Methuselah* (1970 edn), p. 54.
[2]Speech at Glasgow, *The Times*, 5 Feb. 1914, 5b.
[3]Smith, *Wealth of nations*, Cannan edn (1976), Bk. III, ch. iv, p. 441.

small farmers. Rural nostalgia pervaded the labour discontents of the period 1815–1850 and the dream of 'Home Colonisation' and spade husbandry found outlets in many schemes, from Robert Owen's co-operative communities of the 1820s to the Chartist Land Company of the 1840s.[4] John Stuart Mill devoted five chapters of his *Principles* (1848) to peasant tenures, and sang a paean to small ownership. G. J. Holyoake, a linking figure between Owenism and late-Victorian Liberalism, demanded in his election manifesto in 1857,

> that the State should establish well-devised Home Colonies upon the waste lands of the Crown, which might eventually extinguish pauperism – home colonies where the labourer in distress, instead of taking his wallet for the parish loaf, need only take his spade to dig his honest bread ...[5]

Reduced to essentials, Liberal doctrine envisaged the redistribution of large estates among a multitude of small owners and the provision of garden allotments for farm labourers. In Cobden's thinking, this was a means towards the bourgeois revolution. In 1849 he wrote to Bright about his plan for establishing forty-shilling freeholders in the country-side –

> The citadel of privilege in this country is so terribly strong, owing to the concentrated masses of property in the hands of the comparatively few, that we cannot hope to assail it with success unless with the help of the propertied classes in the middle ranks of society, and by raising up a portion of the working-class to become members of a propertied order;

Urging caution, he went on to say,

> The politicians who would propose to break up the estates of this country into smaller properties, will be looked upon as revolutionary democrats aiming at nothing less than the establishment of a Republic upon the ruin of Queen and Lords.[6]

The respective economic merits of small and large farming units were also debated throughout the nineteenth century and into the twentieth,[7]

---

[4]W. Hasbach, *A history of the English agricultural labourer* (1920), *passim* (see index, under allotments, small farms, small holdings); Hall, *Pilgrimage* (1913), *passim* and his contribution to Lord Ernle, *English farming past and present*, ed. A. D. Hall (5th edn 1936) pp. 428–30.

[5]Holyoake, *Sixty years* (1902), ii, 44; and see an illuminating study by C. Dewey, 'The rehabilitation of the peasant proprietor in nineteenth-century economic thought', *History of Political Economy* 6 (1974).

[6]J. Morley, *The life of Richard Cobden* (1881), ii, Cobden to J. Bright, 1 Oct. 1849, 53–4 (compare chapter 9 above, pp. 149–50).

[7]H. Levy, *Large and small holdings* (1911), *passim*.

but whether in or out of tune with economic rationality, the principle of small holdings (henceforth SH) failed to convert the farmers to Liberalism. For this reason, and particularly after the 1884 reform act, SH and allotments became bids for the soul of the English agricultural labourer and a challenge to his traditional masters. Like its contemporary, the bicycle, the SH programme of the 1880s became a Liberal vehicle into the countryside.

Joseph Chamberlain raised allotments and small holdings from the personal crusade of his protegé Jesse Collings to a resonant national political issue. 'Three acres and a cow' became the central (on one opinion, the only) plank of his 1885 'unauthorised programme'.[8] Good Liberal results in English country constituencies in the subsequent election appeared to vindicate the strategy.[9] An exhaustive rehearsal of the supposed pros and cons of the question can be found in a debate that followed on the election – Jesse Collings' amendment to the address in January 1886 – a debate that ended with Salisbury's defeat. Three main questions were involved: (1), was it for the good – of the labourer, the farmer, the landowner, society at large, that the worker should acquire land? (2), what size of plot was best, a part-time allotment or a full-time small holding? (3), given the need, how to meet it – from charity or glebe lands; voluntarily by sympathetic landlords, or by the State compelling the owner? and if the latter, then should the labourer lease the land or buy it? Liberal answers to these questions may be summarised as (1) Yes – the labourer should have access to land; (2) both allotments and SH, depending on the circumstances. Opinions diverged on (3), the mode of provision. Collings favoured compelling the landowner, and selling land to the labourer; Goschen was set against compulsion.[10]

Collings tried to assure the Tories that SH were conservative devices which would help to release the gentry from social isolation. But compulsion threatened to dilute the landowner's property rights and Conservative attitudes to SH remained largely negative. Furthermore, it was feared that farmers would lose labour just when it was most urgently required.[11] But some owners arrived independently at the same con-

[8] J. Collings and J. L. Green, *The life of the right hon. Jesse Collings* (1920), pt. II, chs. XVII–XXII; A. Simon, 'Joseph Chamberlain and the unauthorised programme' (Oxford Univ. D. Phil. thesis 1970), pp. 226–7, 230ff., 444.

[9] Simon, *op. cit.*, pp. 265–6. The contrary argument of Pelling, *Social geography* (1967), p. 16 is not well-documented and is partly contradicted on p. 128.

[10] 302 H.C. deb. 3 ser. 26 Jan. 1886, Collings, 444–5; Goschen, 493–4.

[11] Collings, *Jesse Collings* and see 302 H.C. deb., Captain Verney, 447, H. Chaplin, 448 ff., and M. E. G. Finch-Hatton, 472–9.

clusions as Collings. Many provided allotments and a few even set small-holding schemes in motion.[12] Contrary to popular belief, said Henry Chaplin in debate, the Tory party was in favour of extending land ownership. He invoked the 'ramparts of property' strategy:

> a large increase in the number of owners of land such as I desire is, I think, the surest and perhaps the only safeguard against the predatory instincts of a class whose Socialist schemes have found such powerful exponents in these days ...[13]

Chaplin, a leading agrarian and Chancellor of the Duchy, proposed an act for encouraging the supply of allotments.[14] After the Liberal split the Conservatives conceded compulsory powers to local bodies for the provision of allotments.[15]

Not, however, without the strongest misgivings. Lord Salisbury attempted to convince the Cabinet that with 766,612 agricultural labourers (in 1881) and 691,410 allotments, there was no shortage to meet. His main fear was that allotments would create a precedent for politically-motivated redistributions of property.

> Land has never been taken forcibly by Parliament from one individual merely to benefit another individual. The principle so introduced will spread. The restriction to one acre is purely artificial, and will speedily be overstepped.[16]

About the same time, as we have seen (chapter 9, pp. 153, 156), he embraced the principles of Free Trade in Land and began to extend goodwill towards small holders. If sales remained voluntary, he was willing to regard small owners as bulwarks of property. To this extent, at least, he was prepared to support Chamberlain, and the permissive and ineffective Small Holdings Act of 1892 was an expression of this equivocation.[17] The property press still held SH in almost equal

---

[12] For the activities of the 'Land and glebe association for the voluntary extension of the allotment system' see the Earl of Onslow, *Landlords and allotments* (1886), *passim*. Lord Wantage donated 411 acres to a 'Small farms and labourers' holding company' established on building society lines by a group of landowners and politicians associated with the LPDL in 1886 (Bristow, 'Liberty and property' (1970), pp. 264–6).

[13] 302 H.C. deb. 3 ser. 26 Jan. 1886, 457.

[14] CAB 37/17/11, H. Chaplin, 'Allotments', 14 Jan. 1886, p. 7.

[15] Allotments act, 1887 (50 & 51 Vict. c. 48) see Hasbach, *History* (1920), pp. 315–6.

[16] CAB 37/18/53, Lord Salisbury, 'Allotments bill, note of objections', 6 Dec. 1886, pp. 4 (no. of allotments) and 2 (quotation).

[17] Small holdings act 1892 (55 & 56 Vict. c. 31); see Hasbach, *History* (1920) pp. 316–21.

horror as TLV.[18] But Salisbury was shrewd enough to realise how the former could neutralise the latter:

It is rather the fashion to look upon landowners as a semi-criminal class (laughter) upon which it is quite reasonable to heap every burden you like in the shape of rates. But when we have the alliance of those sturdy yeomen whom we hope to create we may expect to be treated in a very different manner.[19]

Collings, however, was compromised by the Unionist connection. His Rural Labourers' League, set up in 1888, became a Unionist organ, advocating allotments to gain the ear of Liberal labourers. Support came mainly from Liberal Unionists.[20] The league continued to decline and Collings later confessed, 'I had to dip my hands into my own pocket for hundreds of pounds, which I could ill afford, in order to keep the organisation alive'.[21] On the Liberal side land settlement received new impetus from the unco-ordinated action of many different organs. Alfred Russel Wallace, leader of the small but dynamic Land Nationalisation Society, expounded a vision of a toiling, small-holding state tenantry.[22] General Booth made the principle an element in his solution for the social question, and the Salvation Army established a number of farm colonies in the early 1890s.[23] London vestries followed the example, and in addition a number of co-operative colonies under various auspices were established by the mid 1890s.[24] Aspiring young Liberals carried out SH and allotment agitation work in the countryside and two idealistic and wealthy Liberal landowners, Richard Winfrey and Lord Carrington, established successful small-holding schemes in Lincolnshire.[25] Joseph

[18]E.g. 'Lord Salisbury and the land', *EG* (leader), 28 Nov. 1891.

[19]Salisbury, speech at Exeter, *The Times*, 3 Feb. 1892, 6c.

[20]Joseph Chamberlain papers JC 6/5/6/4, 'The truth about allotments' (Rural labourers' league leaflet, n.d. [mid 1890s]); JC 6/5/6/5, 'The rural labourers' league' (typed memo. n.d. [early 1890s?]); Rural labourers' league, *Seventh annual report* (1896), p. 18.

[21]W. Long papers WRO 348, J. Collings to Long, 7 Sept. 1910.

[22]E.g. A. R. Wallace, 'How to cause wealth to be more equally distributed', *Industrial remuneration conference: the report* (1885), pp. 385–92.

[23]W. Booth, *In darkest England and the way out* (1890), pp. 124–42.

[24]J. A. Hobson (ed.), *Co-operative labour upon the land (and other papers)* (1894); *London*, April–Sept. 1895, *passim* (consult index); J. Harris, *Unemployment and politics 1886–1914* (1972), pp. 115–24, 135–44.

[25]See e.g. Herbert Samuel's notebooks on social conditions in Oxfordshire in the 1890s, Samuel papers A/6 and A/7, his pamphlets from this period in A/9 and his *Liberalism* (1902), p. 97 ff. On Lord Carrington's and Winfrey's SH experiments see Peacock, 'Land reform' (1961), pp. 147–9 and L. Jebb, *The small holdings of England* (1907), pp. 214–45.

Fels, whose money fertilised the land reform movement around the turn of the century, fervently believed in rural regeneration and purchased farm colonies for London's unemployed. Keir Hardie and George Lansbury, to name only two of Labour's leaders, shared in Fels' belief in Home Colonisation.[26] Liberalism was moving towards a more collectivist conception of the countryside; even the arid soul of Sidney Webb was willing to assign some room for small holders in the interstices of the municipal sewage farms, 'recreation reserves' and colonies for defectives and incurables which made up his own rural vision.[27]

For the Liberal party, Land Settlement was a mission into uncharted territory. The land reform societies opened the routes with their red and yellow vans in the late 1880s and Liberal agitators followed in their wake for the 1892 election.[28] Youthful Liberal missionary enthusiasm was absorbed and lost in the silence, distance and toil of the countryside. Lives of rural labour present a dull mirror and only a fleeting ray testifies that the mission found its mark. The diary of James Hawker, the untaught Victorian labourer and master poacher, reveals a village personality inwardly committed to the values of late-Victorian Radicalism. Joseph Ashby of Tysoe, Warwickshire, was an articulate labourer who had been active in the Arch campaigns of the 1870s, worked in his village for allotments in the 1880s, joined the Georgian 'Red Van' for a tour in the 1890s and found purpose and dignity in small holding. He acted as unpaid Liberal agent, and served on Parish and District councils, living a life of exemplary Liberal virtue. Another life shaped by Rural Radicalism was that of W. Tuckwell, a 'Radical parson' who risked his income and standing in 1886 when he divided his glebe in Stockton, Warwickshire among small holders and found his reward in a closer human communion with his working-class parishioners, in the face of hostility from gentry and clergy.[29]

The rural mission was also intended to re-vitalise moribund metropolitan heartlands. Campbell-Bannerman's first speech as Prime Minister, on 21 December 1905, could be mistaken for a revivalist meeting. The Albert Hall was filled to its 9,000 capacity and many had to be turned away. 'For an hour before the proceedings began the audience passed the

[26]M. Fels, *Joseph Fels* (1920), esp. ch. 5, and pp. 32ff. and 59.
[27]S. Webb, 'Preface' (1908) in Hasbach, *History* (1920), pp. x–xi.
[28]Peacock, 'Land reform' (1961), pp. 127ff., 153ff.
[29]*James Hawker's journal: A Victorian poacher*, ed. G. Christian (Oxford, 1961), esp. ch. IX; M. K. Ashby, *Joseph Ashby of Tysoe* (1961), *passim.*; W. Tuckwell, *Reminiscences of a radical parson* (n.d.), ch. X.

time in singing with much fervour the familiar political songs'.[30] The whole leadership packed the platform. After dwelling on foreign and fiscal affairs, the Prime Minister turned to the land, singling out Chamberlain as his main target.

> We desire to develop our undeveloped estates in this country (cheers) – to give the farmer greater freedom and greater security in the exercise of his business; to secure a home and career for the labourer who is now in many cases cut off from the soil. We wish to make the land less a pleasure ground for the rich (loud cheers) and more of a treasure house for the nation (Renewed cheers). Now why cannot Mr Chamberlain drop his project of taxing corn and cheese and so forth, and come back to his old love of three acres and a cow? ... After all, the health and stamina of the nation are bound up with the maintenance of a large class of workers on the soil. (Cheers).[30]

After 25 years of depression all was not well with agriculture and much remained that had been unsatisfactory before. Even defenders and spokesmen were prepared to admit this.[31] On the social, economic and regional aspects of the malaise we cannot dwell: it was reflected in the range of meliorations put forward. Liberals were full of genuinely constructive goodwill; they did not lose sight, however, of political ends. Small holdings were given legislative priority. Their diffusion was expected to stem rural depopulation and to alleviate urban overcrowding; to mend deformities that the previous war had exposed in national character and physique, and to build up the latter for the coming war; to secure food for wartime; to replace imports; to make full use of the nation's landed resources; to preserve rural values and virtues; to promote social stability and mitigate class conflict; to improve rural incomes and rural housing; to touch the labourer with the magic wand of property, and to enable him to mount the social ladder; to compel the landlord to accept social responsibility. All this and more was expected by true believers, who were to be found in both parties.[32] Unionists did not dissent; many of these ends and outcomes were

[30] *The Times*, 22 Dec. 1905, 6.
[31] See R. H. Rew, Decline in the agricultural population of Great Britain, 1881–1906. Rep.; P.P. 1906 Cd. 3273 XCVI, esp. pp. 9–21; H. Rider Haggard, *Rural England* (1906), ii, 'Conclusion', pp. 536–7.
[32] C. F. G. Masterman, W. B. Hodgson *et al.*, *To colonise England: a plea for a policy* (1907) was a Liberal SH manifesto; and see the small holdings and allotments bill debates, 174 H.C. deb. 4 ser. 27 May 1907, esp. L. Harcourt, 1377–87 and 175 H.C. deb. 4 ser. 12 June 1907, 1444–1539.

also inscribed in their own books.[33] They only professed to differ on the best way of attaining them.

Party differences crystallised over the question of tenure. Lord Carrington, the Lincolnshire SH enthusiast, was President of the Board of Agriculture. Farmers' security of tenure was greatly extended by two Agricultural Holdings Acts in 1906 and 1908, and much parliamentary time was consumed by the Small Holdings and Allotments Acts in 1907 and the following year. The Small Holdings Acts were closely modelled on A. R. Wallace's proposals of 1885 (p. 354), and were thus tainted as 'Land Nationalisation'. They obliged county councils to establish and satisfy the demand for small holdings and gave them compulsory powers to do so. In particular, the 1908 act enabled councils to compel a landowner to hire out land or sell it (through the local authority) to small-holding tenants. As H. Levy pointed out, such tenants were favoured with the 'three fs' of Gladstone's Irish land acts (fixity of tenure, fair rents and free sale, i.e. compensation (or sale) for improvements). As in Ireland, landowners complained of the deterioration of tenure into 'dual ownership'.[34] As in Ireland, some landowners preferred to be bought out by the state. This conformed with the 'ramparts of property' strategy and A. J. Balfour spoke out for state-aided purchase in September 1909:

> There is no measure with which I am more proud to have been connected that with that giving peasant ownership in such large measure to Ireland, and I hope to see a great extension of such ownership to England. Nothing could be more desirable or important.

The pre-condition of success at SH farming was 'a feeling of ownership and nothing else'.[35] On the Liberal side, great emphasis was placed on the doctrinal superiority of council tenancy over outright ownership.[36] The Land Nationalisers regarded tenancies as an instalment towards their programme, and tenancies also satisfied the collectivist predilections of the 'New Liberals'.[37]

[33] E.g. J. Collings, *Land reform* (1906) and E. A. Pratt, *Small holders: what they must do to succeed* (1909).
[34] Levy, *Small holdings* (1911), p. 140ff.
[35] Balfour, speech at Birmingham, *The Times*, 23 Sept. 1909, 7e. Further developments of this programme are described below, pp. 361–2, 380.
[36] E.g. Mrs. R. Wilkins (L. Jebb), *The small holdings controversy: tenancy v. ownership* (1909).
[37] E.g. J. Hyder, *The case for land nationalization* (2nd edn 1914), p. 259; L. T. Hobhouse, *Liberalism* (n.d. [1911]), pp. 175–6.

Lloyd George was earnest about his vision of rural regeneration, perhaps more so than about any of his other enthusiasms.[38] But he was not inwardly committed to the Liberal Small Holding Peasants' Paradise. In the summer of 1910, during the Budget impasse, the made the well-known coalition proposals to Balfour.[39] The text of this highly confidential memorandum is open to many interpretations, and should certainly not be taken entirely at face value. That part of the memorandum which relates to the land is remarkable chiefly for disavowals and these, in the nature of the document, must have been genuine (the positive content was non-committal and was possibly meant to accommodate the other side). One thing is clear: Lloyd George regarded the small holdings programme as politically divisive and economically dubious.

There is no question which would gain more, by the elimination of Party strife and bitterness, than that of the land. It is admitted on all hands that the land of this country is capable of much more profitable use than is now given to it. Both parties seem to imagine, for the moment, that the real solution lies in the direction of establishing a system of small holdings. I think they have been rather too readily rushed by small, but well organised groups of their own supporters into the acceptance of this doctrine. These groups are inspired by men of no marked intelligence and with little knowledge of land cultivation. The small holdings craze is of a very doubtful utility: and I do not think its devotees have sufficiently considered whether farming on a large scale by competent persons with adequate capital is not more likely to be profitable to the community than a system which divides the land amongst a large number of more or less incompetent small holders... If a mistake is made, it will be irreparable for generations. Once a system of small holdings is rooted in this country, it will be almost impossible for a very long time to substitute for it a system of farming on a large scale with adequate capital, where the state might very well assist, and under intelligent management.[40]

When coalition came to nothing, Lloyd George did not hesitate to fall back on the faddists, and extract the utmost from the partisan potential of the Liberal rural programme.

[38] See *Lloyd George: a diary by Frances Stevenson*, ed. A. J. P. Taylor (1971), pp. 193–4, 262.
[39] Printed in Grigg, *Lloyd George: people's champion* (1978), pp. 362–8.
[40] *Ibid.* p. 366–7, original typescript, Lloyd George papers LG C/3/14/18, untitled, 17 Aug. 1910, pp. 8–9.

What then was the outcome of the SH legislation? It was not entirely negligible. Between 1908 and 1914 more than 14,000 holdings were created, and some 200,000 acres were acquired by Councils for this purpose, despite the misgivings of their agrarian members.[41] But this fell rather short of social revolution. During roughly the same period (from 1909 to 1913) there was actually a net loss of holdings under 50 acres, mainly, it is claimed, because of urban encroachment.[42] Liberal policy was failing to effect a rural transformation. The reason is not far to seek; it may be found in that same Albert Hall speech of December 1905 which painted the glorious vision. Prior to declaiming on the land, Campbell-Bannerman made a commitment to budgetary retrenchment, a pledge he proceeded to honour by cutting expenditure and stepping up the redemption of the national debt.[43] Small holdings were meant to be strictly solvent, and popular demand for a house and holding was frustrated by strict economic tests. Councils, landowners, and farmers also put obstacles in the way.[44] Risks were borne by the Councils. Limited state credit was available, but there was no question of subsidies. SH legislation embodied the old Liberal belief that the shackles of tenure had only to be removed for Free Trade to work its benefits. Despite trappings of 'socialism' in the form of Council tenancies, it remained an essay in Free Trade in Land.

An unbridgeable gap between ends and means characterised Campbell-Bannerman's cautious SH policy. One member of the Cabinet, at least, was impatient. In August 1908 a survey of the rural land problem was hurriedly prepared for the new Chancellor of the Exchequer, Lloyd George. Written by E. S. Montagu, Asquith's Parliamentary secretary, it concentrated on landlord–tenant relations.[45] Dwelling on achievements, it began with the Agricultural Holdings Act of 1908, which extended farmers' security of tenure.[46] 'The object of the Liberal agricultural policy', wrote Montagu, accurately describing the *limits* of that policy, was 'to endeavour to replace a system which depends on the existence of the well-to-do landlord by a system depend-

[41]C. S. Orwin and E. H. Whetham, *History of British agriculture, 1846–1914* (2nd edn Newton Abbot, 1971), pp. 334–5.

[42]J. A. Venn, *The foundations of agricultural economics* (2nd edn Cambridge, 1933), p. 111.

[43]Mallet, *British budgets* (1913), pp. 288–90, 294–5.

[44]See e.g. Ernle, *Whippingham* (1938), pp. 232–3; *The land* (1913), i, 217ff.

[45]AP 24, E.S.M [ontagu]., 'The chancellor of the exchequer', (typed memo.) 22 Aug. 1908, fols. 273–7.

[46]On this subject see Matthews, *Fifty years* (1915), ch. VI.

ing only on the energy and success of the man who tills the soil'.[47] But Lloyd George was concerned not with the salvation of individuals, but with rural society and economy as a whole. For the 1909 Budget he came up with a true innovation, a central, government-financed Development Fund to encourage scientific and practical agricultural research, to promote rural co-operation, marketing and transport, to disseminate practical instruction, to build up technical education, and to initiate afforestation. National intervention was necessary because 'the limit of development possible under our system of local government has been reached'.[48] Lloyd George envisaged a central, rational, and concerted effort. What is more, in a year of severe financial pressures he was willing to find substantial sums, at the expense of the sacred sinking fund. In justification, he invoked the same vitalist metaphor cited at the beginning of this chapter:

> We have drawn on the robust vitality of the rural areas of Great
> Britain, and especially of Ireland, and spent its energies recklessly in
> the devitalising atmosphere of urban factories and workshops as if
> the supply were inexhaustible. We are now beginning to realise that
> we have been spending our capital, and at a disastrous rate, and it is
> time we should make a real concerted, national effort to replenish it.
> I put forward this proposal, not a very extravagant one, as a
> beginning.[49]

II

Unionist responses to the Liberal challenge wavered between two poles. On the one side were those who advocated an accommodation with the new regime; on the other, those who, like Balfour and Bonar Law, believed in outright resistance. But the landed interest, the most directly affected, lacked a firm voice. The Central Chamber of Agriculture had lapsed from its previous pre-eminence as the Parliamentary organ of the agrarians, to the disquiet of its members.[50] At the same time, the other sectional interests were strengthening their organisation. A Land Agents' Society was set up in 1901; agricultural trades unionism was re-

[47]AP 24, Montagu, 'The chancellor' fol. 274.
[48]William Runciman papers, WR/30, E.S.M[ontagu]., 'English development' (typed memo.), April 1909, p. 1.
[49]4 H.C. deb. 5 ser. 29 April 1909, 495.
[50]Discontent came out in the form of demands for an agricultural party in 1907 and 1908 (Matthews, *Fifty years* (1915), ch. XIII).

juvenated in 1906, and from local beginnings early in the century, a National Farmers' Union was established in 1908.[51] On 3 July 1907 a group of (mainly) Unionist politicians met at the Junior Carlton Club and founded the Central Land Association, in order to create a Parliamentary front against the Small Holdings Bill. The Association claimed non-party status and co-opted a number of Liberals on to its executive committee.[52] In three years it grew to more than a thousand landowner members, and aspired to become the landowners' 'Trades Union'.[53]

The President and guiding personality was Walter Long, the foremost political squire in the House of Commons. Long's attitude was not combative. In his heart he had probably given up the fort already. Landed society had had its day, and now was the time to retire with good face and pocket intact. 'The position is very different from what it used to be', he told the founders of the CLA,

Many of the amenities connected with the ownership of land have been largely reduced in value. Some have almost disappeared and there is no doubt that throughout the country there are opportunities for the transfer of land which did not exist in the days that are gone ... If we could agree upon a policy of purchase I believe that would be a very great step in the right direction for all who are concerned with our industry.[54]

Whether for political or for other reasons, large old estates were being dismantled at a growing pace in the late Edwardian period.[55] The Unionist leaders were pestered with would-be reformers who tried to interest them in Land Banks, Co-operation, State purchase and other devices to foster small holdings on supposedly non-Liberal lines.[56] In

[51]Country Landowners Association records, CLA C/1, H. M. Walker, 'The history of the central landowners' association, 1907–1947' (typescript, n.d. c. 1948), p. 8.

[52]CLA A/VII-1, 'Report of the proceedings at the inaugural meeting of the landholders central association', 3 July 1907 (16 pp.); *The Times*, 4 July 1907, 14c; 'A constructive land policy', *EG*, 6 July 1907, 7.

[53]CLA A/VII-2, Lord Onslow, CLA 'Second annual general meeting', 15 July 1909, p. 5.

[54]CLA A/VII-1, CLA, 'Proceedings at the inaugural meeting', p. 3.

[55]Thompson, *Landed society* (1963), pp. 320–6. But Venn (*Agricultural economics* (1933), p. 113) points out that the number of owner-occupied farms in England and Wales actually declined by 12.8 per cent between 1909 and 1913, to 48,760.

[56]E.g. G. Parker, *The land for the people* (1909) with a preface by Balfour. Interesting references to many schemes can be found in WL WRO 947/438, R. D. Blumenfeld [editor of the *Daily Express*] to W. Long, 22 Aug. 1910 and J. Collings to Long, 7 Sept. 1910.

this atmosphere of uncertainty Long embraced Jesse Collings and his state-financed small-ownership scheme, which he repeatedly tried to press upon Balfour.[57] But many landowners and farmers still regarded SH as a threat to the established rural order.[58]

Long was no longer personally committed to the rural order and was more concerned, it appears, to preserve a market for land.[59] Early in September 1910 he wrote to Balfour:

> Even with all its risks I personally am a convert to the system of small ownership, for one reason above all others. I believe it is the only way in which we can resist the march of Socialism, as exemplified, not by Snowden and Keir Hardie, but by the present financial policy of the Government, which must undoubtedly make the ownership of land in large quantities impossible for anybody who has not got other very large sources of income.

He echoed Balfour's idea that the state-financed withdrawal of the aristocracy from Ireland was a suitable precedent for England. State-aided purchase had quenched socialism in Ireland and he urged its adoption in Britain.[60] A few days later he wrote to Collings:

> I am selling a portion of my own estate now simply and solely because I feel that it is impossible for poor men like myself to keep large estates in face of the present burdens.[61]

What was the reality of the 'burdens'?

[57] WL, WRO 947/438, Long to Balfour, carbon copy, n.d. (late 1909?).
[58] *The land* (1913), i. 217ff.
[59] WL WRO 947/438, Long to Balfour, carbon copy, n.d. (late 1909?).
[60] *Ibid.*, n.d. (early Sept. 1910), fols. 2–3.
[61] Balfour was non-committal; See WL WRO 947/438, Long to Collings, 15 Sept. 1910 (quoted).

22

PEOPLE'S BUDGET AND RURAL
LAND CAMPAIGN 1909–1914

I

The 'people's budget' and the 'land campaign' came out of the Cobden tradition of political mobilisation for fiscal reform by platform rhetoric; the very term 'people's budget' was coined by Cobden.[1] Lloyd George's 1909–10 budget acted out Cobden's fantasies, but it went far beyond them: it threw down the gauntlet to the whole tenurial interest of the country. On top of the super-tax, increased death duties, doubled stamp duties, new road and petrol taxes and higher duties on drink the Land Value duties singled out landowners for special severity of treatment. The duties followed on the preamble and took up half the text of this very long finance bill. To the owners, there was an ominous gap between the cumbersome machinery and the meagre revenues expected. In Limehouse, on 30 July 1909, the Chancellor questioned the very legitimacy of landed property,[2] and on 30 October the owners were told that 'the new state valuation must be the basis of all plans for communal purchase'. He also invoked Irish land purchase, but with a different emphasis. Scores of millions of British credit were being pledged to rid Ireland of 'the crippling influences of landlordism'. Was nothing to be done for Britain?[3]

The budget provided for a new valuation of all the land in the kingdom, a veritable Domesday. Grand national valuations were no novelty; they were carried out as a matter of course every five years for income tax Schedule A assessment. Capital valuations were also routinely scrutinised for death duties by the Inland Revenue Valuation Department, which was entrusted with the new valuation. Nevertheless, even apart from the entirely new scale, there was an important difference. The valuation went beyond the market and into the realms of pure theory: beyond rents, beyond selling prices, even beyond capital valuation, to tease out and capitalise the pure rent. This was already implicit in Moulton's original kite of 1889, and was the Achilles' heel of

[1] Morley, *Cobden* (1881), ii, 33–4; Rogers, *Cobden* (1873), p. 73.
[2] *The Times*, 31 July 1909, 9 (esp. c–d).
[3] D. Lloyd George, 'The issues of the budget', *The Nation*, 30 Oct. 1909, 182.

the whole project, for it made the valuers' task doubly difficult and provocative. Five different values had to be established. The most straightforward was the first, the composite selling value of the site and structures ('gross value'), from which mortgages and other charges and rights were deduced to arrive at the 'total value'. Then, in the most controversial procedure, buildings and other improvements were deducted to arrive at 'full site value'; another set of deductions (for improvements affecting the site) reduced this to the 'assessable site value'. All the values were to be establsihed retroactively for 30 April 1909, and not the date of actual valuation. Finally, owners were allowed to substitute for the 'original site value' of 1909 any higher value actually recorded in a transfer up to twenty years previously (effectively neutralising the increment tax in many cases until values had exceeded those of the previous boom).[4] Another 'fifth value' sometimes applicable was the value for agricultural purposes.[5]

At each step, owners could be confronted with debatable valuations which no reference to facts could possibly settle. Every valuation was vulnerable to appeals in sympathetic courts. In spite of the apparent goodwill of the revenue staff, the task was formidable and the valuation got off to a bad start. Between nine and a half and ten and a half million 'hereditaments' (i.e. separate units of tenure) had to be valued. In August 1910 the department sent out 10.5 million copies of the notorious Form 4, which asked owners for detailed particulars of the extent, income, use and tenure of their properties, and allowed them to declare four of the values (see Fig. 22.1). Revenue officials then made their own inquiries and issued a 'provisional valuation' of the five values, which the owner could test on appeal.[6] The Unionist and property press shouted themselves hoarse with protest, and even the Liberal press printed very critical letters from supporters of the government.[7] Failure to return Form 4 carried a penalty of £50. The opposition cried foul play. It was alleged

[4]Text of finance bill, as amended in committee and on report; see D. Lloyd George, *The people's budget* (1909), pp. 135–90 (Pt. I, 2(3), 25).

[5]Land values. Sel. com. ev.; P.P. 1920 Cmd. 556 XIX, App. III, 'Report of the secretary ... of the Land Union', p. 75. This blue book is the main primary printed source on the valuation. The valuation field books (a detailed record of ownership and occupation) were made available to the public in 1979 at the PRO, class no. IR 58, and locally at a number of county record offices.

[6]*IRAR*, 1911, pt. I, p. 159; CAB 37/117/96, [Inland revenue, 'Taxation and rating of site values'], 24 Dec. 1913, p. 10; Land values. Sel. com. (1920), C. J. Howell Thomas, pp. 9–13 (including copies of the forms).

[7]E.g. *The Times*, 16 Aug. 1910, 3a–b *et seq.*, esp. leader 27 Aug. 9d–e. *EG* leaders, 20 Aug. 1910, 325; 3 Sept. 405; 17 Sept. 485; *The Nation* 3 Sept. 1910, 801–2; 17 Sept. 878–9; 24 Sept. 909–10.

PUNCH, OR THE LONDON CHARIVARI. —AUGUST 24, 1910.

THE HOLIDAY TASK.

STUDY OF A FREE-BORN BRITON WHO, WITHIN THE PERIOD USUALLY ALLOTTED TO HIS HOLIDAYS, IS REQUIRED, UNDER THREAT OF A PENALTY OF £50, TO ANSWER A MASS OF OBSCURE CONUNDRUMS RELATING TO LAND VALUES, IN ORDER TO FACILITATE HIS FUTURE TAXATION.

Fig. 22.1. *A cartoon published in* Punch, *24 August 1910.*
Text reset.

that the revenue authorities deliberately wrote down the value of land in order to obtain higher increment duties.[8] In subjecting tenure to such scrutiny, the Liberals were tampering with a large constituency of their own supporters. Even Charles Trevelyan was discomfited by the valuation on his own house in Newcastle (£7,300).[9]

Hundreds of qualified valuation staff had to be recruited in a hurry, and the opposition of property professions gave way to boundary disputes in competition for well-paid employment in a period of market depression.[10] As criticism and dissatisfaction mounted in 1911, the arbitrary values and deductions gave rise to such Alice-in-Wonderland entities as 'minus site values'.[11] Edgar Harper, who had long preached the simplicity and cheapness of valuation, resigned from the LCC in order to advise the government in May 1911, and was given responsibility for the valuation department in September.[12] In the nature of his talents, he only succeeded in making confusion worse confounded. Robert Chalmers' lucid and terse advice gave way to opaque disquisitions of mounting desperation.[13]

Walter Long disapproved of the diehard resistance of the House of Lords, in spite of his distaste for the Budget; the Central Land Association kept up correct relations with the Chancellor of the Exchequer, achieved a considerable concession for its members and retained the Liberals on its executive committee.[14] Other landowners were in a more combative mood, and a 'Land Defence League' was founded in the summer of 1909.[15] Foremost among the militants was Ernest G. Pretyman (1860–1931). He had been an obscure artillery captain until 1889, when an

---

[8]*LUJ*, June 1911, 15; Nov. 1911, 5.

[9]WR 68, C. P. Trevelyan to W. R. Runciman, 14 Jan. 1912; Evidence of Liberal unrest, see WR 35, R. Chalmers to Runciman, 8 Sept. 1910 and CPT 29, letters to Trevelyan from F. Marshall (22 May and 10 June 1912), [illegible signature] (22 Sept. 1912), J. Aynsley (6 Oct.); Also IR 63/31, 'Points likely to be raised on behalf of the small owner of house property', n.d. [1912], fols. 150–3.

[10]See IR 74/146 M3.11, H. Thomas, 'Draft notes on the organisation of the land valuation department', June 1910.

[11]IR 63/25, N19.2, Revenue bill, 1911, 'Minus site values', fols. 411–2; Commissioners of Inland Revenue v. Herbert and others, reported in *LUJ*, June 1913, supplement.

[12]He resigned in order to join the departmental committee on local taxation; see Haward, *LCC from within* (1932), pp. 218–21 and *LUJ*, Oct. 1911, 7.

[13]See e.g. IR 63/31, N21.5, 'Report by the chief valuer ...', 9 Feb. 1912, fol. 59 ff. and T 171/69, 1914 budget papers, Feb. 1914 onwards.

[14]For the concession see Stamp, *British incomes* (1920), p. 63; retention of Liberals, CLA A/II, Executive com. mins. 2, 24 Feb. 1910; moderate Form IV reaction, CLA memo. Oct. 1910, IR 63/31, N21.5, fols. 40–52.

[15]*LUJ*, May 1913, 14. The founder was C. E. Newton-Robinson.

unexpected bequest placed him in possession of a large landed estate near Ipswich, 'said to be twenty-two miles long by six wide' with a promising urban stake in Felixstowe.[16] He used his new-found eminence to embark on a political career, and was elected to Parliament in 1895. Large parties came down from London for shooting on the grand scale and Pretyman also became Master of the Brocklesby Hounds on an outlying part of his estate in Lincolnshire,[17] but despite the trappings of social elevation he did not disdain to descend in pursuit of a political base. In opposition he specialised in tenurial politics, and repeatedly stressed the local tax question.[18]

Pretyman led the Parliamentary resistance to the budget almost from the start,[19] and set out to fan the apprehensions created among the mass of small proprietors by the land value duties. In January 1910 he joined forces with the Land Defence League and on 28 April the first meeting of his 'Land Union' took place. Unlike the Tory magnates, the new association did not stand aloof from the small fry.

The Land Union gives particular attention to the interests of small owners of Land and House property, also to those of Farmers, Builders, and others who without its aid would be unable individually to defend themselves against a powerful government department.[20]

In addition to wealth and position, Pretyman acquired a unique mastery of the detail of the land value duties, and probably understood them better than anyone on the government side, Harper included. He deployed this knowledge with deadly effect and kept up a programme of sniping and harassment in Parliament, the press and direct correspondence.[21] His most effective sphere of operation, however, turned out to be the courts of law.

Lord Eversley described how, by a careful choice of cases, courts and judges, the preservation of many commons was secured between the 1860s and the 1880s. But by the turn of the century, with the middle-class retreat from Liberalism, there was a shift among the judiciary as well. In

[16] *Truth*, 24 Oct. 1901. Other sources: interview with Mr G. Pretyman, 25 Aug. 1977 and three albums of press cuttings in his possession.

[17] Pretyman cuttings, vol. I, fols. 52 (1901), 64 (1903); vol. II fols. 82 (1905), 85 (1905); *The Throne*, 5 Oct. 1907; A. Chamberlain, *Politics from inside* (1936), pp. 107–8.

[18] E.g. speech reported in *Essex Weekly News*, 2 Aug. 1907.

[19] Almost three columns in the *Hansard* index for 1909.

[20] The Land Union, *Objects and policy* (1913), p. 3; *LUJ*, May 1913, 14.

[21] Recorded monthly in the *LUJ*; correspondence, see e.g. IR 63/31 N21.5, E. G. Pretyman to R. Hawtrey, 25 July 1911 *et seq.*

1905 the Commons Preservation Society suffered its first major legal defeat when it failed to secure free access to Stonehenge.[22] From its inception the Land Union subjected the Land Valuation to extensive litigation, and the Inland Revenue suffered numerous embarrassing mishaps in the courts. Two celebrated cases developed into serious reversals.

In the first of these, popularly known as the Lumsden case (1911) the judgement established that speculative builders' profits were liable for increment value duty, thereby confirming builders' and owners' apprehensions and laying a damaging onus for depression in housing on the government.[23] Try as they might to show that other factors were also involved, the Liberals had to admit that those apprehensions had taken root, and had exercised an adverse effect on construction and upon property values and mortgage lending. With incomes on the rise and vacancies decreasing, the stage was set for a repetition of the housing famine of the late 1890s. Lloyd George had explicitly promised immunity for the builders in 1910 – but the tax on new buildings was painful to abandon: it brought in more than half the revenue. The Lumsden decision exposed the inherent contradictions, unintended consequences and careless drafting of the land values taxation.[24]

Even more serious in its effect was the 'Scrutton judgement' of February 1914.[25] Sir Thomas Edward Scrutton (1856–1934), the High Court judge, was a living demonstration of the shift in judicial attitudes from high Victorian Liberalism. In 1887 he published a prize essay on *Commons and Common Fields* which, although it questioned some of the legal assumptions underlying Commons Preservation Society tactics, gave wholehearted support to their aims and suggested additional ways of advancing them.[26] In Commissioners of the Inland Revenue *v.* Smyth

[22]Eversley, *Commons* (1910), pp. 30–1, 302–11.

[23]The legal campaign from the Land Union side, R. B. Yardley, *Land value taxation and rating* (n.d. 1930), pp. 642–55; *IRAR* (1911–14), legal cases; IR 63/32A, N21.6, which deals with the ramifications of the Lumsden case, 1911–13; Lumsden *v.* Commissioners of Inland Revenue, [1914], A.C. 877.

[24]*The land* (1914), ii, *urban*, 80–96; T 171/40, Builders' deputation to the chancellor of the exchequer, 17 April 1913, transcripts and correspondence, esp. printed transcript, pp. 9–13; Bad drafting, IR 63/23A, N21.6, Sir M. Nathan to Sir J. Simon, 18 April 1913, fols. 104–8. Painful to abandon – T 171/28, Land value duties, finance bill 1913, f. 38.

[25]Commissioners of Inland Revenue v. Smyth, [1914] 3 K.B. 423, also known as the 'Norton Maleward case'. It was sponsored by the Land Union.

[26]T. E. Scrutton, *Commons and common fields* (Cambridge, 1887), pp. vi–viii, 174–6.

[1914] he decreed, in effect, that all previous agricultural valuations were invalid, and prescribed an impracticable new method of valuation. This brought the levying of Undeveloped Land Duty, the most productive of the duties, and the original 'Harper Tax' of 1908, to a halt; pending an appeal or new legislation, it placed the whole elaborate valuation project in abeyance.[27] Six years later, in 1920, Lord Justice Scrutton made these observant remarks:

> the habits you are trained in, the people with whom you mix, lead to your having a certain class of ideas of such a nature that, when you have to deal with other ideas, you do not give as sound and accurate judgements as you would wish ... It is very difficult sometimes to be sure that you have put yourself into a thoroughly impartial position between two disputants, one of your own class and one not of your class.[28]

The Scrutton judgement revealed an aspect of the influence of the legal system that was already familiar to Edwardian progressives: the ability of individual judges to divert the political engine from its predetermined path, or even to bring it to a halt.

II

Mounted at a cost of more than £2 million, and bringing in only a quarter of that amount in revenue,[29] the Land Valuation must be judged an abortive and expensive raid on the landed interest's pocket; but it was only one prong of a concerted attack. Lloyd George also aimed at the heart of landed society, at its sport. Sporting rights amounting to almost £1.3 million a year were leased out in Great Britain in 1910, and much shooting land was kept in hand for the entertainment of estate owners and their guests.[30] Large shooting parties would descend on country houses in the autumn and engage in a curious and cruel competition for the largest number of bags. On 18 December 1913, for example, 3,937 pheasants were dispatched by shotgun at Hall Barn,

[27] IR 63/86, Bd. of Inland Revenue, 'Land value duties and the valuation ...', 13 Feb. 1919, fols. 115–16. Land values. Sel. com. ev. (1920). P. Thompson, p. 17 (12.).
[28] T. E. Scrutton, 'The work of the commercial courts', *Cambridge Law Journal* 1 (1921), 8.
[29] IR 63/35, N22.1, E. J. Harper, 'Cost of valuation', 2 May 1914, fol. 168; [M. Nathan], 'Use of valuation ... for local taxation and other purposes', ?2 [sic] May 1914, fol. 172.
[30] *IRAR*, 1912, pp. 105, 113 and Stamp, *British incomes* (1920), pp. 44–8.

Bucks, home of Lord Burnham, setting a British record. The second
Marquess of Ripon exterminated more than half-a-million birds and
beasts in a lifetime of shooting, and more than 10,000 in both 1911 and
1912.[31] Fox-hunting was even more integral to country life and symbolic
of the old regime.[32] In a chapter of his memoirs entitled 'Glorious days
of hunting the fox', Lord Willoughby de Broke, the diehard peer,
exclaimed: 'it is doubtful if France before the revolution was a better place
than Warwickshire before the war'.[33]

The Game Laws were one of the oldest Radical bugbears, and one of
the first initiatives of Gladstone's government in 1880 was the Ground
Game Act, which allowed farmers to destroy rabbits and hares without
reference to the landowners. Radicals were literally spoil-sports.[34] 'A
radical', in Willoughby de Broke's book, 'was a person whose motto was
"Down with everything" and who certainly could not be trusted with a
gun within shooting distance of a fox,

"For I looked into its pages, and I read the book of Fate,
and saw Fox-hunting abolished by the State."'[35]

The memory of the highland clearances made deer forests into an
emotional issue in Scotland. Deer-stalking withdrew vast expanses of
land from grazing and closed them to walkers. James Bryce introduced
the first of many Access To Mountains bills in 1888 and C. P. Trevelyan
renewed the effort in 1908.[36] In England's arable counties shooting was a
serious farmers' grievance and was acknowledged even by Conservative
experts as one of the main reasons for agricultural backwardness.[37] After
the start of the land campaign a farmer wrote to Lloyd George to say,

I am absolutely opposed to you in politics so I have no axe to grind
except I do not like feeding other people's animals at my own
expense and the landlord getting two rents for the same ground.[38]

Small holdings were not granted because landowners feared that small
holders would swamp the game.[39] Even troops on manoeuvre were shut

[31]J. G. Ruffen, *The big shots: Edwardian shooting parties* (n.d. [1978]), pp. 134–5.
[32]See R. Carr, *English fox hunting: a history* (1976), esp. ch. IX.
[33]Willoughby de Broke, *The passing years* (1924), p. 196.
[34]43 & 44 Vict. c. 47. Poaching and Liberalism agreed very well: see *Hawker: Victorian poacher* (1962).
[35]de Broke, *Passing years* (1924), p. 167.
[36]*Scottish land: the report of the Scottish land enquiry committee* (1914), ch. XIII; C. E. M. Joad, *A charter for ramblers* (n.d. ?1935), p. 184.
[37]C. Turnor, *Land problems and national welfare* (n.d. [1911]), pp. 17–8, 38, 55, 108–9; Hall, *Pilgrimage* (1913), p. 147.
[38]LG C/10/1/95, W. H. Cooper to Lloyd George, n.d. (Oct. 1913).
[39]*The land* (1913), i, 220, 224.

off from shooting land, well before the season, in a clash of values that patriotic *Punch* found more distressing than amusing.[40]

For all these reasons Lloyd George chose sport as a central target in his attacks on landowners. 'Are they going to reduce their gamekeepers?' he asked in mocking tones at Limehouse in 1909. At Bedford on 11 October 1913, at the opening of the land campaign, he stated that gamekeepers had increased from 9,000 in 1851 to 23,000 in 1911, while farmworkers had declined by 600,000.[41] But the Liberal *Kulturkampf* was lacking in conviction. Given the opportunity and the means, wealthy Liberals loved to indulge in Tory pleasures. Charles Hobhouse, Postmaster General, was a long-range cyclist but also a passionate rider to hounds and an enthusiastic hunter.[42] C. P. Trevelyan was not content with the man hunt: 'I got 16 brace to my sole gun,' he boasted to Runciman in 1910.[43] After Lloyd George reproached the game tenantry at his Swindon speech, Bonar Law found no difficulty in obtaining a list of Liberal shooting tenants.[44] With a mind peculiarly indifferent to the attractions of the outdoors, he was personally immune to such a line of attack.[45] And while the Chancellor concentrated on the ravages of the grouse and the pheasant, he avoided the subject of fox-hunting, maybe in obedience to the Prime Minister's wife, who demanded in January 1913, 'Promise me you won't mention fox hunting in your land speeches'.[46] Liberals were compromised by their complicity in the culture of the rural ascendancy.[47] But Lloyd George's *concrete* proposals were part of a Rural Land Campaign of much wider scope.

III

The origins of the Liberal land campaign of 1912–14 have been traced, and the story of the campaign is familiar in outline;[48] the internal

[40]'Preserving the country' (cartoon), *Punch*, 21 Sept. 1910, 201.
[41]*The Times*, 31 July, 1909, 9d; 13 Oct. 1913, 13d.
[42]*Inside Asquith's cabinet* (1977), pp. 5–6, 120, 122.
[43]WR 35, Trevelyan to Runciman, 19 Sept. 1910.
[44]BL 30/3/60, W. J. Marshall, 'List of Scottish shootings owned or rented by radicals ...', 27 Oct. 1913.
[45]See Blake, *Unknown prime minister* (1955), pp. 18, 30–1.
[46]LG C/6/12/1, Margot Asquith to Lloyd George, 3 Jan. 1913.
[47]See F. M. L. Thompson, 'Britain' in D. Spring (ed.), *European landed elites in the nineteenth century* (Baltimore, 1977).
[48]See especially A. Briggs, *Social thought and social action: a study of the work of Seebohm Rowntree* (1961), p. 64ff.; H. V. Emy, 'The land campaign: Lloyd George as a social reformer 1906–14' in *Lloyd George: twelve essays*, ed. A. J. P.

coherence of its proposals has not, however, been fully appreciated. First, a massive 'Land Enquiry' was launched in June 1912. Unofficial enquiries had been invented by Joseph Chamberlain: the *Radical Programme* of 1885, and the much more elaborate Tariff Commission of 1905.[49] Following these precedents, the Enquiry was designed to translate an overriding political impulse into detailed practical policies and to give it publicity and impetus. Like the Tariff Commission, the Land Enquiry eventually published a valuable record of economic and social conditions. Unlike the Tariff Commission it avoided public hearings and pronouncements. Instead, it tapped hundreds of informants in every part of the country for private information about tenurial and labour conditions, thoroughly alerting both supporters and opponents and creating a heightened sense of apprehension and expectation.

Practical men, experienced social investigators, idealists and hardened politicians joined together, in an alliance designed to advance social ideals by political means, and to exploit those ideals for political ends.[50] B. S. Rowntree provided the initial spark in 1912, and undertook the methodological, administrative and financial leadership.[51] His own interest arose from the connection between poverty and land tenure which the enthusiasts for SH and decentralisation perceived. Small holdings and better access to the countryside stood near the top of his priorities and a deeply rooted moral preference for the country over the town informed his analysis. It pained him when a town labourer recalled his days in the country and said 'I felt as if I was buried alive'.[52] He rejoiced when another put up with hardship in order to live in the country and cycle for work into town.[53]

Taylor (1971); B. B. Gilbert, 'The reform of British landholding and the budget of 1914', *Historical Journal* 21 (1978); A. S. King, 'Some aspects of the history of the Liberal party in Britain, 1906–14' (Oxford Univ. D. Phil. thesis, 1962), ch. VIII; B. K. Murray, 'Lloyd George and the land: the issue of site-value rating', *Studies in local history*, ed. J. A. Benyon *et al.* (Cape Town, 1976).

[49] See J. Chamberlain, *A political memoir 1880–92* ed. C. H. D. Howard (1953), p. 108 and Amery, *Chamberlain* (1969), vi, 529–34.

[50] See LG C/2 for the enthusiastic commitment of the enquiry workers.

[51] Briggs, *Social thought* (1961); Rowntree's father contributed £10,000 and William Lever another £5,000 (LG C/2/3/16, B. S. Rowntree to Lloyd George, 6 Oct. 1913 and C/10/1/58, W. H. Lever to Lloyd George, 22 Oct. 1913).

[52] B. S. Rowntree, *Land and labour: lessons from Belgium* (2nd edn 1911), p. 540n.; and see pp. v, 542–7.

[53] LG C/2/4/12, B. S. Rowntree to Lloyd George, 2 April 1914, enclosing a letter from S. F. Harrison to Rowntree describing the tribulations of finding a suitable rural dwelling.

372

Lloyd George was by no means so keen on small holdings, and occasionally even failed to distinguish between Unionist and Liberal enthusiasts.[54] Other considerations must have weighed on his mind. After 1910 the English Tory rural constituencies remained the last electoral frontier still open to the Liberal party and their capture could shift the political balance in its favour. 'Half of the seats in England which the Liberals could hope to win in 1915 were rural in character', writes a student of the electoral configuration. Only 35 out of 150-odd English rural constituencies had been held by the Unionists continuously since 1885.[55] It suited the Chancellor that the Enquiry placed rural poverty at the centre of its concern. Wages in agriculture were low, employment often casual or seasonal, the work hard, the hours long. Housing was bad and its tenure insecure.[56] Farmers were becoming restive over Unionist shifts and turns on tariff reform, particularly after food tariffs were abandoned in January 1913. Game leases and insecurity of tenure added to their worries.[57] From these elements of discontent Lloyd George forged a strategy for land. It was masterly in conception, simple in structure and incisive in effect.

'A coming land campaign', announced an *Estates Gazette* headline on 25 May 1912. From the start it was clear to friend and foe that agricultural wages would be the focus of the campaign and the plan was apparently settled in outline in Lloyd George's mind that summer.[58] Asquith gave public consent to a land campaign in October, and private approval in February 1913.[59] Lloyd George kept abreast of the progress of the enquiry but did not wait for its conclusion. A preliminary proposal was circulated to the Cabinet on 21 August 1913, and the principles were acknowledged by two other ministers in important Cabinet papers in September.[60] Yet discussions of detail went on and the plan did not

---

[54]See p. 358. He was impressed by the writings of J. L. Green, Jesse Collings' lieutenant, and in ignorance of his identity, asked whether he could be recruited for the land campaign (LG C/2/1/19, Lloyd George to J. S. G. Heath, 12 Sept. 1912).

[55]King, 'Some aspects' (1962), pp. 325, 326.

[56]*The land* (1913), i, Pt. I.

[57]See B. Gilbert, *Farmers and tariff reform* (1913), *passim* and *The land*, i, Pt. III.

[58]LG C/9/3/9, F. A. Huckle to Lloyd George, 19 July 1912 (a reply to an inquiry about farm labour in agriculture) and C/2/1/22, Lloyd George to J. St G. Heath, secretary of the enquiry, 14 Sept. 1912.

[59]Speech at Ladybank, 5 Oct. 1912 (*Annual register* (1912), 214); WR 82, Lloyd George to Runciman, 10 Feb. 1913.

[60]CAB 37/116/56, 'Land' ('embodies the suggestions of some members of the cabinet'), 21 Aug. 1913; CAB 37/116/58, W. Runciman, 'Rural land', 13 Sept. 1913 and CAB 37/116/64–5, S. Buxton, 'The land question', and 'Figures

The Land Campaign   -   Bedford,October 11th.

1913

Not here to discuss questions which divide

    Home Rule,etc

    Nothing which could not be adjusted

Some people would like to fight election after election

    They can afford luxury

Millions sitting in darkness

    Search Light

    Ernestly praying

No questions ever raised more vitally affecting well-

  being of community

Enters into every necessity of life.- Food,drink,air,

  light, houses, industry, entertainment, necessities

  comforts, amenities

Ownership in hands of half Bedford

If they mishandle authority, disastrous

Cannot conceive more urgent question

    Use made by land-owners

Powers terrible

Landlordism greatest of all monopolies

    Least restricted by conditions

    Time come to inquire into gigantic powers

    and use.

Fig. 22.2. *Blank verse?*

The first sheet of Lloyd George's notes for the opening speech of the
land campaign. Source: Lloyd George papers, LG C/28/1 (House of Lords
Record Office).

come to the Cabinet until 15 October 1913, four days *after* the official launching speech at Bedford.[61] Only at Lloyd George's Swindon speech, on 22 October, was it presented in full.[62]

The Cabinet documents were long, and full of administrative detail. The land speeches were even longer, and clouded by vitalist rhetoric (see Fig. 22.2). The plan which the Chancellor placed before his colleagues was a ramshackle affair which took 'three long Cabinets' to consider.[63] A jumble of concrete proposals without clear priority were piled on top of each other, and even the Chancellor soon needed a list of all his promises.[64] As in previous instances of tenurial policy, the cutting edge was hidden in a sheath of subordinate detail. Nor was obfuscation without a function. It served to tone down the partisan purpose of the proposals; and to very good effect, as we shall see. On 18 October Bonar Law's advisers tendered their own interpretation:

In a few words, *MR. LLOYD GEORGE'S POLICY* is as follows:-

The labourers in this country are getting an insufficient wage, and they must be paid more.

This increase in wages must not come out of the pockets of the farmers, who cannot afford it, and the deficiency must therefore be made up by a deduction from their rent.

The chief point of this policy is the extreme difficulty it presents in combating it from a political point of view.[65]

It could not be better put. The proposals were a crowbar intended to pry the tenures apart and let a Liberal constituency loose; an ancient Radical conviction held that this would also raise production in the countryside and elevate its moral and physical well-being.[66] The essence of the plan was simple: a minimum wage for agricultural labourers, raising it to the level of the best-paying districts and making an increase

relating to the land question', Sept. 1913 (printed 3 Oct.). Lloyd George and the enquiry, see LG C/2/1 – C/2/3/14 (July 1912–Oct. 1913).

[61] *Inside Asquith's cabinet* (1977), pp. 146–8; comp. Runciman's notes, WR 74.

[62] *The Times*, 13 Oct. 1913, 14 and 23 Oct. 1913, 9–10.

[63] *Inside Asquith's cabinet* (1977), pp. 147–8.

[64] LG C/2/3/37, Heath to Lloyd George, 8 Nov. 1913, and enclosure.

[65] BL 30/3/35, H. C. Thornton (on National Union notepaper) to Miss Tugander (B. Law's secretary), 18 Oct. 1913, enclosing a memo. (quoted) by B. Tollemache (secretary of the CLA) prepared for Law.

[66] S. Buxton's preamble (CAB 37/11/65) spoke in similar terms; Runciman's time horizon was bounded by the coming election (CAB 37/116/58, pp. 4, 7–8); the 'Radical conviction' is spelt out in 'Land' (CAB 37/116/56), p. 1.

of from one-quarter to a third or more in most districts. A living wage would enable the labourer to pay an economic rent and end his bondage to the farmer's tied house. To meet the increased wage-bill, farmers could get *pro rata* remissions of rent from the landowners, and were also promised compensation for game damage and greater security of tenure. The policy was to be effected amicably by arbitration and conciliation in Wage Boards and Rent Courts, an extension into agriculture of the old Liberal rent courts in Ireland, and the Wages Boards instituted by Asquith's government in sweated occupations and the coal mines. Arbitration powers were to be vested in a Land Commission.

Whatever its impact, the campaign was not conceived as a flag for labour in its conflict with capital; 'socialism' was only invoked by its enemies. Its principles were not collectivist but Benthamite: an intervention to improve the working of the market and the 'artificial identification of interests', to use Halévy's phrase.[67] Freely-entered individual employment and land rental contracts were to remain the framework of productive relations. But contractual frictions would be cooled by a utilitarian system of adjudication:

> Abuses of the present system show themselves in *unfairness of contract* between the landlord and the tenant or between tenant and labourers or workmen; and the cardinal point of the present proposals is that a Commission should have discretionary power to intervene in any case in which it was alleged that an unfairness of contract existed which prevented land being used *in the best interests of the community*.[68]

As in Bentham's thinking, the overriding constraint was fiscal probity. This was the proposal's decisive virtue: it made few claims on government finance. Like the previous SH legislation, it was going to be cheap, as Asquith assured the party elite: no substantial spending was envisaged.[69] Tenurial adjustment alone would provide the means. In this respect the plan went beyond SH and beyond Bentham too, since a real economic transfer was required to raise real wages. *Someone* had to pay. The plan conformed with the Classical Economic concensus and bore the marks of Liberal animus to landowners: improved wages were to come out of rent,

---

[67] Halévy, *Philosophic radicalism* (1972 edn), p. 17.
[68] CAB 37/116/56, 'Land', 21 Aug. 1913, p. 1. Italics added.
[69] AP 25, 'Mr. Asquith on land policy, at a dinner at the National Liberal Club, Dec. 12 1913 ...', fol. 76a.

not farmers' profit. All the rest of the programme (small holdings and allotments, registration of title, compulsory purchase, education, afforestation, rural transport, law reform etc.) appears, in the light of the political imperatives of the campaign, to be elaboration and dressing. An urban policy on similar lines was also outlined (see p. 390). 'A new ministry of land' was projected to pull all the strands together, a descendant of Brickdale's 'Domesday office' proposals of 1910.[70]

After a sluggish start at Bedford, the rural campaign took off 'like wildfire'. So deep was rural despondency that the promise of decent' wages was irresistible; devotional scenes abounded. Scores of Liberal missionaries poured into the countryside and brought back reassuring messages.[71] Farmers sent in testimonials; Liberal candidates were enthusiastic.[72] At one stage 90 to 120 meetings were being held every day; millions of pamphlets and leaflets were distributed. On 28 May 1914 the Secretary of the campaign organisation took stock of the situation and reported that the rural effort had achieved its goals:

THE RURAL CAMPAIGN: speaking of the country as a whole I may say without exception the Government's proposals are arousing unprecedented enthusiasm in the rural constituencies. In a large number of villages every elector physically capable of doing so has attended the meetings. Men walk five, six and seven miles to be present. The women are as enthusiastic as the men. The people will stand for an hour or more in the drenching rain or piercing wind to hear the proposals explained. For the first time in the history of modern Liberalism farmers who do not support the Liberals are attending Liberal meetings where owing to violent opposition or small population, no meeting has been possible before. I get two reports from each meeting; one from the speaker and one from the local organiser and the story of success is universal ... In the Rural districts we are making friends wholesale among non-Liberals, and the Tories have no sort of reply to make to our case. The farmers are

[70] CAB 37/118/9, 'Ministry of land', 9 Jan. 1914, including a cabinet note of October 1913 (pp. 22–3). 'Domesday office', see p. 76.
[71] LG C/10/1/71, O. Brett (Lib. candidate, Tavistock) to Lloyd George, 26 Oct. 1913 (quoted); C/2/4/23–9 for detailed constituency reports, May 1914.
[72] Farmers' letters, see LG C/10/1/87b, 95; candidates, C/10/1/71, 90 and C/11/1/56. Farmers also wrote in to ask how owner-occupiers could afford higher wages, and to complain of displacement by SH (C/10/2/83, C/11/1/1).

thinking as they have never thought before... [and] I am perfectly sure we are going to get the support of farmers and labourers who are not hopeless Tories. This means that unless some accident happens we shall sweep the rural constituencies.[73]

IV

How well-conceived this policy was is attested by the Unionist response. From the land campaign's very beginning in 1912 it threw the agrarians into disarray. The Earl of Malmesbury, for example, warned Bonar Law on 1 July 1912 that 'there is not the slightest doubt that Mr Lloyd George intends making another violent, uncalled-for and unjust attack upon Land'. He asked Law to commit the party to Jesse Collings' land-purchase proposals.[74] The Unionists were disunited. At least three separate study groups were separately commissioned, by Walter Long, Austen Chamberlain and Arthur Steel-Maitland, chairman of the Party, on top of the existing pressure groups, the CLA, the Land Union and Collings' Rural League.[75] Walter Long's experts made an accurate prediction of Lloyd George's policy: 'We regard it as evident,' they reported, 'that the Chancellor of the Exchequer has his attention directed to the question of Agricultural Wages, and contemplates steps to raise them by Act of Parliament'.[76]

Landowners had already been reacting for two or three years to an atmosphere of apprehension and insecurity at home (and to increased investment opportunities abroad) by selling off estates in whole or part at an increasing pace. Wholesale changes of ownership had a disturbing effect upon tenant farmers, and their discontent gave rise to an official enquiry. A majority of the committee recommended some form of state-aided transfer of ownership to farmers, in order to secure continuous occupation and incidentally, to buoy up the price of land. This eminently conservative committee, with a majority of owners, property pro-

[73]LG C/2/4/20, G. Wallace Carter, 'The plan of campaign', (typed land campaign progress report by the secretary of its official body, the Central Land and Housing Council) to Lloyd George, 28 May 1914, pp. 2, 4.
[74]BL 26/5/1, Malmesbury to Law, 1 July 1912; see 34 H.C. debs. 5 ser. 23 Feb. 1912, B. Stanier, 888–96; J. Collings, 896–903.
[75]WL WRO 947/439, W. H. Trustram Eve to Long, 14 July 1912 (and see[76]).
[76]WL WRO 947/439, 10 pp. typed report on rural and urban land, signature illegible, 1 Aug. 1912, p. 7 (commissioned in letter from Long to B. Peto, MP, 29 June 1912, *ibid.*).

fessionals and farmers, even went so far as to consider the purchase and management of large estates by the state![77]

Henry Trustram Eve, a land agent, surveyor and trusted Unionist agrarian expert, was commissioned by Steel-Maitland to help Alfred Milner in drafting an authorised 'land policy for rural districts'. He advised informally that the Unionist party was defenceless in the face of the Liberal proposals. Labourers had a grievance, and Liberals promised tangible benefits where the Unionists could offer none. In addition to old age pensions, 'the best tangible result of politics they have ever known', the spirit of Limehouse was a source of disaffection.

The whole political atmosphere has been changed since Limehouse, Newcastle, etc. and I suppose it is a fact of history that when once the respect of one class for another is gone, there is no halting place. It is either there or it is gone – like a pebble thrown in a pond.[78]

Lord Milner circulated his authorised report in the winter of 1912–13. It ran to 43 printed pages in the blue covers and cabinet-paper format used by the Unionists for their policy documents. Lord Lansdowne responded on 13 April 1913 in similar format but shorter length.[79] Milner admitted that agricultural wages were 'much too low'.[80] Walter Long's experts had suggested a sliding scale for agricultural wages pegged to the price of produce, on the lines of the tithe commutation index.[81] Milner took up their idea of a bounty on wheat to compensate farmers for higher wages, and put forward a profit-sharing scheme, in line with a contemporary anti-socialist vogue.[82] Unionist hearts were not in higher wages. Eve opined that 'the dignified course is to be patient and wait'.[83] In spite of its acknowledged urgency, the question of rural poverty was given much lower priority in the counsels of the party than

[77]Tenant farmers and sales of estates. Dept. com. rep.; P.P. 1912–13 Cd. 6030 XLVII, esp. pp. 5–16.

[78]Steel-Maitland commission, WL 947/439, Eve to Long, 14 July and 7 Aug. 1912. Quote from H. T. Eve, 'Random notes in June 1912. Suggestions for the Unionist party' (14 pp. typed), pp. 1, 2. Long sent this outspoken survey of rural politics to Bonar Law on 8 Aug. 1912 (BL 27/1/28).

[79]WL WRO 947/439, [Viscount Milner], 'Confidential' [undated, unsigned untitled memo.]; L[ord Lansdowne]., 'Observations on Lord Milner's memorandum – (agricultural reform)', 13 April 1913.

[80]Milner memo p. 35.

[81]WL WRO 947/439, land study group report, 1 Aug. 1912, pp. 6–8.

[82]*Ibid.* p. 8 and Milner memo pp. 35–6. On profit-sharing, see E. Bristow, 'Profit-sharing, socialism and labour unrest' in Brown, *Anti-labour history* (1974).

[83]WL WRO 947/439, Eve, 'Random notes' (1912), p. 4.

reinforcing the bulwarks of property, in the tradition of Salisbury. Lord Milner gave forceful expression to this line of reasoning.

There can be no manner of doubt that the institution of private property is seriously menaced at the present time – more seriously menaced perhaps in Great Britain than anywhere else in the world ... If the present Social Order is to endure, it is simply necessary, at whatever cost, to effect a great increase in the number of people who have a direct personal interest in the maintenance of private property.

There is no bulwark to communism at all equal to that provided by a large number of small property owners and especially small owners of land.[84]

Most of the proposals were designed to further this end: 100 per cent State aid for purchase, co-operative small-holding settlements, credit banks, even 're-enclosure' of villages so as to give labourers some land close at hand.[85] Lansdowne damned these schemes with faint praise.[86] The old landed magnates held back: reluctant to acknowledge or hasten the break-up of their old authority, yet eager to get the best possible deal when sale became desirable or inevitable. Two debates on Collings' state-aided purchase schemes, and Lansdowne's wavering approval for Irish-model purchases reflected this indecision.[87] In the summer of 1913, the party faced the coming onslaught without an agreed strategy. Even Lord Lansdowne had to admit that rural conditions were crying for reform.

We cannot, as politicians, conceal from ourselves the seriousness of the position in the agricultural districts. The farmers are discontented and suspicious. The labourers are unsettled, and attracted by the prospect of a minimum wage; and there is a serious risk that we may lose a number of the seats which we now hold in the rural districts.[88]

Yet in spite of repeated pleas in the first half of 1913, Bonar Law declined to give the party a lead.[89]

The challenge of the 'New Liberalism' provoked populist instincts

[84]Milner memo pp. 1–2.
[85]*Ibid., passim.*
[86]Lansdowne, 'Observations', *passim.*
[87]WL 947/439 Eve, 'Random notes' (1912), pp. 2–3, 14; 34 H.C. deb. 5 ser. 23 Feb. 1912, E. Jardine, 928–32 and 11 H.L. deb. 5 ser. 7 March, esp. Marlborough, 338 and Lansdowne, 380.
[88]Lansdowne, 'Observations' (1913), pp. 1–2.
[89]BL 29/1/24, Lord Selborne to Law, 19 Feb. 1913; 29/6/19, J. Baird MP to Law, 11 July 1913.

within the Unionist party. This movement of dissent over Unionist social policy developed after the 1910 defeat. W. A. S. Hewins, the economist and secretary of the Tariff Commission, lost the contest in Shipley, in the West Riding of Yorkshire. This taught him (he later claimed), that 'Conservatism divorced from its historic policy of social reform had no chance whatever in the country'; soon after, he helped to found a Parliamentary Unionist Social Reform Group, which grew a number of offshoots into different spheres of policy.[90] It was from within this 'Tory democrat' circle that a powerful movement grew in the summer of 1913 with the object of disarming Lloyd George by embracing his proposals. Lord Edmund Talbot, chief Unionist whip, and Leslie Scott, a prominent 'progressive' MP, took a leading part in the movement. In July 1913 'a few members of the young Tory party' met and drafted an agricultural manifesto.[91] In August Talbot was spurred into action by Alexander Thynne, MP and landowner, who recounted in detail how far real wages had declined as prices rose, and how the agrarian revival had passed the labourers by. In a tone of great urgency Thynne called upon Talbot to sponsor a voluntary movement among landowners to encourage wage increases by lowering rents, and threatened a back-bench revolt in support of wage boards if no action was taken.[92] Bonar Law was perturbed, but Lord Lansdowne advised against concessions. Steel-Maitland, the party chairman, warned against any diversion from Ulster, the central conservative cause.[93] In the meanwhile the back-bench group adopted the wage board principle, drafted a wage-board bill, and published their manifesto. Finally, in the face of the party leaders' impassivity, they approached the devil, Lloyd George himself, with an offer of co-operation, in return for a promise not to 'Limehouse' the landlords and the party.[94]

[90]W. A. S. Hewins, *The apologia of an imperialist* (1929), i, 251.

[91]Lord Henry Bentinck, *Tory democracy* (1918), pp. 79–80. See n. [94] below.

[92]BL 30/1/31, E. Talbot to Law, 29 Aug. 1913, encl. letter from A. E. Thynne to Talbot, 22 Aug. 1913.

[93]BL 33/5/53, Law to Lansdowne, 2 Sept. 1913; 33/5/54, Law to Talbot, 2 Sept.; 30/2/4, Talbot to Law, 3 Sept.; 30/2/7, Lansdowne to Law, 4 Sept.; 30/2/17, Lansdowne to Law, 20 Sept.; 33/5/54, Law to Lansdowne, 24 Sept.; 30/2/26, Steel-Maitland to Law, 25 Sept.; 30/2/24, A. E. Weigall MP to Law, 25 Sept.

[94]'A group of Unionists', *A Unionist agricultural policy* (Sept. 1913), esp. pp. 9–11. See also BL 30/2/17, Lansdowne to Law, 20 Sept. 1913 and 30/2/24, A. E. Weigall to Law, 25 Sept. 1913. Scott's pourparlers with Lloyd George are contained in his letters of 29 Sept. and 6 Oct. 1913 (LG C/2/8/1–2). The verb 'limehouse' appears in the second. A letter from 'agricultural policy' group to Law (BL 30/4/12, 8 Nov. 1913) was signed by Waldorf Astor, W. J. Ashley, Stanley Baldwin, Charles Bathurst, Henry Bentinck, J. W. Hills, P. Lloyd-

Rural regeneration was a nostrum that numbed the political reflexes of many Unionists. Lloyd George had successfully invoked that moral heritage which formed the subject of our preceding chapters. Even Milner succumbed to moral frustration under the Welsh wizard's spell. 'I think George's handling of the Land question ... *quite detestable*', he wrote to Bonar Law after the Swindon speech. 'With some of his particular proposals and with what he professes to be his object ... I quite agree'.[95] Lloyd George had no use for Unionist collaboration, and Leslie Scott's group then appealed to their own leader. 'An attempt simply to ignore the Land problem', they wrote early in November, 'cannot in the nature of things meet with success ... the agricultural voter might be inclined to think that he had to choose between sacrificing Ulster and sacrificing his own private interest'.[96]

Late in September, in response to the moderates' manifesto, Trustram Eve came up with a counter-suggestion: a new, impartial inquiry to establish the facts, propose remedies and lift the land question out of the realm of party politics.[97] The conciliation movement gathered strength with the public accession of William Joynson-Hicks, an influential Unionist back-bencher.[98] Even Bonar Law admitted, in a speech at Norwich, that farm wages were unacceptably low.[99] But Pretyman wrote to Law, 'You cannot expect your agricultural followers to accept such a policy as these "social reformers" are putting forward'. And Long warned, 'I am sure you recognise the danger of estranging or even alarming the landowners and farmers who are the backbone of our party'.[100] The alacrity with which the inquiry proposal was taken up on all sides, including the intransigents, amounted to an admission of the unanswerable force of the land campaign.[101] Pretyman wrote, 'If it were

Greame, Lord Malmesbury, Leslie Scott, Edward Strutt, A. Thynne, Christopher Turnor, Fabian Ware, Edward Wood and Maurice Woods.

[95] BL 30/3/50, Milner to Law, 24 Oct. 1913.

[96] BL 30/4/12, Fifteen Unionist MPs and experts to Law, 8 Nov. 1913 (listed above, p. 381, [94]).

[97] BL 30/2/26, A. Steel-Maitland to Lansdowne, 24 Sept. 1913. Eve was secretary of the 'Land Conference', a front body which united the Land Union, Farmers' Club and Rural League with the property professional associations. 'I have reason to believe we could use this body for our purpose', wrote Steel-Maitland, 'and if we got them, we also have the others'.

[98] See his letter, *Pall Mall Gazette*, 27 Oct. 1913 (cutting, LG C/15/1/11). BL 30/3/64, Pretyman to Law, 28 Oct. 1913, contains an angry response.

[99] *The Times*, 14 Nov. 1913, 10b–c.

[100] BL 30/3/66, 77, Pretyman to Law, 29 Oct. 1913 and Long to Law, 31 Oct.

[101] See BL 30/3/50, Milner to Law, 24 Oct. 1913, and [104].

not for our own "Land Reformers" I should propose to fight straight without enquiry, but they make this very difficult'.[102] So an official enquiry became the party line.[103] But dissension continued to rack the landed interest, notably within the Central Land Association, which wavered between conciliation and admiration for Land Union militancy.[104] So despite a plethora of publications and some of the best talent money could buy (notably the writer and historian R. E. Prothero[105]), the Unionist response remained defensive and negative. The land campaign had hit home. There remained the urban sector, where the Unionists had come to grief a decade before. How well did Lloyd George handle the urban question?

[102]BL 30/3/64, 66, Pretyman to Law, 28 and 29 Oct. (quoted), 1913.

[103]See BL 33/6/91, Law to Pretyman, n.d. (reply to 28–29 Oct. letters, n.6 above); 34/1/17, Law to Lord Salisbury, 26 Jan. 1914; 32/3/13, Long to Law, 6 May 1914.

[104]For an abortive move to co-operate with the Land Union, to which the CLA was losing members, see CLA A/II, exec. com. mins. 3, 15 April, 2 June, 7 July 1913. Initiatives for voluntary rent reductions as a counter to the land campaign, *ibid.*, 10 Dec. 1913 and CLA A/VII/3, circular to members from exec. com. chairman (A. H. Smith), 19 Dec. 1913.

[105]See e.g. *The Times*, 31 July 1913, 11; 4 Nov. 1913, 13c–d; WL WRO 947/439, 'Notes on the report (vol. I rural) of Mr Lloyd George's land enquiry committee' ['Confidential', 24 pp. printed, unsigned], Dec. 1913, cites Prothero extensively, esp. the historical outline, Pt. III (pp. 5–7). He also compiled the Land Agents' Society's anti-Liberal *Facts about land* (1915) (Ernle, *Whippingham* (1938), pp. 205–8).

23

THE URBAN QUESTION AGAIN
1910–1914

The urban conundrum would not go away just because governments had changed in 1905. Its essence was unchanged: liabilities were growing faster than resources, and government failed to step into the breach. Education retained its primacy: school meals, medical care, better staffing, higher standards and salaries and a great expansion in 'secondary' education all added to the financial strain on the local authorities. Starting in 1907, a tide of resolutions, reports, pamphlets and deputations exercised never-failing pressure on the government, culminating in the mammoth A.M.C. and County Council Association deputation to the Prime Minister on 18 March 1909.[1] Walter Runciman, who had Cabinet responsibility for education, admitted the justice of the complaints. He told the Cabinet in December 1909 that government expenditure on education had actually declined since their assumption of power; that the share of government grants for elementary education had fallen to half the cost; and that the distribution of grants at a fixed rate per child took no account of enormous disparities in the level of expenditure between different areas. Lloyd George had resisted any increase, but this could not continue: a million pounds were urgently required.

> several Local Authorities are on the brink of revolt; I am constantly hearing from all quarters that the hostility of the ratepayers offers an insuperable obstacle to educational improvements; I have reason to believe that the National Union of Teachers have decided to launch their powerful organisation into an active campaign; and pressure is now being exerted on the county candidates. A movement is developing which it would be difficult for any Government to resist, and there are obvious advantages in dealing with the problem before our hands are forced.[2]

[1] *The Times*, 19 March 1909, 6c; Deputations and reports, 1907–9, see A.M.C. minutes, 1907, –8, –12 (PRO 30/72/37,38,43); *National Federation of Ratepayers, Report of the first public conference ... subject: 'The cost of education.'* (9 June 1909).

[2] CAB 37/101/158, W. Runciman, 'The need for an increase of exchequer grants in aid of elementary education', 12 Dec. 1909.

London again led the municipal agitation, but after the 1907 alternation in metropolitan politics the London boot was on the other foot, and it was a Unionist LCC majority that put the pressure on central government.[3] Municipalities had high expectations from TLV and were angry to discover that the duties were going into the national, not the local chest. Political exigencies had forced this course but the uproar had been foreseen and might have been appeased. An A.M.C. deputation to the Chancellor on 8 July 1909 complained that municipalities had been the pioneers of TLV. 'They have sown the seed, and they have looked to the increasing value of their land as their rightful inheritance.'[4] Instead of giving them their due, the Budget actually harmed the towns by depressing rateable values. 'We are two rival authorities,' the A.M.C. vice-president said, '... whatever rights we ... have to prey upon the public, for goodness sake let us have not right to prey upon the other'.[5]

The towns put in a claim for part of the Land Value revenues. Lloyd George had to concede one-half;[6] moreover, he promised to set aside a substantial portion out of the following year's ample budget surplus 'to relieve the burdens of local authorities'.[7] But this opened another thorny issue: how were the revenues to be distributed between the different towns? The question which suddenly forced itself upon the Chancellor's advisers lay at the very heart of historical Liberal doctrines of local taxation: if the tax was to be collected nationally, was it not right to use it as an instrument of equalisation? This threatened to knock open a hornets' nest of local interests.[8] In 1910 it began to appear that the Budget would decrease the consumption of drink, and local authorities stood to lose on their allocations of 'Whiskey money' (p. 202). Lloyd George now consecrated the local authorities' half-share of the land-value duties to meet this shortfall.[9] In 1911 even the half-share was withdrawn as a trade-off for the indirect relief offered to the ratepayers by making paupers eligible for old-age pensions. In the face of continued local authority discontent a Departmental Committee was appointed,

[3]IR 73/6, Reports of the LCC finance, local govt. and parliamentary committees, 9, 11 and 17 June 1909 respectively, fols. 138–55.
[4]PRO 30/72/39, A.M.C. (1909), 'Deputation to the Right Hon. DAVID LLOYD–GEORGE [sic] ... July 8th 1909', A. H. Scott MP [Lib.], p. 149.
[5]Ibid., Report of the A.M.C. law committee on the finance bill, 30 June 1909, pp. 135–6; deputation, J. Harmood-Banner MP [Cons.], p. 149 (quoted).
[6]6 H.C. deb. 5 ser. 22 June 1909, Lloyd George, 1578.
[7]PRO 30/72/39, A.M.C. (1909), 'Deputation', 8 July 1909, Lloyd George, p. 155.
[8]IR 73/6, Memoranda, fols. 28–31 (early June 1909), 52–6, 57–63 (undated & unsigned); 11 H.C. deb. 5 ser. 27 Sept. 1909, Lloyd George, 940–1, 962–3.
[9]Documented in T 172/27.

and the payment of half the land duties revenue to the towns was postponed until 31 March 1914 by the Revenue Act of 1911.[10]

The agrarians had never abandoned the demand for rate-supporting grants, and urban Unionists took it up in 1911 with redoubled zeal. That old device, the amendment to the address, was pressed into service to make an occasion for raising banners and testing the wind.[11] Powerful support came from the Webbs, who advocated grants-in-aid (subject to tests of efficiency and need) as an instrument of Poor Law and municipal reform, in their minority report and in Sidney's *Grants in aid* (1911). The Webbs, unlike the Unionists, wanted to spend the grants on better services, not in relief of the ratepayers.[12] Nonetheless, Sidney's book was warmly commended by the *Land Union Journal*.[13] The *LUJ*'s rapport with the Webbs was implicitly acknowledged by the insertion of advertisements for the LSE's student journal, the *Clare Market Review* and the LSE's publishers, P.S. King.

That a Departmental Committee on Local Taxation had to be appointed was a sign that Liberal statesmanship had failed to grapple with the problem and was playing for time. Edgar Harper's appointment to this committee hinted at the drift of Lloyd George's designs. Indirectly, the government's social policy had already made an impact on the urban problem. Old-age pensions, when extended to paupers in January 1911, made a discernible dent in Poor Law expenditure in the big towns. National insurance was to have a similar effect. Lloyd George pressed ahead in 1912 with an ambitious campaign against tuberculosis, and the Road Fund first infused £1.4 million into trunk roads in 1911. Asquith's government moved beyond the limitations of Gladstonian finance and undertook a definite obligation for social welfare. But its social policy entailed a neglect of the welfare machinery of local government, and was perceived as an affront to local dignity.

Liberal finance remained true to the Liberal interdict on doles and managed thereby to inflict real damage on town budgets. Between 1907

[10]21 H.C. deb. 5 ser. 20 Feb. 1911, Lloyd George, 1644–5; GLC, LCC Local govt. and taxation com. *Pr.P* 75, 1913, H. E. Haward, *London and the imperial exchequer* (LCC report to the finance committee, no. 1620, 2 July 1913), pp. 37–8.

[11]See e.g. the agrarian deputation to Asquith, *The Times*, 21 March 1908, and the CCA's 'Report on the local taxation committee on exchequer contributions' (1908) (T 172/30); 21 H.C. deb. 5 ser. 13 Feb. 1911, 700–818.

[12]Poor laws and relief of distress. Roy. com. minority rep.; P.P. 1909 Cd. 4499 XXXVII, ch. X, 'Grants-in-aid', esp. pp. 968–76; S. Webb, *What about the rates?* (Fabian tract no. 172, July 1913), pp. 10–12.

[13]*LUJ*, Aug. 1911, 13.

and 1911 the assigned revenues (pp. 201–2) which had guaranteed an expanding grant income for the towns, were gradually replaced by *fixed* allocations from the Consolidated Fund. Two-thirds of government grants-in-aid were 'stereotyped' in this way by 1911.[14] Central government expenditure increased by almost 30 per cent between 1908 and 1913, while grants-in-aid increased by just over two (local authority spending grew by 18 per cent).[15] As house-vacancies began to decline with the onset of employment and prosperity in 1911 the 'housing question' began to press with renewed urgency.[16] But education remained the field of primary liability and of greatest neglect.[17] On 13 December 1913 the President of the Board of Education was moved to warn his Cabinet colleagues in the same terms his predecessor had used four years before. National education was in danger of collapse, he said. 'My own personal view is that, if the Government attempt at the present moment to resist the public demand for some relief in rates during the year 1914–15, public opinion will be too strong for the government'.[18]

Had the Tories been less demoralised they would have been in a better position to exploit the government's procrastination. A conclave of party leaders, including George Wyndham, F. E. Smith and Austen Chamberlain, considered the question in March 1910 as part of a review of party policy. Smith and others, Chamberlain wrote to Balfour, 'say that in the English towns we were beaten by the Land Taxes of the Budget'. They urged that the way to blunt the appeal of the People's Budget and to win back the towns was to grant them local TLV powers.

> a proposal on these lines coming from the leader of the Unionist Party would be very popular with the great Town Councils who had forced Lloyd George to share his plunder and even now grudged the Treasury the half which Lloyd George retained. It is certain that if we do nothing the Radical Party will sooner or later establish their national taxes, and once established in that form any Radical Chancellor in need of money, or any Socialist Chancellor in pursuit

[14]Mallet, *British budgets* (1913), 285–6.
[15]Mitchell and Deane, *Abstract*, pp. 398, 414–8. In 1913 central govt. expenditure was £184M, grants-in-aid £21.9M and local expenditure £140.3M.
[16]See e.g. *Daily Chronicle* special commissioners, *The lost homes of England* (1912); Spensley, 'Urban housing problems' (1918), 169–71; *The Times* series on housing in London, 6, 9, 10 April 1912.
[17]PRO 30/72/44, A.M.C. (1913), 'Imperial and local taxation' (conference minutes, 24 April 1913), esp. pp. 60–1; GLC, Haward, *London* (1913), p. 46.
[18]CAB 37/117/90, J. A. Pease, 'Note on the necessity for increased financial aid to local authorities in 1914–15', 13 Dec. 1913, p. 3, and his two May 1913 memoranda, CAB 37/115/32–3.

of the policy of nationalisation ... will find it an easy task to give a turn to the screw and raise the levy from year to year. On the other hand, if this source of revenue, such as it is, is once given to the municipalities, the Treasury will never be able to put its finger in the pie again and the Chancellor of the Exchequer will have no temptation to screw up taxes from which he derived no advantage ... Those present believed that if it were made clear by someone speaking with authority that this was the Unionist Policy it would produce an enormous effect on the Boroughs.

Bonar Law was alone among those present, very sceptical of the plan.[19] After 1911, however, it was his view that counted.

The urban demand for rate-support grants was doubly embarrassing for the government. First, Lloyd George's social policy gave Insurance and Pensions a higher priority and money was short. Secondly, grants were the old Unionist prescription of 'doles' to which Lloyd George had once led the resistance, and which still raised deep misgivings among many of the Radical faithful. These embarrassments were skilfully exposed by the Unionists in the Housing Bill they introduced in February 1912. The Unionist social reform committee drafted it in consultation with the councils of nine large towns, called for support from the Town Planning and Housing lobbies, and gained the approval of socialists and Labour MPs. The bill provided for a government grant of a million pounds for local authority housing, to be spent under the direction of government Housing Commissioners.[20] The latent affinity between Tory étatisme and State Socialism was revealed once again. John Burns was placed in embarrassing opposition to an ameliorative measure with natural appeal to working-class and municipal sections of the Liberal electorate. The government majority destroyed the bill. Ramsay Macdonald and Snowden remained loyal, but Labour left-wingers voted with the Tories. The episode was played out again in 1913.[21] Land Taxers led in opposition to the Bill; they had their own solution to urban problems.[22]

The Land Taxers' intentions had been restated in a memorial presented by 173 Liberal MPs to the Prime Minister and the Chancellor

[19]Brit. Lib. Add. MSS. 49736, A. J. Balfour papers, memo. (headed 'P.S. to XVI', 9 March 1910, fols. 79–80; reprinted Chamberlain, *Politics* (1936), pp. 228–9.

[20]See F. E. Smith, *Unionist policy and other essays* (1913), pp. 307–12.

[21]It has been described by P. Wilding, 'Towards exchequer subsidies for housing, 1906–1914', *Social and Economic Administration*, 6 (1972), 3–18 and Englander, 'Workmen's national housing council' (1973), pp. 300–9.

[22]E.g. 35 H.C. deb. 5 ser. 15 March 1912, J. C. Wedgwood, 1437–52; J. D. White, 1452–5.

of the Exchequer on 18 May 1911. They asked, specifically, for the valuation to be accelerated; for powers for local authorities to rate on the basis of the valuation; and for a national tax on all Land Values to be used for grants-in-aid for locally-provided 'national services': education, poor relief, roads etc; and in relief of remaining duties on food.[23] Here was the comprehensive, alternative Liberal programme for the reform of local taxation. When Edgar Harper resigned from the LCC the *Property Owners' Journal* put two and two together and anticipated his appointment to head the valuation. 'Assessment of site values, instead of rateable values ... will inevitably follow such an appointment, for Mr Harper's opinions have not been kept exclusively to himself'.[24] After Harper's appointment, in 1912, a plan was drafted in the Inland Revenue (probably by Harper himself) to give effect to the land taxers' memorial.[25] But the single-taxers did not regard the Chancellor as one of their own; repeatedly they swore him to loyalty and brandished the penalties for deviation.[26] In spite of the reverses and disappointments to which the poor conception and conduct of the valuation had already subjected him,[27] Lloyd George was willing. On 25 June 1913, on the eve of the land campaign, he made a compact with the single-taxers which they recorded in writing.

> We understand that the principle [sic] proposals put before us are the complete abolition of the present system of rating which falls upon improvements, industry and houses. In place of this there will be substituted a national land value tax in relief of rates, and a rate levied on the land value alone. It will no longer be open to Local Authorities to raise their ordinary rates on any other basis.

They would co-operate with Lloyd George, but only if rating reform was given precedence in the land campaign.[28] Lloyd George did not renege on this compact; but he also continued on the course of tenurial reform.

[23]Copy of the memorial, LG C/15/1/4.

[24]*POJ*, June 1911, 1.

[25]T 171/39, Finance bill papers 1913, 'Memorandum on land valuation, and the taxation and rating of land values' (4 pp., undated, unsigned). Internal evidence suggests that this was written in 1912.

[26]E.g. LG C/9/3/10, C. Llewellyn Davies to Lloyd George, 4 Aug. 1912.

[27]See Pretyman's attacks, 52 H.C. deb. 5 ser. 28 April 1913, esp. 838–56. The revenue bill, drafted to meet this criticism, had to be withdrawn after some controversy, owing to an adverse speaker's ruling. See the Land Union, *The lost revenue bill of 1913 – and after* (1913), pp. 3–5.

[28]LG C/9/4/62, E. G. Hemmerde, R. L. Outhwaite, J. C. Wedgwood, E. R. Jones, C. E. Price, P. W. Raffan, C. Trevelyan and F. Neilson, 'Note to the Chancellor ... following conversation of June 25th'.

The underlying paradigm of the Land Campaign was arbitration between tenures with a bias in favour of the underdog: labourer against farmer, farmer against landowner. The same principle was also applied to the relations between capitalist leaseholder and urban groundowner. One of the highlights of the Limehouse speech of 1909 had been the grievances of Gorringe, a prosperous draper and tenant of the Duke of Westminster. When his lease expired the Duke increased the ground-rent ten-fold to £4,000 and demanded a fine of £50,000.[29] Liberal urban policy was outlined to a deputation of shopkeepers from the 'Town Tenants' League' on 30 October 1913 and shortly afterwards in a speech at Holloway.[30] Lloyd George promised these capitalists continuity of tenure and compensation for improvements. It was the old Leasehold Enfranchisement constituency all over again (though facilities for purchase were not offered) and a good ploy so far as it went. On 5 December Lloyd George reported to Asquith that the traders were delighted. C. P. Scott had told him 'that the Government proposals had given great satisfaction to the Middle classes, whom we are in danger of losing'.[31] London Conservatives were certainly alarmed; the member for North Islington wrote to Walter Long: 'If we let the Radicals monopolise this policy we should lose both votes and workers, and possibly the seat itself. It would determine the vote of many shop-keepers'.[32] Long came up to the same hall in Holloway and promised the traders everything they had asked for;[33] apparently this was deemed insufficient for Long was urged to go one better and promise leasehold enfranchisement.[34] Yet capitalist leaseholders, as we have seen, could never be more than a marginal constituency: important, perhaps, to tilt the balance but not the solid mass of urban support that both parties needed.

The ground was certainly ready for an urban reform programme. Overcrowding was increasing, private construction was depressed, and a wave of tenant protest began to rise in 1912.[35] In the *Land Union Journal* a 'Unionist working man', in a hard-hitting article, warned the landowners,

[29] *The Times*, 30 July 1909, 9c.
[30] *Ibid.*, 31 Oct. 1913, 9–10; Holloway speech, *ibid.*, 1 Dec. 1913, 65a–b.
[31] AP 25, Lloyd George to Asquith, 5 Dec. 1913, f. 65.
[32] WL WRO 947/441, G. H. Touche MP to Walter Long, 6 Jan. 1914.
[33] On 17 Jan. 1914 (*Birmingham Daily Post*, 19 Jan. 1914, 12, in WRO 947/441).
[34] WRO 947/441, A. Steel-Maitland to Long, 26 June 1914.
[35] D. Englander, 'Landlord and tenant in urban Britain: the politics of housing reform 1838–1924' (Warwick Univ. Ph.D. thesis, 1979), ch. 7. This important study became available too late to be fully utilized.

Despite all we English people say about 'home', hundreds of thousands of us regard it as a good place to be out of, and so we throng the public-house, the music hall, and the picture theatre; while our children, as soon as they can walk, live in the streets. Only our wives really live at home. The rest of our families only sleep and eat there; and so, while it is pretty to read and sing about 'Home, sweet home', what we really feel about home, even if we can express our feelings, is that it is mostly a stuffy old place to go to only when we must. Now, if Mr Lloyd George is going to persuade working men that the result of his policy will be to give us nicer, cleaner, brighter and more comfortable dwellings, working men are going to vote for his proposal to tax land.[36]

The builders, the press and the opposition placed the onus for the building depression, the property slump and the housing shortage squarely on the government's land value duties. Even the Liberals' own urban report (*The land*, vol. ii) admitted that there was a case to answer.

That the Finance (1909–10) Act, 1910, actually had a considerable effect in checking house-building there can be no doubt. It operated in two ways. First, in the political controversy which took place over the Budget, extravagant statements were made by the opponents of that measure, which created a strong feeling of insecurity among property owners generally, and especially those small owners who had not the necessary knowledge to judge whether the Finance Act would really affect them adversely or not. (p. 82.)

Secondly, the government valuation forced the property slump on the notice of owners and mortgagees. Low valuations of property prompted lenders, who lost the margin of security, to call in their loans, and new mortgages were difficult to obtain (*ibid.* p. 83). Furthermore, builders were alarmed by the Lumsden judgement (see p. 368).

When Lloyd George took up the land question in the towns he counter-attacked on the same front, and stressed groundowner responsibility for the shortfalls of supply. Overcrowded dwellings and bad urban facilities were both blamed on monopoly landowners who inflated land prices for private dwellings, municipal housing and public works. A large stock of examples was available for this standard item of the repertoire. In the first 'urban' speech of the campaign at Middlesborough Lloyd George cited the case of a Peer who had sold

[36]'The land and the worker. By a Unionist working man', *LUJ*, Aug. 1912, 82.

some bare and isolated moorland to Leeds City Council for 200 years purchase. 'He demanded a huge sum of money because the construction of the waterworks would disturb the game ... it would interfere with the pheasants when they were attending to the crops. (Laughter)'.[37]

Lawyers and surveyors who administered the compulsory purchase system came under attack for conceding the landowners' extravagant claims and for inflating their own costs, often beyond even the level of the owners' compensation. The land campaign's two instruments were tailor-made to counter those evils. National site valuation would establish fair prices, and the land commissioners would undertake arbitration in cases of compulsory purchase. Land nationalisers were encouraged to hope that these were steps in their direction.[38] Whether urban housing deprivation could really be ascribed to deficiencies of supply alone was another question, which Lloyd George did not properly face. 'A fair day's wage for a fair day's work was also required', he said.[39] Hadn't the social surveys of the decade shown that low wages were the main cause of poor housing? But except for a vague reference to the Trade Boards Act, an urban minimum wage did not form any prominent part of the campaign. Consequently, the urban land campaign failed to ignite the towns.

II

In October 1913, just as Lloyd George began to mount his campaign for higher rural wages, he also gave the signal for another thrust. This second campaign began to take shape in feverish activity behind the scenes as a crash programme to transform the system of local taxation on TLV lines. It was destined to be the climax of the land campaign, and of 65 years of English tenurial politics. Ever since Goschen's ill-fated local government and taxation bills of 1871 no politician had mustered the courage to clean those Augean stables, and piecemeal improvement merely underscored the anomalies of local finance. Considering that discontent over urban finance had helped to bring the Liberals into power in the first place, and in view of their repeated promises and dismal record of support for the towns, reform was long overdue. The urban scissors of rising needs and stagnant revenue (see chapter 18, esp.

[37] *The Times*, 10 Nov. 1913, 4b.
[38] LG C/2/3/47, 49, J. S. G. Heath to Lloyd George, 4 Dec. 1913, enclosing letter (same date) from L. C. Money; Hyder, *Land nationalisation* (1914), pp. 376–7.
[39] *The Times*, 10 Nov. 1913, 4c.

pp. 294–7) presented a domestic priority for government action; such intervention had a further attraction, from a Liberal point of view, of showing no overt bias for capital or labour. It also discharged Lloyd George's undertaking to the single-taxers.

Urban clamour ran high. At a special A.M.C. conference in April 1913 £5 million of grants were demanded. '... we must', said Cyril Jackson (an LCC alderman and veteran educationalist), 'bring before the Chancellor that he has really jeopardized the whole of the local government of England by delaying this matter year after year, and apparently decade after decade'. It was a bumper budget year for the government, 'and if we cannot be relieved now we shall never get any relief at all'.[40]

The project had been long, very long, in the making, but the decision to implement it was sudden, and calls for comment. Lloyd George made his promises to the land taxers on 25 June 1913, but the reform of local taxation was only mentioned off-hand at the end of the August Cabinet memorandum; it formed no part of the land proposals discussed by Cabinet on 15–17 October. The unofficial rural report appeared in October 1913, but the urban report was not due until 1914. The departmental committee report was also expected no earlier than March–April 1914. More important than all, the valuation was only planned for completion on 31 March 1915, i.e. in time for that year's budget.[41] All these signs indicate that the original conception envisaged a gradual build-up of publicity in the summer of 1914, in anticipation of a dramatic reforming budget in 1915, followed perhaps by a general election. With national insurance securely on the statute book and the Marconi scandal safely scotched, local taxation could be the next area of reform.

Both official and unofficial enquiries (the departmental committee on local taxation and the Liberal urban land enquiry) were still in progress. Public opinion had not been canvassed. Cabinet was unconvinced; and civil servants were unprepared if not actually unwilling. But the Chancellor pushed forward. On 16 October, in the midst of Cabinet debates on the land campaign, the courses of action were outlined by Edgar Harper. Harper had already prepared a confidential proposal for the Chancellor a year before, and both documents contained the essence

---

[40]PRO 30/72/44, A.M.C. (1913), 'Imperial and local taxation' (conference minutes), 24 April 1913, pp. 83–4.

[41]Pp. 373–5, 389; Valuation completion date, see Land values. Sel. com. (1920), E. J. Harper, p. 43 (7.).

of the subsequent programme.[42] With some further assistance from Harper, a Cabinet paper was produced on 13 December 1913.[43]

The Liberal promotion of Scottish site value bills in 1907–8 had infused their principles into Liberal rating doctrine, and these were now enunciated by Lloyd George to the Cabinet. 'From both the "revenue" and the "productive" point of view it would clearly be desirable to transfer all rates from the composite hereditaments to sites, and further to levy all rates directly on owners,' he wrote. This was not an addition to taxation, but merely a redistribution of existing rate burdens from the owners of structures to the owners of sites. A 'sudden and complete transference' (such as he had promised to the single-taxers) was out of the question for practical reasons. It would have unacceptably 'drastic results on the fortunes of individuals'. A scheme of partial transference, however, would be both expedient and just. But mere re-distribution was not sufficient any more and a positive contribution was required: 'It is assumed that there is a general agreement that further grants must be made from the Exchequer in relief of local rates'. This was a break with Liberal dogma and Lloyd George went even further by suggesting that part of the money should come from taxes on personalty. The rest was to come from a doctrinally orthodox source: £4–6 million could be raised from a $\frac{1}{2}$d. in the pound national tax on site values. Such a tax could be used to effect a measure of *national* redistribution from sites in the rich districts to structures in the poor.[44]

It had become axiomatic with land-taxers that shifting the rates on to the sites was going to have a beneficial 'productive' effect. Precisely what sort of effect? Harper was given just one day to ponder the question and draw up a Cabinet brief for the Chancellor.[45] A substantial contribution could be expected from certain values which now escape, he wrote, namely vacant land and empty property. The rate burden would be more equitably distributed between high- and low-value districts and investment of capital in improvements upon land would be encouraged.

The probability is that the present rather steep curve of rental value, rising from the suburbs to the centre of the town, would tend to

[42]IR 63/35, N22.1, E. J. Harper, 'Alternative systems for the relief of improvements from taxation', 16 Oct. 1913, fols. 1–5; E. J. Harper to C. J. H. Thomas, 2 Nov. 1913, f. 18; see [25].

[43]CAB 37/117/92, D. Lloyd George, ['Pt. I. The rating of site values' etc.] 13 Dec. 1913.

[44]*Ibid.*, pp. 3, 6, 8, 9.

[45]IR 63/35, N22.1, M. Nathan to Lloyd George, 11 Dec. 1913, f. 33.

become flatter, the large additional burden on the most valuable sites tending to depress their value.[46]

Harper went on to give a quantitative example. No site valuations of cities had been completed yet and the only set of data came from Farnworth, a small town in Lancashire. Given *existing* property values a transfer of rates on to site value would give some relief to industry and working-class dwellings, mostly at the expense of vacant land. But Harper was forced into a fatal qualification: the persistence of existing capital values could not be assumed. Quite the contrary – property values were bound to be affected by the transfer of rates and their new distribution could not be predicted with any confidence.[47]

Paradoxically, valuation created uncertainty about property values. This had already acted to dampen investment in building. Detached consideration of the effects of a site-value rate indicates further that, other things being equal, there would be a shift of rate burdens towards unbuilt development land and towards urban-centre property in areas of particularly high site values. A redistribution of *property* would take place in the other direction: towards property with a lower than average ratio of site to structure. Eventually, the site-value rate might indeed stimulate new construction on the urban fringe, and thus act to moderate the rent gradient.[48] But this depended on the configuration of many other variables; particularly on the strength of demand for accommodation and the effect of the tax on investors' confidence. In any case, Harper's analysis was rudimentary, and failed to make a convincing case from the meagre empirical data he had managed to compile after two years of effort.[49] For on top of the inherent indeterminancy of the project, the valuation still had to be completed and adapted to its new tasks. It had been started in 1910. On 16 October 1913 Harper estimated that '... it is unlikely that the basis of the assessment can be completely ready before 1917 – or at the earliest, in time for use in connection with the fiscal year 1916–17'.[50]

Despite these uncertainties, Lloyd George went ahead. The land

[46]CAB 37/117/96, [E. J. Harper, M. Nathan and C. J. H. Thomas], 'I. National tax on site values', printed 24 Dec. 1913, pp. 3, 5 (various parts are attributed to authors in Nathan's letter, n. [45] above).

[47]*Ibid.* pp. 6–7.

[48]See R. Turvey, *The economics of real property* (1957), ch. VII for an elementary (and indeterminate) economic analysis.

[49]CAB 37/117/96, 'National tax on site values' (1913), pp. 6–7 and IR 63/35, N22.1, Harper to M. Nathan, 5 Dec. 1913, f. 19.

[50]IR 63/35, Harper, 'Alternative systems ...', f. 5.

campaign needed an urban platform and the land taxers continued to pester.[51] Their influence in Scotland had to be taken into account.[52] The Chancellor made a public commitment to a programme of rating reform in Glasgow, on 4 February 1914.[53] Treasury officials got their briefing on 29 January, and more details on 24 February. It was imperative to get at least 6d off the rates, he told them, so some £6 million of grants would be provided. Relief would be given to improvements alone, and the local assessment system would be converted to a site-value basis. A rating bill would see to that; Site valuation would be accelerated.[54] The grants-in-aid would come from an increase in the income tax. At Middlesborough in November Lloyd George had complained of the burden of armaments. Were it not for recent additions, he said, he would 'next year take eighteen pence in the pound off the rates of everybody in the United Kingdom'.[55] This was a reminder of the greatest constraint on social expenditure. He had just passed through a stormy struggle over the Naval estimates and a Cabinet member later explained the Budget in these terms: 'He is taxing heavily in order to meet the claims of his friend at the Admiralty and he aimed at gilding the pill by a heavy set of subsidies to the local authorities'.[56]

So many questions were still unresolved: boundaries would have to be re-drawn, new allocations negotiated with the towns, vested interests placated. The valuation would have to be de-capitalised to fit in with rental-based local assessments, at a large expenditure of money and time. It was still a year off completion and already five years out-of-date.[57] The project would cost £2.8 million to completion in 1915, and another million or so was required for adaptation to rating.[58]

Preparations, like those for the People's Budget in 1909, were muddled and rushed. Valuation had turned out to be a white elephant, unsuitable for burden and bogged down in legal quicksands. Much of the blame lay

[51]Weakness of urban campaign, e.g. LG C/2/4/6, B. S. Rowntree and others to Lloyd George, 4 Feb. 1914; land-taxer pressure, C/2/4/1, W. Raffan, for the Land Values Group, 17 Dec. 1914 and Lloyd George's public commitment, 1 Jan. 1914 (cutting, same item).
[52]LG C/10/2/84, James Pens [?], Glasgow, to Lloyd George, 24 Dec. 1913.
[53]The Times, 5 Feb. 1914, 10c.
[54]4. IR 63/46 (N22.8), M. Nathan, 'Memorandum of interview', 29 Jan. 1914, fols. 24–6; IR 63/35, holograph report of Chancellor's meeting with Treasury officials by R. V. N. Hopkins, fols. 69–75.
[55]The Times, 10 Nov. 1913, 4c.
[56]WR 135, Runciman to Robert Chalmers, 24 June 1914.
[57]IR 63/35, N22.1, Hopkins, fols. 69–75, and [62] below (Nathan).
[58]Ibid. E. J. Harper, 'Cost of valuation', 2 May 1914, f. 168.

with Harper. He had preached for the project for many years, and was allowed, indeed, called in, to show his prowess. Practice showed that the scheme had been less than fully thought out. In retrospect Harper blamed everyone but himself: He invoked poor drafting, cumbrous appeals, insufficient time.[59] All true, but insufficient to absolve him. If the budget was really premature, was it not Harper's task to dissuade the Chancellor? Harper, one has to conclude, failed to rise to the challenge. Treasury and Revenue policy files reveal a poor standard of staff work; one senses the scepticism of the leading civil servants. Chalmers' strong hand, which had firmly guided the People's Budget, was conspicuous by its absence. Sir Matthew Nathan and John Bradbury, the senior Revenue and Treasury officials respectively involved, were cool if not actually hostile. Harper, placed in a subordinate position, with his defects as a communicator, and possibly encumbered by his social origins, could not supply the deficiency.[60] The new projections of revenue and expenditure did not appear in internal Treasury estimates until May.[61] And on the very eve of the budget speech, Lloyd George was reminded by his senior advisers that there was no prospect of a rating bill until the completion of the valuation in 1916, and that the grants he proposed could not be distributed on a site-value basis.[62] Lloyd George was too deeply committed to turn back; he had brought it off once before; perhaps he thought he could do it again. Such was the origin of the budget of 4 May 1914.

Lloyd George gave the project its compulsive drive. He assumed the risks. The 1914 Budget statement was a leap in the dark. Had it been capable of execution (which it was not), it would still contain elements designed to antagonise Unionists, Liberals and municipalities all at once. Rate-support grants financed from the income tax (i.e. from 'personalty')

[59]Land values. Sel. com. ev. (1920), E. J. Harper, p. 43 (7.); Sir Edgar Harper, 'The Lloyd George finance (1909–10) act, 1910: its errors and how to correct them', International Union for Land Value Taxation and Free Trade, *Conference papers presented at the fourth international conference, Edinburgh* (1929), pp. 84–9.

[60]See IR 63/35, Feb. 1914 et seq.; T 171/69–71, Feb. 1914 et seq.; e.g. T 171/69, Harper to Nathan, 22 April 1914 and Nathan to H. P. Hamilton, same date; T 171/71, John Bradbury, 'Reduction of rates on local improvements', 21 April 1914.

[61]T 171/55 contains a series of Treasury projections of the coming budget and the following one, starting 9 Nov. 1913. There is no hint of Lloyd George's new programme before the forecast dated 1 May 1914.

[62]T 171/69, Nathan to Lloyd George, 2 May 1914; IR 63/35, Sir A. Thring, 'Grants to local authorities', ?3 [sic] May 1914, fols. 175–8.

were an old Conservative principle and were not opposed, except, subsequently, by the government's own supporters.[63] The Chancellor indulged in a little rearrangement of history to justify the new departure, and claimed that he had not opposed the Agricultural Rates Act in principle, but only because the grant was fixed and did not rise with expenditure (compare p. 210). Relief for improvements was given prominence. In view of the problems of local stagnation, this relief was particularly apt, but details were put off to a revenue bill. Adapting the valuation for local taxation 'would not be a considerable task', Lloyd George said, less than truthfully.[64] The towns welcomed the grants, but resented a government intervention verging on a takeover of the assessment system.[65] And Conservatives did not relax their suspicion of the valuation.

Perhaps Lloyd George hoped for a good political row over the principle of site-value rating, a re-enactment of the Peers v. the People. In the event, the chance never came. Splitting the measure between a Finance and a Revenue Bill, and making the first conditional on the second was a constitutional irregularity, which Pretyman was the first to identify.[66] Lloyd George then tried to tack the grants on to the Finance Bill, abandoning the principle of a subsidy for improvements, the last purely Liberal element in the bill. When the 'cave' of Liberal right-wing and industrialist MPs ganged upon him, in June, their main complaint was that he was violating the old Liberal interdict on doles for landlords.[67] The grants were then withdrawn and the whole plan came to naught.

For the Chancellor's colleagues the withdrawal of the grants was a shattering fiasco, which they nevertheless took with a pinch of *Schadenfreude*.[68] Runciman sent an account to Robert Chalmers, who had helped to prepare the 'People's Budget' and was now Governor-General in Ceylon:

> You can imagine the blow this has been to Lloyd George and the dreadful muddle we are now in for. Banks and local authorities and electioneering Radicals are all enraged; our programme and legislation are horribly upset ... We are indeed in a precarious plight,

[63]E.g. 62 H.C. deb. 5 ser. 4 May 1914, 62.
[64]62 H.C. deb. 5 ser. 4 May 1914, Lloyd George, 67, 69.
[65]IR 63/35, Birmingham Corporation and Birmingham Assessment Union, 'Memorandum' (printed), June 1914, pp. 1–3 (fols. 238–40).
[66]See Gilbert, 'Budget of 1914' (1978), p. 133 et seq.
[67]*Pall Mall Gazette*, 15 June 1914 (T 171/86); *The Times*, 18 June 1914, 8b.
[68]Gilbert, 'Budget of 1914', 138–41.

and but for the follies of Bonar and his Orange and Tariff Reform colleagues we should be easily displaced.[69]

Chalmers thanked Runciman for information 'as regards the goat's cropper,' and gave his own insider's assessment.

It all springs from the besetting sin of the creature that he will not work at his business beforehand & betimes, and it serves him perfectly right that he has got it 'in the neck'. Yet I am sorry for him in a way because I think his Budget the clearest, if [not] the easiest that he has produced.[70]

Professor Gilbert claims that the Budget might have been fatal to Lloyd George's career.[71] This is difficult to credit. Failure had not been fatal to Goschen, though it had done something to turn the Liberals out in 1874. Local taxation was known to be an intractable problem, and the Chancellor had established his *bona fides*. He had known in advance that little was possible before 1916, and kept a brave face; work on the rating bill proceeded, and the Cabinet was beseeched not to abandon the land campaign.[72] One element at least did reach the Statute Book. At Swindon Lloyd George had promised to apply National Insurance reserve funds to housing, and after the war broke out, £4 million of government housing loans were allocated to local authorities and other agencies.[73] Ironically, a concerted effort in 'rural regeneration', with Agricultural Wages Boards and planned production, was presided over by R. E. Prothero, the land campaign's old bugbear, as coalition President of the Board of Agriculture during the war. To continue the TLV programme after the war, the Scrutton judgement had to be contested in the Lords, or remedied by legislation. In 1920, and despite a Chancellor's reluctance to give up a source of revenue, the valuation was abandoned.[74]

Charles Masterman, Lloyd George's lieutenant in the heady years before the war, pronounced its epitaph:

the valuation of unused site apart from building was recognized by all as being the centre of the whole matter. Landlords or reformers feared or hoped that the valuation would prove the starting-point of

[69] WR 135, Runciman to Chalmers, 24 June 1914.

[70] WR 135, Chalmers to Runciman, 13 July 1914.

[71] Gilbert, 'Budget of 1914', 140–1.

[72] CAB 37/120/77, H. Samuel, 'Rating bill', 29 June 1914; CAB 37/120/78, 'Land policy, declarations of ministers', 29 June 1914.

[73] Housing (No. 2) act, 1914 (4 & 5 Geo. 5, c. 52).

[74] Land values. Sel. com. ev. (1920), P. Thompson, pp. 16–20; IR 63/86, 'Land value duties ...', 13 Feb. 1919, f. 114 ff.

a larger policy. 'This Bill is a beginning', said Mr Lloyd George triumphantly, 'and with God's help it is but a beginning.'

Ten years after, with or without God's help, this Bill was proved to be an end. Liberalism looked on, saddened and amazed, while the new Parliament destroyed all the results of the vigorous campaign. The Coalition dug the grave wide and deep. They flung into it the Land Taxes of Mr Lloyd George, the Land Valuation of Mr Lloyd George, and the Land Policy of Mr Lloyd George. They dumped earth upon it. They stamped down the ground over the grave. They set up a stone to commemorate their victory for testimony to the passing stranger. 'Here, buried for ever, lies the Land Crusade.' And finally – so that there should be no doubt at all as to their triumph – they extorted for the taxpayer of the present every penny which had been paid by the landlords as Land Taxes in the past, and returned two millions of money, as an unexpected windfall to the landlord owners of the increment of the urban lands of Britain. Never, it would seem, was a cause so sensationally and utterly destroyed.[75]

[75]C. F. G. Masterman, *The new liberalism* (1920), pp. 163–4 (quoted in K. O. Morgan, *The age of Lloyd George* (1971), pp. 208–9).

CONCLUSION

Bentham's conception of property provided a point of departure for this study. Property, according to this view, was the pre-condition of prosperity, but possession was precarious. Adam Smith expressed similar ideas with equal force:

> It is only under the shelter of the civil magistrate that the owner of valuable property, which is acquired by the labour of many years, or perhaps of many successive generations, can sleep a single night in security. He is at all times surrounded by unknown enemies whom, though he never provoked, he can never appease, and from whose injustice he can be protected only by the powerful arm of the civil magistrate continually held up to chastise it.[1]

In return, Property must be willing to bear the cost of government and the law. A pamphleteer of 1831 conveyed this relation in a striking metaphor:

> Property and taxation are converse propositions; as much so, as beauty and ugliness, or light and darkness. As taxation is a necessary adjunct for the protection of property, so will the contrast of ugliness convey stronger perceptions of beauty; and the contrast of darkness will give due effect to the lustre of light.[2]

Such, then, is the conception of tenure that we have adopted as a framework of explanation. Property in land was a source of wealth, authority and privilege which depended on the sovereign and the legal system to fend off the populace. But the law was not only a State organ. It was also a private corporation. 'Justice', wrote Smith, '... never was in reality administered gratis in any country .... The fees annually paid to lawyers and attornies amount, in every court, to a much greater sum than the salaries of the judges'.[3] Registration of title was a typical offspring of the Benthamite programme for efficiency and cheapness in administration and justice, and was launched with the blessing of the master himself.

[1]Smith, *Wealth of nations* (Cannan edn 1976), Bk. V. ch. i, pt. ii, p. 232.
[2]Henry Court, *Tithes ... a letter to Lord Chancellor Brougham* (1831), p. 15.
[3]Smith, *Wealth of nations* Bk. V, pp. 239–40.

Victorian Radicals regarded property in a somewhat different light. Adam Smith had distinguished between mercantile and landed property, and his heart was with the landowners. Ricardo reversed the sympathies of economic theory if not his own private preference. His stark opposition of landowners and capitalists was gladly embraced by Victorian manufacturers and merchants. The Cobdenite faction strove to reinforce industry and commerce by mobilising the populace against the landowners, by denying the economic legitimacy of aristocracy and by dismantling its legal defences. It also drew upon the doctrines of natural rights of Rousseau, Spence and John Stuart Mill. These doctrines embodied 'an illogical association of the natural rights of men with a glorified state of society and the not less illogical association of the latter with agrarian pursuits'.[4] Both equity and efficiency were to be served by peasant proprietorship, small holdings and allotments, which were among the practical legacies of this cluster of ideas. So too was the transcendentalism which fired the Commons Preservation movement. The coherence of this romantic strain was more cultural and social than economic. Here also was the Achilles' heel of the Radical programme: it had a strong mental affinity with the ideals of the landed ascendancy which it strove to challenge.

The Radical model of landed property conferred its weaknesses on the causes it inspired: on peasant smallholding, leasehold enfranchisement, registration of title and site-value rating. These programmes failed to take sufficient account of the real distribution of property in England. Peasant smallholdings required a social, economic and tenurial redistribution that went beyond the resources of politics. Leasehold enfranchisement was condemned to remain a minority cause, without any appeal to the masses. The Victorian and Edwardian projectors of registration of title failed to make an allowance for the peculiar property rights acquired by the lawyers in defending the property system. The lawyers' tenure in the land laws was a right that the eighteenth century might recognise, but one which the Radicals failed to acknowledge. The solicitors' instinct for survival proved a more powerful motive than the prospect of savings to the community from greater market rationality.

The unearned increment is always with us. The London Radicals' site-value rating programme was suffused with a vision of greater equality, to be achieved by the taxation of rent. A conflict of interest

---

[4]J. A. Schumpeter, *A history of economic analysis* (1954), pp. 229–30 (a reference to the Physiocrats).

between landed and capitalist tenures was real enough in London and other leasehold towns, but the bulk of urban property, as we have seen, was composite, and was not divided between owners of the ground and enterprising capitalists. The majority of urban capitalist proprietors were more likely to be antagonised than attracted by the policy.

Yet in 1914 the programme arrived at the very threshold of application. Given better management and a more hospitable political and economic climate it might have been established. It foundered on its own inner contradictions: on the difficulties, both political and practical, of isolating rent as a separate, morally repugnant fraction of property. The doctrine was a valuable flag and rallied much support for the Liberal party over many years outside the tenurial interests. But in the final count Henry George's doctrine proved to be a voluntarist heresy, an illusory short-cut on the road of adaptive re-distribution and reform, a destructive worm in the apple of the New Liberalism. Even on a charitable interpretation, it was a case of the best driving out the good. For long years it displaced the equalisation of local taxation which had been part of the original Liberal programmes of the 1860s, and which was so urgently required.

Personalities made a significant difference: the implicit étatisme of Disraeli, the expertise of Wolstenholme, Henry George's utopianism, the earnest activism of C. P. Trevelyan, the energy and perversity of Rubinstein, the misplaced confidence of Edgar Harper; the sway of political doctrines, cultural attitudes and sectional loyalties; the reckless audacity of Lloyd George – all helped to determine the course of events. The Victorian Radical programme was strangled in the anti-Radical backlash of 1919–22. It fell to Lloyd George, who had invested so much political and emotional capital in his budget and land campaigns, to preside over the programme's demise. His reputation never recovered from the compromises of those years. But land reform refused to lie down. The Liberals carried out a post-war land enquiry.[5] Philip Snowden attempted to revive the valuation and prepared for a TLV budget in 1930–31. Labour in power has repeatedly attempted to intercept the unearned increment, with the Town and Country Planning Act of 1947, the Land Commission in 1967 and the Community Land Act of 1974. The inter-war years were the heyday of 'transcendentalism', of the cyclist and the hiker, but this was largely drained of political content. Allotments and smallholdings have likewise continued to flourish while losing their political lustre. Commons preservation has

[5] Liberal Land Committee, *The land and the nation* (n.d. [1923–5]).

sustained its impetus, with the increasing emphasis on recreation, commuter and week-end housing, and tourism, in rural land uses. Registration of title has made a painful comeback which allows it to exist as an accessory to an expensive legal monopoly. Its time may come again.

Local taxation bore on the most fundamental process of social change in nineteenth-century England: the country's final transformation from an agrarian to an urban, imperial, manufacturing and trading society; the extended growth of the economy; and the massive provision of urban collective capital and a measure of education and welfare for a large and growing population. For the owner of urban property (as for the Fabian) local taxation combined the aspects of his two enemies, the populace and the State; hence the catchword 'municipal socialism'. The task of politics was to balance the demands of private property and a popular franchise, internal stability and international order, giving due regard for the changing weighting of internal and international forces.

Disraeli raised the flag of state subsidies after the repeal of the Corn Laws, in order to rally the agrarians. But his programme was also attractive to the towns, and when it was cautiously implemented by Northcote in the 1870s and Goschen in the 1880s, it gave an impetus to the emergence of a centralised welfare state. Balfour and Salisbury preferred to subsidise their clients in the countryside and the Church between 1895 and 1902, and were fortunate to benefit from an urban building boom. After 1906 the Liberal government allowed urban tenure to run down; first, by their failure to mitigate the crisis of local taxation, and later, with their programme of site-value taxation. Property owners did not fail to draw the parallel between their own predicament and that of the solicitors, who were threatened with registration of title. The *Property Owners' Journal* leader lamented in May 1910 (p. 1),

the old order is changing, [and] does not metamorphose without a struggle, so the property owner in the one case and the solicitor in the other curses his luck, just as in the old coaching days, the owners of coaches and postillions were just displaced by the advent of railways, and went out of being with as good grace, as the superseded can ever expect to exhibit in transit.

The surveyor George Head also wondered aloud, in his paper to the auctioneers in 1910, whether the slump was temporary or terminal.

Are we to regard the recent diminution in values [he asked] as one of the normally recurring depressions, to be followed by an equally normal elevation? Is it merely a stage in the periodic rise and fall of values, or has it an element of permanence?

There is no question about the plight of the towns. Both private house-building and public services (education in particular) were depressed in the last Liberal years. Of some of the cyclical and international causes of domestic under-investment the government had little or no cognisance, let alone control. But its commitment to TLV put off the reform of local taxation. Regional inequities persisted and grants remained haphazard and insufficient. The Liberals tolerated high localised rates and rejected the étatiste remedy of grants-in-aid which they regarded as a subsidy for landowners. The small owner of weekly property did not recover from the Edwardian slump. Rent control in wartime transformed the pre-war slump into a capital levy on the small landlord. And the Tory champions of property did not rush, post-war, to salvage this most self-effacing of political interests. Was it because rent control was numbing one of the most painful of social interfaces, the relation between landlord and urban working-class tenant? In other ways as well capitalism found the means to handle the post-war housing shortage; it began to search for those means even before the war.

Disraeli's policy of grants-in-aid to local government from national taxes (endorsed by the Webbs), was to prevail in the long run. Even before the war, it offered a solution for housing the poorly paid, without resorting to a minimum wage. A Unionist publication from the social reform committee, but carrying the National Union imprint, openly embraced the principle of state subsidies to local authorities and builders.

> It has always been the view of [the Tory] Party that where individual enterprise for any reason has failed by itself to achieve the best possible results from a national standpoint, it should be both assisted and regulated by the State ...
>
> The Housing of the people has not been satisfactorily carried out by a system of unassisted and unregulated private competition. The results of that system have been satisfactory neither to the body politic, as existing conditions of Housing prove, nor in the present day to the individuals concerned, who find in the main the building of houses is no longer a profitable form of industry.[6]

The pamphlet proposed grants to make good the deficits of private developers and local authorities. Lord Lansdowne, the Unionist leader in the Lords, endorsed this proposal in a policy speech in June 1913.[7] It was taken up by the Liberals in the Housing Act (no. 2) of August 1914, and more importantly, in Addington's Housing Act of

[6]National Unionist Association ..., *The history of housing reform* (1913), p. 28.
[7]Lord Lansdowne, speech at Matlock Bath, 21 June, *The Times*, 23 June 1913, 4.

1919, which began the great expansion of subsidised council-house building in the inter-war years.

The policy was justified as an extension of Salisbury's 'ramparts of property' strategy to the property-less, a scheme to reconcile property and populace, by guaranteeing a psychological-subsistence standard of tenure for all.

> The maintenance of the principle of property, and of that stability of the body politic without which that principle cannot be maintained, depends in the ultimate resort, on the existence, within these Islands, of the vast majority of its inhabitants living under social conditions which, negatively at least, permit them to believe in and practice the ordinary civic virtues. And this ideal clearly cannot be attained where the homes of the people are in such a condition that nothing but squalor, vice or revolution is likely to issue from them.[8]

Conservatives envisaged an order of large and small proprietors that would transcend the animosities of class and guarantee the survival of great wealth. The Conservative premise of defensive solidarity between all forms of property has proved more durable than the Radical opposition of land and capital. It was rooted in the tenurial realities of England. After the war the resumption of economic growth made it possible to extend owner-occupation gradually down the social scale, and to bolster the old 'landed interest' with a new one, as Salisbury had advocated. An expanding tenurial constituency grew on the fertile soil of building-society finance, and may have acted as an antidote to the extension of the Labour constituency after 1918. The sale of council houses which the Conservative party is promoting in 1980 is a measure of the party's commitment to the 'ramparts' strategy.

Property professionals, the affluent middlemen of the 'property-owning democracy', are another element of stability (not to say rigidity) in this system. A third bulwark of this modern order is the one which was actively canvassed by the advocates and practitioners of 'municipal socialism'. The administrators, councillors, contractors and professionals who manage society's collective capital at the local and national level have appropriated many of the trappings of tenure. Rousseau, in his vision of the strifeless society, did not foresee these prosperous and powerful offspring of the General Will.

[8]National Unionist Assoc. ..., *housing reform* (1913), p. 70.

SELECTED BIBLIOGRAPHY

I. ARCHIVAL SOURCES

Birmingham University Library
Papers of J. Chamberlain.
Bodleian Library, Oxford
Papers of H. H. Asquith, L. Harcourt and A. Milner.
British Library
Papers of W. E. Gladstone, the Earl of Halsbury and A. J. Balfour.
British Library of Political and Economic Science (the London School of Economics)
Papers of Charles Booth,. E. Cannan, G. Lansbury, and B. and S. Webb (Professional Coll. Misc. 248).
Greater London Record Office
Business Papers of Arthur Robert Chamberlayne (solicitor).
L.C.C. Local Government and Taxation Committee Minutes and Presented Papers.
L.C.C. Presented Papers; L.C.C. *Questions.*
London Ground Plan.
House of Lords Record Office
Papers of A. Bonar Law, D. Lloyd George, and H. Samuel.
H.M. Land Registry (Lincoln's Inn Fields, London)
Statistical Department records.
Newcastle University Library
Papers of W. Runciman and C. P. Trevelyan.
Public Record Office
Papers of Lord Cairns, /PRO 30/51.
Inland Revenue IR 63, IR 73, IR 74.
Land Registry records LAR 1, LAR 2.
Lord Chancellor's Office records LCO 1, LCO 2.
Board of Agriculture small holdings policy records, MAF 48.
Treasury papers T 168, T 170, T 171, T 172.
Association of Municipal Corporations minutes and records, PRO 30/72.
Rating and Valuation Association
Metropolitan Rate Collectors' Association minute books.
Reading University, Museum of English Rural Life
Central Land Association records.
Privately held
Papers of C. F. Brickdale.
E. G. Pretyman press cuttings.
Papers of J. C. Wedgwood.
Wiltshire Record Office
Papers of W. Long.

II. UNPUBLISHED THESES AND TYPESCRIPTS

BRISTOW, E. 'The defence of liberty and property in Britain, 1880–1914' (Yale Univ. Ph.D. thesis, 1970).

COWCHER, W. B. 'A dissertation upon the incidence of local rates and taxes upon the unearned increment of land' (Oxford Univ. B.Litt. thesis, 1914).

ENGLANDER, D. 'The Workmen's National Housing Council, 1898–1914,' (Warwick Univ. M.A. thesis, 1973).

ENGLANDER, D. 'Landlord and tenant in urban Britain: The politics of housing reform, 1838–1924' (Warwick Univ. Ph.D. thesis, 1979).

FEINSTEIN, C. H. 'Home and foreign investment 1870–1913' (Cambridge Univ. Ph.D. thesis, 1959).

FISHER, J. R. 'Public opinion and agriculture 1875–1900' (Hull Univ. Ph.D. thesis, 1972).

HAY, J. R. 'British government finance 1906–1914' (Oxford Univ. D.Phil. thesis, 1970).

HO, P. 'Land and state in great Britain 1873–1910: A study of the land reform movement and land policies' (Columbia Univ. Ph.D. thesis, 1952).

KING, A. S. 'Some aspects of the history of the Liberal party in Britain, 1906–14' (Oxford Univ. D.Phil. thesis, 1962).

PEACOCK, A. J. 'Land reform 1880–1919: A study of the activities of the English Land Restoration Leagues and the Land Nationalization Society' (Southampton Univ. M.A. thesis, 1961).

REEDER, D. H. 'Capital investment in the western suburbs of Victorian London' (Leicester Univ. Ph.D. thesis, 1965).

RUBINSTEIN, W. D. 'Men of property: The wealthy in Britain 1809–1939,' (Johns Hopkins Univ. Ph.D. thesis, 1975).

SIMON, A. 'Joseph Chamberlain and the Unauthorized Programme' (Oxford Univ. D.Phil. thesis, 1970).

THOMPSON, F. M. L. 'The economic and social background of the English landed interest 1840–70, with particular reference to the estates of the Dukes of Northumberland' (Oxford Univ. D.Phil. thesis, 1955).

VALLIS, E. A. 'Trends in urban land and building values' (Oxford Univ. B.Litt. thesis, 1971).

WALLER, P. J. 'Democracy and sectarianism: Liverpool 1868–1974' (Typescript, in the press).

WARD, S. B. 'Land reform in England 1880–1914' (Reading Univ. Ph.D. thesis, 1976).

WILDING, P. R. 'Government and housing: A study in the development of social policy 1906–1939' (Manchester Univ. Ph.D. thesis, 1970).

WILKS, W. I. 'Jesse Collings and the 'Back to the land' movement' (Birmingham Univ. M.A. thesis, 1964).

III. PARLIAMENTARY PAPERS

1. Debates

House of Commons and House of Lords Debates, third, fourth, and fifth series, 1842–1925.

2. Annual Reports and Statistical Series in the Sessional Papers

Board of Agriculture. Agricultural Statistics.
Board of Trade. Bankruptcy Acts.
Duchy of Lancaster.
Ecclesiastical Commissioners.
Inland Revenue.
Land Registry.
Local Government Board.
Statistical Abstract for the United Kingdom.
H.M. Woods, Forests and Public Revenues.

3. Other Sessional Papers, in chronological order

Law of real property. R. com. 1st rep.; 1829 (263) X.
Law of real property. R. com. 2nd rep.; 1830 (575) XI.
Burdens affecting real property. Sel. com. H.L. rep.; 1846 (411) VI Pt. I.
Local taxation and government of the metropolis. Sel. com. 1st-3d reps.; 1861 (211, 372, 476) VIII.
Metropolitan local government. Sel. com. 1st and 2nd rep.; 1866 (186, 452) XIII.
Metropolitan local government. 2nd rep.; 1867 (268) XII.
Poor rates assessment. Sel. com. rep.; 1867–8 (348) XIII.
Land transfer. R. com. rep.; 1870 C. 20 XVIII.
Local taxation. Sel. com. rep.; 1870 (294) VIII.
Increase of local taxation. Report of G. J. Goschen; 1870 (470) LV.
Municipal and corporate bodies. Return showing the gross annual value of property assessed to income tax under Schedule A for the year 1870; 1872 (122) XXXVI.
Endowed charities. Explanatory memorandum and tabular summaries; 1877 (261) LXVI.
Land titles and transfer. Sel. com. mins. of ev.; 1878 (291) XV.
Land titles and transfer. Report; 1878–9 (244) XI.
Abstract of a return of all real property held in mortmain etc.; 1882 (274) L.
Housing of the working classes. R. com. 1st rep.; 1884–5 C.4402 XXX.
Town holdings. Sel. com. rep. mins. of ev. etc.; 1886 (213) XII.
Town holdings. Sel. com. rep. mins. of ev. etc.; 1887 (260) XIII.
Town holdings. Sel. com. rep.; 1889 (251) XV.
London streets (Strand improvement) bill. Sel. com. rep.; 1890 (239) XV.
Small holdings. Sel. com. rep.; 1890 (223) XVII.
Town holdings (second part of inquiry. Taxation of ground rents and improvements). Sel. com. rep. and mins. of ev.; 1890 (341) XVIII. 1890–1 (325) XVIII.
Town holdings. Sel. com. rep.; 1892 (214) XVIII.
Labour. R. com. mins. of ev.; 1893–4 C.7603–1 XXXIX Pt. I.
Local taxation H. H. Fowler. Report; 1893–4 (168) LXXVII.
Town improvements (betterment). Sel. com. (H. of Lords) rep.; 1894 (235) XV.
Land transfer bill (H. of Lords). Sel. com. rep. and mins. of ev.; 1895 (364) XI.
Agricultural depression. R. com. 2nd. rep.; 1896 C.7981 XVI.
Agricultural depression. R. com. mins. of ev.; 1896 C. 8021 XVII.
Systems of registration of title now in operation in Germany and Austria-Hungary. Reports of the assistant registrar of the Land Registry; 1896 C.8139 LXXXIV.

Registration of title in Germany and Austria-Hungary. Rep.; 1897 C.8319 LXXXVIII.

Local taxation. R. com. apps. and memos.; 1898 C.8765 XLII.

Local taxation. R. com. 1st rep. Local rates in England and Wales. Valuation and collection; 1899 C. 9141 XXXV.

Local taxation. R. com. 2nd rep. Tithe rentcharge, valuation and rating; 1899 C.9142 XXXV.

Local taxation. R. com. Classification and incidence of imperial and local taxation. Memos. E. Hamilton, A. Marshall and other economists; 1899 C.9528 XXXVI.

Municipal trading. Sel. com. mins. of ev.; 1900 (305) VII.

Local taxation. R. com. vol. iv. mins. of ev.; 1900 Cd. 201 XXXVI.

Local taxation. R. com. final report (England and Wales); 1901 Cd. 638 XXIV.

Municipal trading. Sel. com. rep.; 1903 (270) VII.

British and foreign trade and industry. Memos etc. 2nd ser. Bd. of Trade; 1905 Cd. 2337 LXXXIV.

Small holdings in Great Britain. Dept. com. rep.; 1906 Cd. 3277–8 LV.

Income tax. Sel. com. rep.; 1906 (365) IX.

Land values taxation etc. (Scotland) bill. Sel. com. rep.; 1906 (379) X.

London traffic. R. com. maps etc.; 1906 Cd. 2799 XLVI.

Decline in the agricultural population of Great Britain, 1881–1906. Report by R. H. Rew; 1906 Cd. 3273 XCVI.

Boroughs (rateable value). Return; 1906 (215) CII.

Education rates. Dept. com. rep. and apps.; 1907 Cd. 3313 XXI.

House letting in Scotland. Dept. com. mins. of ev. and appendices; 1908 Cd. 3792 XLVII.

Railway company contributions to institutions and associations of various character not directly controlled by the companies; 1908 (312) XCV.

Cost of living of the working classes. Bd. of Trade report; 1908 Cd. 3864 CVII.

Taxation of land etc. Papers bearing on land taxes and on income taxes etc.; 1909 Cd. 4750, 4845, LXXVI.

Land transfer acts. R. com. 2nd rep.; 1911 Cd. 5483 XXX.

Tenant farmers and sales of estates. Dept. com. rep.; 1912 Cd.6030 XLVII.

Cost of living of the working classes. Report; 1913 Cd. 6955 LXVI.

Local taxation. Dept. com. final rep.; 1914 Cd. 7315 XL.

Rent increases in Scotland. Dept. com. rep.; 1914–16 Cd. 8111 XXXV.

Land values. Sel. com. rep and mins. of ev.; 1920 Cmd. 556 XIX.

IV. PERIODICAL PUBLICATIONS, INCLUDING YEARBOOKS AND ANNUAL REPORTS

Dates in brackets denote the limits of systematic reading. In years outside these limits and in periodicals not delimited reference was not systematic.

Annual Register

Auctioneers' Institute (denotes occasional papers read at the Auctioneers' Institute and published by it)

Auctioneers' Institute, *Yearbook and Diary*

Bristol Daily Times and Mirror (Feb. 1883)

Building Societies' Gazette

Crockford's Clerical Directory

BIBLIOGRAPHY

Dod's Parliamentary Companion
East London Observer (1906)
Estates Chronicle
Estates Gazette (1890–1914)
Holloway, Hornsey and Muswell Hill Press (1907–8)
Incorporated Association for the Protection of Property Owners, *Reports of Council.*
Islington Mercury (Nov. 1902–April 1903)
Journal of the Royal Statistical Society (1900–12)
Land Agents' Record
Land and House Property Year Book (1892–1912)
Land and Labour
Land and Law (Feb.–March 1903)
Land Law Reform Association, *Annual Meeting, Report and Balance Sheet*
Land Roll
Land Union Journal (1911–1914)
Land Values
Law Clerk (1906–1913)
Law Journal
Law Notes
Law Society Registry (*Gazette and Register* from Oct. 1903) (1902–1913)
Incorporated Law Society, *Annual Report of the Council* (1871–1925)
Incorporated Law Society, *Proceedings and Resolutions of the Annual Provincial Meeting* (1879–1923)
Law Times
Leaseholds Enfranchisement Association, *Annual Reports*
London (1893–1898)
London County Council, *Minutes of Proceedings*
London County Council, *London Statistics* (1892–1914)
London Manual
Manchester Guardian
Manual of Electrical Undertakings, ed. E. Garcke (1896–1914)
Metropolitan Rate Collectors' Association, *Annual Reports* (1901–1911)
Municipal Reformer (Oct. 1909–March 1910)
Municipal Yearbook
Municipal Journal (succeeded *London*; 1899–1906)
Nation
New Statesman
Property Market Review
Property Owners' Journal (1903–1914)
Punch
Reformers' Year Book
Rural Labourers' League, *Annual Report* (1889–1900)
Rural World
Single Tax (predecessor of *Land Values*)
Solicitors' Journal
Stoke Newington and Hackney Recorder (1907)
The Times (1870–1914)
Transactions of the Surveyors' Institution (1890–1914)
Who's Who

V. PUBLISHED DIARIES, MEMOIRS AND BIOGRAPHIES

ADDISON, C. *Politics from within, 1911–18* (1924).
ANNAN, N. G. *Leslie Stephen: his thought and character in relation to his time* (1951).
ARCH, J. *Joseph Arch: The story of his life, told by himself*, ed. The Countess of Warwick (1898).
ASHBY, M. K. *Joseph Ashby of Tysoe 1859–1919, a study of English village life* (Cambridge, 1961).
ASQUITH, M. *The diaries of Margot Asquith* (Penguin edn 1936).
ATTLEE, C. R. *As it happened* (1954).
AMERY, J. *The life of Joseph Chamberlain* (1951–1969), iv–vi.
BALFOUR, F. *A memoir of Lord Balfour of Burleigh* (1924).
BARKER, C. A. *Henry George* (New York, 1955).
BEACH, V. H. *Life of Sir Michael Hicks Beach* (1932).
BEAVERBROOK, LORD *Politicians and the war 1914–16* (1929).
BIRNIE, A. *Single-tax George* (1939).
BLAKE, R. *The unknown Prime Minister* (1955).
BLAKE, R. *Disraeli* (1966).
BOWLE, J. E. *Viscount Samuel* (1957).
BRIGGS, A. *Social thought and social action: a study of the work of Seebohm Rowntree 1871–1954* (1961).
BULLOCK, A. *The life and times of Ernest Bevin* (1960), i.
BURGESS, J. *John Burns: the rise and progress of a right honourable* (Glasgow, 1911).
CARPENTER, E. *My days and dreams* (1916).
CECIL, G. *Life of Robert Marquis of Salisbury* (1921).
CHAMBERLAIN, A. *Politics from inside: an epistolary chronicle 1906–14* (1936).
CHAMBERLAIN, J. *A political memoir, 1880–92*, ed. C.H.D. Howard (1953).
CHANNING, F. A. *Memories of midland politics 1885–1910* (1918).
CHURCHILL, R. S. *Winston Spencer Churchill* (1967), ii.
CHURCHILL, W. S. *Lord Randolph Churchill* (2nd edn 1907).
COLLINGS J. & GREEN, J. *The life of the right hon. Jesse Collings* (1920).
Dictionary of National Biography.
DIGBY, M. *Horace Plunkett* (Oxford, 1949).
DUFF, A. G. (ed.), *The life-work of Lord Avebury* (1924).
DUGDALE, B. E. C. *Arthur James Balfour* (1939).
ELLIOT, A. D. *The life of George Joachim Goschen, first Viscount Goschen* (1911).
'EPHESIAN' (B. Roberts), *Lord Birkenhead* (5th edn 1936).
LORD ERNLE (R. E. PROTHERO), *Whippingham to Westminster* (1938).
EVANS, H. *Radical fights of forty years* (1913).
FELS, M. *Joseph Fels* (1920).
FENBY, C. *The other Oxford: the life and times of Frank Gray and his father* (1970).
FIFOOT, C. H. S. *F. W. Maitland: a life* (Cambridge, Mass. 1971).
FIFOOT, C. H. S. *Pollock and Maitland* (Glasgow, 1971).
FISHER, H. A. L. *Frederick William Maitland: a biographical sketch* (1908).
FISHER, H. A. L. *James Bryce (Viscount Bryce of Dechmont, O.M.)* (1927).
FOWLER, E. H. *The life of Henry Fowler* (1912).
FOX, A. W. *The Earl of Halsbury, Lord High Chancellor (1823–1921)* (1929).
GARDINER, A. G. *The life of Sir William Harcourt* (1923).
GARDINER, A. G. *Life of George Cadbury* (1923).
GARDINER, A. G. *John Benn and the Progressive movement* (1925).

GARVIN, J. L. *The life of Joseph Chamberlain* (1932–4), i–iii.

GEORGE, H. Jnr., *The life of Henry George* (1900).

GOSSE, E. *The life of Philip Henry Gosse* (1890).

GREY, Viscount of Fallodon, *Twenty-five years, 1892–1916* (1925).

GRIGG, J. E. P. *The young Lloyd George* (1973).

GRIGG, J. E. P. *Lloyd George: the people's champion* (1978).

GWYNN, S. & TUCKWELL, G. H. *The life of the rt. hon. Sir Charles W. Dilke* (2nd edn 1917).

HAWARD, H. *The London County Council from within: forty years' official recollections* (1932).

James Hawker's journal: a Victorian poacher, ed. G. Christian (Oxford, 1961).

HENDERSON, P. *William Morris: his life, work and friends* (Penguin edn 1973).

HEUSTON, R. F. V. *Lives of the Lord Chancellors 1885–1940* (Oxford, 1964).

HOBHOUSE, C. *Inside Asquith's cabinet: from the diaries of Charles Hobhouse*, ed. E. David (1977).

HEWINS, W. A. S. *The apologia of an imperialist* (1929), i.

HOBHOUSE L. T. & HAMMOND, J. L. *Lord Hobhouse: A memoir* (1905).

HOBSON, J. A. *Confession of an economic heretic: the autobiography of J. A. Hobson*, ed. M. Freeden (1976).

HOLLAND, B. *The life of Spencer Compton, Duke of Devonshire* (1913).

HOLYOAKE, G. J. *Sixty years of an agitator's life* (5th edn 1902).

HORN, P. *Joseph Arch, 1826–1919, the farm workers' leader* (Kineton, 1971).

HUTCHINSON, H. G. *Life of Sir John Lubbock, Lord Avebury* (1914).

HYNDMAN, H. M. *The record of an adventurous life* (1911).

JAMES, R.R. *Lord Randolph Churchill* (1959).

JONES, J. H. *Josiah Stamp: Public servant* (1964).

KOSS, S. E. *Sir John Brunner, Radical plutocrat 1842–1919* (Cambridge, 1970).

LESLIE, C. R. *Memoirs of the life of John Constable composed chiefly of his letters* (2nd edn 1845) ed. J. Mayne (1951).

LONG, W. *Memories* (1923).

MACKAIL, J. W. *The life of William Morris* (World's Classics edn 1950).

MCKENNA, S. M. *Reginald McKenna 1863–1943* (1948).

MAGNUS, P. *Gladstone: A biography* (1963 edn).

MAITLAND, F. W. *The life and letters of Leslie Stephen* (1906).

MARQUAND, D. *Ramsay McDonald* (1977).

MARTIN, K. *Harold Laski* (1953).

MASTERMAN, L. *C.F.G. Masterman: a biography* (1939).

MILL, J. S. *Autobiography* (World's Classics edn 1924).

MONEYPENNY, W. F. & BUCKLE, G. E. *The life of Benjamin Disraeli Earl of Beaconsfield* (1914), iii.

MORGAN, K. O. *Keir Hardie: Radical and socialist* (1975).

MORLEY, J. *The life of Richard Cobden* (1881).

MORLEY, J. *The life of William Ewart Gladstone* (1903).

MORRIS,.A. J. A. *C. P. Trevelyan 1870–1958: portrait of a Radical* (Belfast, 1977).

NEWTON, LORD *Lord Lansdowne: a biography* (1929).

PALMER, R. (EARL OF SELBORNE), *Memorials* (Edinburgh, 2 vols. 1889 and 1892).

PARKER, C. A. *Mr Stubbs, the horse painter* (1971).

PANKHURST, S. *The Suffragette movement* (1931).

PELL, A. *The reminiscences of Albert Pell*, ed. T. MacKay (1908).

PETRIE, C. *Walter Long and his times* (1936).

PETRIE, C. *The life and letters of the rt. hon. Sir Austen Chamberlain* (1939–40).

POSTGATE, R. *The life of George Lansbury* (1951).
RATHBONE, E. F. *William Rathbone: a memoir* (1905).
ROBERTS, R. *The classic slum: Salford life in the first quarter of the century* (Penguin edn 1973).
ROWLAND, P. *Lloyd George* (1974).
RUSSELL, B. *The autobiography of Bertrand Russell* (one-vol. edn 1975).
SAMUEL, VISCOUNT *Memoirs* (1945).
SCOTT, C. P. *The political diaries of C. P. Scott*, ed. T. Wilson (1970).
SIMEY, T. S. & SIMEY, B. *Charles Booth, social scientist* (1960).
SIMS, G. R. *My life: sixty years' recollections of Bohemian London* (1917).
SMITH, S. *My life work* (1903).
SPENDER, J. A. & ASQUITH, C. *Life of Herbert Henry Asquith, Lord Oxford and Asquith* (1932).
SPINNER, T. J. *George Joachim Goschen: the transformation of a Victorian liberal* (Cambridge, 1973).
Lloyd George: a diary by Frances Stevenson, ed. A. J. P. Taylor (1971).
TAYLOR, A. J. P. *Beaverbrook* (1972).
TAYLOR, B. *Stubbs* (1971).
TAYLOR, H. A. *Robert Donald* (1934).
THOMPSON, E. P. *William Morris: romantic to revolutionary* (2nd edn 1977).
THOMPSON, F. *Lark Rise to Candleford* (Penguin edn 1973).
TREVELYAN, G. M. *The life of John Bright* (1913).
UNDERHILL, A. *Change and decay. The recollections and reflections of an octogenarian Bencher* (1938).
VAIZEY, J. S. *The Institute – a club of conveyancing counsel. Memoirs of former members* (1895).
WEBB, B. *My apprenticeship* (1929).
WEBB, B. *Our partnership* ed. M. I. Cole and B. Drake (1948).
WEBB, B. *B. Webb's Diaries 1912–24*, ed. M. I. Cole (1952).
WEDGWOOD, C. V. *The last of the Radicals: Josiah Wedgwood M.P.* (1951).
WEDGWOOD, J. C. *Memoirs of a fighting life* (1940).
WICKSTEED, H. M. *Charles Wicksteed* (1933).
WILLOUGHBY DE BROKE, LORD *The passing years* (1924).

VI. CONTEMPORARY WRITINGS

ADAM, E. *Land values and taxation* (1907).
ADAMS, T. *Garden city and agriculture: how to solve the problem of rural depopulation* (1904).
ADEANE, C. R. W. & SAVILL, E. *The land retort: a study of the land question, with an answer to the report of the secret enquiry committee* (1914).
ARNOLD, A. *Social politics* (1878).
ARNOLD, A. *Free land* (1880).
ARNOLD, M. *Culture and anarchy: an essay in political and social criticism* (1869).
ASHBURNER, W. *A concise treatise on mortgages, pledges and mortgage liens* (2nd edn 1911).
AVEBURY, LORD, *Essays and addresses 1900–1903* (1903).
AVEBURY, LORD, et al., *Speeches delivered at the annual meeting of the Industrial Freedom League* (1905).
AVEBURY, LORD, *On municipal and national trading* (1906).
AVEBURY, LORD, 'Municipal and government trading,' *Political socialism: a remonstrance* ed. M. H. Judge (1908), pp. 106–121.

BAGEHOT, W. *Lombard street* (new edn 1910).

BANFIELD, F. *The great landlords of London* (1890).

BATEMAN, J. *The great landlords of Great Britain and Ireland* (4th edn 1883).

BAXTER, R. D. *Local government and taxation, and Mr Goschen's report* (1874).

BEAUMONT, G. D. B. *Observations on the code for real property proposed by James Humphreys, esq.* (1827).

BEDFORD, DUKE OF *A great agricultural estate* (1897).

BEER, M. *A history of British socialism* (one-vol. edn 1940).

BELL, F. (Lady Bell), *At the works: a study of a manufacturing town* (1907).

BELLAMY, E. *Looking backward, 2000–1887* (1888).

BELLOC, H. *The servile state* (1912).

BENTHAM, J. *The works of Jeremy Bentham* ed. J. Bowring (1838–1843).

BENTHAM, J. 'Principles of the civil code', *Works*, Bowring edn i, 297–364.

BENTHAM, J. 'Commentary on Mr Humphrey's real property code' (1826), *Works*, Bowring edn v, 387–416.

BENTHAM, J. 'Outline of a plan of a general register of real property' (1826), *Works*, Bowring edn v, 417–35.

BENTHAM, J. *Of laws in general* ed. H. L. A. Hart (1970).

BEVERIDGE, W. H. *Unemployment: a problem of industry (1909 and 1930)* (1931).

BIRKENHEAD, VISCOUNT *Points of view* (1922), ii.

BLAKE, E. H. 'Mortgages – some notes on law and practice,' *Auctioneers' Institute* (11 Nov. 1908).

BLATCHFORD, R. (Nunquam), *Merrie England* (1894).

BLUNDEN, G. H. 'Some observation on the distribution and incidence of rates and taxes,' *Journ. Roy. Stat. Soc.* 49 (1895), 644–56.

BOOTH, C. *Improved means of locomotion as a first step towards the cure of the housing difficulties of London* (1901).

BOOTH, C. *Life and labour of the people in London* (1902).

BOOTH, W. *In darkest England and the way out* (1890).

BOURNE, G. *Change in the village* (1912).

BOWLEY, A. L. & BURNETT-HURST, A. R. *Livelihood and poverty* (1913).

BRICKDALE, C. F. *Notes on land transfer in various countries* (1894).

BRICKDALE, C. F. *Methods of land transfer* (1914).

BRIGHT, J. *Selected speeches of the rt. honble. John Bright M.P. on public questions* (Everyman's edn 1907).

BROADHURST, H. & REID, R. T. *Leasehold enfranchisement* (1886).

BRODRICK, G. C. *English land and English landlords* (1881).

BUXTON, S. *Finance and politics: 1783–1885. An historical study* (1888).

CAIRD, J. *English agriculture in 1850–51* (1852).

CAIRD, J. *The landed interest and the supply of food* (4th edn 1880).

CAMPBELL, LORD JOHN, *Speeches of Lord Campbell at the bar and in the House of Commons* (Edinburgh, 1852).

CAMPION, B. 'Bankers' advances upon title deeds to landed property, Pt. I,' *Journ. Inst. Bankers*, 28 (1907), 26–53.

CAMPION, H. *Public and private property in Great Britain* (1939).

CANNAN, E. 'Proposed relief of buildings from local rates,' *Econ. Journ.*, 17 (1907).

CANNAN, E. *The history of local rates in England in relation to the proper distribution of the burden of taxation* (2nd edn 1912).

CHARTERED SURVEYOR, *Auctioneering as a profession* (1909).

CHERRY, B. L. & RUSSELL, A. E. (eds.), *Wolstenholme's conveyancing and settled land acts* (9th edn 1905).

CHILCOTT, T. B. *The law of mortmain* (1905).

CHOMLEY, C. H. & OUTHWAITE, R. L. *The essential reform: land values taxation in theory and practice* (1909).

CHORLTON, J. D. *The rating of land values* (Manchester, 1907).

CHRISTIAN, E. B. V. *A short history of solicitors* (1896).

CHRISTIAN, E. B. V. *Leaves of the lower branch: the attorney in life and letters* (1909).

CHRISTIAN, E. B. V. *Solicitors. An outline of their history* (1925).

COBDEN CLUB, *Essays* 2nd ser. (1872).

COBDEN, R. *Speeches on questions of public policy*, ed. J. Bright & J. E. Thorold Rogers (1878).

COLLINGS, J. *Land reform, occupying ownership, peasant proprietary and rural education* (1906).

COLLINGS, J. *The colonization of rural Britain: a complete scheme for the regeneration of British rural life* (1914).

COSTELLOE, B. F. C. *The incidence of taxation* (1893).

COX, H. *Land nationalization and land taxation* (1892, 2nd edn 1906).

CURTLER, W. H. *The enclosure and redistribution of our land* (1920).

Daily News (G. Haw), *No room to live* (1900).

DALTON, H. *Some aspects of the inequality of incomes in modern communities* (2nd edn 1925).

DARWIN, L. *Municipal trade: the advantages and disadvantages resulting from the substitution of representative bodies for private proprietors in the management of industrial undertakings* (1903).

DAVIES, C. E. *Reports of land valuation appeals: Finance (1909–10) Act* (1913–14).

DAVIES, D. H. *The cost of municipal trading* (Read before the Society of Arts, London, 1899).

DAWSON, W. H. *The unearned increment* (1890).

DEWSNUP, E. R. *The housing problem in England, Its statistics, legislation and policy* (Manchester, 1907).

DICEY, A. V. 'The paradox of the land law,' *Law Quart. Rev.* 21 (1905), 221–32.

DICEY, A. V. *Lectures on the relation between law and public opinion in England during the nineteenth century* (2nd edn 1914).

DONE, J. J. 'Valuation for mortgage.' *Trans. Surv. Inst.*, 38 (1905–6), 67–110.

DOWSETT, C. F. (ed.), *Land: its attractions and riches, by fifty-seven writers* (1892).

ENGELS, F. 'The housing question' in K. Marx and F. Engels, *Selected works* (Moscow, 1970), ii.

ERNEST, R. *How to become a successful estate agent* (1904).

EVANS, H. *Our old nobility* (6th edn 1909).

EVERSLEY, LORD *Commons, forests and footpaths* (revised edn. 1910).

FABIAN SOCIETY (S. Webb and G. B. Shaw), 'To your tents, oh Israel!' *Fortnightly Review* 40 (1893), 569–89.

FARRER, T. H. *Mr Goschen's finance 1887–1890* (1891).

FAWCETT, H. *Manual of political economy* (6th edn 1883).

FINLASON, W. F. *An essay on the history and effects of the law of mortmain and the laws against testamentary disposition for pious purposes* (1853).

FIRTH, J. B. F. *Reform of London government and of the City guilds* (1888).

FOX, A. W. *The rating of land values* (2nd edn 1908).

GALSWORTHY, J. *The man of property* (1906).

GARCKE, E. *The limitations of municipal enterprise* (read before the National Liberal Club Political and Economic Circle, 24 Oct. 1900).

GARCKE, E. *The progress of electrical enterprise* (1907).

GEDDES, P. *Cities in evolution: an introduction to the town planning movement and to the study of ethics* (1915).

GEORGE, D. L. 'The issues of the budget,' *The Nation*, 30 Oct. 1909, 180–2.

GEORGE, D. L. *The people's budget explained* (1909).

GEORGE, H. & HYNDMAN, H. M. *The single tax versus social democracy* (1889, rep. 1906).

GEORGE, H. *Progress and poverty* (Everyman's edn 1911).

GIBBS, V. *Municipal trading* (read at the Westminster Palace Hotel, 19 Nov. 1902).

GIDE, C. & RIST, C. *A history of economic doctrines from the time of the physiocrats to the present day* (1915).

GIFFEN, R. *Essays in finance* (1880).

GIFFEN, R. *The growth of capital* (1889).

The political correspondence of Mr Gladstone and Lord Granville 1868–1876, ed. A. Ramm (1952), ii. 1871–76.

GOSCHEN, G. J. *Essays and speeches on local taxation* (1872).

GOSCHEN, G. J. *Addresses* (Edinburgh, 1885).

GOSCHEN, G. J. *Essays and addresses on economic questions, 1865–1893* (1905).

GRICE, J. W. *National and local finance* (1910).

GRIFFIN, H. 'Weekly property as an investment,' *Trans. Surv. Inst.*, 26 (1893–4), 331–76.

GRISEWOOD, H. & ROBINS, E. *Land and the politicians, being an enquiry into the report of the Land Enquiry Committee* (1914).

HAGGARD, H. R. *Rural England* (2nd edn 1906).

HALL, A. D. *A pilgrimage of British farming* (1913).

HALL, C. P. 'Local taxation and the compound householder,' *Trans. Surv. Inst.* 42 (1909–10), 73–116.

HARPER, E. J. 'The bases of local taxation in England,' *Journ. Roy. Stat. Soc.* 81 (1918), 397–448.

HARRIS, W. J. & LAKE, K. A. 'Estimation of the realisable wealth of the U.K. based mostly on the estate duty returns,' *Journ. Roy. Stat. Soc.* 69 (1906), 709–45.

HASBACH, W. *A history of the English agricultural labourer*, trans. R. Kenyon (1920).

HEAD, G. J. 'Giant London: the evolution of a great city in size and value', *Trans. Surv. Inst.* 41 (1908–9), 309–38.

HEAD, G. J. 'The property market – retrospect and outlook', *Auctioneers' Institute* (12 Jan. 1910).

HILL, O. *Our common land* (1877).

HOBHOUSE, A. *The dead hand* (1880).

HOBHOUSE, A. *London government* (1892).

HOBHOUSE, L. T. *Liberalism* (n.d. 1911).

HOBSON, J. A. (ed.), *Co-operative labour upon the land (and other papers)* (1895).

HOGG, J. E. *Registration of title to land throughout the empire* (Toronto, 1920).

HORSFALL, T. C. *The improvement of the dwellings and surroundings of the people. The example of Germany* (Manchester, 1904).

The house famine and how to relieve it (Fabian Tract no. 101, 1900).

HOWARD, E. *Garden cities of to-morrow* (1902), ed. F. J. Osborn (1965 edn).

HOWARTH, E. G. & WILSON, M. *West Ham: a study in social and industrial problems* (1907).

HUEFFER, F. M. *The soul of London* (1905).

HUMPHREYS, J. *Observations on the actual state of the English laws of real property with the outlines of a code* (1826).

HUMPHREYS, J. *A letter to Edward B. Sugden in reply to his remarks on the alterations proposed by James Humphreys, esq. in the English laws of real property* (1827).

HYDER, J. *The case for land nationalisation* (2nd edn 1914).

HYNDMAN, H. M. *England for all* (1881).

IMPEY, F. *Three acres and a cow: successful small holdings and peasant proprietors in England: and the right of the labourer to allotments and small holdings* (Birmingham, 1890).

IMPEY, F. *Small holdings in England* (Birmingham 1909).

Industrial remuneration conference: report and proceedings (1885).

JEBB, L. *The small holdings of England: a survey of various existing systems* (1907).

JEFFERIES, R. *Hodge and his masters* (new edn 1890).

JEFFERIES, R. 'The king of acres', *Fraser's Magazine* (Jan. 1884), rep. in *idem. The hills and the vale*, ed. E. Thomas (1909).

KAUFMAN, M. *The housing of the working classes and of the poor* (1907).

KAY, J. *The social condition and education of the people in England and Europe* (1850).

KENNY, C. S. *The history of the law of primogeniture in England and its effect upon landed property* (Cambridge, 1878).

KROPOTKIN, P. *Fields, factories and workshops* (1898).

KROPOTKIN, P. 'Natural selection and mutual aid,' *Humane science lectures* (by various authors) (1897), 182–6.

Land and the people (1913).

LAND AGENT'S SOCIETY, *Facts about land. A reply to 'The land', the report of the unofficial Land Enquiry Committee* (1915).

LAND ENQUIRY COMMITTEE, *The land. The report of the Land Enquiry Committee* i. rural (1913) ii. urban (1914).

LAND LAW REFORM ASSOCIATION (HERBERT SAMUEL), *The ratepayer and the landowner: a statement of the case for the rating of ground values in towns* (1898).

LAND LAW REFORM ASSOCIATION, *The rating of ground values* (conference at the Westminster Palace Hotel, 8 Dec. 1898).

LAND TENURE REFORM ASSOCIATION, *Report of the inaugural public meeting* (15 May 1871).

THE LAND UNION, *The Land Union's reasons for repeal of the new land taxes and land valuation* (1910).

THE LAND UNION, *Objects and policy* (1913).

THE LAND UNION, *The lost revenue bill of 1913 and after* (1913).

INCORPORATED LAW SOCIETY, *Statement on the land laws* (1886).

INCORPORATED LAW SOCIETY, *Law, practice and usage in the Solicitors Profession* (1909).

INCORPORATED LAW SOCIETY, Reports of committees and miscellaneous papers, (1900–8) (Bodleian Law Library X Cw UK 670 L415p).

LAWRENCE, N. T. *Facts and suggestions as to the law of real property* (1879).

Lawyers and their clients: a practical guide for the latter (1901).

LAYARD, G. S. 'Family budget II. A lower middle-class-budget,' *Cornhill Mag.* new ser. 49 (1901), 656–66.

LENNARD, R. G. *Economic notes on English agricultural wages* (1914).

LESLIE, T. E. C. *Land systems and industrial economy of Ireland, England and continental countries* (1870).

BIBLIOGRAPHY

LEVY, H. J. *Large and small holdings: a study of English agricultural economics* (1911).

LIBERTY AND PROPERTY DEFENCE LEAGUE, *The dangers of municipal trading* (1899).

LIVERPOOL LAND AND HOUSE OWNERS ASSOCIATION, *Memorial to the right hon. W. E. Gladstone, M.P. on local taxation* (Liverpool, 1882).

LLOYD, J. *London municipal government: history of a great reform 1880–88* (2nd edn 1911).

LOANE, M. *An Englishman's castle* (1909).

LONDON COUNTY COUNCIL, *Comparative municipal statistics 1912–13* (1915).

LOWTHER, J. *Local taxation* (1901).

LUBBOCK, J. (Lord Avebury), *The pleasures of life* (1887).

MACDONALD, J. R. *Socialism and society* (2nd edn 1905).

MACDONALD, J. R. *The socialist movement* (n.d. 1911).

MAITLAND, F. W. 'The law of real property,' (1879) *Collected Papers*, ed. H.A.L. Fisher (Cambridge, 1911), i, 162–201.

MALLET, B. *British budgets 1887–88 to 1912–13* (1913).

MALLET, B. & GEORGE, C. O. *British budgets, 2nd ser. 1913–14 to 1920–21* (1929).

MALLET, B. & STRUTT, H. C. 'The multiplier and capital wealth,' *Journ. Roy. Stat. Soc.* 78 (1915), 555–99.

MALLOCK, W. H. 'Phantom millions – an inquiry into the actual amount of the annual increment of land values,' *Nineteenth Century and after*, 65 (1909), 757–76.

MALLOCK, W. H. *The nation as a business firm* (1910).

MARR, T. R. *Housing conditions in Manchester and Salford* (Manchester, 1904).

MARRIOT, J. A. R. *The English land system* (1914).

MARSHALL, A. *Principles of economics* (8th edn 1920).

MARX, K. *Capital* (Moscow, 1959), iii.

MASTERMAN, C. F. G. (ed.), *The heart of the empire: discussions of problems of modern city life in England* (1902 edn).

MASTERMAN, C. F. G. *The condition of England* (1909).

MATTHEWS, A. H. H. *Fifty years of agricultural policy, being the history of the Central Chamber of Agriculture* (1915).

MILL, J. S. *Principles of political economy with some of their applications to social philosophy*, ed. W. J. Ashley (1909).

MONEY, L. G. C. *Riches and poverty* (1905).

MORRIS, R. R. *A Summary of the law of land and mortgage registration* (1895).

MORRIS, W. 'News from nowhere,' *The collected works of William Morris*, ed. May Morris (1912), xvi.

MOULTON, J. F. *The taxation of ground values* (1889).

NORTHCOTE, S. *Twenty years of financial policy* (1862).

OLDERSHAW, L. (ed.) *England: a nation* (1904).

ONSLOW, EARL OF *Landlords and allotments: the history and present condition of the allotment system* (1886).

PALEY, W. 'Natural theology' (1802) *The works of William Paley* (1828), ii.

PALGRAVE, R. H. I. *The local taxation of Great Britain and Ireland* (1871).

PALGRAVE, R. H. I. (ed.), *Dictionary of political economy* (1900 edn).

PARKER, G. *The land for the people* (1909).

POLLOCK, F. *The land laws* (2nd edn 1887).

PRATT, E. A. *The organization of agriculture* (1905).

PRATT, E. A. *Small holders: what they must do to succeed* (1909).

PROBYN, J. W. (ed.) *Systems of land tenure in various countries* (1871; new edn 1881).

PROBYN, J. W. (ed.), *Local government and taxation in the United Kingdom* (1882).

PROPERTY PROTECTION SOCIETY, *Taxes on land* (1889).

PROPERTY PROTECTION SOCIETY, *The truth about the rating of vacant building land* (1891).

PROPERTY PROTECTION SOCIETY, *A catechism on land values* (1905).

PROTHERO, R. E. (Lord Ernle), *English farming: Past and present* ed. A. D. Hall (1936).

The Radical Programme (1885).

RAE, G. *The country banker: his clients, cares and work* (4th edn 1885).

RAFFAN, P. W. *The policy of the land values group in the House of Commons* (1912).

RATHBONE, W., PELL, A. & MONTAGUE, F. C. *Local government and taxation* (1885).

READE, W. *The martyrdom of man* (1872, repr. 1923).

REDMAN, J. H. *Pratt and Redman's income tax law* (9th edn 1910).

REEVES, M. P. *Round about a pound a week* (1913).

RICARDO, D. 'On the principles of political economy and taxation,' *The works and correspondence of David Ricardo*, ed. P. Sraffa and M. H. Dobb (Cambridge, 1951), i.

ROBERTSON, J. W. *England's green and pleasant land* (1925, Penguin edn 1947).

ROGERS, J. E. T. *The laws affecting landed property* (read before the Manchester Reform Club, 1869).

ROGERS, J. E. T. *Cobden and modern political opinion* (1873).

ROGERS, J. E. T. *The economic interpretation of history* (1888).

ROUSSEAU, J-J. *The social contract and discourses*, ed. & transl. G. D. H. Cole (Everyman's edn 1913).

ROW-FOGO, J. *Local taxation in England* (Edinburgh, 1902).

ROWNTREE, B. S. *Poverty: a study of town life* (4th edn 1902).

ROWNTREE, B. S. *Land and labour. Lessons from Belgium* (2nd edn 1911).

ROWNTREE, B. S. *The human needs of Labour* (1918).

RUSKIN, J. *Modern painters* (pop. edn 1906).

RUSKIN, J. *Unto this last and other essays on art and political economy* (Everyman's edn 1907).

RUSKIN, J. *The stones of Venice* (Everyman's edn 1907), ii.

RYDE, W. C. *The law and practice of rating* (3rd edn 1912).

Lord Salisbury on politics, ed. P. Smith (Cambridge, 1972).

SAMUEL, H. *Liberalism* (1902).

SARGANT, C. H. *Ground-rents and building leases* (1886).

SARGANT, C. H. *Urban rating* (1890).

SAUNDERS, A. M C. & WILSON, P. A. *The professions* (Oxford, 1933).

SAUNDERS, W. *History of the first London County Council 1889–1890–1891* (1892).

SCHEFTEL, Y. *The taxation of land value* (Boston, 1916).

Scottish land: the report of the Scottish land enquiry committee (1914).

SCRUTTON, T. E. *Land in fetters or the history and policy of the laws restricting alienation and settlement of land in England* (Cambridge, 1886).

SCRUTTON, T. E. *Commons and common fields or the history and policy of the laws relating to commons and enclosure in England* (Cambridge, 1887).

SELIGMAN, E. R. A. *Essays in taxation* (1903).

SELIGMAN, E. R. A. *The shifting and incidence of taxation* (5th edn New York, 1926).

BIBLIOGRAPHY

SHADWELL, A. *Industrial efficiency: A comparative study of industrial life in England, Germany and America* (one-vol. edn 1909).
SHAW, G. B. (ed.), *Fabian essays in socialism* (1908 edn).
SHAW, G. B. 'Widowers' houses,' *Plays Unpleasant* (Penguin edn 1946).
SHAW, G. B. *Man and superman* (Penguin edn 1946).
SHAW, G. B. *Back to Methuselah* (Penguin edn 1970).
SHAW, G. B. *The commonsense of municipal trading* (1908).
SHAW, G. B. *Fabianism and the empire: a manifesto by the Fabian society* (1900).
SHAW-LEFEVRE, G. *Agrarian tenures* (1893).
SHEARMAN, T. G. *Natural taxation* (1895).
SHELFORD, L. *A practical treatise on the law of mortmain* (1836).
SIMS, G. R. *How the poor live* (1883).
SMITH, A. *An inquiry into the nature and causes of the wealth of nations*, ed. E. Cannan (Chicago, 1976).
SMITH, F. E. (Viscount Birkenhead), *Unionist policy and other essays* (1913).
SPENCER, H. 'The coming slavery,' *The man and the state*, ed. D. MacRae (Penguin edn 1969).
SPENSLEY, J. C. 'Urban housing problems,' *Journ. Roy. Stat. Soc.* 81 (1918), 161–228.
STAMP, J. C. *British incomes and property* (1920 edn).
Stanford's indexed atlas of the County of London (1911).
STEAD, W. T. 'Character sketches I. The labour party and the books that helped to make it,' *Review of Reviews*, 33 (1906), 568–82.
STEPHEN, L. 'Wordsworth's ethics,' *Hours in a library* 3rd ser. (1879), 178–225.
STEPHEN, L. *The playground of Europe* (new edn 1894).
'A STOCKBROKER', 'The depreciation of British home investments,' *Econ. Journ.*, 22 (1912), 219–30.
SUGDEN, R. *A letter to James Humphreys, esq. on his proposal to repeal the laws of real property and substitute a new code* (1826).
SUTHERS, R. B. *Mind your own business: the case for municipal management* (1905).
SWEET, C. 'The land transfer acts', *Law Quart. Rev.* 24 (1908).
THOMPSON, G. C. *A neglected aspect of the land question* (1883).
THOMPSON, R. J. 'An inquiry into the rent of agricultural land in England and Wales during the nineteenth century,' *Journ. Roy. Stat. Soc.* 70 (1907), 587–624.
THOMPSON, W. *The housing handbook up-to-date* (1907).
TOKE, L. A. St. L. *A list of some recent works on housing and on rural problems* (1908).
TOLLEMACHE, B. *The occupying ownership of land* (1913).
TORRENS, R. *An essay on the transfer of land by registration* (1882).
TOYNBEE, A. *'Progress and poverty'. A criticism of Mr Henry George.* (1883).
TOYNBEE, A. *Lectures on the industrial revolution in England, popular addresses, notes and other fragments* (1884).
TRESSELL, R. *The ragged trousered philanthropists* (1965).
TREVELYAN, C. & HIRST, F. W. *The renewal of the doles. A handbook for political speakers* (1901).
TREVELYAN, G. M. 'The call and claims of natural beauty' (1931) in *idem. An autobiography and other essays* (1949).
TURNOR, C. *Land problems and national welfare* (1911).
UNDERHILL, A. *Should entails be abolished? A popular essay on the land law reform question* (1879).

421

UNDERHILL, A. *'Freedom of land' and what it implies* (1882).
URLIN, R. D. *A handbook of investment in houses and lands* (3rd edn 1902).
URLIN, R. D. *A handy book on the investment of trust funds* (3rd edn 1902).
WALLAS, G. *Human nature in politics* (3rd edn 1920).
WEBB, C. A. *Valuation of real property* (1909).
WEBB, S. *A plea for the taxation of ground rents* (1887).
WEBB, S. *Wanted a programme: an appeal to the Liberal party* (1888).
WEBB, S. *Socialism in England* (1890).
WEBB, S. *The London programme* (1891).
WEBB, S. *Grants in aid: a criticism and a proposal* (1911).
WEBB, S. *What about the rates? Or, municipal finance and municipal autonomy* (1913).
WEDGWOOD, J. C. 'The principle of land value taxation,' *Econ. Journ.* 22 (1912), 388–97.
WELLS, H. G. *A modern utopia* (1905).
WELLS, H. G. *Tono-Bungay* (1909).
WELLS, H. G. *The new Machiavelli* (1911).
WICKSTEED, C. *Our mother earth* (1893).
WICKSTEED, C. *The land for the people* (2nd edn 1894).
VON WIESER, F. 'The theory of urban ground rent,' *Essays in European economic thought*, ed. L. Sommer (1960), 39–80.
WILLIAMS, A. *Co-Partnership and profit-sharing* (1914).
WILKINS, MRS R. (L. Jebb), *The small holdings controversy: tenancy v. ownership* (1909).
WILLIAMS, J. *Principles of the law of real property*, ed. T. C. Williams (18th edn 1896).
WOLSTENHOLME, E. P. 'Simplification of title to land preferable to the introduction of novel modes of assurance, with an outline of a plan', *Papers read before the Juridical Society*, 2, no. 27 (1862).
YARDLEY, R. B. *Land value taxation and rating* (n.d. 1930).

VII. SECONDARY STUDIES

ABEL-SMITH, B. & STEVENS, R. *Lawyers and the courts: a sociological study of the English legal system 1760–1965* (1967).
ALBROW, M. *Bureaucracy* (1970).
ALLEN, D. E. *The naturalist in Britain* (Pelican edn 1978).
ANDERSON, G. *Victorian clerks* (Manchester, 1976).
ANNAN, N. G. 'The Victorian intellectual aristocracy,' *Studies in social history: a tribute to G. M. Trevelyan* ed. J. H. Plumb (1953).
ARMYTAGE, W. H. G. *Heavens below: utopian experiments in England 1560–1960* (1961).
ASHWORTH, W. *The genesis of modern British town planning* (1954).
ASHWORTH, W. *An economic history of England 1870–1939* (1960).
BANKS, J. A. *Prosperity and parenthood* (1954).
BARKER, E. *Political thought in England, 1848 to 1914* (2nd edn 1928).
BARKER, M. *Gladstone and Radicalism. The reconstruction of Liberal policy 1885–1894* (Brighton, 1975).
BARKER, T. C. & ROBBINS, M. *A history of London Transport* (1963 and 1974).
BARRY, E. E. *Nationalisation in British Politics. The historical background* (1965).

BEST, G. F. A. *Temporal pillars: Queen Anne's Bounty, the Ecclesiastical Commissioners, and the Church of England* (Cambridge, 1964).

BIRKS, M. *Gentlemen of the law* (1960).

BLACKMAN, J. E. & SIGSWORTH, E. M. 'The home boom of the 1890s,' *Yorks. Bull. Econ. Soc. Res.*, 17 (1965), 75–97.

BLAKE, R. *The Conservative party from Peel to Churchill* (1970).

BLAUG, M. *Economic theory in retrospect* (2nd edn 1968).

BLEWETT, N. 'The franchise in the United Kingdom, 1885–1918,' *Past and Present*, no. 32 (1965), 27–56.

BLEWETT, N. *The peers, the parties and the people: The general election of 1910* (1972).

BOWLES, R. & PHILLIPS, J. 'Solicitors' remuneration: a critique of recent developments in conveyancing', *Modern Law Review* 40 (1977), 639–50.

BOWLEY, A. L. *Wages and income in the United Kingdom since 1860* (Cambridge, 1937).

BOWLEY, M. *Housing and the state, 1919–1944* (1945).

BRIGGS, A. *History of Birmingham* (1952), ii.

BRIGGS, A. 'The welfare state in historical perspective,' *Archives Européennes du Sociologie*, 2 (1961), 221–58.

BRIGGS, A. *Victorian cities* (Penguin edn 1968).

BRISTOW, E. 'The Liberty and Property Defence League and individualism,' *Hist. Journ.*, 18 (1965), 761–89.

BROWN, J. 'Scottish and English land legislation, 1905–11,' *Scot. Hist. Journ.* 46 (1968), 72–85.

BROWN, K. D. (ed.), *Essays in anti-labour history: responses to the rise of labour in Britain* (1974).

BURNETT, J. *A social history of housing, 1815–1970* (Newton Abbot, 1978).

CAIRNCROSS, A. K. *Home and foreign investment 1870–1913* (Cambridge, 1953).

CANNADINE, D. 'Aristocratic indebtedness in the nineteenth century: The case re-opened,' *Econ. Hist. Rev.* 2nd ser. XXX (1977), 624–50.

CAPLAN, M. 'The new poor law and the struggle for union chargeability', *International Review of Social History*, 23 (1978), 267–300.

CHALKLIN, C. W. *The provincial towns of Georgian England: a study of the building process 1750–1820* (1974).

CHAMBERS, J. D. & MINGAY, G. E. *The agricultural revolution 1750–1880* (1966).

CHAPMAN, D. H. *The Chartered Auctioneers' and Estate Agents' Institute. A short history* (1970).

CHAPMAN, S. D. (ed.), *The history of working class housing* (Newton Abbot, 1971).

CHERRY, G. E. *The evolution of British town planning* (1974).

CLAPHAM, J. H. *An economic history of modern Britain* (Cambridge, 1926–1938).

CLARK, C. *Population growth and land use* (1967).

CLARKE, P. F. *Lancashire and the New Liberalism* (Cambridge, 1971).

CLARKE, P. F. 'Electoral sociology of modern Britain,' *History* 57 (1972), 31–55.

CLARKE, P. F. 'The Progressive movement in England,' *Trans. Roy. Hist. Soc.* 5th ser. 24 (1974), 159–81.

CLARKE, P. F. *Liberals and social democrats* (Cambridge, 1979).

CLEARY, E. J. *The building society movement* (1965).

COASE, R. H. 'The problem of social cost,' *Journ. Law & Econ.* 3 (1960), 1–44.

COOKE, A. B. & VINCENT, J. R. *The governing passion: Cabinet government and party politics in Britain 1885–6* (Brighton, 1973).

COONEY, E. W. 'Long waves in building in the British economy of the nineteenth century' *Econ. Hist. Rev.* 13 (1960).

CORD, S. B. *Henry George: Dreamer or realist?* (Philadelphia, 1965).

CORNFORD, J. 'The transformation of conservatism in the late nineteenth century,' *Vict. Stud.* 7 (1963), 35–65.

CROSSICK, G. (ed.) *The lower middle class in Britain, 1870–1914* (1977).

DAUNTON, M. J. *Coal Metropolis: Cardiff 1870–1914* (Leicester, 1977).

DEANE, P. & COLE, W. H. *British economic growth, 1688–1959* (2nd edn Cambridge, 1967).

DEMSETZ, H. 'Towards a theory of property rights,' *Amer. Econ. Rev.*, 55 (1967), 347–59.

DEWEY, C. 'The rehabilitation of the peasant proprietor in nineteenth-century economic thought,' *History of Political Economy* 6 (1974).

DONNISON D. V. *The government of housing* (1967).

DOUGLAS, R. *Land, people and politics: A history of the land question in the United Kingdom, 1878–1952* (1976).

DUNBABIN, J. P. D. 'Oxford and Cambridge finances, 1871–1913,' *Econ. Hist. Rev.* 27 (1975), 631–647.

DYOS, H. J. *Victorian suburb: a study of the growth of Camberwell* (Leicester, 1961).

DYOS, H. J. 'The speculative builders and developers of Victorian London,' *Vict. Stud.* 11 (supplement, 1968), 641–77.

DYOS, H. J. & WOLFF, M. (eds), *The Victorian city* (1973).

DYOS, H. J. 'A castle for everyman,' *London Journ.* 1 (1975), 118–134.

EDEL, M. 'The theory of rent in radical economics,' *Boston Studies in Urban Political Economy* No. 12 (1974).

EMY, H. V. 'The land campaign: Lloyd George as a social reformer 1906–14' in *Lloyd George: twelve essays*, ed. A. J. P. Taylor (1971), 35–68.

EMY, H. V. 'The impact of financial policy on English party politics before 1914,' *Hist. Journ.* 15 (1972), 103–31.

EMY, H. V. *Liberals, radicals and social politics 1892–1914* (Cambridge, 1973).

ENSOR, R. C. K. *England 1870–1914* (1936).

ENSOR, R. C. K. 'Some political and economic interactions in later Victorian England,' *Trans. Roy. Hist. Soc.* 4th ser. 31 (1949), 17–28.

EVANS, E. J. *The contentious tithe: The tithe problem and English agriculture, 1750–1850* (1976).

FEDDEN, R. *The continuing purpose: A history of the national trust, its aims and work* (1968).

FEINSTEIN, C. H. *National income, expenditure and output of the United Kingdom, 1855–1965* (Cambridge, 1972).

FORD, P. & G. *Select list of British parliamentary papers 1833–1899* (Oxford, 1953).

FORD, P. & G. *A breviate of parliamentary papers 1900–1916* (Oxford, 1957).

FREEDEN, M. *The New Liberalism: An ideology of social reform* (Oxford, 1978).

FRIEDMAN, W. *Law in a changing society* (2nd Penguin edn 1972).

FULFORD, R. *Five decades of B.E.T.* (1946).

FUROBORTON, E. G. & PEJOVICH, S. 'Property rights and economic theory: A survey of recent literature,' *Journ. Econ. Literature*, 10 (1972), 1137–62.

GAULDIE, E. *Cruel habitations. A history of working-class housing 1780–1918* (1974).

GEIGER, G. R. *The philosophy of Henry George* (1933).

GILBERT, B. B. 'David Lloyd George: Land, the budget and social reform,' *Amer. Hist. Rev.* 81 (1976), 1058–66.

GILBERT, B. B. 'David Lloyd George: The reform of British landholding and the budget of 1914,' *Hist. Journ.* 22 (1978), 117–41.

GIROUARD, M. *Victorian pubs* (1975).

GIROUARD, M. *Sweetness and light: The 'Queen Anne' movement 1860–1900* (1977).

GIROUARD, M. *Life in the English country house* (New Haven, 1978).

GOSDEN, P. H. J. H. *Self-help: Voluntary associations in nineteenth-century Britain* (1973).

GOTTLIEB, M. *Long swings in urban development* (New York, 1976).

HABAKKUK, H. J. 'Fluctuation in house-building in Britain and the United States in the nineteenth century,' *Journ. Econ. Hist.* 22 (1962), 198–230.

HALÉVY, E. *History of the English people in the nineteenth century* (2nd edn 1951), v–vi.

HANHAM, H. J. *Elections and party management: Politics in the time of Disraeli and Gladstone* (1959).

HARDING, A. *A social history of English law* (1965).

HARRIS, J. *Unemployment and politics: A study in English social policy 1886–1914* (Oxford, 1972).

HARRISON, R. 'The land and labour league,' *Bull. Intl. Inst. Soc. Hist.* no. 3 (1953).

HARRISON, R. *Before the socialists* (1965).

HAY, J. R. *The origins of the Liberal welfare reforms* (1975).

HENNOCK, E. P. *Fit and proper persons: Ideal and reality in nineteenth century urban government* (1973).

HICKS, U. K. *British public finances: Their structure and development 1880–1952* (1954).

HICKS, U. K. *Public finance* (2nd edn Cambridge, 1955).

History of the Times (1947), iii. 1884–1912.

HOBSBAWM, E. *Labouring men: Studies in the history of labour* (1968 edn).

HOLDSWORTH, W. S. *An historical introduction to the land law* (Oxford, 1927).

Housing and class in Britain: A second volume of papers presented at the political economy of housing workshop (1976).

HOWARD, C. H. D. 'Joseph Chamberlain and the 'unauthorized programme',' *Eng. Hist. Rev.* no. 254 (1950), 477–91.

HOWELL, D. W. *Land and people in nineteenth-century Wales* (1977).

HUSSEY, C. *The picturesque: Studies in a point of view* (1927).

HYDE, R. F. L. A. 'Mapping London's landlords: *The ground plan of London: 1892–1915,' Guildhall Studies in London History* 1 (1973), 28–34.

IONESCO, G. & GELLNER, E. (eds), *Populism* (1969).

JACKSON, A. A. *Semi-detached London: Suburban development, life and transport, 1909–39* (1973).

JENKINS, R. *Mr Balfour's poodle* (1954).

JENKINS, S. *Landlords to London* (1975).

JONES, G. L. *History of the law of charity 1537–1827* (Cambridge, 1969).

JONES, G. S. *Outcast London* (Penguin edn 1976).

JONES, P. d'E. *The Christian Socialist revival 1877–1914. Religion, class and social conscience in late-Victorian England* (Princeton, 1968).

KIERNAN, V. G. 'Private property in history,' *Family and inheritance: rural society in Western Europe*, ed. J. Goody *et al.* (Cambridge, 1976).

KIRK, H. *Portrait of a profession: A history of the solicitors' profession, 1100 to the present day* (1976).

KNOEPFLMACHER, U. C. & TENNYSON, G. B. (eds) *Nature and the Victorian imagination* (Berkeley, Calif. 1977).

KNOX, D. M. 'The development of the tied house system in London,' *Oxford Economic Papers* 10 (1958), 55–83.

LAWRENCE, E. P. *Henry George in the British Isles* (East Lansing, Mich., 1957).

LEWIS, J. P. *Building cycles and Britain's growth* (1965).

LOWNDES, G. A. N. *The silent social revolution* (1937).

LYND, H. M. *England in the eighteen-eighties* (New York, 1945).

MCBRIAR, A. M. *Fabian socialism and English politics 1884–1918* (Cambridge, 1962).

MACKENZIE, J. & N. *The first Fabians* (1977).

MARDER, A. J. *The anatomy of British sea power 1880–1905* (1940).

MARDER, A. J. *From Dreadnought to Scapa Flow* (1961), i.

MATTHEW, H. C. G. *The Liberal imperialists. The ideals and politics of a post-Gladstonian elite* (1973).

MITCHELL, B. R. & DEANE, P. *Abstract of British historical statistics* (Cambridge, 1962).

MORGAN, K. O. *Wales in British politics 1868–1922* (Cardiff, 1963).

MORRIS, A. J. A. (ed.), *Edwardian Radicalism* (1974).

MURRAY, B. K. 'The politics of the 'People's Budget',' *Hist. Journ.* 16 (1973), 555–70.

MURRAY, B. K. 'Lloyd George and the land: The issue of site-value rating,' *Studies in local history* ed. J. A. Benyon *et al.* (Capetown, 1976).

MUSGROVE, F. 'Middle-class education and employment in the nineteenth century,' *Econ. Hist. Rev.* 2nd ser. 12 (1959), 99–111.

NEEDLEMAN, L. *The economics of housing* (1965).

NEVITT, A. A. *Housing, taxation and subsidies* (1966).

NOYES, C. R. *The institution of property* (New York, 1936).

NEW YORK PUBLIC LIBRARY, *Henry George and the single tax. A catalogue of the collection* (New York, 1926).

OFFER, A. 'The origins of the law of property acts 1910–25' *Modern Law Review* 40 (1977), 505–22.

OFFER, A. 'Ricardo's paradox and the movement of rents in England, c. 1870–1910' *Econ. Hist. Rev.* 33 (1980), 236–52.

OLSEN, D. J. *Town planning in London: the eighteenth and nineteenth centuries* (New Haven, 1964).

OLSEN, D. J. *The growth of Victorian London* (1976).

ORWIN, C. S. & WHETHAM, E. *History of British agriculture 1846–1914* (2nd edn Newton Abbot, 1971).

OWEN, D. *English philanthrophy 1660–1960* (Cambridge, Mass., 1965).

PARRIS, L. *Landscape in Britain c. 1750–1850* (1973).

PEACOCK, A. T. & WISEMAN, J. V. *The growth of public expenditure in the United Kingdom* (2nd edn 1967).

PELLING, H. *The origins of the Labour party 1880–1900* (2nd edn 1965).

PELLING, H. *A social geography of British elections, 1885–1910* (1967).

PELLING, H. *Popular politics and society in late Victorian England* (1968).

PERKIN, H. J. 'Middle-class education and employment in the nineteenth century. A critical note,' *Econ. Hist. Rev.* 2nd ser. 14 (1961).

PERKIN, H. J. 'Land reform and class conflict in Victorian Britain,' *The Victorians and social protest*, ed. J. Butt and I. F. Clarke (Newton Abbot, 1973).

PERRY, P. J. (ed.), *British agriculture 1875–1914* (1973).

Political economy and the housing question: Papers presented at the housing workshop of the Conference of Socialist Economists (1975).

POSNER, R. A. *Economic analysis of law* (Boston, 1972).

PREST, A. R. & ADAMS, A. A. *Consumers' expenditure in the United Kingdom 1900–19* (Cambridge, 1954).

PRICE, J. S. *Building societies, their origins and history* (1958).

PRITCHARD, R. M. *Housing and the spatial structure of the city: Residential mobility and the housing market in an English city since the industrial revolution* (Cambridge, 1976).

RAMSDEN, J. *A history of the Conservative party, vol. 3: The age of Balfour and Baldwin, 1902–1940* (1978).

READER, W. J. *Professional men: The rise of the professional classes in nineteenth-century England* (1966).

REEDER, D. A. 'The politics of urban leaseholds in late Victorian England,' *Intl. Rev. Soc. Hist.* 6 (1961), 413–30.

RHEE, H. A. *The rent of agricultural land in England and Wales 1870–1946* (1949).

ROBERTSON, D. 'Mid-Victorians amongst the alps', in Knoepflmacher & Tennyson (eds) *Nature and the Victorian imagination* (1977), 113–36.

ROBSON, R. *The attorney in eighteenth-century England* (Cambridge, 1959).

ROSEVEARE, H. *The Treasury: The evolution of a British institution* (1968).

ROWLAND, P. *The last Liberal governments* (1971).

RUBINSTEIN, D. 'Cycling in the 1890s,' *Vict. Stud.* 21 (1977), 47–71.

RUFFER, J. G. *The big shots: Edwardian shooting parties* (n.d. 1978).

RUSSELL, A. K. *Liberal landslide: The general election of 1906* (Newton Abbot, 1973).

SABINE, B. E. V. *A History of income tax* (1966).

SAUL, S. B. 'House-building in England 1890–1914,' *Econ. Hist. Rev.* 2nd ser. 15 (1962), 119–37.

SAVILLE, J. *Rural depopulation in England and Wales 1851–1951* (1957).

SAVILLE, J. 'Henry George and the British labour movement,' *Science and Society* 24 (1960), 321–33.

SAVILLE, J. & BRIGGS, A. (eds), *Essays in labour history 1886–1923* (1971).

SEMMEL, B. *Imperialism and social reform. English social-imperial thought 1895–1914* (1960).

SHEHAB, F. *Progressive taxation* (Oxford, 1953).

SHEPPARD, D. K. *The growth and role of U.K. financial institutions 1880–1962* (1971).

SHEPPARD, F. *London 1808–1870: The infernal wen* (1971).

SIMON, B. *Education and the labour movement 1870–1920* (1965).

SIMPSON, A. W. B. *An introduction to the history of the land law* (1961).

SIMPSON, M. A. & LLOYD, T. H. (eds), *Middle-class housing in Britain* (Newton Abbot, 1977).

SIMPSON, S. R. *Land law and registration* (Cambridge, 1976).

SPRING, D. 'English landownership in the nineteenth century: A critical note,' *Econ. Hist. Rev.* 2nd ser. 9 (1957), 472–84.

SPRING, D. *The English landed estate in the nineteenth century* (1963).

SPRING, E. 'The settlement of land in nineteenth-century England', *American Journal of Legal History* 8 (1964), 209–23.

SPRING, E. 'Landowners, lawyers and land law reform in nineteenth-century England', *American Journal of Legal History* 21 (1977), 40–59.

STANSKY, P. *Ambitions and strategies: The struggle for the leadership of the Liberal party in the 1890s* (1964).

STEARNS, P. N. *Lives of labour: Work in a maturing society* (1975).

SUMMERSON, J. N. *Georgian London* (Penguin edn 1962).

BIBLIOGRAPHY

SUTHERLAND, G. *Policy-making in elementary education, 1870–1895* (1973).

TARN, J. N. *Working class housing in 19th-century Britain* (1971).

TARN, J. N. *Five per cent philanthropy: An account of housing in urban areas between 1840 and 1914* (1973).

TAYLOR, A. J. P. *Politics in wartime and other essays* (1964).

THOMAS, B. *Migration and urban development* (1972).

THOMAS, B. *Migration and economic growth* (2nd edn Cambridge, 1973).

THOMAS, J. A. *The House of Commons* (Cardiff, 2 vols. 1939, 1958).

THOMPSON, F. M. L. 'The end of a great estate,' *Econ. Hist. Rev.* 2nd ser. 8 (1955), 36–52.

THOMPSON, F. M. L. 'The land market in the nineteenth century,' *Oxford Economic Papers* new ser. 9 (1957), 285–308.

THOMPSON, F. M. L. *English landed society in the nineteenth century* (1963).

THOMPSON, F. M. L. 'Land and politics in England in the nineteenth century,' *Trans. Roy. Hist. Soc.* 5th ser. 15 (1965).

THOMPSON, F. M. L. *Chartered surveyors: The growth of a profession* (1968).

THOMPSON, F. M. L. *Victorian England: The horse-drawn society* (1970).

THOMPSON, F. M. L. *Hampstead: Building a borough 1650–1964* (1974).

THOMPSON, F. M. L. 'Britain' in D. Spring (ed.), *European landed elites in the nineteenth century* (Baltimore, 1977).

THOMPSON, P. R. *Socialists, Liberals and Labour – the struggle for London 1885–1914* (1967).

VENN, J. A. *The foundations of agricultural economics* (2nd edn Cambridge, 1933).

VINCENT, J. R. *Pollbooks: How Victorians voted* (Cambridge, 1967).

VINCENT, J. R. *The formation of the British Liberal party 1857–68* (Penguin edn 1972).

WARD, J. T. & WILSON, R. G. (eds), *Land and industry: The landed estate and the industrial revolution* (Newton Abbot, 1971).

WEDGWOOD, J. *The economics of inheritance* (2nd edn 1939).

WILDING, P. 'Towards Exchequer subsidies for housing 1906–1914,' *Soc. & Econ. Admin.* (1972), 3–18.

WILLIAMS, R. *The country and the city* (1973).

YOUNG, G. M. *Victorian England: Portrait of an age* (2nd edn 1953).

YOUNG, K. *Local politics and the rise of party* (Leicester, 1976).

INDEX

434

369–71; borrowing of, 138–40; capitalists and, 33, 106, 113–18, 151–2, 165–6, 169, 189, 203, 297, 300, 390, 402–3; death duties and, 206; dissolution of large estates, 112–13, 361–2, 378–9; economic role of, 113–18, 152; ground property and, 272–3; 'groundowners', 4, 390; income data not available, 108; intangible vs. economic benefits, 329; large variance in estate duty a signature of large estates, 109, 111, 139; law of property and, 24–6, 34, 40–44; lawyers and, 12, 24–6, 27, 32, 42, 45, 47; of London, 154, 157, 189, 200, 300–1, 303; and middle classes, 94; overseas investment and, 146; peasant proprietors and, 150; Radicals and, 33, 41–2, 76, 105–8, 148–50; ratepayers associations and, 297, 301; reaction to Liberal challenge, 1906–10, 360–2, 366–9; share of the national income, 114; and the state, 152, 154; taxation and, 165, 189, 325–6; urban, 151–2, 165, 189 (also under 'tenures')

Lansbury, George (Labour politician), 303, 310–11, 345, 355

Lansdowne, 5th Marquess (Unionist politician), 379–81, 405

Laveleye, Emile de (Belgian economist), 150

law: natural, 3; and property, 1–2, 5, 11, 401

Law, A. Bonar (Unionist politician), 322, 371, 378, 380, 381–2, 388, 399

law cases: Commissioners of Inland Revenue v. Smythe, 368–9; Lumsden v. Commissioners of Inland Revenue, 368

Law Clerk, the, 15, 58–60

Law Notes, 72, 73

Lawrence, N. T. (solicitor), 38, 44–5, 48

law-writers, 21–2, 58–9, 120

Law Society, Incorporated: and conveyancing barristers, 77; council of, and rank-and-file, 68–9; cut-price conveyancing and, 87; examinations, 14, 51, 61–3; 'Officialism', reports on (1892, 1893), 45; Presidents, 55–7, 60, 61, 101, 223; professional ethics and, 57–8; registration of title and, 36, 38–9, 43–5, 47, 60, 68–87; Registry, 15n, 16–18, 51, 59, 61; 'ten year men' and, 14, 60; 'Wolstenholme scheme' and, 47–8, 78–82

Lawson, R. G. (solicitor), 55–6, 63

lawyers and land-law reform, 32 (see also 'barristers' and 'solicitors')

Lay, George W. (solicitor), 13n, 14

leases, leasehold, see under 'tenures'

leasehold enfranchisement, 42, 151–8, 230, 300, 390, 402

Leaseholds Enfranchisement Association, 153–7; and J. S. Rubinstein, 70

Leeds, 175, 332, 392

Leicester, 119–20, 299

Letchworth Garden City, 346, 347

Lever, William (Liberal industrialist), 346

Levy, H. (German social scientist), 357

Lewis, Harvey (Liberal MP), 172–3, 174

Liberal party: differences with Fabian society, 157, 195–7; doctrines of local taxation, 162–6, 170–3, 180, 186–200, 203–4, 210, 211, 230, 246–7, 252–3, 318, 385, 386, 403; education

bill, 1902, and, 215–16; Edwardian, 245; financial policy in government (1910–14), 386–7; Gladstone ministries (1868–74) 35, 176–80, (1880–5) 42, 181–2, 203–4 (1892–4) 205–6; government (1906–14) 317–27, 355–400 passim, 404–5; Henry George and, 186–200, 325, 345, 403; law of property and, 43, 155; land settlement and, 354–5 (see also 'Home Colonisation'); and landowners, 76, 376–7; leasehold enfranchisement and, 154, 156–8; and Lord Salisbury, 43, 155; and natural rights, 3; Newcastle programme (1891), 194; policies for countryside, 350–60; railway political subscriptions and, 299; and ratepayers' associations, 301; registration of title and, 33, 44, 76–80; rural land campaign and, 373–8; socialism and, 245–6, 310, 312, 322, 376; solicitors and, 33–48, 76; TLV and, 172, 194–7, 230–1, 217–27

Liberal Unionists, 354

'Liberalism, New' (Edwardian), 245, 301, 337, 343, 357, 380, 403; outdoors attitudes, 336–42

Liberator Building Society, failure of, 45

Liberty and Property Defence League (LPDL), 41, 152, 156, 224, 234–5, 297, 301

Limehouse, see under 'George, David Lloyd'

'limpet and the registrar, The' (poem), 73–4

Lincoln, 234

Liverpool: compounding for rates in, 287; corporation council, 300; electrical generation, Merseyside, 234; gardens closed on Sundays, 332; Land and House Owners' Association, 298, 300; politicians, 80–1, 175; poor law guardians, 175; rating of owners, 226, 230, 248; tenure in, 118; United Property Owners' Association, 230, 298, 299, 300

Livery companies (London), 93, 95, 96

Lloyd George, David, see 'George, David Lloyd'

Lloyd, John (London government reformer), 272

local government: annual loan charges, 161; exchequer grants-in-aid, 165; 'national' (or 'imperial') services and, 162, 165; property ownership, 108, 161; registration of title, 72; sanitary inspectors, 123; taxation and, 161–6, 215–15 (see also 'grants-in-aid', municipal corporations', 'municipal enterprise', 'taxation, local')

Local Government Board, 237, 241, 304

London, see also 'City of London', 'embankment', 'Metropolitan Board of Works';

London (Progressive weekly), 228, 229, 234

London: administrative county of, 68–9, 73–4, 256; Auction Mart (q.v.); banks in, lending on mortgage, 142; Bedford estate, 151; 'bitter cry' poverty agitation (1883–4), 186; borough and council elections, 1906–7, 301–9; breweries, 264–5; capital projects, 171–3; clubs, 93, 96; coal and wine duties, 171, 190, 302; commercial property in, 264–5; compounding for rates in, 287; Conservative party in, 301–7; corporate property in, 96; distribution of property in, 273; distribution of tenures in, 276–7; Duke of Westminister's Pimlico estate, 274; dwelling-house property, 264–78; dwelling-

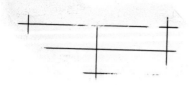